New General Mathematics

for Junior Secondary Schools 3
UBE Edition

M F Macrae
A O Kalejaiye
Z I Chima
G U Garba
J B Channon
A McLeish Smith
H C Head

Pearson Education Limited
Edinburgh Gate
Harlow
Essex CM20 2EJ
England
and Associated Companies throughout the World

20 19 18 17 16 15 14 13 12
IMP 15 14 13 12 11 10 9 8

ISBN: 978-1-4058-7000-9

Prepared for publication by Fakenham Photosetting

Printed in Malaysia, KHL

Preface

New General Mathematics

This widely popular series has been revised to reflect the 2007 Nigerian Educational Research and Development Council (NERDC) National Mathematics Curriculum for the junior secondary level.[1]

A survey of schools indicated that, in addition to coverage of the NERDC mathematics curriculum and general updating, the inclusion of chapter objectives and suggestions for teaching and learning materials would strengthen the series. We have also used the opportunity to ensure that examples and exercises contain, where appropriate, references to emerging issues such as information and communications technology, social awareness, the environment and health. In addition, at various places within the books, there are challenges and puzzle corners to encourage quantitative reasoning and non-routine problem solving. While making these revisions, care has been taken to retain the style and rigour of the previous *New General Mathematics* course books.

Book 3 is the final book of the Junior Secondary course. We have therefore included a revision course (Chapters R1 to R4) and four full-scale practice examinations as preparation for the Junior Secondary Certificate of Education (JSCE) in mathematics.

The authors wish to express their appreciation to the many students and teachers who have corresponded with them over the years. In addition we would like to acknowledge our debt to Dotun Kalejaiye, John Channon, Alex McLeish Smith and Henry Head, whose inputs to earlier versions helped to create such a sound foundation for this highly respected series.

MFM, ZIC, GUG
Lagos 2008

---

[1] The National Curriculum covers the 9-year Universal Basic Education cycle. The Junior Secondary level, or Upper Basic level, is the last three years of this cycle. The NGM course covers the mathematics component of Junior Secondary/Upper Basic schooling.

Each chapter contains the following:

- **Chapter objectives**

  This tells you what you will be able to do if you work carefully through the chapter.

- **Teaching and learning materials**

  This section suggests what the teacher and student should bring to the lesson. We realise that it will not always be possible to bring everything that is listed. However, we wish to stress that mathematics is a 'doing' subject. Therefore every student will need at least an exercise book, a pen, a mathematical set and, when appropriate, graph paper.

- **Worked examples**

  These provide guidelines and models on setting out mathematical work.

- **Graded exercises**

  For the new edition we have graded the exercises by writing the question numbers in up to three different ways:

  ① You must do all of these questions if you are to understand the topic.

  ② You should do these questions if possible.

  ③ If you want a challenge, then you could do these questions.

  Where you see *QR* beside an exercise or a question, this stands for *Quantitative Reasoning*. You should do and discuss these questions with your teacher and classmates. They give special practice at improving your number-work and your ability to calculate.

- **Chapter summary**

  This appears at the end of the chapter and lists the main learning outcomes.

- **Puzzle corners**

  Throughout the book you will find occasional puzzle corners. Try the puzzles in your spare time. To keep you guessing, we have deliberately *not* included the answers.

> **PUZZLE CORNER**
>
> Arrange these Digits:
>
> 1, 1, 2, 2, 3, 3, 4, 4
>
> ... so that
> the 1's are four digits apart,
> the 2's are three digits apart,
> the 3's are two digits apart,
> and the 4's are one digit apart.

Contents

CURRICULUM MATCHING CHART

Chapter	Chapter Title	NERDC JS 3 Curriculum Themes and Topics	NERDC JS3 Performance Objectives
Prelim	Review of previous coursework	*Number and Numeration* *Algebraic Processes* *Geometry and Mensuration* *Everyday Statistics*	
1	Binary system: Operations and Applications	*Number & Numeration, p 31* *Topic 1: Whole numbers*	Recall and use binary number concepts Add, subtract, multiply binary numbers Convert binary numbers to other bases and vice versa
2	Word problems	*Number & Numeration, p 31* *Topic 1: Whole numbers*	Translate word problems into numerical expressions
3	Factorisation: Common factors	*Algebraic Processes, p 34*	Factorise simple algebraic expressions
4	Geometrical constructions	*Geometry & Mensuration, p 28* *Topic 5: Construction*	Bisect a line segment Bisect an angle Construct angles of 90°, 45°, 60°, 30° Copy a given angle Solve construction problems
5	Calculation using standard form	*Number & Numeration*	Add, subtract, multiply, divide numbers in standard form
6	Formulae: Substitution and change of subject	*Algebraic Processes*	Substitute values in a formula Change the subject of a formula
7	Similarity and enlargement	*Geometry & Mensuration, p 37* *Topic 1: Similar shapes*	Identify similar plane shapes and solid shapes Enlarge a shape by a given scale factor
8	Tangent of an angle	*Geometry & Mensuration, p 38* *Topic 2: Trigonometry*	Determine the tangent of an acute angle Apply the tangent ratio to finding distances, lengths and angles
9	Factorisation of quadratic expressions	*Algebraic Processes, p 34* *Topic 1: Factorisation*	Factorise quadratic expressions Solve word problems related to factorisation
10	Equations involving fractions	*Algebraic Processes, p 35* *Topic 2: Equations involving fractions*	Solve simple equations involving fractions Solve word problems leading to equations involving fractions
11	Compound interest	*Number & Numeration, p 32* *Topic 1: Whole numbers*	Solve compound interest problems Relate compound interest methods to real life situations
12	ICT and computers	*Number & Numeration, p 31* *Topic 1: Whole numbers*	List the uses of ICT Use a computer to perform mathematical calculations

Chapter	Chapter Title	NERDC JS 3 Curriculum Themes and Topics	NERDC JS3 Performance Objectives
13	Proportion: Direct, inverse and reciprocals	**Number & Numeration, p 32** **Topic 1: Whole numbers**	Solve problems involving direct and inverse proportion and reciprocals Solve word problems involving direct and inverse proportion
14	Simultaneous linear equations	**Algebraic Processes, pp 35–36** **Topic 3: Simultaneous linear equations**	Compile tables of values Solve simultaneous linear equations graphically Solve simultaneous linear equations by methods of substitution and elimination
15	Sine and cosine of angles	**Geometry & Mensuration, p 38** **Topic 2: Trigonometry**	Determine the sine and cosine of acute angles Apply the sine and cosine ratios to finding distances, lengths and angles
16	Everyday statistics	**Everyday Statistics, pp 41–42** **Topic 1: Measures of central tendency** **Topic 2: Data presentation**	Find the mean, median, mode and range of given data Represent numerical information on pie charts, bar charts and pictograms Apply everyday statistics to topical issues such as substance abuse and voting patterns
17	Area of plane shapes	**Geometry & Mensuration, pp 38–39** **Topic 3: Area of plane figures**	Find the area of a triangle, parallelogram, trapezium, circle Apply area to real situations in the home, the environment and in relation to land measure
18	Areas and volumes of similar shapes	**Geometry & Mensuration, p 37** **Topic 1: Similar shapes**	Calculate lengths, areas and volumes of similar shapes Use scale factor (k, k^2, k^3) in relation to areas and volumes of similar shapes
19	Variation	**Number & Numeration, p 32** **Topic 1: Whole numbers**	Solve numerical and word problems involving direct, indirect, joint and partial variation
20	Rational and non-rational numbers	**Number & Numeration, p 32** **Topic 1: Whole numbers**	Distinguish between rational and non-rational numbers Determine approximate values of square roots and pi (π)
R1	Number and numeration	**Number & Numeration (all topics JS1 to JS3)**	NERDC Performance Objectives in number and numeration for JS1 to JS3
R2	Algebraic processes	**Algebraic Processes (all topics JS1 to JS3)**	NERDC Performance Objectives in algebra for JS1 to JS3
R3	Geometry and mensuration	**Geometry & Mensuration (all topics JS1 to JS3)**	NERDC Performance Objectives in geometry and mensuration for JS1 to JS3
R4	Statistics, averages, probability, graphs, tables	**Everyday Statistics**	NERDC Performance Objectives in statistics for JS1 to JS3

Preliminary chapter
Review of previous coursework

OBJECTIVES

By the end of this chapter you should be able to recall, from Books 1 and 2 of *New General Mathematics*, the facts and methods that relate to the following themes:

1 Number and numeration
2 Algebraic processes
3 Geometry and mensuration
4 Everyday statistics.

Teaching and learning materials

Teacher: Addition and multiplication wall charts; 1–100 number square; metre rule, measuring tape, chalk board instruments (ruler, set square, compasses), solid shapes

Students: Mathematics set

To make the best use of Book 3 of *New General Mathematics*, readers should be familiar with the contents of Books 1 and 2. This chapter contains those themes and topics from Books 1 and 2 that are necessary to understand Book 3.

P-1 Number and numeration

a Numbers are usually written in the decimal **place value** system (Fig. P1).

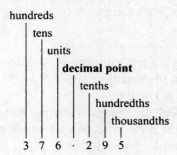

Fig. P1

The symbols 0, 1, 2, 3, 4, 5, 6, 7, 8, 9 are called **digits**.

b The words **thousand**, **million**, **billion**, **trillion** are used for large numbers:

1 thousand	$= 1\,000$	$= 10^3$
1 million	$= 1$ thousand $\times 1\,000$	$= 10^6$
1 billion	$= 1$ million $\times 1\,000$	$= 10^9$
1 trillion	$= 1$ billion $\times 1\,000$	$= 10^{12}$

Similarly, **thousandth**, **millionth**, **billionth**, ..., are used for small decimal fractions:

1 thousandth	$- 0{\cdot}001$	$= 10^{-3}$
1 millionth	$= 0{\cdot}000\,001$	$= 10^{-6}$
1 billionth	$= 0{\cdot}000\,000\,001$	$= 10^{-9}$

When writing large and small numbers, group the digits in threes from the decimal point, e.g. $9\,560\,872\,143$ and $0{\cdot}067\,482$.

c $28 \div 7 = 4$. 7 is a **whole number** which divides exactly into another whole number, 28. 7 is a **factor** of 28. 28 is a **multiple** of 7.

d A **prime number** has only two factors, itself and 1. 1 is *not* a prime number. 2, 3, 5, 7, 11, 13, 17, ..., are prime numbers. They continue without end. The **prime factors** of a number are those factors which are prime. For example, 2 and 5 are the prime factors of 40. 40 can be written as a **product of prime factors**: either $2 \times 2 \times 2 \times 5 = 40$, or, in **index form**, $2^3 \times 5 = 40$.

e The numbers 18, 24 and 30 all have 3 as a factor. 3 is a **common factor** of the numbers. The **highest common factor (HCF)** is the largest of the common factors of a given set of numbers. For example, 2, 3 and 6 are the common factors of 18, 24 and 30; 6 is the HCF.

The number 48 is a multiple of 4 and a multiple of 6. 48 is a **common multiple** of 4 and 6. The **lowest common multiple (LCM)** is the smallest of the common multiples of a given set of numbers. For example, 12 is the LCM of 4 and 6.

f A **fraction** is the number obtained when one number (the **numerator**) is divided by another number (the **denominator**). The fraction $\frac{5}{8}$ means $5 \div 8$ (Fig. P2).

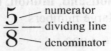

$$\frac{5}{8} \begin{array}{l} \text{— numerator} \\ \text{— dividing line} \\ \text{— denominator} \end{array}$$

Fig. P2

Fractions are used to describe parts of quantities (Fig. P3).

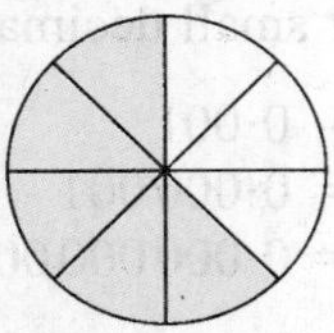

Fig. P3 $\frac{5}{8}$ of the circle is shaded

The fractions $\frac{5}{8}, \frac{10}{16}, \frac{15}{24}$ all represent the same amount; they are **equivalent fractions**. $\frac{5}{8}$ is the **simplest form** of $\frac{15}{24}$, i.e. $\frac{15}{24}$ in its **lowest terms** is $\frac{5}{8}$.

To add or subtract fractions, change them to equivalent fractions with a **common denominator**. For example:

$$\frac{5}{8} + \frac{2}{3} = \frac{15}{24} + \frac{16}{24} = \frac{15 + 16}{24} = \frac{31}{24} \left(= 1\frac{7}{24}\right)$$

$$\frac{13}{16} - \frac{5}{8} = \frac{13}{16} - \frac{10}{16} = \frac{13 - 10}{16} = \frac{3}{16}$$

To multiply fractions, multiply numerator by numerator and denominator by denominator. For example:

$$\frac{5}{8} \times \frac{2}{3} = \frac{5 \times 2}{8 \times 3} = \frac{10}{24} \left(= \frac{5}{12} \text{ in simplest form}\right)$$

$$12 \times \frac{5}{8} = \frac{12}{1} \times \frac{5}{8} = \frac{12 \times 5}{1 \times 8} = \frac{60}{8} \left(= \frac{15}{2} = 7\frac{1}{2}\right)$$

To divide by a fraction, multiply by the **reciprocal** of the fraction. For example:

$$35 \div \frac{5}{8} = \frac{35}{1} \times \frac{8}{5} = \frac{35 \times 8}{1 \times 5} = \frac{7 \times 8}{1} = 56$$

$$\frac{5}{8} \div 3\frac{3}{4} = \frac{5}{8} \div \frac{15}{4} = \frac{5}{8} \times \frac{4}{15} = \frac{5 \times 4}{8 \times 15}$$
$$= \frac{20}{120} \left(= \frac{1}{6}\right)$$

g $x\%$ is short for $\frac{x}{100}$. 64% means $\frac{64}{100}$. To change a fraction to an equivalent **percentage**, multiply the fraction by 100. For example, $\frac{5}{8}$ as a percentage $= \frac{5}{8} \times 100\% = \frac{125}{2}\% = 62\frac{1}{2}\%$

h To change a fraction to a **decimal fraction**, divide the numerator by the denominator. For example:

$$\frac{5}{8} = 0{\cdot}625$$

$$\begin{array}{r} 0{\cdot}625 \\ 8\overline{)5{\cdot}000} \\ \underline{4\ 8} \\ 20 \\ \underline{16} \\ 40 \\ \underline{40} \end{array}$$

When adding or subtracting decimals, write the numbers in a column with the decimal points exactly under each other. For example, *add 2·29, 0·084 and 4·3, then subtract the result from 11·06.*

$$\begin{array}{r} 2{\cdot}29 \\ 0{\cdot}084 \\ +\ 4{\cdot}3 \\ \hline 6{\cdot}674 \end{array} \qquad \begin{array}{r} 11{\cdot}06 \\ -\ 6{\cdot}674 \\ \hline 4{\cdot}386 \end{array}$$

To multiply decimals, first ignore the decimal points and multiply the numbers as if they are whole numbers. Then place the decimal point so that the answer has as many digits after the point as there are in the question. For example, $0{\cdot}08 \times 0{\cdot}3$:

$$8 \times 3 = 24$$

There are three digits after the decimal points in the question, so, $0{\cdot}08 \times 0{\cdot}3 = 0{\cdot}024$.

To divide by decimals, change the division so that the divisor becomes a whole number. For example, $5{\cdot}6 \div 0{\cdot}07$:

$$5 \cdot 6 \div 0 \cdot 07 = \frac{5 \cdot 6}{0 \cdot 07} = \frac{5 \cdot 6 \times 100}{0 \cdot 07 \times 100} = \frac{560}{7} = 80$$

i Numbers may be positive or negative. Positive and negative numbers are called **directed numbers**. Directed numbers can be shown on a **number line** (Fig. P4).

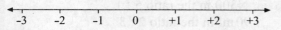

Fig. P4

The following examples show how to add, subtract, multiply and divide directed numbers.

addition

$(+8) + (+3) = +11$
$(+8) + (-3) = +5$
$(-8) + (+3) = -5$
$(-8) + (-3) = -11$

subtraction

$(+9) - (+4) = +5$
$(+9) - (-4) = +13$
$(-9) - (+4) = -13$
$(-9) - (-4) = -5$

multiplication

$(+2) \times (+7) = +14$
$(+2) \times (-7) = -14$
$(-2) \times (+7) = -14$
$(-2) \times (-7) = +14$

division

$(+6) \div (+3) = +2$
$(+6) \div (-3) = -2$
$(-6) \div (+3) = -2$
$(-6) \div (-3) = +2$

An **integer** is any positive or negative *whole* number as shown in Fig. P4.

j The number $3 \cdot 7 \times 10^4$ is in **standard form**. The first part of the product is a number between 1 and 10. The second part is a power of 10.

k When **rounding off** numbers, the digits 1, 2, 3, 4 are rounded down and the digits 5, 6, 7, 8, 9 are rounded up. For example:

3425 = 3430 to 3 **significant figures**
= 3400 to the **nearest hundred**

$7 \cdot 283$ = $7 \cdot 28$ to 2 **decimal places**
= $7 \cdot 3$ to 1 **decimal place**
= 7 to the **nearest whole number**

l The everyday system of numeration uses ten digits and is called a **base ten**, or **denary** system. The **base two**, or **binary**, system of numeration uses only two digits, 0 and 1. To **convert between bases** ten and two, express the given numbers in powers of two:

43_{ten}
$= 32 + 8 + 2 + 1$
$= 2^5 + 2^3 + 2^1 + 2^0$
$= 1 \times 2^5 + 0 \times 2^4 + 1 \times 2^3 +$
$\quad 0 \times 2^2 + 1 \times 2^1 + 1 \times 2^0$
$= 101011_{\text{two}}$

10110_{two}
$= 1 \times 2^4 + 0 \times 2^3 + 1 \times 2^2 +$
$\quad 1 \times 2^1 + 0 \times 2^0$
$= 16 + 0 + 4 + 2 + 0$
$= 22_{\text{ten}}$

Use the following identities when adding, subtracting and multiplying binary numbers:

Addition:

$0 + 0 = 0 \qquad 1 + 0 = 1$
$0 + 1 = 1 \qquad 1 + 1 = 10$

Multiplication:

$0 \times 0 = 0 \qquad 1 \times 0 = 0$
$1 \times 0 = 0 \qquad 1 \times 1 = 1$

Detailed coverage of number and numeration is given in *NGM* Book 1, Chapters 1, 2, 3, 4, 9, 12, 23, 24; and *NGM* Book 2, Chapters 1, 2, 4, 5, 8, 9, 15.

Review test 1 *(Number and numeration)*
Allow 30 minutes for this test. Use the answers at the back of the book to check your work. If you do not understand why some of your answers are incorrect, ask a friend or your teacher. Then try Test 2.

(1) Express each of the following as a product of factors. Hence find their square roots.
a 4900 b 1296
c 3969 d 5625

(2) Express the following in standard form.
a $5\,000\,000$ b $40\,000$
c $0 \cdot 0005$ d $0 \cdot 000\,007$

(3) Round off the following to
i 1 s.f., ii 2 s.f., iii 3 s.f.
a 9405 b 20062
c $29 \cdot 604$ d $0 \cdot 005\,207$

(4) Round off the following to
i 1 d.p., ii 2 d.p., iii 3 d.p.
a $14 \cdot 9028$ b $0 \cdot 0072$
c $3 \cdot 8765$ d $0 \cdot 0077$

(5) Simplify the following.
a $(-6) \times (-3)$ b $22 \times (-2)$

3

c $-38 \div 19$ d $(-15) \div (-3)$

⑥ A college has 778 students. The average mass of a student is approximately 52 kg. Estimate, to 1 significant figure, the total mass in tonnes of all the students in the college.

⑦ Divide the following quantities in the given ratios.
   a ₦1 500 in the ratio 1 : 2
   b 400 mm in the ratio 4 : 1
   c 44 oranges in the ratio 7 : 4

⑧ Find the discount price if:
   a 10% is given on a cost price of ₦500
   b 25% is given on a cost price of ₦4 400

⑨ Use tables to find:
   a 190^2 b $8 300^2$
   c $\sqrt{3 998}$ d $\sqrt{705}$

⑩ Round off the following to the nearest
   i whole number, ii tenth, iii hundredth.
   a $1 \cdot 054$ b $89 \cdot 845$

Review test 2 *(Number and numeration)*
Allow 30 minutes for this test. Use the answers at the back of the book to check your work. If you do not understand why some of your answers are incorrect, ask a friend or your teacher.

① Express each of the following as a product of factors. Hence find their square roots.
   a 3 600   b 5 184
   c 4 356   d 6 561

② Express the following in standard form.
   a 8 000   b 200 000 000
   c 0·000 04   d 0·009

③ Round off the following to
   i 1 s.f., ii 2 s.f., iii 3 s.f.
   a 546·52   b 8·028 6
   c 39 447   d 0·044 55

④ Round off the following to
   i 1 d.p., ii 2 d.p., iii 3 d.p.
   a 35·228 8   b 2·096 5
   c 0·058 4   d 0·009 2

⑤ Simplify the following.
   a $(-72) \times (-9)$ b -5×12
   c $65 \div -5$ d $(-80) \div (-8)$

⑥ A typist can type about 33 words per minute. Estimate, to 1 significant figure, how long it will take her to type a letter that is 682 words long.

⑦ Divide the following quantities in the given ratios.
   a ₦300 in the ratio 5 : 1
   b 90 ml in the ratio 2 : 3
   c 60 eggs in the ratio 5 : 7

⑧ Find the discount price if:
   a 5% is given on a cost price of ₦2 000
   b 20% is given on a cost price of ₦420

⑨ Use tables to find:
   a 57^2 b $1 050^2$
   c $\sqrt{8 005}$ d $\sqrt{664}$

⑩ Round off the following to the nearest
   i whole number, ii tenth, iii hundredth.
   a $0 \cdot 975$ b $6 \cdot 295$

P-2 Algebraic processes

a $3y^2 + 2x - 7x$ is an example of an **algebraic expression**. The letters y and x stand for numbers. $3y^2$, $2x$, $7x$ are the **terms** of the expression. $3y^2$ is short for $3 \times y \times y$. 3 is the **coefficient** of y^2. Algebraic terms may be **simplified** by combining **like terms**. Thus $3y^2 + 2x - 7x = 3y^2 - 5x$ since $2x$ and $7x$ are like terms (i.e. both terms in x).

b $3(5x - 2) = 11x$ is an **algebraic sentence** containing an equals sign; it is an **equation** in x. x is the **unknown** of the equation. To **solve an equation** means to find the value of the unknown which makes the equation true.
Use the **balance method** to solve equations.
For example,

$$3(5x - 2) = 11x$$

Clear brackets.

$$15x - 6 = 11x$$

Subtract $11x$ from both sides.

$$15x - 11x - 6 = 11x - 11x$$
$$4x - 6 = 0$$

Add 6 to both sides.

$$4x - 6 + 6 = 0 + 6$$
$$4x = 6$$

Divide both sides by 4.
$$\frac{4x}{4} = \frac{6}{4}$$
$$x = 1\frac{1}{2}$$

In general, when solving equations, i first clear brackets and fractions, ii using equal additions and/or subtractions, collect unknown terms on one side of the equals sign and known terms on the other, iii where necessary divide or multiply both sides of the equation by the same number to find the unknown.

c An **inequality** is an algebraic sentence which contains an inequality sign:

$<$ is less than
$\leqslant$ is less than or equal to
$>$ is greater than
$\geqslant$ is greater than or equal to

Inequalities are solved in much the same way as equations. However, when both sides of an inequality are multiplied or divided by a negative number, the inequality sign is *reversed*. For example,

If $-3a \leqslant 12$
Divide both sides by -3 and reverse the inequality
Then $a \geqslant -4$

d A **graph** of an algebraic sentence is a picture representing the meaning of the sentence. Graphs of equations and inequalities in one variable can be shown on the number line (Fig. P5).

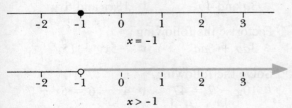

Fig. P5

For graphs connecting two variables, two **axes** are drawn at right angles to each other to give a **cartesian plane**. The horizontal **x-axis** and the vertical **y-axis** cross at their zero-point, the **origin** of the plane. Fig. P6 is the graph of the equation $y = 2x - 3$.

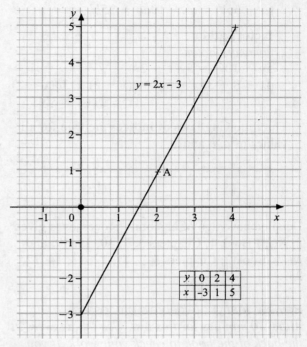

Fig. P6

To draw a straight-line graph, plot at least three points which satisfy the given equation. See the table of values in Fig. P6. At point A in Fig. P6, $x = 2$ and $y = 1$. The **coordinates** of A are A(2, 1). The *order* of the coordinates is important: the **x-coordinate** is given first, the **y-coordinate** second.

Straight-line graphs can be drawn to represent any two connected variables: for example, cost and quantity, distance and time, temperature and time. Straight-line graphs can also be drawn to show conversions between currencies or between marks and percentages.

e Algebraic expressions may be **factorised** or **expanded** using the basic rules of arithmetic. Some examples are given below.

expansion

$3(a - 2b) = 3a - 6b$

$(5 + 8x) x = 5x + 8x^2$

$(a + b) (c + d) = c(a + b) + d(a + b)$
$$= ac + bc + ad + bd$$

$(3x + 2) (x - 4) = 3x^2 + 2x - 12x - 8$
$$= 3x^2 - 10x - 8$$

$(a - 5b)^2 = a^2 - 10ab + 25b^2$

factorisation

common factor

$5y - 10y^2 = 5y(1 - 2y)$

$4x - 8 + 3bx - 6b = 4(x - 2) + 3b(x - 2)$
$$= (x - 2) (4 + 3b)$$

f The following **laws of indices** are true for all values of a, b and x.

$$x^a \times x^b = x^{a + b} \qquad x^a \div x^b = x^{a - b}$$

$$x^0 = 1 \qquad x^{-a} = \frac{1}{x^a}$$

Detailed coverage of algebraic processes is given in *NGM* Book 1, Chapters 5, 7, 10, 15, 19; and *NGM* Book 2, Chapters 5, 7, 11, 12, 13, 14, 22, 23.

Review test 3 (Algebraic processes)

Allow 30 minutes for this test. Use the answers at the back of the book to check your work. If you do not understand why some of your answers are incorrect, ask a friend or your teacher. Then try Test 4.

1 State the additive inverse of:
   a -5 b $+14$
   c -514 d $+\frac{3}{7}$

2 State the multiplicative inverse of:
   a $+7$ b $-\frac{6}{7}$
   c $+34$ d $-0·15$

3 Remove brackets and simplify.
   a $7(a - b) - 8(a - 2b)$
   b $y(y - 3) - 6(y - 3)$

4 Expand the following.
   a $(6 - x) (3 + y)$ b $(5x - y) (x - 3y)$

5 State the HCF of the following.
   a $10x^2$ and $15x^2$ b $24ax^2$ and $3a^2x$

6 State the LCM of the following.
   a pq and qr b $3a^2$ and $8ab$

7 Factorise the following.
   a $2a^2 - 9ab$ b $-18pq - 12p$

8 Solve the following.
   a $51 = 3 + 8x$ b $6x + 1 = 26 - 2x$

9 Which symbol, $<$ or $>$, goes in the box to make the statement true?
   a $15 \square 18 - 8$ b $3 \times 6·2 \square 18·8$

10 Solve the following.
   a $2x < 9$ b $-12 > 5x$
   c $3x - 8 < 5x$

Review test 4 (Algebraic processes)

Allow 30 minutes for this test. Use the answers at the back of the book to check your work. If you do not understand why some of your answers are incorrect, ask a friend or your teacher.

1 State the additive inverse of:
   a $+3$ b -7
   c $+118$ d $-0·27$

2 State the multiplicative inverse of:
   a 4 b $\frac{1}{5}$
   c -9 d $-0·7$

3 Remove brackets and simplify.
   a $x(x + 4) - 5(x - 2)$
   b $a(a + b) - b(a + b)$

4 Expand the following.
   a $(x + 6) (y - 9)$ b $(x - 2) (3x + 7)$

5 State the HCF of the following.
   a $18xy$ and $6xy$ b $12xy^2$ and $3xy$

6 State the LCM of the following.
   a $3a$ and $4b$ b $18xy$ and $6xy$

7 Factorise the following.
   a $3ab + 6ac$ b $-5xy + 15y$

8 Solve the following.
   a $10g - 7 = 47$ b $4x - 6 = 5x - 7$

9 Which symbol, $<$ or $>$, goes in the box to make the statement true?
   a $7 + 5 \square 10$ b $31 \div 10 \square 3·2$

⑩ Solve the following.

  a $2x > 10$ b $-7 < 4x$

  c $x + 4 \geqslant 10x - 23$

P-3 Geometry and mensuration

a Fig. P7 gives sketches and names of some common **solids**.

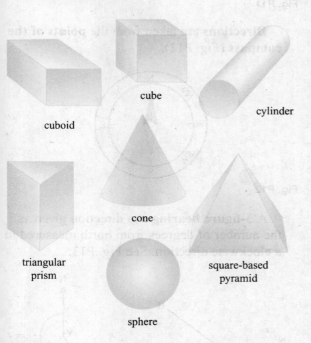

cube

cylinder

cuboid

cone

triangular prism

square-based pyramid

sphere

Fig. P7

All solids have **faces**; most solids have **edges** and **vertices** (Fig. P8).

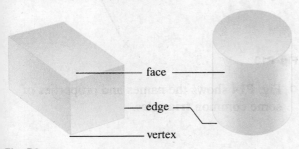

face

edge

vertex

Fig. P8

Formulae for the **surface area** and **volume** of common solids are given in Table P1.

The **net** of a solid is the plane shape which can be folded to make the solid.

	surface area	volume
cube edge s	$6s^2$	s^3
cuboid length l, breadth b, height b	$2(lb + bh + hl)$	lbh
prism height h, base area A		Ah
sphere radius r	$4\pi r^2$	$\frac{4}{3}\pi r^3$
cylinder base radius r, height h	$2\pi r(r + h)$	$\pi r^2 h$
cone base radius r, height h, slant height l	$\pi r(r + l)$	$\frac{1}{3}\pi r^2 h$

Table P1

b **Angle** is a measure of rotation or turning.

  1 **revolution** = 360 **degrees** (1 rev = 360°)

The names of angles change with their size. See Fig. P9.

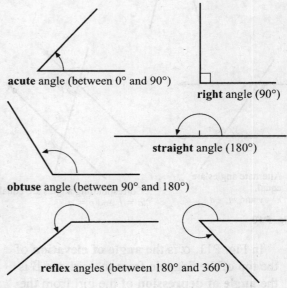

acute angle (between 0° and 90°)

right angle (90°)

straight angle (180°)

obtuse angle (between 90° and 180°)

reflex angles (between 180° and 360°)

Fig. P9

Angles are measured and constructed using a **protractor**.

Fig. P10 shows some properties of angles formed when straight lines meet.

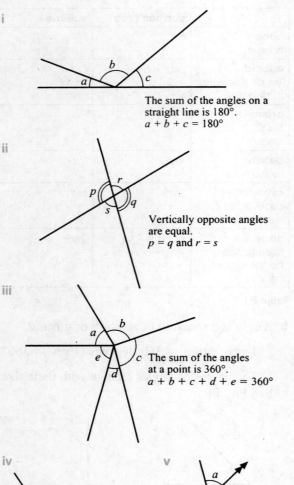

i

b

a   *c*

The sum of the angles on a straight line is 180°.
$a + b + c = 180°$

ii

r

p   *q*

s

Vertically opposite angles are equal.
$p = q$ and $r = s$

iii

a   *b*

e   *c*

d

The sum of the angles at a point is 360°.
$a + b + c + d + e = 360°$

iv

m *x*

y *n*

Alternate angles are equal.
$x = y$ and $m = n$

Fig. P10

v

a

p

b

q

Corresponding angles are equal.
$a = b$ and $p = q$

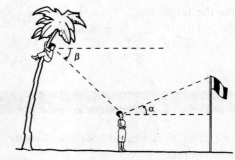

Fig. P11

Directions are taken from the **points of the compass** (Fig. P12).

Fig. P12

A **3-figure bearing** is a direction given as the number of degrees from north measured in a clockwise direction. See Fig. P13.

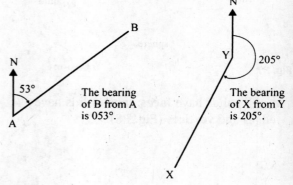

The bearing of B from A is 053°.

The bearing of X from Y is 205°.

Fig. P13

In Fig. P11, α is the **angle of elevation** of the top of the flagpole from the girl and β is the **angle of depression** of the girl from the boy.

c Fig. P14 shows the names and properties of some common **triangles**.

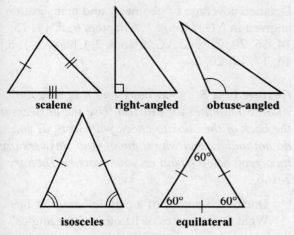

scalene   right-angled   obtuse-angled

isosceles   equilateral

Fig. P14 Some common triangles

Fig. P15 shows the names and properties of some common **quadrilaterals**.

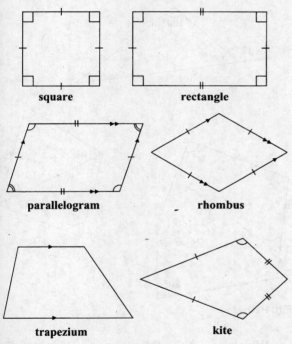

square   rectangle

parallelogram   rhombus

trapezium   kite

Fig. P15

Fig. P16 gives the names of lines and regions in a **circle**.

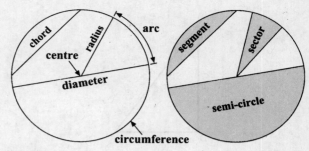

chord   radius   arc
centre
diameter   segment   sector

semi-circle

circumference

Fig. P16

A **polygon** is a plane shape with three or more straight sides. A **regular polygon** has all its sides of equal length and all its angles of equal size. Fig. P17 gives the names of some common regular polygons.

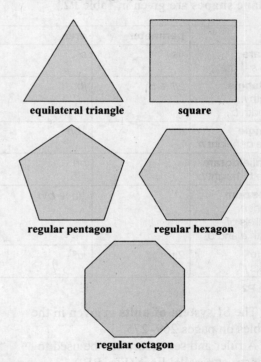

equilateral triangle   square

regular pentagon   regular hexagon

regular octagon

Fig. P17

The **sum of the angles of an *n*-sided polygon** is $(n - 2) \times 180°$. In particular, the sum of the angles of a triangle is 180° and the sum of the angles of a quadrilateral is 360°.

To **solve a triangle** means to calculate the sizes of its sides and angles. Right-angled triangles can be solved using **Pythagoras' rule**.

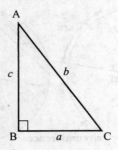

Fig. P18

In Fig. P18, $\triangle ABC$ is right-angled at B; side $\overline{AC}$ is the **hypotenuse**.

Pythagoras' rule: $b^2 = a^2 + c^2$

Formulae for the **perimeter** and **area of plane shapes** are given in Table P2.

	perimeter	area
square side s	$4s$	s^2
rectangle length l, breadth b	$2(l + b)$	lb
triangle base b, height h		$\frac{1}{2}bh$
parallelogram base b, height h		bh
trapezium height h, parallels of length a and b		$\frac{1}{2}(a + b)h$
circle radius r	$2\pi r$	πr^2

Table P2

The **SI system of units** is given in the tables on pages 269–275.

A ruler and set-square can be used to construct parallel lines (Fig. P19).

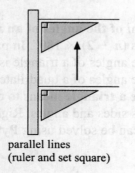

parallel lines
(ruler and set square)

Fig. P19

10

Detailed coverage of geometry and mensuration is given in *NGM* Book 1, Chapters 6, 8, 11, 13, 14, 16, 20, 21; and *NGM* Book 2, Chapters 3, 6, 16, 17, 19, 20, 24.

Review test 5 *(Geometry and mensuration)*
Allow 30 minutes for this test. Use the answers at the back of the book to check your work. If you do not understand why some of your answers are incorrect, ask a friend or your teacher. Then try Test 6.

1 One of the angles of a parallelogram is 119°. What are the sizes of its other three angles?

2 How many lines of symmetry does a kite have?

3 Find the values of m, n, p, q, s, in Fig. P20.

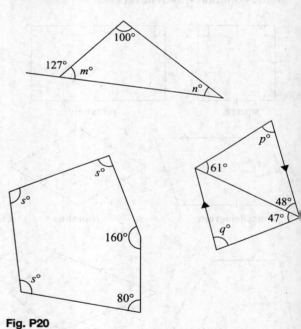

Fig. P20

4 Which one of the following is a Pythagorean triple?
a 3, 8, 9   b 4, 10, 11   c 5, 12, 13

5 Calculate to 2 s.f. the length of a diagonal of a 30 mm by 20 mm rectangle

6 Copy and complete the following table of cylinders. Use the value 3 for π.

	radius	height	curved surface area	volume
a	8 cm	6 cm		
b	5·5 cm	16 cm		
c		11 cm	198 cm²	
d	4 cm			336 cm³

⑦ In Fig. P21, BC is horizontal. Measure:
a the angle of elevation of A from B,
b the angle of depression of C from A.

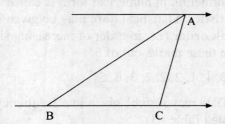

Fig. P21

⑧ In Fig. P22, state the bearings of A, B, C and D from X.

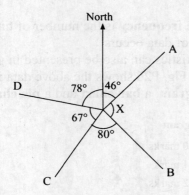

Fig. P22

⑨ Copy and complete the following table of cones. Complete only the unshaded spaces. Use the value 3 for π.

	slant height	angle of sector	curved surface area	base radius	height	volume
a	10 cm	150°				
b	4 cm	240°				
c				5 cm	18 cm	
d				4 cm	10 cm	

Allow 30 minutes for this test. Use the answers at the back of the book to check your work. If you do not understand why some of your answers are incorrect, ask a friend or your teacher.

① One of the angles of a rhombus is 42°. What are the sizes of its other three angles?

② How many lines of bilateral symmetry does a square have?

③ Find the values of p, q, r, s, t, x in Fig. P23.

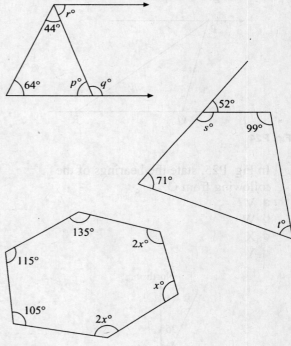

Fig. P23

④ Which one of the following is a Pythagorean triple?
a 2, 3, 4   b 3, 4, 5   c 4, 5, 6

⑤ Calculate to 2 s.f. the length of the longest straight line that can be drawn on a rectangular chalkboard that measures 1·2 m by 3·0 m.

⑥ Copy and complete the following table of cylinders. Use the value 3 for π.

	radius	height	curved surface area	volume
a	4 cm	10 cm		
b	2·5 cm	12 cm		
c		7 cm	126 cm²	
d	5 cm			300 cm³

	slant height	angle of sector	curved surface area	base radius	height	volu
a	8 cm	210°				
b	5 cm	135°				
c				7 cm	20 cm	
d				3·5 cm	12 cm	

7. In Fig. P24, QR is horizontal. Measure:
   a the angle of elevation of P from Q.
   b the angle of depression of R from P.

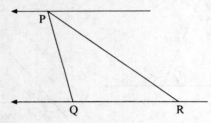

Fig. P24

8. In Fig. P25, state the bearings of the following from O.
   a V
   b W
   c X
   d Y

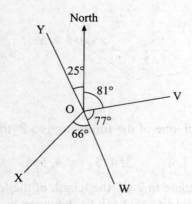

Fig. P25

9. Copy and complete the following table of cones. Complete only the unshaded spaces. Use the value 3 for π.

P-4 Everyday statistics

a Information in numerical form is called **statistics**. Statistical **data** may be given in **rank order** (i.e. in order of increasing size) like these marks out of 5:

0, 1, 1, 2, 2, 2, 3, 3, 5

Data may also be given in a **frequency table** (Table P3).

mark	0	1	2	3	4	5
frequency	1	2	3	2	0	1

Table P3

The **frequency** is the number of times each piece of data occurs.

Statistics can also be presented in **graphical** form. Fig. P26 shows the above data in a **pictogram**, a **bar chart** and a **pie chart**.

pictogram

bar chart

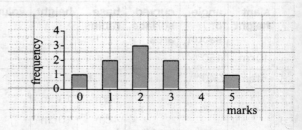

pie chart

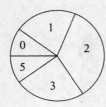

Fig. P26

b **Probability** is a measure of the likelihood of a required event happening.

$$\text{probability} = \frac{\text{number of required events}}{\text{number of possible events}}$$

If an event *must* happen, probability = 1
If an event *cannot* happen, probability = 0

Hence the probability of something happening is a fraction whose value lies between 0 and 1. If the probability of something happening is x, then the probability of it *not* happening is $1 - x$.

Detailed coverage of statistics is given in *NGM* Book 1, Chapters 17, 18, 22; and *NGM* Book 2, Chapters 18, 21.

Review test 7 (Everyday statistics)
Allow 20 minutes for this test. Use the answers at the back of the book to check your work. If you do not understand why some of your answers are incorrect, ask a friend or your teacher. Then try Test 8.

1 For each set of numbers, calculate the mean.
   a 12, 14, 1   b 9, 10, 14
   c 1, 8, 6, 8, 7   d 7, 7, 3, 2, 11

2 Find the mode, median and mean of each set of numbers.
   a 7, 7, 9, 12, 15
   b 0, 1, 4, 4, 5, 5, 5, 6, 6, 7
   c 10, 8, 5, 12, 8, 11
   d 5, 3, 9, 5, 10, 6, 4, 7, 5

3 Table P4 shows the results of a survey of vehicles on a city road in one hour.

	cars	lorries	buses	others	total
number	28	5	7	10	

Table P4

a How many vehicles altogether?
b What is the probability that the next vehicle is a car?
c What is the probability that the next vehicle is *not* a car?
d What is the probability that the next vehicle is not a car, a lorry or a bus?

Review test 8 (Everyday statistics)
Allow 20 minutes for this test. Use the answers at the back of the book to check your work. If you do not understand why some of your answers are incorrect, ask a friend or your teacher.

1 For each set of numbers, calculate the mean.
   a 18, 6, 8, 12
   b 3, 11, 6, 8
   c 2, 9, 0, 6, 7, 0
   d 9, 10, 12, 13, 16, 18

2 Find the mode, median and mean of each set of numbers.
   a 4, 5, 5, 7, 8, 10
   b 4, 8, 11, 11, 12, 12, 12
   c 3, 1, 17, 1, 8, 12
   d 4, 3, 1, 4, 1, 0, 2, 4, 2, 3, 4, 2

3 A school enters candidates for the JSC examination. Table P5 shows the results for the years 2005–2008.

	2005	2006	2007	2008
candidates entered	86	95	109	110
number gaining JSC	56	57	65	70

Table P5

During the four years:
a How many candidates were entered for JSC?
b How many candidates gained a JSC?
c What is the school's success rate (as a percentage)?
d What is the approximate probability (as a decimal to 1 s.f.) of a student at this school getting a JSC?

OBJECTIVES

By the end of this chapter you should be able to:

1 Express numbers in bases other than ten
2 Convert numbers from base ten to other bases and vice versa
3 Express numbers using the binary system
4 Convert numbers from base ten to base two and vice versa
5 Add, subtract and multiply binary numbers
6 Use the binary system in computer applications such as punch cards and punch tape.

Teaching and learning materials

Teacher: Counters (e.g. bottle tops, matchsticks, pebbles); punch cards (as in Fig. 1.3 to 1.6)
Students: Bottle tops, pebbles

1-1 Number bases

Bases other than ten

Most people count in tens. Fig. 1.1 shows the place value of the digits in number 4956 in this system.

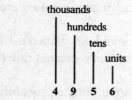

Fig. 1.1

The place values are in powers of ten. It is called the **base ten** system.

$$4956 = 4 \times 1000 + 9 \times 100 + 5 \times 10 + 6 \times 1$$
$$= 4 \times 10^3 + 9 \times 10^2 + 5 \times 10^1 + 6 \times 10^0$$

Some people traditionally count in 5s, others in 20s. Using the method of the base ten system, a **base five** system is in powers of five. So, for example, in base five, 342 would be

$$342_{five} = 3 \times 25 + 4 \times 5 + 2 \times 1$$
$$= 3 \times 5^2 + 4 \times 5^1 + 2 \times 5^0$$

Notice that 342_{five} is short for 342 in base five.

Example 1

Expand a 320745_{eight}, b 11101_{two} *in powers of their bases.*

a 320745_{eight}
$$= 3 \times 8^5 + 2 \times 8^4 + 0 \times 8^3$$
$$+ 7 \times 8^2 + 4 \times 8^1 + 5 \times 8^0$$

b 11101_{two}
$$= 1 \times 2^4 + 1 \times 2^3 + 1 \times 2^2$$
$$+ 0 \times 2^1 + 1 \times 2^0$$

Exercise 1a [Oral]

[QR] ① What should go in the boxes?

a $2379_{ten} = \square \times 10^3 + \square \times 10^2 + \square \times 10^1 + \square \times 10^0$

b $533_{seven} = \square \times 7^2 + \square \times 7^1 + \square \times 7^0$

c $24103_{five} = \square \times 5^4 + \square \times 5^3 + \square \times 5^2 + \square \times 5^1 + \square \times 5^0$

d $30213_{four} = \square \times 4^4 + \square \times 4^3 + \square \times 4^2 + \square \times 4^1 + \square \times 4^0$

e $10011_{two} = \square \times 2^4 + \square \times 2^3 + \square \times 2^2 + \square \times 2^1 + \square \times 2^0$

[QR] ② What should go in the boxes?

a $3572_{ten} = 3 \times \square + 5 \times \square + 7 \times \square + 2 \times \square$

b $604_{eight} = 6 \times \square + 0 \times \square + 4 \times \square$

c $25140_{six} = 2 \times \square + 5 \times \square + 1 \times \square$
$+ 4 \times \square + 0 \times \square$

d $1110_{two} = 1 \times \square + 1 \times \square + 1 \times \square$
$+ 0 \times \square$

e $22012_{three} = 2 \times \square + 2 \times \square + 0 \times \square$
$+ 1 \times \square + 2 \times \square$

3) Expand the following in the powers of their bases.

a 3402_{five} b 22011_{four}
c 35732_{eight} d 1011_{two}
e 4312_{six} f 34208_{ten}
g 101101_{two} h 20201_{three}
i 603_{seven} j 11110_{two}

Converting base ten numbers to other bases

To convert from base ten to another base, express the given number in powers of the new base.

Example 2

Convert 37_{ten} *a to base eight,*   *b to base five.*

a Since $37 < 64$, there are no sixty-fours in 37. To find the number of eights in 37, divide by 8.

$37 \div 8 = 4$, remainder 5
$37 = 4$ eights $+ 5$ units
$37_{ten} = 45_{eight}$
Check: $45_{eight} = 4 \times 8 + 5 \times 1$
$= 32 + 5$
$= 37$

b Since $37 > 25$, there must be a twenty-five in 37.

$37 \div 25 = 1$, remainder 12
$37 = 1$ twenty-five $+ 12$ units.

Consider the 12 units. Since $12 > 5$, there must be some fives in 12.

$12 \div 5 = 2$, remainder 2
$12 = 2$ fives $+ 2$ units
$\therefore 37 = 1$ twenty-five $+ 2$ fives $+ 2$ units
$= 1 \times 5^2 + 2 \times 5^1 + 2 \times 1$
$37_{ten} = 122_{five}$

Check: $122_{five} = 1 \times 25 + 2 \times 5 + 2 \times 1$
$= 25 + 10 + 2$
$= 37$

The method in part **b** of Example 2 can be shortened as follows:

$$
\begin{array}{r|l}
5 & 37 \\
\hline
5 & 7 + 2 \quad \text{(i.e. } 7 \times 5 + 2 \times 1) \\
5 & 1 + 2 \quad \text{(i.e. } 1 \times 5^2 + 2 \times 5^1) \\
5 & 0 + 1 \quad \text{(i.e. } 0 \times 5^3 + 1 \times 5^2)
\end{array}
$$

Continued division by 5 gives remainders. Reading the remainders *upwards* gives $37_{ten} = 122_{five}$ (see the arrows above).

To change from base ten to another base:

1 Divide the base ten number by the new base number.
2 Continue dividing until 0 (zero) is reached, writing down the remainder each time.
3 Start at the last remainder and read upwards to get the answer.

Example 3

Convert 75_{ten} *a to base four,*   *b to base two.*

a
$$
\begin{array}{r|l}
4 & 75 \\
\hline
4 & 18 + 3 \\
4 & 4 + 2 \\
4 & 1 + 0 \\
4 & 0 + 1
\end{array}
$$
$75_{ten} = 1023_{four}$

b
$$
\begin{array}{r|l}
2 & 75 \\
\hline
2 & 37 + 1 \\
2 & 18 + 1 \\
2 & 9 + 0 \\
2 & 4 + 1 \\
2 & 2 + 0 \\
2 & 1 + 0 \\
 & 0 + 1
\end{array}
$$
$75_{ten} = 1001011_{two}$

Example 3 shows that if a remainder is 0, it must be written down.

Notice that a base eight number cannot contain an 8 or a 9. In the same way, a base five number contains no digits greater than 4. In base two, the only digits are 0 and 1.

Exercise 1b

① Convert the following base ten numbers to base eight.
   | a 15 | b 27 | c 128 |
   | d 569 | e 1 239 | f 5 046 |

② Change the following base ten numbers to base five.
   | a 20 | b 76 | c 99 |
   | d 115 | e 256 | f 733 |

③ Convert the following base ten numbers to base two.
a 11	b 18	c 35
d 25	e 17	f 31
g 29	h 39	i 17
j 43	k 23	l 27

④ Change the following base ten numbers to base six.
   | a 12 | b 31 | c 49 |
   | d 68 | e 725 | f 1 000 |

⑤ Convert the following base ten numbers to base two.
a 63	b 64	c 65
d 49	e 100	f 129
g 54	h 72	i 101
j 120	k 89	l 94

Converting from other bases to base ten

Example 4

Convert $1 264_{eight}$ to base ten.

1st method: By expanding the given number:

$$1 264_{eight} = 1 \times 8^3 + 2 \times 8^2 + 6 \times 8 + 4 \times 1$$
$$= 1 \times 512 + 2 \times 64 + 6 \times 8 + 4 \times 1$$
$$= 512 + 128 + 48 + 4$$
$$= 692_{ten}$$

2nd method: By repeated multiplication:

$$
\begin{array}{cccc}
1 & 2 & 6 & 4 \\
\times 8 & \downarrow & & \\
8 + 2 = 10 & & & \\
& \times 8 & & \\
& 80 + 6 = & 86 & \\
& & \times 8 & \\
& & 688 + 4 = & 692
\end{array}
$$

$$1 264_{eight} = 692_{ten}$$

Notice that the method of repeated multiplication is the inverse of the repeated division method for conversion from base ten.

Example 5

Convert the following to base ten.

a 432_{five} *b* $11 101_{two}$

a By repeated multiplication,

$$
\begin{array}{ccc}
4 & 3 & 2 \\
\times 5 & \downarrow & \\
20 + 3 = 23 & & \\
& \times 5 & \\
& 115 + 2 = 117_{ten} &
\end{array}
$$

b By expanding in powers,

$$11 101_{two} = 1 \times 2^4 + 1 \times 2^3 + 1 \times 2^2$$
$$+ 0 \times 2^1 + 1 \times 1$$
$$= 1 \times 16 + 1 \times 8 + 1 \times 4$$
$$+ 0 \times 2 + 1 \times 1$$
$$= 16 + 8 + 4 + 0 + 1$$
$$= 29_{ten}$$

Exercise 1c

Convert the following to base ten.

① 17_{eight}	② 31_{eight}	③ 231_{eight}
④ 472_{eight}	⑤ 631_{eight}	⑥ 63_{seven}
⑦ 45_{seven}	⑧ 126_{seven}	⑨ 324_{seven}
⑩ 616_{seven}	⑪ 32_{four}	⑫ 130_{four}
⑬ 231_{four}	⑭ 301_{four}	⑮ $1 023_{four}$
⑯ 212_{three}	⑰ $1 122_{three}$	⑱ $2 120_{three}$

1-2 The binary system (revision)

Binary numbers

In *NGM Book 1* we defined **base two** numbers as belonging to the **binary system**. So, for example, $11\,010_{two}$ and 111_{two} are binary numbers. The binary system is important because of its relationship to computer circuits. Binary numbers only have two digits: 0 and 1. Likewise a computer circuit can only be in two states, either off (0) or on (1).

Table 1.1 shows the first ten binary numbers.

binary number	value in powers of 2	base ten number
1	1×1	1
10	$1 \times 2^1 + 0 \times 1$	2
11	$1 \times 2^1 + 1 \times 1$	3
100	$1 \times 2^2 + 0 \times 2^1 + 0 \times 1$	4
101	$1 \times 2^2 + 0 \times 2^1 + 1 \times 1$	5
110	$1 \times 2^2 + 1 \times 2^1 + 0 \times 1$	6
111	$1 \times 2^2 + 1 \times 2^1 + 1 \times 1$	7
1000	$1 \times 2^3 + 0 \times 2^2 + 0 \times 2^1 + 0 \times 1$	8
1001	$1 \times 2^3 + 0 \times 2^2 + 0 \times 2^1 + 1 \times 1$	9
1010	$1 \times 2^3 + 0 \times 2^2 + 1 \times 2^1 + 0 \times 1$	10

Table 1.1

Example 6

Convert 105_{ten} to a binary number.

```
2 | 105
2 |  52 + 1
2 |  26 + 0
2 |  13 + 0
2 |   6 + 1
2 |   3 + 0
2 |   1 + 1
  |   0 + 1
```

Thus, $105_{ten} = 1\,101\,001_{two}$

Example 7

Convert $100\,110_{two}$ to   *a a base ten number*
b a base eight number.

a $100\,110_{two}$
$$= 1 \times 2^5 + 0 \times 2^4 + 0 \times 2^3$$
$$+ 1 \times 2^2 + 1 \times 2^1 + 0 \times 2^0$$
$$= 32 + 0 + 0 + 4 + 2 + 0$$
$$= 38_{ten}$$

b $38_{ten} = 32 + 6$
$$= 4 \times 8^1 + 6 \times 8^0$$
$$= 46_{eight}$$

Therefore $100\,110_{two} = 46_{eight}$

Example 7b shows that when converting between bases, it is usually easiest to find the equivalent **denary** (base ten) number as an intermediate step.

Example 8 shows how to convert a binary number to a denary number using repeated multiplication.

Example 8

Use repeated multiplication to convert $11\,001_{two}$ to a base ten number.

```
 1    1      0       0        1
×2    ↓      ↓       ↓        ↓
   2 + 1 = 3
           ×2
        6 + 0 = 6
                ×2
             12 + 0 = 12
                      ×2
                   24 + 1 = 25_ten
```

The method in Example 7a is probably quicker. However, to use this method successfully needs a good knowledge of the values of powers of two.

Example 9

Find the value of a $(101_{two})^3$,
b *square root of* $100\,100_{two}$, *in base two.*

Work in base ten.

a $(101_{two})^3 = (5_{ten})^3 = 125_{ten}$
$\qquad = 64 + 32 + 16 + 8 + 4 + 1$
$\qquad = 1 \times 2^6 + 1 \times 2^5 + 1 \times 2^4$
$\qquad \quad + 1 \times 2^3 + 1 \times 2^2 + 0 \times 2$
$\qquad \quad + 1 \times 1$
$\qquad = 1\,111\,101_{two}$

b $100\,100_{two} = 1 \times 2^5 + 0 \times 2^4 + 0 \times 2^3$
$\qquad\qquad\quad + 1 \times 2^2 + 0 \times 2 + 0 \times 1$
$\qquad\qquad = 32_{ten} + 4_{ten} = 36_{ten}$
Square root of $36_{ten} = 6_{ten}$
$\qquad\qquad\qquad\quad = 110_{two}$

Note: In Examples 7 and 9, it is easier to work in base ten, converting as required.

Exercise 1d

1. Fig. 1.2 shows how to use a piece of paper and three bottle tops to represent the binary number $1\,011_{two}$.

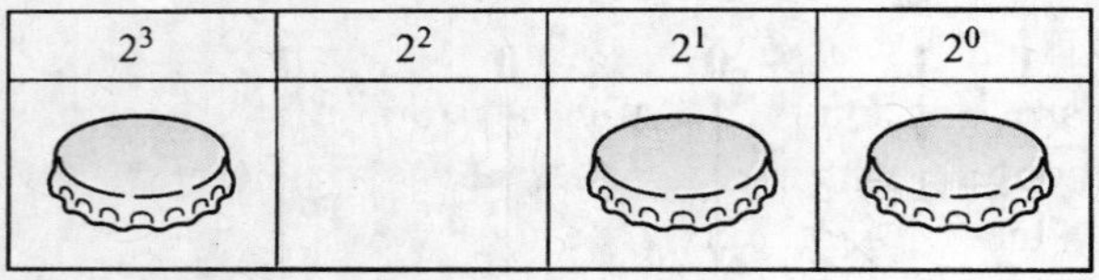

2^3	2^2	2^1	2^0

Fig. 1.2

Draw a piece of paper like this and collect some counters (bottle tops, pebbles).
   a Using one counter, represent as many different binary numbers as possible on the paper.
   b Repeat with two counters.
   c Repeat with three counters.
   d Repeat with four counters.
   e Arrange your binary numbers in order of size.

2. Table 1.1 on page 18 contains the first ten binary numbers. Extend the table to include the first twenty binary numbers.

3. a Convert 10_{ten} to a binary number.

b Convert $(10_{ten})^2$ to a binary number.

4. Use repeated division to convert the following denary numbers into binary numbers.
   a 28   b 27   c 38   d 41
   e 50   f 59   g 63   h 77

5. Convert the following binary numbers into base ten numbers.
   a 1001   b 1011   c 10101
   d 11110   e 11010   f 110101

6. Convert $111\,110_{two}$ to   a a base ten number,
   b a base eight number.

7. Find the value of the following, leaving your answers in base two.
   a the square of 111_{two} b $(1011_{two})^2$

8. Find the square root of the following. Give your answers in base two.
   a $1\,000\,000_{two}$ b $1\,010\,001_{two}$

Operations with binary numbers (revision)

To add, subtract and multiply binary numbers, use the methods that you use with base ten numbers. However, you must remember that you are working with powers of two, not powers of ten. The following identities are very useful:

Addition:

$0 + 0 = 0 \qquad 1 + 0 = 1$
$0 + 1 = 1 \qquad 1 + 1 = 10$

Multiplication:

$0 \times 0 = 0 \qquad 1 \times 0 = 0$
$0 \times 1 = 0 \qquad 1 \times 1 = 1$

Example 10 shows how to use these identities when operating with binary numbers. Follow the notes carefully.

Example 10

Calculate the following.

a
$$
\begin{array}{r}
1\,001 \\
+\ 1\,011 \\
\end{array}
$$

b
$$
\begin{array}{r}
1\,110 \\
-\ 101 \\
\end{array}
$$

c
$$
\begin{array}{r}
110 \\
\times\ 101 \\
\end{array}
$$

a
$$
\begin{array}{r}
1\,001 \\
+\ 1\,011 \\
\hline
10\,100 \\
\end{array}
$$

Note: 1st column: $1 + 1 = 10$; write down
0, carry 1
2nd column: as above
3rd column: $1 + 0 + 0 = 1$
4th column: $1 + 1 = 10$; write down
0, carry 1

b
$$
\begin{array}{r}
1\,110 \\
-\ 101 \\
\hline
1\,001 \\
\end{array}
$$

Note: 1st column: 1 from 0 'won't go'.
Move the 1 in the 2nd
column to the 1st
column: $10 - 1 = 1$;
write down 1
2nd column: the 1 has been removed,
leaving 0; $0 - 0 = 0$;
write down 0
3rd column: $1 - 1 = 0$; write down 0
4th column: $1 - 0 = 1$;
write down 1

c
$$
\begin{array}{r}
110 \\
\times\ 101 \\
\hline
110 \\
0\,00 \\
110 \\
\hline
11\,110 \\
\end{array}
$$

Note: Set out as in a normal long
multiplication, multiplying by 1 or 0
as necessary.
Take care with placing the digits
Add as explained in part *a*

All calculations may be checked by converting
to base ten. E.g. part *c* of Example 10 is
equivalent to $6 \times 5 = 30$.

Exercise 1e

1. Calculate the following in base two,
checking your results by converting to base
ten.

a
$$
\begin{array}{r}
1\,101 \\
+\ 1\,011 \\
\end{array}
$$

b
$$
\begin{array}{r}
10\,110 \\
+\ 111 \\
\end{array}
$$

c
$$
\begin{array}{r}
11\,101 \\
\div\ 1\,011 \\
\end{array}
$$

d
$$
\begin{array}{r}
11\,110 \\
-\ 111 \\
\end{array}
$$

e
$$
\begin{array}{r}
1\,101\,101 \\
+\ 11\,011 \\
\end{array}
$$

f
$$
\begin{array}{r}
10\,100 \\
-\ 1\,110 \\
\end{array}
$$

g
$$
\begin{array}{r}
1\,100 \\
\times\ 11 \\
\end{array}
$$

h
$$
\begin{array}{r}
10\,011 \\
\times\ 101 \\
\end{array}
$$

i
$$
\begin{array}{r}
1\,111 \\
\times\ 110 \\
\end{array}
$$

j
$$
\begin{array}{r}
10\,111 \\
\times\ 1\,011 \\
\end{array}
$$

2. Calculate:
   a $111_{two} \times (1\,111_{two} + 1\,010_{two})$,
   b $111_{two} \times (1\,111_{two} - 1\,010_{two})$.

3. Use long multiplication to check that:
   $(11_{two})^4 = (1\,001_{two})^2 = 1\,010\,001_{two}$.

1-3 Applications of the binary system

Punch cards

Cards are sometimes used to store information
about people or things. These use a binary
system of a hole punched out (0) or a slot cut
out (1). Fig. 1.3 shows a card for a student, Ita
Akpan. In a survey, it is found that Isa plays
volleyball and hockey but *not* football or
tennis.

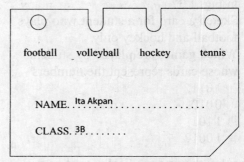

football   volleyball   hockey   tennis

NAME. Ita Akpan . . . .

CLASS. 3B . . . .

Fig. 1.3

If 1 represents a game played and 0 a game *not* played, each possible combination of games can be represented by a binary number. The number for the games played by Ita is 0110.

To find those who play football, the cards for the class are stacked together, perhaps in a box as in Fig. 1.4.

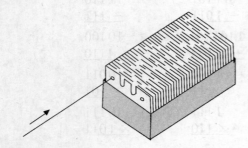

Fig. 1.4

A thin rod, e.g. a knitting needle or a straight piece of wire, is put through the first hole, representing football. The rod is lifted up. It will hold all the cards of those who do *not* play football. The cards for those who play football will be left in the box.

If those who play football *and* volleyball are required, the rod is passed through the second hole of the football players' cards (i.e. those left in the box). The cards of the footballers who do not play volleyball will be lifted up, leaving the cards of those who play both football and volleyball in the box.

Exercise 1f

1. Look at Fig. 1.3.
   a Why has the corner been cut off the card in Fig. 1.3?
   b Sketch a card for a student who plays football and hockey only.
   c Which games are played by students whose cards represent the numbers
      i 1011,
      ii 0010,
      iii 1101,
      iv 1001?

2. Fig. 1.5 shows a medical record card.
   a What binary number represents Mary Olode's medical record?

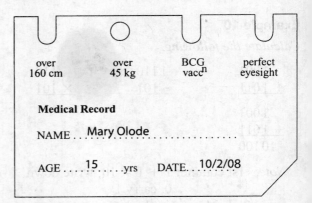

over 160 cm   over 45 kg   BCG vacc^n perfect eyesight

Medical Record

NAME . . . Mary Olode . . . .

AGE . . . . 15 . . . . . yrs   DATE . . . 10/2/08

Fig. 1.5

   b Sketch a card for someone who is 158 cm tall, 48 kg in mass, has had a BCG vaccination and wears glasses.
   c A wire is pushed through the 'over 160 cm' hole in a box of medical record cards. Which of the following cards will be lifted out? A(1010), B(0001), C(0101), D(1101), E(1000), F(0011).

3. a Make a blank medical record card like that of Fig. 1.5. (The teacher may give you one.)
   b Complete your own medical record on the card by cutting slots where necessary. (Use a sharp knife or scissors to cut the slot.)
   c Give your card to the teacher. The teacher will show the class how punch cards are used.

4. a Sketch a punch card which could be used in Biology to record the following information about living things:
      i able to fly, ii has feathers, iii has fur, iv has four legs.
   b With the order given in part a, what binary number would represent
      i a vulture, ii a cockroach, iii a dog, iv a fish, v a lizard?

5. You will need a sheet of paper, a paper punch and a pair of scissors for this question.
   a Cut up a sheet of paper to make a set of punch cards like those in Fig. 1.6. Notice that the numbers on the cards correspond to the binary numbers punched on them.
   b Mix the cards and stack them together in

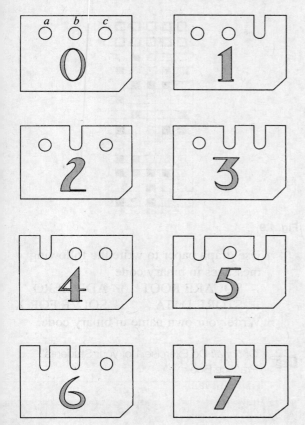

Fig. 1.6

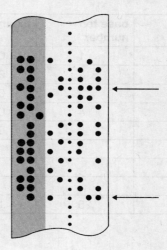

Fig. 1.7

any order so that they all face the same way.

c Push the point of a pair of compasses through the holes and slots in position *a* and lift carefully. Place the cards which are lifted at the front of the stack.

d Now push the point of your compasses through the holes and slots in position *b* and lift carefully. Again place the cards which are lifted at the front of the stack.

e Repeat for the holes and slots in position *c*.

f Look at the order of the cards when you have finished. What has happened?

Punch tape

There are many ways in which computers receive instructions. Punch cards were sometimes used in the past. Sometimes cards are used on which pencil marks are made, e.g. those used by the

West African Examinations Council in exams. Another way is to use a paper tape which has been punched with holes. Fig. 1.7 shows part of a **punch tape**.

The punch tape has eight columns. Each column may contain a hole (1) or may be left unpunched (0). The first three columns on the left contain special instructions for the computer; they have been shaded in Fig. 1.7. The other five columns contain the computer **program**. The small holes are to guide the tape through the computer; they are not part of the program.

Each row of holes represents a binary number. In Fig. 1.7 the arrowed rows represent the numbers 1111_{two} and 10011_{two}.

Exercise 1g

① The code for the computer program shown in Fig. 1.7 is given by numbers standing for letters: A = 1, B = 2, C = 3, etc. However, the numbers are converted to binary numbers.

Make a table like Table 1.2 and include all the letters of the alphabet.

letter	base ten number	binary number
A	1	00001
B	2	00010
C	3	00011
D	4	00100
E	5	00101
.	.	.
.	.	.
.	.	.
Z	26	11010

Table 1.2

② Fig. 1.7 is part of a computer program for finding prime numbers. Use the table you made in question 1 to find out what the tape says.

③ Fig. 1.8 shows four messages written in computer code (the three left-hand columns have not been included).

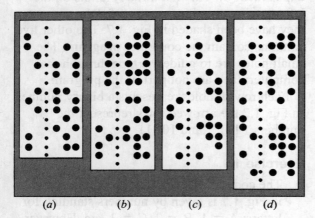

(a)   (b)   (c)   (d)

Fig. 1.8

Use the table you made in question 1 to find out what each message says.

④ Fig. 1.9 shows how a strip of graph paper may be used as a punch tape. The first two rows show how to space the 'holes'.
Find out what the message is in Fig. 1.9.

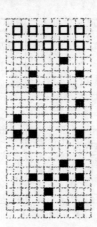

Fig. 1.9

⑤ a Use graph paper to write the following messages in binary code.
   i SQUARE ROOT   ii ADD ZERO
  iii STORE DATA   iv SOLVE FOR X
  b Write your own name in binary code.

 Optional: Do Exercise 1 of your Students' Practice Book.

SUMMARY

1 Most people count in tens, using the digits 1, 2, 3, 4, 5, 6, 7, 8, 9 and 0 (zero). This is called the *base ten* system.

2 It is possible to represent numbers using other systems, e.g. *base two, base five, base eight* and so on. Base two is called the *binary system*; it uses only two digits: 1 and 0.

3 To convert a number from base ten to another base, use repeated division as follows:
  a divide the base ten number by the new base number;
  b continue dividing until 0 is reached, writing down any remainders each time;
  c start at the last remainder and read upwards to get the new number. See Examples 3 and 6.

4 To convert a number from another base to base ten, either expand the given number or use repeated multiplication. See Examples 4 and 5.

5 The binary system is important because of its applications to computing, including punch cards, punch tape and binary code systems.

2 Word problems

OBJECTIVES

By the end of this chapter you should be able to:

1 Use appropriate symbols for words such as *sum*, *difference*, *product*
2 Solve word problems involving whole numbers and fractions
3 Create an equation from a word problem and solve it.

> **Teaching and learning materials**
> **Teacher:** Flash cards with words and symbols

2-1 Sum and difference

The **sum** of a set of numbers is the result when the numbers are added together.

Example 1

The sum of four consecutive numbers is 58. Find the numbers.

Let the numbers be n, $n + 1$, $n + 2$, $n + 3$.

$$n + (n + 1) + (n + 2) + (n + 3) = 58$$
$$4n + 6 = 58$$

Subtract 6 from both sides.

$$4n = 58 - 6$$
$$4n = 52$$

Divide both sides by 4.

$$4n = \frac{52}{4}$$
$$n = 13$$

The numbers are 13, 14, 15, 16.

The **difference** between two numbers is the result of subtracting one from the other. It is usual to subtract the smaller number from the larger. This gives a positive difference.

Example 2

The difference between 8 and another number is 17. Find two possible values for the number.

Let the number be x.

i Assuming $x > 8$, then
$$x - 8 = 17$$
Add 8 to both sides
$$x = 17 + 8$$
$$= 25$$

ii Assuming $x < 8$, then
$$8 - x = 17$$
Add x to both sides
$$8 = 17 + x$$
Subtract 17 from both sides
$$8 - 17 = x$$
$$x = -9$$

Thus, the number could be 25 or -9.

Exercise 2a

1. Find the sum of 12 and 9.
2. Find the sum of 82 and 148.
3. Find the positive difference between 19 and 8.
4. Find the sum of 23, 27 and 33.
5. Find the positive difference between 6·7 and 9·8.
6. Find the sum of all the odd numbers between 10 and 20.
7. Find the positive difference between $3\frac{3}{4}$ and $2\frac{2}{3}$.
8. Find the sum of 0·8 and 1·2.
9. Find the sum of $\frac{3}{4}$ and $\frac{5}{7}$.
10. Find the sum of -2 and $-3\cdot4$.
11. Find the positive difference between -7 and -12.
12. Find the positive difference between 16 and -2.

(13) Find the sum of -14 and $+18$.

(14) Find the positive difference between $3 \cdot 8$ and $-3 \cdot 8$.

(15) The sum of a certain number and 13 is 30. What is the number?

(16) The sum of three consecutive numbers is 63. Find the numbers.

(17) The sum of four consecutive odd numbers is 80. Find the numbers.

(18) The difference between two numbers is 7. If the smaller number is 7, find the other.

(19) The difference between $12 \cdot 6$ and a number is $5 \cdot 4$. Find two possible values for the number.

(20) The difference between -3 and a number is 8. Find two possible values for the number.

2-2 Product

The **product** of two or more numbers is the result when the numbers are multiplied together.

Example 3

Find the product of -6, $0 \cdot 7$ *and* $6\frac{2}{3}$.

$$\begin{aligned} \text{product} &= -6 \times 0 \cdot 7 \times 6\frac{2}{3} \\ &= -6 \times \frac{7}{10} \times \frac{20}{3} \\ &= \frac{-6 \times 7 \times 20}{10 \times 3} \\ &= -2 \times 7 \times 2 \\ &= -28 \end{aligned}$$

Example 4

The product of two numbers is $8\frac{4}{9}$. *If one of the numbers is* $\frac{1}{4}$, *find the other*.

Let the number be x.
$$\frac{1}{4} \times x = 8\frac{4}{9}$$

Multiply both sides by 4.
$$\begin{aligned} x &= 8\frac{4}{9} \times 4 \\ &= 33\frac{7}{9} \end{aligned}$$

Exercise 2b

(1) Find the product of 8 and 6.

(2) Find the product of 2, 3 and 9.

(3) Find the product of -4 and -7.

(4) Find the product of -2, -5 and $+9$.

(5) Find the product of $0 \cdot 4$ and $0 \cdot 5$.

(6) Find the product of $0 \cdot 3$ and $0 \cdot 3$.

(7) Find the product of $3\frac{3}{8}$ and $3\frac{5}{9}$.

(8) Find the product of $0 \cdot 9$ and $3\frac{1}{3}$.

(9) Find the product of $\frac{1}{2}$ and 22.

(10) Find the product of 12, $0 \cdot 6$ and $6\frac{1}{4}$.

(11) The product of two numbers is 54. If one of the numbers is 27, find the other.

(12) The product of two numbers is -18. If one of the numbers is 6, find the other.

(13) The product of two numbers is 13. If one of the numbers is $\frac{1}{2}$, find the other.

(14) A number is multiplied by itself. The product is $5\frac{4}{9}$. Find the number.

(15) The product of three numbers is $0 \cdot 084$. If two of the numbers are $0 \cdot 7$ and $0 \cdot 2$, find the third number.

Combining products with sums and differences

Example 5

Find the positive difference between 31 *and the product of* 4 *and* 14.

$$\begin{aligned} \text{product of 4 and 14} &= 4 \times 14 \\ &= 56 \\ \text{difference between 31 and 56} &= 56 - 31 \\ &= 25 \end{aligned}$$

Notice that the problem is to find the *difference* between 31 and a product. Therefore find the product first. $(4 \times 14) - 31$ is equivalent to 'the positive difference between 31 and the product of 4 and 14'.

Example 6

Find the product of 11 *and the positive difference between* 4 *and* 10.

$$\begin{aligned} \text{positive difference between 4 and 10} &= 10 - 4 \\ &= 6 \end{aligned}$$

product of 11 and 6 = 11 × 6
= 66

Notice that the problem is to find the *product* of 11 and a difference. Therefore, find the difference first. $11 \times (10 - 4)$ is equivalent to 'the product of 11 and the positive difference between 4 and 10'.

Example 7

Find the sum of 0·9 and the product of 1·7 and 3.

sum = $0.9 + (1.7 \times 3)$
= $0.9 + 5.1$
= 6

Example 8

Find the product of $\frac{1}{7}$ and the sum of $\frac{3}{5}$ and $1\frac{1}{2}$.

product = $\frac{1}{7} \times (\frac{3}{5} + 1\frac{1}{2})$
= $\frac{1}{7} \times (\frac{3}{5} + \frac{3}{2})$
= $\frac{1}{7} \times (\frac{6}{10} + \frac{15}{10})$
= $\frac{1}{7} \times \frac{21}{10}$
= $\frac{3}{10}$

Example 9

Find the positive difference between the sum of 1·6 and 2 and the product of 7 and 0·4.

difference = $(1.6 + 2) - (7 \times 0.4)$
= $3.6 - 2.8$
= 0.8

☞ *Optional:* Do Exercise 2 of your Students' Practice Book.

Exercise 2c

In this exercise, take 'difference' to mean 'positive difference'.

① Find the difference between 63 and the product of 10 and 5.

② Find the difference between 27 and the product of 8 and 9.

③ Find the product of 5 and the difference between 15 and 7.

④ Find the product of 21 and the difference between $1\frac{1}{2}$ and $-\frac{1}{2}$.

⑤ Find the sum of 16 and the product of 2 and 7.

⑥ Find the sum of 0·14 and the product of 0·9 and 0·4.

⑦ Find the product of 6 and the sum of $2\frac{1}{2}$ and $4\frac{1}{2}$.

⑧ Find the product of 0·25 and the sum of 13 and 11.

⑨ Find the sum of the product of 9 and 5 and the product of 10 and 6.

⑩ Find the sum of the product of $\frac{3}{5}$ and $\frac{5}{9}$ and the product of $\frac{5}{9}$ and $\frac{3}{20}$.

⑪ Find the difference between the sum of 16 and 17 and the product of 8 and 4.

⑫ Find the difference between the product of 0·6 and 0·4 and the sum of 0·6 and 0·4.

⑬ Find the product of the sum of −2 and 9 and the difference between −8 and −5.

⑭ Find the product of the difference between 2 and 7 and the sum of 2 and 7.

⑮ Find the sum of 29, the product of 2 and 9 and the difference between 2 and 9.

2·3 Expressions with fractions

Example 10

Find one-quarter of the positive difference between 29 and 11.

required value = $\frac{1}{4}(29 - 11)$
= $\frac{1}{4}(18)$
= $\frac{18}{4}$
= $4\frac{1}{2}$

Example 11

Divide 40 by the sum of 3 and 5.

required value = $\frac{40}{3 + 5}$
= $\frac{40}{8}$
= 5

Example 12

Find one-ninth of the positive difference between 55 and the sum of 12 and 7.

$$\text{required value} = \frac{55 - (12 + 7)}{9}$$

$$= \frac{55 - 19}{9}$$

$$= \frac{36}{9}$$

$$= 4$$

Notice that the dividing line of a fraction acts like a bracket on the expressions above or below the line. For example,

$$\frac{40}{3 + 5} = \frac{40}{(3 + 5)}$$

Always simplify the expressions above or below the line before dividing out the fraction.

Example 13

From the product of 10 and 6, subtract 24; then divide the result by 4.

$$\text{required value} = \frac{(10 \times 6) - 24}{4}$$

$$= \frac{60 - 24}{4}$$

$$= \frac{36}{4}$$

$$= 9$$

Exercise 2d

In this exercise, take 'difference' to mean 'positive difference'.

1. Find one-ninth of the difference between 49 and 13.
2. Find one-eighth of the sum of 14, 15 and 19.
3. Find one-third of the product of 12 and 5.
4. Add 4, 9 and 22; then divide the result by 5.
5. From 38 subtract 17; then divide the result by 7.
6. Subtract 9 from 65; then find one-eighth of the result.
7. Divide 48 by the sum of 4 and 8.
8. Divide 48 by the product of 4 and 8.
9. Divide 48 by the difference between 4 and 8.
10. Find one-third of the difference between 29 and the sum of 11 and 6.
11. Find one-quarter of the difference between 17 and the square of 3.
12. Find one-seventh of the sum of 19 and the product of 4 and 11.
13. Subtract 18 from the product of 4 and 10; then divide the result by 2.
14. From 50 subtract the sum of 3 and 5; then divide the result by 6.
15. Add 6·2 to the difference between 4·1 and 1·9; then divide the result by 3.
16. To −9 add −11; divide the result by the product of −2 and 5.
17. Find one-tenth of the difference between the product of 3 and 1·4 and the sum of 0·6 and 0·4.
18. Divide 52 by the sum of 1 and the product of 2 and 6.
19. Subtract the square root of 9 from the square of 9; divide the result by 13.
20. Divide 36 by the difference between the product of 3 and 6 and the square root of 36.

2-4 From numbers to words

Example 14

Change the following numerical expressions into word statements.

a $(2 + 7) - 3$ b $5(9 - 6)$

c $\dfrac{(2 + 7) - 3}{9}$ d $\dfrac{26 + 7 \times 2}{8}$

a $(2 + 7)$ is 'the sum of 2 and 7'.
   $(2 + 7) - 3$ is 'the positive difference between the sum of 2 and 7 and the number 3'
   or 'from the sum of 2 and 7, subtract 3'.

b $5(9 - 6)$ is 'the product of 5 and $(9 - 6)$'.
   But, $(9 - 6)$ is 'the positive difference between 9 and 6'.
   $5(9 - 6)$ is 'the product of 5 and the positive difference between 9 and 6'.

c Notice that the numerator is the same as in part *a*.

$$\frac{(2 + 7) - 3}{9} = \frac{1}{9} \text{ of } \{(2 + 7) - 3\}$$

$\dfrac{(2 + 7) - 3}{9}$ is 'one-ninth of the positive difference between the sum of 2 and 7 and the number 3'.

d Similarly,

$\dfrac{26 + 7 \times 2}{8}$ is 'one-eighth of the sum of 26 and the product of 7 and 2'.

There can be many different correct answers when changing from numbers to words. For example, part *d* of Example 14 could also be 'add 26 to the product of 7 and 2 and then divide the result by 8'.

Exercise 2e

Change the following expressions into words.

1. $19 + 8$
2. $-7 + -3$
3. $-8 + 2 + 5$
4. $16 - 2$
5. $-5 - (-20)$
6. $6 - 11$
7. 3×14
8. -6×5
9. $5 \times 4 \times 9$
10. $4(2 + 7)$
11. $5(8 - 3)$
12. $(7 + 9)8$
13. $(5 + 8) - 2$
14. $20 - (3 + 9)$
15. $5 \times 4 - (8 + 11)$
16. $\dfrac{4}{9 + 2}$
17. $\dfrac{10}{6 \times 5}$
18. $\dfrac{13}{12 - 7}$
19. $\dfrac{(9 + 14) - 8}{3}$
20. $\dfrac{5 \times 11 + 9}{4}$

2-5 Problems involving equations

Example 15

The product of a certain number and 5 is equal to twice the number subtracted from 20. Find the number.

Let the number be x.

the product of x and 5 is $5x$
twice x subtracted from 20 is $20 - 2x$
thus, $5x = 20 - 2x$
Add $2x$ to both sides.
$\quad 7x = 20$
Divide both sides by 7.

$$x = \frac{20}{7} = 2\frac{6}{7}$$

The number is $2\frac{6}{7}$.

Example 16

The sum of 35 and a certain number is divided by 4. The result is equal to double the number. Find the number.

Let the number be n.

the sum of 35 and n is $35 + n$

the sum divided by 4 is $\dfrac{35 + n}{4}$

double the number is $2n$

thus, $\dfrac{35 + n}{4} = 2n$

Multiply both sides by 4.

$\quad 35 + n = 8n$

Subtract n from both sides.

$\quad 35 = 7n$

Divide both sides by 7.

$\quad 5 = n$

The number is 5.

Example 17

The sum of 9 and a certain number is one and a half times the original number. Find the number.

Let the number be z.

$$z + 9 = 1\frac{1}{2}z$$

Subtract z from both sides.

$$9 = \frac{1}{2}z$$

Multiply both sides by 2.

$$18 = z$$

The number is 18.

Example 18

The sum of two numbers is 22. The sum of $\frac{3}{4}$ of one of the numbers and $\frac{1}{5}$ of the other number is 11. Find the two numbers.

Let the numbers be t and $22 - t$.

$$\frac{3}{4}t + \frac{1}{5}(22 - t) = 11$$

20 is the LCM of 4 and 5; multiply both sides by 20:

$$20 \times \tfrac{3}{4}t + 20 \times \tfrac{1}{5}(22 - t) = 20 \times 11$$
$$15t + 4(22 - t) = 220$$
$$15t + 88 - 4t = 220$$
$$11t = 220 - 88$$
$$= 132$$
$$t = \frac{132}{11} = 12$$

The numbers are 12 and 10.

Exercise 2f

1. The sum of 8 and a certain number is equal to the product of the number and 3.
Find the number.

2. Four times a certain number is equal to the number subtracted from 40. Find the number.

3. Twice a certain number is subtracted from 9 times the number. The result is 21.
Find the number.

4. 13 is subtracted from the product of 4 and a certain number. The result is equal to the sum of 5 and the original number.
Find the number.

5. When 8 is added to a certain number and the sum is multiplied by 3, the result is 57.
Find the number.

6. I add 7 to a certain number. I double the result. My final answer is 34.
What was my number?

7. I subtract 14 from a certain number. I multiply the result by 3. The final answer is 3.
What was the number?

8. From a certain number 3 is subtracted. The result is divided by 2. The final answer is 5.
What is the number?

9. When I add 45 to a certain number and divide the sum by 2, the result is the same as 5 times the number. What is the number?

10. The sum of two numbers is 21. Five times the first number added to 2 times the second number is 66. Find the two numbers.

11. 2 is added to twice a certain number and the sum is doubled. The result is 10 less than 5 times the original number.
Find the original number.

12. The sum of two numbers is 38. When 8 is added to twice one of the numbers, the result is 5 times the other number.
Find the two numbers.

13. 14 is added to $\tfrac{2}{3}$ of a number. The result is $1\tfrac{1}{4}$ times the original number. Find the number.

14. $\tfrac{1}{3}$ of a number is added to 5. The result is one and a half times the original number.
Find the number.

15. The sum of two numbers is 21. $\tfrac{3}{4}$ of one of the numbers added to $\tfrac{2}{3}$ of the other gives a sum of 15. Find the two numbers.

16. The sum of two numbers is 31. $\tfrac{2}{3}$ of one of the numbers is equal to $\tfrac{5}{8}$ of the other.
Find the two numbers.

17. I add 12 to a number and then double their sum. The result is one and a half times what I get when I double the original number and add 12. Find the number.

18. Find the number such that when $\tfrac{3}{4}$ of it is added to $3\tfrac{1}{2}$, the sum is the same as when $\tfrac{2}{3}$ of it is subtracted from $6\tfrac{1}{2}$.

19. $\tfrac{1}{4}$ of a certain number is added to $4\tfrac{1}{3}$. The sum is the same as when $\tfrac{1}{3}$ of it is subtracted from $20\tfrac{2}{3}$. Find the number.

20. $\tfrac{5}{12}$ of a number is subtracted from $\tfrac{3}{4}$ of the number. Their positive difference is 7 less than $\tfrac{5}{6}$ of the number. Find the number.

SUMMARY

The following words have mathematical meanings.

word	meaning
sum	the result of addition
difference	the result of subtraction
positive difference	larger number minus smaller number
product	the result of multiplication

Factorisation: Common factors

OBJECTIVES

By the end of this chapter you should be able to:

1 Remove brackets from algebraic expressions
2 Factorise algebraic expressions by taking common factors
3 Use factorisation to simplify calculations
4 Use grouping to factorise expressions with four terms.

Teaching and learning materials

Teacher: Factorisation charts (similar to those in QR Box 1 on page 30); Dienes blocks (if available)

3-1 Removing brackets (revision)

The expression $3(2x - y)$ means three times $(2x - y)$.

Example 1

Remove brackets from:
a $3(2x - y)$,
b $(3a + 8b)5a$,
c $-2n(7y - 4z)$.

a $3(2x - y) = 3 \times 2x - 3 \times y$
$\qquad\qquad\quad = 6x - 3y$
b $(3a + 8b)5a = 3a \times 5a + 8b \times 5a$
$\qquad\qquad\qquad = 15a^2 + 40ab$
c $-2n(7y - 4z) = (-2n) \times 7y - (-2n) \times 4z$
$\qquad\qquad\qquad\quad = -14ny - (-8nz)$
$\qquad\qquad\qquad\quad = -14ny + 8nz$
$\qquad\qquad\qquad\quad = 8nz - 14ny$

Exercise 3a [Oral revision]
Remove brackets from the following:
1 $2(x + y)$
2 $5(7 - a)$

3 $(n + 9)3$
4 $8(2a - b)$
5 $5(-x - 3y)$
6 $(-3p + q)4$
7 $-2(m + n)$
8 $-3(a - b)$
9 $(p + q)(-4)$
10 $-7(3d - 2)$
11 $-9(-2k - 3r)$
12 $(-7s + t)(+6)$
13 $x(x + 2)$
14 $y(y - 1)$
15 $(a + b)a$
16 $n(3n - 2)$
17 $p(2s + 3t)$
18 $(5 - 3n)m$
19 $2a(5a - 8b)$
20 $3x(x + 9)$
21 $5p(9r - 8s)$
22 $-6a(2a - 7b)$
23 $(3a - 4b)3b$
24 $2\pi r(r + h)$

If you had difficulty with Exercise 3a, revise Chapter 7 in Book 2.

3-2 Common factors

Example 2
Find the HCF of $6xy$ and $18x^2$.

$6xy = 6 \times x \times y$
$18x^2 = 3 \times 6 \times x \times x$
The HCF of $6xy$ and $18x^2$ is $6 \times x = 6x$

Exercise 3b [Oral revision]
Find the HCF of the following:
1 $5a$ and $5z$
2 $6x$ and $15y$
3 $7mnp$ and mp
4 $5xy$ and $15x$
5 $12a$ and $8a^2$
6 $13ab$ and $26b$
7 ab^2 and a^2b
8 $6d^2e$ and $3de^2$
9 $8pq$ and $24p^2$
10 $10ax^2$ and $14a^2x$
11 $9xy$ and $24pq$
12 $30ad$ and $28ax$

Common factors of binomial expressions

A **binomial expression** has two terms. To **factorise** an expression is to write it as a product of its factors.

Example 3

Factorise the following binomial expressions.

a $9a - 3z$
b $5x^2 + 15x$
c $2mh - 8m^2h$

a The HCF of $9a$ and $3z$ is 3.
$$9a - 3z = 3\left(\frac{9a}{3} - \frac{3z}{3}\right)$$
$$= 3(3a - z)$$

b The HCF of $5x^2$ and $15x$ is $5x$.
$$5x^2 + 15x = 5x\left(\frac{5x^2}{5x} + \frac{15x}{5x}\right)$$
$$= 5x(x + 3)$$

c The HCF of $2mh$ and $8m^2h$ is $2mh$.
$$2mh - 8m^2h = 2mh\left(\frac{2mh}{2mh} - \frac{8m^2h}{2mh}\right)$$
$$= 2mh(1 - 4m)$$

Examples 2 and 3 show that factorisation is the opposite of removing brackets. *Note*: It is not necessary to write the first line of working as shown; this has been included to show the method.

Exercise 3c   [Oral revision]

Factorise the following. Questions 1–10 correspond to questions 1–10 in Exercise 3b.

1. $5a + 5z$
2. $6x - 15y$
3. $7mnp - mp$
4. $5xy + 15x$
5. $12a + 8a^2$
6. $13ab - 26b$
7. $ab^2 - a^2b$
8. $6d^2e - 3de^2$
9. $8pq + 24p^2$
10. $10ax^2 + 14a^2x$
11. $5am - 20bm$
12. $5a^3 - 3a^2b$
13. $\pi r^2 + \pi rs$
14. $7d^2 - d$
15. $33bd - 3de$
16. $9pq + 12t$
17. $ab - 2b$
18. $3dh + 15dk$
19. $x^2 + 9xy$
20. $2a^2 + 10a$

1

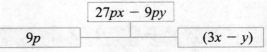

QR – Factorisation

The following '*binomial box*' shows a binomial and its two factors

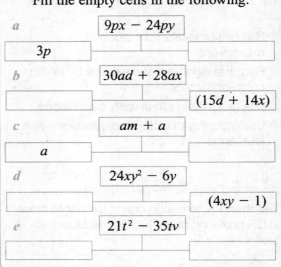

Fill the empty cells in the following:

If you had difficulty with Exercise 3b or 3c or QR Box 1, revise Chapter 11 in Book 2.

Common factors with larger expressions

Example 4

Factorise $2x(5a + 2) - 3y(5a + 2)$.

This expression is of the same kind as $2xm - 3ym$, in which m is common to both terms, so that:
$$2xm - 3ym = m(2x - 3y)$$
In the given expression,
$$2x(5a + 2) = 2x \text{ times } (5a + 2)$$
and $\quad 3y(5a + 2) = 3y$ times $(5a + 2)$
Hence the products $2x(5a + 2)$ and $3y(5a + 2)$ have the factor $(5a + 2)$ in common. Thus,
$$2x(5a + 2) - 3y(5a + 2) = (5a + 2)(2x - 3y)$$

Example 5

Factorise $2d^3 + d^2(3d - 1)$.

$2d^3$ and $d^2(3d - 1)$ have the factor d^2 in
common. Thus,

$$2d^3 + d^2(3d - 1) = d^2[2d + (3d - 1)]$$
$$= d^2[2d + 3d - 1]$$
$$= d^2(5d - 1)$$

Example 6

Factorise $(a + m)(2a - 5m) - (a + m)^2$.

The two parts of the expression have the factor
$(a + m)$ in common. Thus,

$$(a + m)(2a - 5m) - (a + m)^2$$
$$= (a + m)\{(2a - 5m) - (a + m)\}$$
$$= (a + m)\{2a - 5m - a - m\}$$
$$= (a + m)(a - 6m)$$

Example 7

Factorise $(x - 2y)(z + 3) - x + 2y$.

Notice that -1 is a factor of the last two
terms. The given expression may be written as
follows.

$$(x - 2y)(z + 3) - x + 2y$$
$$= (x - 2y)(z + 3) - 1(x - 2y)$$

The two parts of the expression now have
$(x - 2y)$ as a common factor.

$$\text{RHS} = (x - 2y)\{(z + 3) - 1\}$$
$$= (x - 2y)(z + 3 - 1)$$
$$= (x - 2y)(z + 2)$$

 Optional: Do Exercise 3 of your Students'
Practice Book.

Exercise 3d
Factorise the following.

1. $3m + m(u - v)$
2. $2a - a(3x + y)$
3. $x(3 - a) + bx$
4. $(4m - 3n)p - 5p$
5. $a(m + 1) + b(m + 1)$

6. $a(n + 2) - b(n + 2)$
7. $ax - x(b - 4c)$
8. $5x(a - b) - 2y(a - b)$
9. $3h(5u - v) + 2k(5u - v)$
10. $m(u - v) + m^2$
11. $d(3h + k) - 4d^2$
12. $5a^2 + a(b - c)$
13. $4x^2 - x(3y + 2z)$
14. $3d^3 - d^2(e - 4f)$
15. $a(3u - v) + a(u + 2v)$
16. $(5x - y)\,a - (3x + 5y)a$
17. $3(3u + 2v) - a(3u + 2v)$
18. $(4a - b)3x + (4a - b)2y$
19. $h(2a - 7b) - 3k(2a - 7b)$
20. $m(3m - 2) + 2m^2$
21. $a^2(5a - 3b) - 3a^3$
22. $5x^2 - x(x + 4)$
23. $2d(3m - 4n) - 3e(3m - 4n)$
24. $(a + 2b)(x - y) - 3(x - y)$
25. $p(2m + n) + (q - r)(2m + n)$
26. $(h + k)(r + s) + (h + k)(r - 2s)$
27. $(3x - y)(u + v) + (x + 2y)(u + v)$
28. $(b - c)(3d + e) - (b - c)(d - 2e)$
29. $(a + 2b)^2 - 3(a + 2b)$
30. $(3m - 2n)^2 + 5p(3m - 2n)$
31. $(2u - 3v)(3m - 4n) - (2u - 3v)(m + 2n)$
32. $a(x + 2y) + (x + 2y)^2$
33. $3u(2x + y) - (2x + y)^2$
34. $(f - g)4e - (f - g)^2$
35. $(a - 3b)(2u - v) + (a - 3b)(u + 7v)$
36. $(5m + 2n)(6a + b) - (5m + 2n)(a - 4b)$
37. $(x + 3y)(m - n) + x + 3y$
38. $(2a - 3b)(c + d) - 2a + 3b$
39. $7u - 2v + (7u - 2v)^2$
40. $(2u - 7v)^2 + 7v - 2u$

3-3 Simplifying calculations by factorisation

Example 8

By factorising, simplify $79 \times 37 + 21 \times 37$.

37 is a common factor of 79×37 and 21×37.
$$79 \times 37 + 21 \times 37 = 37(79 + 21)$$
$$= 37 \times 100$$
$$= 3\,700$$

Example 9

Factorise the expression $\pi r^2 + 2\pi rh$. *Hence find the value of* $\pi r^2 + 2\pi rh$ *when* $\pi = \frac{22}{7}$, $r = 14$ *and* $h = 43$.

$$\pi r^2 + 2\pi rh = \pi r(r + 2h)$$
when $\pi = \frac{22}{7}$, $r = 14$ and $h = 43$,
$$\pi r^2 + 2\pi rh = \pi r(r + 2h)$$
$$= \frac{22}{7} \times 14(14 + 2 \times 43)$$
$$= 22 \times 2(14 + 86)$$
$$= 44 \times 100$$
$$= 4\,400$$

Exercise 3e

Simplify questions 1–15 by factorising.

1. $34 \times 48 + 34 \times 52$
2. $61 \times 87 - 61 \times 85$
3. $128 \times 27 - 28 \times 27$
4. $693 \times 7 + 693 \times 3$
5. $\frac{8}{13} \times 125 + \frac{5}{13} \times 125$
6. $\frac{22}{7} \times 10 + \frac{22}{7} \times 4$
7. $121 \times 67 + 79 \times 67$
8. $67 \times 23 - 67 \times 13$
9. $\frac{22}{7} \times 3\frac{1}{4} - \frac{22}{7} \times 2\frac{1}{4}$
10. $53 \times 49 - 53 \times 39$
11. $\frac{3}{4} \times 133 - \frac{3}{4} \times 93$
12. $35 \times 29 + 35 \times 11$
13. $27 \times 354 + 27 \times 646$
14. $\frac{22}{7} \times 1\frac{1}{4} + \frac{22}{7} \times 2\frac{3}{4}$
15. $762 \times 87 - 562 \times 87$
16. Factorise the expression $\pi R^2 - \pi r^2$.
    Hence find the value of the expression
    when $\pi = \frac{22}{7}$, $R = 9$ and $r = 5$.

17. Factorise the expression $2\pi r^2 + 2\pi rh$.
    Hence find the value of the expression when
    $\pi = \frac{22}{7}$, $r = 5$, and $h = 16$.
18. Factorise the expression $\pi r^2 h + \frac{1}{3}\pi r^2 H$.
    Hence find the value of the expression when
    $\pi = \frac{22}{7}$, $r = 3$, $h = 10$ and $H = 12$.

3-4 Factorisation by grouping

Example 10

Factorise $cx + cy + 2dx + 2dy$.

The terms cx and cy have c in common.
The terms $2dx$ and $2dy$ have $2d$ in common.
Grouping in pairs in this way,
$$cx + cy + 2dx + 2dy = (cx + cy) + (2dx + 2dy)$$
$$= c(x + y) + 2d(x + y)$$

The two products now have $(x + y)$ in
common.
$$c(x + y) + 2d(x + y) = (x + y)(c + 2d)$$
Hence $cx + cy + 2dx + 2dy = (x + y)(c + 2d)$

Example 11

Factorise $3a - 6b + ax - 2bx$.

$$3a - 6b + ax - 2bx = 3(a - 2b) + x(a - 2b)$$
$$= (a - 2b)(3 + x)$$

Notice in Examples 10 and 11, the same bracket
must occur twice in the first line of the working.
If the given expression is to be factorised, there
must be a repeated bracket. For this reason, it
is often easiest to write this bracket down again
immediately, as soon as it has been found. See
Example 12.

Example 12

Factorise $2x^2 - 3x + 2x - 3$.

$$2x^2 - 3x + 2x - 3 = x(2x - 3) \ldots (2x - 3)$$

The terms $+2x - 3$ in the given expression are
obtained by multiplying $(2x - 3)$ by $+1$. Thus,

$$2x^2 - 3x + 2x - 3 = x(2x - 3) + 1(2x - 3)$$
$$= (2x - 3)(x + 1)$$

Optional: Do Exercise 4 of your Students' Practice Book.

Exercise 3f
Factorise the following by grouping in pairs.

1. $ax + ay + 3bx + 3by$
2. $7a + 14b + ax + 2bx$
3. $x^2 + 5x + 2x + 10$
4. $pq + qr + ps + rs$
5. $a^2 - 9a + 3a - 27$
6. $8m - 2 + 4mn - n$
7. $5x^2 - 10x + 3x - 6$
8. $ab - bc + ad - cd$
9. $2ab - 5a + 2b - 5$
10. $3m - 1 + 6m^2 - 2m$

In many cases it is only possible to get a repeated second bracket if a negative common factor is taken. See Example 13.

Example 13
Factorise $2am - 2m^2 - 3ab + 3bm$.

$$2am - 2m^2 - 3ab + 3bm$$
$$= 2m(a - m) \dots (a - m)$$

The terms $-3ab$ and $+3bm$ in the given expression are obtained by multiplying $(a - m)$ by $-3b$. Hence,

$$2am - 2m^2 - 3ab + 3bm$$
$$= 2m(a - m) - 3b(a - m)$$
$$= (a - m)(2m - 3b)$$

 Optional: Do Exercise 5 of your Students' Practice Book.

Exercise 3g
Factorise the following.

1. $ab + bc - am - cm$
2. $9x + 6 - 3x^2 - 2x$
3. $2ax - 2ay - 3bx + 3by$
4. $x^2 - 7x - 2x + 14$

5. $5a - 5b - ac + bc$
6. $3pq + 12pr - qy - 4ry$
7. $a^2 - 3a - 3a + 9$
8. $2ps + 5pt - 2rs - 5rt$
9. $x^2 - 6x - x + 6$
10. $3k + 1 - 3hk - h$

Sometimes the first attempt at grouping the terms does not give a common factor. In these cases, regroup the terms and try again. See Example 14.

Example 14
Factorise $cd - de + d^2 - ce$.

$$cd - de + d^2 - ce = d(c - e) \dots (\ )$$

d^2 and ce have no common factors. Regroup the given terms.

Either

$$cd - de + d^2 - ce = cd + d^2 - ce - de$$
$$= d(c + d) - e(c + d)$$
$$= (c + d)(d - e)$$

or

$$cd - de + d^2 - ce = cd - ce + d^2 - de$$
$$= c(d - e) + d(d - e)$$
$$= (d - e)(c + d)$$

Four terms can be grouped in pairs in three ways. If the expression factorises, two of these ways will give the required result and one will not.

 Optional: Do Exercise 6 of your Students' Practice Book.

Exercise 3h
Regroup then factorise the following.

1. $6a + bm + 6b + am$
2. $pr + qs + qr + ps$
3. $15 - xy + 5y - 3x$
4. $ac - bd - bc + ad$
5. $ax - xy + x^2 - ay$

⑥ $ad - cm - am + cd$

⑦ $x^2 + 15 - 3x - 5x$

⑧ $8a + 15by + 12y + 10ab$

⑨ $3a - cb - 3b + ac$

⑩ $t + 6sz + 3s + 2tz$

If *all* the terms contain a common factor, it should be taken out *first* as in Example 15. *This should always be the rule when factorising any type of expression.*

Example 15

Factorise $2sru + 6tru - 4srv - 12trv$.

$2r$ is a factor of every term in the given expression.

$$2sru + 6tru - 4srv - 12trv$$
$$= 2r\{su + 3tu - 2sv - 6tv\}$$
$$= 2r\{u(s + 3t) - 2v(s + 3t)\}$$
$$= 2r(s + 3t)(u - 2v)$$

 Optional: Do Exercise 7 of your Students' Practice Book.

Exercise 3i

Factorise the following where possible. If there are no factors, say so.

① $mx + nx + my + ny$

② $ax - ay + bx - by$

③ $hu + hv - ku - kv$

④ $au - bu - av + bv$

⑤ $am + 2bm + 2bn + an$

⑥ $cx - dx + 2cy - 2dy$

⑦ $2ce + 4df - de - 2cf$

⑧ $ab + 4xy - 2bx - 2ay$

⑨ $am - an + m - n$

⑩ $u + v - dv + du$

⑪ $a^3 + a^2 + a + 1$

⑫ $2mh - 3nh - 3nk + 2mk$

⑬ $3sx - 5ty + 5tx - 3sy$

⑭ $abx^2 + bxy + axy + y^2$

⑮ $hk - 2km + 3hn - 6mn$

⑯ $mn - 6xy - 3nx + 3my$

⑰ $2gk - 3gl + 2hk - 3hl$

⑱ $2fh + 4gh - fk - 2gk$

⑲ $3eg - 4eh - 6fg + 2fh$

⑳ $hl + 2kl - 3hm - 6km$

㉑ $3ce + 4df - 2de - 6cf$

㉒ $xy - 2ny - 6n^2 + 3nx$

㉓ $ab + 2b^2 - 2ac - 4bc$

㉔ $cd - ce + d^2 + de$

㉕ $8uv - 2v^2 + 12uw - 3vw$

㉖ $mn - 6pn + 3pm - 2n^2$

㉗ $3xy - 2ay - 3ax + 2y^2$

㉘ $3ab - 3bu + 3av - 3uv$

㉙ $ab + 6mn - 2bm - 3bn$

㉚ $8ce + 12de - 2cf - 3df$

㉛ $nuv - muv + mnu^2 - v^2$

㉜ $5mx - 5nx - 5my + 5ny$

㉝ $3ab + 3cd - bc - 9ad$

㉞ $6ab - 15bc - 10cd + 4ad$

㉟ $2amu + 2anu - 2amv - 2anv$

㊱ $abm^2 + 2bm - 3am - 6$

㊲ $4ax + 2bx + 8ay + 4by$

㊳ $21mn - xy - 3nx + 7my$

㊴ $3ax - 2a - 6bx + 2b$

㊵ $2am - 3m^2 + 4an - 6mn$

㊶ $10uv + 5u - 2v - 1$

㊷ $a^2m + am^2 - mn - an$

㊸ $2x^2y - xy^2 + 2ax - ay$

㊹ $1 + 3x - 5a - 15ax$

㊺ $2d^2x + 4dx^2y - 3dy - 6xy^2$

34

1 To *factorise* an expression is to write it as a product of its factors.

2 Algebraic factors may be numerical or a combination of numbers and letters.

 For example, 1, 2, 3, 6, *a*, 2*a*, 3*a*, 6*a*, *x*, 2*x*, 3*x*, 6*x*, *ax*, 2*ax*, 3*ax*, 6*ax* are all factors of 6*ax*.

3 In algebra, *factorisation* is the opposite of removing brackets.

4 If the terms in an algebraic expression have a *common factor*, the expression can be written as a product that includes the common factor. For example,

 $$ax + bx = x(a + b)$$

 where x and $(a + b)$ are the factors of $ax + bx$, x being the common factor of the two terms.

5 Factorisation can be used to simplify calculations. See Examples 8 and 9.

6 Larger algebraic expressions can sometimes be factorised by grouping. See Examples 10 to 15.

PUZZLE CORNER

The Inheritance

A farmer gives the above plot to his four children provided they can divide it so that:
a) all pieces are equal in area,
b) each shape is similar to the original.
How can they divide the plot?

PUZZLE CORNER

17's round a Hexagon

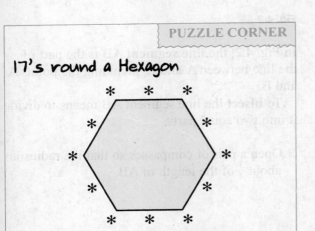

Replace the stars by the numbers 1 to 12 so that there are three numbers totalling 17 along each side of the hexagon.

PUZZLE CORNER

Crossing the River

Two teachers weigh 60 kg each.
Two students weigh 30 kg each.
They all wish to cross a river in a boat that can only carry 60 kg.
Describe how they can manage it.
[Assume they can all paddle.]

Geometrical constructions

Teaching and learning materials

Teacher: Chalk board instruments (especially ruler and compasses); plain paper; old newspapers (for Exercises 4a and 4b)

Student: Mathematical set (especially ruler, compasses, sharp pencil)

Using ruler and compasses

Remember the following when making geometrical constructions.

1 Use a hard pencil with a sharp point. This gives thin lines which are more accurate.
2 Check that your ruler has a good straight edge. A damaged ruler is useless for construction work.
3 Check that your compasses are not too loose. Tighten loose compasses with a small screwdriver.
4 All construction lines must be seen. Do not rub out anything which leads to the final result.
5 Always take great care, especially when drawing a line through a point.
6 Where possible, arrange that the angles of intersection between lines and arcs are about 90°.

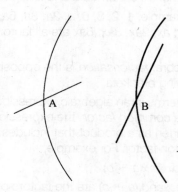

Fig. 4.1

In Fig. 4.1 there is a clear point of intersection at A. At B there is a large 'area of intersection'; this is because the lines are too thick and the angle between them is too small.

4-1 To bisect a straight line segment

Fig. 4.2

In Fig. 4.2, the **line segment** AB is the part of the line between A and B, including the points A and B.

To **bisect** the line segment AB means to divide it into two equal parts.

a Open a pair of compasses so that the radius is about $\frac{3}{4}$ of the length of AB.

b Place the sharp point of the compasses on A. Draw two arcs, one above, the other below the middle of AB, as in Fig. 4.3.

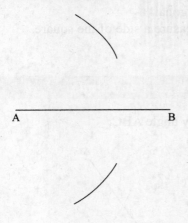

Fig. 4.3

c *Keep the same radius* and place the sharp point of the compasses on B. Draw two arcs so that they cut the first arcs at P and Q as in Fig. 4.4.

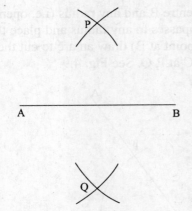

Fig. 4.4

d Draw a straight line through P and Q so that it cuts AB at M.

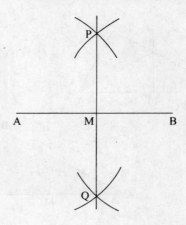

Fig. 4.5

M is the mid-point of AB. PQ meets AB perpendicularly. PQ is the **perpendicular bisector** of AB. Use a ruler and protractor to check that AM = MB and $\hat{AMP} = \hat{BMP} = 90°$ in Fig. 4.5.

 Optional: Do Exercise 8 of your Students' Practice Book.

Exercise 4a

Use ruler and compasses **only** in this exercise.

1. Draw any line segment AB. Use the above method to find the mid-point of AB. Check by measurement that your answer is correct.

2. Fig. 4.6 represents a paper triangle, ABC.

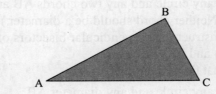

Fig. 4.6

△ABC is folded so that A meets C. This gives a fold line PM as shown in Fig. 4.7.

37

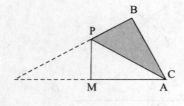

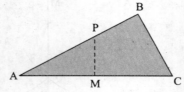

Fig. 4.7

a What can be said about the point M?
b What can be said about line PM?

3 a Use a sheet of newspaper to make a large
   paper triangle, ABC (as in Fig. 4.6).
   △ABC should be scalene and acute angled.
b Fold △ABC so that A meets C.
c Open out △ABC, then make a second fold
   so that B meets C.
d In the same way, make a third fold so that
   A meets B.
e What do you notice about the three folds?
f What can be said about each fold?

4 Draw any triangle ABC.
a Construct the perpendicular bisector of
   each side.
b What do you notice?

5 Draw any circle and any two chords AB and
   XY. (Neither chord should be a diameter.)
a Construct the perpendicular bisectors of
   AB and XY.
b What do you notice?

6 Draw any circle and any diameter AB.
a Construct the perpendicular bisector of
   AB and extend it if necessary to cut the
   circumference at P and Q.
b What kind of chord is PQ?
c Join AP, PB, BQ, QA. What kind of
   quadrilateral is APBQ?

7 Draw any triangle ABC.
a Construct the mid-point, M, of AB.
b Construct the mid-point, N, of BC.
c Measure MN and AC.

d What do you notice?
8 a Draw a line 10 cm long.
  b Construct a square with this line as
    diagonal.
  c Measure a side of the square.

4-2 To bisect any angle

Given any angle ABC:

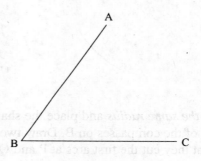

Fig. 4.8

a With centre B and any radius (i.e. open a pair
of compasses to any radius and place the
sharp point at B) draw an arc to cut the arms
BA, BC at P, Q. See Fig. 4.9.

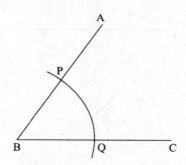

Fig. 4.9

b With centres P, Q and equal radii, draw arcs to cut each other at R. See Fig. 4.10.

c Join BR (Fig. 4.11).

BR bisects AB̂C. BR is the **bisector** of AB̂C. Use a protractor to check that AB̂R = CB̂R in Fig. 4.11.

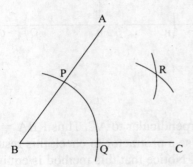

Fig. 4.10

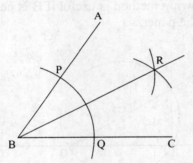

Fig. 4.11

☞ *Optional:* Do Exercise 9 of your Students' Practice Book.

Exercise 4b

Use ruler and compasses **only** in this exercise.

① Draw any angle ABC. Use the above method to construct the bisector of AB̂C. Use a protractor to check your result.

② A paper triangle like that of Fig. 4.6 is folded so that AB lies along AC. This gives a fold line AR as shown in Fig. 4.12.

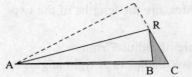

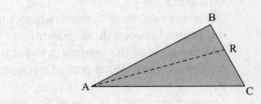

Fig. 4.12

a What can be said about angles BAR and CAR?

b What is the correct name for the line AR?

③ a Use newspaper to make a large paper triangle, ABC, like that of Fig. 4.6.

b Fold △ABC so that AB lies along AC.

c Open out △ABC, then make a second fold so that BC lies along BA.

d In the same way, make a third fold so that CB lies along CA.

e What do you notice about the three folds?

④ a Draw a scalene triangle PQR such that Q is obtuse.

b Construct the bisectors of P̂, Q̂ and R̂.

c If necessary, extend each bisector so that it cuts the other two.

d What do you notice about the three bisectors?

⑤ a Construct an isosceles triangle XYZ such that XY = YZ = 8 cm.

b Construct the bisector of Ŷ.

c Construct the perpendicular bisector of side XZ.

d What do you notice?

⑥ a Draw any obtuse angle ABC.

b RB is the bisector of AB̂C. Construct RB.

c SB is the bisector of RB̂C. Construct SB.

d TB is the bisector of SB̂C. Construct TB.

e What fraction of AB̂C is TB̂C?

⑦ a Draw a triangle with sides 6, 8, 10 cm.

b Bisect the smallest angle.

c The bisector cuts the opposite side into

two parts. Measure the lengths of the two parts.

8 a Draw a circle of radius 75 mm.
   b Construct two diameters at right angles to each other.
   c Construct two more diameters bisecting the angles between those drawn first.
   d Join the ends of the diameters to form a regular polygon. What sort of polygon is it?
   e Measure the length of one of the sides of the polygon.

4-3 To construct angles of 90° and 45°

90°

Given a point B on a straight line AC:

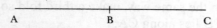

Fig. 4.13

It is required to construct a line BR through B such that $R\hat{B}A = R\hat{B}C = 90°$.

a With centre B and any radius draw arcs to cut AC at P and Q. See Fig. 4.14.

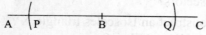

Fig. 4.14

b With centres P, Q and equal radii, draw arcs to cut each other at R, as in Fig. 4.15.

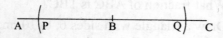

Fig. 4.15

c Join BR.

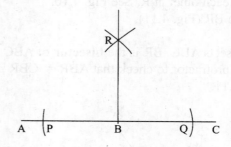

Fig. 4.16

BR is perpendicular to AC. Thus $R\hat{B}A = R\hat{B}C = 90°$. Use a protractor to check this result in Fig. 4.16. Notice that this method is equivalent to bisecting an angle of 180°.

The following method is useful if B is near the edge of the paper.

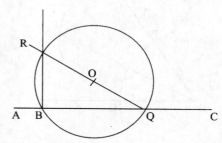

Fig. 4.17

In Fig. 4.17,
a Draw any circle to pass through B and cut AC at Q. Mark the centre of the circle, O.
b Join QO. Extend QO to cut the circle again at R.
c Join BR. $R\hat{B}C = 90°$.
   Use a protractor to check that $R\hat{B}C = 90°$ in Fig. 4.17.

45°

$45° = \frac{1}{2}$ of 90°. To construct an angle of 45°, first construct an angle of 90° and then bisect it. This is shown in Fig. 4.18.

40

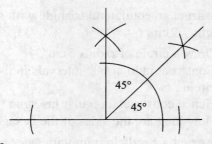

Fig. 4.18

Use a protractor to check the data in Fig. 4.18.

 Optional: Do Exercise 10 of your Students' Practice Book.

Exercise 4c

Use ruler and compass **only** in this exercise.

① Construct angles of 90° and 45°.

② Construct an angle of 135°.

③ a Construct a square with sides each 83 mm long.
  b Measure the length of a diagonal.

④ a Construct a rectangle measuring 7·4 cm by 10·3 cm.
  b Measure the length of a diagonal.

⑤ a Construct △PQR such that $\hat{Q} = 90°$, PQ = 5 cm and QR = 6 cm.
  b Measure the length of its hypotenuse PR.

⑥ a Draw any circle and any chord AB. (AB should *not* be a diameter.)
  b Construct another chord BC such that $\hat{ABC} = 90°$.
  c Join AC. What do you notice about the line AC?

⑦ a Construct △XYZ such that $\hat{X} = \hat{Z} = 45°$ and XZ = 8 cm.
  b Measure either of the sides XY or YZ.

⑧ a Construct an isosceles triangle with the equal sides 9 cm long and the angle between them 45°.
  b Measure the third side.

⑨ **(Discussion)**

Explain how you could use a sheet of paper to check the accuracy of the 45°, 90° and 135° angles you have constructed in this exercise.

4-4 To construct angles of 60° and 30°

60°

Given a straight line BC:

Fig. 4.19

To construct a point A such that $\hat{ABC} = 60°$:

a With centre B and any radius, draw an arc to cut BC at X. Notice in Fig. 4.20 that the arc is extended well above BC.

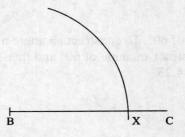

Fig. 4.20

b With centre X and the *same* radius as in a, draw an arc to cut the first arc at A.

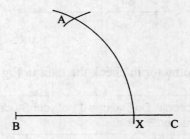

Fig. 4.21

c Join AB.

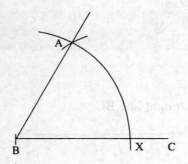

Fig. 4.22

AB̂C = 60°. Use a protractor to check that
AB̂C = 60° in Fig. 4.22. Notice that the
points A, B and X form an equilateral triangle.
Compare Fig. 4.22 with Fig. 11.11 in Book 1.

30°

30° = ½ of 60°. To construct an angle of 30°,
first construct an angle of 60° and then bisect it.
See Fig. 4.23.

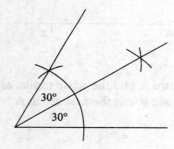

Fig. 4.23

Use a protractor to check the data in Fig. 4.23.

☞ *Optional:* Do Exercise 11 of your Students'
Practice Book.

Exercise 4d
Use ruler and compasses **only** in this exercise.

① Construct angles of 60°, 30°, 15°.
② Construct angles of 120°, 105°.

③ Construct an equilateral triangle with sides of
length 7·2 cm.

④ a Draw a circle of radius 5 cm.
   b Construct radii at 60° intervals in the
     circle.
   c Hence construct a regular hexagon.
   d How long are the sides of the hexagon?

⑤ Construct a parallelogram with sides 6 cm
   and 9 cm, the angle between these sides being
   60°. Measure the diagonals.

⑥ a Construct a rhombus with sides 6 cm such
     that one of its acute angles is 75°.
   b Measure the diagonals of the rhombus.

⑦ a Construct △LMN in which
     LM = 105 mm, M̂ = 60° and N̂ = 90°.
   b Measure LN and MN.

⑧ a Construct a kite ABCD in which
     AB = 5 cm, AD = 8 cm and Â = Ĉ = 105°.
   b Measure the diagonal AC.

4-5 To copy any angle

Given any angle ABC:

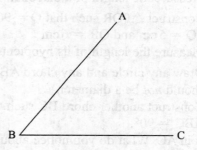

Fig. 4.24

To make a copy of AB̂C,

a Draw any line XY. Mark a point B′ on XY.
  With centre B and any radius, draw an arc to
  cut BA, BC at P, Q. Then with centre B′ and
  the *same* radius, draw an arc to cut XY at Q′.
  See Fig. 4.25 on page 44.

QR – Constructing angles

The sketches below show some angles constructed using ruler and compasses.

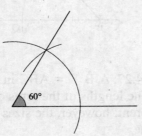

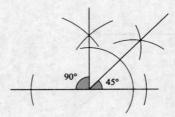

Study the following constructions and work out the sizes of each angle marked in green.

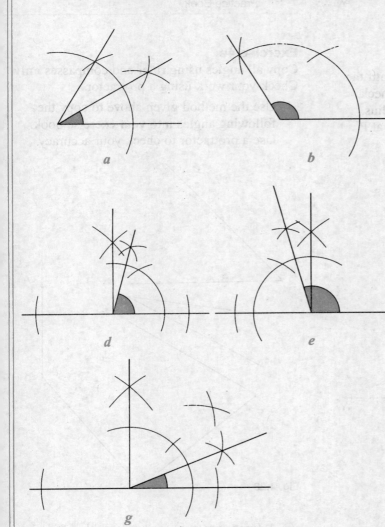

a

b

c

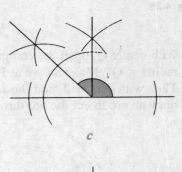

d

e

f

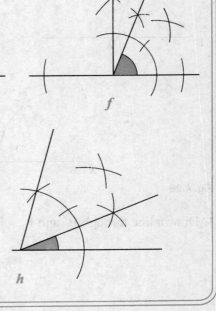

g

h

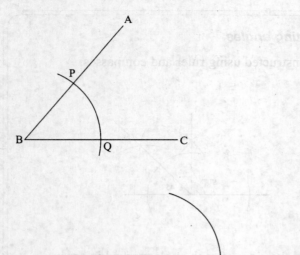

Fig. 4.25

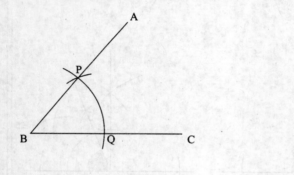

b With centre Q, open the compasses until the radius = QP. Make an arc at P as a check. Then with centre Q' and the *same* radius, draw an arc to cut the arc through Q' at P'.

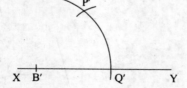

Fig. 4.26

c Draw a line through B' and P'.

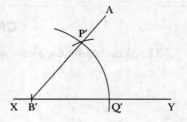

Fig. 4.27

In Fig. 4.27, A'B̂'Y = AB̂C in Fig. 4.24.
Note: The lengths of the arms of the angles may be different; however, the sizes of the angles are the same.

👉 *Optional:* Do Exercise 12 of your Students' Practice Book.

Exercise 4e

Copy all angles using ruler and compasses **only**. Check your work using a protractor.

1 Use the method given above to copy the following angles into your exercise book. Use a protractor to check your accuracy.

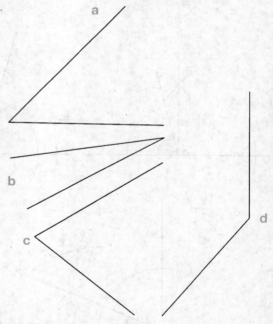

Fig. 4.28

2 a Exchange exercise books with a friend. Draw three angles of any size in your

friend's book. (Your friend will draw three angles in your book.)

b Get your own book back. Copy the three angles your friend has drawn.

c Use a protractor to check the accuracy of your work.

Example 1

Construct a parallelogram ABCD with AB = 72 mm, BC = 96 mm and $\hat{B}$ = 60°. Measure AC.

Fig. 4.29 is a scale drawing of the required construction.

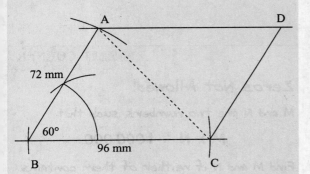

Fig. 4.29

By measurement, AC = 87 mm.

Example 2

Construct a trapezium PQRS in which PS is parallel to QR, $\hat{Q}$ = 30°, $\hat{R}$ = 45°, PQ = 80 mm and QR = 135 mm. Measure PS.

Fig. 4.30 is a scale drawing of the required construction.

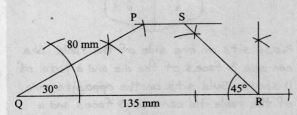

Fig. 4.30

By measurement, PS = 26 mm.

Exercise 4f   [Further practice]

In this exercise draw a rough figure first. This will give you an idea of the shape of the final drawing. All construction lines should be left in your work.

1 a Construct an isosceles △ABC so that AB = AC, BC = 75 mm and the length of the perpendicular from A to BC is 60 mm.
   b Measure AB.

2 a Construct △ABC with sides 7 cm, 8 cm, 9 cm.
   b Draw the perpendicular bisectors of all three sides. These should meet at one point O.
   c With centre O and radius OA, draw a circle.
   d What is the radius of the circle? Does the circle also pass through B and C?

3 a Draw a triangle PQR with sides 69 mm, 102 mm, 135 mm.
   b Use the method of question 2 to construct the circle passing through P, Q and R.
   c Measure the radius of the circle.

4 a Construct a triangle with sides 6 cm, 8 cm, 9 cm.
   b Use ruler and compasses to find the mid-point of each side.
   c Join each vertex to the mid-point of the opposite side.
     (These three lines are called **medians**.)
   d Do the three medians meet at a point?
   e By careful measurement, find the ratio in which this point divides the length of each median.

5 a Use the method of question 4 with a triangle of any size.
   b Do the three medians behave in the same way as before?

6 a Construct △XYZ in which XY = 8·3 cm, YZ = 11·9 cm and XŶZ = 60°.
   b Construct M, the mid-point of XZ.
   c Measure YM.

7 a Construct △ABC with AB = 68 mm, AC = 102 mm and $\hat{B}$ = 120°.
   b Construct the perpendicular bisectors of AB and BC and let them meet at O.
   c Measure OA, OB, OC.

45

8 a Construct △ABC in which AB = 9 cm,
      BC = 12 cm, AB̂C = 60°.
   b Construct the bisector of Â and let it meet
      BC at D.
   c Measure DC.

9 a Construct △ABC in which AB = 99 mm,
      BC = 114 mm, CA = 126 mm.
   b Use ruler and compasses to find the
      position of M, the mid-point of BC.
   c Through M, construct lines parallel to AC,
      AB to meet AB, AC in H, K respectively.
   d Measure HK.

10 a Construct a parallelogram ABCD with
      BD = 104 mm, DC = 48 mm and
      BD̂C = 30°.
   b Measure AC.

11 a Construct a trapezium PQRS in which PQ
      is parallel to SR, PQ = 6 cm, PS = 5 cm,
      SR = 11 cm and QS = 9 cm.
   b Measure QR.

12 a The diagonals of a parallelogram bisect
      each other. Construct a parallelogram with
      one side 10 cm long, and diagonals 15 cm
      and 10 cm long. (Draw a sketch first.)
   b Measure the length of the side that is not
      given.

SUMMARY

1 The chapter shows how to:
   • *bisect a line segment*   page 36
   • *bisect an angle*   page 38
   • *construct a 90° angle*   page 40
   • *construct a 45° angle*   page 40
   • *construct a 60° angle*   page 41
   • *construct a 30° angle*   page 42
   • *copy an angle*   page 42

2 Always make a rough freehand sketch
   before attempting to draw an accurate
   construction.

3 Make sure your construction is accurate by:
   • using a sharp pencil and a ruler with a
      good edge;
   • checking that your compasses are not
      too loose.

4 Always leave all construction lines on your
   final drawing.

PUZZLE CORNER

Zeros Not Allowed!

M and N are two numbers such that

$$M \times N = 1\,000\,000$$

Find M and N if neither of them contains
any zeros.

PUZZLE CORNER

Rose, Sule and the Die

A die rests on a table:

Rose sits on one side of the table. She
can see 3 faces of the die and a total of
11 spots. Sule sits on the opposite side
of the table. He can see 3 faces and a
total of 7 spots.

How many spots are there on the bottom
face of the die?

5 Calculation using standard form

OBJECTIVES

By the end of this chapter you should be able to:

1 Add and subtract numbers in standard form
2 Multiply and divide numbers in standard form
3 Solve mixed problems using standard form.

5-1 Standard form (revision)

$$1\,000 = 10^3$$
$$100 = 10^2$$
$$10 = 10^1$$
$$1 = 10^0$$

$$0\cdot1 = \frac{1}{10} = 10^{-1}$$

Divide both sides of the previous line by 10.

$$0\cdot01 = \frac{1}{100} = \frac{1}{10^2} = 10^{-2}$$

$$0\cdot001 = \frac{1}{1\,000} = \frac{1}{10^3} = 10^{-3}$$

The above pattern continues for higher and lower powers of 10.

$$234 = 2\cdot34 \times 100$$
$$= 2\cdot34 \times 10^2$$
$$4\,231 = 4\cdot231 \times 1\,000$$
$$= 4\cdot231 \times 10^3$$
$$0\cdot23 = 2\cdot3 \times 0\cdot1$$
$$= 2\cdot3 \times 10^{-1}$$
$$0\cdot031 = 3\cdot1 \times 0\cdot01$$
$$= 3\cdot1 \times 10^{-2}$$

A number in the form $A \times 10^n$, where A is a number between 1 and 10 and n is an integer, is said to be in **standard form**.

Example 1

Express the numbers 737 500 and 0·066 28 in standard form.

$$737\,500 = 7\cdot375 \times 100\,000$$
$$= 7\cdot375 \times 10^5$$
$$0\cdot066\,28 = 6\cdot628 \times 0\cdot01$$
$$= 6\cdot628 \times 10^{-2}$$

Example 2

Express the numbers $3\cdot06 \times 10^4$ and $4\cdot931 \times 10^{-6}$ in ordinary form.

$$3\cdot06 \times 10^4 = 3\cdot06 \times 10\,000$$
$$= 30\,600$$
$$4\cdot931 \times 10^{-6} = 4\cdot931 \times 0\cdot000\,001$$
$$= 0\cdot000\,004\,931$$

Exercise 5a [Revision]

Express the following in standard form.

1 32·4
2 0·471
3 3 472 000
4 0·000 613 1
5 4576
6 51 720
7 0·043 81
8 0·000 000 231
9 623 000 000
10 0·003 471 21

Express the following in ordinary form.

11 $3\cdot13 \times 10^2$
12 $7\cdot834 \times 10^{-1}$
13 $4\cdot29 \times 10^{-2}$
14 $9\cdot14 \times 10^5$
15 $8\cdot67 \times 10^1$
16 $5\cdot73 \times 10^{-3}$
17 $1\cdot36 \times 10^4$
18 $6\cdot474 \times 10^{-4}$
19 $2\cdot43 \times 10^{-6}$
20 $8\cdot25 \times 10^7$

If you had difficulty with Exercise 5a, revise Chapter 2 in Book 2.

Example 3

Find the sum of $6 \cdot 28 \times 10^3$ and $9 \cdot 5 \times 10^4$.
Give the sum in standard form.

Either change to ordinary form:

$$6 \cdot 28 \times 10^3 + 9 \cdot 5 \times 10^4 = 6280 + 95\,000$$
$$= 101\,280$$
$$= 1 \cdot 0128 \times 100\,000$$
$$= 1 \cdot 0128 \times 10^5$$

or factorise:

$$6 \cdot 28 \times 10^3 + 9 \cdot 5 \times 10^4 = 10^3(6 \cdot 28 + 9 \cdot 5 \times 10)$$
$$= 10^3(6 \cdot 28 + 95)$$
$$= 10^3(101 \cdot 28)$$
$$= 10^3 \times 1 \cdot 0128 \times 10^2$$
$$= 1 \cdot 0128 \times 10^5$$

Example 4

Find the value of $2 \cdot 9 \times 10^6 - 3 \cdot 8 \times 10^5$. Give the answer in standard form.

Either change to ordinary form:

$$2 \cdot 9 \times 10^6 - 3 \cdot 8 \times 10^5 = 2\,900\,000 - 380\,000$$
$$= 2\,520\,000$$
$$= 2 \cdot 52 \times 10^6$$

or factorise:

$$2 \cdot 9 \times 10^6 - 3 \cdot 8 \times 10^5 = 10^5(2 \cdot 9 \times 10 - 3 \cdot 8)$$
$$= 10^5(29 - 3 \cdot 8)$$
$$= 10^5 \times 25 \cdot 2$$
$$= 10^5 \times 2 \cdot 52 \times 10$$
$$= 2 \cdot 52 \times 10^6$$

Example 5

Express $1 \cdot 6 \times 10^{-2} - 8 \cdot 4 \times 10^{-3}$ as a single number in standard form.

Either change to ordinary form:

$$1 \cdot 6 \times 10^{-2} - 8 \cdot 4 \times 10^{-3} = 0 \cdot 016 - 0 \cdot 0084$$
$$= 0 \cdot 0076$$
$$= 7 \cdot 6 \times 10^{-3}$$

or factorise:

$$1 \cdot 6 \times 10^{-2} - 8 \cdot 4 \times 10^{-3}$$
$$= 10^{-2}(1 \cdot 6 - 8 \cdot 4 \times 10^{-1})$$
$$= 10^{-2}(1 \cdot 6 - 0 \cdot 84)$$
$$= 10^{-2} \times 0 \cdot 76$$
$$= 10^{-2} \times 7 \cdot 6 \times 10^{-1}$$
$$= 7 \cdot 6 \times 10^{-3}$$

Numbers in standard form can be added or subtracted by taking out the power of 10 which is a common factor. If necessary, check the working by changing the given numbers to ordinary form.

☞ *Optional:* Do Exercise 13 of your Students' Practice Book.

Exercise 5b

Simplify the following.
Give all answers in standard form.

1. $3 \cdot 4 \times 10^3 + 6 \cdot 2 \times 10^3$
2. $5 \cdot 7 \times 10^8 + 1 \cdot 8 \times 10^8$
3. $4 \cdot 62 \times 10^9 + 3 \cdot 75 \times 10^9$
4. $8 \cdot 7 \times 10^4 - 3 \cdot 5 \times 10^4$
5. $4 \cdot 3 \times 10^2 - 2 \cdot 8 \times 10^2$
6. $9 \cdot 37 \times 10^4 - 6 \cdot 51 \times 10^4$
7. $9 \cdot 9 \times 10^5 + 6 \cdot 8 \times 10^5$
8. $4 \cdot 1 \times 10^6 + 5 \cdot 9 \times 10^6$
9. $7 \cdot 95 \times 10^3 + 3 \cdot 06 \times 10^3$
10. $5 \cdot 8 \times 10^4 - 5 \cdot 2 \times 10^4$
11. $1 \cdot 75 \times 10^9 - 1 \cdot 25 \times 10^9$
12. $8 \cdot 49 \times 10^6 - 8 \cdot 44 \times 10^6$
13. $3 \cdot 6 \times 10^{-2} + 4 \times 10^{-2}$
14. $2 \cdot 9 \times 10^{-4} + 3 \cdot 5 \times 10^{-4}$
15. $7 \cdot 8 \times 10^{-3} - 3 \cdot 4 \times 10^{-3}$
16. $8 \cdot 65 \times 10^{-5} - 5 \cdot 76 \times 10^{-5}$
17. $1 \cdot 7 \times 10^4 + 6 \cdot 5 \times 10^3$
18. $9 \cdot 17 \times 10^5 + 7 \cdot 45 \times 10^6$
19. $6 \cdot 9 \times 10^{-2} + 5 \times 10^{-3}$
20. $8 \cdot 31 \times 10^3 - 9 \cdot 73 \times 10^2$

㉑ $6.4 \times 10^5 - 1.5 \times 10^4$

㉒ $5.9 \times 10^{-4} - 4.1 \times 10^{-5}$

㉓ $3.18 \times 10^{-2} + 9.73 \times 10^{-1}$

㉔ $1.1 \times 10^{-3} - 8.7 \times 10^{-4}$

5-3 Multiplying and dividing numbers in standard form

Use the laws of indices when simplifying powers of 10 that are multiplied or divided.

$$10^a \times 10^b = 10^{a+b}$$
$$10^a \div 10^b = 10^{a-b}$$

Example 6

Simplify $(6 \times 10^9) \times (8 \times 10^2)$.

$$\begin{aligned}
(6 \times 10^9) \times (8 \times 10^2) &= 6 \times 8 \times 10^9 \times 10^2 \\
&= 48 \times 10^{9+2} \\
&= 48 \times 10^{11} \\
&= 4.8 \times 10 \times 10^{11} \\
&= 4.8 \times 10^{12}
\end{aligned}$$

Example 7

Divide 6×10^3 *by* 8×10^{-2}.

$$\begin{aligned}
(6 \times 10^3) \div (8 \times 10^{-2}) &= \frac{6 \times 10^3}{8 \times 10^{-2}} \\
&= \frac{6}{8} \times 10^{3-(-2)} \\
&= 0.75 \times 10^5 \\
&= 7.5 \times 10^{-1} \times 10^5 \\
&= 7.5 \times 10^4
\end{aligned}$$

Example 8

Simplify $(1.4 \times 10^{-5}) \times (2.4 \times 10^6)$.

$$\begin{aligned}
(1.4 \times 10^{-5}) \times (2.4 \times 10^6) \\
&= 1.4 \times 2.4 \times 10^{-5} \times 10^6 \\
&= 3.36 \times 10^{-5+6} \\
&= 3.36 \times 10^1 \\
&= 33.6
\end{aligned}$$

Working:
```
    14
  ×24
  ‾‾‾‾
    56
    28
  ‾‾‾‾
   336
```

 Optional: Do Exercise 14 of your Students' Practice Book.

Exercise 5c

Simplify the following.
Give all answers in standard form.

① $(3 \times 10^8) \times (2 \times 10^3)$

② $(2.8 \times 10^6) \div (1.4 \times 10^2)$

③ $(2 \times 10^{-5}) \times (4 \times 10^{-2})$

④ $(6.3 \times 10^{-2}) \div (2.1 \times 10^4)$

⑤ $(5 \times 10^2) \times (8 \times 10^5)$

⑥ $(4.8 \times 10^7) \div (8 \times 10^3)$

⑦ $(7 \times 10^6) \times (4 \times 10^{-4})$

⑧ $(3.6 \times 10^2) \div (9 \times 10^{-5})$

⑨ $(9 \times 10^{-7}) \times (5 \times 10^4)$

⑩ $(4.2 \times 10^{-9}) \div (7 \times 10^5)$

⑪ $(6 \times 10^{-3}) \times (6 \times 10^{-3})$

⑫ $(5.4 \times 10^{-3}) \div (2.7 \times 10^{-7})$

⑬ $(8.7 \times 10^2) \times (5 \times 10^2)$

⑭ $(8 \times 10^3) \times (1.5 \times 10^{-3})$

⑮ $(1.6 \times 10^8) \div (6.4 \times 10^7)$

⑯ $(1.3 \times 10^{-5}) \times (1.9 \times 10^4)$

⑰ $(9.1 \times 10^{-2}) \div (1.3 \times 10^{-2})$

⑱ $(5.5 \times 10^{-6}) \times (4.2 \times 10^{-4})$

⑲ $(1.92 \times 10^{-6}) \div (1.6 \times 10^{-3})$

⑳ $(1.05 \times 10^{-7}) \div (1.68 \times 10^{-9})$

㉑ $(6.2 \times 10^{-5}) \times (8.1 \times 10^6)$

㉒ $(1.404 \times 10^3) \div (2.6 \times 10^{-2})$

㉓ $(1.12 \times 10^{-1}) \times (2.43 \times 10^5)$

㉔ $(8.51 \times 10^{-3}) \div (3.7 \times 10^{-1})$

QR – Calculation with standard form

The boxes below show two calculations with the answers in standard form.

$$\boxed{2 \times 10^3} + \boxed{4 \times 10^3} = \boxed{8} \times \boxed{10^3}$$

$$\boxed{7 \times 10^{-5}} \div \boxed{2 \times 10^{-2}} = \boxed{3.5} \times \boxed{10^{-3}}$$

The following boxes obey the same rules. Fill the gaps.

a $\boxed{3 \times 10^2} + \boxed{4.5 \times 10^2} = \boxed{} \times \boxed{10^2}$

b $\boxed{8 \times 10^{-4}} - \boxed{6 \times 10^{-4}} = \boxed{} \times \boxed{10^{-4}}$

c $\boxed{6.2 \times 10^{-6}} + \boxed{2.7 \times 10^{-6}} = \boxed{8.9} \times \boxed{}$

d $\boxed{7 \times 10^5} - \boxed{4.3 \times 10^5} = \boxed{2.7} \times \boxed{}$

e $\boxed{4 \times 10^3} \times \boxed{6 \times 10^7} = \boxed{} \times \boxed{10^{11}}$

f $\boxed{8.8 \times 10^{-3}} \div \boxed{4 \times 10^{-3}} = \boxed{} \times \boxed{10^0}$

g $\boxed{3 \times 10^{-2}} \times \boxed{5 \times 10^{-2}} = \boxed{1.5} \times \boxed{}$

h $\boxed{1.8 \times 10^4} \div \boxed{9 \times 10^9} = \boxed{2} \times \boxed{}$

5-4 Mixed problems and standard form

In science and astronomy, many measurements use very small or very large numbers. For this reason, most scientists prefer to do calculations in standard form. Scientists use standard form so often that it is sometimes called **scientific notation**.

Example 9

The density of hydrogen is $8.89 \times 10^{-5}\,\text{g/cm}^3$.

a *Find the mass of $1\,\text{m}^3$ of hydrogen.*
b *Argon is approximately 20 times as dense as hydrogen. Find the density of argon, giving the answer in standard form correct to 3 s.f.*

a
$$1\,\text{m}^3 = 10^6\,\text{cm}^3$$
$$\begin{aligned}\text{mass of }1\,\text{m}^3\text{ hydrogen} &= 8.89 \times 10^{-5} \times 10^6\,\text{g} \\ &= 8.89 \times 10^1\,\text{g} \\ &= 88.9\,\text{g}\end{aligned}$$

b density of argon
$$\begin{aligned} &= 20 \times 8.89 \times 10^{-5}\,\text{g/cm}^3 \\ &= 2 \times 10^1 \times 8.89 \times 10^{-5}\,\text{g/cm}^3 \\ &= 2 \times 8.89 \times 10^{-4}\,\text{g/cm}^3 \\ &= 17.78 \times 10^{-4}\,\text{g/cm}^3 \\ &= 1.778 \times 10^{-3}\,\text{g/cm}^3 \\ &= 1.78 \times 10^{-3}\,\text{g/cm}^3 \text{ to 3 s.f.}\end{aligned}$$

Rounding off

Remember when rounding off numbers:

round down digits 1, 2, 3, 4, and
round up digits 5, 6, 7, 8, 9.

Significant figures count from the first non-zero digit at the left of a number. Decimal places count after the decimal point. In Example 9 the answer, 1.78×10^{-3}, is correct to 3 significant figures where the 1, 7 and 8 are significant. However, also notice that:

$$1.78 \times 10^{-3} = 0.001\,78$$

Here $0.001\,78$ is correct to *both* 5 decimal places *and* 3 significant figures. See pages 3 and 52 for further revision notes on rounding off.

Example 10

The diameters of the earth and moon are $1.28 \times 10^4\,\text{km}$ and $3.5 \times 10^3\,\text{km}$ respectively. Find the ratio, diameter of earth : diameter of moon, in the form n : 1 where n is correct to 2 s.f.

$$\begin{aligned}\frac{\text{diameter of earth}}{\text{diameter of moon}} &= \frac{1.28 \times 10^4}{3.5 \times 10^3} \\ &= \frac{1.28}{3.5} \times 10 \\ &= \frac{128}{35} \\ &= \frac{3.65\ldots}{1}\end{aligned}$$

$$\text{ratio} = 3.7 : 1$$

$$\begin{array}{r} 3.65\ldots \\ 35\overline{)128.00} \\ \underline{105} \\ 23\ 0 \\ \underline{21\ 0} \\ 2\ 00 \\ \underline{1\ 75} \\ 75 \end{array}$$

Example 11

Togo has an estimated population of 5.04×10^6 *people and a land area of* $5.6 \times 10^4 \, km^2$. *Calculate the population density of Togo.*

$$\text{population density} = \text{average number of people per km}^2$$

$$= \frac{5.04 \times 10^6}{5.6 \times 10^4}$$

$$= \frac{5.04}{5.6} \times 10^2$$

$$= \frac{5\,040}{56}$$

$$= 90 \text{ (people/km}^2)$$

Exercise 5d

Give all answers in standard form unless told otherwise.

1. An atom of *caesium 133* vibrates 9 192 631 770 times per second. Give this number in standard form correct to 2 s.f.

2. The area of Nigeria is 923 770 km². Express this area in standard form correct to 3 s.f.

3. 1 hectare (ha) = $10^4 \, m^2$.
   a Find the number of ha in 1 km².
   b Use the data of question 2 to find the area of Nigeria in hectares in standard form correct to 3 s.f.

4. In a State budget, the following allocations were made:
   Posts and Telecommunications ₦294 260 000
   Education   ₦301 400 000
   Health   ₦49 573 000
   a Find the sum of the three amounts.
   b Express the sum in standard form correct to 3 s.f.

5. The populations of two cities are 5.77×10^6 and 3.66×10^6. Find the difference between the two populations.

6. The distance of the moon from the earth varies between $3.843 \times 10^5 \, km$ and $3.563 \times 10^5 \, km$. Find the difference between these two distances.

7. Mount Everest is the highest point on the earth's surface: $8.848 \times 10^3 \, m$ above sea level. The lowest point on the earth's surface is in the Mariana Trench: $1.103 \times 10^4 \, m$ *below* sea level. Find the vertical distance between the lowest and highest points on the earth's surface.

8. The wavelength of sodium light is 5 893 Å, where 1 Å = 10^{-10} m. Give the wavelength of sodium light in metres in standard form.

9. The diameters of the sun and earth are approximately $1.4 \times 10^6 \, km$ and $1.3 \times 10^4 \, km$ respectively. Express both numbers correct to 1 s.f. and hence find the approximate ratio,
   diameter of the sun : diameter of the earth.

10. Express 1 hour in seconds in standard form.

11. The velocity of light is approximately $3 \times 10^5 \, km/s$. Use your answer to question 10 to find the distance travelled by light in 1 hour.

12. Atmospheric pressure at the earth's surface is approximately $1.013 \times 10^5 \, newton/m^2$. At a height of 6 km, the atmospheric pressure is about half of that at the surface of the earth. Find the atmospheric pressure at this height, giving your answer correct to 2 s.f.

13. A room measures 4 m by 3 m by $2\frac{1}{2}$ m. Calculate its volume in cm³ in standard form.

14. The density of air is $1.3 \times 10^{-3} \, g/cm^3$. Calculate the mass of air in the room in question 13. Give your answer in kg in ordinary form.

15. The masses of the earth and the sun are approximately $6 \times 10^{24} \, kg$ and $2 \times 10^{30} \, kg$ respectively. Express the ratio, mass of earth : mass of sun in the form $x : 1$, where x is a number in standard form.

16. One barrel of oil has a capacity of $1.65 \times 10^{-1} \, m^3$. Find the total volume, in m³, of 6.7×10^7 barrels of oil. Give the volume in standard form correct to 2 s.f.

17. The pages of a dictionary are numbered from 1 to 1 322. The dictionary is 7 cm thick (neglecting the covers).
    a How many thicknesses of paper make 1 322 numbered pages?
    b Find the thickness of one sheet of paper.

Give your answer in metres in standard form correct to 1 s.f.

18. Table 5.1 gives the approximate populations and areas of five countries of West Africa.

country	population	area (km²)
The Gambia	$1 \cdot 5 \times 10^6$	$1 \cdot 1 \times 10^4$
Ghana	$2 \cdot 8 \times 10^7$	$2 \cdot 4 \times 10^5$
Liberia	$3 \cdot 6 \times 10^6$	$1 \cdot 1 \times 10^5$
Nigeria	$1 \cdot 4 \times 10^8$	$9 \cdot 2 \times 10^5$
Sierra Leone	$5 \cdot 3 \times 10^6$	$7 \cdot 2 \times 10^4$

Table 5.1

a Find the total population of the five countries correct to 3 s.f.
b Find the population density (i.e. the number of people per km²) of each country. Give each answer in ordinary form correct to 2 s.f.

SUMMARY

1 A number in *standard form* is written as $A \times 10^n$, where A is a number between 1 and 10, and n is a positive or negative whole number.

2 *Significant figures* begin from the first non-zero digit at the left of a number. For example:

   18 329   = 18 000 to 2 significant figures

   0·092 752   = 0·092 8 to 3 significant figures

3 *Decimal places* are counted from the decimal point. Zeros after the point are significant. For example:

   2·0816 = 2·1 to 1 decimal place

   = 2·08 to 2 decimal places

   = 2·082 to 3 decimal places

4 *Add* and *subtract* numbers in standard form *either* by changing to ordinary form or by factorising out the powers of 10. See Examples 3, 4 and 5.

5 *Multiply* and *divide* numbers in standard form by using the laws of indices to simplify the powers of 10. See Examples 6, 7, 8, 10 and 11.

How Many People?

In a village there are exactly
   10% more boys than girls,
   15% more women than men, and
   20% more children than adults.
How many boys, girls, men and women are there? [The population of the village is less than 6000.]

Opposite but Equal Pairs

Copy this diagram ... but ... arrange the numbers so that any two numbers that are side by side have the same total as the pair opposite.
[In the given diagram this is only true for 1 + 10 = 5 + 6]

By the end of this chapter you should be able to:

1 Substitute values in a formula
2 Change the subject of a formula.

Teaching and learning materials
Teacher: Flash cards with formulae for discussion

6-1 Formulae and substitution

A **formula** is an equation with letters which stand for quantities. For example,

$$c = 2\pi r$$

is the formula which gives the circumference, c, of a circle of radius r.

In science,

$$I = \frac{V}{R}$$

is the formula which shows the relation between the current, I amps, voltage, V volts, and resistance, R ohms, in an electrical circuit. In arithmetic,

$$I = \frac{PRT}{100}$$

is the formula which gives the interest, I, gained on a principal, P, invested at R% per annum for T years.

Sometimes the same letter can stand for different quantities in different formulae. For example, I stands for current in the science formula and I stands for interest in the arithmetic formula. **Formulae** is the plural of formula.

Substitution

To **substitute** in a formula means to replace letters by their values. This makes it possible to calculate other values.

Example 1

A gas at a temperature of $\theta°C$ has an absolute temperature of T K, where $T = \theta + 273$.
a Find the absolute temperature of a gas at a temperature of $68°C$.
b If the absolute temperature of a gas is 380 K, find its temperature in $°C$.

a
$$T = \theta + 273$$
when $\theta = 68$,
$$T = 68 + 273 = 341$$
The absolute temperature is 341 K.

b
$$T = \theta + 273$$
when $T = 380$,
$$380 = \theta + 273$$
Subtract 273 from both sides.
$$380 - 273 = \theta$$
$$107 = \theta$$
The temperature of the gas is $107°C$.

Example 2

The formula $W = VI$ gives the power, W watts, used by an electrical item when a current of I amps flows through a circuit of V volts.
a An air conditioner on maximum power needs a current of 25 amps in a 120 volt circuit. Find the power being used.
b An electric light bulb is marked 100 watts, 240 volts. Find the current required to light the bulb.

a
$$W = VI$$
when $V = 120$ and $I = 25$,
$$W = 120 \times 25$$
$$= 3\,000$$
The maximum power is $3\,000$ watts.

b
$$W = VI$$
when $W = 100$ and $V = 240$,
$$100 = 240I$$
Divide both sides by 240.

$$\frac{100}{240} = I$$

$$I = \frac{10}{24} = \frac{5}{12}$$

The current required is $\frac{5}{12}$ amp.

Exercise 6a

1. A gas at a temperature of $\theta\,°C$ has an absolute temperature of $T\,K$, where $T = \theta + 273$.
   a Find the absolute temperature of a gas at a temperature of $36\,°C$.
   b If the absolute temperature of a gas is $400\,K$, find its temperature in $°C$.

2. The perimeter of a rhombus of side d cm is p cm, where $p = 4d$.
   a Find the perimeter of a rhombus of side $3\cdot2$ cm.
   b Find the length of a side of a rhombus of perimeter 14 cm.

3. Two quantities x and y are connected by the formula $y = 7 - 9x$.
   a Find the value of y when $x = 0$.
   b Find the value of x when $y = 0$.

4. A rectangle l units long and b units wide has an area of A square units, where $A = lb$.
   a Find the floor area of a room 5 m long and 3 m wide.
   b Find the width of a postcard of area $112\,cm^2$, the length being 14 cm.
   c Find the length of a rectangular piece of plastic of area $171\,cm^2$ and width $9\frac{1}{2}$ cm.
   d The area of a picture is $3\cdot125\,m^2$ and its width is $1\cdot25$ m. Find its length.

5. The simple interest formula $I = \dfrac{PRT}{100}$ gives the interest I on a principal P invested at a rate of $R\%$ per annum for T years.
   a Find the interest when ₦$150\,000$ is invested at 5% per annum for 4 years.
   b Find the principal that gains an interest of ₦$16\,100$ in 5 years at 7% per annum.

6. A circuit of voltage V volts and resistance R ohms has a current of I amps, where $I = \dfrac{V}{R}$.
   a Find the current when the voltage is 240 volts and the resistance is 80 ohms.
   b Find the voltage when the current is $0\cdot6$ amps and the resistance is 5 ohms.
   c Find the resistance when the current is $0\cdot1$ amp and the voltage is 9 volts.

7. A rectangular room l m long and b m wide has a perimeter p, where $p = 2l + 2b$.
   a Find the perimeter of a room which is $3\cdot5$ m long and 2 m wide.
   b Find the length of a room of perimeter 20 m and width 3 m.

8. The mass of water in a rectangular tank l m long, b m wide and h m deep is M kg, where $M = 1\,000\,lbh$.
   a What is the mass of water in a tank 5 m long, 4 m wide and 3 m deep?
   b How deep is the water in a tank 4 m long and 3 m wide if its mass is $24\,000$ kg?
   c How wide is a tank 3 m long and $0\cdot5$ m deep if it holds exactly one tonne of water?

9. The circumference, C units, of a circle of radius r units is given by the formula
   $C = 2\pi r$, where $\pi = \frac{22}{7}$.
   a What is the circumference of a circle of radius 7 cm?
   b What is the radius of a circle whose circumference is 22 m?
   c What is the circumference of a circle of radius one metre?
   d What is the radius of a circle of circumference $2\cdot75$ m?

10. The speed s km/h of a car t seconds after starting is given by the formula $s = 12t$.
    a Find the speed of the car 5 seconds after starting.
    b How long does it take the car to reach a speed of 75 km/h?

Example 3

If $y = 3 - x$, find the values of y when $x = 1$, 2, 3, 4, 5.

when $x = 1$, $y = 3 - 1 = 2$
when $x = 2$, $y = 3 - 2 = 1$
when $x = 3$, $y = 3 - 3 = 0$
when $x = 4$, $y = 3 - 4 = -1$
when $x = 5$, $y = 3 - 5 = -2$

The working and results in Example 3 can be set out more neatly in a **table of values** as shown in Table 6.1.

x	1	2	3	4	5
3	3	3	3	3	3
$-x$	-1	-2	-3	-4	-5
$y = 3 - x$	2	1	0	-1	-2

Table 6.1 $y = 3 - x$

Example 4

If $y = 2x - 5$, *make a table of values of y for*
$x = -1, 0, 1, 2, 3$.

x	-1	0	1	2	3
$2x$	-2	0	2	4	6
-5	-5	-5	-5	-5	-5
y	-7	-5	-3	-1	1

Table 6.2 $y = 2x - 5$

Example 5

*The weekly cost, c naira, of running a
household of n people is given by the formula*
$c = 180n + 450$.
a *Find the weekly cost for five people.*
b *How many people are there if the weekly
cost is ₦1 170?*

a There are five people, thus, $n = 5$.
$$c = 180n + 450$$
When $n = 5$,
$$c = 180 \times 5 + 450 = 900 + 450$$
$$= 1\,350$$
The weekly cost = ₦1 350.

b The weekly cost is ₦1 170,
thus, $c = 1\,170$.
$$c = 180n + 450$$
When $c = 1\,170$,
$$1\,170 = 180n + 450$$
Subtract 450 from both sides.
$$720 = 180n$$
Divide both sides by 180.
$$4 = n$$
There are four people.

Exercise 6b

① If $y = 5 - x$, find the values of y when
$x = 1, 2, 3, 4, 5$.

② If $d = c + 3$, find the values of d when
$c = -2, -1, 0, 1, 2$.

③ If $y = 2x + 1$, find the values of y when
$x = 0, 1, 2, 3, 4$.

④ Given that $y = 3x + 2$, copy and complete
Table 6.3 to show values of y for
$x = -1, 0, 1, 2, 3$.

x	-1	0	1	2	3
$3x + 2$	$+2$	$+2$	$+2$	$+2$	$+2$
y					

Table 6.3

⑤ If $y = 17 - 6x$, make a table of values of y
for $x = 0, 1, 2, 3, 4, 5$.

⑥ The cost, c naira, of hiring a car for a journey
of d km is given by the formula $c = 5d + 850$.
a Find the cost of hiring a car for a journey
of 420 km.
b How long is a journey if the cost of car-
hire is ₦1 580?

⑦ The time, t min, to cook meat is given by the
formula $t = 40m + 25$, where m is the mass
of the meat in kg.
a Find how long it takes to cook a piece of
meat of mass 1·2 kg.
b Find the mass of a piece of meat which
takes 2 h 9 min to cook.

⑧ On a certain island the tax, T, paid on an
income of I is given by the formula
$T = 0·2I - 50$. How much tax is paid
on an income of a $1 000, b $6 225?
c What income would have a tax of $450?

⑨ A car starts a journey with a full petrol tank.
The amount of petrol, p litres, left in the tank
after travelling for t hours is given by the
formula $p = 63 - 10t$.
a Find the amount of petrol left after
travelling for $2\frac{1}{2}$ hours.
b If there are 18 litres of petrol left, how
long has the car been travelling?
c How long will it take the car to run out of
petrol? (i.e. find t when $p = 0$.)

⑩ A closed cylinder of height h cm and base
radius r cm has a surface area, A cm^2, where A
$= 2\pi r^2 + 2\pi rh$. Use the value $\frac{22}{7}$ for π to find:
a the surface area of a closed cylinder of
height 9 cm and base radius 5 cm;

b the height of a closed cylinder of base radius 7 cm and surface area 1 012 cm².

Example 6

If $y = 5x^2 - 1$, find a the value of y when $x = -3$, b the values of x when $y = 79$.

a
$$y = 5x^2 - 1$$
When $x = -3$
$$y = 5 \times (-3)^2 - 1$$
$$= 5 \times (+9) - 1$$
$$= 45 - 1$$
$$= 44$$

b
$$y = 5x^2 - 1$$
When $y = 79$
$$79 = 5x^2 - 1$$
Add 1 to both sides.
$$80 = 5x^2$$
Divide both sides by 5.
$$16 = x^2$$
Take the square root of both sides
$$\sqrt{16} = x$$
$$x = +4 \text{ or } -4$$

Notice that there are two possible values for x. We can shorten this to $x = \pm 4$ where $\pm$ is short for '+ or −'.

Example 7

From a height of h metres above sea level it is possible to see a distance of approximately d kilometres, where d and h are connected by the formula $2d^2 = 25h$.
a From what height is it possible to see a distance of 10 km?
b What distance can be seen from a height of 18 m?

a
$$2d^2 = 25h$$
The distance is 10 km. Thus, when $d = 10$,
$$2 \times 10^2 = 25h$$
$$2 \times 100 = 25h$$
$$200 = 25h$$
Divide both sides by 25.
$$8 = h$$
The height is 8 metres.

b The height is 18 m. Thus, when $h = 18$,
$$2d^2 = 25h$$

becomes
$$2d^2 = 25 \times 18$$
$$2d^2 = 450$$
Divide both sides by 2.
$$d^2 = 225$$
Take the square root of both sides.
$$d = 225$$
$$= \pm 15$$

In this example the value $d = -15$ would not be sensible; the distance that can be seen is 15 km.

Exercise 6c

1 If $y = 40x^2$, find
  a y when $x = 0, 1, 2, 3, 4, 5$,
  b x when $y = 10, 360, 1\,000, 4\,000$.

2 If $y = 16 - x^2$, find
  a y when $x = -4, -2, 0, 2, 4$,
  b x when $y = 0, 7, 12, 15$.

3 If $m = \dfrac{100}{n^2}$, find
  a m when $n = 1, 5, 10, 20$,
  b n when $m = 1, 4, 9, 25$.

4 The area, A square units, of a circle of radius r units is given by the formula $A = \pi r^2$, where $\pi = \frac{22}{7}$.
  a What is the area of a circle of radius 7 m?
  b What is the radius of a circle of area 616 cm²?
  c What is the radius of a circle of area 38·5 m²?

5 The volume, V cm³, of a cylinder of base radius r cm and height h cm is given by the formula $V = \pi r^2 h$. Use the value $\frac{22}{7}$ for π to find:
  a the volume of a cylinder of base radius $3\frac{1}{2}$ cm and height 8 cm;
  b the height of a cylinder of volume 1 100 cm³ and radius 5 cm;
  c the base radius of a cylinder of volume 770 cm³ and height 45 cm.

6 If a stone is dropped, the distance, d m, which it falls in t seconds is given by the formula $d = 4·9t^2$.
  a How far does it fall in 3 seconds?
  b How far does it fall in $1\frac{1}{7}$ seconds?
  c How long does it take to fall 490 m?
  d How long does it take to fall $122\frac{1}{2}$ m?
  e How far does it fall in the fifth second?

7. The time, t minutes, taken over a committee meeting is given by the formula $t = 5n^2 + 15$ when n people are present.
   a How long does the meeting take if there are four people?
   b How many people are present if the meeting takes 2 h 20 min?

8. The visible distance, D km, of the horizon from a height of h m is given by the formula $h = \frac{2}{25}D^2$.
   a How high must a cliff be if a ship $12\frac{1}{2}$ km away is visible from it?
   b How high is an observation tower on the top of the cliff in a if a ship 15 km away is visible from it?
   c What is the distance of the visible horizon from the top of a wireless mast 200 m high?

9.

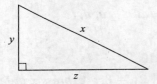

Fig. 6.1

In the right-angled triangle in Fig. 6.1, the length of the hypotenuse, x cm, is given by the formula $x = \sqrt{y^2 + z^2}$.
   a Find the value of x when $y = 2\frac{1}{2}$ cm and $z = 6$ cm.
   b Find the value of y when $x = 16$ and $z^2 = 60$.

10. If there are n numbers in a uniformly increasing series (like 2, 5, 8, 11 ...), starting with a and ending with l, the sum of the numbers is S, where $S = \frac{1}{2}n(a + l)$.
   a What is the sum of all whole numbers from 1 to 50 inclusive?
   b How many numbers are there in the series 2, ..., 20 if the sum is 143?
   c What is the last term of a series of 10 numbers beginning with 7 if their sum is 85?

6-2 Change of subject

The letter I is the **subject** of the formula $I = \frac{PRT}{100}$.

The subject stands on its own. Its value can be found directly by substituting the values of the other letters in the formula.

It is often necessary to **change the subject** of a formula. This means to rearrange the order of the letters in the formula so that one of the other letters becomes the subject.

Example 8

Make P, R and T in turn the subject of the formula
$$I = \frac{PRT}{100}.$$
$$I = \frac{PRT}{100}$$

Multiply both sides by 100
$$100I = PRT \tag{1}$$

Dividing both sides of equation (1) by RT gives
$$P = \frac{100I}{PT} \tag{2}$$

Dividing both sides of equation (1) by PT gives
$$R = \frac{100I}{PT} \tag{3}$$

Dividing both sides of equation (1) by PR gives
$$T = \frac{100I}{PR} \tag{4}$$

Equations (2), (3) and (4) show P, R and T respectively as subjects of the given formula.

Example 9

Make x the subject of the following.

a $y = x - 9$ b $N = 7x$ c $\frac{x}{a} = 8$

d $\frac{h}{x} = k$ e $y = 2x + 1$

a
$$y = x - 9$$
Add 9 to both sides.
$$y + 9 = x$$
$$x = y + 9$$

b $N = 7x$
Divide both sides by 7.
$$\frac{N}{7} = x \text{ or } x = \frac{N}{7}$$

c $\frac{x}{a} = 8$

Multiply both sides by a.

$x = 8a$

d $\dfrac{h}{x} = k$

Multiply both sides by x.

$h = kx$

Divide both sides by k.

$\dfrac{h}{k} = x$ or $x = \dfrac{h}{k}$

e $y = 2x + 1$

Subtract 1 from both sides.

$y - 1 = 2x$

Divide both sides by 2.

$\dfrac{y - 1}{2} = x$

$\qquad x = \dfrac{y - 1}{2}$

To change the subject of a formula:
1 treat the formula as an algebraic equation;
2 solve the equation for the letter which is to be the subject of the formula.

 Optional: Do Exercise 15 of your Students' Practice Book.

Exercise 6d   [QR]

In each question a formula is given. A letter is printed in heavy type after it. Make that letter the subject of the formula. If more than one letter is given, make each the subject in turn.

① $y = x + 8$ **x**

② $y = x - 3$ **x**

③ $b = a + c$ **a, c**

④ $y = 3x$ **x**

⑤ $y = \dfrac{x}{4}$ **x**

⑥ $b = ac$ **a, c**

⑦ $n = 5ax$ **a, x**

⑧ $\dfrac{x}{y} = 9$ **x**

⑨ $\dfrac{y}{x} = 2$ **x**

⑩ $\dfrac{m}{n} = p$ **m, n**

⑪ $y = 6x + 11$ **x**

⑫ $y = 7x - 2$ **x**

⑬ $b = 5a - c$ **a**

⑭ $x + y = 13$ **x, y**

⑮ $2p - q = 0$ **q, p**

⑯ $2x - y = d$ **x, y**

⑰ $p = 4d$ **d**

⑱ $c = 2\pi r$ **r**

⑲ $T = \theta + 273$ **θ**

⑳ $W = VI$ **V, I**

㉑ $A = \pi r l$ **r, l**

㉒ $V = lbh$ **l, b, h**

㉓ $A = 2\pi r h$ **r, h**

㉔ $s = \frac{1}{2}vt$ **v, t**

㉕ $A = \frac{1}{2}bh$ **b, h**

㉖ $V = \frac{1}{2}lbh$ **l, b, h**

㉗ $I = \dfrac{PRT}{100}$ **R**

㉘ $I = \dfrac{V}{R}$ **V, R**

㉙ $s = 2l + 2b$ **l, b**

㉚ $v = u + at$ **u, a, t**

Example 10

Given $3x - 2y = 8$, a express x in terms of y and find x when $y = 11$, b obtain a formula for y and find y when $x = 2$.

a 'Express x in terms of y' means 'make x the subject of the formula'.

$3x - 2y = 8$

Add $2y$ to both sides.

$\qquad 3x = 8 + 2y$

Divide both sides by 3.

$\qquad x = \dfrac{8 + 2y}{3}$

When $y = 11$,

$\qquad x = \dfrac{8 + 2 \times 11}{3}$

$\qquad = \dfrac{8 + 22}{3}$

$\qquad = \dfrac{30}{3}$

$\qquad = 10$

b 'Obtain a formula for y' means 'make y the subject of the formula'.

$3x - 2y = 8$

Add $2y$ to both sides.

$\qquad 3x = 8 + 2y$

Subtract 8 from both sides.

$3x - 8 = 2y$

Divide both sides by 2.

$$\frac{3x - 8}{2} = y$$

When $x = 2$,

$$y = \frac{3 \times 2 - 8}{2}$$

$$= \frac{6 - 8}{2}$$

$$= \frac{-2}{2}$$

$$= -1$$

Exercise 6e

1. If $y = 2x - 9$,
   a express x in terms of y,
   b find x when $y = 5$.

2. If $3x + y = d$,
   a express x in terms of y and d,
   b find x when $d = 1$ and $y = 13$.

3. A cylinder of radius r cm and height h cm has a curved surface area A cm², where $A = 2\pi rh$.
   a Obtain a formula for h.
   b Find the value of h when $A = 93$, $r = 2 \cdot 5$ and $\pi = 3 \cdot 1$.

4. A triangle of base b cm and height h cm has an area A cm², where $A = \frac{1}{2}bh$.
   a Express b in terms of A and h.
   b Hence find the value of b when $A = 135$ and $h = 18$.

5. The wage, w naira, of a person who works r hours of overtime is given by the formula $w = 200r + 5\,900$.
   a Make r the subject of this formula.
   b Hence find the number of hours of overtime worked by someone whose total wage is ₦8 200.

6. a Make P the subject of the simple interest formula $I = \frac{PRT}{100}$.
   b Hence find the principal which earns an interest of ₦29 750 in 7 years at a rate of 5% per annum.

7. a Make T the subject of the simple interest formula $I = \frac{PRT}{100}$.
   b Hence find how long it takes for a principal of ₦25 000 to earn an interest of ₦2 625 at 3% per annum.

8. a Make R the subject of the simple interest formula $I = \frac{PRT}{100}$.
   b Hence find the rate of interest if ₦16 200 earns an interest of ₦2 160 in 4 years.

9. If $p = \frac{c}{d}$,
   a express d in terms of p and c,
   b find d when $p = 3$ and $c = 5 \cdot 7$.

10. In an electrical circuit, the current, I amps, the voltage, V volts, and the resistance, R ohms, are connected by the formula $I = \frac{V}{R}$.
    a Make V the subject of the formula and find the voltage when $I = 2$ and $R = 6$.
    b Express R in terms of I and V and find the resistance when $V = 240$ and $I = 0 \cdot 1$.

Example 11

Make r the subject of the formula $V = \frac{1}{3}\pi r^2 h$.

$V = \frac{1}{3}\pi r^2 h$

Multiply both sides by 3.

$3V = \pi r^2 h$

Divide both sides by πh.

$$\frac{3V}{\pi h} = r^2$$

Take the square root of both sides.

$$\sqrt{\frac{3V}{\pi h}} = r$$

Example 12

Make v the subject of the formula $\frac{1}{f} = \frac{1}{u} + \frac{1}{v}$.

Either:

fuv is the LCM of f, u and v. Multiply each term by fuv.

$uv = fv + fu$

Collect terms in v to one side of the equation. In this case, subtract fv from both sides.

$uv - fv = fu$

Factorise the LHS.

$v(u - f) = fu$

Divide both sides by $(u - f)$.

$$v = \frac{fu}{u - f}$$

Or:

First make $\frac{1}{v}$ the subject of the formula,

$$\frac{1}{v} = \frac{1}{f} - \frac{1}{u} = \frac{u - f}{fu}$$

then take the reciprocal of both sides.

$$v = \frac{fu}{u - f}$$

Example 13

Given $S = \frac{1}{2}n(a + l)$, express l in terms of S, n and a.

$$S = \tfrac{1}{2}n(a + l)$$

Multiply both sides by 2.

$$2S = n(a + l)$$

Divide both sides by n.

$$\frac{2S}{n} = a + l$$

Subtract a from both sides.

$$2\frac{S}{n} - a = l$$

Example 14

The time of oscillation, T, of a simple pendulum is given by the formula $T = 2\pi\sqrt{\dfrac{l}{g}}$, where l is the length of the pendulum and g is the constant of gravitation. Make l the subject of the formula.

$$T = 2\pi\sqrt{\frac{l}{g}} \quad \text{(from the first sentence)}$$

Square both sides of the formula.

$$T^2 = 4\pi^2\frac{l}{g}$$

Multiply both sides by g.

$$gT^2 = 4\pi^2 l$$

Divide both sides by $4\pi^2$.

$$l = \frac{gT^2}{4\pi^2}$$

It is impossible to give general rules for rearranging formulae and equations. However, the following points should be remembered.

1 Begin by clearing fractions, brackets and square root signs.
2 Rearrange the resulting equation so that all the terms which contain the subject are on one side and the rest on the other.
3 Simplify the side containing the subject until it remains as a single term.

 Optional: Do Exercise 16 of your Students' Practice Book.

Exercise 6f

① Write down the squares of the following.

   a xy b $\dfrac{a}{t}$ c $\dfrac{x^2}{y}$

   d $x + y$ e $\sqrt{\dfrac{d}{g}}$ f $a\sqrt{m}$

   g $2\pi\sqrt{a}$ h $\dfrac{3}{\sqrt{b}}$ i $\dfrac{\pi}{3}\sqrt{2g}$

② Write down the square roots of the following.

   a $9b^2$ b b^2x^2 c $3m^2$

   d $\dfrac{16}{9}t^2m^2$ e xy f $a - b$

   g $a^2 + b^2$ h $\dfrac{A}{\pi}$ i $\dfrac{2s}{g}$

③ Write down the reciprocals of the following.

   a x b $\dfrac{x}{y}$ c $\dfrac{1}{x}$

   d $\dfrac{1}{xy}$ e $\dfrac{1}{3}m$ f $\dfrac{1}{3m}$

   g $\dfrac{b - 1}{b}$ h $\dfrac{ab}{a + b}$ i $\dfrac{2f - v}{fv}$

Exercise 6g

Each question gives an equation or a formula. A letter is printed in heavy type after the formula. Make that letter the subject of the formula.

① $\sqrt{x} = a$ **x**

② $\sqrt{2x} = a$ **x**

③ $2\sqrt{x} = a$ **x**

④ $x^2 = a$ **x**

⑤ $y = 4ax^2$ **x**

⑥ $\dfrac{a}{b} = \dfrac{c}{d}$ **b**

⑦ $3(2a - b) = a$ **b**

⑧ $x(x + a) = ab$ **a**

⑨ $\frac{a}{x} + b = c$ **x**

⑩ $\frac{1}{a} = 1 + \frac{1}{b}$ **a**

⑪ $P = \frac{N + 2}{D}$ **N**

⑫ $D = \sqrt{\frac{3h}{2}}$ **h**

⑬ $W = I^2R$ **I**

⑭ $s = \frac{1}{2}gt^2$ **t**

⑮ $h = \frac{2d^2}{25}$ **d**

⑯ $V = \pi r^2 h$ **r**

⑰ $s = \frac{1}{2}(u + v)t$ **u**

⑱ $S = 2\pi r(r + h)$ **h**

⑲ $x = \sqrt{y^2 + z^2}$ **z**

⑳ $\frac{1}{u} + \frac{1}{v} = \frac{2}{f}$ **u**

Exercise 6h

① The mean, m, of two numbers a and b is given by $m = \frac{1}{2}(a + b)$.
   a Express a in terms of m and b.
   b Hence find a when $m = 19$ and $b = 23$.

② If $x = \frac{1}{4}\sqrt{\frac{y}{a}}$,
   a express y in terms of a and x,
   b find y when $a = 3$ and $x = \frac{1}{2}$.

③ The area A of a circle is given by the formula $A = \pi r^2$, where r is the radius of the circle.
   a Obtain a formula for r.
   b Hence find the radius of a circle of area $38 \cdot 5\,\text{cm}^2$, taking π to be $\frac{22}{7}$.

④ The surface area of a sphere of radius r is S, where $S = 4\pi r^2$.
   a Express r in terms of S and π.
   b Find the radius of a sphere which has a surface area of $616\,\text{cm}^2$. (Use the value $3\frac{1}{7}$ for π.)

⑤ In a right-angled triangle, the hypotenuse is h cm long and the other two sides are f cm and g cm in length.
   a Write down a formula which connects f, g and h.
   b Make f the subject of your formula.
   c Find f when $g = 2\,\text{cm}$ and $h = 2 \cdot 5\,\text{cm}$.

⑥ If $\frac{n^2 - 1}{m} = 4$,
   a express n in terms of m,
   b hence find n when $m = 12$.

⑦ The energy, E, possessed by an object of mass m kg travelling with a speed of v m/s is $\frac{1}{2}mv^2$ joules.
   a Express v in terms of E and m.
   b If the energy of a 50 kg mass is $4\,900$ joules, how fast is it moving?

⑧ The volume V of a cone of height h and base radius r is $\frac{1}{3}\pi r^2 h$.
   a Obtain a formula for r.
   b Find the base radius of a cone of height 14 cm and volume $91\frac{2}{3}\,\text{cm}^3$. (Use the value $\frac{22}{7}$ for π.)

⑨ The total resistance, R ohms, of two resistances x ohms and y ohms connected in parallel is given by the formula $\frac{1}{R} = \frac{1}{x} + \frac{1}{y}$.
   a Obtain a formula for y in terms of R and x.
   b Find y if $x = 2\frac{2}{3}$ and $R = 2\frac{1}{4}$.

⑩ The curved surface area A of a cone of height h and base radius r is $\pi r \sqrt{h^2 + r^2}$.
   a Make h the subject of the formula.
   b Find the height of a cone of area $550\,\text{cm}^2$ and base radius 7 cm, taking π to be $\frac{22}{7}$.

SUMMARY

1 A *formula* is an equation with letters that stand for quantities.

2 The *subject* of a formula stands on its own. The subject can be evaluated by substituting given values.

3 To *change the subject* of a formula:
   • treat the formula like an algebraic equation;
   • solve the equation for the letter that is to be the new subject of the formula.

   Remember to:
   • begin by clearing fractions, brackets and square root signs;
   • rearrange the resulting equation so that all the terms that contain the subject are on one side (and the rest on the other);
   • simplify the side containing the subject until it remains as a single term.

<table>
<tr><td>

7 Similarity and enlargement

</td></tr>
</table>

OBJECTIVES

By the end of this chapter you should be able to:

1 Decide whether plane shapes are similar or not

2 Decide whether solid shapes are similar or not

3 Recall and apply the properties of similar triangles

4 Name similar figures correctly

5 Draw an enlargement of a shape, given the centre of enlargement and the scale factor of the enlargement

6 Identify the centre of enlargement and scale factor from a given enlargement.

Teaching and learning materials
Teacher: Models of similar solids; charts of similar plane shapes

---

7-1 Similarity

Look at the photographs in Fig. 7.1.

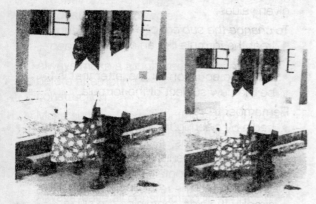

Fig. 7.1

Both photographs show the same picture but the pictures are different sizes. We say that the pictures are **similar** to each other. Fig. 7.2 shows further examples of similar shapes.

a similar cuboids

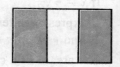

b similar flags

c similar symbols

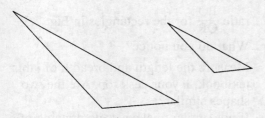

d similar triangles

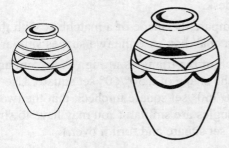

e similar jars

Fig. 7.2

Notice that the pairs of shapes in Fig. 7.2 are the same but their sizes are different.

Fig. 7.3 shows two rectangles ABCD and PQRS.

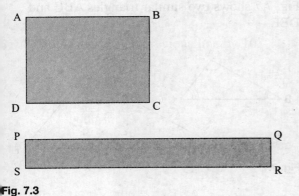

Fig. 7.3

ABCD has a shape like that of an envelope. PQRS has a shape like that of a ruler. Although the shapes are both rectangles, they are *not* similar. PQRS is long and thin, but ABCD is not.

Example 1

a *Measure the length and breadth of the flags in Fig. 7.2b.*
b *Find the ratio* length : breadth *for each flag.*
c *What do you notice?*

a Large flag:
length = 35 mm, breadth = 21 mm
Small flag:
length = 25 mm, breadth = 15 mm

b Large flag: $\dfrac{\text{length}}{\text{breadth}} = \dfrac{35}{21} = \dfrac{5}{3}$

Small flag: $\dfrac{\text{length}}{\text{breadth}} = \dfrac{25}{15} = \dfrac{5}{3}$

c The ratio of corresponding sides in each figure is the same, $\dfrac{5}{3}$.

Example 2

a *Measure the lengths of all the sides of both shapes in Fig. 7.4. What do you notice?*
b *Measure the angles of the shapes in Fig. 7.4.*
c *Are the two shapes similar? Give reasons.*

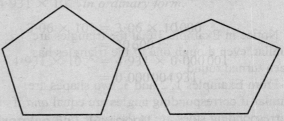

Fig. 7.4

a In both shapes, the sides are each 2 cm. Both shapes have sides of the same length.
b Each angle in the first shape = 108°. In the second figure there are two angles of 114°, two angles of 90° and one angle of 132°.
c The shapes are *not* similar. Although the sides in both figures are of equal length, their angles are different.

Example 3

a *Use measurement to find the ratio* longest side : shortest side *for the two triangles in Fig. 7.5. What do you notice?*
b *Measure the angles of both triangles. What do you notice?*
c *Are the two triangles similar? Give reasons.*

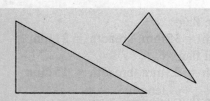

Fig. 7.5

a Large triangle: $\dfrac{\text{longest side}}{\text{shortest side}} = \dfrac{4\,\text{cm}}{2\,\text{cm}} = \dfrac{2}{1}$

Small triangle: $\dfrac{\text{longest side}}{\text{shortest side}} = \dfrac{22\,\text{mm}}{11\,\text{mm}} = \dfrac{2}{1}$

The ratio of corresponding sides in each triangle is the same.

b In each triangle the angles are 30°, 60°, 90°. The angles are the same in both triangles.

c The triangles are similar. Their angles are equal and their corresponding sides are in the same ratio.

Notice in Example 3 that the triangles are similar, even though one of the triangles has been turned round.

From Examples 1, 2 and 3, two shapes are similar if corresponding angles are equal *and* if corresponding sides are in the same ratio.

Exercise 7a

① a Measure the heights of the cuboids in Fig. 7.2a, on page 64, and find the ratio of the two heights.

  b Measure the widths of the cuboids in Fig. 7.2a, on page 64. Find the ratios of the two widths.

② Measure the angles of the triangles in Fig. 7.2d. What do you notice?

③ Use a ruler to find the ratio *longest side* : *smallest side* for each of the triangles in Fig. 7.2d. What do you notice?

④ a In Fig. 7.3 write down the sizes of the angles of ABCD and PQRS. What do you notice?

  b Use a ruler to find the ratio $\dfrac{AB}{BC}$ and the

ratio $\dfrac{PQ}{QR}$ for the rectangles in Fig. 7.3.
What do you notice?

⑤ a Measure the length and breadth of i this textbook, ii your desk top. Are the two shapes similar?

  b If not similar, make a scale drawing of a shape which is similar to the shape of your desk.

⑥ Compare the shape of a matchbox with that of a chalkbox. Are the two shapes similar?

⑦ Each of the triangles in Fig. 7.5 is similar to the shape of a 30°/60° set square. Use a 30°/60° set square to check that the two triangles are similar. (You may have to slide the set square and turn it over.)

 Optional: Do Exercise 17 of your Students' Practice Book.

7.2 Similar triangles

Fig. 7.7 shows two similar triangles ABC and DEF.

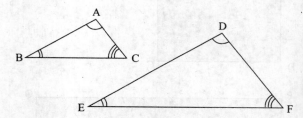

Fig. 7.7

Notice that Â, B̂, Ĉ in △ABC are equal respectively to D̂, Ê, F̂ in △DEF. The two triangles are **equiangular**. This means that the angles of one are equal to the angles of the other. Equiangular triangles are always similar. This is true even if one of the triangles is turned round as in Fig. 7.8.

QR – Similarity

Look at each pair of diagrams in Fig. 7.6. Say whether they are similar or not. Use measurement to help you if you are not sure.

a

b

c

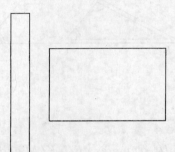

d

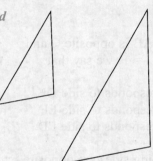

e

f

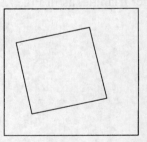

g

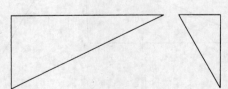

h

 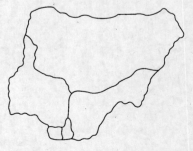

Fig. 7.6

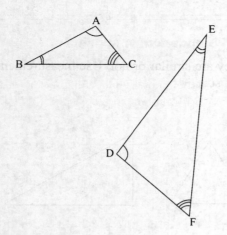

Fig. 7.8

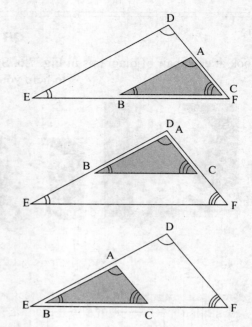

Fig. 7.9

Corresponding sides

In both Figs 7.7 and 7.8, AB is opposite $\hat{C}$ and DE is opposite $\hat{F}$. Since $\hat{C} = \hat{F}$, we say that:

        side AB corresponds to side DE

similarly side BC corresponds to side EF

and   side CA corresponds to side FD.

Notice that corresponding sides are opposite equal angles. This can be checked by making a tracing of the smaller triangle and sliding it within the larger triangle, as in Fig. 7.9.

Example 4

In Fig. 7.10, triangles ABC, KLM and XYZ are similar. Write down the sides in triangles KLM and XYZ which correspond to sides AB, BC and CA in △ABC.

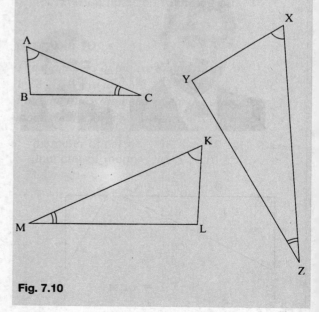

Fig. 7.10

Notice that the triangles are in various positions. Corresponding sides are opposite equal angles.

In △KLM and △ABC,

$\hat{M} = \hat{C}$, thus KL corresponds to AB
$\hat{K} = \hat{A}$, thus LM corresponds to BC
$\hat{L} = \hat{B}$, thus MK corresponds to CA

In △XYZ and △ABC,

$\hat{Z} = \hat{C}$, thus XY corresponds to AB
$\hat{X} = \hat{A}$, thus YZ corresponds to BC
$\hat{Y} = \hat{B}$, thus ZX corresponds to CA

Naming similar figures

Take care to name similar figures with the letters in the correct corresponding order. For example if △GHK is similar to △ABC, then since the letters are in corresponding order, side GH of the first triangle corresponds to side AB of the second, HK to BC, and GK to AC. It is not necessary to draw the triangles.

Notice that if two angles of a triangle are respectively equal to two angles of another, then the third angles must be equal, since the sum of the angles of any triangle is 180°.

5

QR – Similar triangles

In each pair of triangles in Fig. 7.11, state the sides which correspond to sides AB, BC and CA in △ABC.

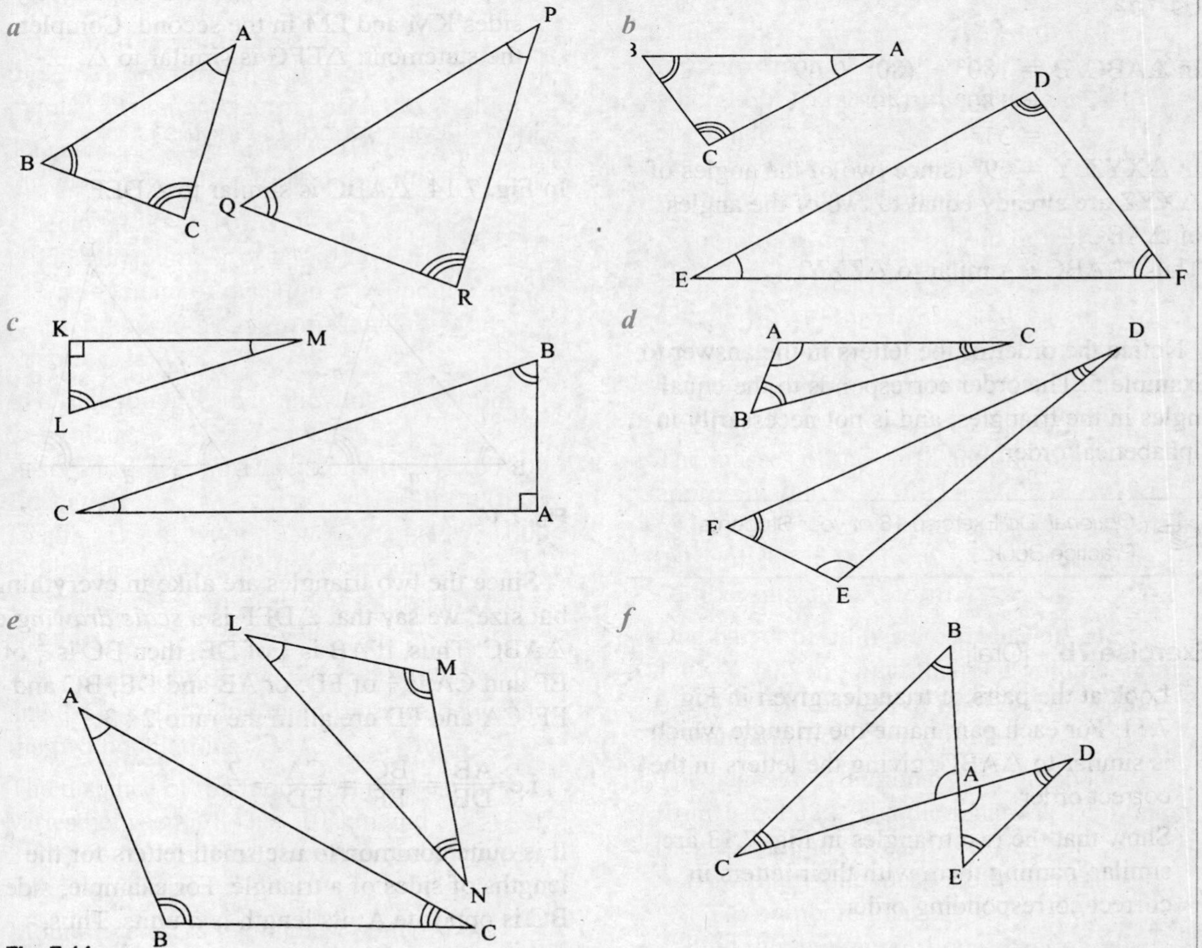

Fig. 7.11

Example 5

Calculate the missing angles in the triangles given in Fig. 7.12. Hence show that the triangles are similar, naming them with their letters in correct corresponding order.

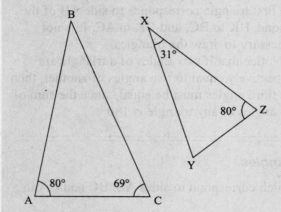

Fig. 7.12

In $\triangle ABC$, $\hat{B} = 180° - (80° + 69°)$
$$= 180° - 149°$$
$$= 31°$$

In $\triangle XYZ$, $\hat{Y} = 69°$ (since two of the angles of $\triangle XYZ$ are already equal to two of the angles of $\triangle ABC$).

Thus, $\triangle ABC$ is similar to $\triangle ZXY$.

Notice the order of the letters in the answer to Example 5. The order corresponds to the equal angles in the triangles, and is not necessarily in alphabetical order.

 Optional: Do Exercise 18 of your Students' Practice Book.

Exercise 7b   [Oral]

① Look at the pairs of triangles given in Fig. 7.11. For each pair, name the triangle which is similar to $\triangle ABC$, giving the letters in the correct order.

② Show that the two triangles in Fig. 7.13 are similar, naming them with their letters in correct corresponding order.

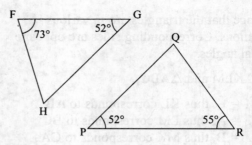

Fig. 7.13

③ If $\triangle DEF$ is similar to $\triangle QRP$, which side corresponds to **a** DE, **b** FE, **c** PQ, **d** DF?

④ Rectangle ABCD is similar to rectangle NOPM. Name the line which corresponds to **a** side BC, **b** side MN, **c** diagonal AC, **d** diagonal MO, **e** side AD.

⑤ Two similar triangles are such that sides FE and GE in the first correspond respectively to sides KM and LM in the second. Complete the statement: $\triangle EFG$ is similar to $\triangle ....$

Ratio of corresponding lengths

In Fig. 7.14, $\triangle ABC$ is similar to $\triangle DEF$.

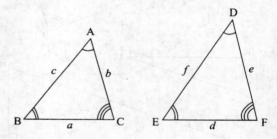

Fig. 7.14

Since the two triangles are alike in everything but size, we say that $\triangle DEF$ is a *scale drawing* of $\triangle ABC$. Thus, if AB is $\frac{2}{3}$ of DE, then BC is $\frac{2}{3}$ of EF and CA is $\frac{2}{3}$ of FD; or AB and DE, BC and EF, CA and FD are all in the ratio 2 : 3.

i.e. $\dfrac{AB}{DE} = \dfrac{BC}{EF} = \dfrac{CA}{FD} = \dfrac{2}{3}$

It is quite common to use small letters for the lengths of sides of a triangle. For example, side BC is opposite A; its length is *a* units. Thus,

$$\frac{c}{f} = \frac{a}{d} = \frac{b}{e} = \frac{2}{3}$$

Also, since $\frac{c}{f} = \frac{a}{d}$, multiplying both sides by fd

$$\frac{c}{f} \times fd = \frac{a}{d} \times fd$$

$$cd = af$$

Divide both sides by ad.

$$\frac{cd}{ad} = \frac{af}{ad}$$

$$\frac{c}{a} = \frac{f}{d}$$

i.e. $\dfrac{AB}{BC} = \dfrac{DE}{EF}$

Similarly, $\dfrac{BC}{CA} = \dfrac{EF}{FD}$ and $\dfrac{CA}{AB} = \dfrac{FD}{DE}$

These results can be more easily seen by using numbers. See Fig. 7.15.

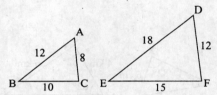

Fig. 7.15

If AB, BC, CA are 12, 10, 8 cm respectively, then, since AB is $\frac{2}{3}$ of DE, etc., DE, EF, FD are 18, 15, 12 cm respectively.

Hence $\dfrac{AB}{BC} = \dfrac{12}{10} = \dfrac{6}{5}$ and $\dfrac{DE}{EF} = \dfrac{18}{15} = \dfrac{6}{5}$

$\therefore \dfrac{AB}{BX} = \dfrac{DE}{EF}$

Similarly, $\dfrac{BC}{CA} = \dfrac{EF}{FD}$ and $\dfrac{CA}{AB} = \dfrac{FD}{DE}$

Example 6

In Fig. 7.16, show that the two triangles are similar. Name the triangles, giving the letters in corresponding order. Hence calculate BC and RQ.

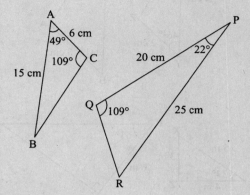

Fig. 7.16

$\hat{B} = 180° - 49° - 109° = 22°$
$\hat{R} = 180° - 22° - 109° = 49°$

Since the triangles are equiangular, they are similar. A corresponds to R, B to P, and C to Q. Hence $\triangle ABC$ is similar to $\triangle RPQ$.

Thus, $\dfrac{AB}{RP} = \dfrac{AC}{RQ} = \dfrac{BC}{PQ}$

$\dfrac{15}{25} = \dfrac{6}{RQ} = \dfrac{BC}{20}$

Thus, $\dfrac{3}{5} = \dfrac{6}{RQ}$ and $\dfrac{3}{5} = \dfrac{BC}{20}$

$3RQ = 30$ and $5BC = 60$
$RQ = 10\,cm$ and $BC = 12\,cm$

 Optional: Do Exercise 19 of your Students' Practice Book.

Exercise 7c

In each part of Fig. 7.17 **a** name the triangle which is similar to $\triangle XYZ$, giving the letters in the right order, **b** calculate those sides and angles which are not given.

69

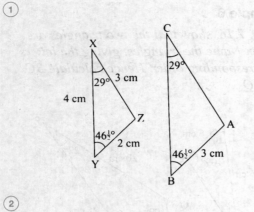

①

②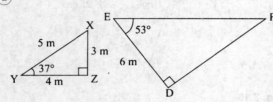

③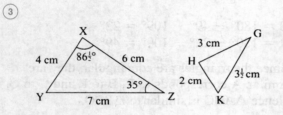

④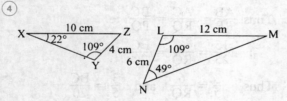

⑤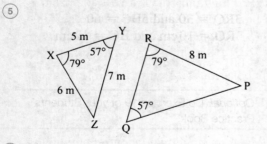

⑥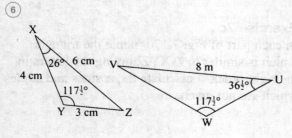

⑦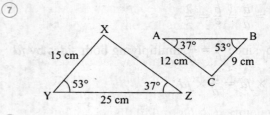

⑧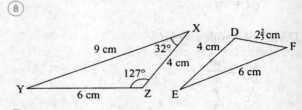

⑨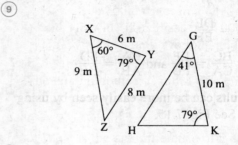

⑩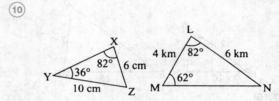

Fig. 7.17

Example 7

In Fig. 7.18, calculate MN *and* YM.

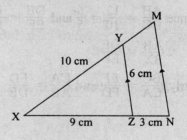

Fig. 7.18

Since YZ ∥ MN,
XŶZ = XM̂N and XẐY = XN̂M
(corresponding angles)
Thus, triangles XYZ and XMN are equiangular
and similar.

70

Thus $\dfrac{XY}{XM} = \dfrac{XZ}{XN} = \dfrac{YZ}{MN}$

$$\dfrac{10}{XM} = \dfrac{9}{12} = \dfrac{6}{MN}$$

Thus $\dfrac{10}{XM} = \dfrac{3}{4}$ and $\dfrac{6}{MN} = \dfrac{3}{4}$

$3XM = 40$ and $3MN = 24$

$XM = 13\frac{1}{3}$ cm and $MN = 8$ cm

Hence $YM = 3\frac{1}{3}$ cm and $MN = 8$ cm

Exercise 7d

① Measure the sides of both triangles in Fig. 7.11a. Hence find the values of:

a $\dfrac{AB}{PQ}$, b $\dfrac{BC}{QR}$, c $\dfrac{CA}{RP}$, giving each answer

as a fraction in its simplest terms.

② Measure the sides of both triangles in Fig. 7.11b. Hence complete the following:

$\dfrac{AB}{EF} = \dfrac{BC}{\square} = \dfrac{\square}{DE} = \dfrac{\square}{\square}$,

giving the final answer as a fraction in its simplest terms.

③ Measure the sides of both triangles in Fig. 7.11c. Hence complete the following:

$\dfrac{AB}{KL} = \dfrac{BC}{\square} = \dfrac{CA}{\square} = \dfrac{\square}{\square}$,

giving the final answer as a whole number.

④ Measure the sides of both triangles in Fig. 7.11d. Hence complete the following:

$\dfrac{AB}{EF} = \dfrac{\square}{\square} = \dfrac{\square}{\square} = \dfrac{\square}{\square}$,

giving the final answer as a fraction in its simplest terms.

⑤ Measure the sides of both triangles in Fig. 7.11e. Hence complete the following:

$\dfrac{AB}{\square} = \dfrac{BC}{\square} = \dfrac{CA}{\square} = \dfrac{\square}{\square}$,

giving the final answer as an improper fraction in its simplest terms.

⑥ Measure the sides of both triangles in Fig. 7.11f. Hence complete the following:

$\dfrac{\square}{AD} = \dfrac{\square}{DE} = \dfrac{\square}{EA} = \dfrac{\square}{\square}$,

giving the final answer as a whole number.

⑦ Construct triangles ABC, PQR as in Fig. 7.19 so that $\hat{B} = \hat{Q} = 35°$, $\hat{C} = \hat{R} = 80°$, $BC = 8$ cm and $QR = 10$ cm.

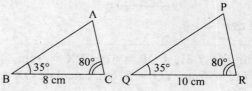

Fig. 7.19

Measure AB, AC, PQ, PR and complete the following:

$\dfrac{BC}{QR} = \dfrac{8}{10} = 0{\cdot}8$, $\dfrac{AB}{PQ} = \dfrac{\square}{\square} = \square$,

$\dfrac{AC}{PR} = \dfrac{\square}{\square} = \square$.

⑧ Construct triangles with angles as in Fig. 7.19 but with $BC = 6$ cm, $QR = 9$ cm. Measure AB, AC, PQ, PR and complete the following in decimal form.

a $\dfrac{AB}{BC} = \dfrac{\square}{6} = \square$, $\dfrac{PQ}{QR} = \dfrac{\square}{9} = \square$

b $\dfrac{AC}{BC} = \dfrac{\square}{6} = \square$, $\dfrac{PR}{QR} = \dfrac{\square}{9} = \square$

c $\dfrac{AB}{AC} = \dfrac{\square}{\square} = \square$, $\dfrac{PQ}{PR} = \dfrac{\square}{\square} = \square$

⑨ Construct two triangles with sides of 6, 8, 10 cm and 9, 12, 15 cm respectively. Measure all the angles. What can you say about the two triangles?

⑩ In Fig. 7.20, state why triangles ABC and ADE are similar. If $AB = 8$ m, $AC = 9$ m, $BC = 6$ m, $AD = 12$ m, calculate AE and DE.

Fig. 7.20

⑪ In Fig. 7.20, if $AB = 8$ cm, $BD = 2$ cm, $AC = 10$ cm, $DE = 6\frac{1}{4}$ cm, calculate AE and BC.

⑫ In Fig. 7.21, which triangle is similar to $\triangle YOQ$, and why? If $OP = 4$ m, $OX = 7$ m, $PX = 6$ m, $YQ = 4\frac{1}{2}$ m, calculate OY and OQ.

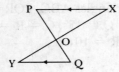

Fig. 7.21

13 In Fig. 7.21, if OP = 6 cm, PX = 9 cm, OY = 6 cm, YQ = $5\frac{2}{5}$ cm, calculate OX and OQ.

14 In Fig. 7.22, name the triangle which is similar to △OAB, and give reasons. If OA = 10 cm, OB = 8 cm, OK = 6 cm, AB = 7 cm, calculate OH and HK.

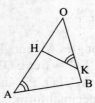

Fig. 7.22

15 In Fig. 7.22, if OH = 9 m, HA = 5 m, HK = 6 m, AB = 8 m, calculate OK and KB.

7-3 Similar plane shapes and solids

For triangles to be similar, it is sufficient that their corresponding angles should be equal. For all other plane shapes to be similar, their corresponding angles must be equal *and* the ratio of corresponding sides must be constant.

Example 8

Rectangle ABCD is similar to rectangle WXYZ. AB = 4 cm and WX = 5 cm. If BC = 9 cm, calculate the length of XY.

Assume that the letters of the rectangles are given in corresponding order.

The ratio $\frac{WX}{AB} = \frac{5}{4}$

The ratio $\frac{XY}{BC}$ must also be $\frac{5}{4}$

Hence $\frac{XY}{9} = \frac{5}{4}$

$$XY = \frac{5 \times 9}{4} \text{cm}$$

$$= \frac{45}{4} \text{cm} = 11\frac{1}{4} \text{cm}$$

For two solids to be similar, their corresponding angles must be equal *and* the ratio of the lengths of corresponding edges must be constant.

Example 9

A matchbox is in the shape of a cuboid 6 cm long, 3 cm wide and 2 cm high. Matchboxes are packed in a similar box, a cuboid 45 cm wide. Calculate the length and height of the box.

Comparing the widths of the matchbox and packing box:

$$\frac{\text{width of packing box}}{\text{width of matchbox}} = \frac{45 \text{cm}}{3 \text{cm}} = \frac{15}{1}$$

Each edge on the packing box is 15 times the corresponding edge on the matchbox.
length of box = 15 × 6 cm = 90 cm
height of box = 15 × 2 cm = 30 cm

See Chapter 18 for further treatment of similar plane shapes and solids.

Exercise 7e

1 Fig. 7.23 shows two sets of rectangles.

Use a ruler to find which set contains rectangles that are similar to each other.

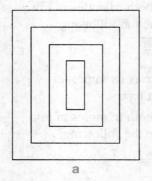
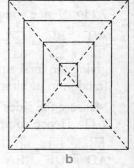

a   b

Fig. 7.23

② Rectangles ABCD and PQRS are similar. CD = 3 cm and RS = 5 cm. If AD = 12 cm, calculate the length of PS.

③ Rectangles ABCD and WXYZ are such that AB = 5 cm, BC = 15 cm, WX = 8 cm, XY = 18 cm. Is ABCD similar to WXYZ? Give reasons.

④ A cuboid is 4 cm long, 7 cm wide and 10 cm high. A similar cuboid is 25 cm high. Calculate its length and width.

⑤ Milk powder is sold in similar cylindrical tins. The small tins are of height 12 cm and diameter 10 cm. If the radius of a large tin is 7·5 cm, calculate its height.

⑥ Write down the dimensions of any two cubes. Are the two cubes similar?

⑦ A car is 4·30 m long and 1·72 m wide. If a toy model of the car is 2·6 cm long, calculate the width of the model.

⑧ A water tank is in the shape of a cuboid 2 m high, 3 m wide and 4 m long. A similar tank is 1·2 m high. Calculate the width and length of the smaller tank.

⑨ A rectangle is such that the lengths of two of its adjacent sides are in the ratio 1 : 3. A similar rectangle has one side of length 6 cm. Find two possible values for the length of its adjacent side.

⑩ State whether the following are *true* or *false*.
  a All equiangular triangles are similar.
  b All isosceles triangles are similar.
  c All equilateral triangles are similar.
  d All squares are similar.
  e All rectangles are similar.
  f All cubes are similar.
  g All cuboids are similar.

7-4 Enlargement and scale factor

Fig. 7.24 shows a method of drawing a $\triangle A_1B_1C_1$ which is similar to a given $\triangle ABC$.

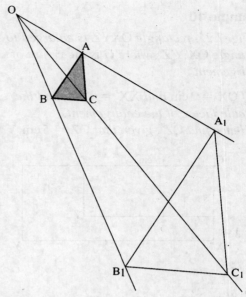

Fig. 7.24

Given $\triangle ABC$, choose any point O. O can be anywhere; in Fig. 7.24 O is outside $\triangle ABC$. From O, draw lines through A, B and C. The point A_1 is on OA extended such that $OA_1 = 3OA$. Similarly B_1 and C_1 are such that $OB_1 = 3OB$ and $OC_1 = 3OC$. Join $A_1B_1C_1$.

$\triangle A_1B_1C_1$ is similar to $\triangle ABC$. We say that $\triangle A_1B_1C_1$ is an **enlargement** of $\triangle ABC$. O is the **centre of enlargement**. In Fig. 7.24,

$$\frac{OA_1}{OA} = \frac{OB_1}{OB} = \frac{OC_1}{OC} = 3$$

The fraction $\frac{OA_1}{OA}\left(= \frac{OB_1}{OB} = \frac{OC_1}{OC}\right)$ is the **scale factor** of the enlargement. In this case the scale factor is 3.

The sides of $\triangle A_1B_1C_1$ are three times longer than the corresponding sides of $\triangle ABC$. Check this by measuring corresponding sides in Fig. 7.24. Thus,

$$\frac{A_1B_1}{AB} = \frac{B_1C_1}{BC} = \frac{C_1A_1}{CA} = 3$$

Thus the ratio of the lengths of corresponding sides is equal to the scale factor.

Example 10

In Fig. 7.25, rectangle OXYZ is enlarged to rectangle OX′Y′Z′ where O is the centre of enlargement.

a *If OX = 2 cm and XX′ = 1 cm, find the scale factor of the enlargement.*

b *Hence find OZ′, given that OZ = 5 cm.*

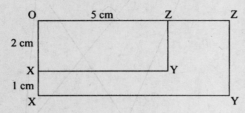

Fig. 7.25

a OX′ = 2 cm + 1 cm = 3 cm

scale factor $= \dfrac{OX′}{OX} = \dfrac{3}{2}$

b OZ′ = OZ × scale factor

$= 5 × \dfrac{3}{2}$ cm

$= 7\dfrac{1}{2}$ cm

 Optional: Do Exercise 20 of your Students' Practice Book.

Exercise 7f

1 On graph paper, draw a square ABCD and points X and Y as shown in Fig. 7.26.

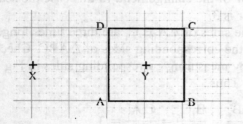

Fig. 7.26

Enlarge the square:

a by scale factor 3 with centre of enlargement at X,

b by scale factor 2 with centre Y,

c by scale factor $1\dfrac{1}{2}$ with centre A.

2 In Fig. 7.27, APQR is an enlargement of ABCD.

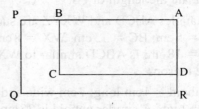

Fig. 7.27

a Which point is the centre of enlargement?

b Use measurement to find the scale factor of enlargement.

3 In Fig. 7.28, △OAB is enlarged to △OA′B′.

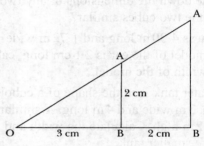

Fig. 7.28

a Which point is the centre of enlargement?

b If OB = 3 cm and BB′ = 2 cm, find the scale factor.

c If AB = 2 cm, calculate the length of A′B′.

4 The coordinates of the vertices of △ABC are A(1, 1), B(3, 1), C(1, 4).

a Choose a suitable scale and draw △ABC on graph paper.

b With the origin (0, 0) as centre of enlargement, enlarge △ABC by scale factor 2.

c Write down the coordinates of A′, B′, C′, the vertices of the enlargement.

5 The rectangle A(3, $3\dfrac{1}{2}$), B(2, 3), C(3, 1), D(4, $1\dfrac{1}{2}$) is enlarged to rectangle A′ (2, 4), B′ (0, 3), C′ (2, −1), D′ (4, 0).

a Choose a suitable scale and draw these rectangles on graph paper.

b Hence find the scale factor and the coordinates of the centre of enlargement.

Exercise 7f shows that if the scale factor is k, each length on the enlarged figure is k times as big as the corresponding length on the original figure.

Fig. 7.29 shows that k can be fractional, positive or negative.

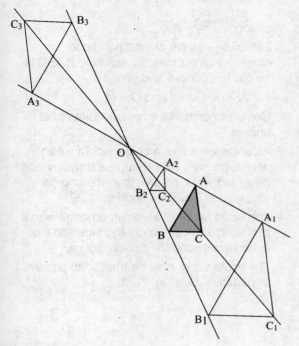

Fig. 7.29

$\triangle ABC$ is the original triangle.

$\triangle A_1B_1C_1$: $k = 2$ the enlargement is bigger than $\triangle ABC$

$\triangle A_2B_2C_2$: $k = \frac{1}{2}$ the enlargement is smaller than $\triangle ABC$

$\triangle A_3B_3C_3$: $k = -1\frac{1}{2}$ a negative scale factor means that the enlargement is on the other side of the centre of enlargement from $\triangle ABC$

Example 11

In Fig. 7.30, P′Q′ is an enlargement of PQ with centre O.

a If OP = 5 cm and OP′ = 2 cm find the scale factor of the enlargement.

b If PQ = 3 cm, calculate P′Q′.

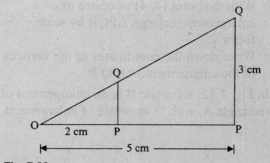

Fig. 7.30

a   scale factor $= \dfrac{OP'}{OP}$

$$= \frac{2}{5}$$

b   P′Q′ $=$ scale factor $\times$ PQ

$$= \frac{2}{5} \times 3 \text{ cm}$$

$$= \frac{6}{5} \text{ cm}$$

$$= 1\cdot2 \text{ cm}$$

Exercise 7g

1. Make a copy of Fig. 7.26 on graph paper. Enlarge square ABCD:
   a by scale factor $-\frac{1}{2}$ with centre of enlargement X,
   b by scale factor $\frac{4}{5}$ with centre Y,
   c by scale factor $-1\frac{1}{2}$ with centre A.

2. In Fig. 7.31, the **p** is an enlargement of the **d**. Use measurement to find the scale factor of the enlargement.

Fig. 7.31

3. The coordinates of the vertices of $\triangle PQR$ are P(0, 2), Q(4, 6), R(8, 1).
   a Choose a suitable scale and draw $\triangle PQR$ on graph paper.

b With the point (4, 4) as centre of enlargement, enlarge △PQR by scale factor $\frac{1}{2}$.

c Write down the coordinates of the vertices of the enlargement, △P′Q′R′.

④ In Fig. 7.32, rectangle B is an enlargement of rectangle A, with O as centre of enlargement.

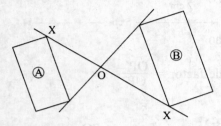

Fig. 7.32

a If OX = 8 cm and OX′ = 10 cm, find the scale factor of the enlargement.

b If the diagonals of rectangle A are 12 cm long, calculate the length of the diagonals of rectangle B.

⑤ Square A(−2, −1), B(1, −1), C(1, −4), D(−2, −4) is enlarged to square A′(4, 1), B′(3, 1), C′(3, 2), D′(4, 2).

a Choose a suitable scale and draw these squares on graph paper, labelling the vertices carefully.

b Hence find the scale factor and the coordinates of the centre of enlargement.

SUMMARY

1 *Similar shapes* have *corresponding angles* equal and *corresponding sides* in the same ratio. That is if △ABC is similar to △XYZ, then

$$\hat{A} = \hat{X}, \hat{B} = \hat{Y}, \hat{C} = \hat{Z} \text{ and}$$

$$\frac{AB}{XY} = \frac{BC}{YZ} = \frac{AC}{XZ}$$

2 Similar figures are always named in corresponding order, for example △ABC is similar to △XYZ, if and only if

$$\hat{A} = \hat{X}, \hat{B} = \hat{Y} \text{ and } \hat{C} = \hat{Z}.$$

3 Corresponding sides are opposite equal angles.

4 An *enlargement* of a shape about a *centre of enlargement* will produce a similar shape, either bigger or smaller than the original shape. See Fig. 7.24 and Fig. 7.29.

5 The *scale factor* of an enlargement is equal to the ratio of corresponding sides on the enlargement and the original figure.

6 The scale factor may be fractional, positive or negative. See Fig. 7.29.

PUZZLE CORNER

Enter PIN Code

Etim changed his mobile phone PIN code from 0000 but he has now forgotten it. He remembers that if you multiply it by 4, the answer is the PIN code in reverse.
Can you help Etim?

8 Tangent of an angle

OBJECTIVES

By the end of this chapter you should be able to:

1 Define the tangent of an angle in a right-angled triangle
2 Use measurement to find the tangent of an angle
3 Use tangents of angles to calculate lengths and angles in a right-angled triangle
4 Define and use the complement of an angle
5 Use tangent tables to find the tangents of angles from 0° to 90°
6 Solve practical problems using tangents of angles and tangent tables.

Teaching and learning materials

Teacher: Cardboard models of right-angled triangles (as in Fig. 8.2); tangent tables (provided on page 271)

Student: Tangent tables (provided on page 271).

8-1 Tangent of an angle

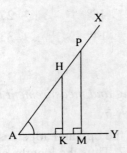

Fig. 8.1

Fig. 8.1 shows an angle A with arms AX and AY. H and P are any two points on AX. HK and PM meet

AY perpendicularly at K and M. Thus, △AHK is equiangular and therefore similar to △APM.

Thus, $\dfrac{HK}{KA} = \dfrac{PM}{MA}$

If any number of points are taken on AX and the perpendiculars drawn, the ratio

$\dfrac{\text{length of perpendicular}}{\text{length of base-line}}$ is the same for each.

Hence the value of the ratio $\dfrac{HK}{KA}$ depends only on the size of Â.

The ratio $\dfrac{HK}{KA}$ is called the **tangent** of the angle A. This is usually shortened to **tan A**. Fig. 8.2 shows △AHK in various positions.

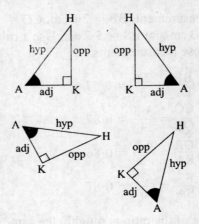

Fig. 8.2

The sides of the triangle are as follows.

AH   the **hypotenuse**
HK   the side **opposite** to Â
KA   the side **adjacent** to Â

These are abbreviated to **hyp, opp, adj** respectively, so that

$$\textbf{tan A} = \frac{\textbf{opp}}{\textbf{adj}}$$

In Fig. 8.3, $X\hat{A}Y = 41°$, perpendiculars BP, CQ, DR, ES have been drawn so that AP = 3 cm, AQ = 4 cm, AR = 5 cm and AS = 6 cm.

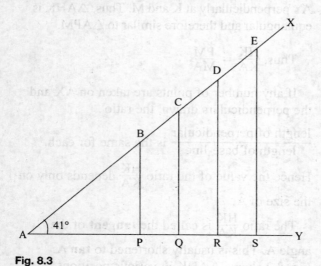

Fig. 8.3

By measurement, BP = 2·6 cm, CQ = 3·5 cm, DR = 4·3 cm and ES = 5·2 cm. Use a ruler to check these measurements.

Hence $\dfrac{BP}{PA} = \dfrac{2·6}{3} = 0·87$

$\dfrac{CQ}{QA} = \dfrac{3·5}{4} = 0·87$

$\dfrac{DR}{RA} = \dfrac{4·3}{5} = 0·86$

$\dfrac{ES}{SA} = \dfrac{5·2}{6} = 0·87$

The value of the ratio is roughly the same each time, i.e. tan 41° ≃ 0·87.

The working is made easier if the base-line (adj) is a convenient length such as 10 cm.

☞ *Optional:* Do Exercise 21 of your Students' Practice Book.

Exercise 8a [Class assignment]

① Copy Fig. 8.3, making $X\hat{A}Y = 30°$, AP = 7 cm, PQ = QR = RS = 1 cm. Measure BP, CQ, DR, ES. Hence calculate the values of tan 30° by the above method.

② Use the method of question 1 with $X\hat{A}Y = 51°$. Hence find four values of tan 51°.

Example 1

Find the value of tan 57° by drawing and measurement.

Fig. 8.4 is a scale drawing of the method.

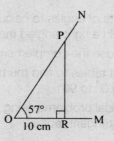

Fig. 8.4

Draw an angle $M\hat{O}N = 57°$. On OM, mark off OR equal to 10 cm. From R, draw a line perpendicular to OM to meet ON at P. Measure RP. It is found that RP = 15·4 cm (approx).

$$\tan 57° = \frac{PR}{RO} = \frac{15·4}{10} = 1·54 \text{ (approx)}$$

Exercise 8b

Find the tangents of the following angles by drawing and measurement.

① 42° ② 62° ③ 38°
④ 71° ⑤ 45° ⑥ 27°
⑦ 77° ⑧ 14° ⑨ 33°

Example 2

Find by drawing and measurement the angle whose tangent is $\frac{3}{7}$.

The lengths of the opp and adj sides are to be in the ratio 3 : 7. Thus the lengths could be 3 cm and 7 cm, or 6 cm and 14 cm, and so on. The bigger the drawing, the better the chance of accurate measurement.

Fig. 8.5 is a scale drawing of the required triangle.

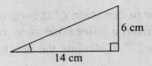

Fig. 8.5

By measurement, the angle whose tangent is $\frac{3}{7}$ is 23° (approx).

 Optional: Do Exercise 22 of your Students' Practice Book.

Exercise 8c
Find by drawing and measurement the angles whose tangents are as follows.

① $\frac{5}{9}$ ② $\frac{2}{7}$ ③ $\frac{4}{3}$

④ $\frac{8}{5}$ ⑤ $\frac{11}{4}$ ⑥ $\frac{5}{8}$

⑦ $\frac{9}{10}$ ⑧ $\frac{10}{9}$ ⑨ $\frac{5}{7}$

8-3 Use of tangent of an angle

The use of tables for finding the tangent of an angle will be explained later in this chapter. Meanwhile, Table 8.1 gives the tangents of some chosen angles.

angle A	tan A
25°	0·4663
30°	0·5774
35°	0·7002
40°	0·8391
45°	1·000
50°	1·192
55°	1·428
60°	1·732
65°	2·145
70°	2·747

Table 8.1

The values in Table 8.1 are correct to 4 significant figures.

Example 3
The angle of elevation of the top of a building is 25° from a point 70 m away on level ground. Calculate the height of the building.

In Fig. 8.6, HK represents the height of the building; AK is on level ground.

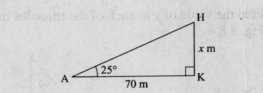

Fig. 8.6

$\dfrac{HK}{KA} = \tan 25°$.

Let HK be x m. KA = 70 m and, from Table 8.1, $\tan 25° = 0·4663$. Hence:

$$\frac{x}{70} = 0·4663$$
$$x = 0·4663 \times 70$$
$$= 4·663 \times 7$$
$$= 32·641$$

However, the answer cannot be given to this **degree of accuracy**. Since the data are given to 2 significant figures, the answer should also be to 2 s.f.

The height of the building is 33 m to 2 s.f.

Exercise 8d
Use the values in Table 8.1 in this exercise. Give all answers correct to 2 s.f.

① Find the value of x in each of the triangles in Fig. 8.7.

79

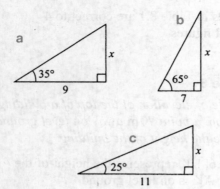

Fig. 8.7

② Find the value of y in each of the triangles in Fig. 8.8.

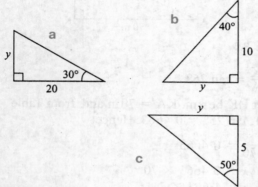

Fig. 8.8

③ Find the value of z in each of the triangles in Fig. 8.9.

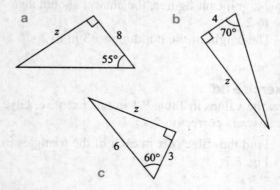

Fig. 8.9

④ When the angle of elevation of the sun is 45°, a student's shadow on level ground is 1·6 m long. Find the height of the student.

⑤ An aerial mast has a shadow 40 m long on level ground when the elevation of the sun is 70°. Calculate the height of the mast.

⑥ The angle of elevation of the top of a building from a point 80 m away on level ground is 25°. Calculate the height of the building.

Complement of an angle

In Exercise 8d, the given length was always *adjacent* to the given angle. The side to be found was always *opposite* the given angle.

Suppose, as in Fig. 8.10, the opposite side is given and the adjacent side is to be found.

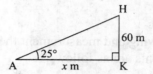

Fig. 8.10

In Fig. 8.10, $\hat{A} = 25°$, HK = 60 m and AK = x m. Then, as before,

$$\tan 25° = \frac{60}{x}$$

Multiply both sides by x.

$$x \times \tan 25° = 60$$

Divide both sides by $\tan 25°$.

$$x = \frac{60}{\tan 25°}$$

$$= \frac{60}{0·4663}$$

This involves difficult calculation. A different method, involving easier calculation, would be better. See below.

Since $\triangle$AHK is right-angled at K, $\hat{H} = 90° - 25° = 65°$

80

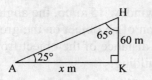

Fig. 8.11

With the data of Fig. 8.11,

$$\frac{x}{60} = \tan 65°$$

$$x = 60 \tan 65°$$
$$= 60 \times 2·145$$
$$= 128·7$$
$$= 130 \text{ to 2 s.f.}$$

Thus, AK = 130 m.

65° is the **complement** of 25°, i.e. 65° + 25° = 90°. To avoid dividing by the tangent of an angle, find the complement of the angle and use its tangent.

Example 4

A post is standing vertically in horizontal ground such that 80 cm of the post is above ground. Find the length of its shadow when the elevation of the sun is 40°.

In Fig. 8.12, AB is the post and BC, *d* cm long, is its shadow.

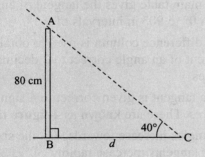

Fig. 8.12

If Ĉ = 40°, then Â = 90° − 40° = 50°

$$\frac{BC}{AB} = \tan 50°$$

$$\frac{d}{80} = 1·192$$

$$d = 1·192 \times 80$$
$$= 95·36$$
$$= 95 \text{ to 2 s.f.}$$

The shadow is 95 cm long.

Example 5

A student walks 5 km due north from O and then 8 km due east. Find his bearing from O.

In Fig. 8.13, the bearing of the student from his original position (point O) is given by angle PÔQ.

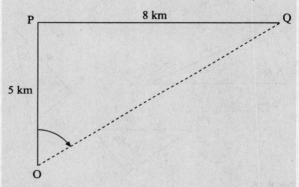

Fig. 8.13

$$\tan PÔQ = \frac{8}{5} = 1·600$$

$$PÔQ = 58° \text{ (using 4-figure tables)}*$$

Thus, the student's bearing from O is 058°.

*Section 8-4 explains how to use 4-figure tangent tables.

Exercise 8e

Use the values in Table 8.1 in this exercise. Give all answers correct to 2 s.f.

(1) Find the value of *a* in each of the triangles in Fig. 8.14.

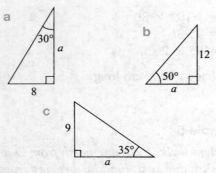

Fig. 8.14

② Find the value of *b* in each of the triangles in Fig. 8.15.

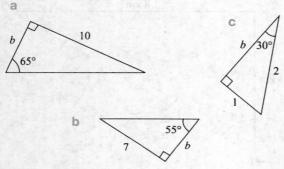

Fig. 8.15

③ Find the value of *c* in each of the triangles in Fig. 8.16.

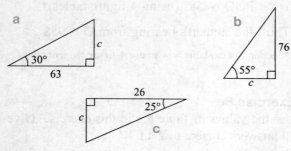

Fig. 8.16

④ Calculate the length of the shadow cast on level ground by a radio mast 90 m high when the elevation of the sun is 40°.

⑤ From a window 15 m up, the angle of depression of an object on the ground is 20°. Find the distance of the object from the base of the building.

⑥ Point A is 5 km due east of point B. B is due north of a point C and A is on a bearing 025° from C. Calculate the distance between B and C.

⑦ A ship steams 4 km due east from O and then 5 km due north. What is the bearing of its final position from O?

⑧ A point Q is 8 km east of P. If another point R is 7 km south of P, find the bearing of Q from R.

⑨ A point R is *x* km north of a point P. Another point, Q, is 10 km east of R. If the bearing of Q from P is 32°, calculate the distance between P and R.

Use the tangent tables on page 271 to find the tangents of angles from 0° to 90°. Table 8.2 shows three lines taken from the tangent table.

Notice the following:

① The main table gives the tangent of any angle from 0° to 90° in intervals of 0·1°.

② The difference column is used to obtain the tangent of an angle correct to 2 decimal places.

③ Each tangent is given correct to 4 significant figures. These are known as **4-figure tables**.

④ As angles increase towards 90°, the sizes of their tangents increase rapidly.

x	·0	·1	·2	·3	·4	·5	·6	·7	·8	·9	Add difference								
											1	2	3	4	5	6	7	8	9
32	0·6249	0·6273	0·6297	0·6322	0·6346	0·6371	0·6395	0·6420	0·6445	0·6469	2	5	7	10	12	15	17	20	22
59	1·644	1·671	1·678	1·684	1·691	1·698	1·704	1·711	1·718	1·725	1	1	2	3	3	4	5	5	6
71	2·904	2·921	2·937	2·954	2·971	2·989	3·006	3·024	3·042	3·060	2	3	5	7	9	10	12	14	16

Table 8.2 Tangent tables

Example 6

Use tables to find the tangents of angles
a 32°   *b* 59·6°   *c* 71·38°.

a Looking within the table entries, the number opposite 32° and under 0·0° is 0·6249. Thus, tan 32° = 0·6249.

b The number opposite 59° and under 0·6° is 1·704. Thus, tan 59·6° = 1·704.

c The number opposite 71° and under 0·3° is 2·954. The number opposite 71° and under 8 (0·08°) in the difference column is 14. The tangent of 71·38° is 2·954 + 0·014 = 2·968. Thus, tan 71·38° = 2·968.

Always add the number in the difference column to the rightmost digits of the main table entry.

Exercise 8f   [Oral or written]

Use the tables on page 271 to find the tangents of the following.

① 13°   ② 64°   ③ 35°   ④ 56°

⑤ 74°   ⑥ 88°   ⑦ 23·1°   ⑧ 36·1°

⑨ 45·1°   ⑩ $32\frac{1}{2}$°   ⑪ 42·5°   ⑫ 19·5°

⑬ 56·2°   ⑭ 63·8°   ⑮ 18·3°   ⑯ 27·7°

⑰ 48·6°   ⑱ 67·4°   ⑲ 78·6°   ⑳ 78·8°

㉑ 25·9°   ㉒ 87·1°   ㉓ 87·2°   ㉔ 87·3°

㉕ 68·12°   ㉖ 39·45°   ㉗ 11·18°   ㉘ 71·92°

㉙ 80·4°   ㉚ 55·77°   ㉛ 85·6°   ㉜ 81·8°

㉝ 3·28°   ㉞ 12·53°   ㉟ 42·42°   ㊱ 45·54°

Example 7

Use tables to find the angles whose tangents are:
a 0·9556   *b* $\frac{7}{3}$ *c* 0·6398.

a Let the angle be A, then tan A = 0·9556. Looking within the table entries, 0·9556 is opposite 43° and under 0·7°. Thus, A = 43·7°.

b Let the angle be B, then tan B = $\frac{7}{3}$ = 2·333 to 4 s.f. Thus, B = 66·8°.

c Let the angle be C, then tan C = 0·6398. Look at Table 8.2. There is no 0·6398 in the table. We therefore look for a number close to it, and not more than it. In this case the number is 0·6395. The difference between 0·6398 and 0·6395 is 0·0003. We now look for a value in the difference column (opposite 0·6395) that is close to 3. In this case the value is 2. Thus, the nearest value to 0·6398 is 0·6395 + 0·0002 = 0·6397. 0·6395 is opposite 32° and under 0·6°, and the 'extra' 2 is under 0·01°. Thus, C = 32·61°.

Exercise 8g

Use the tables on page 271 to find the angles whose tangents are as follows.

① 0·9325   ② 0·4452   ③ 0·5543   ④ 1·881

⑤ 2·356   ⑥ 19·08   ⑦ 1·570   ⑧ 0·8816

⑨ 0·8847   ⑩ 2·194   ⑪ 0·0524   ⑫ 1·711

⑬ 0·3581   ⑭ 3·582   ⑮ 35·80   ⑯ 0·1016

⑰ 10·20   ⑱ 13   ⑲ $\frac{5}{8}$ ⑳ $\frac{8}{5}$

㉑ $\frac{7}{9}$ ㉒ $\frac{5}{2}$ ㉓ $\frac{2}{5}$ ㉔ $\frac{17}{9}$

㉕ 0·4997   ㉖ 0·683   ㉗ 2·765   ㉘ 0·940

㉙ 0·941   ㉚ 150

8-5 Applications to practical problems

In geometry, we use capital letters for naming points and angles. Small letters often stand for the lengths of lines. We often use Greek letters for sizes of angles. Some of the most common Greek letters are α (alpha), β (beta), γ (gamma), δ (delta), θ (theta) and ϕ (phi).

Example 8

A cone is 6 cm high and its vertical angle is 54°. Calculate the radius of its base.

In Fig. 8.17, the **vertical angle** is the angle between opposite slant heights VA and VB.

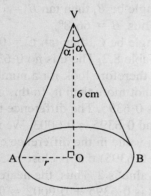

Fig. 8.17

Thus, with the lettering of the diagram, the vertical angle is 2α.

$$2\alpha = 54°$$
$$\text{thus } \alpha = 27°$$

In $\triangle$AVO, $\tan \alpha = \dfrac{r}{6}$

$$r = 6 \tan 27°$$
$$= 6 \times 0.5095$$
$$= 3.057$$
$$= 3.1 \text{ to 2 s.f.}$$

The radius of the base of the cone is 3.1 cm.

Example 9

An aerial is $83\frac{1}{2}$ m high. Calculate the angle of elevation of its top from a point 120 m away on level ground.

Let the angle of elevation be θ.

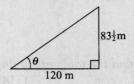

Fig. 8.18

From Fig. 8.18,

$$\tan \theta = \frac{83.5}{120}$$
$$= \frac{8.35}{12} = \frac{4.175}{6}$$
$$= 0.6958 \text{ to 4 s.f.}$$

From tables, $\theta = 34.8°$ to nearest $0.1°$.
The angle of elevation is approximately $34.8°$.

Exercise 8h

Give all lengths correct to 2 significant figures. Give all angles correct to the nearest $0.1°$.

1 Calculate the lengths marked x in the triangles shown in Fig. 8.19, all lengths being in metres.

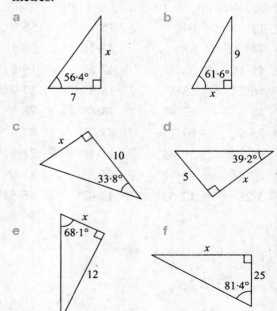

Fig. 8.19

84

② Calculate the angles marked θ in the triangles in Fig. 8.20.

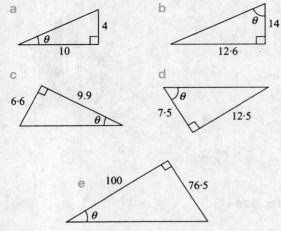

a

b

c

d

e

Fig. 8.20

③ Calculate the angles marked α and β in the triangles in Fig. 8.21.

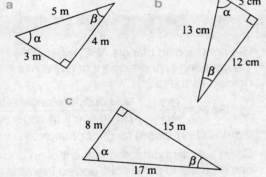

a

b

c

Fig. 8.21

④ A cone is 8 cm high and its vertical angle is 62°. Find the diameter of its base.

⑤ An isosceles triangle has a vertical angle of 116°, and its base is 8 cm long. Calculate its height.

⑥ Find the angle of elevation of the top of a flagpole 31·9 m high from a point 55 m away on level ground.

⑦ The gradient of a road is 1 (vertically) in $4\frac{1}{2}$ (horizontally). See Fig. 8.22.

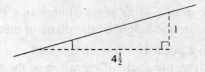

$4\frac{1}{2}$

Fig. 8.22

Calculate the angle that the road makes with the horizontal.

⑧ From a point on level ground 40 m away, the angle of elevation of the top of a tree is $32\frac{1}{2}$°. Calculate the height of the tree.

⑨ In question 8, if the tree had been 21·6 m high, what would have been the angle of elevation?

⑩ A rectangle has sides of length 2·2 m and 8 m. Calculate the angle between a diagonal and a longer side.

⑪ A student travels 8 km north and then 5 km east. What is then her bearing from her starting point?

⑫ Find the angle of elevation of the sun when a mosque tower 93 m high has a shadow 62 m long.

⑬ The roof of a round house 3·6 m in diameter rises symmetrically to a vertex. If the roof slopes at 48° to the horizontal, calculate the height of the vertex above the top of the house's wall.

⑭ In Fig. 8.23, O is the centre of the circle.

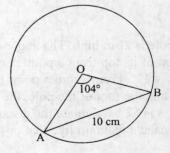

Fig. 8.23

Calculate the perpendicular distance of O from AB.

⑮ An aeroplane, coming in to land, passes over a point 1 km away from its landing place on level ground. If its angle of elevation is 15°, calculate the height of the plane in metres.

16 From a point 100 m from the foot of a building, the angle of elevation of the top of the building is 18·7°. Find the height of the building.

17 Fig. 8.24 shows how a student finds the width of a river. He places a stone at P on one bank directly opposite a post Q on the other bank. From P he walks 200 m along the bank to R. He finds that $P\hat{R}Q = 23\frac{1}{2}°$. Calculate the width of the river.

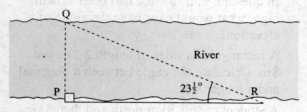

Fig. 8.24

18 Given the data of Fig. 8.25, calculate the length of AB. (*Hint*: first find FA, then FB, and subtract.)

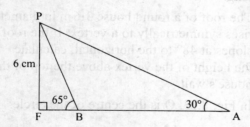

Fig. 8.25

19 A flagpole is 20 m high. The angle of elevation of its top from a point A on level ground is 37°. From another point B, in line with A and the foot of the pole, the angle of elevation is 52°. Calculate the distance AB. (*Hint*: make a diagram like that of Fig. 8.25.)

20 Fig. 8.26 represents a football player, P, kicking at goal AB.

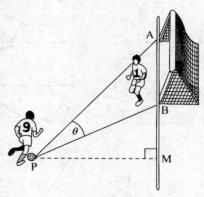

Fig. 8.26

If AB = 7·2 m, BM = 4·8 m, PM = 12 m, find the angle θ which the goal subtends at P. (*Hint*: find the difference between $A\hat{P}M$ and $B\hat{P}M$.)

Revision exercise 1   (Chapters 1, 2, 5)

1. Find the greater of 21_{seven} and 10101_{two}.

2. With the help of Table 1.2 on page 23, write FIND UNKNOWN in binary code.

3. Use Table 1.2 on page 23 to decode the following.

   a 10011
      10100
      01111
      00011
      01011

   b 00011
      01111
      01110
      10100
      10010
      01111
      01100

4. Find the sum of 11 and the product of 3 and 13.

5. Find one-third of the sum of 23 and the square of 5.

6. If $\dfrac{0 \cdot 0001 \times 1 \cdot 11}{0 \cdot 1 \times 10^4}$ simplifies to $A \times 10^n$, where A is a number between 1 and 10 and n is an integer, find the values of A and n.

7. Find the sum of $8 \cdot 55 \times 10^3$ and $4 \cdot 15 \times 10^3$ and express the answer in standard form.

8. Simplify the following. Give the answers in standard form.

   a $(5 \cdot 3 \times 10^4) - (2 \cdot 4 \times 10^4)$
   b $(4 \cdot 21 \times 10^{-3}) + (3 \cdot 72 \times 10^{-3})$
   c $(5 \cdot 2 \times 10^2) + (6 \cdot 24 \times 10^3)$
   d $(7 \times 10^{-3}) - (8 \times 10^{-4})$

9. Simplify the following. Give the answers in standard form.

   a $(2 \times 10^3) \times (3 \cdot 8 \times 10^2)$
   b $(6 \cdot 5 \times 10^8) \div (1 \cdot 3 \times 10^5)$
   c $(4 \times 10^{-4}) \times (8 \times 10^5)$
   d $(5 \cdot 4 \times 10^2) \div (9 \times 10^{-3})$

10. The populations of two countries are $5 \cdot 9 \times 10^7$ and $8 \cdot 7 \times 10^6$ respectively. Find the total population of the two countries correct to 2 significant figures.

Revision test 1   (Chapters 1, 2, 5)

1. Change 342_{six} to a number in base ten.
   A 34·2   B 44   C 57   D 134
   E 3 420

2. Change the number 10010_{two} to base ten.
   A 40_{ten} B 34_{ten} C 18_{ten} D 10_{ten}
   E 36_{ten}

3. Express in base two, the square of 11_{two}.
   A 1001   B 1010   C 1011   D 1 101
   E 1 100

4. The sum of three consecutive even numbers is 72. The highest of the three numbers is:
   A 12   B 14   C 22   D 24   E 26

5. Calculate $82 \cdot 5 \div 0 \cdot 025$, expressing the answer in standard form.
   A $3 \cdot 3 \times 10^{-3}$ B $3 \cdot 3 \times 10^{-2}$
   C $3 \cdot 3 \times 10^1$ D $3 \cdot 3 \times 10^2$
   E $3 \cdot 3 \times 10^3$

6. Change the following base ten numbers to base two.
   a 30   b 57   c 100

7. The product of two numbers is $7\frac{1}{5}$. If one of the numbers is 9, find the other.

8. Find one-sixth of the positive difference between 36 and 63.

9. Simplify the following. Give the answers in standard form.
   a $(6 \cdot 3 \times 10^{-3}) + (3 \times 10^{-4})$
   b $(7 \cdot 42 \times 10^4) - (6 \cdot 8 \times 10^3)$
   c $(4 \times 10^5) \times (3 \cdot 9 \times 10^{-1})$
   d $(9 \cdot 1 \times 10^{-5}) \div (7 \times 10^{-3})$

10. A lorry is loaded with 500 boxes. Each box contains 24 bottles. Express the number of bottles on the lorry in standard form.

Revision exercise 2 (Chapters 3, 6)

① Factorise the following.
  a $9a - 27$ b $3r - 8rt$
  c $42x^3 - 28xy$ d $42a^2b - 51ab^2$

② Factorise the following, simplifying brackets where possible.
  a $x(1 - 3x) - 4x^2$
  b $(x + a)(3y - b) + (x + a)(2y - b)$

③ Factorise the following by grouping in pairs.
  a $an + am - 3m - 3n$
  b $a^2 - 7a + 3a - 21$
  c $3xy - 6xz - 5ay + 10az$

④ In each of the following, regroup the given terms, then factorise.
  a $3ay - 2bx + 2xy - 3ab$
  b $ds + rt - dt - rs$

⑤ If $n = 37^2 + 37 \times 63$, use factorisation to find the value of n.

⑥ If $y = 3x - 7$, find y when x is a 5, b −5.

⑦ If $y = 3x^2$, find a y when $x = 2$, b x when $y = 147$.

⑧ A triangle of base b cm and height h cm has an area A cm² given by $A = \frac{1}{2}bh$.
  a Find the area when $b = 5$ and $h = 7$.
  b Find the height of a triangle which has a base 6 cm long and an area of 33 cm².

⑨ Make x the subject of each of the following.
  a $y = 8x$ b $\frac{x}{3} = z$
  c $y = 5x - 3$ d $2\pi x = c$

⑩ a Make r the subject of the formula $A = 2\pi rh$.
  b Hence find r when $A = 264$, $\pi = \frac{22}{7}$ and $h = 14$.

Revision test 2 (Chapters 3, 6)

① The highest common factor of $10a^2b$ and $8ab$ is:
  A $80a^2b$ B $2ab$ C $5a$ D $1\frac{1}{4}a$ E 4

② Which of the following are factors of $6x^2 - 21xy$? I, 3; II, x; III, $(2x - 7y)$.
  A I only   B II only   C I and II only
  D All of them   E None of them

③ If $y = \dfrac{x + 9}{x - 3}$, find the value of y when $x = 5$.
  A −5   B −2   C 5   D 6   E 7

④ If $a = 2b - c$, find the value of b when $a = 11$ and $c = -3$.
  A 4   B 7   C 8   D 14   E 16

⑤ If $A = \frac{1}{2}(a + b)h$, express h in terms of A, a and b, $h =$
  A $A - \frac{1}{2}(a + b)$ B $\frac{1}{2}(a + b)A$
  C $\dfrac{2A}{a + b}$ D $\dfrac{A}{2(a + b)}$ E $\dfrac{a + b}{2A}$

⑥ Factorise the following.
  a $7x - 28$
  b $5m + 8mn$
  c $27ab + 36b^2$
  d $35p^2q - 14pq^2$

⑦ Factorise the following, simplifying where possible.
  a $3a^2 + a(2a + b)$
  b $(5x - 2y)(a - b) - (2x - y)(a - b)$
  c $pq - pr + 8q - 8r$
  d $5x + ky + 5y + kx$

⑧ a Factorise $\pi r^2 + 2\pi rh$.
  b Hence find the value of the expression when $\pi = \frac{22}{7}$, $r = 4$ and $h = 5$.

⑨ Given that $y = 9 - 2x$, copy and complete Table R1.

x	−2	−1	0	1	2
$9 - 2x$	9	9	9	9	9
y					

Table R1

⑩ The cost, c naira, of having a car repaired is given by the formula $c = 250 + 150t$, where t is the number of hours the work takes.
  a Find the cost when the work takes $2\frac{1}{2}$ hours.
  b If the cost of repairs is ₦850, how long did the work take?

Revision exercise 3 (Chapters 4, 7, 8)

In this exercise, construct all figures using ruler and compasses only.

① Construct angles of a 45°, b 60°, c 150°, d 75°. (*Note:* 150° = 180° − 30°, 75° = 45° + 30°.) Leave all construction lines on your drawings.)

② Draw *any* quadrilateral such that its four sides are of different lengths. Find, by construction, the mid-point of each side. Join the mid-points to form a new quadrilateral. What kind of quadrilateral is it?

③ a Construct △XYZ such that $\hat{Y} = 90°$, XY = 8 cm and YZ = 5 cm.
   b Measure the length of the hypotenuse XZ.

④ In Fig. R1, △ABC is similar to △PQR. From the data in the figure, calculate the length of
   a QR, b PR.

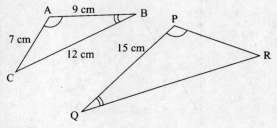

Fig. R1

⑤ In Fig. R2, △APQ is an enlargement of △AXY.

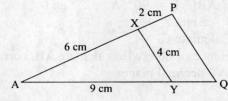

Fig. R2

   a What is the scale factor of the enlargement?
   b Calculate the length of PQ.

⑥ With the data as given in Fig. R3, calculate the length of YZ.

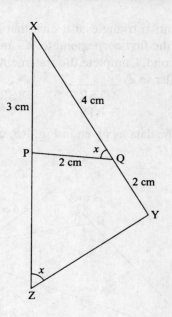

Fig. R3

⑦ Find the tangent of 60° by construction and measurement.

⑧ Find the value of x and z in the triangles in Fig. R4.

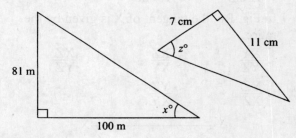

Fig. R4

⑨ When the angle of elevation of the sun is 64°, a student's shadow on level ground is 80 cm long. Calculate the height of the student to the nearest 5 cm.

⑩ AB is a chord of a circle, centre O. AB = 16 cm and AÔB = 110°. Calculate the distance between O and the mid-point of AB.

Revision test 3 (Chapters 4, 7, 8)

① Which one of the following angles can be constructed using ruler and compasses only?
   A 115°   B 125°   C 135°
   D 145°   E 155°

② Two similar triangles are such that AB and CB in the first correspond to RT and ST in the second. Complete the statement: △ABC is similar to △ _____ .

A RST   B TSR   C SRT
D TRS   E RTS

③ With the data as given in Fig. R5, calculate YQ.

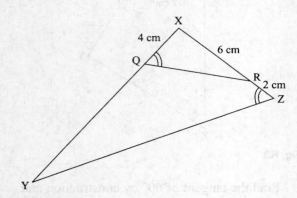

Fig. R5

A 6 cm   B 8 cm   C 10 cm
D 12 cm   E 16 cm

④ In Fig. R6, the tangent of $\hat{X}$ is given by the ratio:

A $\dfrac{XY}{YZ}$ B $\dfrac{XZ}{XY}$ C $\dfrac{XZ}{YZ}$

D $\dfrac{YZ}{XZ}$ E $\dfrac{YZ}{XY}$

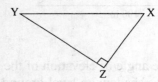

Fig. R6

⑤ Using 4-figure tables, find the angle with a tangent equal to 0·2796.
A 15·3°   B 15·4°   C 15·6°   D 15·7°
E 15·8°

⑥ a Draw a line AB 6 cm long.
  b Construct the perpendicular bisector of AB.
  c Hence construct an isosceles triangle ACB such that CA = CB = 8 cm.
  d Measure $\hat{C}$.

⑦ Construct △ABC such that BC = 6·5 cm, $\hat{B}$ = 45° and BA = 7·5 cm. Measure AC.

⑧ In Fig. R7, name the triangle which is similar to △OAB. If OA = 3 cm, OX = 7·5 cm and AB = 4 cm, calculate XY.

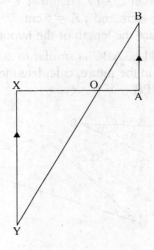

Fig. R7

⑨ Find, by drawing and measurement, the angle whose tangent is $\frac{3}{5}$.

⑩ In △ABC, $\hat{B}$ = 90°, $\hat{A}$ = 23° and BC = 6 cm.
  a Calculate $\hat{C}$.
  b Hence or otherwise calculate AB, correct to 2 decimal places.

General revision test A   (Chapters 1–8)

① Find the value of $(101_{two})^2$ in base two.
A 1010   B 1111   C 10100
D 10101   E 11001

② Find the product of the square of $\frac{1}{2}$ and the sum of 13 and 19.
A 8   B 16   C 32   D 64   E 128

③ Calculate 72 × 8 000, giving the answer in standard form.
A 9×10^{-3} B $5 \cdot 76 \times 10^{3}$ C 9×10^{3}
D $5 \cdot 76 \times 10^{4}$ E $5 \cdot 76 \times 10^{5}$

④ Which of the following are factors of $6a^2 - 2ab - 3ab + b^2$?
I, $(3a - b)$;   II, $(2a + b)$;   III, $(2a - b)$.
A I only   B I and II only
C I and III only   D II and III only
E None of them

5. If $S = 2(n - 2)$, find n when $S = 18$.
   A 7   B 10   C 11   D 18   E 32

6. If $P = 2(l + b)$, express b in terms of P and l. $b =$
   A $2(l + P)$ B $P - 2l$ C $\dfrac{P}{2} - l$
   D $2P - l$ E $\dfrac{P - 2}{l}$

7. If $\triangle$RXS is similar to $\triangle$TPQ, which one of the following angles must equal $\hat{X}$?
   A $\hat{P}$ B $\hat{Q}$ C $\hat{R}$ D $\hat{S}$ E $\hat{T}$

8. In Fig. R8, calculate the length of BX.
   A 7·5 cm   B 8 cm   C 10·8 cm
   D 13 cm   E 18 cm

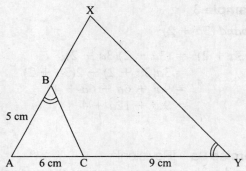

Fig. R8

9. Using 4-figure tables, find $X°$ where $\tan X° = 0·4549$.
   A 24·3°   B 24·4°   C 24·5°
   D 24·6°   E 24·7°

10. Using 4-figure tables, the value of $\tan 37·7°$ is:
    A 0·7536   B 0·7563   C 0·7646
    D 0·7701   E 0·7729

11. a Starting at 001, write down the first seven binary numbers as 3-digit numerals. Label these A, B, C, D, E, F, G.
    b Hence find the words that the following represent.
    i 010   ii 011   iii 110
       001   001   101
       111   110   101
                   101   100

12. The difference between two numbers is 10. If one of the numbers is 7, find two possible values for the other number.

13. Simplify the following, giving the answers in standard form.
    a $(5·8 \times 10^4) + (7·7 \times 10^4)$
    b $(8·2 \times 10^{-2}) - (4 \times 10^{-2})$
    c $(5·1 \times 10^{-3}) \times (3 \times 10^{-2})$
    d $(5 \times 10^5) \div (8 \times 10^{-2})$

14. Factorise the following, simplifying brackets where necessary.
    a $18ab - 63$
    b $52x - 8x^2$
    c $5a^2 + a(2b - 3a)$
    d $(2x + y)(2a + b) - (2a + b)(x - 5y)$

15. Factorise the following.
    a $22ab - 11ac + 6rb - 3rc$
    b $x^2 + 5x - 9x - 45$
    c $6ax - 2by + 4ay - 3bx$

16. Factorise $\pi rs + \pi r^2$. Hence find the value of the expression when $\pi = \frac{22}{7}$, $r = 5$ and $s = 16$.

17. Given that $3x + 4y = 26$,
    a express x in terms of y and thus find x when $y = 5$,
    b express y in terms of x and thus find y when $x = 10$.

18. Using ruler and compasses only, construct $\triangle$PQR such that PQ = 8·4 cm, $\hat{Q} = 60°$ and QR = 4·2 cm. Measure $\hat{P}$ and find the length of PR.

19. The two shorter sides of a right-angled triangle are 12 cm and 15 cm long. Calculate the sizes of the acute angles in the triangle.

20. From a point on level ground 60 m away, the angle of elevation of the top of a tree is $24\frac{1}{2}°$.
    Calculate the height of the tree to the nearest metre.

9 Factorisation of quadratic expressions

OBJECTIVES

By the end of this chapter you should be able to:

1 Multiply two binomials together to give a quadratic expression

2 Expand products directly

3 Factorise quadratic expressions where the coefficient of x^2 is 1

4 Expand and factorise expressions involving perfect squares

5 Expand and factorise expressions involving difference of two squares

6 Use factorisation to solve simple word problems.

Teaching and learning materials

Teacher: Cardboard models of Fig. 9.1 and Fig. 9.2; factorisation chart; quadratic equation boxes

---

9-1 Expansion of algebraic expressions (revision)

The expression $(x + 2)(x - 5)$ means $(x + 2) \times (x - 5)$. The product of the two binomials $(x + 2)$ and $(x - 5)$ is found by multiplying each term in the first binomial by each term in the second binomial. Read the following examples carefully.

Example 1

Find the product of $(x + 2)$ and $(x - 5)$.

$$\begin{aligned}(x + 2)(x - 5) &= x(x + 2) - 5(x + 2)\\ &= x^2 + 2x - 5x - 10\\ &= x^2 - 3x - 10\end{aligned}$$

We say that $(x + 2)(x - 5)$ is **expanded** to $x^2 - 3x - 10$. Notice that the terms in x, $+2x$ and $-5x$, are added together in the final line of working in Example 1.

Example 2

Expand $(2c - 3m)(c - 4m)$.

$$\begin{aligned}(2c - 3m)(c - 4m) &= c(2c - 3m) - 4m(2c - 3m)\\ &= 2c^2 - 3cm - 8cm + 12m^2\\ &= 2c^2 - 11cm + 12m^2\end{aligned}$$

Example 3

Expand $(3a + 2)^2$.

$$\begin{aligned}(3a + 2)^2 &= (3a + 2)(3a + 2)\\ &= 3a(3a + 2) + 2(3a + 2)\\ &= 9a^2 + 6a + 6a + 4\\ &= 9a^2 + 12a + 4\end{aligned}$$

Exercise 9a   [Revision]

Expand each expression. Arrange the working as in Examples 1, 2 or 3.

1. $(a + 2)(a + 3)$
2. $(c + 6)(c - 1)$
3. $(e - 3)(e + 2)$
4. $(d - 6)(d + 3)$
5. $(x - 1)(x - 2)$
6. $(a + 3)^2$
7. $(b - 5)^2$
8. $(m + 4)(m - 4)$
9. $(n + 5)(n - 4)$
10. $(d + 3)(d - 7)$
11. $(b - 5)(b + 6)$
12. $(p - 3)(p - 5)$
13. $(q - 3)(q + 3)$
14. $(u - 9)(u + 5)$
15. $(v - 4)(v - 9)$
16. $(2a + 1)(a + 3)$
17. $(b + 4)(3b + 2)$
18. $(2c - 5)(c - 3)$
19. $(d - 9)(2d + 3)$
20. $(2x + 1)^2$
21. $(5x + 2)(2x - 3)$
22. $(3y - 5)(2y + 1)$
23. $(m + 4n)^2$
24. $(u + 2v)(u + 3v)$
25. $(3d - 2e)(3d + 2e)$
26. $(3b + 2c)(2b - c)$
27. $(2s - 5t)(3s + t)$
28. $(2c - 3d)^2$
29. $(4m - n)(3m - 3n)$
30. $(2c - 9e)(4c + 5e)$

If you had difficulty with Exercise 9a, revise Chapter 7 of Book 2.

With practice, it is not necessary to write down all the working as in Exercise 9a. The product of an expansion can be written down directly.

For example, in the product

$$(c - 3)(c - 4) = c^2 - 7c + 12$$

notice that

1 the first term in the expansion is the product of the first two terms in the brackets:

$$(c - 3)(c - 4) = c^2 - 7c + 12$$

2 the last term in the expansion is the product of the last two terms in the brackets:

$$(c - 3)(c - 4) = c^2 - 7c + 12$$

3 the middle term in the expansion is found by adding the products of the inner and outer pairs of terms:

$$(c - 3)(c - 4) = c^2 - 7c + 12$$

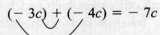

$$(- 3c) + (- 4c) = - 7c$$

Fig. 9.1 shows these steps in one diagram.

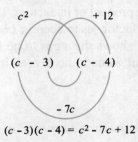

$$(c - 3)(c - 4) = c^2 - 7c + 12$$

Fig. 9.1

We can remember the method in Fig. 9.1 as "eyebrow, eyebrow, nose and mouth".

Example 4

Expand $(d - 2)(d + 5)$ directly.

$$(d - 2)(d + 5) = d^2 + 3d - 10$$

In the answer,
d^2 is the product of d and d,
$+3d$ is the result of adding $-2 \times d = -2d$ to $d \times +5 = +5d$,
-10 is the product of -2 and $+5$.

Example 5

Expand $(x + 7)^2$.

$$(x + 7)^2 = (x + 7)(x + 7)$$
$$= x^2 + 14x + 49$$

Example 6

Expand $(10 + x)(10 - x)$ without showing any working.

$$(10 + x)(10 - x) = 100 - x^2$$

Notice in this example that the middle term reduces to zero.

$$+10x + (-10x) = 0$$

Exercise 9b

Expand the following without showing any working.

① $(a + 1)(a + 2)$ ② $(a + 2)(a + 3)$
③ $(a + 3)(a + 4)$ ④ $(b + 1)(b - 2)$
⑤ $(b + 2)(b - 3)$ ⑥ $(b + 3)(b - 4)$
⑦ $(c - 3)(c - 4)$ ⑧ $(d + 7)(d + 1)$
⑨ $(e + 2)(e + 9)$ ⑩ $(f - 5)(f - 4)$
⑪ $(x - 7)(x - 1)$ ⑫ $(y - 2)(y - 9)$
⑬ $(h + 6)^2$ ⑭ $(k - 5)^2$
⑮ $(z + 2)(z - 9)$ ⑯ $(a + 4)(a + 6)$
⑰ $(a - 4)(a - 6)$ ⑱ $(a - 4)(a + 6)$
⑲ $(a + 4)(a - 6)$ ⑳ $(b + 6)(b - 3)$
㉑ $(c - 1)(c - 2)$ ㉒ $(m - 1)^2$
㉓ $(n + 1)^2$ ㉔ $(f + 9)(f + 11)$
㉕ $(e - 3)(e - 5)$ ㉖ $(d - 2)(d + 10)$

㉗ $(h + 3)(h - 8)$ ㉘ $(a + 3)^2$

㉙ $(a - 3)^2$ ㉚ $(a + 3)(a - 3)$

㉛ $(b - 5)(b + 5)$ ㉜ $(c + 7)(c - 7)$

Coefficients of terms

The **coefficient** of an algebraic term is the number which multiplies the unknown. For example,

in $3x^2$, the coefficient of x^2 is 3
in $-2y$, the coefficient of y is -2
in $\frac{2}{3}d$, the coefficient of d is $\frac{2}{3}$

Example 7

Find the coefficient of x in the expansion of
$(x + 9)(x + 3)$.

It is not necessary to expand the expression fully. The middle term is the term in x,
    middle term $= (+9x) + (+3x) = +12x$.
The coefficient of x in the expansion is $+12$.

Example 8

Find the coefficient of ab in the expansion of
$(5a + 2b)(4a - 3b)$.

The terms containing ab are

$$2b \times 4a = 8ab$$

and $5a \times (-3b) = -15ab$.
These add to give $-7ab$.
The coefficient of ab in the expansion is -7.

With practice, it should be possible to write down coefficients without any written working.

Exercise 9c

① Find the coefficient of d in the expansion of:
  a $(d + 2)(d + 7)$ b $(d - 4)(d + 6)$
  c $(d - 3)(d - 1)$ d $(d - 8)(d + 3)$
  e $(d + 7)^2$

② Find the coefficient of x in the expansion of:

  a $(x - 5)(x + 4)$ b $(x + 8)(x - 11)$
  c $(x - 3)(x + 5)$ d $(x - 4)(x + 4)$
  e $(x - 5)^2$

③ Find the coefficient of u in the expansion of:
  a $(u + 2)(2u + 3)$ b $(u - 4)(3u + 5)$
  c $(2u - 5)(3u + 5)$ d $(4u - 5)(2u - 7)$
  e $(3u - 4)^2$

④ Find the coefficient of ab in the expansion of:
  a $(3a + b)(a + 2b)$ b $(a - b)(3a - 2b)$
  c $(4a + 3b)(5a - 3b)$
  d $(5a + 2b)(5a - 2b)$ e $(a - 3b)^2$

9-2 Factorisation of quadratic expressions

A **quadratic** expression is one in which 2 is the highest power of the unknown(s) in the expression. For example, $x^2 - 4x - 12$, $16 - a^2$, $3x^2 + 17xy + 10y^2$ are all quadratic expressions.

Since $(x + 2)(x - 6) = x^2 - 4x - 12$,

$(x + 2)$ and $(x - 6)$ are the **factors** of $x^2 - 4x - 12$. Just as in arithmetic, $5 \times 7 = 35$ where 5 and 7 are the factors of 35.
    A quadratic expression may *not* have factors. In arithmetic, 13 is said to be prime since it has no factors other than itself and 1. Similarly, $x^2 + 2x - 6$ has no factors (other than itself and 1).
    To **factorise** a quadratic expression is to express it as a product of its factors. Thus, $x^2 - 4x - 12$ factorises to become $(x + 2)(x - 6)$.
    Example 9 shows the steps to be followed when factorising quadratic expressions.

Example 9

Factorise the quadratic expression
$x^2 + 7x + 10$.

The problem is to fill the brackets in the statement $x^2 + 7x + 10 = ($ $)($ $)$.

1st step: Look at the *first* term in the given expression, x^2. From work done in expanding brackets (as in Exercise 9b), when the first

94

term in the expansion is x^2, x appears first in each bracket: $x^2 + 7x + 10 = (x \qquad)(x \qquad)$.

2nd step: Look at the *last* term in the given expression, $+10$. The *product* of the last terms in the two brackets must be $+10$. Number pairs which have a product of $+10$ are:

a $+10$ and $+1$
b $+5$ and $+2$
c -10 and -1
d -5 and -2

These give four possible answers:

a $(x + 10)(x + 1)$
b $(x + 5)(x + 2)$
c $(x - 10)(x - 1)$
d $(x - 5)(x - 2)$

3rd step: Look at the coefficient of the *middle* term in the given expression, $+7$. The *sum* of the last terms in the two brackets must be $+7$. Adding the number pairs in turn:

a $(+10) + (+1) = +11$
b $(+5) + (+2) = +7$
c $(-10) + (-1) = -11$
d $(-5) + (-2) = -7$

Of these, only *b* gives $+7$. Thus,

$$x^2 + 7x + 10 = (x + 5)(x + 2)$$

Note: **1** The answer can be checked by expanding the brackets.
      2 The order of the brackets is not important.
$$(x + 5)(x + 2) = (x + 2)(x + 5)$$

In Example 9, both the last term and the coefficient of x were positive. It was not really necessary to consider the possibility of having negative factors of $+10$. Example 10 shows how the method to shorten.

Example 10

Factorise $d^2 + 11d + 18$.

1st step: $d^2 + 11d + 18 = (d \qquad)(d \qquad)$.

2nd step: Find two numbers such that their *product* is $+18$ and their sum is $+11$. Since the 18 is positive *and* the 11 is positive, consider positive factors only.

	factors of $+18$	sum of factors
a	$+1$ and $+18$	$+19$
b	$+2$ and $+9$	$+11$
c	$+3$ and $+6$	$+9$

Of these, only *b* gives the required result. Thus,

$$d^2 + 11d + 18 = (d + 2)(d + 9)$$

The method of Examples 9 and 10 is called a **trial and improvement** method. It is necessary to try various number pairs in turn, until the correct pair is found. To begin with, this will take time. With practice, it will be possible to factorise quadratic expressions quite quickly.

 Optional: Do Exercise 23 of your Students' Practice Book.

Exercise 9d
Factorise the following quadratic expressions.

1. $x^2 + 6x + 5$
2. $x^2 + 12x + 11$
3. $a^2 + 14a + 13$
4. $b^2 + 8b + 7$
5. $y^2 + 9y + 8$
6. $z^2 + 6z + 8$
7. $c^2 + 8c + 15$
8. $d^2 + 13d + 22$
9. $n^2 + 8n + 12$
10. $r^2 + 9r + 20$
11. $s^2 + 10s + 16$
12. $t^2 + 8t + 16$

Example 11

Factorise $x^2 - 9x + 8$.

1st step: $x^2 - 9x + 8 = (x \qquad)(x \qquad)$.

2nd step: Find two numbers such that their product is $+8$ and their sum is -9.
List the possible pairs and find their sums:

	factors of $+8$	sum of factors
a	$+8$ and $+1$	$+9$
b	$+4$ and $+2$	$+6$
c	-8 and -1	-9
d	-4 and -2	-6

Of these, only c gives the required result. Thus,

$$x^2 - 9x + 8 = (x - 8)(x - 1)$$

In Example 11, the last term is positive and the coefficient of x is negative. This gives a negative sign in both brackets.

Example 12

Factorise $t^2 - 10t + 24$.

1st step: $t^2 - 10t + 24 = (t \quad)(t \quad)$.

2nd step: Find two numbers such that their product is $+24$ and their sum is -10. Since the 24 is positive and the 10 is negative, consider negative factors only.

	factors of $+24$	sum of factors
a	-1 and -24	-25
b	-2 and -12	-14
c	-3 and -8	-11
d	-4 and -6	-10

Of these, only d gives the required result. Thus,

$$t^2 - 10t + 24 = (t - 4)(t - 6)$$

 Optional: Do Exercise 24 of your Students' Practice Book.

Exercise 9e

Factorise the following.

1. $x^2 - 4x + 3$
2. $y^2 - 3y + 2$
3. $z^2 - 18z + 17$
4. $a^2 - 8a + 7$
5. $b^2 - 5b + 6$
6. $c^2 - 7c + 6$
7. $d^2 - 9d + 14$
8. $n^2 - 7n + 10$
9. $p^2 - 11p + 24$
10. $q^2 - 10q + 21$
11. $f^2 - 16f + 28$
12. $x^2 - 10x + 25$

So far, the given quadratic expressions have all contained a positive last term. Examples 13 and 14 show what happens when the last term is negative.

Example 13

Factorise the expression $x^2 + 2x - 15$.

1st step: $x^2 + 2x - 15 = (x \quad)(x \quad)$.

2nd step: Find two numbers such that their product is -15 and their sum is $+2$. List the possible pairs and find their sums.

	factors of -15	sum of factors
a	-15 and $+1$	-14
b	$+15$ and -1	$+14$
c	-5 and $+3$	-2
d	$+5$ and -3	$+2$

Of these, only d gives the correct result. Thus,

$$x^2 + 2x - 15 = (x + 5)(x - 3)$$

Example 14

Factorise $x^2 - 4x - 12$.

Find two numbers such that their product is -12 and their sum is -4.

	factors of -12	sum of factors
a	-12 and $+1$	-11
b	$+12$ and -1	$+11$
c	-6 and $+2$	-4
d	$+6$ and -2	$+4$
e	-4 and $+3$	-1
f	$+4$ and -3	$+1$

Of these, only c gives the required result. Thus,

$$x^2 - 4x - 12 = (x - 6)(x + 2)$$

Notice, in Examples 13 and 14, that if the last term in the given expression is negative, the signs inside the brackets are different: one positive and one negative.

☞ *Optional:* Do Exercise 25 of your Students' Practice Book.

Exercise 9f

Factorise the following.

① $x^2 + 4x - 5$ ② $a^2 - 4a - 5$

③ $x^2 + 6x - 7$ ④ $b^2 + 6b - 7$

⑤ $n^2 + n - 2$ ⑥ $r^2 - 2r - 3$

⑦ $x^2 - 10x - 11$ ⑧ $y^2 + 12y - 13$

⑨ $x^2 - 2x - 15$ ⑩ $x^2 + 14x - 15$

⑪ $s^2 + 5s - 6$ ⑫ $t^2 - 5t - 6$

⑬ $u^2 - u - 6$ ⑭ $v^2 + v - 6$

⑮ $z^2 + z - 20$ ⑯ $c^2 - 8c - 20$

⑰ $x^2 - 49$ ⑱ $x^2 - 4$

9-3 Perfect squares

$$(a + b)^2 = (a + b)(a + b) = a^2 + ab + ab + b^2$$
$$\therefore (a + b)^2 = a^2 + 2ab + b^2$$

$$(a - b)^2 = (a - b)(a - b) = a^2 - ab - ab + b^2$$
$$\therefore (a - b)^2 = a^2 - 2ab + b^2$$

These results are very important and should be remembered. They are given in words below:

The square of the *sum* of two quantities is equal to the sum of their squares *plus* twice their product.

The square of the *difference* of two quantities is equal to the sum of their squares *minus* twice their product.

Fig. 9.2 gives a geometrical representation of $(a + b)^2 = a^2 + 2ab + b^2$.

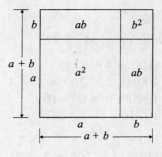

Fig. 9.2

Example 15

Expand the following:
a $(3m + 7n)^2$, b $(4u - 5v)^2$.

a $(3m + 7n)^2$ is equal to the (square of $3m$) + (twice the product of $3m$ and $7n$) + (the square of $7n$).
Thus, $(3m + 7n)^2$
$$= (3m)^2 + (2 \times 3m \times 7n) + (7n)^2$$
$$= 9m^2 + 42mn + 49n^2$$

b Similarly, $(4u - 5v)^2$
$$= (4u)^2 + (2 \times 4u \times 5v) + (5v)^2$$
$$= 16u^2 - 40uv + 25v^2$$

Notice that the squared terms are *always positive*.

Exercise 9g

Write down the expansions of the following.

① $(a + 4)^2$ ② $(b - 3)^2$

③ $(5 + c)^2$ ④ $(2 - d)^2$

⑤ $(1 + m)^2$ ⑥ $(2n + 1)^2$

⑦ $(3x + y)^2$ ⑧ $(u - 2v)^2$

⑨ $(5h - k)^2$ ⑩ $(p + 4q)^2$

⑪ $(2a + 3d)^2$ ⑫ $(3b - 5c)^2$

⑬ $(7e - 2f)^2$ ⑭ $(10x - 1)^2$

⑮ $(1 + 12y)^2$ ⑯ $(3a + 7b)^2$

⑰ $(c - 8d)^2$ ⑱ $(9u + v)^2$

The expansion of a perfect square can sometimes be used to shorten the working when squaring numbers. See Example 16.

Example 16

Find the value of a 104^2, b 97^2.

a $104^2 = (100 + 4)^2$
$ = 100^2 + 2 \times 100 \times 4 + 4^2$
$ = 10\,000 + 800 + 16$
$ = 10\,816$

b $97^2 = (100 - 3)^2$
$ = 100^2 - 2 \times 100 \times 3 + 3^2$
$ = 10\,000 - 600 + 9$
$ = 9\,409$

Exercise 9h

Find the squares of the following numbers.

1. 101
2. 99
3. 103
4. 98
5. 1 001
6. 999
7. 1 005
8. 996
9. 995
10. 72
11. 83
12. 79

Example 17

Factorise the following:
a $h^2 + 12h + 36$, b $25h^2 - 30hk + 9k^2$.

a Notice that h^2 is the square of h, 36 is the square of 6 and $12h$ is twice the product of h and 6. Thus,
$h^2 + 12h + 36 = (h + 6)(h + 6)$
$ = (h + 6)^2$

b $25h^2$ is the square of $5h$
$9k^2$ is the square of $3k$
$30hk$ is twice the product of $5h$ and $3k$
$\therefore 25h^2 - 30hk + 9k^2 = (5h - 3k)^2$

Exercise 9i   [Oral or written]

Give the following as the square of an expression in brackets.

1. $a^2 + 10a + 25$
2. $b^2 + 8b + 16$
3. $c^2 + 6c + 9$
4. $d^2 + 20d + 100$
5. $m^2 - 6m + 9$
6. $n^2 - 12n + 36$
7. $x^2 - 4x + 4$
8. $y^2 - 2y + 1$
9. $z^2 + 16z + 64$
10. $k^2 - 14k + 49$
11. $4 - 4b + b^2$
12. $81 + 18d + d^2$
13. $x^2 + 6xy + 9y^2$
14. $4u^2 - 12u + 9$

15. $1 - 2a + a^2$
16. $25n^2 - 30nv + 9v^2$
17. $9a^2 - 24ab + 16b^2$
18. $121 - 22y + y^2$

9-4 Difference of two squares

$(a + b)(a - b) = a^2 + ab - ab - b^2 = a^2 - b^2$
Hence $a^2 - b^2 = (a + b)(a - b)$

or in words:

The difference of the squares of two quantities is equal to the product of their sum and their difference.

Fig. 9.3 shows how to make a cardboard model to demonstrate that:

$$a^2 - b^2 = (a + b)(a - b).$$

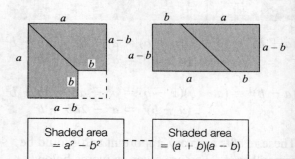

Fig. 9.3

☞ *Optional:* Do Exercise 47 of your Students' Practice Book.

Example 18

Factorise the following:
a $y^2 - 4$, b $36 - 9a^2$, c $25m^2 - 16n^2$.

a $y^2 - 4 = (y)^2 - (2)^2$
$ = (y + 2)(y - 2)$
b $36 - 9a^2 = (6)^2 - (3a)^2$
$ = (6 + 3a)(6 - 3a)$
c $25m^2 - 16n^2 = (5m)^2 - (4n)^2$
$ = (5m + 4n)(5m - 4n)$

Example 19

Factorise $5a^2 - 45$.

The two terms have the factor 5 in common.
Take this out first:

$$5a^2 - 45 = 5(a^2 - 9)$$
$$= 5(a^2 - 3^2)$$
$$= 5(a + 3)(a - 3)$$

~~Ex~~ercise 9j   [Oral or written]

~~F~~actorise the following.

1. $x^2 - 1$
2. $1 - y^2$
3. $4m^2 - n^2$
4. $u^2 - 16v^2$
5. $1 - a^2b^2$
6. $9 - 4c^2$
7. $4d^2 - 9e^2$
8. $3 - 3f^2$
9. $4g^2 - 4$
10. $4h^2 - 25$
11. $25k^2 - 16$
12. $49m^2 - n^2$
13. $p^2q^2 - 9$
14. $25 - u^2v^2$
15. $81 - w^2$
16. $100x^2 - 1$
17. $16y^2 - 4z^2$
18. $16h^2 - k^2$
19. $4c^2 - 49d^2$
20. $e^2 - 4f^2$
21. $36a^2 - 49b^2$
22. $5c^2 - 45d^2$
23. $x^2y^2 - z^2$
24. $100 - w^2$

---

6) QR – Factorising quadratics

The following *'quadratic box'* shows a quadratic and its binomial factors.

$$x^2 + 4x - 5$$

$(x - 1)$ ———— $(x + 5)$

Fill the empty boxes in the following.

a $x^2 - 3x - 18$

$(x + 3)$ ————

b $x^2 + 6x + 5$

———— $(x + 5)$

c $x^2 - 8x + 15$

$(x - 5)$ ————

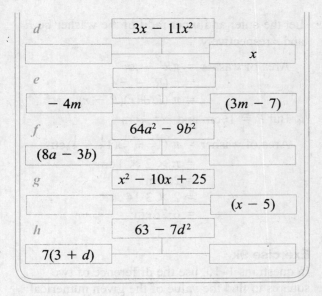

d $3x - 11x^2$

———— x

e

$- 4m$ ———— $(3m - 7)$

f $64a^2 - 9b^2$

$(8a - 3b)$ ————

g $x^2 - 10x + 25$

———— $(x - 5)$

h $63 - 7d^2$

$7(3 + d)$ ————

Calculations and word problems

The difference of two squares can sometimes shorten calculations and simplify word problems. Read Examples 20 and 21 carefully.

Example 20

Find the value of $173^2 - 127^2$.

$$173^2 - 127^2 = (173 + 127)(173 - 127)$$
$$= 300 \times 46$$
$$= 13\,800$$

Example 21

Fig. 9.4 shows a circular metal washer. If the diameters of the washer and its hole are 3 cm and 1 cm respectively, find the area of the washer. Use the value 3·14 for π.

Fig. 9.4

Let the outer and inner radii of the washer be R and r respectively.

$$\text{Area of washer} = \pi R^2 - \pi r^2$$
$$= \pi (R^2 - r^2)$$
$$= \pi (R + r)(R - r)$$

But $R = 1\frac{1}{2}$ cm and $r = \frac{1}{2}$ cm.

$$\text{Area of washer} = \pi (1\frac{1}{2} + \frac{1}{2})(1\frac{1}{2} - \frac{1}{2}) \text{ cm}^2$$
$$= \pi \times 2 \times 1 \text{ cm}^2$$
$$= 2\pi \text{ cm}^2$$
$$= 2 \times 3 \cdot 14 \text{ cm}^2$$
$$= 6 \cdot 28 \text{ cm}^2$$

Exercise 9k

In questions 1–10, use the difference of two squares to find the value of the given numerical expressions.

1. $96^2 - 4^2$
2. $118^2 - 18^2$
3. $73^2 - 71^2$
4. $98^2 - 4$
5. $103^2 - 9$
6. $52^2 - 48^2$
7. $63^2 - 37^2$
8. $57^2 - 55^2$
9. $1\,004^2 - 16$
10. $997^2 - 9$

11. Make a copy of Fig. 9.3. Calculate the shaded area if $a = 8$ cm and $b = 5$ cm.

12. Fig. 9.5 shows an ornament made by cutting a square hole in a silver square.

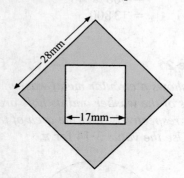

Fig. 9.5

Use the dimensions in Fig. 9.5 to calculate the area of silver in the ornament.

13. A husband is 3 years older than his wife. The sum of their ages is 73 years. Calculate the difference between the squares of their ages.

14. A metal washer has an outer diameter of 14 mm and an inner diameter of 6 mm. Use the value $3 \cdot 14$ for π to find the area of the metal washer in mm^2.

15. A cylindrical metal pipe, 1 m long, has inner and outer radii of $3 \cdot 7$ cm and $2 \cdot 3$ cm respectively. Use the value $\frac{22}{7}$ for π to find the volume of metal in the pipe in cm^3.

Exercise 9l [General practice]

Factorise the following where possible. If there are no factors say so.

1. $a^2 + 4a + 3$
2. $b^2 + 5b + 6$
3. $c^2 + 3c + 2$
4. $d^2 + 7d + 10$
5. $e^2 + 7e + 12$
6. $f^2 - 6f + 5$
7. $g^2 - 3g + 2$
8. $h^2 - 8h + 15$
9. $m^2 - 7m + 12$
10. $n^2 - 8n + 7$
11. $p^2 + 2p - 3$
12. $q^2 - 2q - 3$
13. $r^2 + 3r - 10$
14. $s^2 - 3s - 10$
15. $t^2 - t - 6$
16. $u^2 + u - 6$
17. $v^2 + v + 1$
18. $w^2 - 5w - 14$
19. $x^2 + 5x - 14$
20. $y^2 + y + 14$
21. $z^2 + 5z - 6$
22. $z^2 - 5z - 6$
23. $m^2 + 13m + 12$
24. $n^2 + 11n - 12$
25. $a^2 + a - 12$
26. $d^2 + 4d + 5$
27. $b^2 - 8b + 12$
28. $x^2 - 4x - 12$
29. $u^2 + 3u - 2$
30. $d^2 - 2d + 4$
31. $b^2 - 9b + 20$
32. $a^2 - 12a + 20$
33. $e^2 - e - 20$
34. $w^2 + 7w - 20$
35. $x^2 + 8x - 20$
36. $y^2 + 21y + 20$
37. $z^2 + 6z + 9$
38. $m^2 - 8m + 16$
39. $n^2 - 3n + 16$
40. $p^2 + 6p - 16$
41. $q^2 + 3q - 18$
42. $b^2 - 7b - 18$
43. $c^2 + 10c + 25$
44. $a^2 - 14a + 49$
45. $f^2 - 10f + 21$
46. $x^2 - 9$
47. $y^2 - 25$
48. $h^2 - 2h - 35$
49. $l^2 - 7l - 7$
50. $u^2 - 12u + 32$
51. $v^2 + 13v + 36$
52. $w^2 + 8w + 9$
53. $a^2 - 6a + 4$
54. $b^2 - 16$
55. $c^2 - 36$
56. $d^2 + 14d + 40$

57. $c^2 + 13e + 40$
58. $f^2 + 8f - 48$
59. $g^2 - 2g - 48$
60. $h^2 - 26h + 48$

SUMMARY

1. To *expand* an expression in the form
   $$(a + b)(c + d)$$
   means to find the product that results from multiplying each term in the first binomial bracket by each term in the second binomial bracket.

2. The *coefficient* of an algebraic term is the number that multiplies the unknown.
   For example
   in $-5y^2$, the coefficient of y^2 is -5.

3. A *quadratic expression* is one in which 2 is the highest power of the unknown.
   For example
   $$y^2 - 3y + 2$$
   is a quadratic expression in y.

4. Since
   $$(y - 1) \times (y - 2) = y^2 - 3y + 2,$$
   we say that $(y - 1)$ and $(y - 2)$ are the *factors* of $y^2 - 3y + 2$.

5. To *factorise* a quadratic expression $x^2 + bx + c$, means to find values m and n such that
   $$x^2 + bx + c = (x + m)(x + n).$$

6. Quadratic expressions are usually factorised by using *trial and improvement* methods. See Examples 9–14.

7. Remember the following identities for *perfect squares*.
   $$(a + b)^2 = a^2 + 2ab + b^2 \text{ and}$$
   $$(a - b)^2 = a^2 - 2ab + b^2$$

8. The *difference of two squares* factorises as follows:
   $$a^2 - b^2 = (a + b)(a - b)$$

9. The identities for perfect squares and difference of two squares may be used to simplify calculations. See Examples 16, 18, 19, 20 and 21.

PUZZLE CORNER

How Many Triangles? (1)

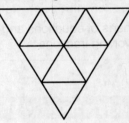

How many equilateral triangles are in this 3 x 3 triangular grid?

How many would there be in a 4 x 4 triangular grid? ... a 10 x 10 grid?

PUZZLE CORNER

Hexagon in a Hexagon

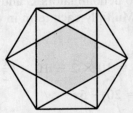

What fraction of the area of the big hexagon, does the small hexagon cover?

101

10 Equations involving fractions

Teaching and learning materials

Teacher: Charts of equations and word problems involving fractions

---

10-1 Clearing fractions (revision)

Always clear fractions before beginning to solve an equation. To clear fractions, multiply each term in the equation by the LCM of the denominators of the fraction.

Example 1

Solve the equation $\dfrac{x-4}{5} = 2 - \dfrac{x}{2}$.

$$\frac{x-4}{5} = 2 - \frac{x}{2}$$

There are two denominators, 5 and 2. Their LCM is 10. Multiply each term in the equation by 10.

$$\frac{10(x-4)}{5} = 10 \times 2 - 10 \times \left(\frac{x}{2}\right)$$

$$2(x-4) = 20 - 5x$$

Clear brackets.

$$2x - 8 = 20 - 5x$$

Add $5x$ to both sides.

$$7x - 8 = 20$$

Add 8 to both sides.

$$7x = 28$$

Divide both sides by 7.

$$x = 4$$

Check: when $x = 4$,

$$\text{LHS} = \frac{4-4}{5} = \frac{0}{5} = 0$$

$$\text{RHS} = 2 - \frac{4}{2} = 2 - 2 = 0 = \text{LHS}$$

Exercise 10a [Revision]
Solve the following equations.

1. $\dfrac{x}{9} = 2$

2. $\dfrac{3}{4} = \dfrac{a}{20}$

3. $\dfrac{d-7}{2} = 5$

4. $h = \dfrac{18 + 5h}{7}$

5. $n - \dfrac{n}{6} = \dfrac{5}{2}$

6. $\dfrac{r}{2} = \dfrac{1}{2} + \dfrac{2r}{5}$

7. $\dfrac{7 + 3x}{2} = \dfrac{5x}{3}$

8. $\dfrac{x+9}{5} + \dfrac{2+x}{2} = 0$

9. $\dfrac{2(4x-1)}{3} = \dfrac{9(x+1)}{4}$

10. $2x = \dfrac{5x+1}{7} + \dfrac{3x-5}{2}$

If you had difficulty with Exercise 10a, revise Chapter 13 in Book 2.

Example 2

Solve $2\frac{3}{4} + \frac{33}{2x} = 0$

$$2\frac{3}{4} + \frac{33}{2x} = 0$$

Express $2\frac{3}{4}$ as an improper fraction.

$$\frac{11}{4} + \frac{33}{2x} = 0$$

The denominators are 4 and $2x$. Their LCM is $4x$. Multiply each term in the equation by $4x$.

$$4x\left(\frac{11}{4}\right) + 4x\left(\frac{33}{2x}\right) = 4x \times 0$$

$$11x + 66 = 0$$

$$11x = -66$$

$$x = -6$$

Check: when $x = -6$,

$$\text{LHS} = 2\frac{3}{4} + \frac{33}{-12} = 2\frac{3}{4} - \frac{11}{4} = 0 = \text{RHS}$$

Example 3

Solve $\frac{1}{3a} + \frac{1}{2} = \frac{1}{2a}$.

$$\frac{1}{3a} + \frac{1}{2} = \frac{1}{2a}$$

The denominators are $3a$, 2 and $2a$. Their LCM is $6a$. Multiply each term in the equation by $6a$.

$$6a \times \left(\frac{1}{3a}\right) + 6a \times \frac{1}{2} = 6a \times \left(\frac{1}{2a}\right)$$

$$2 + 3a = 3$$

$$3a = 1$$

$$a = \frac{1}{3}$$

Check: when $a = \frac{1}{3}$

$$\text{LHS} = \frac{1}{3 \times \frac{1}{3}} + \frac{1}{2} = 1 + \frac{1}{2} = 1\frac{1}{2}$$

$$\text{RHS} = \frac{1}{2 \times \frac{1}{3}} = \frac{3}{2} = 1\frac{1}{2} = \text{LHS}$$

Examples 2 and 3 show that when unknowns, such as x or a, appear in the denominator, they are treated like numbers. Clear fractions by multiplying each term of the equation by the LCM of the denominators of the fractions. Then solve the equation in the usual way.

Exercise 10b

Solve the following equations.

(1) $\frac{1}{x} = \frac{1}{5}$ (2) $\frac{1}{9} = \frac{1}{r}$

(3) $\frac{1}{m} - \frac{1}{4} = 0$ (4) $\frac{1}{y} = \frac{2}{7}$

(5) $2\frac{1}{2} = \frac{1}{s}$ (6) $2\frac{3}{4} + \frac{1}{n} = 0$

(7) $\frac{2}{t} = \frac{6}{11}$ (8) $\frac{9}{10} = \frac{3}{z}$

(9) $\frac{4}{9} - \frac{2}{p} = 0$ (10) $\frac{10}{3} = \frac{5}{a}$

(11) $\frac{13}{x} = 5\frac{1}{5}$ (12) $\frac{8}{q} + 3\frac{3}{7} = 0$

(13) $\frac{1}{5b} = \frac{1}{30}$ (14) $\frac{1}{40} = \frac{1}{8y}$

(15) $\frac{1}{3r} - \frac{1}{24} = 0$ (16) $\frac{7}{3c} = \frac{21}{2}$

(17) $\frac{3}{10} = \frac{9}{2d}$ (18) $\frac{16}{9} + \frac{4}{3s} = 0$

(19) $3\frac{3}{5} = \frac{12}{25z}$ (20) $\frac{33}{2r} = 3\frac{1}{7}$

(21) $3\frac{3}{4} - \frac{5}{2t} = 0$ (22) $\frac{1}{x} = \frac{1}{4} + \frac{1}{12}$

(23) $\frac{1}{y} + \frac{1}{5} = \frac{1}{3}$ (24) $\frac{1}{9} = \frac{1}{d} - \frac{1}{18}$

(25) $\frac{1}{f} + \frac{1}{2} = \frac{5}{6}$ (26) $2 = \frac{7}{2x} - \frac{1}{3}$

(27) $\frac{3}{h} = \frac{1}{5} + \frac{8}{35}$ (28) $\frac{5}{2x} - \frac{1}{x} = \frac{1}{6}$

(29) $\frac{2}{x} + \frac{3}{2x} = \frac{7}{8}$ (30) $\frac{9}{4x} - \frac{5}{x} + \frac{11}{3} = 0$

Example 4

The students in a class have a total mass of 1717 kg. If the average mass per student is $50\frac{1}{2}$ kg, find the number of students in the class.

The number of students is the unknown. Let there be n students in the class. Then,

$$\text{average mass per student} = \frac{1717}{n} \text{kg}$$

(from first sentence in question).

Thus,

$$50\frac{1}{2} = \frac{1717}{n}$$

(from second sentence in question).

$$\frac{101}{2} = \frac{1717}{n}$$

Multiply throughout by $2n$.

$$101n = 2 \times 1717$$

$$n = \frac{2 \times 1717}{101}$$

$$= 2 \times 17$$

$$n = 34$$

There are 34 students in the class.

The problem in Example 4 could have been solved by simple arithmetic. The algebraic method was not really necessary. However, Example 5 shows a problem which is best solved by using algebra.

Example 5

A cow costs seven times as much as a goat. For ₦84 000 I can buy 18 more goats than cows. How much does a goat cost?

The cost of a goat is the unknown. Let a goat cost ₦h. Thus, a cow costs ₦$7h$ (from first sentence in question). For ₦84 000 I can buy $\frac{84\,000}{h}$ goats or $\frac{84\,000}{7h}$ cows.

Thus, $\quad \frac{84\,000}{h} - \frac{84\,000}{7h} = 18$

(from second sentence).

Multiply throughout by $7h$.

$$7h \times \frac{84\,000}{h} - 7h \times \frac{84\,000}{7h} = 7h \times 18$$

$$7 \times 84\,000 - 1 \times 84\,000 = 7 \times 18 \times h$$

$$6 \times 84\,000 = 7 \times 18 \times h$$

$$\frac{6 \times 84\,000}{7 \times 18} = h$$

$$h = \frac{12\,000}{3}$$

$$= 4\,000$$

Thus, a goat costs ₦4 000 (and a cow costs ₦28 000).

When solving problems of this kind:
1 find out what the unknown is;
2 choose a letter to stand for the unknown quantity;
3 change the statements in the question into algebraic expressions and make an equation;
4 solve the equation, leaving any numerical simplification until the last step of the working.

In Exercise 10c below, some questions give a letter for the unknown; in other questions you must choose a letter for yourself.

Exercise 10c

① A fisherman catches n fish. Their total mass is 15 kg.
  a Write down the average mass of a fish in terms of n.
  b If the average mass of a fish was $\frac{3}{4}$ kg, find the number of fish caught.

② A trader buys x calculators (all alike) for ₦6 720.
  a Write down the cost of one calculator in terms of x.
  b If the calculators cost ₦960 each, find the number of calculators bought.

③ A student walks 3 km at a speed of v km/h.

a Write down the time taken, in hours, in terms of v.

b If the journey takes 35 min, find the value of v.

④ A trader sells a number of books and takes in ₦57 400 altogether. If the average selling price of a book is ₦700, find the number of books sold.

⑤ A bag of mangoes has a total mass of 56 kg. If the average mass of a mango is $1\frac{3}{5}$ kg, find the number of mangoes in the bag. (Ignore the mass of the bag.)

⑥ A car travels 120 km at a certain average speed. If the journey takes $2\frac{1}{2}$ h, find the average speed.

⑦ A pencil costs ₦x and a notebook costs ₦$4x$. I spend ₦100 on pencils and ₦100 on notebooks.

a Write down the number of pencils I get in terms of x.

b Write down the number of notebooks I get in terms of x.

c If I get 15 more pencils than notebooks, how much does a pencil cost?

⑧ A table costs five times as much as a chair. For ₦40 000 a trader can buy 20 more chairs than tables. Find the cost of a chair.

⑨ A boy walks 8 km at v km/h. He then cycles 15 km at $2v$ km/h. In terms of v, write down the time taken in hours **a** when walking, **b** when cycling. **c** If the total time for the journey is 2 h 35 min, find the boy's walking speed.

⑩ A car travels for 15 km in a city at a certain speed. Outside the city it travels 72 km at twice its former speed. If the total travelling time is 1 h 8 min, find the average speed in the city.

⑪ Mariamu has n oranges of total mass 14·5 kg. Anna has $2n$ oranges of total mass 21 kg.

a What is the average mass of one of Mariamu's oranges in terms of n?

b What is the average mass of one of Anna's oranges in terms of n?

c If the average mass of Anna's oranges is 0·1 kg less than the average mass of Mariamu's oranges, find the number of oranges that Mariamu has.

⑫ A fisherman caught 15 kg of fish on Monday and 23 kg on Tuesday. On Tuesday there were twice as many fish as on Monday, but their average mass was $\frac{1}{8}$ kg less. How many fish did the fisherman catch on Monday?

10-4 Fractions with binomials in the denominator

Example 6

Solve the equation $\dfrac{5}{x-3} = 2$.

$$\frac{5}{x-3} = 2$$

There is *one* denominator, $x - 3$. Notice that the *whole* of the binomial $x - 3$ is the denominator; it cannot be split into parts. Multiply both sides by $(x - 3)$.

$$(x-3) \times \frac{5}{x-3} = 2(x-3)$$

On the LHS, the $(x - 3)$s divide, leaving 5; clear brackets on the RHS.

$$5 = 2x - 6$$

Add 6 to both sides.

$$11 = 2x$$

Divide both sides by 2.

$$5\tfrac{1}{2} = x$$

Check: when $x = 5\frac{1}{2}$,

$$\text{LHS} = \frac{5}{5\frac{1}{2} - 3} = \frac{5}{2\frac{1}{2}} = 2 = \text{RHS}$$

Example 7

Solve $\dfrac{5}{7a-1} - \dfrac{4}{9} = 0$.

$$\frac{5}{7a-1} - \frac{4}{9} = 0$$

The denominators are $(7a - 1)$ and 9. Their LCM is $9(7a - 1)$. Multiply each term by $9(7a - 1)$.

$$9(7a - 1) \times \frac{5}{7a - 1} - 9(7a - 1) \times \frac{4}{9}$$
$$= 9(7a - 1) \times 0$$
$$9 \times 5 - 4(7a - 1) = 0$$

Clear brackets and collect terms.

$$45 - 28a + 4 = 0$$
$$49 - 28a = 0$$
$$49 = 28a$$
$$a = \frac{49}{28} = \frac{7}{4}$$
$$a = 1\frac{3}{4}$$

The solution is $a = 1\frac{3}{4}$.
The check is left as an exercise.

In a fraction like $\frac{7}{2r + 3}$, the division line acts like a bracket on the terms in the denominator: $\frac{7}{(2r + 3)}$. Examples 6 and 7 show that this bracket must be kept in the working until it can be cleared properly.

Exercise 10d

Solve the following equations.

1. $\dfrac{12}{x - 1} = 3$
2. $\dfrac{4}{1 + x} = 1$
3. $2 = \dfrac{7}{y + 2}$
4. $\dfrac{4}{t - 2} = 3$
5. $\dfrac{1}{z + 4} = 1$
6. $5 = \dfrac{15}{1 - r}$
7. $\dfrac{6}{x + 7} + 3 = 0$
8. $2 - \dfrac{1}{k - 2} = 0$
9. $2 = \dfrac{2}{4 - 3a}$
10. $\dfrac{13}{2x + 1} = 5$
11. $\dfrac{1}{x + 3} = \dfrac{1}{5}$
12. $\dfrac{1}{7} = \dfrac{1}{a - 3}$
13. $\dfrac{1}{2} - \dfrac{1}{y - 5} = 0$
14. $\dfrac{1}{b + 5} + \dfrac{1}{4} = 0$
15. $\dfrac{3}{2 - e} = \dfrac{3}{8}$
16. $\dfrac{4}{9} = \dfrac{2}{c - 8}$
17. $\dfrac{5}{2n - 5} = \dfrac{3}{2}$
18. $2\dfrac{1}{2} = \dfrac{10}{3d + 7}$
19. $\dfrac{2}{5} + \dfrac{3}{a - 8} = 0$
20. $\dfrac{5}{3x + 2} - \dfrac{1}{4} = 0$

Example 8

Solve $\dfrac{7}{x - 2} = \dfrac{5}{x}$.

$$\frac{7}{x - 2} = \frac{5}{x}$$

The denominators are $(x - 2)$ and x. Their LCM is $x(x - 2)$. Multiply both sides by $x(x - 2)$.

$$x(x - 2) \times \frac{7}{x - 2} = x(x - 2) \times \frac{5}{x}$$
$$7x = 5(x - 2)$$
$$7x = 5x - 10$$
$$2x = -10$$
$$x = -5$$

Check: when $x = -5$,

$$\text{LHS} = \frac{7}{-5 - 2} = \frac{7}{-7} = -1$$
$$\text{RHS} = \frac{5}{-5} = -1 = \text{LHS}$$

Example 9

Solve $\dfrac{x + 4}{2x - 5} = \dfrac{2}{3}$.

$$\frac{x + 4}{2x - 5} = \frac{2}{3}$$

The denominators are $(2x - 5)$ and 3. Their LCM is $3(2x - 5)$. Multiply both sides by $3(2x - 5)$.

$$3(2x - 5) \times \frac{x + 4}{2x - 5} = 3(2x - 5) \times \frac{2}{3}$$
$$3(x + 4) = 2(2x - 5)$$

Clear brackets and collect terms.

$$3x + 12 = 4x - 10$$
$$12 + 10 = 4x - 3x$$
$$22 = x$$

The solution is $x = 22$.
The check is left as an exercise.

Example 10

Solve $\dfrac{1}{a + 2} = \dfrac{8}{3a + 1}$.

$$\frac{1}{a + 2} = \frac{8}{3a + 1}$$

The denominators are $(a + 2)$ and $(3a + 1)$. Their LCM is $(a + 2)(3a + 1)$. Multiply both sides by $(a + 2)(3a + 1)$.

$$(a + 2)(3a + 1) \times \frac{1}{a + 2}$$
$$= (a + 2)(3a + 1) \times \frac{8}{3a + 1}$$

$$1(3a + 1) = 8(a + 2)$$
$$3a + 1 = 8a + 16$$
$$1 - 16 = 8a - 3a$$
$$-15 = 5a$$
$$-3 = a$$

The solution is $a = -3$.
The check is left as an exercise.

Exercise 10e
Solve the following equations.

1. $\dfrac{4}{a + 1} = \dfrac{3}{a}$

2. $\dfrac{3}{y} = \dfrac{2}{y - 5}$

3. $\dfrac{2}{x} = \dfrac{1}{x + 2}$

4. $\dfrac{5}{3 - a} = \dfrac{3}{a}$

5. $\dfrac{2}{n - 3} = \dfrac{1}{n}$

6. $\dfrac{2}{3 - n} = \dfrac{1}{n}$

7. $\dfrac{x}{x + 9} = \dfrac{3}{4}$

8. $\dfrac{x}{x - 6} = \dfrac{5}{2}$

9. $\dfrac{x}{x + 5} = \dfrac{4}{9}$

10. $\dfrac{x}{x + 5} = \dfrac{9}{4}$

11. $\dfrac{4}{2x + 1} = \dfrac{2}{3x}$

12. $\dfrac{4}{7t} = \dfrac{3}{5t - 2}$

13. $\dfrac{7}{3k + 1} - \dfrac{2}{k} = 0$

14. $\dfrac{1}{2a} + \dfrac{2}{a - 25} = 0$

15. $\dfrac{2}{a + 8} = \dfrac{1}{a + 1}$

16. $\dfrac{3}{x - 1} = \dfrac{2}{x + 4}$

17. $\dfrac{5}{3 + n} = \dfrac{2}{4 - n}$

18. $\dfrac{5}{a - 4} = \dfrac{3}{a - 5}$

19. $\dfrac{6}{y + 3} = \dfrac{11}{y - 2}$

20. $\dfrac{3}{1 - c} = \dfrac{1}{1 + c}$

21. $\dfrac{2x + 3}{2x - 3} = \dfrac{3}{5}$

22. $\dfrac{2t + 5}{t - 2} = \dfrac{7}{3}$

23. $\dfrac{1}{a + 2} = \dfrac{3}{a - 3}$

24. $\dfrac{5}{3d - 1} = \dfrac{3}{2d + 7}$

25. $\dfrac{5}{2r + 1} = \dfrac{4}{r - 7}$

26. $\dfrac{3}{5p + 1} = \dfrac{1}{3p - 4}$

27. $\dfrac{4}{w + 3} - \dfrac{3}{w + 2} = 0$

28. $\dfrac{3}{a - 8} + \dfrac{2}{a - 3} = 0$

29. $\dfrac{1}{x - 2} - \dfrac{3}{2x + 1} = 0$

30. $\dfrac{3}{2b - 5} - \dfrac{4}{b - 3} = 0$

Further word problems involving fractions

Example 11
A student cycles 12 km at a certain average speed. He then increases his speed by 4 km/h and takes the same time to travel 15 km. Find his speeds for both parts of the journey.

The problem is to find the student's speed. Let his speed for the first part of the journey be v km/h. Then his speed for the second part of the journey is $v + 4$ km/h (from second sentence of question).

$$\text{Time taken for first part} = \frac{12}{v} \text{ h}$$
$$\text{Time taken for second part} = \frac{15}{v + 4} \text{ h}$$

The two times are the same. Thus,

$$\frac{12}{v} = \frac{15}{v + 4}$$

Multiply both sides by $v(v + 4)$.

$$12(v + 4) = 15v$$
$$12v + 48 = 15v$$
$$48 = 15v - 12v = 3v$$
$$16 = v$$

His speed for the first part of the journey was 16 km/h and for the second part, 20 km/h.

Example 12
A man is 5 years older than his wife. Four years ago the ratio of their ages was 7 : 6. Find their present ages.

The problem is to find their ages. Let the age of the man be y years. Then the age of his wife is $y - 5$ years (from the first sentence of question). Four years ago their ages were as follows:

man's age = $y - 4$ years
wife's age = $(y - 5) - 4 = y - 9$ years.

107

Thus, $\dfrac{y-4}{y-9} = \dfrac{7}{6}$ (from second sentence of question). Multiply both sides by $6(y-9)$.

$$6(y-4) = 7(y-9)$$
$$6y - 24 = 7y - 63$$
$$63 - 24 = 7y - 6y$$
$$39 = y$$

The man's age is 39 years and his wife's age is 34 years.

Example 13

A trader bought two boxes of ball-point pens, each pen costing the same amount and each box containing the same number of pens. In one box, eight pens were faulty; she sold the rest for ₦600. In the other box, all the pens were good; she kept five for herself and sold the rest for ₦645. How many pens were in each box to start with?

Let there be n pens in each box.

In the first box, $n - 8$ pens were sold for ₦600 (second sentence of question).

$$\text{Average cost of a pen} = \frac{600}{n-8} \text{ naira.}$$

In the second box, $n - 5$ pens were sold for ₦645 (third sentence of question).

$$\text{Average cost of a pen} = \frac{645}{n-5} \text{ naira.}$$

Thus, $\dfrac{600}{n-8} = \dfrac{645}{n-5}$ (first sentence of question: each pen cost the same).

Multiply both sides by $(n-8)(n-5)$.

$$600(n-5) = 645(n-8)$$
$$600n - 3\,000 = 645n - 5\,160$$
$$5\,160 - 3\,000 = 645n - 600n$$
$$2\,160 = 45n$$
$$n = \frac{2\,160}{45} = \frac{432}{9}$$
$$n = 48$$

There were 48 pens in each box to start with.

As with other word problems, choose a letter to stand for the unknown quantity. Then use the data in the question to make an equation.

In Exercise 10f, some questions give a letter for the unknown; in other questions, choose a letter for yourself.

Exercise 10f

1. 20 is divided by the sum of 2 and n. If the result is 4, find n.

2. When 48 is divided by the sum of 5 and a certain number, the result is 3. What is the number?

3. I think of a number and subtract 5 from it. I divide 72 by the result. If my answer is 4, what number did I think of?

4. A full roll of cloth contains d metres. When 18m have been sold, the value of the remaining cloth is ₦12 800.
   a How many metres of cloth are worth ₦12 800?
   b Express the selling price of 1 metre of cloth in terms of d.
   c If the selling price is ₦400 per metre, find the length of a full roll of cloth.

5. When full, a cinema has seats for n people. When 280 people have taken seats, the cost of the tickets for the remaining seats comes to ₦38 400.
   a Express the cost of a ticket in terms of n.
   b If tickets cost ₦120 each, find the number of seats in the cinema.

6. When full, a car's petrol tank holds k litres. After using 15 litres, the remaining petrol is enough for the car to travel 344 km.
   a Express the amount of petrol left in the tank in terms of k.
   b Hence express the distance that the car travels on 1 litre of petrol in terms of k.
   c If the car travels 8 km/litre, find the value of k.

7. During a football season, a team scores 42 goals. If the team had played two matches less, its goal average would have been exactly three goals per game. How many games did the team play?

8

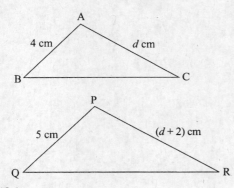

Fig. 10.1

In Fig. 10.1, △ABC is similar to △PQR. Use the data in the figure to find the lengths of AC and PR.

9 A rectangle is such that the lengths of two of its adjacent sides differ by 5 cm. A similar rectangle measures 18 cm by 28 cm. Find the length and breadth of the first rectangle.

10 A father is 24 years older than his son.
   a If the son is x years old, how old is the father?
   b If the ratio of their ages is 5 : 2, find the age of the son.

11 The masses of a mother and daughter differ by 27 kg, and are in the ratio of 8 : 5. Find the mass of each.

12 A man drives 156 km from P to Q at an average speed of v km/h. He then drives 180 km from Q to R. Between Q and R his average speed increases by 8 km/h.
   a Express the time taken between P and Q in terms of v.
   b Give the average speed between Q and R in terms of v.
   c Hence express the time taken between Q and R in terms of v.
   d If the times for each part of the journey are the same, find the value of v.

13 A motorist drives 146 km at a certain average speed. She then increases this speed by 9 km/h and takes the same time to travel the next 164 km. Find her speeds for both parts of the journey.

14 A motorist travels 29 km on an open road at a certain average speed. In the city, he reduces his average speed by 42 km/h, and he finds that it takes him the same time to cover 15 km. Find his average speed, a on the open road, b in the city.

15 A mother is 20 years older than her daughter.
   a If the daughter is y years old, how old is the mother?
   b In terms of y, how old was the daughter 4 years ago?
   c In terms of y, how old was the mother 4 years ago?
   d Four years ago, the ratio of their ages was 7 : 3. Find the present age of the daughter.

16 A brother is 3 years older than his sister. Five years ago, the ratio of their ages was 4 : 3. Find their present ages.

17 A car is travelling at a steady speed.
   a It travels 100 m in $t - 4$ seconds. Write down an expression for the car's speed in m/s.
   b It travels 200 m in $t + 1$ seconds. Write down another expression for the car's speed.
   c Hence find the value of t and the speed of the car in m/s.

18 A piece of brass has a volume V cm³.
   a If there were 6 cm³ more brass, its mass would be 200 g. Write down an expression in V for its density (g/cm³).
   b If there were 4 cm³ less brass, its mass would be 120 g. Write down another expression in V for its density.
   c Hence find the volume of brass and its density in g/cm³.

19 A woman makes n baskets and sells them all at the same price.
   a If she sells all but three of the baskets, she will get ₦5 700. Express the selling price of a basket in terms of n.
   b If she makes three more baskets and sells them all, she will get ₦7 500. Write down another expression in n for the selling price of a basket.
   c Hence find n and the selling price of each basket.

20 Two traders, Ali and Baba, each started with the same number of mangoes. Ali ate two mangoes and sold the rest for a total of ₦700. Baba found that 11 of his mangoes were bad; he sold the rest for ₦600. If their average selling prices per mango were the same, how many mangoes did they each have to start with?

SUMMARY

1 *To solve an equation with fractions*, always clear fractions.

2 *To clear fractions*, multiply each term on both sides of the equation by the LCM of the denominators of the fractions.

3 After the fractions have been cleared, clear brackets, collect like terms and solve in the usual way.

4 When solving word problems:
- find out what the unknown is;
- choose a letter to stand for the unknown quantity;
- change the statements in the question into algebraic expressions and make an equation;
- solve the equation, leaving any numerical simplification until the last step of the working.

PUZZLE CORNER

Birthday Girl

Two days ago she said she was 10.
Next year she will be 13.
What is the date today and when is her birthday?

PUZZLE CORNER

A Cutting Problem

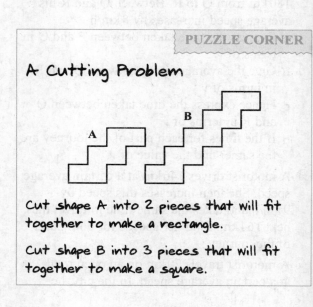

Cut shape A into 2 pieces that will fit together to make a rectangle.

Cut shape B into 3 pieces that will fit together to make a square.

110

11 Compound interest

OBJECTIVES

By the end of this chapter you should be able to:

1 Recall and use the simple interest formula
2 Find the amount that a principal will reach over a given time period and rate of simple interest
3 Find the amount that a principal will reach over a given time period and rate of compound interest
4 Apply the principles of compound interest to daily life problems, including inflation and depreciation.

Teaching and learning materials

Teacher: Simple interest and compound interest charts; newspaper advertisements for mortgage loans, savings accounts, pension schemes; newspaper articles on inflation and depreciation

11-1 Simple interest (revision)

Interest is a payment given for saving money. It can also be the price paid for borrowing money. When interest is calculated on the basic sum of money saved (or borrowed) it is called **simple interest**.

Simple interest, I, can be calculated using the formula

$$I = \frac{PRT}{100}$$

where P is the **principal** (the sum of money saved or borrowed), R is the annual **rate** of interest (given as a percentage) and T is the **time** for which the money is saved (or borrowed).

Example 1

Find the simple interest on ₦12 000 for $7\frac{1}{2}$ years at 6% per annum.

$$I = \frac{PRT}{100}$$

$$= ₦\frac{12\,000 \times 6 \times 7\frac{1}{2}}{100}$$

$$= ₦\frac{12\,000 \times 6 \times 15}{100 \times 2}$$

$$= ₦5\,400$$

The simple interest is ₦5 400.

Exercise 11a

Find the simple interest on the following.

1. ₦3 000 for 4 years at 8%
2. ₦5 200 for 5 years at 7%
3. ₦2 250 for 4 years at 9%
4. ₦1 250 for 3 years at 8%
5. ₦1 600 for $3\frac{1}{2}$ years at 6%
6. ₦3 800 for 4 years at $7\frac{1}{2}$%
7. ₦8 200 for 6 years at $7\frac{1}{2}$%
8. ₦1 500 for 32 years at $4\frac{1}{2}$%
9. ₦6 880 for 2 years at 5%
10. ₦616.50 for 4 years at 5%
11. ₦21 210 for $3\frac{1}{2}$ years at 6%
12. ₦29 275 for 2 years at 10%
13. $475.20 for 6 years at $6\frac{1}{4}$%
14. $787 for 3 years at 9%
15. $131.70 for 6 yr 8 mo at $4\frac{1}{2}$%

If you had difficulty with Exercise 11a, revise Chapter 10 in Book 2.

The **amount** is the sum of the principal and the interest. In Example 1, a principal of ₦12 000 makes an interest of ₦5 400; the amount is ₦12 000 + ₦5 400 = ₦17 400.

Example 2

Find the amount of ₦34 320 in 5 years at $6\frac{1}{4}\%$ per annum.

$$I = \frac{PRT}{100}$$

$$= ₦ \frac{34\,320 \times 6\frac{1}{4} \times 5}{100}$$

$$= ₦ \frac{34\,320 \times 25 \times 5}{100 \times 4}$$

$$= ₦ \frac{8\,580 \times 5}{4} = ₦ \frac{42\,900}{4}$$

$$= ₦10\,725$$

interest = ₦10 725
principal = ₦34 320
amount = ₦45 045

Exercise 11b

Find the amount of the following.

1. ₦500 for 1 year at 6%
2. ₦800 for 1 year at 8%
3. ₦4 000 for 3 years at 6%
4. ₦7 000 for 2 years at $7\frac{1}{2}\%$
5. ₦45 000 for 4 years at 4%
6. ₦15 000 for 20 years at $6\frac{1}{4}\%$
7. ₦360 for $5\frac{1}{2}$ years at 7%
8. ₦1 350 for 1 yr 6 mo at 8%
9. $84 for 2 yr 5 mo at 10%
10. ₦21 300 for 10 years at 5%
11. ₦5 736 for 5 years at $6\frac{2}{3}\%$
12. ₦43 250 for 2 yr 8 mo at 9%
13. $112.80 for $7\frac{1}{2}$ years at $7\frac{1}{2}\%$
14. $172.35 for 3 yr 4 mo at 8%
15. $423.68 for 6 yr 3 mo at $2\frac{1}{2}\%$

11-2 Compound interest

When money is saved with simple interest, the interest is paid at regular intervals and the principal remains the same.

With **compound interest**, the interest is added to the principal at the end of each interval. Thus, the principal increases and so the interest becomes greater for each interval.

Most savings schemes give compound interest, *not* simple interest.

Example 3

Find the compound interest on ₦60 000 for 2 years at 8% per annum.
Note: 'per annum' means 'each year'.

The interest is added at 1 year intervals.
1st year:

$$I_1 = ₦ \frac{60\,000 \times 8 \times 1}{100}$$

$$= ₦4\,800$$

Amount at end of
1st year $= ₦60\,000 + ₦4\,800$
$= ₦64\,800$

2nd year:
The principal is now ₦64 800.

$$I_2 = ₦ \frac{64\,800 \times 8 \times 1}{100}$$

$$= ₦648 \times 8$$
$$= ₦5\,184$$

Amount at end of
2nd year $= ₦64\,800 + ₦5\,184$
$= ₦69\,984$

Compound
interest $= ₦69\,984 - ₦60\,000$
$= ₦9\,984$

The working is easier if arranged in a table. The annual interest can be calculated by inspection. For example, 6% of ₦21 000 is found by multiplying ₦21 000 by 6, and moving the digits two places to the right (to divide by 100); i.e.

$$6\% \text{ of } ₦21\,000 = ₦210 \times 6 = ₦1\,260$$

Example 4 shows how to arrange the working.

Example 4

Find the amount that ₦5000 becomes if saved for 3 years at 6% per annum compound interest.

1st year: Principal   ₦5000
          6% Interest $+300$ $\left(\frac{6}{100} \times 5000\right)$
2nd year: Principal   5300
          6% Interest $+318$ $\left(\frac{6}{100} \times 5300\right)$
3rd year: Principal   5618
          6% Interest $+337.08$ $\left(\frac{6}{100} \times 5618\right)$
          Amount   ₦5955.08

Exercise 11c

Find **a** the amount, **b** the compound interest, for each of the following.

1. ₦40000 for 2 years at 8% per annum
2. ₦60000 for 2 years at 7% per annum
3. ₦50000 for 2 years at 6% per annum
4. ₦30000 for 2 years at 8% per annum
5. ₦6000 for 2 years at 5% per annum
6. ₦87000 for 2 years at 10% per annum
7. ₦12000 for 2 years at 5% per annum
8. ₦35000 for 2 years at 6% per annum
9. ₦5000 for 2 years at 8% per annum
10. $80 for 2 years at 5% per annum
11. ₦1000 for 3 years at 10% per annum
12. ₦6000 for 3 years at 5% per annum
13. ₦5000 for 3 years at 8% per annum
14. ₦10000 for 3 years at 7% per annum
15. ₦2300 for 4 years at 10% per annum

When calculating compound interest, the arithmetic often gives final answers to many decimal places. Final answers should be rounded to the nearest naira. Such rounding should be left to the last line of the working. If possible, use a calculator to calculate interest.

Example 5

Find the sum to which ₦14300 amounts in 2 years at $5\frac{1}{2}$% per annum compound interest.

1st year:
Principal   ₦14300
Interest $\begin{cases} 5\% \\ \frac{1}{2}\% \end{cases}$ $\begin{matrix} 715 \\ 71\cdot50 \end{matrix}$ $\left(\frac{1}{10} \text{ of } 5\%\right)$
2nd year:
Principal   15086·50
Interest $\begin{cases} 5\% \\ \frac{1}{2}\% \end{cases}$ $\begin{matrix} 754\cdot32 \\ 75\cdot43 \end{matrix}$
Amount =   15916·25
₦15916 to the nearest naira

When money is borrowed, interest must be paid back as well as the principal. When a large sum of money is paid back over a number of years, the principal gradually reduces. Example 6 shows how this works when paying back on a **mortgage** (i.e. a loan) for house purchase.

Example 6

A man borrows ₦900000 to buy a house at 8% per annum compound interest. He repays ₦92000 at the end of each year. How much does he still owe at the end of 3 years?

Calculate the amount with interest added for each year, then subtract the repayment. Carry this amount on to the next year.

1st year: Principal   ₦900000
          8% Interest $+72000$ $\left(\frac{8}{100} \times 900000\right)$
                   972000
          Repayment -92000
2nd year: Principal   880000
          8% Interest $+70400$ $\left(\frac{8}{100} \times 880000\right)$
                   950400
          Repayment -92000
3rd year: Principal   858400
          8% Interest $+68672$ $\left(\frac{8}{100} \times 858400\right)$
                   927072
          Repayment -92000
                   835072

Total owed after 3 years = ₦835072.

Depreciation

Many items, such as cars, clothes, electrical goods, lose value as time passes. This loss in value is called **depreciation**. Depreciation is usually given as a percentage of the item's value at the beginning of the year. For example, if a radio costing ₦10 000 depreciates by 20% per annum, then its value will be ₦8 000 at the end of the first year. At the end of the second year, its value will be ₦8 000 less 20% of ₦8 000, i.e. ₦8 000 − ₦1 600 = ₦6 400.

Example 7

A car costing ₦680 000 depreciates by 25% in its first year and 20% in its second year. Find its value after 2 years.

1st year:

Value of car	₦680 000	
25% depreciation	−170 000	$\left(\frac{1}{4} \text{ of } 680\,000\right)$

2nd year:

Value of car	510 000	
20% depreciation	−102 000	$\left(\frac{1}{5} \text{ of } 510\,000\right)$

Value after 2 yr = ₦408 000

Inflation

Due to rising prices, money loses its value as time passes. Loss in value of money is called **inflation**. Inflation is usually given as the percentage increase in the cost of buying things from one year to the next. For example, if the rate of inflation is 15% per annum, then a CD player which cost ₦10 000 a year ago will now cost ₦11 500. Money has lost its value since it now costs more to buy the same thing. Table 16.4 on page 156 gives an example of the effect of inflation on the price of groundnuts.

Example 8

How long will it take for prices to double if the rate of inflation is 20% per annum?

Start with an initial cost of 100 units.

initially, cost =	100	
rise =	20	
after 1 year, cost =	120	
rise =	24	(i.e. 20% of 120)
after 2 years, cost =	144	
rise =	28.8	(20% of 144)
after 3 years, cost =	172.8	
rise =	34.56	(20% of 172.8)
after 4 years, cost =	207.36	

The cost after 4 years is a little more than double the initial cost. Hence prices will double in just under 4 years.

Exercise 11d

Unless told otherwise, give all answers to the nearest naira.

1. ₦24 000 is saved in an account which gives 7% per annum compound interest. Find the amount after 2 years.

2. Find the sum to which ₦10 000 will amount in 3 years at 6% per annum compound interest.

3. Find the compound interest on ₦31 600 in 3 years if the interest rate is 5% per annum.

4. Find the amount when ₦48 400 is saved for 2 years at $5\frac{1}{2}$% per annum compound interest.

5. A man borrows ₦200 000 to buy a car. He is charged compound interest at 9% per annum. He repays ₦128 000 after one year. How much should he repay at the end of the second year to clear his debt?

6. A woman borrows ₦75 000 at 8% per annum compound interest. At the end of the first year she pays back ₦31 000. At the end of the second year she repays ₦30 000. At the end of the third year she clears her debt completely. What is her final payment?

7. A man borrows ₦7 million to buy a house.

He is charged compound interest at 8% per annum. He repays ₦960 000 at the end of each year. How much does he still owe at the end of 3 years?

8. A person saves $650 at 4% compound interest and adds $150 to the amount at the end of each year. What are the total savings after 3 years, to the nearest cent?

9. The population of a town increases by 2% each year. Three years ago the population was 447 000. What is the population now? (Give your answer to 3 s.f.)

10. A car loses value each year by 20% of its value at the beginning of the year. If a car cost ₦540 000, find its value 2 years later.

11. A new car costs $64 000. It depreciates by 25% in the first year, 20% in the second year, and 15% in each of the following years. Find the value of the car to the nearest $50 after 4 years.

12. A person saves ₦3 000 at $4\frac{1}{2}$% compound interest. She adds ₦800 to her amount at the end of each year.
Find her total savings after 2 years.

13. A man borrows ₦185 000 at 6% compound interest. He pays back ₦45 000 at the end of each year. How much does he still owe after he has made his second repayment?

14. Members of a family estimate that they will need ₦700 000 to improve their house in 3 years' time. They deposit ₦550 000 at 5% per annum compound interest. They add ₦25 000 at the end of the first year and a further ₦35 000 at the end of the second.
a Find their total savings after 3 years.
b By how much are their savings greater or less than the ₦700 000 needed?

15. A piece of land increases in value by 10% each year. By what percentage does its value increase over 3 years? (*Hint:* Let the land have an initial value of 100 units.)

16. A CD player costs ₦10 000. Find the cost of buying the same kind of CD player in 2 years' time if the rate of inflation is 15% per annum.

17. Show that prices will double in less than 3 years if the rate of inflation is 30% per annum.
(*Hint:* Start with an initial cost of 100 units).

18. The present cost of a radio is ₦4 800. If the rates of inflation for the next two years are 25% and 15% respectively, find the cost of buying the same kind of radio in 2 years' time.

SUMMARY

1 *Interest* is a payment given (or charged) for saving (or borrowing) money.

2 *Simple interest* is calculated on a basic sum of money saved (or borrowed).

3 The *simple interest formula* is
$$I = \frac{PRT}{100}$$
where
- I is the interest, P is the *principal* (the basic sum of money saved, or borrowed);
- R is the annual *rate of interest* (given as a percentage);
- T is the time (in years) for which the money is saved (or borrowed).

4 The *amount* is the sum of the principal and the interest.

5 Normally *compound interest* is given (or charged): this is where interest is added to the principal at the end of each time interval. (The principal increases and so the interest becomes greater for each successive interval.)

6 Due to wear and tear, most items lose value as time passes. The loss in value is called *depreciation*.

7 Due to rising prices and/or poor financial management, money loses value as time passes. Loss in value of money is called *inflation*.

8 Calculation of depreciation and inflation is similar to the calculation of compound interest.

12 ICT and computers

12-1 Overview of ICT

In the past few decades the impact of **Information and Communications Technology (ICT)** on many people's personal and professional lives has been immense. Mobile phones, computers and computer programs have played a central role in ICT development and will play an even greater role in the future.

Although computers were originally developed to speed up calculation, a huge leap forward in ICT development took place when it became possible to connect them to the **internet** on a **world wide web (www)** via telephone, satellite and radio systems. Think of the internet as a global communication network that provides national and international access to information and to other people. Millions of people use the internet on a daily basis to access information, to purchase and provide goods and services, and to communicate with each other by electronic mail (**email**).

Nowadays, to meet ICT demands, computers have become smaller, faster, more versatile, more reliable and more affordable. Computer chips are used in cars, mobile phones, television sets, music players, cameras and are carried by many people in the form of bank cards. The tendency for greater portability, greater connectivity and 'more power for less cost' will continue throughout this century. For example, many mobile phones now have considerable computing, photographic, entertainment and internet capability.

ICT is mainly used for 'connecting people', usually by the spoken or written word. Fig. 12.1 shows some of the kinds of computers available, and Fig. 12.2 shows some of the functions and programs that demonstrate the computer's central place in ICT.

(a) desk top computer

(b) lap top computer

(c) mobile phone with in-built computer

Fig. 12.1

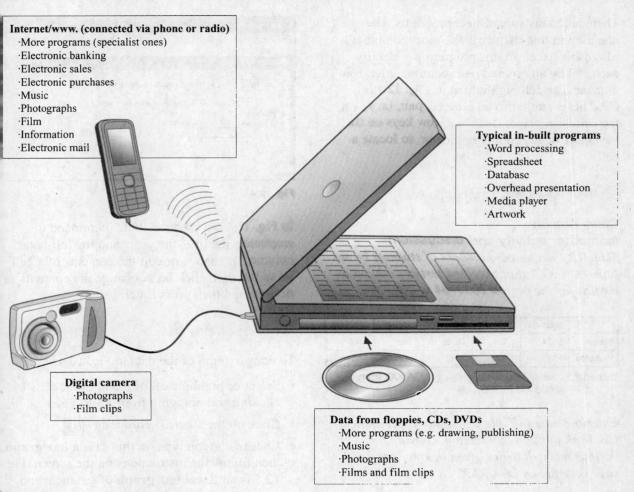

Internet/www. (connected via phone or radio)
- More programs (specialist ones)
- Electronic banking
- Electronic sales
- Electronic purchases
- Music
- Photographs
- Film
- Information
- Electronic mail

Typical in-built programs
- Word processing
- Spreadsheet
- Database
- Overhead presentation
- Media player
- Artwork

Digital camera
- Photographs
- Film clips

Data from floppies, CDs, DVDs
- More programs (e.g. drawing, publishing)
- Music
- Photographs
- Films and film clips

Fig. 12.2

12-2 Computers and mathematics

This section will only be meaningful if you have access to a computer that has a spreadsheet program, preferably Microsoft Excel as used here.
Follow through the Class Activities on your computer.

As already mentioned, computers had a historically important role in speeding up calculation and handling numerical information. Of the software listed in Fig. 12.2, **spreadsheet** programs currently have the greatest everyday application to mathematics, statistics and economics.

A spreadsheet has the appearance of an extensive matrix of cells (Fig. 12.3). Data, either written or numerical, are entered into each cell.

Fig. 12.3

There are many spreadsheet programs. The one used in this chapter is the most common: Microsoft Excel. In this program we identify each cell by an ordered pair: column letter, row number. The cell highlighted in Fig. 12.3 is C7. This is similar to an ordered pair, (x, y), on the cartesian plane. Use the arrow keys on the keyboard, or the computer mouse, to locate a cell.

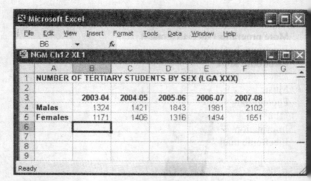

Fig. 12.4

In Fig. 12.4 we used the 'bold' command to emphasise the title, the years and the left-hand column. To change or edit the contents of a cell, go to that cell, click on it, change the contents as desired, and then press Enter.

Entering data into a spreadsheet

Class Activity
(computer activity and discussion)

Table 12.1 shows the numbers of students by sex from LGA XXX that obtained tertiary education awards for the period 2003–04 to 2007–08.

	2003–04	2004–05	2005–06	2006–07	2007–08
Males	1324	1421	1843	1981	2102
Females	1171	1406	1316	1494	1651

Table 12.1 Tertiary students by sex in LGA XXX from 2003–04 to 2007–08

Enter the data in Table 12.1 onto a spreadsheet file. Work through this section, copying the various methodologies given below. At the end, save your file as LGA XXX.

Method:
Open a blank spreadsheet.

- Go to Cell A1. Type in the table title. Press Enter.
- Go to Cell B3. Enter **2003–04**. Then, move across to cells C3, D3, E3, F3 one at a time, entering the years from **2004–05** to **2007–08**.
- Go to Cell A4. Enter the title **Males**. Move across from B4 to F4; enter the numerical data for males from Table 12.1. [Do not put spaces between the digits.]
- Go to Cell A5. Enter the title **Females**, then move across from B5 to F5, entering the numerical data for females from Table 12.1.

Your spreadsheet should now look like Fig. 12.4.

Drawing graphs

To draw a graph of the data in Fig. 12.4:

- Select or highlight all of the relevant cells by clicking and dragging from A3 to F5.
- Click on the *Chart Wizard* icon .
- Choose a graph type, in this case a **bar graph**, then follow the instructions on the screen. Fig. 12.5 is an Excel **bar graph** of the male and female tertiary students for the given years.

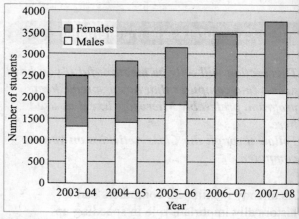

Fig. 12.5

Alternatively, you may wish to draw a **pie chart** that shows the proportion of male to female students in a given year, e.g. 2003/04:

Select the data for 2003/04 (cells B4 to B5). Follow the steps under the *Chart Wizard*, this time selecting the instructions for a pie chart. Fig. 12.6 shows one of many kinds of pie chart that Excel can draw.

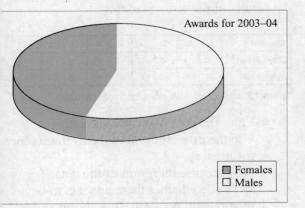

Fig. 12.6

Depending on the data, we can use the spreadsheet program to draw other graphs, such as a line graph or a scattergram. For example, Fig. 12.7 is a **line graph** of the data, drawn by selecting cells B3 to F5, then following the instructions in the *Chart Wizard*.

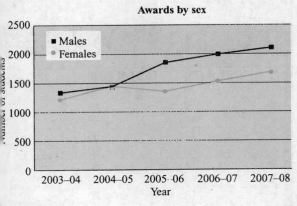

Fig. 12.7

Using formulae functions

Sum

To find the **sum** of the numbers in cells B4 to F4 and place the total in Cell G4:

- First click in Cell G4
- Then type =SUM(B4:F4) and press Enter.

Notice that =SUM(B4:F4) is short for 'the sum of the values in cells B4 to F4'. Another way to find this sum is to select cells B4 to F4 and press the Σ icon (Σ is the Greek letter S, which is short for 'sum'). Try this for cells B5 to F5.

Use both of these methods to check the data in the **Totals (1)** row and **Totals (2)** column in Fig. 12.8.

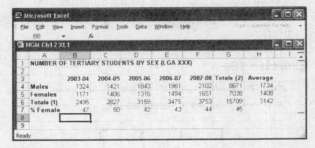

Fig. 12.8

Average

To find the **average** of the numbers from B4 to F4 on the spreadsheet:

- Click the cell where you want the average to go (H4)
- Type =AVERAGE(B4:F4), then press Enter.

The result is shown in Cell H4 in Fig. 12.8. Similarly, cells H5 and H6 give the averages of cells B5 to F5 and B6 to F6 respectively.

Percentage

The spreadsheet program allows you to make up your own formula. For example, to find the **percentage** of females in 2003–04:

- Click in Cell B7
- Type =B5*100/B6, then press Enter.

The outcome, 47, is the percentage of females to the nearest whole number. Note that the formula =B5*100/B6 is short for (B5 $\times$ 100) $\div$ B6, i.e. B5 as a percentage of B6. On a computer * and / are the symbols for multiplication and division.

Check the percentage formulae in the other boxes.

Notes:

1. The spreadsheet program that produced Fig.

12.4 to Fig. 12.8 was adjusted to give data to the nearest whole number.

2. When writing a formula, always begin with an = sign.

3. The above is a simplified account of some basic operations with a spreadsheet. There are many other operations, clever shortcuts and other ways of working with data on a spreadsheet. Practise on your computer and don't be too proud to ask for tips from other users.

Exercise 12a

① *Puzzle: magic square.* Work on a 3 cell × 3 cell grid on a spreadsheet.

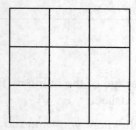

Fig. 12.9

Enter the digits 1 to 9, one to each cell, so that the three numbers in every row, every column *and* in the two main diagonals all have the same total.

② Table 12.2 gives similar data to Table 12.1 for LGA YYY.

	2003–04	2004–05	2005–06	2006–07	2007–08
Males	2504	2701	2855	3019	3186
Females	2399	2650	2777	2982	3177

Table 12.2 Tertiary students by sex in LGA YYY from 2003–04 to 2007–08

a Make a copy of the file you worked on for LGA XXX.
Rename the copy LGA YYY.

b Replace the written and numerical data in cells A1 to F5 with the data in Table 12.2. (Do not touch the other cells.)

c Notice what happens automatically to the data in the **Totals**, **Average** and **% Female** rows and columns.

d What does this tell you about the power of the spreadsheet program?

③ Table 12.3 shows the attendances (days absent) of 10 students during a school term. The table also shows the end of term test results of the same students.

Student	A	B	C	D	E	F	G	H	I	J
Days absent	0	4	0	0	2	15	8	0	10	5
Test result	71	66	80	56	61	43	50	74	44	60

Table 12.3 Student absences and test results

a Enter the data on a spreadsheet.

b Use the program to find the average score for the test.

c Produce a scattergram of the data. Try to decide whether there appears to be a relationship between days absent and test results.

④ Fig. 12.10 shows the results of two tests: Test A out of 25 and Test B out of 100, as presented on a spreadsheet.

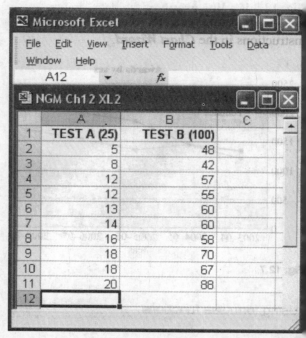

Fig. 12.10

Test A was on the geography of Nigeria and was given *before* any teaching had taken place. The teacher then taught about the geography of Nigeria and afterwards gave the class Test B. The data show corresponding marks of ten of the students: i.e. the student in Row 4 got 12/25 in Test A and 57/100 in Test B.

a In Column C, scale up the scores in Test A to marks out of 100.
E.g. try =A3*4 for Cell C3 and so on for the rest of the column.

b Produce a scattergram for the data.

c Use the scattergram to decide whether the teacher had been effective.

⑤ A school uses its office computer to keep its accounts. Fig. 12.11 shows part of the stationery account.

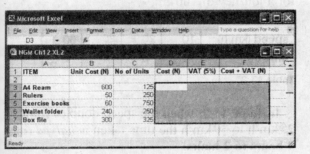

Fig. 12.11

a Open a spreadsheet and enter the data as in Fig. 12.11.

b In Row 3, the formulae for the *Cost*, *VAT* and *Cost + VAT* columns are, respectively: =B3*C3 (entered into D3), =D3*0.05 (entered into E3) and =D3+E3 (entered into F3). Apply these formulae to all the rows.

c Use the program to complete the shaded cells, showing the total costs of the stationery.

d How would you change the VAT formula if the Government increases VAT to 12%?

⑥ *Challenge.* In this challenge you can use a spreadsheet to record your work.

<table>
<tr><td>a</td><td></td><td></td><td></td></tr>
<tr><td>1</td><td></td><td></td><td></td></tr>
<tr><td></td><td></td><td>4</td><td></td></tr>
<tr><td></td><td>2</td><td></td><td></td></tr>
<tr><td></td><td></td><td></td><td>3</td></tr>
</table>

Fig. 12.12

The challenge is to complete Fig. 12.12 so that the cells in every row, every column *and* every 2 × 2 box each contain the digits 1 to 4 once and once only. The digits can be in any order. [This puzzle can be done by logic. As in question 1, you can try this with pencil and paper.]

b Make up a similar puzzle of your own. (But make up the answer first!)

SUMMARY

1 The development of dependable, cheaper computers and mobile phones has given rise to the growth of *ICT (Information and Communications Technology)*. ICT enables people to interact using the spoken and written word.

2 Historically, computers were developed to improve computation, but nowadays most people use them for creating, sending and storing written files and emails.

3 A *spreadsheet program* enables numerical data to be stored and operated upon. The outcomes of the operations may be numerical or graphical.

4 A spreadsheet looks like an extended *matrix of cells,* each of which may contain written or numerical data.

5 Data within the spreadsheet are operated upon by *formulae* such as those shown in the Class Activity.

OBJECTIVES

By the end of this chapter you should be able to:

1 Solve problems on direct and inverse proportion
2 Draw and interpret graphical representations of direct and inverse proportion
3 Find and apply reciprocals of numbers, using four-figure tables where necessary
4 Use reciprocals to simplify calculations.

Teaching and learning materials
Teacher: Charts on direct and inverse proportion; reciprocal tables (page 272)
Student: Reciprocal tables (page 272)

13-1 Direct and inverse proportion

Direct proportion

If a student walks with a steady speed, then the more time taken, the greater the distance walked. Table 13.1 gives corresponding times and distances for a student walking with a steady speed of 5 km/h.

time (h)	1	2	3	4	5
distance (km)	5	10	15	20	25

Table 13.1

In Table 13.1, the ratio of any two times is equal to the ratio of the corresponding distances. For example, in 5 hours the student travels 25 km and in 2 hours the student travels 10 km:

$$\frac{5\,h}{2\,h} = \frac{5}{2} \text{ and } \frac{25\,km}{10\,km} = \frac{5}{2}$$

Thus, the distance travelled is in **direct proportion** to the time taken, or distance **varies directly** with time.

Inverse proportion

If a student travels a certain distance, then the greater the speed, the *less* time it will take. Table 13.2 gives the corresponding speeds and times for a journey of 100 km.

speed (km/h)	10	20	25	50
time (h)	10	5	4	2

Table 13.2

In Table 13.2, when the speed doubles from 25 km/h to 50 km/h the time taken is *halved* from 4 hours to 2 hours:

$$\frac{50\,km/h}{25\,km/h} = \frac{2}{1} \text{ and } \frac{2\,h}{4\,h} = \frac{1}{2}$$

The ratio of any two speeds is equal to the **reciprocal** of the ratio of the corresponding times. This is an example of **inverse proportion**. The time taken is **inversely proportional** to the speed, or time **varies inversely** with speed.

Example 1

Two boxes of matches cost ₦20 and five boxes of matches cost ₦100.
a Does the cost of the matches vary directly or inversely with the number of boxes?
b Find the cost of eight boxes of matches.

a Find the ratios of the corresponding numbers of boxes and costs.

$$\frac{5 \text{ boxes}}{2 \text{ boxes}} = \frac{5}{2} \text{ and } \frac{₦100}{₦20} = \frac{5}{2}$$

Thus, the cost is in direct proportion to the number of boxes.

Let the cost of eight boxes be x naira.

Then $\dfrac{x}{20} = \dfrac{8}{2}$.

$$x = \dfrac{8 \times 20}{2} = 80$$

Eight boxes cost ₦80.

Example 1 could easily be answered by finding the cost of one box. However, the method given above shows that it is not necessary to find the cost of one box.

 Optional: Do Exercise 28 of your Students' Practice Book.

Example 2

A cyclist travels 40 km *between two villages.*

a *Make a table showing the speed if the journey takes* 1 h, 2 h, 4 h.

b *Is the speed directly or inversely proportional to the time taken?*

c *If the cyclist travels at* 18 km/h *find how long the journey takes.*

a Table 13.3 is the required table.

time (h)	1	2	4
speed (km/h)	40	20	10

Table 13.3

b From the table, if the time is doubled, the speed is halved. Thus, speed is inversely proportional to time.

c *Either*

Let the time be t hours. Then comparing a time of t hours and a speed of 18 km/h with a time of 4 hours and a speed of 10 km/h,

$\dfrac{t}{4} = \dfrac{1}{\frac{18}{10}}$ (The ratio of corresponding times is equal to the reciprocal of the ratio of corresponding speeds.)

$$\dfrac{t}{4} = \dfrac{10}{18}$$

$$t = \dfrac{4 \times 10}{18} = \dfrac{20}{9} = 2\tfrac{2}{9}$$

The journey takes $2\tfrac{2}{9}$ hours.

Or

Using time $= \dfrac{\text{distance}}{\text{speed}}$

Time taken $= \dfrac{40}{18} = 2\tfrac{2}{9}$ hours

 Optional: Do Exercise 29 of your Students' Practice Book.

Example 3

A length of wire can be cut into five pieces each 24 cm *long. How many pieces each* 15 cm *long can be cut from the wire?*

First decide whether the example is one of direct proportion or inverse proportion.

From the data of the question, the greater the number of pieces, the smaller their length. The number of pieces is inversely proportional to the length of each piece. Let there be n pieces. Then,

$$\dfrac{n}{5} = \dfrac{1}{\frac{15}{24}} = \dfrac{24}{15}$$

$$n = \dfrac{5 \times 24}{15} = \dfrac{24}{3} = 8$$

There will be eight pieces.

Exercise 13a

1 In each of the following, say whether the two quantities in *italics* are in direct proportion or inverse proportion to each other:

a the *radius* and *diameter* of a circle;

b the *number* and *cost* of pencils;

c the *number* and *size of angle* of equal sectors in a circle;

d the *time* and *distance* when travelling at a steady speed;

e the *speed* and *time* when travelling a certain distance;

f the *cost* per item and the *number* of items that can be bought for a fixed sum of money;

g the *volume* and *cost* of petrol;

h two numbers x and y such that their product is always 100.

2 Five rubbers cost ₦120 and eight rubbers cost ₦192.
   a Does the cost of the rubbers vary directly or inversely with the number bought?
   b Find the cost of nine rubbers.

3 A bottle of water can fill five cups of capacity 200 mℓ, or four cups of capacity 250 mℓ.
   a Does the number of cups vary directly or inversely with their capacity?
   b How many cups of capacity 100 mℓ could the bottle fill?

4 One metre of cloth costs ₦450.
   a Make a table showing the cost of 2 m, 4 m, 8 m of cloth.
   b Is the cost of cloth directly or inversely proportional to the length?

5 A woman has ₦3 000 to spend. She buys items which cost the same amount each.
   a Make a table showing the number of items she can buy if they cost ₦200, ₦300, ₦600 each.
   b Is the cost per item directly or inversely proportional to the number of items?

6 A cake has a mass of 2 kg. It is cut into pieces of equal mass.
   a Make a table showing the number of pieces if they are each of mass 200 g, 125 g, 50 g.
   b Does the number of pieces vary directly or inversely with the mass of each piece?

7 A roll of cloth is cut into pieces of equal length. Table 13.4 shows the length of each piece and the corresponding number of pieces that can be cut from the roll.

length (m)	5	8	20
number	8	5	2

Table 13.4

   a How many pieces of length 4 m could be cut from the roll?
   b If 80 pieces are cut from the roll, what is the length of each piece?

8 A lorry travels a distance of 50 km.
   a Make a table showing its speed if the journey takes 2 h, 5 h, 10 h.
   b If the journey takes 3 hours, find its speed.

9 A boy cycles a distance of 30 km.
   a Make a table to show the time he takes if his speed is 10 km/h, 15 km/h, 20 km/h.
   b If he cycles at 18 km/h, find the time he takes.

10 A roll of cloth is 40 m long. It is cut into pieces of equal length.
    a Make a table to show the number of pieces if they are each of length 5 m, 8 m, 20 m.
    b If the cloth is cut into 16 pieces of equal length, find the length of each piece.

11 A car travels 42 km on 7 litres of petrol. How far will it travel on 12 litres?

12 A length of string can be cut into nine pieces of length 20 cm. How many pieces each 6 cm long can be cut from the string?

13 A student has enough money to buy 8 pens at ₦30 each. How many rubbers costing ₦24 each can she buy for the same money?

14 A car factory produces 700 cars in five work days. How many cars will it produce in 12 work days?

15 A lorry can safely carry 90 sacks each of mass 75 kg. How many boxes each of mass 27 kg can it safely carry?

16 A bus, travelling at a steady speed, takes $2\frac{1}{2}$ hours for a certain journey. How long will a car take if it travels at three times the speed of the bus?

See Section 19-1, pages 185 to 189, for further coverage of direct and inverse proportion.

13-2 Graphical representation

Direct proportion

Using the data of Table 13.1 (on page 124), Fig. 13.1 is a distance/time graph for a person walking with a steady speed of 5 km/h.

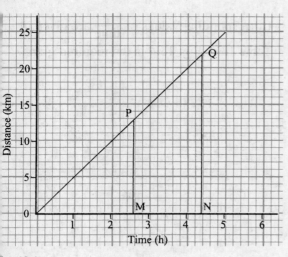

Fig. 13.1

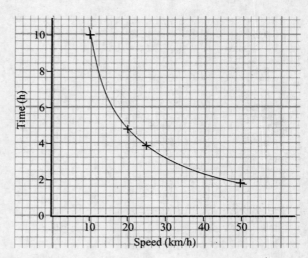

Fig. 13.2

Since distance is directly proportional to time, Fig. 13.1 is a straight line graph through the origin. If P and Q are two points on the graph, then △OPM is similar to △OQN and

$$\frac{PM}{OM} = \frac{QN}{ON}$$

Similarly,

$$\frac{PM}{QN} = \frac{OM}{ON}$$

The first of these ratios gives the person's speed; the second shows that distance is directly proportional to time. The graph can be used as a ready reckoner since corresponding times and distances can be read directly from it.

Inverse proportion

Using the data of Table 13.2 (on page 122), Fig. 13.2 is a speed/time graph for a journey of 100 km.

Notice that as the speed increases, the time decreases. This gives a graph in the shape of a curve. This can be difficult to draw accurately, especially if only a few points are given.

However, since speed and time are inversely proportional, speed is *directly* proportional to $\frac{1}{time}$. Thus a straight line graph will be obtained by plotting $\frac{1}{time}$ against speed.

Table 13.5 gives the values of $\frac{1}{time}$ which correspond to the given speeds.

speed (km/h)	10	20	25	50
time (h)	10	5	4	2
$\frac{1}{time}$	0·1	0·2	0·25	0·5

Table 13.5

Fig. 13.3 is the corresponding graph of $\frac{1}{time}$ against speed.

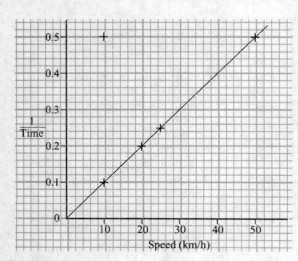

Fig. 13.3

The advantage of a straight line graph is that it is much easier to draw accurately. Also, only three points need to be plotted (i.e. two necessary points and a third point as a check).

Example 4

Four workers can do a piece of work in 10 days.
a *Make a table of values showing the time it would take four, eight, twenty workers to do the work.*
b *Find the corresponding values of $\frac{1}{time}$ and plot these values against number of workers to give a straight line graph.*
c *Use the graph to find the number of days it would take 16 workers to do the work.*

It is assumed that all workers work at the same rate.

a If four workers take 10 days, then eight workers would take half as long, 5 days. Twenty workers would take one-fifth as long, 2 days. These values are shown in Table 13.6.

no. of workers	4	8	20
time (days)	10	5	2
$\frac{1}{time}$	0·1	0·2	0·5

Table 13.6

b Corresponding values of $\frac{1}{time}$ are given in Table 13.6. Fig. 13.4 is the required graph.

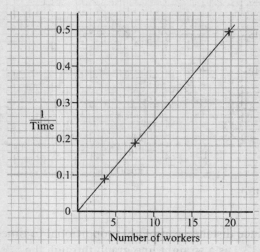

Fig. 13.4

c From the graph, when the number of workers = 16,
$$\frac{1}{time} = 0·4$$
Take the reciprocal of both sides.
$$time = \frac{1}{0·4} = \frac{10}{4} = 2\frac{1}{2} \text{ days}$$

☞ *Optional:* Do Exercise 30 of your Students' Practice Book.

Exercise 13b

① Given that ₦100 is equivalent to 625 fr CFA, draw a graph to exchange amounts up to ₦100 into fr CFA.

Use the graph to find the value of
a ₦21, ₦46 in fr CFA;
b 120 fr CFA, 280 fr CFA in naira.

② Three cyclists start together and travel at speeds of 5 km/h, 15 km/h and 18 km/h respectively.
a On one set of axes, draw graphs to show the distances they travel for any time up to 5 hours. (Take time in hours on the

horizontal axis and distance in km on the vertical axis.)

b Find the distance that each one has travelled after $3\frac{1}{2}$ hours.

3) Three students travel a distance of 60 km at speeds of 12 km/h, 15 km/h and 20 km/h respectively, starting together.

a On one set of axes, draw graphs to show their positions at any time.

b Find the time that each one takes to travel 24 km.

4) Given that 50 litres of kerosene costs ₦4 250, draw a graph and from it read off:

a the cost of 11, 32, 45 litres;

b the number of litres that can be bought for ₦1 615, ₦2 295, ₦3 485.

5) Given that the mass of 100 cm³ of a certain metal is 254 g, draw a graph connecting mass with volume up to 100 cm³. Read off:

a the mass of 37 cm³, 64 cm³ of the metal;

b the volume which has a mass of 100 g, 208 g.

6) Table 13.7 gives the average speeds and corresponding times for a journey.

speed (km/h)	30	60	90
time (h)	4	2	$1\frac{1}{2}$

Table 13.7

a Copy Table 13.7 and add an extra line for $\frac{1}{\text{time}}$. Complete your table by calculating the corresponding values of $\frac{1}{\text{time}}$.

b Taking speed on the horizontal axis and $\frac{1}{\text{time}}$ on the vertical axis, draw a graph connecting speed and reciprocal of time.

c Use your graph to find the time taken if the speed is 48 km/h.

7) A lorry travels a distance of 60 km.

a Copy and complete Table 13.8.

speed (km/h)	6	12	60
time (h)			
$\frac{1}{\text{time}}$			

Table 13.8

b Draw a graph connecting speed and reciprocal of time.

c Use your graph to find i the time taken at a speed of 15 km/h, ii the speed that corresponds to a time of $7\frac{1}{2}$ hours.

8) A car travels a distance of 80 km.

a Copy and complete Table 13.9.

time (h)	8	4	2
speed (km/h)			
$\frac{1}{\text{speed}}$			

Table 13.9

b Draw a graph connecting time with reciprocal of speed.

c Use your graph to find i the speed if the time taken was 5 hours, ii the time at a speed of 25 km/h.

9) A woman spends ₦6 000. She buys n items, each costing the same price.

a Copy and complete Table 13.10.

price/item	₦300	₦600	₦1 000
n			
$\frac{1}{n}$			

Table 13.10

b Draw a graph connecting price/item with $\frac{1}{n}$.

c Use your graph to find i the number of items that can be bought if they cost ₦240 each, ii the price/item when $n = 15$.

10) ₦20 000 is shared equally between n people.

a Make a table of values of n and $\frac{1}{n}$ corresponding to each person getting ₦2 000, ₦4 000, ₦5 000.

b Draw a graph connecting the amount of money each person gets with the reciprocal of n.

c Use the graph to find i n when each person gets ₦2 500, ii the amount each person gets when there are nine people.

13-3 Reciprocals of numbers

Table 13.11 shows the reciprocals of some numbers and the product of the numbers and their reciprocals.

number	reciprocal	product of number and reciprocal
4	$\frac{1}{4}$	$4 \times \frac{1}{4} = 1$
$\frac{1}{4}$	4	$\frac{1}{4} \times 4 = 1$
$-\frac{3}{4}$	$-\frac{4}{3}$	$-\frac{3}{4} \times \left(-\frac{4}{3}\right) = 1$
$-\frac{4}{3}$	$-\frac{3}{4}$	$-\frac{4}{3} \times \left(-\frac{3}{4}\right) = 1$
$\frac{7}{10}$	$\frac{10}{7}$	$\frac{7}{10} \times \frac{10}{7} = 1$
$\frac{9}{26}$	$\frac{26}{9}$	$\frac{9}{26} \times \frac{26}{9} = 1$
$0 \cdot 03$	$\frac{1}{0 \cdot 03}$	$0 \cdot 03 \times \frac{1}{0 \cdot 03} = 1$

Table 13.11

1 The reciprocal of 4 is $\frac{1}{4}$. Similarly, the reciprocal of $\frac{1}{4}$ is 4. Thus, if the reciprocal of x is y, then the reciprocal of y is x.

2 The product of any number and its reciprocal is 1. Thus, the reciprocal of any number is its **multiplicative inverse**.

3 If a number is *multiplied by a power of 10*, its reciprocal is *divided by that power of 10*. Table 13.12 shows the products of 4 and some powers of 10 and their corresponding reciprocals.

number	reciprocal
$0 \cdot 04 = \frac{4}{10^2}$	$\frac{10^2}{4} = \frac{1}{4} \times 10^2 = 25$
$0 \cdot 4 = \frac{4}{10}$	$\frac{10}{4} = \frac{1}{4} \times 10^1 = 2 \cdot 5$
$4 = 4 \times 10^0$	$\frac{1}{4} \times 10^0 = \frac{1}{4} \times 1 = 0 \cdot 25$
$40 = 4 \times 10^1$	$\frac{1}{40} = \frac{1}{4 \times 10^1} = \frac{1}{4} \times 10^{-1} = 0 \cdot 025$
$400 = 4 \times 10^2$	$\frac{1}{400} = \frac{1}{4 \times 10^2} = \frac{1}{4} \times 10^{-2} = 0 \cdot 0025$

Table 13.12

Example 5

Find the reciprocals of the following.

a 6   b 25   c $3\frac{1}{3}$ d $0 \cdot 0002$

a Reciprocal of 6 is $\frac{1}{6} = 0 \cdot 1\dot{6} = 0 \cdot 167$ to 3 s.f.

b Reciprocal of 25 is $\frac{1}{25} = \frac{4}{100} = 0 \cdot 04$.

c Reciprocal of $3\frac{1}{3}$ is $\frac{1}{3\frac{1}{3}} = \frac{1}{\frac{10}{3}} = \frac{3}{10} = 0 \cdot 3$.

d Reciprocal of $0 \cdot 002$ is $\frac{1}{0.002} = \frac{1\,000}{2} = 500$.

Reciprocals can also be calculated by long division. See Example 6.

Example 6

Calculate the reciprocal of $0 \cdot 58$.

Reciprocal of $0 \cdot 58$ is $\frac{1}{0.58} = \frac{100}{58}$

$$\text{working: } 58 \overline{)100 \cdot 000 \ldots} \quad 1 \cdot 724 \ldots$$

```
       1·724...
58)100·000...
   58
   42 0
   40 6
    1 40
    1 16
      240
      232
      ...
```

Reciprocal of $0 \cdot 58$ is $1 \cdot 72$ to 3 s.f.

1. Copy and complete Table 13.13. Give each reciprocal as a decimal number correct to 3 s.f.

n	$\frac{1}{n}$	n	$\frac{1}{n}$	n	$\frac{1}{n}$
1		10		0·1	
2		20		0·2	
3		30		0·3	
4		40		0·4	
5		50		0·5	
6		60		0·6	
7		70		0·7	
8		80		0·8	
9		90		0·9	

Table 13.13

2. Find the reciprocals of the following. Give each answer as a decimal, rounding off to 3 s.f. where necessary.

a 2   b 0·2   c 0·02

d 8   e 80   f 800

g $\frac{2}{3}$ h $1\frac{2}{3}$ i $6\frac{2}{3}$

j $\frac{1}{4}$ k $1\frac{1}{4}$ l $6\frac{1}{4}$

m $1\frac{1}{2}$ n $\frac{3}{4}$ o $4\frac{1}{2}$

p 0·05   q 0·625   r 15

3. Use long division to find the reciprocals of the following correct to 3 s.f.

a 0·32   b 0·47   c 8·9

d 65   e 0·018   f 290

Reciprocal tables

The reciprocal of any number given to 4 or fewer significant figures can be obtained by using the reciprocal table on page 272. Table 13.14 shows some lines from the 4-figure reciprocal table.

Notice the following:

1 Each reciprocal is given to 4 significant figures.
2 As the numbers increase, their reciprocals decrease.
3 Use inspection to place the decimal point.

x	0	1	2	3	4	5	6	7	8	9	SUBTRACT Differences								
											1	2	3	4	5	6	7	8	9
10	1000	9901	9804	9709	9615	9524	9434	9346	9259	9174	9	18	28	37	46	55	64	74	83
11	9091	9009	8929	8850	8772	8696	8621	8547	8475	8403	8	15	23	31	38	46	53	61	69
12	8333	8264	8197	8130	8065	8000	7937	7874	1813	7752	7	13	20	26	33	39	46	52	59
13	7692	7634	7576	7519	7463	7407	7353	7299	7246	7194	6	11	17	22	28	33	39	44	50
14	7143	7092	7042	6993	6944	6897	6849	6803	6757	6711	5	10	14	19	24	29	33	38	43
15	6567	6623	6579	6536	6494	6452	6410	6369	6329	6289	4	8	13	17	21	25	29	33	38
16	6250	6211	6173	6135	6098	6051	6024	5988	5952	5917	4	7	11	15	18	22	26	29	33
17	5882	5848	5814	5780	5747	5714	5682	5650	5618	5587	3	7	10	13	16	20	23	26	29
18	5556	5525	5495	5464	5435	5405	5376	5348	5319	5291	3	6	9	12	15	17	20	23	26
19	5263	5236	5208	5181	5155	5128	5102	5076	5051	5025	3	5	8	11	13	16	18	21	24

continued

											SUBTRACT Differences								
X	0	1	2	3	4	5	6	7	8	9	1	2	3	4	5	6	7	8	9
55	1818	1815	1812	1808	1805	1802	1799	1795	1792	1789	0	1	1	1	2	2	2	3	3
56	1786	1783	1779	1776	1773	1770	1767	1764	1761	1757	0	1	1	1	2	2	2	3	3
57	1754	1751	1748	1745	1742	1739	1736	1733	1730	1727	0	1	1	1	1	2	2	2	3
58	1724	1721	1718	1715	1712	1709	1706	1704	1701	1698	0	1	1	1	1	2	2	2	3
59	1695	1692	1689	1686	1684	1681	1678	1675	1672	1669	0	1	1	1	1	2	2	2	3
60	1667	1664	1661	1658	1656	1653	1650	1647	1645	1642	0	1	1	1	1	2	2	2	3
61	1639	1637	1634	1631	1629	1626	1623	1621	1618	1616	0	1	1	1	1	2	2	2	2
62	1613	1610	1608	1605	1603	1600	1597	1595	1592	1590	0	1	1	1	1	2	2	2	2
63	1587	1585	1582	1580	1577	1575	1572	1570	1567	1565	0	0	1	1	1	1	2	2	2
64	1562	1560	1558	1555	1553	1550	1548	1546	1543	1541	0	0	1	1	1	1	2	2	2

Table 13.14 Reciprocals, $x \to \frac{1}{x}$

Example 7

Use Table 13.14 to find the reciprocal of:
a 6·3   *b* 1·76   *c* 1·256   *d* 5·748.

a To find the reciprocal of 6·3.
In Table 13.14, locate 63 in the left-hand column marked x. Read across from 63 and under the column 0.
The number is 1587.
We place the decimal point by inspection. In this example, all the numbers, x, are such that

$$1 < x \leqslant 10.$$

Their reciprocals, $\frac{1}{x}$, are such that

$$1 > \frac{1}{x} \geqslant 0{\cdot}1.$$

Notice that as a number increases, its reciprocal *decreases*. Thus

$$\frac{1}{6{\cdot}3} = 0{\cdot}1587$$

b To find the reciprocal of 1·76.
In Table 13.14, locate 17 in the left-hand column marked x. Read across from 17 and under the column 6.
The number is 5682.
The reciprocal of 1·76 is 0·5682.

Thus, $\dfrac{1}{1{\cdot}76} = 0{\cdot}5682$

c To find the reciprocal of 1·256.
In Table 13.14, locate 12 in the left-hand column marked x. Read across from 12 and under the column 5.
The number is 8000.
Read across the row of 12 and under 6 in the difference column. The number is 39. The value will now be 8000 *minus* 39, because as numbers increase, their reciprocals decrease.

Thus, $\dfrac{1}{1{\cdot}256}$
$$\begin{aligned} &= \quad 0{\cdot}8000 \\ &- \quad 0{\cdot}0039 \\ &= \quad 0{\cdot}7961 \end{aligned}$$

d To find the reciprocal of 5·748.
Locate 57 in the left-hand column marked x. Read across from 57 and under the column 4.
The number is 1742.
Read across the row of 57 and under 8 in the difference column. The number is 2. The reciprocal of 5·748 is given by

$\dfrac{1}{5{\cdot}748}$
$$\begin{aligned} &= \quad 0{\cdot}1742 \\ &- \quad 0{\cdot}0002 \\ &= \quad 0{\cdot}1740 \end{aligned}$$

Example 8

Use the table on page 272 to find the reciprocal of:
a 761   *b* 2235   *c* 0·4037   *d* 0·03678.

If the given number is greater than 10 or less

than 1, express the number in standard form before beginning.

a To find the reciprocal of 761.

$$761 = 7.61 \times 10^2$$

Thus, $\dfrac{1}{761} = \dfrac{1}{7.61 \times 10^2}$

$$= \dfrac{1}{7.61} \times \dfrac{1}{10^2}$$

$$= \dfrac{1}{7.61} \times 10^{-2}$$

$$= 0.1314 \times 10^{-2}$$

$$= 0.001314$$

b To find the reciprocal of 2 235.

$$2235 = 2.235 \times 10^3$$

Thus, $\dfrac{1}{2235} = \dfrac{1}{2235 \times 10^3}$

$$= \dfrac{1}{2.235} \times \dfrac{1}{10^3}$$

$$= \dfrac{1}{2.235} \times 10^{-3}$$

$$= 0.4474 \times 10^{-3}$$

$$= 0.0004474$$

c To find the reciprocal of 0.403 7.

$$0.4037 = 4.037 \times 10^{-1}$$

Thus, $\dfrac{1}{0.4037} = \dfrac{1}{4.037 \times 10^{-1}}$

$$= \dfrac{1}{4.037} \times \dfrac{1}{10^{-1}}$$

$$= \dfrac{1}{4.037} \times 10^1$$

$$= 0.2477 \times 10^1$$

$$= 2.477$$

d To find the reciprocal of 0.036 78.

$$0.03678 = 3.678 \times 10^{-2}$$

Thus, $\dfrac{1}{0.03678} = \dfrac{1}{3.678 \times 10^{-2}}$

$$= \dfrac{1}{3.678} \times \dfrac{1}{10^{-2}}$$

$$= \dfrac{1}{3.678} \times 10^2$$

$$= 0.2719 \times 10^2$$

$$= 27.19$$

With practice, you will be able to omit many of the above steps.

Exercise 13d   [Oral or written]
Use four-figure tables to find the reciprocals of the following.

① 1.7   ② 4.0   ③ 5.2   ④ 9.0   ⑤ 6.9
⑥ 3.8   ⑦ 1.75   ⑧ 4.06   ⑨ 8.13
⑩ 7.52   ⑪ 2.49   ⑫ 6.06
⑬ 15   ⑭ 22   ⑮ 93
⑯ 0.35   ⑰ 0.58   ⑱ 0.71
⑲ 2.893   ⑳ 2 895   ㉑ 0.002 894
㉒ 48.36   ㉓ 4 837   ㉔ 0.483 9
㉕ 7.754   ㉖ 0.129 8   ㉗ 3.165
㉘ 0.897 2   ㉙ 1.117   ㉚ 0.303 1

Calculations using reciprocals

Example 9
Find the value of $\dfrac{4}{7.41}$.

Treat $\dfrac{4}{7.41}$ as $4 \times \dfrac{1}{7.41}$.

$\dfrac{4}{7.41} = 4 \times 0.1350$ (from reciprocal tables)

$$= 0.5400$$

$$= 0.54 \text{ (to 2 s.f.)}$$

It is possible to find the value of $\dfrac{4}{7.41}$ by long division. However, this would mean a long and tiring calculation. By using reciprocal tables, the work can be done mentally. Notice that the final answer is correct to 2 s.f. only. This is accurate enough for most purposes.

Example 10
Find the value of f, if $\dfrac{1}{f} = \dfrac{1}{9.5} + \dfrac{1}{4.4}$.

$$\dfrac{1}{f} = \dfrac{1}{9.5} + \dfrac{1}{4.4}$$

Using tables to find the reciprocals of the RHS.

$$\dfrac{1}{f} = 0.1053 + 0.2273$$

$$\dfrac{1}{f} = 0.3326$$

Take the reciprocal of both sides.

$$f = 3.007$$

$$= 3.0 \text{ to 2 s.f.}$$

Formulae such as that given in Example 10 are often found in science. Use of reciprocal tables can make the calculation much simpler.

Example 11

The volume of a right-angled triangular prism is $6.0 \, \text{cm}^3$ and the base area is $1.208 \, \text{cm}^2$. Calculate the height of the prism.

Volume = base area × height

$6.0 \, \text{cm}^3 = 1.208 \, \text{cm}^2 \times$ height

$$\text{Height} = \frac{6.0 \, \text{cm}^3}{1.208 \, \text{cm}^2}$$

$$= \frac{1}{1.208} \times 6 \, \text{cm}$$

$$= 0.8281 \times 6 \, \text{cm} \text{ (using reciprocal tables)}$$

$$= 4.9686$$

$$= 5.0 \text{ to 2 s.f.}$$

Notice in Example 11 how the use of reciprocals makes it easy to divide by 'difficult' numbers. To divide by a number is the same as to multiply by its reciprocal.

Exercise 13e

Use reciprocal tables to simplify any calculation. Give all answers correct to 2 s.f.

① Use tables to find the value of the following.

a $\dfrac{5}{6.6}$ b $\dfrac{2}{0.34}$ c $\dfrac{4}{170}$

d $\dfrac{2}{2.38}$ e $\dfrac{3}{0.477}$ f $\dfrac{6}{\pi}$

② A car travels 80 km in 1·17 hours. Calculate its average speed.

③ A trader sells 7 oranges to a woman for ₦100. Find the average cost of an orange to the nearest 10 kobo.

④ A car uses 12·8 litres of petrol to travel 100 km. Find the number of kilometres the car travels on 1 litre.

⑤ A circle has a circumference of 40 cm. Use the value 3·14 for π to calculate its radius.

⑥ A rectangle has an area of $50 \, \text{cm}^2$. Calculate its length if its breadth is 8·33 cm.

⑦ A machine makes 5000 pencils in 42 hours. Calculate its production rate in pencils/hour.

⑧ A boarding school uses an average of 30 000 litres of water per week. Find the average number of litres/hour used.

⑨ Find the value of f if $\dfrac{1}{f} = \dfrac{1}{19} + \dfrac{1}{26}$.

⑩ Find the value of R if $\dfrac{1}{R} = \dfrac{1}{2.7} + \dfrac{1}{6.4}$.

⑪ 27·65 metres of string costs ₦700. What is the cost of a metre of string?

⑫ The product of two numbers is 20. If one of the numbers is 1·245, find the other number.

⑬ $x = 3.152y$ is an equation connecting x and y. If $x = 8$, find the value of y.

⑭ Find the value of

a $\dfrac{6}{1.405}$ b $\dfrac{90}{15.05}$ c $\dfrac{12}{0.2104}$

⑮ The fare for a journey of 884 km is ₦2500. What is the fare per kilometre?

SUMMARY

1 Two quantities are in *direct proportion* if they are related in such a way that if one changes by a factor k, the other also changes by factor k. We say they *vary directly* with each other.

2 Two quantities are in *inverse proportion* if they are related in such a way that if one changes by a factor m, the other changes by factor $\dfrac{1}{m}$. We say they *vary inversely* with each other.

3 The *reciprocal* of a number is its *multiplicative inverse*.

For example, y and $\dfrac{1}{y}$ are reciprocals of each other, since

$$y \times \frac{1}{y} = 1.$$

4 Page 272 contains a Table of Reciprocals. Notice that as a number increases, its reciprocal decreases.

14 Simultaneous linear equations

Teaching and learning materials

Teacher: Charts of tables of values; graph board and ruler; graph paper for class use

Student: Graph paper or graph exercise book; ruler

14-1 The graph of an equation

$y = 3x - 4$ is called an **equation in x and y**. For any value of x there is a corresponding value of y. For example, if $x = 1$, then $y = -1$, and if $x = 3$, $y = 5$.

Before drawing a graph, make a **table of values**. Points on the graph can be plotted from values in the table. In the equation $y = 3x - 4$, x and y are often called the **variables**. The equation gives a connection between the variables. A table of values can be calculated from the equation. See Example 1 below.

Example 1

Draw the graph of $y = 3x - 4$ for values of x from -3 to $+3$. Read off:

a the value of y when $x = 2 \cdot 5$,
b the value of x when $y = -2$,
c the coordinates of the points where the line cuts the axes.

Begin by making a table of values. Calculate values of y which correspond to whole-number values of x within the given range.

When $x = -3$, $y = 3(-3) - 4 = -9 - 4 = -13$,

when $x = -2$, $y = 3(-2) - 4 = -6 - 4 = -10$,

and so on. Table 14.1 gives the corresponding values of x and y for values of x in whole numbers from -3 to $+3$.

x	-3	-2	-1	0	1	2	3
y	-13	-10	-7	-4	-1	2	5

Table 14.1

The table gives seven ordered pairs: $(-3, -13)$, $(-2, -10)$,…,$(3, 5)$. The pairs can be plotted as points on a cartesian plane.

x is called the **independent variable**. Values of x are given on the horizontal axis. y is called the **dependent variable**. Values of y are given on the vertical axis.

Fig. 14.1 is the graph of the equation $y = 3x - 4$.

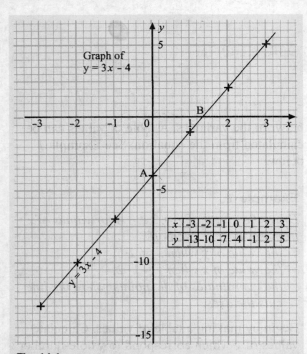

Fig. 14.1

The line in Fig. 14.1 is the **graph of the equation** $y = 3x - 4$. $y = 3x - 4$ is **the equation of the line**.

$y = 3x - 4$ is a **linear equation** in x and y. The variables in a linear equation are always separate and have a power of 1 (i.e. there are no terms such as xy, x^2, y^3, etc.). The graph of a linear equation is always a straight line. Thus, it is sufficient to plot only two points to be able to draw the line. In practice it is better to plot *three* points. If the three points lie in a straight line, the working is probably correct.

Notice that the seven points lie in a straight line. They can be joined by using a ruler. The equation and table of values are also given on the graph paper.

a From the graph, when $x = 2 \cdot 5$, $y = 3 \cdot 5$.
b Similarly, when $y = -2$, $x \simeq 0 \cdot 7$.
c The line cuts the axes at A(0, −4) and B(1·3, 0).

 Optional: Do Exercise 31 of your Students' Practice Book.

134

Exercise 14a

1. Table 14.2 gives corresponding values of x and y for the equation $y = x + 2$.

x	−4	0	+4
y	−2	2	+6

Table 14.2

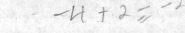

a Using a scale of 2 cm to 1 unit on both axes, draw the graph of $y = x + 2$.
b Find the value of y when $x = 3$.
c Find the value of x when $y = 1$.
d Write down the coordinates of the points where the line cuts the axes.

2. Using a scale of 1 cm to 1 unit on both axes, draw the graphs of the following equations for values of x from −2 to +2.
   a $y = x + 3$ b $y = 2x - 1$
   c $y = 5x$ d $y = 3x - 2$

3. a Draw the graph of $y = 2x - 3$ for values of x from −1 to +3. Use a scale of 2 cm to 1 unit on both axes.
   b On the *same axes*, draw the lines $y = 2x$ and $y = 2x + 1$.
   c What do you notice about the three lines you have drawn?

4. a Draw the line $2y = 3x + 1$ for values of x from −2 to +3. Use $y = \frac{1}{2}(3x + 1)$ to make a table of values.
   b Write down the coordinates of the points where the line crosses the axes.

5. a Draw the graphs of $y = x + 1$ and $y = 3x - 2$ on the *same axes* for values of x from 0 to +3.
   b Write down the coordinates of the point where the two lines cross.

6. a Within the *same axes*, draw the lines $y = 2 - x$ and $y = x + 4$.
   b Find the coordinates of the point where the two lines cross.

7. a On the *same axes*, draw the graphs of $y + 2x = 0$ and $2y = x + 5$ for values of x from 0 to 3.
   b Extend the lines until they cross each

other. Find the coordinates of the point where they cross.

c What is the angle between the lines?

8 Find the coordinates of the points where the following pairs of lines cross.

a $y = x - 3$
$3y = 1 - 2x$

b $y = x - 2$
$y = 7 - 2x$

c $3x - 4y = 0$
$5x - 2y = 7$

d $2x + y = -1$
$3x - y = -10$

14-2 Simultaneous linear equations

Consider the equation $2x + y = 7$.

For any value of x there is a corresponding value of y. If $x = 0$, $y = 7$; if $x = 1$, $y = 5$; and so on. Table 14.3 gives some of these pairs of values.

x	0	1	2	3	4	5	...
y	7	5	3	1	−1	−3	...

Table 14.3

Similarly, consider the equation $x - y = 2$.

Table 14.4 sets out pairs of values for this equation in the same way.

x	0	1	2	3	4	5	...
y	−2	−1	0	1	2	3	...

Table 14.4

Look at the pairs of values in Tables 14.3 and 14.4. Notice that the pair $x = 3$, $y = 1$ appears in *both* tables. This is the *only* pair that appears in both tables. This means that this pair of values satisfies both equations *simultaneously* (i.e. at the same time). Hence the solution of the **simultaneous linear equations** $2x + y = 7$ and $x - y = 2$ is $x = 3$ and $y = 1$.

This result can be shown by drawing the graphs of the two lines as in Fig. 14.2.

The two lines *intersect* (i.e. cut each other) at the point (3, 1). This is the only point which is on both lines. The coordinates of the point of intersection give the solution of the simultaneous equations.

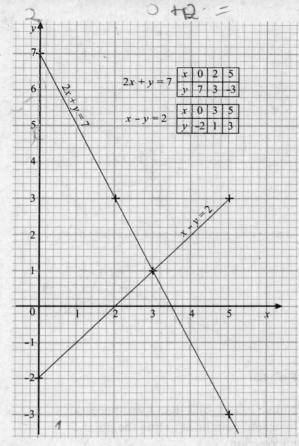

Fig. 14.2

Example 2

Solve graphically the simultaneous linear equations
$2x - y = -1$, $x - 2y = 4$.

1st step: Make tables of values for each equation. Three pairs of values are sufficient for each:

$2x - y = -1$

x	0	1	2
y	1	3	5

$x - 2y = 4$

x	0	1	2
y	−2	$-1\frac{1}{2}$	−1

2nd step: Choose a suitable scale and plot the points. Draw both lines. Extend the lines if necessary so that they intersect. Fig. 14.3 shows the graphs of the two lines.

135

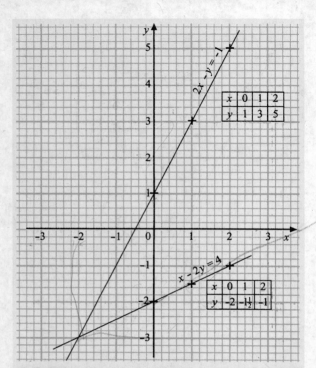

Fig. 14.3

Notice in Fig. 14.3 that it was necessary to extend both lines to find the point of intersection.

3rd step: Find the coordinates of the point of intersection. From the graphs, the lines intersect at $(-2, -3)$.

The solution of the simultaneous linear equations is $x = -2$ and $y = -3$.

 Optional: Do Exercise 32 of your Students' Practice Book.

Exercise 14b

Solve graphically the following pairs of simultaneous equations.

1. $x + y = 3$
   $3x - y = 1$

2. $x - y = 1$
   $x + 2y = 7$

3. $x - 2y = 1$
   $2x + y = 2$

4. $y = 2x + 2$
   $3x + 2y = 4$

5. $3y = 2x + 8$
   $x + y = 1$

6. $x + 3y = 0$
   $x - 3y = 6$

136

7. $x - y = 0$
   $3x - y + 2 = 0$

8. $4x - 2y = 7$
   $x + 3y = 7$

9. $x + y = 3$
   $5x - 5y = 1$

10. $2x - 2y = 5$
    $2x + 3y + 1 = 0$

11. $3x + 7y = 11$
    $x - y + 4 = 0$

12. $5x - 2y = 1$
    $4x + 3y = -10 \cdot 7$

13. $y - 2x = 9$
    $y + x = 6$

14. $y - 4x = 0$
    $2x + y = 12$

15. $y - 3x = 8$
    $y - x = 2$

16. $4x = 3y$
    $6y - 5x = 18$

17. $2x - y = 3$
    $3x - 5y = 15$

18. $2x - y = 7$
    $4x + 3y = -1$

19. $3y + 2x = 16$
    $4y + 3x = 24$

20. $3x + 2y = 4$
    $2x + 3y = 1$

14-3 Method of substitution

The graphical method is time consuming and can often be inaccurate. It is quicker and more accurate to use an algebraic method to solve simultaneous linear equations. Read Example 3 carefully.

Example 3

Solve the equations $2x + y = 7$, $x - y = 2$.

Note: When asked to solve two equations with two unknowns, assume that they are simultaneous linear equations.

Write out the equations, one below the other. Label the equations (1) and (2).

$$2x + y = 7 \quad (1)$$
$$x - y = 2 \quad (2)$$

From equation (2),
$$x = 2 + y \quad (3)$$

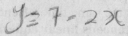

Substitute $(2 + y)$ for x in equation (1).

$$2(2 + y) + y = 7$$

Clear brackets and collect terms.

$$4 + 2y + y = 7$$
$$3y = 3$$
$$y = 1$$

Substitute the value 1 for y in equation (3).

$x = 2 + 1 = 3$

Thus, $x = 3$ and $y = 1$.

Check: substitute 3 for x and 1 for y in (1) and (2).
(1) $2x + y = 2 \times 3 + 1 = 6 + 1 = 7 = $ RHS
(2) $x - y = 3 - 1 = 2 = $ RHS

Use the method of **substitution** when the coefficient of one of the unknowns in the given equations is 1.

Example 4

Solve the equations
$3a + b = 10, 2a + 4b = 0$.

$3a + b = 10$ (1)
$2a + 4b = 0$ (2)

From (1),

$b = 10 - 3a$ (3)

Substitute $(10 - 3a)$ for b in (2).

$2a + 4(10 - 3a) = 0$

Clear brackets and collect terms.

$2a + 40 - 12a = 0$
$\qquad -10a = -40$
$\qquad\qquad a = 4$

Substitute 4 for a in (3).

$b = 10 - 3 \times 4 = 10 - 12$
$b = -2$

Thus, $a = 4$ and $b = -2$.

Check: substitute 4 for a and -2 for b in (1) and (2).
(1) $3a + b = 3 \times 4 + (-2) = 12 - 2 = 10$
$\qquad\qquad = $ RHS
(2) $2a + 4b = 2 \times 4 + 4(-2) = 8 - 8 = 0$
$\qquad\qquad = $ RHS

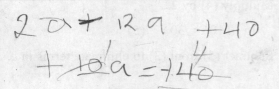

Example 5

Solve the equations $2x - y = 6, 3x + 2y = 2$.

$2x - y = 6$ (1)
$3x + 2y = 2$ (2)

From (1),

$2x = 6 + y$
$2x - 6 = y$
$\qquad y = 2x - 6$ (3)

Substitute $(2x - 6)$ for y in (2).

$3x + 2(2x - 6) = 2$

Clear brackets and collect terms.

$3x + 4x - 12 = 2$
$\qquad\quad 7x = 14$
$\qquad\quad\; x = 2$

Substitute 2 for x in (3).

$y = 2(2) - 6$
$\; = -2$

Thus, $x = 2$ and $y = -2$.

Check: substitute 2 for x and -2 for y in (1) and (2).
(1) $2x - y = 2 \times 2 - (-2) = 4 + 2 = 6$
$\qquad\qquad = $ RHS
(2) $3x + 2y = 3 \times 2 + 2 \times (-2) = 6 - 4$
$\qquad\qquad = 2 = $ RHS

Always check the accuracy of the answers by substituting the values into the original equations.

 Optional: Do Exercise 33 of your Students' Practice Book.

Exercise 14c

Use the method of substitution to solve the following pairs of simultaneous equations.

① $y = x + 1$
   $x + y = 3$

② $y = 2x - 4$
   $3x + y = 11$

③ $a = 5 - 2b$
   $5a + 2b = 1$

④ $2m + n = 0$
   $m + 2n = 3$

⑤ $x + y = 4$
$2x - y = 5$

⑥ $y - 2x = 1$
$3x - 4y = 1$

⑦ $a - 2b = 9$
$2a + 3b = 4$

⑧ $3x + 2y = 10$
$4x - y = 6$

⑨ $x + 2y = 7$
$3x - 2y = -3$

⑩ $2a + b = 19$
$3a - 2b = 11$

⑪ $4x - 3y = 1$
$x - 2y = 4$

⑫ $4x = y + 7$
$3x + 4y + 9 = 0$

⑬ $2a + b = 3$
$3a + 2b = 0$

⑭ $3x + y = 8$
$5x - 3y = 4$

⑮ $2x + 7y = 3$
$2x - y = 3$

⑯ $5m + 10n = 10$
$2m - n - 1 = 0$

⑰ $6a + 3b = 4$
$a + b = 1$

⑱ $2x + y = -5$
$3x + 2y = -8$

⑲ $5m - 2n = 4$
$m - 4n = -1$

⑳ $3x + 5y = 11$
$2x - y = 3$

14-4 Method of elimination

When none of the coefficients of the unknowns is 1, use the method of **elimination**. The aim of this method is to get rid of (eliminate) one of the unknowns by making its coefficient the same in both equations. Then add or subtract the equations as necessary. Read Example 6 carefully.

Example 6

Solve the equations
$3x + 2y = 12, 5x - 3y = 1$.

$3x + 2y = 12$ (1)
$5x - 3y = 1$ (2)

The coefficients of y can be made the same if (1) is multiplied by 3 and (2) is multiplied by 2.*

(1) ×3: $9x + 6y = 36$
(2) ×2: $10x - 6y = 2$
Adding: $19x = 38$
           Thus, $x = 2$

Substitute 2 for x in (1).

$3 \times 2 + 2y = 12$
$2y = 12 - 6 = 6$
$y = 3$

Thus, $x = 2$ and $y = 3$.

Check: substitute 2 for x and 3 for y in (1) and (2).
(1) $3x + 2y = 3 \times 2 + 2 \times 3 = 6 + 6 = 12$
               $=$ RHS
(2) $5x - 3y = 5 \times 2 - 3 \times 3 = 10 - 9 = 1$
               $=$ RHS

*Remember that an equation remains the same if every term is multiplied or divided by the same number.

In the above example, instead of substituting 2 for x to find y, it may be simpler to start again with the original equations and eliminate x to find y. For example,

(1) ×5: $15x + 10y = 60$
(2) ×3: $15x - 9y = 3$
Subtracting: $19y = 57$
            $y = 3$

This method can be very useful when the first value found is a fraction, since fractions often give difficult working when substituted.

Example 7

Solve the equations
$3f = 4 - 4e, 2e = 5f + 15$.

$3f = 4 - 4e$ (1)
$2e = 5f + 15$ (2)

Arrange the equations so that unknowns are in alphabetical order on the LHS and numbers are on the RHS.

$4e + 3f = 4$ (3)
$2e - 5f = 15$ (4)

Multiply (4) by 2.

$4e - 10f = 30$ (5)

Subtract (5) from (3) to eliminate terms in e.

$$13f = -26$$
$$f = -2$$

Substitute -2 for f in (2).

$$2e = 5(-2) + 15$$
$$2e = -10 + 15 = 5$$
$$e = 2\tfrac{1}{2}$$

The check is left as an exercise.

Note: (1) Where necessary, always arrange the given equations so that the unknowns are in alphabetical order on the LHS and the numbers are on the RHS.

(2) Add the equations if the coefficients of the variable to be eliminated are equal but of different signs. Subtract the equations if the coefficients of the variables to be eliminated are equal and of the same sign.

 Optional: Do Exercise 34 of your Students' Practice Book.

Exercise 14d

Use the method of elimination to solve the following pairs of simultaneous equations.

① $5a - 2b = 14$
$2a + 2b = 14$

② $4p + 3q = 9$
$2p + 3q = 3$

③ $2x + 5y = 4$
$2x - 2y = 18$

④ $5x + 2y = 2$
$2x + 3y = -8$

⑤ $5x + 3y = 1$
$2x + 3y = -5$

⑥ $4x + 3y = 9$
$2x + 5y = 15$

⑦ $4a = 5b + 5$
$2a = 3b + 2$

⑧ $2x + 5y = 0$
$3x - 2y = 19$

⑨ $3x - 2y = 4$
$2x + 3y = -6$

⑩ $6h = 2k + 9$
$3h + 4k = 12$

⑪ $2p - 5q = 8$
$3p - 7q = 11$

⑫ $2r + 3s = 29$
$3r + 2s = 16$

⑬ $2x - 5y = -6$
$4x - 3y = -12$

⑭ $2x + 5y + 1 = 0$
$3x + 7y = 1$

⑮ $3a = 2b + 1$
$3b = 5a - 3$

⑯ $5v = 11 + 3u$
$2u + 7v = 3$

⑰ $5d = 2e - 14$
$5e = d + 12$

⑱ $6x - 5y = -7$
$3x + 4y = 16$

⑲ $3f - 4g = 1$
$6f - 6g = 5$

⑳ $8y + 4z = 7$
$6y - 8z = 41$

14-5 Word problems

Example 8

Four pens and six pencils cost ₦272 altogether. Six pens and five pencils cost ₦328. Find the cost of one pen and one pencil.

Let one pen cost x naira and one pencil cost y naira.
Then 4 pens cost $4x$ naira
6 pencils cost $6y$ naira

Thus, $\quad 4x + 6y = 272 \quad$ (1)
$\quad\quad\quad$ (1st sentence in question)
Similarly, $\quad 6x + 5y = 328 \quad$ (2)
$\quad\quad\quad$ (2nd sentence in question)
(1) $\times 3$: $12x + 18y = 816$
(2) $\times 2$: $\underline{12x + 10y = 656}$
Subtracting: $\quad\quad 8y = 160$
$\quad\quad\quad\quad\quad y = 20$
Substitute 20 for y in (1).
$4x + 120 = 272$
$\quad\quad 4x = 272 - 120 = 152$
$\quad\quad\ x = 38$

Thus, a pen costs ₦38 and a pencil costs ₦20.

Check:
4 pens cost ₦152 $\quad\quad$ 6 pens cost $\quad$ ₦228
6 pencils cost ₦120 $\quad\quad$ 5 pencils cost ₦100
$\quad\quad\quad$ ₦272 $\quad\quad\quad\quad\quad\quad\quad\quad$ ₦328

Example 9

Uche's age and Omo's age add up to 24 years. Six years ago, Uche was three times as old as Omo. What are their ages?

Let Uche's age be a years and Omo's age be b years.

Then

$\quad a + b = 24 \quad$ (1) $\quad$ (1st sentence in question)

Six years ago, Uche was $(a - 6)$ and Omo was $(b - 6)$. Hence

$(a - 6) = 3(b - 6)$ (2nd sentence in question)

Clear brackets and collect terms.

$a - 6 = 3b - 18$
$a - 3b = -12$ (2)

Subtract (2) from (1).

$a + b = 24$ (1)
$a - 3b = -12$ (2)

Subtracting: $4b = 36$
$b = 9$

Substitute 9 for b in (1).

$a + 9 = 24$
$a = 15$

Thus, Uche is 15 and Omo is 9.

Check: Sum of ages $= 15 + 9 = 24$ years;
6 years ago, Uche was 9 and Omo was 3;
$9 = 3 \times 3$.

Note: In both of these examples, the given facts are checked and *not* the equations.

To solve word problems, follow the strategy below.

1 Starting from the last sentence of the question, identify what are required in the problem. These are the two unknowns.
2 Choose two letters to represent the unknowns.
3 Translate the first sentence in the question into an algebraic equation.
4 Also translate the second sentence into an algebraic equation.
5 Solve the two equations simultaneously for the values of the unknowns.
6 Check the result using the information given in the question.

Exercise 14e

1 The sum of two numbers is 19. Their difference is 5. Find the numbers.

2 A father is 25 years older than his son. The sum of their ages is 53 years. Find their ages.

3 The sum of two numbers is 17. The difference between twice the larger number and three times the smaller is 4. Find the numbers.

4 Uzezi and Jaja have ₦600 between them. Jaja has ₦240 more than Uzezi. How much does each have?

5 A newspaper and a magazine cost ₦110 together. The newspaper costs ₦70 less than the magazine. Find the cost of each.

6 A pencil and a rubber cost ₦54 together. Four pencils cost the same as five rubbers. Find the cost of each.

7 I have x ₦5 notes and y ₦10 notes. There are eight notes altogether and their total value is ₦55. How many of each note do I have?

8 Dupe's age and Olu's age add up to 25 years. Eight years ago, Dupe was twice as old as Olu. How old are they now?

9 The sides of the rectangle in Fig. 14.4 are given in cm.

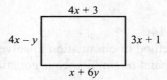

Fig. 14.4

Find x and y and the area of the rectangle.

10 The sides of the equilateral triangle in Fig. 14.5 are given in cm.

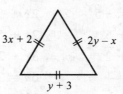

Fig. 14.5

Find x and y and the perimeter of the triangle.

11 Six pencils and three rubbers cost ₦234. Five pencils and two rubbers cost ₦184. How much does each cost?

12 Three nuts and six bolts have a mass of 72 g.

Four nuts and five bolts have a mass of 66 g. Find the mass of a nut and of a bolt.

13 The average of two numbers is 11. The difference between them is 4. Find the numbers.

14 A cyclist travels for x hours at 5 km/h and for y hours at 10 km/h. He travels 35 km altogether and his average speed is 7 km/h. Find x and y.

15 In 10 years' time a father will be twice as old as his daughter. 10 years ago he was six times as old as his daughter. How old is each now?

16 The sides of the parallelogram in Fig. 14.6 are given in cm.

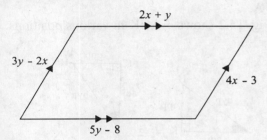

Fig. 14.6

Find x and y and the perimeter of the parallelogram.

17 The sides of the square in Fig. 14.7 are given in cm.

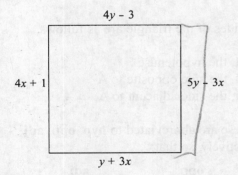

Fig. 14.7

Find x and y and the area of the square.

18 The sum of the digits of a two-digit number is 10. The result of subtracting twice the units digit from three times the tens digit is 15. Find the number.

19 The perimeter of a rectangle is 84 cm and its length is 6 cm longer than its breadth. Find the length and breadth of the rectangle.

20 The sum of the digits of a two-digit number is 12. If the digits are interchanged, the number is increased by 36. Find the number.

SUMMARY

1 In an equation such as
$$y = 3x - 4$$
the unknowns x and y are called *variables*.

2 Corresponding pairs of values of x and y can be calculated and plotted on a graph. See Fig. 14.1. Since values of y depend on the values of x, y is called the *dependent variable*. x is called the *independent variable*.

3 $y = 3x - 4$ is called a *linear equation* in x and y. The equation can be represented by a graph in the form of a continuous straight line. Again, see Fig. 14.1.

4 If two linear equations in x and y are both satisfied by a pair of values, x and y, we say they are *simultaneous linear equations*.

5 Simultaneous linear equations can be solved graphically by drawing the graphs of the two equations on the same axes; their point of intersection gives the solution. See Example 2.

6 Simultaneous equations can also be solved algebraically: either by *substitution* (see Examples 3, 4 and 5) or by *elimination* (see Examples 6 and 7).

OBJECTIVES

By the end of this chapter you should be able to:

1 Define the sine and cosine of an angle in a right-angled triangle

2 Use measurement to find the sine and cosine of acute angles

3 Use sines and cosines of angles to calculate lengths and angles in right-angled triangles

4 Use four-figure tables to find the sines and cosines of angles from 0° to 90°

5 Solve practical problems using sines and cosines of angles

6 Solve right-angled triangles using Pythagoras' rule and the three trigonometrical ratios (sine, cosine, tangent).

Teaching and learning materials

Teacher: Cardboard models of right-angled triangles (as in Fig. 15.2); trigonometrical tables (see pages 269 to 271)

Student: Trigonometrical tables (see pages 269 to 271)

15-1 Sine and cosine

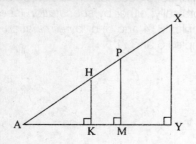

Fig. 15.1

In Fig. 15.1, triangles HAK, PAM, XAY are similar.

Thus, $\dfrac{KH}{AH} = \dfrac{MP}{AP} = \dfrac{YX}{AX}$

The value of this ratio depends only on the size of Â. The ratio is called the **sine of Â**, usually shortened to **sin A**.

Similarly, $\dfrac{AK}{AH} = \dfrac{AM}{AP} = \dfrac{AY}{AX}$ is a ratio whose size depends only on the size of Â. This ratio is called the **cosine of A**, usually shortened to **cos A**.

Fig. 15.2 shows △AHK in various positions.

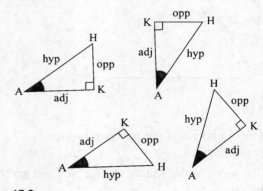

Fig. 15.2

The sides of the triangle are as follows.

AH, the hypotenuse
KH, the side opposite to Â
AK, the side adjacent to Â

These are abbreviated to **hyp, opp, adj**, respectively, so that:

$$\sin A = \frac{opp}{hyp} \qquad \cos A = \frac{adj}{hyp}$$

Example 1

Find, by drawing and measurement, approximate values for sin 25°, cos 25°, sin 48°, cos 48°, sin 70°, cos 70°.

On graph paper, draw a quadrant of a circle of radius 10 units.

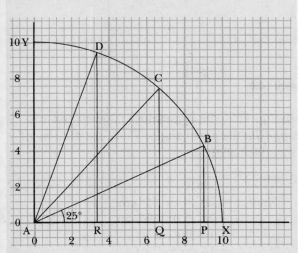

Fig. 15.3

Note: In Fig. 15.3, to save space, a scale of 1 cm to 2 units has been used. In practice, it is better to use a scale of 1 cm to 1 unit.

Draw BÂX = 25°. Construct P on AX so that BP̂A = 90°. Then, in △APB,

$$\sin 25° = \frac{PB}{AB} = \frac{4·2}{10} = 0·42$$

$$\cos 25° = \frac{AP}{AB} = \frac{9}{10} = 0·9$$

Similarly, in △ACQ, CÂQ = 48° and

$$\sin 48° = \frac{QC}{AC} = \frac{7·4}{10} = 0·74$$

$$\cos 48° = \frac{AQ}{AC} = \frac{6·7}{10} = 0·67$$

In △ADR, DÂR = 70° and

$$\sin 70° = \frac{RD}{AD} = \frac{9·4}{10} = 0·94$$

$$\cos 70° = \frac{AR}{AD} = \frac{3·4}{10} = 0·34$$

Example 2

Find by drawing
a the angle whose sine is 0·56,
b the angle whose cosine is 0·60.

a $$0·56 = \frac{5·6}{10}$$

It is necessary to construct a right-angled triangle with a hypotenuse of 10 units and a side of 5·6 units. Draw an arc of a circle centre O and radius 10 cm. Draw perpendicular radii OX and OY. Draw a line parallel to OX and 5·6 cm from OX to cut the arc at A. Draw AB perpendicular to OX.

Fig. 15.4 is a scale drawing of the construction.

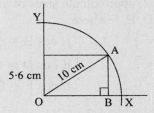

Fig. 15.4

In Fig. 15.4,

$$\sin AÔB = \frac{BA}{OA} = \frac{5·6}{10} = 0·56$$

By measurement, AÔB ≃ 34°.

b $$0·60 = \frac{6}{10}$$

Draw an arc of radius 10 cm and perpendicular radii OX and OY as before. Mark off OB = 6 cm along OX. Construct BA perpendicular to OX to cut the arc at A.

Fig. 15.5 is a scale drawing of the construction.

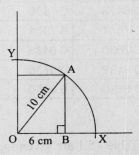

Fig. 15.5

143

In Fig. 15.5,

$$\cos A\hat{O}B = \frac{6}{10} = 0.60$$

By measurement, $A\hat{O}B \simeq 53°$.

Note that in Examples 1 and 2, a radius of 10 units has been chosen to simplify calculations.

Exercise 15a   [Class project]

1. Find by drawing and measurement, as in Example 1, approximate values for:
   a sin 20°, cos 20°,   c sin 40°, cos 40°,
   c sin 65°, cos 65°.

2. Find by drawing and measurement, as in Example 2, approximate sizes of angles A, B, C, D, E, F where:
   a $\sin A = \frac{1}{2}$ b $\cos B = \frac{3}{8}$
   c $\sin C = \frac{3}{5}$ d $\cos D = 0.95$
   e $\sin E = 0.26$ f $\cos F = 0.34$

 Optional: Do Exercise 35 of your Students' Practice Book.

15-2 Use of sine and cosine

Sines and cosines of angles are used to find the lengths of unknown side in triangles. Table 15.1 gives the sines and cosines of some chosen angles.

angle A	sin A	cos A
30°	0.5000	0.8660
35°	0.5736	0.8192
40°	0.6428	0.7660
45°	0.7071	0.7071
50°	0.7660	0.6428
55°	0.8192	0.5736
60°	0.8660	0.5000

Table 15.1

The values in Table 15.1 are given to 4 significant figures.

Example 3
Calculate the value of x in Fig. 15.6.

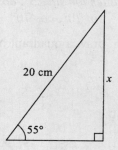

Fig. 15.6

In Fig. 15.6, the hypotenuse is given and x is *opposite* the given angle. Thus, use the *sine* of the given angle.

$$\sin 55° = \frac{x}{20}$$

Thus, $x = 20 \times \sin 55°$ cm
$= 20 \times 0.8192$ cm
$= 16.384$ cm
$= 16$ cm to 2 s.f.

Example 4
Calculate the value of y in Fig. 15.7.

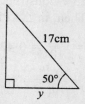

Fig. 15.7

In Fig. 15.7, the hypotenuse is 17 cm and y is *adjacent to* the given angle. Thus use the *cosine* of the given angle.

$$\cos 50° = \frac{y}{17}$$

Thus, $y = 17 \times \cos 50°$ cm
$= 17 \times 0.6428$ cm
$= 10.93$ cm
$= 11$ cm to 2 s.f.

Example 5

A village is 8 km on a bearing of 040° from a point O. Calculate how far the village is north of O.

Fig. 15.8 shows the position of the village, V, in relation to O.

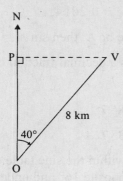

Fig. 15.8

It is required to find the length of OP. OP is *adjacent to* the known angle. Use the *cosine* of 40°.

$$\cos 40° = \frac{OP}{8}$$

Thus, OP $= 8 \times \cos 40°$ km
$= 8 \times 0{\cdot}7660$ km
$= 6{\cdot}128$ km
$= 6{\cdot}1$ km to 2 s.f.

The village is 6·1 km north of O.

Notice that if the unknown side is *opposite* the given angle, use the *sine* of the angle; if the unknown side is *adjacent to* the given angle, use the *cosine* of the angle.

Exercise 15b

Use the values in Table 15.1 in this exercise. Give all answers correct to 2 s.f.

① Find the value of x in each of the triangles in Fig. 15.9.

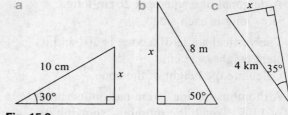

Fig. 15.9

② Find the value of y in each of the triangles in Fig. 15.10.

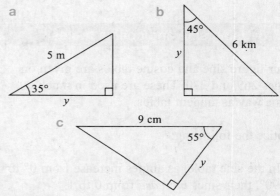

Fig. 15.10

③ Find the value of z in each of the triangles in Fig. 15.11.

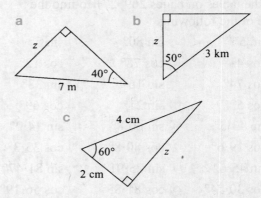

Fig. 15.11

④ A ladder, 5 cm long, leans against a wall so that it makes an angle of 60° with the horizontal ground. Calculate how far up the wall the ladder reaches.

⑤ A village is 10 km on a bearing 050° from a point O. Calculate how far the village is north of O.

6. A diagonal of a square is 20 cm long. How long is each side?

7. The vertical angle of a cone is 70° and its slant height is 11 cm. Calculate the height of the cone.

8. A rhombus of side 10 cm has obtuse angles of 110°. Sketch the rhombus, showing its diagonals and as many angles as possible. Hence calculate the lengths of the diagonals of the rhombus.

15-3 Using sine and cosine tables

Four-figure sine and cosine tables are given on pages 269 and 270. These are used in much the same way as tangent tables.

Notice the following:

1. In the sine table, as angles increase from 0° to 90°, their sines *increase* from 0 to 1.
2. In the cosine table, as angles increase from 0° to 90°, their cosines *decrease* from 1 to 0.

Exercise 15c   [Oral or written]
Use the tables on pages 269–271 to find the value of the following.

1. sin 56°
2. sin 80°
3. sin 5°
4. cos 41°
5. cos 78°
6. cos 12°
7. cos 74°
8. sin 16°
9. sin 38°
10. cos 52°
11. sin 21°
12. cos 69°
13. sin 43·5°
14. sin 60·8°
15. sin 14·2°
16. cos 19·6°
17. cos 80·8°
18. cos 33·3°
19. sin 45·62°
20. sin 25·91°
21. sin 81·47°
22. cos 30·54°
23. cos 81·85°
24. cos 56·19°
25. cos 54·76°
26. sin 35·36°
27. sin 28·64°
28. cos 61·48°
29. cos 66·44°
30. sin 23·65°

Example 6
Use tables to find the angle:

a whose sine is $\frac{2}{7}$,

b whose cosine is 0·4478,

c whose sine is 0·6492,

d whose cosine is 0·5682,

e whose cosine is 0·2614.

a Let the angle be A, then sin A = $\frac{2}{7}$.

Express $\frac{2}{7}$ as a decimal fraction correct to 4 d.p.

$$\frac{2}{7} = 0·2857$$

sin A = 0·2857

Looking within the sine table entries, 0·2857 is opposite 16° and under 0·6°. Thus, A = 16·6°.

b Let the angle be B, then cos B = 0·4478.
Looking within the cosine table entries, 0·4478 is opposite 63° and under 0·4°. Thus, B = 63·4°.

c Let the angle be x, then sin x = 0·6492.
Looking within the sine table entries, the nearest value to 0·6492 is 0·6481. 0·6481 is opposite 40° and under 0·4°.
The difference between 6492 and 6481 is 11. Look for 11 in the difference column along the row of 40°. 11 is under 8.
Thus, $x = \quad 40·40°$
$$\underline{+ \ 0·08°}$$
$$x = \quad 40·48°$$

d Let the angle be y, then cos y = 0·5682.
Looking within the cosine table entries, the nearest value to 0·5682 is 0·5678. 0·5678 is opposite 55° and under 0·4°.
The difference between 5682 and 5678 is 4. Look for 4 in the difference column along the row of 55°. 4 is under 3. As the angles increase, their cosines decrease, therefore *subtract* the difference.
Thus, $y = \quad 55·40°$
$$\underline{- \ 0·03°}$$
$$y = \quad 55·37°$$

e Let the angle be P, then cos P = 0·2614.

Looking within the cosine table entries, the nearest value to 0·2614 is 0·2605. 0·2605 is opposite 74° and under 0·9°.

The difference between 2614 and 2605 is 9. Look for 9 in the difference column along the row of 74°. 9 lies equally between 8 and 10. In such cases, take the higher of the two values. 10 is under 6. As the angles increase their cosine decreases, therefore *subtract* the difference.

Thus, P =   74·90°
            − 0·06°
      P =   74·84°

Exercise 15d   [Oral or written]

Use tables to find the angles whose **a** sines, **b** cosines are as follows.

① 0·5878   ② 0·7986   ③ 0·3584

④ 0·6018   ⑤ 0·5299   ⑥ 0·4067

⑦ 0·8339   ⑧ 0·1685   ⑨ 0·5165

⑩ 0·5990   ⑪ 0·7312   ⑫ 0·0736

⑬ $\frac{3}{8}$ ⑭ $\frac{7}{9}$ ⑮ $\frac{2}{5}$

⑯ $\frac{2}{3}$ ⑰ $\frac{9}{25}$ ⑱ $\frac{4}{7}$

⑲ 0·2235   ⑳ 0·5648   ㉑ 0·6327

Applications of sine and cosine

Example 7

A wire 12 m long goes from the top of a 6 m pole to a point on a vertical wall 10 m above the ground. What is the angle between the wire and the wall? (Assume that the wire is stretched tight.)

Fig. 15.12 represents the data of the question. θ is the required angle.

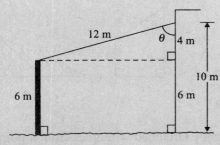

Fig. 15.12

Add the construction line shown dotted in Fig. 15.12.

$$\cos \theta = \frac{4}{12} = \frac{1}{3} = 0·3333$$
$$\theta = 70·53°$$

Example 8

Calculate the length of the hypotenuse of the triangle in Fig. 15.13.

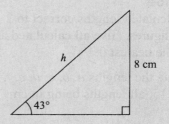

Fig. 15.13

In Fig. 15.13,

$$\sin 43° = \frac{8}{h}$$
$$h \times \sin 43° = 8$$
$$h = \frac{8}{\sin 43°} \text{cm} = \frac{8}{0·6820} \text{cm}$$

From reciprocal tables, $\frac{1}{0·6820} = 1·466$.

Thus, $h = 8 \times 1·466 \text{cm}$
$$= 11·728 \text{cm}$$
$$= 12 \text{cm to 2 s.f.}$$

Example 9

A car travels 120 m along a straight road which is inclined at 8° to the horizontal. Calculate the vertical distance through which the car rises.

Fig. 15.14 is a sketch of the road.

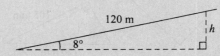

Fig. 15.14

In Fig. 15.14, h is the vertical distance.

$$\sin 8° = \frac{h}{120}$$

147

$$h = 120 \times \sin 8° \, \text{m}$$
$$= 120 \times 0{\cdot}1392 \, \text{m}$$
$$= 16{\cdot}70 \, \text{m}$$
$$= 17 \, \text{m to 2 s.f.}$$

 Optional: Do Exercise 36 of your Students' Practice Book.

Exercise 15e

Give all calculated lengths correct to 2 significant figures. Give all calculated angles correct to the nearest 0·1°.

① Calculate the lengths *a, b, c, d, e, f, g, h* in Fig. 15.15, all lengths being in cm.

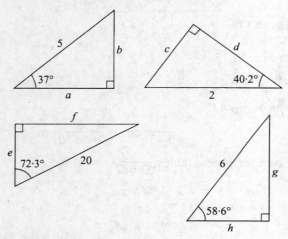

Fig. 15.15

② Calculate the angles α, β, γ, δ in Fig. 15.16.

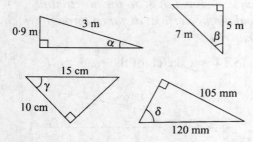

Fig. 15.16

③ Calculate the length of the hypotenuse in each of the following triangles, all lengths being in cm.

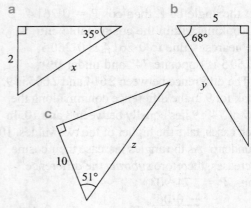

Fig. 15.17

④ Make suitable construction lines, then calculate the lengths BC, XY and PQ in Fig. 15.18.

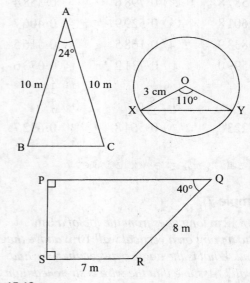

Fig. 15.18

⑤ Calculate the angles α, β, γ, δ in Fig. 15.19.

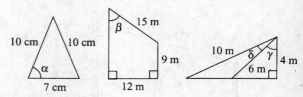

Fig. 15.19

⑥ A tightly stretched wire goes from a point on horizontal ground to the top of a vertical pole. If the wire is 8 m long and is inclined at 68° to the horizontal, calculate the height of the pole.

7. A point P is 40 km from Q on a bearing 061°. Calculate the distance that P is **a** north of Q, **b** east of Q.

8. Fig. 15.20 is a side view of a table which is supported by legs inclined at θ to the horizontal.

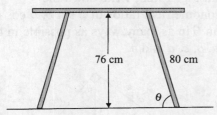

Fig. 15.20

If the table is 76 cm high and each leg is 80 cm long, calculate the value of θ.

9. The roof of a house is made from sheets of corrugated iron of length 2 m, inclined at 18° to the horizontal. (See Fig. 15.21.)

Calculate the width of the house.

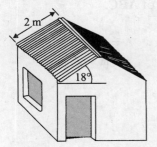

Fig. 15.21

10. A stone rolls 300 m down a slope. As it falls, it drops 120 m vertically.

Calculate the angle of the slope (α in Fig. 15.22).

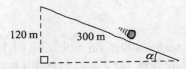

Fig. 15.22

11. A stone is suspended from a point P by a piece of string 50 cm long. It swings back and forward. (See Fig. 15.23.)

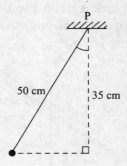

Fig. 15.23

Calculate the angle the string makes with the vertical when the stone is 35 cm vertically below P.

12. An aeroplane is flying at a height of 200 m. Its angle of elevation to an observer on the ground is 23°. (See Fig. 15.24.)

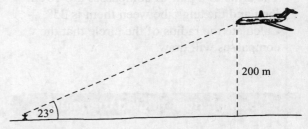

Fig. 15.24

Calculate the distance of the aeroplane from the observer.

13. Fig. 15.25 shows some men using a board to slide loads from a platform onto a lorry.

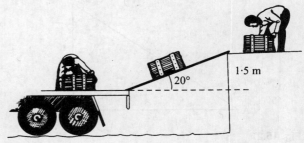

Fig. 15.25

The platform is 1·5 m higher than the lorry. The best position for the board is when it is

inclined at 20° to the horizontal.
Calculate the length of the board.

(14) A 5-metre plank rests on a wall 2 m high, so
that 1·5 m of the plank projects beyond the
wall. (see Fig 15.26.)

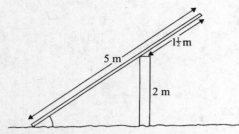

Fig. 15.26

a What angle does the plank make with the
wall?
b How high is the end of the plank above the
ground?

(15) The arms of a pair of compasses are 10 cm
long and the angle between them is 35°.
Calculate the radius of the circle that the
compasses will draw.

15-4 Solving right-angled triangles

Sines, cosines and tangents of angles are known
as **trigonometrical** ratios. **Trigonometry**
means the measurement of lengths and angles.
Right-angled triangles can be solved by using
Pythagoras' rule and the trigonometrical
ratios.

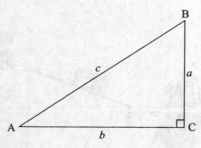

Fig. 15.27

In Fig. 15.27, △ABC is any triangle right-angled
at C.

1 $c^2 = a^2 + b^2$

2 $\sin A = \dfrac{a}{c}$, $\sin B = \dfrac{b}{c}$

3 $\cos A = \dfrac{b}{c}$, $\cos B = \dfrac{a}{c}$

4 $\tan A = \dfrac{a}{b}$, $\tan B = \dfrac{b}{a}$

Exercise 15f

(1) From Fig. 15.28, write down the
trigonometrical ratios of a sin θ, b cos θ,
c tan θ in as many ways as possible in terms
of a, b, c, d and e.

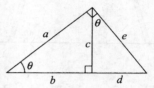

Fig. 15.28

(2) Find, to the nearest cm, the length of the
shadow of a 1-metre vertical stick when the
elevation of the sun is 33°.

(3) In Fig. 15.29, calculate α and β. Hence find
the size of AB̂C.

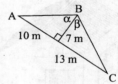

Fig. 15.29

(4) In Fig. 15.30, find the size of QR̂S.

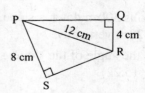

Fig. 15.30

(5) A girl walks 800 m on a bearing of 129°.
Calculate how far a east, b south she is from
her starting point.

(6) An equilateral triangle has three sides of

length 2 m. Calculate the height of the triangle **a** using Pythagoras' rule, **b** using a trigonometrical ratio.

⑦ In Fig. 15.31, **a** find HL, **b** hence find LN̂H.

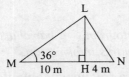

Fig. 15.31

⑧ A regular pentagon is such that its vertices lie on the circumference of a circle of radius 4·5 cm. Find the length of a side of the pentagon to the nearest mm.

⑨ A rhombus of side 5 cm has acute angles of 84°. Find the lengths of the diagonals of the rhombus.

⑩ A rectangular table has sides 2 m and 1·2 m. It is pushed into the corner of a room so that one of the long sides makes 20° with a wall. Fig. 15.32 shows a plan of the corner.

Find the distance of the corner B from each wall.

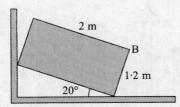

Fig. 15.32

SUMMARY

1. In a right-angled triangle ABC (where B is the right angle), the *sine of angle A* and the *cosine of angle A* are defined as the ratios:

$$\sin A = \frac{BC}{AC} = \frac{\text{side opposite angle A}}{\text{hypotenuse}}$$

$$\cos A = \frac{AB}{AC} = \frac{\text{side adjacent to angle A}}{\text{hypotenuse}}$$

2. The terms *sin A* and *cos A* are short for *the sine of angle A* and *the cosine of angle A* respectively.

3. Given sufficient data, the sine or cosine of an angle can be used to solve right-angled triangles (often in problems involving gradients, bearings and angles of elevation and depression).

4. Values for the sine and cosine ratios of angles from 0° to 90° are provided in the Sine and Cosine tables on pages 269 and 270 of this book.

5. Sines, cosines and tangents are called *trigonometrical ratios*. Trigonometry means the measurement of lengths and angles. Right-angled triangles can be fully solved by using Pythagoras' rule and the trigonometrical ratios.

PUZZLE CORNER

Patterns from Cubes

$1^3 = 1$

$2^3 = 3 + 5$

$3^3 = 7 + 9 + 11$

$4^3 = 13 + 15 + 17 + 19$

What would be the line of numbers for 100^3?

Use this to help you to calculate
$1^3 + 2^3 + 3^3 + 4^3 + \ldots + 99^3 + 100^3$

16

OBJECTIVES

By the end of this chapter you should be able to:

1 Present data in frequency tables, pictograms, bar charts and pie charts
2 Interpret statistical graphs
3 Find the mean, median and mode of given data sets
4 Apply measures of central tendency (mean, median, mode) to everyday issues
5 Find the range of a given set of data.

Teaching and learning materials

Teacher: Charts on mean, median and mode; frequency tables; bar charts; pie charts; real statistics from newspapers and official publications; chalk-board instruments (compasses, protractor, ruler)

Student: Mathematical set; numerical data collected from newspapers

16-1 Presentation of data (revision)

Example 1 revises four important ways of presenting data:

    a **frequency table**,
    a **pictogram**,
    a **bar chart**, and
    a **pie chart**.

Example 1

Table 16.1 shows how class 3A travel to school.

method	bicycle	walk	bus	car
frequency	9	15	7	5

Table 16.1

Draw a a pictogram, b a bar chart, c a pie chart to show this information.

Table 16.1 is a **frequency table**. The frequency is the number of students using each method of transport.

    Fig. 16.1 shows the required graphs.

a

Each symbol represents 5 students.

b

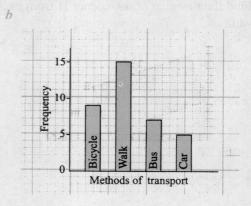

c

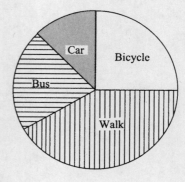

Fig. 16.1

Pictogram: Each method of transport is represented by a suitable picture. In this case each complete picture represents five students.

Bar chart: Each bar represents a method of transport. The height of each bar is proportional to the number of students using that method of transport.

Pie chart: Each sector represents a method of transport. The angle of each sector is proportional to the number of students who use the method of transport shown in that sector. See Table 16.2.

method	frequency	angle of sector
bicycle	9	$\frac{9}{36} \times 360° = 90°$
walk	15	$\frac{15}{36} \times 360° = 150°$
bus	7	$\frac{7}{36} \times 360° = 70°$
car	5	$\frac{5}{36} \times 360° = 50°$
total	**36**	**360°**

Table 16.2

ercise 16a [Revision]

) Fig. 16.2 is a pictogram of a traffic survey.

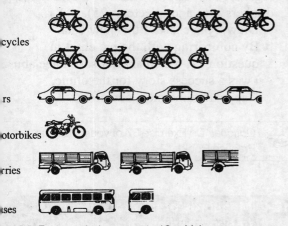

cycles

rs

otorbikes

rries

ses

Fig. 16.2 Each symbol represents 10 vehicles

a Which kind of vehicle is the most common?
b Which kind of vehicle is the least common?

c Approximately how many bicycles were counted?
d Approximately how many lorries were counted?

2 Fig. 16.3 is a bar chart showing the heights and names of the highest mountains of the continents of Asia, South America, North America, Africa and Europe respectively.

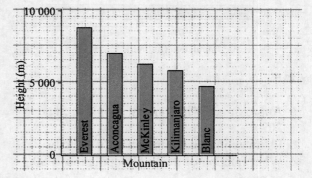

Fig. 16.3

a What is the height of Mount Kilimanjaro?
b What is the height of Mount McKinley?
c Which mountain is 4 800 m high?
d Find the difference in height between Mount Everest and Mount Aconcagua.

3 Fig. 16.4 is a pie chart showing how someone spent the first hour of a day after getting out of bed.

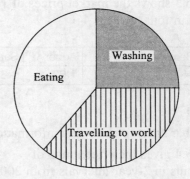

Fig. 16.4

a What fraction of the hour was spent eating?
b What percentage of the hour was spent washing?
c How many minutes were spent travelling to work?

④ Fig. 16.5 is a bar chart showing the estimated population of a city by age group.

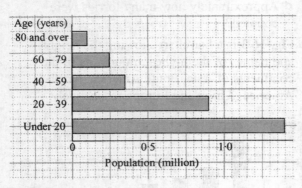

Fig. 16.5

a Approximately how many people are under 20?

b Estimate the total population of the city.

c What fraction of the total population is 80 or over?

d Find the percentage of the total population that is 20–39 years old.

⑤ A farmer has 100 cows, 40 sheep and 65 goats. Draw a pictogram to show the animals that he has. (Let one symbol represent 10 animals.)

⑥ 117 people travel from Kano to Lagos. 55 go by car, 39 go by air, and 23 go by train. Show this information on a pictogram.

⑦ Table 16.3 shows the market prices of 1 kg of plantain in four towns.

town	Benin	Auchi	Agbor	Sapele
price	₦48	₦42	₦62	₦80

Table 16.3

Draw a bar chart to show this information.

⑧ Table 16.4 gives the price/tonne of groundnuts in 2-year intervals from 2000 to 2008.

year	2000	2002	2004	2006	2008
price	₦22 400	₦27 200	₦32 400	₦66 000	₦100 000

Table 16.4

Draw a bar chart to show how the price increased.

⑨ To support a 'Clean Our Village' campaign, the local UBE school collected and burned used plastic bags that were lying around. The Primary classes collected 60 kg of bags; the JS classes collected 48 kg of bags.

a Draw a pie chart that compares the performance of the two sets of classes.

b Discuss the performance with your teacher.

⑩ During a 24-hour period in Kaduna, the sun shone for 10 hours, it was cloudy for 3 hours and it was dark for the remainder of the time. Draw a pie chart to show the periods of sunshine, cloudiness and darkness during the day.

⑪ 180 people attend a voluntary substance-abuse rehabilitation clinic. 100 of them are registered for smoking-related problems (tobacco, cannabis), 50 for drink-related problems (alcohol dependency) and 30 for drug injection (heroin, cocaine, others). Draw a a pictogram, b a pie chart, to represent this data.

⑫ After 1 year, half of the people in question 11 are rehabilitated. The remaining 90 are registered as follows: smokers (30 in total), drinkers (35) and injectors (25).

a Draw a pie chart of this new data.

b By comparing with the pie chart in question 11, which area of substance abuse
  i was a success story for the clinic,
  ii appears to be most addictive?

 Optional: Do Exercise 37 of your Students' Practice Book.

16-2 Measures of central tendency (mean, median, mode)

An **average** is a single number that represents a large set of data. The common averages are the **mean**, **median** and **mode**. These averages are often called **measures of central tendency**, since an average usually has a central value within the data set. Example 2 revises the common averages and also emphasises the importance of placing data in **rank order**.

Example 2

Nine boys take a test. Their marks are: Ali 4, Ben 8, Dan 7, Isa 9, Joe 4, Kam 3, Mbu 6, Olu 4, Sam 7. Place the marks in rank order. Hence find the mean, median and mode for the test.

Table 16.5 gives the names, marks and positions of the boys in rank order.

name	mark	position
Isa	9	1
Ben	8	2
Dan	7	3=
Sam	7	3=
Mbu	6	5
Ali	4	6=
Joe	4	6=
Olu	4	6=
Kam	3	9

Table 16.5

$$\text{mean} = \frac{9 + 8 + 7 + 7 + 6 + 4 + 4 + 4 + 3}{9}$$

$$= \frac{52}{9} = 5\frac{7}{9}$$

The median is the middle mark when the marks are arranged in rank order. In this case, Mbu is in the fifth (or middle) position; his mark is 6.

$$\text{median} = 6$$

The mode is the mark which appears most often. Three of the boys score 4 marks.

$$\text{mode} = 4$$

Example 3

The ages of people attending two drug-abuse clinics are given below:
a Young persons' clinic:
   15, 18, 18, 15, 12, 15, 19

b Adult clinic:
   28, 33, 45, 32, 37, 35, 27, 33, 36, 37

Find the mean, median and modal age for each clinic.

a mean age

$$= \frac{15 + 18 + 18 + 15 + 12 + 15 + 19}{7}$$

$$= \frac{112}{7} = 16 \text{ years}$$

Arrange the ages in rank order:

   19, 18, 18, 15, 15, 15, 12

There are seven ages.

   Median = middle age (i.e. the 4th age)
       = 15 years
   Mode = age appearing most often
       = 15 years

b mean age

$$= \frac{28 + 33 + 45 + 32 + 37 + 35 + 27 + 33 + 36 + 37}{10}$$

$$= \frac{343}{10} = 34 \cdot 3 \text{ years}$$

Arrange the ages in rank order:

   45, 37, 37, 36, 35, 33, 33, 32, 28, 27

There are ten ages.

$$\text{Median} = \frac{\text{5th} + \text{6th}}{2} = \frac{35 + 33}{2}$$

$$= 34 \text{ years}$$

   Mode = age appearing most often

Ages 37 and 33 both appear twice.

The data are **bimodal** (37 years and 33 years).

Notice in Example 3b, when there is no single middle value in the data set, the median is calculated as the average of the middle two pieces of data. Notice also that data may be bimodal.

Example 4

A woman buys three bottles of palm oil at ₦180 per bottle. Next week she buys two bottles of palm oil at ₦200 per bottle. Find the average cost per bottle for the two weeks.

3 bottles at ₦180 cost 3 × ₦180 = ₦540
2 bottles at ₦200 cost 2 × ₦200 = ₦400
total cost of 5 bottles   = ₦940

average cost of 1 bottle $= ₦\dfrac{940}{5}$

                              $= ₦188$

Example 5

A motorist travelled 96 km at an average speed of 60 km/h. She returned at an average speed of 48 km/h. What was her average speed for the whole journey?

96 km at 60 km/h takes $\dfrac{96}{60}$ hours = 1·6 h

96 km at 48 km/h takes $\dfrac{96}{48}$ hours = 2·0 h

Altogether she travelled 192 km in 3·6 h.

average speed $= \dfrac{192}{3·6}$ km/h $= \dfrac{1920}{36}$ km/h

              $= \dfrac{160}{3}$ km/h $= 53\frac{1}{3}$ km/h

Always remember that

$$\text{average speed} = \frac{\textbf{total distance travelled}}{\textbf{total time taken}}$$

Example 6

Table 16.6 gives the scores of 20 students in a mathematics test.

score	11	12	13	14	15	16
frequency	2	1	3	6	5	3

Table 16.6

Find:
a the mean score,
b the median score,
c the modal score.

a mean

$$= \frac{2 \times 11 + 1 \times 12 + 3 \times 13 + 6 \times 14 + 5 \times 15 + 3 \times 16}{2 + 1 + 3 + 6 + 5 + 3}$$

$$= \frac{22 + 12 + 39 + 84 + 75 + 48}{20}$$

$$= \frac{280}{20}$$

$$= 14$$

b There are 20 students. The median score is the mean of the scores of the 10th and 11th students. The 10th and 11th students both scored 14.

     median score = 14

c The mode is the score that occurs most often. Six students scored 14.

     mode = 14

Notice, in Example 6, that it is not necessary to make an ordered list of all the scores. Also note that it is possible for some or all of the averages to be equal to each other.

Exercise 16b   [Revision]

① A motorist drives 80 km at an average speed of 63 km/h. Which average is this: mean, median or mode?

② Twenty people apply for jobs as police officers. There are only 10 jobs available. They are given to the 10 people who are above the average height of those who applied. Which average is this: mean, median or mode?

③ A trader sells shoes. He wants to know the average size of shoe that people buy. Which average is most useful?

④ Arrange the following sets of numbers in order of size. Find the mean, median and mode of each set.
a 7, 10, 7, 9, 7
b 5, 3, 0, 7, 3, 6
c 1, 9, 5, 6, 1, 4
d 8, 3, 1, 7, 3, 4, 8, 3, 4, 9, 5
e 0·1, 0, 1·5, 0, 0·6, 1·1
f 159·5, 155·8, 153·7, 157·2, 155·8

⑤ The wages of five local government trainees are ₦4 166, ₦4 618, ₦3 742, ₦5 838, ₦5 366.
Find a the mean, b the median wage.

⑥ Six people together have a mass of $\frac{1}{2}$ tonne. What is the average mass of the people in kg?

⑦ A man caught four fish of mass 1·9 kg, 1·1 kg, 0·9 kg, 0·7 kg. Find a the mean, b the median mass of the fish.

⑧ The mean age of four women is 19 yr 11 mo. When a fifth woman joins them, the average age of all five is 20 yr 7 mo. How old is the fifth woman?

⑨ There are eight men and a woman in a boat. The average mass of the nine people is 79 kg. Without the woman, the average is 81·5 kg. What is the mass of the woman?

⑩ A trader mixes 3 kg of sugar at ₦172/kg with 2 kg of sugar at ₦152/kg. What is the cost/kg of the mixture?

⑪ The mean daily rainfall for a week was 5·5 mm. For the first six days the mean rainfall was 1 mm. How much rain fell on the seventh day?

⑫ A bridge $1\frac{1}{4}$ km long cost ₦750 million. What was the average cost per metre?

⑬ The ages of a family of six children are 16·4, 14·8, 13·6, 11·10 and the twins are 9·1. Find the mean, median and modal ages of the family. (Take 16·4 to mean 16 years 4 months.)

⑭ A man travelled 30 km in a car at an average speed of 40 km/h. He returned at an average speed of 60 km/h. Find his average speed for the whole journey.

⑮ A woman travelled for $\frac{1}{2}$ hour in a car at an average speed of 40 km/h. For the next $\frac{1}{2}$ hour her average speed was 60 km/h. What was her average speed for the whole time?

⑯ Of a journey of 216 km, 56 km were on untarred road. For this part of the journey, a motorist could only average 28 km/h. If his average speed for the whole journey was 48 km/h, what was his average speed for the part of the journey on tarred road?

⑰ A lorry travelled 80 km at 40 km/h, 64 km at 48 km/h and 40 km at 60 km/h. Find its average speed for the whole distance.

⑱ In a test the average marks for three classes were 74, 58 and 51. If the classes contained 25, 22 and 23 students respectively, what was the average mark for the three classes together?

⑲ Some students were asked how many brothers and sisters they had. The bar chart in Fig. 16.6 shows the number of students who had 0, 1, 2, 3, 4, 5, 6, 7, or 8 brothers and sisters.

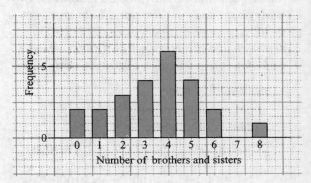

Fig. 16.6

Find:
a the number of students in the survey,
b the modal number of brothers and sisters,
c the median,
d the mean number of brothers and sisters.

⑳ Five students took a test in four subjects. Their results are given in Table 16.7.

	English	History	Maths	Science
Rose	52	69	54	57
Efosa	68	60	67	73
Mfon	80	73	49	42
Emem	26	14	37	35
Vera	34	44	38	48

Table 16.7

Find:
a the mean mark of each student,
b the mean mark in each subject,
c the median mark in each subject.

If you had difficulty with Exercise 16b, revise Chapter 22 in Book 1.

16-3 Interpretation of averages

Remember that an average, such as a mean, median or mode, is a number which represents a whole set of numbers. Sometimes averages can be misleading.

Example 7

A construction company has 20 labourers, two supervisors and two directors. Labourers get ₦6 000 per week, supervisors get ₦20 000 per week and directors get ₦40 000 per week. Calculate the company's average weekly wage.

mean weekly wage

$$= \frac{\text{total money earned}}{\text{number of employees}}$$

$$= \frac{20 \times ₦6\,000 + 2 \times ₦20\,000 + 2 \times ₦40\,000}{20 + 2 + 2}$$

$$= \frac{₦120\,000 + ₦40\,000 + ₦80\,000}{24}$$

$$= \frac{₦240\,000}{24} = ₦10\,000$$

A labourer joining the company in Example 7 is told that the average wage is ₦10 000. He will be disappointed when he gets only ₦6 000. In this case it may be more helpful to give the average wage in terms of the mode, ₦6 000.

Range

The **range** of a set of numbers is the difference between the largest and the smallest numbers in the set.

Example 8

Find the range of the following percentages: 84%, 56%, 72%, 64%, 33%, 49%.

Arranging the set in rank order:
84%, 72%, 64%, 56%, 49%, 33%
The range is 84% − 33% = 51%.

Example 9

The midday temperatures in °C for a week in towns A and B are given below:
Town A: 23, 24, 22, 23, 22, 24, 23
Town B: 29, 29, 26, 23, 19, 18, 17

a *Calculate the mean midday temperature for each town.*
b *Compare the results with the weather for each town.*

a Town A: mean temperature

$$= \frac{23 + 24 + 22 + 23 + 22 + 24 + 23}{7}\,°C$$

$$= \frac{161}{7}\,°C = 23\,°C$$

Town B: mean temperature

$$= \frac{29 + 29 + 26 + 23 + 19 + 18 + 17}{7}\,°C$$

$$= \frac{161}{7}\,°C = 23\,°C$$

b The mean temperature is the same for both towns. However, the weather is *different*. In town A the temperature remained steady at around 23 °C. In town B the week began with hot weather, but the temperature fell daily so that the weather was cool by the end of the week.

In Example 9, the temperatures for town A range from 22 °C to 24 °C and those for town B range from 17 °C to 29 °C. The **range** of temperatures is different in each case. However, the results of Example 9 show that it is possible to get the same mean from different ranges of numbers.

Example 10

The same test was given to two groups of 20 students. The test was marked out of 5. The results of the groups are given in Table 16.8.

1st group

mark	0	1	2	3	4	5
frequency	2	5	6	4	2	1

2nd group

mark	0	1	2	3	4	5
frequency	1	1	2	4	7	5

Table 16.8

a *Draw bar charts for each group.*
b *Find the mode and mean for each group.*
c *Explain the difference between the two results.*

a Fig. 16.7 gives the required bar charts.

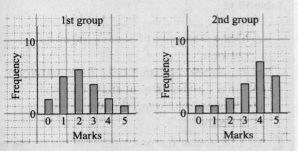

Fig. 16.7

b The mode is the mark with the highest frequency.

1st group: mode = 2 marks
2nd group: mode = 4 marks

1st group: mean
$$= \frac{2 \times 0 + 5 \times 1 + 6 \times 2 + 4 \times 3 + 2 \times 4 + 1 \times 5}{20}$$
$$= \frac{0 + 5 + 12 + 12 + 8 + 5}{20}$$
$$= \frac{42}{20} = 2 \cdot 1 \text{ marks}$$

2nd group: mean
$$= \frac{1 \times 0 + 1 \times 1 + 2 \times 2 + 4 \times 3 + 7 \times 4 + 5 \times 5}{20}$$
$$= \frac{0 + 1 + 4 + 12 + 28 + 25}{20}$$
$$= \frac{70}{20} = 3 \cdot 5 \text{ marks}$$

c The results show that the second group did better on the test than the first group. There are a number of possible reasons for this: they may be older and had covered the subject matter of the test many times before; the first group may not have been taught the subject matter of the test.

Notice in Example 10 that the range of marks is the same for each group: from 0 to 5. However, the mode and mean are different for both groups. This shows that it is possible to get different averages from the same range of numbers. In Fig. 16.7, notice the position of the mode in each group: in general, the higher the mode, the higher the mean.

Exercise 16c

1 Find the range and mean of:
    a 1, 3, 5, 7, 9;
    b 1, 5, 7, 8, 9.

    Compare the two results.

2 Find the range and mean of:
    a 35, 37, 39, 41, 48;
    b 21, 27, 28, 29, 95.

    Compare the two results.

3 A trader buys 200 ball-point pens at ₦28 each and 10 gold pens at ₦4 900 each.
    a Find the mean cost per pen.
    b Is this a sensible value to give for the average cost of a pen?

4 A factory employs 100 workmen, 16 supervisors and four directors. The workmen get ₦4 800 per week, the supervisors get ₦16 000 per week and the directors get ₦36 000 per week.
    a Calculate the mean weekly wage at the factory.
    b Is this average representative of the wages that the people get?

5 The daily rainfall in mm for two weeks is given below:

    Week 1: 13, 12, 10, 14, 17, 12, 13

    Week 2: 28, 32, 21, 10, 0, 0, 0
    a Find the mean daily rainfall for each week.
    b Compare your results with the weather for each week.

6 In a five-a-side basketball match between teams A and B, the points scored by the players are as follows:

    Team A: 8, 8, 10, 26, 30

    Team B: 14, 15, 17, 18, 18
    a Find the mean score/player for each team.

b Compare your results with the actual scores of the players in the two teams.

7 The numbers of days absent during a term for a class of 30 students is given in Table 16.9.

days absent	0	1	2	3	5	35
frequency	14	5	4	3	3	1

Table 16.9

Find a the mode, b the median, c the mean number of days absent.

d Which average is most representative of the data?

8 A club collected money from its members to buy a DVD player. 30 members of the club made the following contributions.

amount in ₦	100	200	500	1 000	5 000
frequency	4	10	8	5	3

Table 16.10

a Find the mean, median and modal amounts of money contributed.

b Which average is most representative of the data? Give reasons.

9 The label on a box of *Strike* matches states, 'Average Contents 40 Matches'. The contents of 30 boxes of *Strike* matches were counted and the results are given in Table 16.11.

no. of matches	37	38	39	40	41	42	43
frequency	4	5	6	7	2	4	2

Table 16.11

a Find the mean, median and modal number of matches per box.

b Is the statement on the box true or not?

10 In a survey, two groups of 20 women were asked how many children they had. The results are given in Table 16.12.

1st group

no. of children	0	1	2	3	4	5
frequency	8	5	3	2	1	1

2nd group

no. of children	0	1	2	3	4	5
frequency	2	2	4	5	4	3

Table 16.12

a Draw a bar chart for each group of women.

b Find the mode and mean for each group.

c Give a possible explanation for the difference between the two sets of averages.

11 In an election the percentage of the registered voters who vote is called the 'average turn-out'. Table 16.13 shows the numbers registered and those who actually voted in a LGA election.

	Men	Women	Total
Number registered	1 808	1 377	3 185
Number who voted	1 419	1 165	2 584

Table 16.13

a What is the total average turn-out in the election (nearest whole percent)?

b Who has the higher average turn-out: the men or the women?

c Give possible explanations why the number of women registered is so much lower than the number of men.

SUMMARY

1 Statistical information is called *data*.

2 Data can be represented pictorially or graphically by *pictograms*, *bar charts* and *pie charts*.

3 An *average* is a single number that is representative of a larger set of numbers.

4 *Mean*, *median* and *mode* are three kinds of average.
  - The mean is the value obtained by dividing the sum of the numbers in a set of data by the total number of numbers in the data.
  - The median is middle value when the numbers are arranged in order of size.
  - The mode is the value with the highest frequency.

5 The *range* of a set of numbers is the difference between the largest and smallest number in the set.

PUZZLE CORNER

Think of a Number

1 2 3 4 5 6 7 8 9

Choose any number from 1 to 9.
Multiply it by 10 and add 1.
Then multiply the answer by 10 and add 7.
Make a note of your answer.

Do it again with a different number.
. What do you notice?

[Now you can pretend to be a mind reader with your friends.]

PUZZLE CORNER

How Many Triangles? (2)

How many equilateral triangles have their corners at the dots of this
3 x 3 triangular lattice?

What about a 4 x 4 lattice, ... etc?

PUZZLE CORNER

Remainders

What is the smallest number that has a remainder of

1 when divided by 5,

5 when divided by 6, and

3 when divided by 7?

Can you find a pattern for all the higher numbers?

1

Chapters 9–16 Revision exercises and tests

Revision exercise 4 (Chapters 9, 10, 14)

1. Expand the following.
   a $(x - 3)(x - 4)$ b $(a + 2b)(a - 3b)$
   c $(3p - 2q)^2$ d $(4x + 1)(4x - 1)$

2. Expand the brackets in $(x + 5)(x - 3) = x(x - 2)$ and hence solve the equation.

3. Factorise the following.
   a $x^2 + 10x + 24$ b $x^2 - 8x + 15$
   c $x^2 - 11x - 26$ d $2ax^2 - 24ax + 22a$

4. Factorise the following.
   a $1 - 25x^2$ b $x^2 - 18x + 81$
   c $9 + 6a + a^2$ d $(5a - 2)^2 - 9a^2$

5. a Expand $(a - b)^2$.
   b Using the fact that $995^2 = (1\,000 - 5)^2$, find the exact value of 995^2 without long multiplication.

6. Solve the following.
   a $\dfrac{18}{2x - 1} = 3$ b $\dfrac{7}{a - 4} = \dfrac{5}{a - 2}$

7. A girl walks 6 km at a speed of v km/h.
   a Write the time taken in hours in terms of v.
   b Find the value of v if her journey takes 1 h 20 min.

8. Solve graphically the simultaneous equations $y = 15 - 4x$ and $y = 2x$. (*Hint*: Make tables of values of y corresponding to $x = 0, 2, 4$.)

9. Solve the following pairs of simultaneous equations.
   a $3x + 2y = 12, 5x - 3y = 1$
   b $2a - 3b = 7, 4a + 5b = 3$

10. Two pencils and one rubber cost ₦66; five pencils and three rubbers cost ₦174. How much does each cost?

Revision test 4 (Chapters 9, 10, 14)

1. The coefficient of x in the expansion of $(x - 2)(x + 9)$ is:
   A -18 B -2 C $+1$ D $+7$ E $+9$

2. The exact value of $285^2 - 215^2$ is:
   A 70   B 140   C 500   D 4 900
   E 35 000

3. If $\dfrac{6}{5} = \dfrac{3}{d}$ then $d =$
   A $\dfrac{5}{18}$ B $\dfrac{2}{5}$ C $2\frac{1}{2}$ D $3\frac{3}{5}$ E 90

4. A girl gets x marks in a test. Her friend gets 4 marks less. The ratio of the two marks is $4 : 3$. Which one of the following equations can be solved for x?

   A $\dfrac{x}{x - 4} = \dfrac{4}{3}$ B $\dfrac{x - 4}{x} = \dfrac{4}{3}$ C $\dfrac{x}{x + 4} = \dfrac{4}{3}$

   D $\dfrac{x + 4}{x} = \dfrac{4}{3}$ E $\dfrac{x + 4}{x - 4} = \dfrac{4}{3}$

5. If $x + 3y = 7$ and $x - 3y = 7$, then $y =$
   A $-4\frac{2}{3}$ B $-2\frac{1}{3}$ C 0   D $2\frac{1}{3}$ E $4\frac{2}{3}$

6. Simplify $(a + 5b)(a - 2b) + (a - 3b)(a - 4b)$.

7. Factorise the following.
   a $x^2 + 10x + 16$ b $r^2 - 16r + 28$
   c $m^2 - 7m - 18$ d $y^2 - 8y - 20$
   e $a^2 + 8a + 16$ f $\pi a^2 - \pi b^2$

8. Solve the following.
   a $\dfrac{2}{x - 10} + \dfrac{1}{3} = 0$ b $\dfrac{23 - 3x}{x + 1} = \dfrac{4}{3}$

9. Solve the following pairs of simultaneous equations.
   a $8y + 4z = 7, 6y - 8z = 41$
   b $2y = 3x + 2, 9x + 8y = 1$

10. A nut and a bolt together have a mass of 98 g. The mass of four bolts and two nuts is 336 g. Find the mass of a nut and of a bolt.

Revision exercise 5 (Chapters 11, 13, 15, 16)

1. ₦40 000 is saved for 2 years at 9% compound interest per annum. Find:
   a the amount,   b the interest.

② The population of a town increases by about 4% each year. Two years ago the population was 38 000. What is the population now? (Give your answer correct to 2 s.f.)

③ A year ago a new refrigerator cost ₦36 000. Today the same kind costs ₦41 400.
  a Calculate the percentage rate of inflation.
  b If inflation stays at the same rate, what will the same kind of refrigerator cost next year?

④ A boy walks at a steady speed and takes 90 min for a certain journey. How many minutes will a girl take if she cycles at $2\frac{1}{2}$ times the speed of the boy?

⑤ In 2007 £1 sterling was equivalent to about ₦250.
  a Draw a graph connecting £ to ₦ for amounts up to ₦4 000.
  b Read off the equivalent amounts in the other currency of:
    i £15, £11, £8
    ii ₦2 500, ₦1 900, ₦3 600.

⑥ Find the value of R if $\frac{1}{R} = \frac{1}{15} + \frac{1}{23}$. Give your answer correct to 2 s.f.

⑦ By drawing and measurement find approximately:
  a the value of cos 44°,
  b the size of the angle whose sine is $\frac{4}{5}$.

⑧ Use 4-figure tables to find the value of:
  a sin 38·2°   b cos 51·7°
  b cos 63·24°   d sin 82·63°

⑨ In △ABC, Â = 38°, B̂ = 90° and AC = 9 cm. Calculate a Ĉ, b AB, c BC.

⑩ The diagonals of a rectangle are 10 cm long and intersect at an angle of 120°. Make a sketch of the rectangle. Hence use trigonometry to calculate the length and breadth of the rectangle.

⑪ A man's average wage for four weeks was ₦6 152. In the first three weeks his wages were ₦5 560, ₦6 672 and ₦6 024. Calculate his wage in the fourth week.

⑫ A motorist averages 48 km/h for the first 30 km of a journey and 64 km/h for the next 120 km. What is the average speed for the whole journey?

⑬ The midday temperatures in °C for a week in a certain town were 27, 29, 29, 33, 28, 24, 26.
  a What is the modal temperature?
  b State the range of temperatures.
  c What is the median temperature?
  d Calculate the mean temperature.
  e What is the greatest deviation from the mean i above, ii below?

⑭ Table R2 gives the estimated number of students (in thousands) between the ages of 15 and 18 in a certain country.

age	15	16	17	18
number (× 1 000)	228	206	152	134

Table R2

Show this information a in a pie chart, b in a bar chart.

Revision test 5 (Chapters 11, 13, 15, 16)

① A new table costs ₦10 000. Find the cost of buying the same kind of table in 2 years' time if the rates of inflation for those years are 20% and 10%.
  A ₦10 000   B ₦11 500   C ₦12 000
  D ₦13 000   E ₦13 200

② A bookshelf can hold 84 books each 3 cm wide. How many books of width 4 cm can it hold?
  A 56   B 63   C 84   D 105   E 112

③ The reciprocal of 0·02 is
  A 500   B 50   C 5   D 0·5   E 0·05

Use Fig. R9 to answer questions 4 and 5.

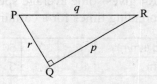

Fig. R9

④ In Fig. R9, sin P̂ =
  A $\frac{p}{q}$ B $\frac{q}{p}$ C $\frac{r}{q}$ D $\frac{p}{r}$ E $\frac{r}{p}$

163

5. Which of the following statements is (are) true in Fig. R9?

   I $\sin \hat{P} = \cos \hat{R}$
  II $\cos \hat{P} = \sin \hat{R}$
 III $\tan \hat{P} = \tan \hat{R}$

  A none of them   B I and II only
  C II and III only D I and III only
  E all of them

6. The average age of 21 students is 14 years 3 months. If the oldest student is not counted, the average drops to 14 years 2 months. The age of the oldest student is:

  A 14 years 4 months   B 14 years 5 months
  C 15 years 11 months D 16 years
  E 21 years

7. Fig. R10 is a pie chart of the information in Table R3.

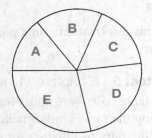

Fig. R10

shoe size	6	7	8	9	10
number of people	5	6	9	10	6

Table R3

Which sector in Fig. R10 represents the people who wear size 8 shoes?

8. ₦200 000 is saved at 10% per annum compound interest. Find a the amount, b the interest, after 3 years.

9. Table R4 gives some average speeds and corresponding times for a certain journey.

speed (km/h)	15	30	50
time (h)	10	5	3

Table R4

a Copy Table R4 and add an extra line for values of $\frac{1}{\text{time}}$.

b Draw a graph connecting speed and reciprocal of time.
c Use your graph to find the time taken when the speed is 45 km/h.

10. a Use reciprocal tables to find the value of $\frac{1}{3\cdot69}$ correct to 2 s.f. Hence write down t values of b $\frac{1}{369}$ and c $\frac{1}{0\cdot369}$.

11. By drawing and measurement, find approximately a the value of sin 37°, b the size of the angle whose cosine is $\frac{7}{10}$.

12. A ladder 6 m long leans against a vertical wall and makes an angle of 80° with the horizontal ground. Calculate, to 2 s.f., how far up the wall the ladder reaches.

13. The ages of 14 students in years and month are:

15,5; 15,0; 15,3; 14,5; 14,7; 15,4; 15,10; 14,9; 15,2; 13,11; 15,1; 16,1; 15,5; 14,11.

a State the range of these ages.
b Calculate the average of the highest and lowest ages and use this as a working mean to find the average age of all the students.
c What is the greatest deviation from the mean, i above, ii below?

14. After 12 games a basketball player's points average was 18·5. How many points must h score in the next game to raise his average t 20?

General revision test B (Chapters 9–16)

1. If $x^2 + 14x + k$ is a perfect square, then $k =$
  A 4 . B 7   C 28   D 49   E 1

2. Which of the following is (are) factors of $3x^2 - 6x - 9$?
  I 3
  II $(x - 3)$
 III $(x + 1)$
  A I only   B II only   C III only
  D I and II only   E I, II and III

3. If $\frac{5}{f} = 4 - \frac{7}{f}$, then $f =$
  A -1 B $\frac{1}{3}$ C $\frac{1}{2}$ D 1   E

4. A herdsman bought a cow for ₦25 000. He sold it to a butcher at a profit of 20%. The

butcher then sold it at a profit of 20%. What was the final selling price of the cow?

A ₦29 000   B ₦29 200   C ₦32 000
D ₦35 000   E ₦36 000

When a sum of money is shared between 40 people they each get ₦800. If the same money is shared equally between 50 people, how much will each get?

A ₦600   B ₦640   C ₦810
D ₦960   E ₦1 000

The reciprocal of 0·08 is 12·5. The reciprocal of 80 is

A 0·001 25   B 0·012 5   C 0·125
D 1·25   E 125 000

If $x = 2y - 1$ and $2x = 3y + 2$, then $x =$

A −9   B −4   C 4   D 7   E 9

Two of the angles of a triangle are $x°$ and $(90 - x)°$. Which of the following is (are) correct?

  I $\sin x° = \cos(90 - x)°$
  II $\cos x° = \sin(90 - x)°$
  III $\tan x° = \dfrac{1}{\tan(90 - x)°}$

A I only   B I and II only   C III only
D all of them   E none of them

ble R5 gives the approximate hand spans of 20 dents.

and span (cm)	19	20	21	22	23
equency	3	2	5	8	2

ble R5

e Table R5 to answer questions 9 and 10.

) What is the median size of hand span?
  A 20·8 cm   B 21 cm   C 21·2 cm
  D 21·5 cm   E 22 cm

) What is the mean hand span?
  A 20·8 cm   B 21 cm   C 21·2 cm
  D 21·5 cm   E 22 cm

) Expand the brackets in $(4a + 3)(a - 2) - (2a - 3)(2a + 3) = 0$ and hence solve the equation.

) Factorise the following.
  a $n^2 + 12n + 32$ b $x^2 - 14x + 33$

  c $z^2 + 11z - 26$ d $y^2 - 9y - 36$
  e $16 + 8h + h^2$ f $9 - (a + 2)^2$

(13) Solve the following.

  a $\dfrac{15}{k} = \dfrac{3}{k} + 3$ b $\dfrac{15}{k} = \dfrac{3}{k + 2}$

  c $\dfrac{1}{x + 5} - \dfrac{1}{4x - 7} = 0$

(14) A motor bike costs ₦750 000. It depreciates by 20% in the first year and by 15% in each of the following years. Find the value of the motor bike to the nearest ₦10 000 after 3 years.

(15) A man saves ₦200 000 at 6% per annum compound interest. At the end of each year he adds ₦18 000 to his total savings. Find his total amount after 3 years.

(16) A long straight road makes an angle of 7° with the horizontal. Two posts are 1 km apart on the road. Calculate in metres:
  a the horizontal distance between the posts,
  b the difference in height between the posts.

(17) First simplify, then solve, the following simultaneous equations:
$3(2x - y) = x + y + 5$
$5(3x - 2y) = 2(x - y) + 1$

(18) A cyclist travels for x hours at 20 km/h and then for y hours at 12 km/h. Altogether she travels 60 km in 4 hours.
  a Express the total time taken in terms of x and y.
  b Express the total distance travelled in terms of x and y.
  c Hence find x and y.

(19) The acute angles of a rhombus are 76°. If the shorter diagonal is of length 8 cm, calculate the length of the sides of the rhombus to the nearest mm. (First make a good sketch.)

(20) A small factory employs 10 workers, two supervisors and one manager. The workers get ₦7 000 per week, the supervisors get ₦11 000 per week and the manager gets ₦17 200 per week
  a Calculate the mean weekly wage at the factory.
  b Compare this result with the modal wage. Which average is most representative of the weekly wages?

17 Area of plane shapes

OBJECTIVES

By the end of this chapter you should be able to:

1 Recall, use and apply the formulae for the area of triangles, quadrilaterals and circles
2 Use trigonometry to solve area problems
3 Calculate the area of sectors and segments of a circle
4 Use addition and subtraction methods to find the areas of composite shapes
5 Apply area formulae to real-life problems in the home, in the environment and in relation to land measure.

Teaching and learning materials

Teacher: Cardboard models of plane shapes; charts with area formulae

---

17-1 Area of basic shapes

The formulae for the areas of some basic shapes are given in Fig. 17.1. These were previously found in Book 1, Chapter 14.

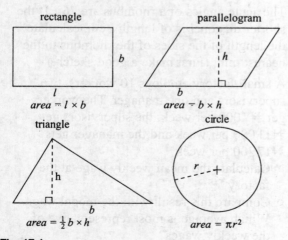

Fig. 17.1

166

Exercise 17a [Revision]

In this exercise, use the value $\frac{22}{7}$ for π unless told otherwise.

① Calculate the areas of the shapes in Fig. 17.2.

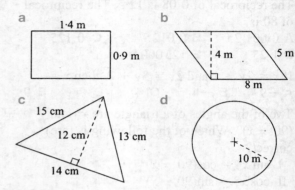

Fig. 17.2

② Calculate the areas of the parallelograms in Fig. 17.3.

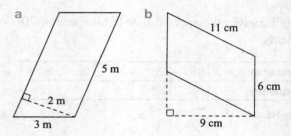

Fig. 17.3

③ Calculate the area of the shapes in Fig. 17.4.

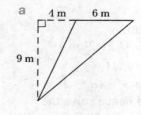
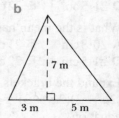

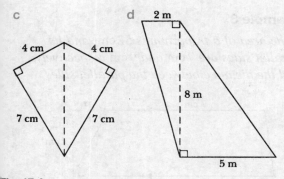

Fig. 17.4

(4) Use subtraction or addition to calculate the shaded areas in Fig. 17.5. Use the value 3·1 for π. All dimensions are in cm.

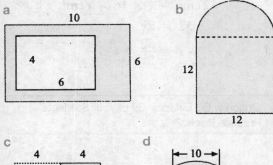

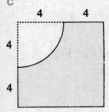

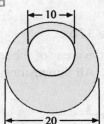

Fig. 17.5

(5) A wooden door is 2·1 m high and 0·8 m wide. Find:
  a the area of the door,
  b the cost of the door if the wood costs ₦3 500 per m².

(6) A page in a photograph album measures 30 cm by 20 cm. It contains six square photos each of side 6 cm. Calculate the area of the page which is *not* covered by the photos.

(7) The seconds hand on a watch is 14 mm long. What area does it sweep through in 30 seconds?

(8) A goat is tied by a rope 2½ m long to a peg in some grass. The goat eats 1 m² of grass in 28 min. How long will it take to eat all that it can reach?

(9) A thin gold disc 10 cm in diameter costs ₦3 300. What is the cost per m²?

(10) 6− cm diameter discs are cut from a sheet 130 cm long and 70 cm wide as shown in Fig. 17.6.

Fig. 17.6

  a How many discs can be cut in this way?
  b What area of the sheet is wasted?

17-2 Area of a trapezium

In Fig. 17.7, ABCD is a trapezium with AB//DC.

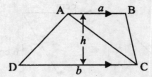

Fig. 17.7

Let the lengths of AB and DC be a and b respectively. Let their perpendicular distance apart be h. Join AC.

Area of ABCD = area of △ABC + area of △ACD

$$= \tfrac{1}{2}ah + \tfrac{1}{2}bh$$

$$= \tfrac{1}{2}h(a + b) \text{ or } \tfrac{1}{2}(a + b)h$$

The area of a trapezium is the product of the average length of its parallel sides and the perpendicular distance between them.

167

Example 1

Find the area of the trapezium in Fig. 17.8.

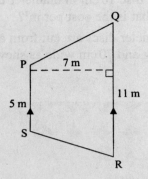

Fig. 17.8

In Fig. 17.8, SP//RQ.

$$\text{Area of PQRS} = \tfrac{1}{2}(5 + 11) \times 7\,\text{m}^2$$
$$= \tfrac{1}{2} \times 16 \times 7\,\text{m}^2$$
$$= 8 \times 7\,\text{m}^2 = 56\ \text{m}^2$$

Example 2

If the area of the trapezium in Fig. 17.9 is $40\tfrac{1}{2}\,cm^2$, find the value of x.

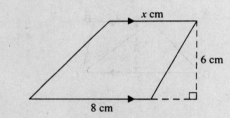

Fig. 17.9

$$\text{Area of trapezium} = \tfrac{1}{2}(x + 8) \times 6\,\text{cm}^2$$
$$= 3(x + 8)\,\text{cm}^2$$

Thus, $\quad 3(x + 8) = 40\tfrac{1}{2}$

$$x + 8 = 40\tfrac{1}{2} \div 3 = 13\tfrac{1}{2}$$
$$x = 13\tfrac{1}{2} - 8 = 5\tfrac{1}{2}$$

Example 3

If the area of a trapezium is $52\,cm^2$ and its parallel sides are 7 cm and 9 cm respectively, find the distance between the parallel sides.

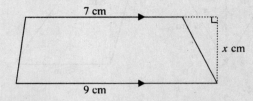

Fig. 17.10

Let the distance be x cm.

$$\text{Area of trapezium} = \tfrac{1}{2}(7 + 9) \times x\,\text{cm}^2$$
$$52\,\text{cm}^2 = \tfrac{1}{2} \times 16 \times x\,\text{cm}^2$$
$$52 = 8x$$
$$x = \frac{52}{8} = 6\cdot5$$

☞ *Optional:* Do Exercise 39 of your Students' Practice Book.

Exercise 17b

① Find the areas of the trapeziums in Fig. 17.11. All dimensions are in cm.

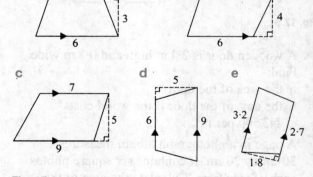

Fig. 17.11

② In each of the trapeziums in Fig. 17.12, find the value of x.

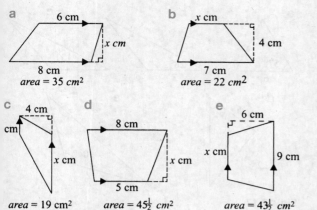

a
6 cm
x cm
8 cm
area = 35 cm²

b
x cm
4 cm
7 cm
area = 22 cm²

c
4 cm
cm
x cm
area = 19 cm²

d
8 cm
x cm
5 cm
area = 45½ cm²

e
6 cm
x cm
9 cm
area = 43½ cm²

Fig. 17.12

17-3 Using trigonometry in area problems

Example 4

Find the area of △ABC to the nearest cm² if BA = 6 cm, BC = 7 cm and B̂ = 34°.

Let the height of the triangle be x cm (see Fig. 17.13).

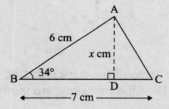

Fig. 17.13

In △ABD, $\frac{x}{6}$ = sin 34°

x = 6 sin 34°

= 6 × 0·5592

= 3·3552

area of △ABC = $\frac{1}{2}$ × BC × AD

= $\frac{1}{2}$ × 7 × 3·3552 cm²

= $\frac{1}{2}$ × 23·4864 cm²

= 11·7432 cm²

= 12 cm² to the nearest cm².

Example 5

Calculate the area of parallelogram PQRS if QR = 5 cm, RS = 6 cm, QR̂S = 118°.

In Fig. 17.14, QD is the height of the parallelogram.

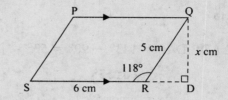

Fig. 17.14

Let QD be x cm.
In △QRD, QR̂D = 180° − 118° = 62°

$\frac{x}{5}$ = sin 62°

x = 5 sin 62°

= 5 × 0·8829

= 4·4145

area of PQRS = SR × QD

= 6 × 4·4145 cm²

= 26·487 cm²

= 26 cm² to the nearest cm².

In Examples 4 and 5, since the data of the questions are given in whole numbers of cm and degrees, it is suitable to give the results to the nearest whole number of cm².

Example 6

Calculate the area of the trapezium in Fig. 17.15.

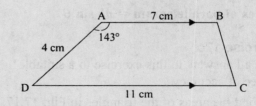

Fig. 17.15

Construct the height AP of the trapezium as in Fig. 17.16.

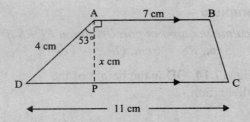

Fig. 17.16

In $\triangle ADP$, $D\hat{A}P = 143° - 90° = 53°$

$$\frac{x}{4} = \cos 53°$$

$$x = 4 \cos 53°$$
$$= 4 \times 0{\cdot}6018$$
$$= 2{\cdot}4072$$

area of ABCD $= \frac{1}{2}(AB + DC) \times AP$
$= \frac{1}{2}(7 + 11) \times 2{\cdot}4072 \, \text{cm}^2$
$= \frac{1}{2} \times 18 \times 2{\cdot}4072 \, \text{cm}^2$
$= 9 \times 2{\cdot}4072 \, \text{cm}^2$
$= 21{\cdot}6648 \, \text{cm}^2$
$= 22 \, \text{cm}^2$ to 2 s.f.

Notice in Examples 4, 5 and 6 that rounding off is only done at the *last* stage of the working. Do not round off at an earlier stage.

Trigonometrical formulae

In general, for a triangle with sides a, b containing an angle θ,

area of triangle $= \frac{1}{2} ab \sin \theta$

and for a parallelogram with non-parallel sides a, b containing an angle θ,

area of parallelogram $= ab \sin \theta$

Exercise 17c

Give all answers in this exercise to a suitable degree of accuracy.

① Find the areas of the triangles in Fig. 17.17. All dimensions are in cm.

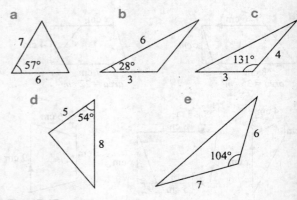

Fig. 17.17

② Find the areas of the parallelograms in Fig. 17.18. All dimensions are in cm.

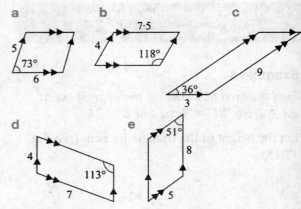

Fig. 17.18

③ Find the areas of the trapeziums in Fig. 17.19. All dimensions are in metres.

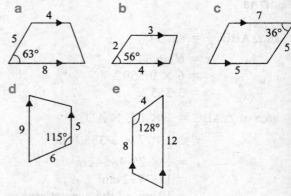

Fig. 17.19

170

In Chapter 6 we found how to change the subject of a formula. Example 7 shows how to change the subject of a formula to find a length from a given area.

Example 7

What is the diameter of a circle of area $3\,850\,m^2$?

$$\text{area} = \pi r^2 = 3\,850\,\text{m}^2$$
$$\text{Thus,}\ \tfrac{22}{7}r^2 = 3\,850$$
$$r^2 = 3\,850 \times \tfrac{7}{22}$$
$$= 175 \times 7$$
$$= 5^2 \times 7^2$$
$$r = 5 \times 7 = 35$$
$$\text{diameter} = 2 \times 35\,\text{m} = 70\,\text{m}$$

Rings

Use subtraction to find the area of a flat ring. See Examples 8 and 9.

Example 8

What is the area of a flat washer 4·8 cm *in outside diameter, the hole being of diameter* 2·2 cm?

The required area is shaded in Fig. 17.20.

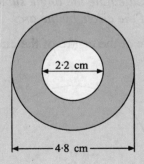

Fig. 17.20

$$\text{area} = \pi(2\cdot4)^2 - \pi\,(1\cdot1)^2\,\text{cm}^2$$
$$= \pi\,(2\cdot4^2 - 1\cdot1^2)\,\text{cm}^2$$
$$= \pi\,(2\cdot4 + 1\cdot1)(2\cdot4 - 1\cdot1)\,\text{cm}^2$$
$$= \tfrac{22}{7} \times 3\cdot5 \times 1\cdot3\,\text{cm}^2$$
$$= 14\cdot3\,\text{cm}^2$$

Example 9

Find the area between two circles with the same centre and of radii 5 cm *and* 9 cm *respectively.*
$(\pi = \tfrac{22}{7})$

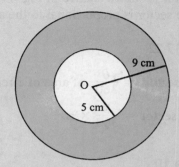

Fig. 17.21

$$\text{area} = \pi(9)^2 - \pi\,(5)^2\,\text{cm}^2$$
$$= \pi\,(9^2 - 5^2)\,\text{cm}^2$$
$$= \pi\,(9 + 5)(9 - 5)\,\text{cm}^2$$
$$= \tfrac{22}{7} \times \tfrac{14}{1} \times \tfrac{4}{1}\,\text{cm}^2$$
$$= 176\,\text{cm}^2$$

Notice that use of factors makes the arithmetic easier. The common factor, π, is taken outside a bracket as soon as possible. The use of 'the difference of two squares' (see Chapter 9) makes the simplification easier in the next line. The numerical value of π is substituted only when the brackets have been simplified.

☞ Optional: Do Exercise 40 of your Students' Practice Book.

Area of a sector of a circle

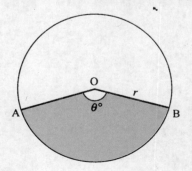

Fig. 17.22

In Fig. 17.22, AOB is a sector of a circle of radius *r* units, centre O. A **sector** is a region bounded by two radii and an arc. $\theta°$ is the angle subtended at the centre of the circle by the arc AB.

The sector is shown shaded in Fig. 17.22. The area of the sector is proportional to the angle of the sector.

In Fig. 17.22,

area of sector $= \dfrac{\theta°}{360°}$ of area of circle

area of sector $= \dfrac{\theta}{360} \times \pi r^2$

Example 10

Find the area of a sector of a circle of radius 7 cm, the angle at the centre of the circle being 108°.

The required area is shaded in Fig. 17.23.

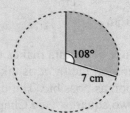

Fig. 17.23

area $= \dfrac{108}{360}$ of $\pi \times 7^2 \, cm^2$

$= \dfrac{108}{360} \times \dfrac{22}{7} \times 7 \times 7 \, cm^2$

$= \dfrac{3}{10} \times 22 \times 7 \, cm^2$

$= 46 \cdot 2 \, cm^2$

Example 11

The area of a sector of a circle is 44 cm². What is the radius of the circle if the angle at the centre of the circle is 140°?

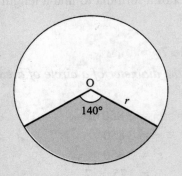

Fig. 17.24

area $= \dfrac{140}{360} \times \dfrac{22}{7} \times r^2 \, cm^2$

$44 = \dfrac{11 \times r^2}{9}$

$11 \times r^2 = 44 \times 9$

$r^2 = \dfrac{44 \times 9}{11}$

$r^2 = 36$

$r = 6 \, cm$

Example 12

The area of a sector of a circle of radius 15 cm is 110 cm². Calculate the angle subtended at the centre of the circle by the arc.

Let the angle at the centre of the circle be $\theta°$.

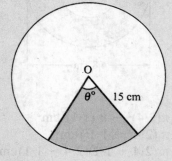

Fig. 17.25

area of sector $= \dfrac{\theta°}{360°} \times \pi r^2$

$110\,\text{cm}^2 \quad = \dfrac{\theta}{360} \times \dfrac{22}{7} \times \dfrac{15}{1} \times \dfrac{15}{1} \times \text{cm}^2$

$110\,\text{cm}^2 \quad = \dfrac{55 \times \theta°}{28}\,\text{cm}^2$

$55 \times \theta \quad = 110 \times 28$

$\theta \quad = \dfrac{110 \times 28}{55} = 56°$

Example 13

Find the area of the shaded segment for a quadrant of radius 14 cm.

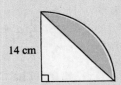

14 cm

Fig. 17.26

A **quadrant** is a sector of a circle with an angle of 90°.

area of quadrant $= \frac{1}{4} \times \pi \times 14^2$

$= \frac{1}{4} \times \frac{22}{7} \times 14 \times 14\,\text{cm}^2$

$= 11 \times 14 = 154\,\text{cm}^2$

area of triangle $= \frac{1}{2} \times 14 \times 14\,\text{cm}^2$

$= 98\,\text{cm}^2$

area of segment $= 154\,\text{cm}^2 - 98\,\text{cm}^2$

$= 56\,\text{cm}^2$

 Optional: Do Exercise 41 of your Students' Practice Book.

Exercise 17d

Throughout this exercise, take π to be $\frac{22}{7}$.

1) Find the area of each of the rings whose outside and inside diameters are as follows.
   a 8 m and 6 m
   b 22 cm and 20 cm
   c 15 m and 6 m
   d 8·6 cm and 8·2 cm

2) Complete Table 17.1 for sectors of circles. Make a rough sketch of each.

	radius	angle at centre	area
a	7 cm	90°	
b	35 m	72°	
c	4·2 cm	120°	
d	5·6 cm	135°	
e	14 m	300°	
f		108°	4 620 cm²
g		120°	462 cm²
h	14 m		77 m²
i		140°	99 m²
j	35 m		770 cm²

Table 17.1

3) Find the area of the shaded part in each of the following. All dimensions are in cm.

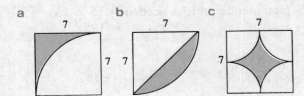

a   b   c

Fig. 17.27

4) Find the radii of circles with the following areas: a 154 cm², b 1 386 cm², c $86\frac{5}{8}$ m², d 6·16 ha.

5) Two circular bronze discs of radii 3 cm and 4 cm are melted down and cast into a single disc of the same thickness as before. What is the radius of the new disc?

17-5 Area in the home and environment

We need to consider area when maintaining and renovating homes, offices and the environment. Floor coverings, cloth, roofing materials and paint are usually sold in units that involve area.

Tiles are often used to cover the floor of a room. The number of tiles needed can be calculated from the dimensions of the room.

There is usually some wastage since tiles are sold in whole numbers.

Example 14

Square tiles, 30 cm × 30 cm, are used to cover a floor. How many tiles are needed for a floor 4·4 m long and 3·8 m wide?

length of room = 4·4 m = 440 cm

number of tiles = $\frac{440}{30} = 14\frac{2}{3}$

Thus, 15 tiles are needed along each length of the room. (The last tile will be cut.)

width of room = 3·8 m = 380 cm

number of tiles = $\frac{380}{30} = 12\frac{2}{3}$

Thus, 13 tiles are needed across each width of the room.

total number of tiles needed = 15 × 13
= 195

Land measure

The **hectare (ha)** is the basic unit of land measure.

1 hectare = 10 000 m²

Since 10 000 m² = 100 m × 100 m (or 2 × 100 m × 50 m) we can think of a hectare as being about the size of two football pitches.

Example 15

A village is roughly in the shape of a circle of diameter 400 m. Use the value 3 for π to find the approximate area of the village in hectares.

Radius of village = $\frac{1}{2}$ of 400 m = 200 m

Area of village ≈ π × 200² m²
≈ 3 × 40 000 m²
≈ 3 × 4 hectares
≈ 12 hectares

The area of the village is about 12 ha.

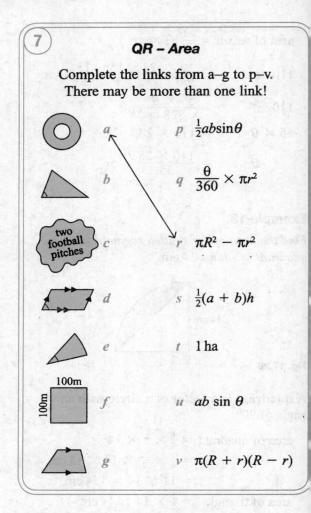

7 **QR – Area**

Complete the links from a–g to p–v.
There may be more than one link!

a	p $\frac{1}{2}ab\sin\theta$
b	q $\frac{\theta}{360} \times \pi r^2$
two football pitches c	r $\pi R^2 - \pi r^2$
d	s $\frac{1}{2}(a + b)h$
e	t 1 ha
f	u $ab \sin \theta$
g	v $\pi(R + r)(R - r)$

Exercise 17e contains questions involving area in the home, in the work place and the environment. The exercise gives practice in using area formulae and the methods covered in this chapter, and applying them to real-life situations. The Exercise is split into three parts.

Exercise 17e
Area in the home and work place

(1) How many tiles, each 30 cm by 30 cm, will be needed for floors with the following dimensions?

a 6 m by 4·2 m   b 3·6 m by 3 m
c 5 m by 4·2 m   d 9 m by 6·2 m
e 10 m by 8·4 m   f 5·2 m by 4·1 m
g 2·9 m by 3·4 m   h 5·83 m by 3·44 m

(2) Square polystyrene tiles, 50 cm by 50 cm,

are used to cover the ceiling of a classroom measuring 7·4 m by 4·5 m.
  a Find the number of tiles that are needed.
  b Find the cost at ₦130 per tile.

③ The walls of a bathroom are to be covered with wall tiles 15 cm by 15 cm. How many tiles are needed for a bathroom 2·7 m long, 2·25 m wide and 3 m high? (Do not allow for doors and windows.)

④ An open rectangular box, 1 m long, 70 cm wide and 50 cm deep is painted inside and outside. Find the cost at ₦90 per m².

⑤ How many paving stones, each 1 m long and 80 cm wide, are needed to cover a compound 13·6 m long and 11 m wide?

⑥ Fig. 17.28 is a sketch of a building with a corrugated roof.

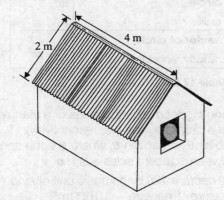

Fig. 17.28

Corrugated iron is sold in sheets measuring 2 m by 60 cm. Find the number of sheets that are needed for the building.

⑦ The walls of a toilet 2·5 m long, 2·05 m wide and 3 m high are to be covered with tiles 15 cm by 15 cm. A saving of 108 tiles is made on doors and windows. How many tiles will be needed altogether? (Note that some tiles will have to be cut.)

⑧ A rectangular compound, 8·55 m long by 5·89 m wide, is to be paved with the largest possible square tiles which will fit in exactly. How many tiles will there be? (*Hint*: express 855 and 589 as products of prime numbers.)

⑨ An office 5 m long, 4 m wide and 2·5 m high

is to have its walls covered with plywood panels. The plywood is sold in sheets 3 m long and 1·5 m wide. If there are no horizontal joins in the panels between floor and ceiling, how many sheets will be needed? Allow a saving of 1 sheet for doors and windows which are not panelled.

⑩ A room 4·38 m long, 3·74 m wide and 2·36 m high has two doorways, each 76 cm by 198 cm, and three windows, each 88 cm by 106 cm. Find the cost, to the nearest naira, of painting the walls of this room at ₦74 per m².

Circular problems (use $\frac{22}{7}$ for π)

⑪ The disc brake in a car is a flat metal ring 22 cm in diameter with a 6-cm diameter hole in the middle. Calculate the area of the metal.

⑫ The friction pad in a motorcycle disc brake is a flat ring of fibre 10 cm in diameter with a 3-cm diameter hole in the middle. What is the area of the fibre?

⑬ The cloth for a wedding dress is cut in the form of a 210° sector of a 3-m radius circle. What is the area of the cloth used?

⑭ Find the cross-sectional area of a round metal pipe if its outside diameter is 13·5 cm and the metal is 0·25 cm thick.

⑮ The windscreen wiper of a car sweeps through an angle of 150°. The blade of the wiper is 21 cm long and the radius of the unswept sector is 6 cm. See Fig. 17.29.

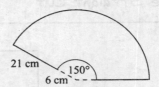

Fig. 17.29

What area of the windscreen is swept clean?

Land measure

⑯ How many hectares are there in 1 km²?

⑰ A hockey pitch measures 90 m by 55 m. Express its area as a fraction of a hectare.

Would you say that this is roughly half a hectare?

18. A town is roughly in the shape of an equilateral triangle of side 600 m. What is the approximate area of the town in hectares? (Use the value 0·9 for sin 60°.)

19. A 58 km highway is part of a national development scheme. On average the highway is 66 m wide (allowing for two carriageways, a central reservation and safety verge). How many hectares (to 2 s.f.) are required for this highway?

20. A City Council makes available 4·2 ha for a housing development. The Council stipulates that 25% of the land should be for roads. Also there should be no more than 40 building plots, each of size 650 m², and some land should be set aside for recreation. What is the minimum area of land for recreation?

SUMMARY

1. Table 17.2 contains the area formulae for some common shapes.

shapes	formulae for area
square side s	s^2
rectangle length l, breadth b	lb
triangle base b, height h	$\frac{1}{2}bh$
parallelogram base b, height h	bh
trapezium height h, parallels a and b	$\frac{1}{2}(a+b)h$
circle radius r	πr^2
sector of circle radius r, angle θ	$\frac{\theta}{360}\pi r^2$

Table 17.2

2. Using *trigonometry*, the areas of a triangle and a parallelogram are, respectively, $\frac{1}{2}ab\sin\theta$ and $ab\sin\theta$, where θ is the angle between adjacent sides a and b.

3. The *hectare (ha)* is the basic unit of *land measure*. 1 hectare = 10 000 m².

4. *Subtraction methods* are often used to find the areas of composite shapes. See Examples 8, 9 and 13.

18 Areas and volumes of similar shapes

OBJECTIVES

By the end of this chapter you should be able to:

1 Use scale factors to find the areas of similar plane shapes

2 Use scale factors to find the volumes of similar solid shapes

3 Derive area and volume factors from given scale factors and vice versa.

Teaching and learning materials

Teacher: Similar plane shapes; similar solid shapes; graph paper

Student: Graph paper; mathematical set

18-1 Areas of similar shapes

Fig. 18.1 represents two similar rectangles, one 7 cm × 3 cm, the other 28 cm × 12 cm.

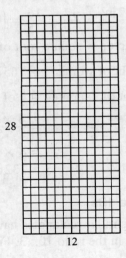

Fig. 18.1

Scale factor of the big rectangle to the small rectangle = ratio of their corresponding sides

$$= \frac{28\,\text{cm}}{7\,\text{cm}} \text{ or } \frac{12\,\text{cm}}{3\,\text{cm}}$$

$$= 4 \text{ in both cases}$$

Area factor of the big rectangle to the small rectangle = ratio of their areas

$$= \frac{28 \times 12\,\text{cm}^2}{7 \times 3\,\text{cm}^2} = 4 \times 4$$

$$= 4^2$$

Hence the area factor is the *square* of the scale factor of the rectangles. $4^2 = 16$. Notice in Fig. 18.1 that the small rectangle fits 16 times into the big rectangle.

Fig. 18.2 represents two circles with radii 5 cm and 3 cm.

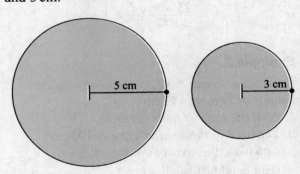

Fig. 18.2

Scale factor of the small circle to the big circle
= ratio of the radii

$$= \frac{3\,\text{cm}}{5\,\text{cm}} = \frac{3}{5}$$

Area factor of the small circle to the big circle
= ratio of their areas

$$= \frac{\pi \times 3^2\,\text{cm}^2}{\pi \times 5^2\,\text{cm}^2} = \frac{3^2}{5^2}$$

$$= \left(\frac{3}{5}\right)^2 \text{ or } \frac{9}{25}$$

Again, the ratio of the areas is the square of the scale factor of the given circles.

In general, **the ratio of the areas of two similar shapes is the square of the scale factor of the two shapes.**

☞ *Optional:* Do Exercise 42 of your Students' Practice Book.

Example 1

A map is drawn to a scale of 1 : 5 000. *On the map, a school has an area of* 6 cm². *Find the true area of the school in hectares.*
(1 ha = 10 000 m².)

scale factor $= 5\,000$

area factor $= (5\,000)^2$

$= 25\,000\,000$

area of school $= 25\,000\,000 \times 6\,\text{cm}^2$

$= \dfrac{25\,000\,000 \times 6}{100 \times 100}\,\text{m}^2$

$= \dfrac{25\,000\,000 \times 6}{10\,000 \times 100 \times 100}\,\text{ha}$

$= \dfrac{25 \times 6}{100}\,\text{ha} = 1 \cdot 5\,\text{ha}$

Example 2

Two similar cones have corresponding slant heights of 8 cm *and* 12 cm.
a *Find the ratio of their areas.*
b *The area of the smaller cone is* 102 cm². *Calculate the area of the larger cone.*

a
$\dfrac{\text{slant height of smaller cone}}{\text{slant height of larger come}} = \dfrac{8\,\text{cm}}{12\,\text{cm}} = \dfrac{2}{3}$

$\dfrac{\text{area of smaller cone}}{\text{area of larger cone}} = \left(\dfrac{2}{3}\right)^2 = \dfrac{4}{9}$

b
$\dfrac{\text{area of smaller cone}}{\text{area of larger cone}} = \dfrac{4}{9}$

$\dfrac{102\,\text{cm}^2}{\text{area of larger cone}} = \dfrac{4}{9}$

area of larger cone $= \dfrac{102 \times 9}{4}\,\text{cm}^2$

$= 229 \cdot 5\,\text{cm}^2$

Example 3

The ratio of the areas of two rectangular fields is $\frac{25}{9}$.
a *Find the ratio of their lengths.*
b *The smaller field is* 120 m *long. Find the corresponding length of the larger field.*

a
$\dfrac{\text{area of larger field}}{\text{area of smaller field}} = \dfrac{25}{9}$

$\dfrac{\text{length of larger field}}{\text{length of smaller field}} = \sqrt{\dfrac{25}{9}} = \dfrac{5}{3}$

b
$\dfrac{\text{length of larger field}}{120\,\text{m}} = \dfrac{5}{3}$

length of larger field $= \dfrac{120 \times 5}{3}\,\text{m}$

$= 200\,\text{m}$

Example 4

A woman uses 5 m² *and* 3·2 m² *of cloth when making similar dresses for herself and her daughter respectively. The woman is* 165 cm *tall. How tall is the daughter?*

Assume that the woman and daughter are similar in build.

area factor of daughter's dress to woman's dress

$= \dfrac{3 \cdot 2\,\text{m}^2}{5\,\text{m}^2} = \dfrac{32}{50} = \dfrac{16}{25} = \left(\dfrac{4}{5}\right)^2$

scale factor = square root of area factor $= \frac{4}{5}$

height of woman $= 165\,\text{cm}$

height of daughter $= \frac{4}{5}$ of 165 cm

$= \dfrac{4 \times 165}{5}\,\text{cm}$

$= 4 \times 33\,\text{cm}$

$= 132\,\text{cm}$

Exercise 18a

1. Two similar rectangles have corresponding sides in the ratio 10 : 3. Find the ratio of their areas.

2. Two similar triangles have corresponding sides of length 4 cm and 7 cm. Find the ratio of their areas.

③ Two similar hexagons have corresponding sides of 2 cm and 5 cm.
  a Find the ratio of their areas.
  b The area of the larger hexagon is 150 cm². Find the area of the smaller one.

④ The ratio of the areas of two circles is $\frac{4}{9}$.
  a Find the ratio of their radii.
  b The smaller circle has a radius of 12 cm. Find the radius of the larger one.

⑤ Two similar triangular prisms have surface areas of 64 cm², and 144 cm².
  a Find the ratio of their heights.
  b The height of the smaller prism is 49 cm. Find the heights of the larger prism.

⑥ Two similar cuboids have corresponding widths of 11 cm and 9 cm.
  a Find the ratio of their surface areas.
  b The surface area of the larger cuboid is 363 cm². Find the surface area of the smaller cuboid.

⑦ A map of Kano is drawn to a scale 1 : 50 000. On the map the airport covers an area of 8 cm². Find the true area of the airport in hectares.

⑧ A sports stadium covers an area of 6 hectares. Find the area in cm² of the sports stadium when drawn on a map of scale 1 : 5 000.

⑨ A photograph measuring 8 cm by 10 cm costs ₦44. What will be the cost of an enlargement measuring 20 cm by 25 cm?

⑩ Two square floor tiles are made of the same material. One costs ₦90 and its edge is 30 cm long. Find the cost of the other if its edge is 50 cm long.

⑪ Two rectangular flags are similar in shape. Their areas are 5 m² and 0·8 m². The height of the larger flag is 180 cm. Find the height of the smaller flag.

⑫ The area of the windscreen of a bus is 1·21 m². In a photograph of the bus, the windscreen appears as a rectangle 12 cm by 3 cm. Find the length and breadth of the real windscreen.

18-2 Volumes of similar shapes

Fig. 18.3 represents two similar cuboids, one 5 cm × 2 cm × 1 cm, the other 15 cm × 6 cm × 3 cm.

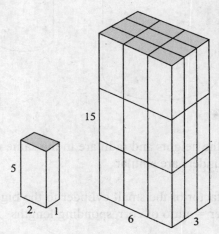

Fig. 18.3

Scale factor of the big cuboid to the small cuboid = ratio of their corresponding edges

$$= \frac{15\,\text{cm}}{5\,\text{cm}} \text{ or } \frac{6\,\text{cm}}{2\,\text{cm}} \text{ or } \frac{3\,\text{cm}}{1\,\text{cm}}$$

= 3 in each case

Volume factor of the big cuboid to the small cuboid = ratio of their volumes

$$= \frac{15 \times 6 \times 3\,\text{cm}^3}{5 \times 2 \times 1\,\text{cm}^3} = 27$$

$$= 3^3$$

Hence the volume factor is the *cube* of the scale factor of the cuboids. In Fig. 18.3 it should be possible to see that the small cuboid will fit 27 times into the big cuboid.

Fig. 18.4 represents two cylinders, one of height 2h and radius 2r, the other of height h and radius r.

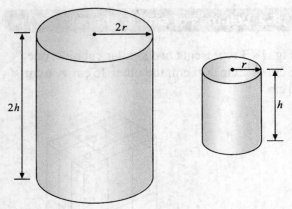

Fig. 18.4

Since the heights and radii are in the same ratio, the cylinders are similar.

Scale factor of the small cylinder to the big cylinder = ratio of corresponding lengths

$$= \frac{h}{2h} \text{ or } \frac{r}{2r}$$

$$= \tfrac{1}{2} \text{ in both cases}$$

Volume factor of the small cylinder to the big cylinder = ratio of their volumes

$$= \frac{\pi r^2 h}{\pi (2r)^2 2h} = \frac{1}{8}$$

$$= \left(\tfrac{1}{2}\right)^3$$

Again, the ratio of the volumes is the cube of the scale factor of the two shapes.

   In general, **the ratio of the volumes of similar solids is the cube of the scale factor of the two solids.**

Example 5

Two pots, similar in shape, are respectively 21 cm *and* 14 cm *high. The smaller pot holds* 1·2 litres. *Find the capacity of the larger one.*

$$\text{scale factor} = \frac{21}{14} = \frac{3}{2}$$

$$\text{Thus, volume factor} = \left(\frac{3}{2}\right)^3 = \frac{27}{8}$$

The smaller pot holds 1·2 litres
The larger pot holds $1·2 \times \frac{27}{8}$ litres
   $= 0·15 \times 27$ litres
   $= 4·05$ litres

Example 6

Two heaps of rice are of similar shape and contain 128 kg *and* 250 kg *of rice respectively. The height of the bigger heap is* 70 cm. *Find the height of the smaller one.*

Mass is proportional to volume, thus,
ratio of volumes = ratio of masses

$$= \frac{128}{250} = \frac{64}{125}$$

$$= \frac{4^3}{5^3} = \left(\frac{4}{5}\right)^3$$

scale factor $= \frac{4}{5}$
height of bigger heap $= 70$ cm
height of smaller heap $= \frac{4}{5}$ of 70 cm
   $= 4 \times 14$ cm
   $= 56$ cm

8 QR – Area and volume factors

The following boxes link scale factor to corresponding area and volume factors.

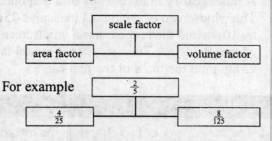

Fill the empty boxes in the following.

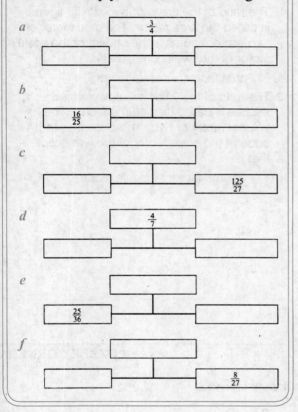

Exercise 18b

① Two similar cups have heights in the ratio 2 : 3. Find the ratio of their capacities.

② Two similar blocks have corresponding edges of length 10 cm and 20 cm.
Find the ratio of their masses.

③ A soap bubble 4 cm in diameter is blown out until its diameter is 8 cm.

By what ratio has the volume of air in the bubble increased?

④ Two metal bolts are similar in shape and have diameters of 5 mm and 15 mm.
   a Find the ratio of their masses.
   b The smaller bolt's mass is 12 g. Find the mass of the larger bolt.

⑤ Two similar buckets hold $13\frac{1}{2}$ litres and 4 litres respectively.
   a Find the ratio of their heights.
   b The height of the larger bucket is 36 cm. Find the height of the smaller bucket.

⑥ Two similar pots have heights of 16 cm and 10 cm. The smaller pot holds 0·75 litres. Find the capacity of the larger pot.

⑦ A sports trophy is in the shape of a cup 30 cm high. The winners are each given copies of the cup, $7\frac{1}{2}$ cm high. One of the copies holds 100 ml.
Find the capacity of the trophy in litres.

⑧ A cup of beans costs ₦80. How much would a similar tin, three times the height and diameter, full of beans cost?

⑨ A pencil manufacturer makes a giant model pencil, 3 m long, as a factory symbol. A real pencil is 18 cm long and has a volume of 9 cm³. Find the volume in m³ of the giant model.

⑩ A builder makes a scale model of a real house. The volumes of air in the scale model and the real house are 27 500 cm³ and 220 m³ respectively. The height of the door in the real house is 2·4 m. Find the height of the door in the scale model.

Example 7

Two similar tins contain 960 g and 405 g of margarine respectively. The area of the base of the larger tin is 120 cm². Find the area of the base of the smaller tin.

ratio of volumes = ratio of masses

$$= \frac{960}{405} = \frac{64}{27}$$

$$= \frac{4^3}{3^3} = \left(\frac{4}{3}\right)^3$$

181

Thus, scale factor $= \frac{4}{3}$

and the area factor $= \left(\frac{4}{3}\right)^2 = \frac{16}{9}$

area of larger base $= 120 \text{ cm}^2$

area of smaller base $= \frac{9}{16}$ of 120 cm^2

$= 67\frac{1}{2} \text{ cm}^2$

Notice in Example 7 that the scale factor must be found before the areas can be compared.

Exercise 18c   [Mixed practice]

1. A metal tray measuring 40 cm by 30 cm costs ₦256. What should be the price of a tray which is similar but 50 cm long?

2. Two plastic cups are similar in shape and their heights are 7·5 cm and 12·5 cm. If the plastic needed to make the first cost ₦72, find the cost for the second.

3. In question 2, if the second cup holds $1\frac{7}{8}$ litres, find the capacity of the first cup in ml.

4. A cylindrical oil drum 70 cm long is made of sheet metal which costs ₦750. Find the cost of the metal for a similar oil drum 84 cm long.

5. A statue stands on a base of area 1·08 m². A scale model of the statue has a base of area 300 cm². Find the mass of the statue (in tonnes) if the scale model is of mass 12·5 kg.

6. A railway engine is of mass 72 tonnes and is 11 m long. An exact scale model is made of it and is 44 cm long. Find the mass of the model.

7. In question 6, if the tanks of the model hold 0·8 litres of water, find the capacity of the tanks of the railway engine.

8. A compound has an area of 3 025 m², and it is represented on a map by an area of 16 cm².
   a Find the scale of the map.
   b Find the true length of a wall which is represented on the map by a line 2·8 cm long.

9. In a scale drawing of a school compound, a path 120 cm wide is shown to be 15 mm wide.
   a Find the scale of the drawing.
   b Find the area of the compound if the corresponding area on the plan is 2 025 cm².

10. A model car is an exact copy of a real one. The windscreen of the model measures 35 cm by 10 cm and the real car has a windscreen of area 0·315 m². The mass of the model is 25 kg. Find the mass of the real car.

SUMMARY

1 The *scale factor* of two shapes is the ratio of two corresponding lengths

2 The ratio of the areas of two similar figures is called the *area factor*. The area factor of two similar figures is the square of the scale factor of the two figures, that is

area factor = (scale factor)².

3 The ratio of the volumes of two similar shapes is called the *volume factor*. The volume factor of two similar solids is the cube of the scale factor of the two solids, that is

volume factor = (scale factor)³.

PUZZLE CORNER

Four Nines

$\frac{9}{9} + \frac{9}{9} = 2$

$9 - 9 + \frac{9}{\sqrt{9}} = 3$

What other numbers can you make with four 9's and mathematical symbols?

Try other numbers: e.g. four 4's.

19 Variation

OBJECTIVES

By the end of this chapter you should be able to:

1 Solve numerical and word problems involving direct and indirect variation

2 Solve numerical and word problems involving joint and partial variation.

Teaching and learning materials

Teacher: Wall charts with examples of the four kinds of variation

19-1 Direct and inverse variation

This section extends the work covered in Section 3-1 on pages 122 to 124.

Direct variation

If a person buys some packets of sugar, the total cost is proportional to the number of packets bought.

The cost of 2 packets at ₦x per packet is ₦$2x$.
The cost of 3 packets at ₦x per packet is ₦$3x$.
The cost of n packets at ₦x per packet is ₦nx.

The ratio of total cost to number of packets is the same for any number of packets bought.

Similarly, Fig. 19.1 shows a new pencil cut into a number of pieces.

Fig. 19.1

The mass of each piece is proportional to its length. The ratio of mass to length is the same for all the pieces.

These are both examples of **direct variation**, or direct proportion. In the first example, the cost, C, varies directly with the number of packets, n. In the second example, the mass, M, varies directly with the length, L.

The symbol $\propto$ means 'varies with' or 'is proportional to'. The statements in the previous paragraph are written:

$$C \propto n$$
$$M \propto L$$

$M \propto L$ really means that the ratio $\frac{M}{L}$ is **constant** (i.e. stays the same).

Example 1

1 packet of sugar costs x naira. What will be the cost of 20 *packets of sugar?*

Cost varies directly with the number of packets bought.

cost of 1 packet $= x$ naira
cost of 20 packets $= 20 \times x$ naira
$= 20x$ naira

Example 2

$C \propto n$ *and* $C = 5$ *when* $n = 20$. *Find the formula connecting C and n.*

$C \propto n$ means $\frac{C}{n}$ is constant.

Let this constant be k.

Then, $\frac{C}{n} = k$

or $C = kn$

$C = 5$ when $n = 20$

hence $5 = k \times 20$

$k = \frac{1}{4}$

Thus, $C = \frac{1}{4}n$ is the formula which connects C and n.

A formula such as $C = \frac{1}{4}n$ is often known as a **relationship** between the variables C and n.

183

Example 3

$M \propto L$ and $M = 6$ when $L = 2$. Find
a the relationship between M and L,
b the value of L when $M = 15$.

a If $M \propto L$, then $M = kL$ when k is a constant.
(See Example 2.)

$$M = kL$$
When $M = 6$, $L = 2$,
thus, $6 = k \times 2$
$$k = 3$$
Therefore $M = 3L$ is the relationship
between M and L.

b $M = 3L$ and $M = 15$,
thus, $15 = 3L$
$$L = 5$$

Note: $M \propto L$ means that $M = kL$ or $L = \frac{1}{k} M$.

Thus, L also varies directly with M.
In general, if $a \propto b$ then also $b \propto a$.

Exercise 19a

1. 1 m of wire has a mass of x g.
   What is the mass of 25 m of the same wire?

2. One jar of coffee costs ₦y.
   What will be the cost of four jars of coffee?

3. A man cycles 15 km in 1 hour.
   How far will he cycle in t hours if he keeps
   up the same rate?

4. Eggs cost ₦25 each.
   How much will n eggs cost?

5. A cup holds d ml, of water.
   How much water will eight of these cups hold?

6. $C \propto n$ and $C = 28$ when $n = 4$.
   Find the formula connecting C and n.

7. $D \propto t$ and $D = 32$ and $t = 2$.
   Find the relationship between D and t.

8. $x \propto y$ and $x = 3$ when $y = 12$.
   Find the relationship between x and y.

9. $d \propto s$ and $d = 120$ when $s = 30$.
   Find the formula connecting d and s.

10. $a \propto b$ and $a = 2 \cdot 4$ when $b = 3$.
    Find the relationship between a and b.

11. $D \propto S$ and $D = 140$ when $S = 35$. Find:
    a the relationship between D and S,
    b the value of S when $D = 176$.

12. $x \propto y$ and $x = 30$ when $y = 12$. Find:
    a the formula connecting x and y,
    b x when $y = 10$,
    c y when $x = 14$.

13. $P \propto Q$ and $P = 4 \cdot 5$ when $Q = 12$. Find:
    a the relationship between P and Q,
    b P when $Q = 16$,
    c Q when $P = 2 \cdot 4$.

14. $A \propto B$ and $A = 1\frac{7}{8}$ when $B = \frac{5}{6}$. Find:
    a A when $B = 0 \cdot 4$,
    b B when $A = 7 \cdot 5$.

15. $d \propto P$ and $d = 0 \cdot 2$ when $P = 10$. Find:
    a d when $P = 18$,
    b P when $d = 1 \cdot 1$.

Inverse variation

Fig. 19.2 shows a circle cut into:
a 5 equal sectors,   b 12 equal sectors.

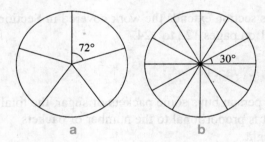

Fig. 19.2

In Fig. 19.2a, there are 5 equal sectors in the
circle. The angle of each sector is 72°.

In Fig. 19.2b, there are 12 equal sectors in the
circle. The angle of each sector is 30°.

If there are 18 sectors, the angle of each sector
would be 20°.

Therefore, the greater the number of sectors,
the smaller the angle of each sector.

Similarly, if a car travels a certain distance,
the greater its average speed, the less time it will
take.

These are both examples of **inverse variation**,
or inverse proportion. In the first example, the
size of the angle, θ, varies inversely with the

number of sectors, n. In the second, the time taken, T, is inversely proportional to the average speed, S. These statements are written:

$$\theta \propto \frac{1}{n} \qquad T \propto \frac{1}{S}$$

Example 4

$x \propto \frac{1}{y}$ and $x = 9$ when $y = 4$. *Find the formula that connects x and y.*

$$x \propto \frac{1}{y}$$

i.e. $x = K \times \frac{1}{y}$, where K is a constant.

Thus, $x = \dfrac{K}{y}$

$x = 9$ when $y = 4$

Thus, $9 = \dfrac{K}{4}$

$$K = 36$$

$x = \dfrac{36}{y}$ is the formula that connects x and y.

Note: $x \propto \frac{1}{y}$ means that $x = \dfrac{K}{y}$ or $y = \dfrac{K}{x}$.
Thus, y also varies inversely with x.
In general, if $a \propto \frac{1}{b}$ then also $b \propto \frac{1}{a}$.

Example 5

$\theta \propto \frac{1}{n}$ and $\theta = 72$ when $n = 5$. *Find:*
a θ when $n = 12$, b n when $\theta = 8$.

First: find the relation between θ and n.

$\theta \propto \frac{1}{n}$ means $\theta = \dfrac{K}{n}$ where K is a constant.

$$\theta = \frac{K}{n}$$

When $\theta = 72$, $n = 5$

Thus, $72 = \dfrac{K}{5}$

$$K = 5 \times 72 = 360$$

Thus, $\theta = \dfrac{360}{n}$ is the relation

a $\theta = \dfrac{360}{n}$

When $n = 12$,

$$\theta = \frac{360}{12} = 30$$

b If $\theta = \dfrac{360}{n}$ then $n = \dfrac{360}{\theta}$.

When $\theta = 8$,

$$n = \frac{360}{8}$$

$$= 45$$

 Optional: Do Exercise 43 of your Students' Practice Book.

Exercise 19b

1. d varies inversely as t. Use the symbol $\propto$ to show a connection between d and t.

2. A piece of string is cut into n pieces of equal length l.
   a Does n vary directly or inversely with l?
   b Use the symbol $\propto$ to show a connection between n and l.

3. A rectangle has a constant area, A. Its length is l and its breadth is b.
   a Write a formula for l in terms of A and b.
   b Write a formula for b in terms of A and l.
   c Does l vary inversely or directly with b?

4. $x \propto \frac{1}{y}$ and $x = 22$ when $y = 3$.
   Find the relationship between x and y.

5. $R \propto \frac{1}{T}$ and $T = 8$ when $R = 4$.
   Find the relationship between R and T.

6. $m \propto \frac{1}{n}$ and $m = 70$ when $n = 100$.
   Find the formula which connects m and n.

7. $T \propto \frac{1}{S}$ and $T = 2$ when $S = 60$.
   a Find the relationship between T and S.
   b Find the value of T when $S = 90$.
   c Find S when $T = 2\frac{1}{2}$.

8. $r \propto \frac{1}{h}$ and $r = 5$ when $h = 12$.
   a Find r when $h = 20$.
   b Find h when $r = 45$.

9. $t \propto \frac{1}{d}$ and $t = 0{\cdot}15$ when $d = 120$.
   a Find t when $d = 45$.
   b Find d when $t = 0{\cdot}12$.

10. $b \propto \frac{1}{h}$ and $b = 8$ when $h = 5$.
    a Find b when $h = 4$.
    b Find h when $b = \frac{1}{4}$.

Example 6

The mass, M g, of a piece of wood varies directly with its volume, V cm³. 200 cm³ of the wood has a mass of 160 g. Find the relationship between M and V. Hence find the volume of a piece of wood of mass 1 kg.

From the wording of the first sentence,

$$M \propto V$$
$$\text{or } M = kV$$

In the second sentence, $M = 160$ when $V = 200$.

Thus, $160 = k \times 200$

$$k = \frac{160}{200} = 0.8$$

Thus, $M = 0.8V$

$1\,\text{kg} = 1000\,\text{g}$

When $M = 1000$,
$$1000 = 0.8V$$
$$V = \frac{1000}{0.8} = \frac{10000}{8} = 1250$$

Thus, 1 kg of wood has a volume of 1 250 cm³.

Example 7

When travelling between two towns, the time taken varies inversely with the average speed. When the average speed is 42 km/h, the journey takes 4 hours. Find the average speed if the journey takes 2 hours 20 minutes.

Let T be the time in hours and S be the average speed in km/h.

Then, from the first sentence, $T \propto \dfrac{1}{S}$

$$\text{or } T = \frac{K}{S}$$

In the second sentence, $T = 4$ when $S = 42$.

Thus, $4 = \dfrac{K}{42}$

$$K = 4 \times 42 = 168$$

Thus, $T = \dfrac{168}{S}$

$2\,\text{h}\,20\,\text{min} = 2\frac{1}{3}\,\text{h}$

When $T = 2\frac{1}{3}$

$$2\frac{1}{3} = \frac{168}{S}$$
$$S = \frac{168}{2\frac{1}{3}}$$
$$= 168 \div \frac{7}{3}$$
$$= 168 \times \frac{3}{7} = 24 \times 3$$
$$= 72$$

When the journey takes $2\frac{1}{3}$ h, the average speed is 72 km/h.

Exercise 19c

1 When exchanging pounds for naira, the number of naira (₦) varies directly with the number of pounds (£). 1 300 naira is exchanged for 5 pounds. Find the formula connecting ₦ and £. Hence find the number of naira that is exchanged for 28 pounds.

2 When travelling at a constant speed, the distance travelled, D km, varies directly with the time taken, T hours. 81 km takes $1\frac{1}{2}$ h. Find the relationship between D and T. Hence find the distance travelled in 5 hours.

3 The height, h cm, of mercury in a thermometer varies directly with the temperature, T°C, of the mercury. When $T = 45$, $h = 6.75$. Find the relationship between h and T. Hence find h when $T = 76$.

4 The thickness of a book varies directly with the number of pages in the book. A book is 1·8 cm thick and contains 350 pages. What is the thickness of the first 84 pages of the book?

5 If a car travels for a certain time, the distance travelled varies directly with the average speed. When the average speed is 35 km/h, the distance travelled is 115 km. What distance is travelled when the average speed is 84 km/h?

6 The number of bricks, b, that a man can carry varies inversely with the mass of each brick, m kg. The man can carry 14 bricks of mass 4 kg. Find the relationship between b

and m. Hence find the number of $3\frac{1}{2}$ kg bricks that he can carry.

⑦ When repaying a loan, the number of monthly payments, m, varies inversely with the amount of each payment, ₦a. The loan can be repaid by 10 monthly payments of ₦1 350. Find the formula which connects m and a. Hence find how long it takes to repay the loan with monthly payments of ₦750.

⑧ The mass of rice that each woman gets when sharing a sack varies inversely with the number of women. When there are 20 women, each gets 6 kg of rice. If there are nine women, how much does each get?

⑨ The membership fee of a club varies inversely with the number of members. When there are 80 members the fee is ₦490. What is the fee when there are 56 members?

⑩ When travelling between two towns, the time taken varies inversely with the average speed. When the average speed is 48 km/h the time taken is $3\frac{1}{4}$ hours. Find the time taken when the average speed is 65 km/h.

⑪ In science, Gay-Lussac's law states that for a given mass of an ideal gas at a constant pressure, its volume (V m³) is proportional to its absolute temperature (T K). At an absolute temperature of 300 K a certain mass of gas occupies 1 m³. Find the volume of the gas when the absolute temperature is 375 K.

⑫ Boyle's law states that for a given mass of an ideal gas at a constant temperature, its pressure (p N/m²) is inversely proportional to its volume (V m³). At a certain temperature, 3 m³ of a gas exerts a pressure of 10^5 N/m². If the gas expands to 12 m³, calculate its pressure, giving your answer in standard form.

19-2 Joint variation

The mass of a sheet of metal is proportional to both the area *and* the thickness of the metal. Therefore $M \propto At$ (where M, A and t are the mass, area and thickness). This is an example of

joint variation. The mass **varies jointly** with the area and thickness.

At midday, the temperature, $T°C$, inside a house is proportional to the outside temperature, $S°C$, *and* is inversely proportional to the thickness of the house walls, t cm. In this case, $T \propto \frac{S}{t}$. This is another example of joint variation.

The inside temperature varies directly with the outside temperature and inversely with the wall thickness.

Example 8

$x \propto \frac{y}{z}$. When $y = 7$ and $z = 3$, $x = 42$.

a Find the relation between x, y and z.
b Find x when $y = 5$ and $z = 9$.

a $x \propto \frac{y}{z}$

Thus, $x = \frac{ky}{z}$, where k is a constant.

When $y = 7$ and $z = 3$, $x = 42$.

Thus, $42 = \frac{k \times 7}{3}$

$$k = \frac{3 \times 42}{7} = 18$$

Hence $x = \frac{18y}{z}$

b When $y = 5$ and $z = 9$,

$$x = \frac{18 \times 5}{9} = 2 \times 5$$

$x = 10$

Exercise 19d

① $x \propto yz$. When $y = 2$ and $z = 3$, $x = 30$.
  a Find the relation between x, y and z.
  b Find x when $y = 4$ and $z = 6$.
② $x \propto \frac{y}{z}$. $x = 27$ when $y = 9$ and $z = 2$.
  a Find the relation between x, y and z.
  b Find x when $y = 14$ and $z = 12$.
③ $A \propto BC$. When $B = 4$ and $C = 9$, $A = 6$.
  a Find the formula that connects A, B and C.
  b Find A when $B = 3$ and $C = 10$.
  c Find C if $A = 20$ and $B = 15$.
④ $T \propto \frac{S}{t}$. When $S = 36$ and $t = 16$, $T = 27$.
  a Find the formula that connects T, S and t.
  b Find T when $S = 33$ and $t = 18$.

(5) The mass of a sheet of metal varies jointly with its area and its thickness. A sheet of metal of area 250 cm² and thickness 1 mm has a mass of 200 g.

  a Find the formula which connects the mass M g, the area A cm² and the thickness t mm.

  b Hence find the mass of a piece of metal of area 400 cm² and thickness 3 mm.

(6) The universal gas law states that the volume (V m³) of a given mass of an ideal gas varies directly with its absolute temperature (T K) and inversely with its pressure (p N/m²). A certain mass of gas at an absolute temperature 275 K and pressure 10^5 N/m² has a volume 0·022 5 m³.

  a Find the formula that connects p, V and T.

  b Hence find the pressure of the gas when its absolute temperature is 374 K and its volume is 0·018 m³.

19-3 Partial variation

When a tailor makes a dress, the total cost depends on two things: first the cost of the cloth; secondly the amount of time it takes to make the dress. The cost of the cloth is constant, but the time taken to make the dress can vary. A simple dress will take a short time to make; a dress with a difficult pattern will take a long time. This is an example of **partial variation**. The cost is partly constant and partly varies with the amount of time taken. In algebraic form, $C = a + kt$, where C is the cost, t the time taken and a and k are constants.

Example 9

R is partly constant and partly varies with E. When $R = 530$, $E = 1\,600$ and when $R = 730$, $E = 3\,600$.

a Find the formula which connects R and E.

b Find R when $E = 1\,300$.

a From the first sentence,
$R = c + kE$ where c and k are both constants.

Substituting the given values gives two equations.

$$530 = c + 1\,600k \quad (1)$$
$$730 = c + 3\,600k \quad (2)$$

These are simultaneous equations.
Subtract (1) from (2).

$$200 = 2\,000k$$
$$k = \frac{200}{2\,000} = \frac{1}{10}$$

Substituting in (1),

$$530 = c + 1\,600 \times \tfrac{1}{10}$$
$$530 = c + 160$$

Thus, $c = 370$

Thus, $R = 370 + \frac{1}{10}E$ is the required formula.

b $R = 370 + \dfrac{E}{10}$

When $E = 1\,300$,

$$R = 370 + \frac{1\,300}{10}$$
$$= 370 + 130$$
$$= 500$$

Example 10

The charge C of a cell phone company is partly constant and partly varies as the number of units of call, U. The cost of 90 units is ₦1 120 and the cost of 120 units is ₦1 216.

a *Find a formula which connects C and U.*

b *Find C when $U = 150$ units.*

a From the first sentence,

$$C = a + bU, \text{ where } a \text{ and } b \text{ are constants}$$

Substituting the values
$$C = 1\,120, U = 90$$
and $C = 1\,216, U = 120$

gives the equations

$$1\,120 = a + 90b \quad (1)$$
$$1\,216 = a + 120b \quad (2)$$

Solve simultaneously.

$$96 = 30b \text{ (subtracting (1) from (2))}$$
$$b = 3\cdot2$$

Substitute $3 \cdot 2$ for b in (1).

$$1\,120 = a + 90 \times 3 \cdot 2$$
$$1\,120 = a + 288$$
$$a = 1\,120 - 288$$
$$a = 832$$

The required formula is

$$C = 832 + 3 \cdot 2U$$

b When $U = 150$,

$$C = 832 + 3 \cdot 2 \times 150$$
$$= 832 + 480$$
$$= 1\,312$$

The cost of 150 units is ₦1 312.

Exercise 19e

① x is partly constant and partly varies as y.
When $y = 2$, $x = 30$, and when $y = 6$,
$x = 50$.
  a Find the relationship between x and y.
  b Find x when $y = 3$.

② x is partly constant and partly varies with y.
When $y = 3$, $x = 11$, and when $y = 4$,
$x = 14$.
  a Find the relationship between x and y.
  b Find x when $y = 10$.

③ x is partly constant and partly varies with y.
When $y = 3$, $x = 7$, and when $y = 6$, $x = 9$.
  a Find the relationship between x and y.
  b Find x when $y = 4$.

④ D is partly constant and partly varies with V.
When $V = 40$, $D = 150$, and when $V = 54$,
$D = 192$.
  a Find the formula connecting D and V.
  b Hence find D when $V = 73$.

⑤ The cost of making a dress is partly constant
and partly varies with the amount of time it
takes to make the dress. If the dress takes 3
hours to make, it costs ₦2 700. If it takes
5 hours to make the dress, it costs ₦3 100.
Find the cost if it takes $1\frac{1}{2}$ hours to make the
dress.

⑥ The cost of a car service is partly constant
and partly varies with the time it takes to
do the work. It costs ₦9 400 for a $5\frac{1}{2}$-hour
service and ₦8 200 for a 4-hour service.
  a Find the formula connecting cost, ₦C
    with time, T hours.
  b Hence find the cost of a $7\frac{1}{2}$-hour service.

⑦ A telephone company makes up its monthly
bills as follows: a fixed charge of ₦800 plus
a charge proportional to the number of units
of call on the telephone. If it charges ₦2 per
unit of call, calculate the total charge on a 80
units, b 150 units, c 782 units.

⑧ The charge for telephone calls, T, is partly
constant and partly varies with the number
n of units of call. The bill for 420 units of
call is ₦806, while the bill for 200 units is
₦410.
  a Obtain the charge per unit of call.
  b Find a formula for T.

⑨ An electricity company charges per quarter
as follows: a fixed charge of ₦500 and a
charge of ₦35 per unit of current used.
  a Calculate the charge for 46 units of
    electricity.
  b If VAT of 5% is paid on the bill, calculate
    the amount to be paid.

⑩ The charge for electricity consumption, E,
is partly constant and partly varies as the
number N of units used. The charge for 82
units is ₦3 655 while the charge for 42 units
is ₦2 055.
  a Calculate the charge per unit of electricity.
  b Obtain a formula for E in terms of N.

1 *Direct variation* between related quantities means that they vary proportionally to one another. As one grows, the other grows; as one decreases, the other decreases. '*C* varies directly as *n*' is written as

$$C \propto n \text{ or } C = kn$$

where *k* is a constant.

2 *Inverse variation* between related quantities means that they vary inversely with each other. As one grows, the other decreases; as one decreases the other grows. '*T* varies inversely as *s*' is written as

$$T \propto \frac{1}{s} \text{ or } T = \frac{k}{s}$$

where *k* is a constant.

3 *Joint variation* is when a quantity varies directly and/or inversely with two or more other quantities. For example, if *G* varies directly with *M* and *m* and inversely with *d²*, then

$$G \propto \frac{Mm}{d^2} \text{ or } G = \frac{kMm}{d^2}$$

where *k* is a constant.

4 *Partial variation* is when a quantity is partly constant and partly varies with another quantity. For example, $P = a + bQ$, where *P* and *Q* are variables and *a* and *b* are constants. We often use simultaneous equations to solve such problems. See Examples 9 and 10.

Number Chain

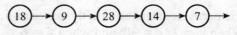

The rules for the above number chain are:
i) if the number is even, divide by 2
ii) if the number is odd, multiply by 3 and add 1.

What happens when you ...
a) continue the above chain?
b) start with a different number?
c) change the rules?

Mini Sudoku*

1			
		4	
	2		
			3

Complete the diagram so that every row, every column and every 2 x 2 box each contains the digits 1 to 4 once and once only.
[* This is small version of a 9 x 9 Sudoku puzzle – see the daily Newspapers!]

Rational and non-rational numbers

OBJECTIVES

By the end of the chapter you should be able to:

1 Distinguish between rational and non-rational numbers
2 Use trial and improvement methods to calculate approximate values of square roots
3 Find an approximate value for π.

Teaching and learning materials

Teacher: Number chart showing rational and non-rational numbers; poster based on Figs 20.2 an 20.3; various bottles and empty tins; thread or string; chalk-board instruments; graph paper

Students: At least one empty tin or bottle; thread or string; mathematical set

---

20-1 Rational and non-rational numbers

We can write numbers such as 8, $4\frac{1}{2}$, $\frac{1}{5}$, $0\cdot211$, $\sqrt{\frac{49}{16}}$, $0\cdot3$ as exact fractions or ratios:

$$\frac{8}{1}, \quad \frac{9}{2}, \quad \frac{1}{5}, \quad \frac{211}{1\,000}, \quad \frac{7}{4}, \quad \frac{1}{3}.$$

Such numbers are called **rational numbers**.

Numbers which cannot be written as exact fractions are called **non-rational numbers**, or irrational numbers. $\sqrt{7}$ is an example of a non-rational number. $\sqrt{7} = 2\cdot645\,751\ldots$, the decimals extending without end and without recurring.

π is another example of a non-rational number. $\pi = 3\cdot141\,592\ldots$, again extending forever without repetition. The fraction $\frac{22}{7}$ is often used for the value of π. However, $\frac{22}{7}$ is a rational number and is only an *approximate value* of π.

All recurring decimals are rational numbers. Read the following example carefully.

Example 1

Write $3\cdot1\dot{7}$ as a rational number.

Let $n = 3\cdot1\dot{7}$
i.e. $n = 3\cdot17\ 17\ 17\ \ldots\ldots$ (1)

Multiply both sides by 100

$100n = 317\cdot17\ 17\ 17\ \ldots.$ (2)

Subtract (1) from (2),

$99n = (317\cdot17\ 17\ \ldots) - (3\cdot17\ 17\ \ldots)$
$99n = 314$

$$n = \frac{314}{99}$$

Thus, $3\cdot1\dot{7} = \frac{314}{99}$, a rational number.

A non-rational number extends forever *and* is non-recurring.

☞ *Optional:* Do Exercise 43 of your Students' Practice Book.

Exercise 20a

① Which of the following are rational and which are non-rational?

a 9 b $\frac{1}{9}$ c $\sqrt{9}$ d $0\cdot9$

e $2\frac{2}{3}$ f $5\frac{3}{4}$ g $\frac{11}{19}$ h $0\cdot815$

i $\sqrt{16}$ j $\sqrt{17}$ k $\sqrt{10}$ l $\sqrt{100}$

m $\frac{22}{7}$ n $3\cdot142$ o π p $\sqrt{8}$

q $\sqrt{49}$ r $\sqrt{4\cdot9}$ s $4\cdot9^2$ t $\frac{1}{4\cdot9}$

u $0\cdot\dot{6}$ v $0\cdot\dot{2}$ w $6\cdot\dot{7}$ x $0\cdot8\dot{3}$

y $\sqrt{2\frac{1}{4}}$ z $\sqrt{5}$

2 Write the following recurring decimals as rational numbers.

a $8\cdot\dot{3}$ b $6\cdot\dot{6}$ c $4\cdot\dot{7}$
d $3\cdot1\dot{9}$ e $3\cdot\dot{2}\dot{8}$ f $1\cdot\dot{6}\dot{1}$

20-2 Square roots

Some square roots are rational:

$$\sqrt{4} = 2, \quad \sqrt{6\cdot25} = 2\cdot5 = \frac{5}{2}$$

Other square roots are non-rational:

$$\sqrt{11} = 3\cdot316\,624\ldots, \quad \sqrt{3\cdot6} = 1\cdot897\,366\ldots$$

The fact that many square roots are non-rational was first discovered by Pythagoras around 500 BC. He tried to find the length of a diagonal of a 'unit square'. Fig. 20.1 is a unit square, a square with side 1 unit.

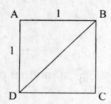

Fig. 20.1

In △ABD, using Pythagoras' rule,

$$BD^2 = AB^2 + AD^2$$
$$BD^2 = 1^2 + 1^2 = 2$$
$$BD = \sqrt{2}$$

Pythagoras was unable to find a rational value for $\sqrt{2}$. Thus, although it is possible to draw the diagonal of a unit square, it is impossible to measure its length accurately! This troubled Pythagoras so much that he called non-rational numbers 'unspeakables'.

It is possible to find the approximate value of non-rational square roots by using a 'trial and improvement' method. See Examples 2 and 3.

Example 2

Find the value of $\sqrt{2}$ correct to 2 significant figures.

Since 2 lies between 1 and 4, $\sqrt{2}$ lies between $\sqrt{1}$ and $\sqrt{4}$, i.e. $\sqrt{2}$ lies between 1 and 2:

Try 1·5: $1\cdot5^2 = 2\cdot25$ (too large)
Try 1·4: $1\cdot4^2 = 1\cdot96$ (too small)

Thus, $\sqrt{2}$ lies between 1·4 and 1·5. Since 1·96 is much closer to 2 than 2·25:

Try 1·41: $1\cdot41^2 = 1\cdot9881^*$ (too small)
Try 1·42: $1\cdot42^2 = 2\cdot0164^*$ (too large)

Thus, $\sqrt{2}$ lies between 1·41 and 1·42.
Thus, $\sqrt{2} = 1\cdot4$ to 2 s.f.
(*Check the calculation of these squares.)

Example 3

Find the value of $\sqrt{94}$ correct to 1 decimal place.

$\sqrt{94}$ lies between $\sqrt{81}$ and $\sqrt{100}$, i.e. $\sqrt{94}$ lies between 9 and 10.

Try 9·5: $9\cdot5^2 = 90\cdot25$ (too small)
Try 9·6: $9\cdot6^2 = 92\cdot16$ (too small)
Try 9·7: $9\cdot7^2 = 94\cdot09$ (just too large)

94·09 is very close to 94. $\sqrt{94} = 9\cdot7$ to 1 d.p.

To find the first digit of a square root, notice the following:
1 Every non-square number lies between two consecutive perfect squares (e.g. 23 lies between 16 and 25).
2 The square root of that number must lie between the square roots of the squares (e.g. $\sqrt{23}$ lies between $\sqrt{16}$ and $\sqrt{25}$, i.e. between 4 and 5).
3 The lower value gives the first digit of the required square root (e.g. $\sqrt{23} = 4\cdot$ 'something').

Further digits are found by trying values as in Examples 2 and 3.

Optional: Do Exercise 45 of your Students' Practice Book.

Exercise 20b

Write down the first digit of the square roots of the following.

a 22	b 6	c 29
d 54	e 14	f 71
g 42	h 88	i 3

Use the method of Examples 2 and 3 to find the value of the following correct to 2 significant figures.

a $\sqrt{3}$	b $\sqrt{8}$	c $\sqrt{13}$
d $\sqrt{23}$	e $\sqrt{52}$	f $\sqrt{69}$

20-3 Pi (π)

As we have seen earlier in the course, **pi**, or π, the ratio of the circumference of a circle to its diameter:

$$= \frac{\text{length of circumference of circle}}{\text{length of diameter of circle}} = \frac{c}{d} = \frac{c}{2r}$$

where r is the radius of the circle.

The problem of finding the value of π has occupied mathematicians through the ages. The most famous attempt to find π was by Archimedes, around 250 BC. His method, using the fact that the area of a circle is πr^2, was as follows.

In Fig. 20.2, squares are drawn inside and outside a circle of radius r.

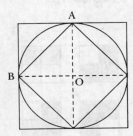

Fig. 20.2

In Fig. 20.2, the area of the circle is about halfway between the area of the inner square and that of the outer square.

Area of inner square $= 4 \times \triangle AOB$
$$= 4 \times \tfrac{1}{2}r^2 = 2r^2$$

Area of outer square $= 8 \times \triangle AOB$
$$= 8 \times \tfrac{1}{2}r^2 = 4r^2$$

Thus, the area of the circle lies between $2r^2$ and $4r^2$. It follows that the value of π must lie between 2 and 4, probably around 3.

Archimedes worked in this way, using regular polygons with more and more sides.

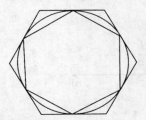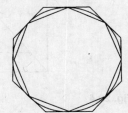

Fig. 20.3

In Fig. 20.3 it can be seen that the greater the number of sides of the polygons, the closer their area is to that of the circle. Using polygons of 96 sides, Archimedes showed that the value of π lies between $3\frac{10}{71}$ and $3\frac{1}{7}$. Both of these values are correct to 2 decimal places.

Class assignment

Do this experiment to find the value of π.

Either

(a) Collect some tins and bottles of various diameters.

(b) Measure the diameter, d, of each object. (An easy way is to place the object on a ruler; then take readings at opposite ends of a diameter.)

(c) Use a piece of string or a strip of paper to measure the circumference, C, of each object.

(d) Make a table of values of d and C.

(e) Draw a graph of d (on the horizontal axis) against C (on the vertical axis). Your graph should look like the sketch in Fig. 20.4.

(f) Construct a suitable triangle as in Fig. 20.4

193

Measure the height of the triangle, C, and the base of the triangle, d. Hence find the value of $\dfrac{C}{d}$ correct to 2 d.p.

(*Note*: $C = 2\pi r = \pi d$; hence $\pi = \dfrac{C}{d}$.)

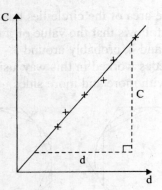

Fig. 20.4

Or

☞ *Optional:* Do Exercise 46 of your Students' Practice Book.

SUMMARY

1 A *rational number* is one that can be expressed as an exact fraction, or ratio. For example, whole numbers (-1, 1, 2, 3, 4, ...), common fractions ($\frac{1}{2}$, $\frac{3}{4}$, $\frac{5}{7}$, $\frac{1}{32}$, $\frac{3}{8}$, ...) and terminating and recurring decimals (7·2, 3·6, 0·$\overline{714258}$, ...) are all rational numbers.

2 A *non-rational number* (sometimes called an *irrational number*) is one that cannot be expressed as an exact fraction or ratio. For example $\sqrt{5}$, $\sqrt{12}$ and π are non-rational numbers.

PUZZLE CORNER

A Problem of Symmetry

Cut out three pieces of cardboard as shown –

Arrange them to make shapes with bilateral symmetry. For example:

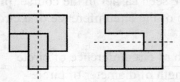

How many symmetrical shapes can you make from the three pieces?

PUZZLE CORNER

Three-colour Squares

Here are some 2 x 2 squares which have been shaded using up to 3 colours:

black
white
orange

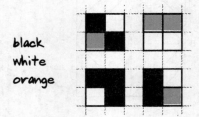

In how many ways can a 2 x 2 square be shaded like this – i.e. using up to 3 colours?

Revision exercise 6 (Chapters 17, 18)

1. Calculate the area of a trapezium in which the parallel sides are 7 cm and 13 cm long and 9 cm apart.

2. Calculate the area of $\triangle ABC$ if AB = 8 cm, BC = 3 cm and $\hat{B}$ = 56°. Give your answer to 2 s.f.

3. Calculate the area of a parallelogram if two of its adjacent sides are 6 cm and 10 cm long and the angle between them is 76°. (First make a sketch; give your answer to the nearest whole number of cm².)

4. How many tiles each 30 cm by 30 cm are needed to cover the floor of a rectangular room 4·2 m by 3·3 m?

5. Find the area of a path 2 m wide which surrounds a circular plot 12 m in diameter. (Make a sketch; use the value $3\frac{1}{7}$ for π.)

6. The dial on an old telephone is a plastic ring 8 cm in diameter with a 4 cm diameter hole in the centre. Ten small dialling holes, each of diameter 1·2 cm, are cut out of the ring. See Fig. R11.

   Use the value $\frac{22}{7}$ for π to calculate the area of plastic in the dial (shaded in Fig. R11).

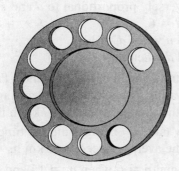

Fig. R11

7. The ratio of the areas of two similar rectangles is $\frac{8}{50}$.
   a Find the ratio of their lengths.

   b If the width of the smaller rectangle is 11 cm, find the width of the other rectangle.

8. A plan of a house is drawn on a scale of 1 : 80. On the plan, the biggest room has an area of about 30 cm². Find the true area of the room to the nearest m².

9. A gas cylinder is 75 cm long and holds 18 kg of liquid gas when full. How much gas will a similar cylinder, 50 cm long, hold when full?

10. Two similarly shaped cooking pots are made from metal of the same thickness. They have capacities of 20 and 2·5 litres respectively. The mass of the small pot is 1·5 kg when empty. What is the mass of the big pot when empty? (*Note*: The mass is proportional to the area of metal in the pot.)

Revision test 6 (Chapters 17,18)

1.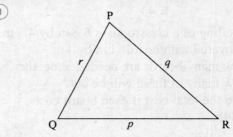

   Fig. R12

   In Fig. R12, which of the following give(s) the perpendicular distance of P from QR?

   I $r \sin \hat{Q}$

   II $q \sin \hat{R}$

   III $p \sin \hat{R}$

   A I only   B II only   C III only

   D I and II only   E I and III only

2. A sector of a circle of radius 12 cm has an angle of 160°. In terms of π, the area of the sector is

$$\text{A } \frac{16\pi}{3} \text{ cm}^2 \qquad \text{B } \frac{32\pi}{3} \text{ cm}^2 \qquad \text{C } 16\pi \text{ cm}^2$$

$$\text{D } 64\pi \text{ cm}^2 \qquad \text{E } 144\pi \text{ cm}^2$$

③

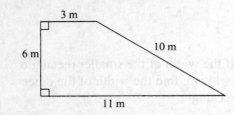

Fig. R13

The area of the trapezium in Fig. R13 is

A 33 m²   B 42 m²   C 56 m²

D 66 m²   E more information is needed

④ The scale of a map is 1 : 2 500.
How many m² does an area of 1 cm² on the map represent?

A 5   B 25   C 625

D 2 500   E 62 500

⑤ Two similar cones have base diameters of 10 cm and 35 cm. The small cone is used to fill the big cone with rice. Approximately how many small cones will it take to fill the big cone?

A 4   B 7   C 12

D 16   E 43

⑥ The ceiling of a classroom is 6·8 m by 4·7 m. It is covered with boards 1 m by 1 m.
   a How many boards are needed altogether?
   b How many of these will be cut?
   c Find the total cost if each board costs ₦348.

⑦

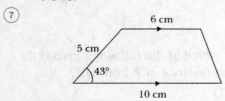

Fig. R14

   a Calculate the perpendicular distance between the parallel sides of the trapezium in Fig. R14.
   b Hence calculate the area of the trapezium to the nearest cm².

⑧ Two circular metal discs are of radius 9·9 cm and 13·2 cm respectively.
   a Express the ratio of their areas in its simplest terms.
   b The discs are melted down and recast as a single disc of the same thickness as before. Find the radius of this disc.

⑨ A road sign is in the shape of a metal triangle of height 70 cm and costs ₦2 695. How much will a similar road sign of height 1 m cost?

⑩ A 350 g packet of soap powder is of height 14 cm. Find the mass of soap powder contained in a similar packet 28 cm high.

Revision exercise 7 (Chapters 19, 20)

① $x \propto y$ and $x = 7$ when $y = 35$.
Find the relationship between x and y.

② $I \propto E$ and $I = 3$ when $E = 240$.
Find the formula connecting I and E. Hence find I when $E = 400$.

③ The number of matchsticks made by a machine is proportional to the time that the machine is working. The machine can make 20 000 matchsticks in $\frac{1}{2}$ hour.
   a Find the number of matchsticks that the machine makes in 2 h 36 min.
   b Find how long the machine takes to make 1 million matchsticks.

④ $I \propto \frac{1}{R}$ and $I = 2$ when $R = 120$.
Find the relationship between I and R.

⑤ n is inversely proportional to d and $n = 100$ when $d = 6$.
   a Find n when $d = 30$.
   b Find d when $n = 400$.

⑥ When travelling a certain distance, the time taken varies inversely with the average speed. When the average speed is 57 km/h the journey takes $3\frac{2}{3}$ hours. Find the time taken when the average speed is 55 km/h.

⑦ $p \propto \frac{m}{n}$ and $p = 6$ when $m = 15$ and $n = 1$.
   a Find the formula which connects p, m and n.
   b Hence find p when $m = 45$ and $n = 24$.

⑧ c is partly constant and partly varies with n. $c = 30$ when $n = 12$, and $c = 54$ when $n = 20$.
  a Find the formula connecting c and n.
  b Hence find c when $n = 27$.

⑨ Express $5 \cdot 2\dot{9}$ as a rational number.

⑩ Use a trial and improvement method to find $\sqrt{74}$ correct to 2 s.f.

Revision test 7 (Chapters 19, 20)

① If $V \propto T$ and $V = 6$ when $T = 2$, then the formula connecting V and T is

  A $V = \dfrac{T}{12}$ **B** $V = \dfrac{T}{3}$ **C** $V = 3T$

  D $V = 4T$ **E** $V = 12T$

② x varies inversely with y and $x = 9$ when $y = 8$. When $y = 12$, $x =$

  A 6   **B** $10\frac{2}{3}$ **C** 11

  D 13   **E** $13\frac{1}{2}$

③ R varies directly with t and inversely with m. Which of the following is the relationship between R, t and m, k being a constant in each case?

  A $R = \dfrac{km}{t}$ **B** $R = t + \dfrac{k}{m}$ **C** $R = ktm$

  D $R = k + \dfrac{t}{m}$ **E** $R = \dfrac{kt}{m}$

④ Which of the following is (are) non-rational?

  I $\sqrt{10}$ **II** $\sqrt{100}$ **III** $\sqrt{1000}$
  A I only   **B** I and II only
  C I and III only   **D** II and III only   **E** II only

⑤ The first digit of the square root of 79 is
  A 2   **B** 4   **C** 7
  D 8   **E** 9

⑥ The extension, e cm, of an elastic string varies directly with the tension, T newtons, in the string. When $T = 2$, $e = 5$.
  a Find the extension when $T = 7$.
  b Find the tension when $e = 20$.

⑦ A triangle has a constant area, k. Its base length is l and its corresponding height is h.
  a Write a formula for l in terms of k and h.
  b Does l vary directly or inversely with h?

⑧ The length of a pencil, l cm, varies directly with its mass, m g, and inversely with its area of cross-section, A cm². When $m = 4$ and $A = 0 \cdot 4$, $l = 18$.
  a Find the formula connecting l, m and A.
  b Hence find the length of a pencil which has a mass of 3 g and a cross-sectional area of 0·5 cm².

⑨ x is partly constant and partly varies with y. When $y = 5$, $x = 19$ and when $y = 10$, $x = 34$.
  a Find the relationship between x and y.
  b Hence find x when $y = 7$.

⑩ Express $1 \cdot 7\dot{5}$ as a rational number in its lowest terms.

PUZZLE CORNER

A Row of Numbers

6	9	15	24	39

To make the above row of numbers; start with 6 and 9 and add them to get 15. Then add 9 and 15 to get 24; finally, 15 + 24 = 39.

The same rule has been used below

5				43

What are the missing numbers?

PUZZLE CORNER

A Number Chain

Here is a number chain made by starting with two single-digit numbers 4 and 9.

$$4 \rightarrow 9 \rightarrow 3 \rightarrow 2 \rightarrow 5 \rightarrow 7 \rightarrow 2 \rightarrow$$

a) How is the chain made?
b) Continue the chain. What happens?
c) What if you started with two other numbers?

End of course review

The following section of this book contains a 4-chapter review course to help you to prepare for the Junior School Certificate Examination (JSCE) in mathematics.

We assume that you have already studied the preceding chapters and course work in the *New General Mathematics* series. Therefore there is minimum explanation in this section. The review course mainly uses worked examples to show how to solve problems.

The order in which the topics are studied is not very important. Arrange the chapters to suit your needs. However, it is important to allow enough time for doing practice examples. Answers are provided to help you. The section closes with a Course Revision Test.

You should attempt the four JSCE-level practice examinations on pages 241 to 264 only after completing the review course.

R1 Number and numeration

The first part of this book contains detailed coverage of the following topics in number and numeration:

R1-1 Fractions, decimals, percentages, approximations

Example 1

Simplify $\frac{5}{9} \div (1\frac{3}{8} - \frac{1}{3})$.

First, simplify the brackets.

$$1\frac{3}{8} - \frac{1}{3} = \frac{11}{8} - \frac{1}{3}.$$

$$= \frac{3 \times 11}{24} - \frac{8 \times 1}{24}$$

$$= \frac{33 - 8}{24} = \frac{25}{24}$$

Then, $\frac{5}{9} \div (1\frac{3}{8} - \frac{1}{3}) = \frac{5}{9} \div \frac{25}{24}$

$$= \frac{5}{9} \times \frac{24}{25}$$

$$= \frac{5 \times 3 \times 8}{3 \times 3 \times 5 \times 5}$$

$$= \frac{8}{15}$$

Example 2

4·8 m of cloth costs ₦2 232. Find the cost of 1 m of cloth.

4·8 m costs ₦2 232

1 m costs ₦ $\frac{2232}{4·8}$ = ₦ $\frac{22320}{48}$

working:

$$
\begin{array}{r}
465 \\
48)\overline{22320} \\
\underline{192} \\
31\,2 \\
\underline{28\,8} \\
2\,40 \\
\underline{2\,40} \\
\end{array}
$$

1 m of cloth costs ₦465.

Example 3

In one year, a hospital admitted 1 525 patients. 671 of these were treated for malaria. What percentage is this?

Fraction with malaria = $\frac{671}{1525}$

Percentage with malaria = $\frac{671}{1525} \times 100$

$$= \frac{671 \times 4}{61}$$

$$= 11 \times 4 = 44$$

44% had malaria.

Example 4

Round off the following numbers to 2 decimal places: *a*   62·0937,   *b*   0·0850.

a   62·0937 = 62·09 (2 d.p.)
b   0·0850 = 0·09 (2 d.p.)

Example 5

Round off the following numbers to 2 significant figures:
a   0·05386,   *b*   6175·28.

a   0·05386 = 0·054 (2 s.f.)
b   6175·28 = 6200 (2 s.f.)

Exercise R1a

① Simplify the following.

   a $1\frac{4}{5} + 3\frac{1}{2}$ b $5\frac{2}{3} - 3\frac{1}{4}$

   c $6\frac{7}{8} + 1\frac{2}{3}$ d $4\frac{1}{6} - 2\frac{5}{8}$

② Simplify the following.

   a $3\frac{3}{4} \times 2\frac{2}{5}$ b $\frac{3}{4}$ of $9\frac{1}{3}$

   c $1\frac{1}{2} \times 1\frac{1}{3}$ d $\frac{7}{8}$ of $5\frac{1}{3}$

③ Simplify the following.

   a $4\frac{1}{3} \div 1\frac{1}{12}$ b $\frac{8}{15} \div \frac{2}{3}$

   c $3\frac{1}{7} \div 3\frac{2}{3}$ d $1\frac{3}{5} \div 2\frac{2}{3}$

④ Simplify the following.

   a $\frac{4}{5}$ of $\left(\frac{1}{2} + \frac{2}{3}\right)$ b $1\frac{3}{11} \times \left(1\frac{1}{2} + \frac{6}{7}\right)$

   c $\frac{4}{9} \div \left(\frac{1}{5} + 1\frac{2}{3}\right)$ d $6\frac{1}{3} \div \left(4\frac{5}{6} - 3\frac{1}{4}\right)$

⑤ Complete the following.

   a   ₦470 + ₦145 =   b   1·207 + 3·995 =
   c   6·4 − 0·57 =   d   ₦1550 − ₦999 =

⑥ Find the value of the following.

   a   0·3 × 15   b   ₦945 × 8
   c   6·5 × 2·6   d   3·92 × 0·44

⑦ Find the value of the following.

   a   26 ÷ 1·3   b   6 ÷ 0·015
   c   0·612 ÷ 3·4   d   14·56 ÷ 0·52

⑧ Find:

   a   28% of 675   b   15% of $8\frac{1}{3}$

   c   8% of ₦2750   d $2\frac{1}{2}$% of 6kg

⑨ Express the following fractions as percentages.

   a $\frac{3}{5}$ b $\frac{19}{25}$

   c $\frac{5}{8}$ d $\frac{2}{3}$

   e   0·54   f   0·03
   g   0·225   h $0·\dot{3}$

⑩ Express
   a   9mm as a percentage of 2cm,
   b   ₦12 as a percentage of ₦400,
   c   165g as a percentage of 1kg,
   d   20min as a percentage of 2h.

⑪ a   Express 0·275 as a fraction in its lowest terms.
   b   Calculate the exact value of $\frac{6·75 \times 7·5}{0·375}$.

⑫ a   Express 15 as a percentage of 40.
   b   Increase 80 by 20 per cent.

⑬ Find the exact value of the following.

   a $\frac{60 \times 217}{868}$ b $\frac{0·05 \times 50}{2·5}$

⑭ Simplify a $\frac{0·01 \times 0·4}{0·0002}$, b $1\frac{1}{2} + 2\frac{1}{3} \times \frac{3}{4} - \frac{1}{2}$.

⑮ a   Simplify $\frac{1}{2}$ of $\frac{3}{4} + \frac{5}{12}$.
   b   A person's salary increases from ₦185000 to ₦207200. Find the increase per cent.

⑯ Arrange the following fractions in order from lowest to highest: $\frac{4}{5}, \frac{9}{10}, \frac{3}{4}, \frac{17}{20}$.

⑰ Find the product of $1\frac{3}{8}$ and the reciprocal of the positive difference between 9 and $\frac{3}{4}$.

⑱ A woman spends $\frac{1}{3}$ of her pay on food and $\frac{1}{5}$ on rent. What fraction of her pay is left?

⑲ A school day consists of eight lessons of 40 minutes. Each day an average of 28min is spent walking between classes.
What percentage of the school day is used this way?

⑳ The population of a UBE school increases from 400 to 1000. What is the percentage increase in the population of the school?

㉑ Round off the following numbers to 2 decimal places:

   a   2·753   b   35·289
   c   157·0648

㉒ Round off to 2 s.f.:
  a 0·00345   b 59·0742
  c 2·175   d 61248

㉓ Round off to 1 s.f.:
  a 59·7   b 18·02
  c 16984   d 0·06873

㉔ Approximate to 3 s.f.:
  a 0·002438   b 54295·7124
  c 0·021638

㉕ Round off each of the following numbers to the degree of accuracy shown in the brackets:
  a 7·3849 (3 d.p.)   b 56·0582 (2 d.p.)
  c 144 (1 s.f.)   d 43·628 (3 s.f.)
  e 43·628 (2 s.f.)

R1·2 Ratio, rate, proportion

Example 6

Two sons are aged 19 years and 17 years. 216 cows are shared between them in the ratio of their ages. How many cows does each get?

Ratio of sons' ages $= 19 : 17$
Thus, number of shares $= 19 + 17 = 36$

$$1 \text{ share} = \frac{216}{36} \text{ cows}$$
$$= 6 \text{ cows}$$

19 shares $= 19 \times 6$ cows $= 114$ cows
17 shares $= 17 \times 6$ cows $= 102$ cows
The sons get 114 and 102 cows respectively.

Example 7

A car uses petrol at the rate of 1 litre per 7 km travelled. When petrol was ₦70 per litre, what was the cost of petrol for a journey of 265 km?

7 km need 1 ℓ, of petrol
1 km needs $\frac{1}{7}$ ℓ, of petrol

265 km need $\frac{265}{7}$ ℓ, of petrol

1 litre cost ₦70

$\frac{265}{7}$ l cost $\frac{265}{7} \times$ ₦70

$$= \frac{265 \times 70}{7} \text{ naira}$$
$$= 265 \times 10 \text{ naira}$$
$$= ₦2650$$

The petrol cost ₦2650.

Example 8

A bucket, when full, contains enough water to fill 27 cups, each of capacity 400 ml. How many cups, each of capacity 360 ml, will the bucket fill?

This is an example of inverse proportion (the smaller the capacity of the cups, the greater the number of cups). Comparing capacities,

big cup : small cup $= 400 \text{ m}\ell : 360 \text{ m}l$
$$= 40 : 36$$
$$= 10 : 9$$

number of 400 mℓ cups $= 27$

number of 360 mℓ cups $= \frac{10}{9} \times 27$
$$= 10 \times 3$$
$$= 30$$

Exercise R1b

① Two traders share a 50 kg sack of rice in the ratio 14 : 11. How much does each get?

② Two women share 54 eggs in the ratio 2 : 7. How many eggs does each get?

③ The number of boys in a mixed school is 280. The ratio of boys to girls is 4 : 5. Find the total number of students in the school.

④ A map has a scale of 1 cm to 5 km. The scale is given as the ratio 1 : n.
What is the value of n?

⑤ A rubber band of length 9·5 cm is stretched to a length of 20·9 cm. Find the ratio, *stretched length : unstretched length*, in its simplest terms.

⑥ Ali and Ojo invest ₦70 000 and ₦140 000 in a business. The profit is shared between them in the ratio of their investment. The profit in the first year is ₦51 840.
How much does each get?

⑦ A metal is made of copper and zinc in the

ratio 3 : 2 by volume. 1 cm³ of copper has a mass of 8·9 g and 1 cm³ of zinc has a mass of 7·1 g. Find the mass of 100 cm³ of the metal.

8 A car uses 30 litres of petrol for a journey of 240 km. How many litres will it use for a journey of 300 km?

9 In 2008, US$1 was equivalent to ₦120. What was the value, in dollars and cents, of ₦5 700?

10 1 cm³ of a metal has a mass of 7·29 g. Find the mass of 200 cm³ of the metal in kg.

11 A container holds 20 litres. It is filled with liquid of density 0·8 kg per litre. What is the mass of the liquid?

12 I can ride a bicycle at a rate of 5 m/s. How many minutes will it take me to ride 12 km at the same rate?

13 The pace of a student is 0·625 m. She walks at the rate of 84 paces per minute.
a How far does she walk in 1 minute?
b How long does she take to walk 7·2 km, to the nearest minute?

14 Muhammad cycled for x km and then walked for $\frac{1}{2}$ hour at a rate of 6 km/h. At the end of that time he had gone 10 km altogether. Find the value of x.

15 A car uses petrol at the rate of 1 litre for every 6 km travelled. When petrol cost ₦66 per litre, the car used ₦7 920 worth of petrol for a certain journey.
How long was the journey?

16 The time taken to do a piece of work is inversely proportional to the number of people doing it. 25 people take 6 days. How long will 10 people take?

17 Five people can do a piece of work in 6 days. How many days, to the nearest whole number, should eight people take to do it?

18 A roll of wire can be cut into six pieces, each of length 24 m. How many pieces, each 9 m long, can be cut from the wire?

19 A hotel lift can safely carry eight adults of average mass 85 kg. How many children of average mass 34 kg can it carry?

20 A girl cycles a certain distance at 16 km/h and takes 2 h 30 min. How long does she take if her speed is 15 km/h?

R1-3 Standard form

Example 9
Express 0·000 33 in standard form.

$$0·000 33 = \frac{3·3}{10 000} = \frac{3·3}{10^4} = 3·3 \times 10^{-4}$$

Example 10
Divide $6·3 \times 10^3$ by $8·0 \times 10^{-5}$, giving the answer in standard form correct to 2 significant figures.

$$(6·3 \times 10^3) \div (8·0 \times 10^{-5})$$
$$= \frac{6·3}{8} \times 10^{3 - (-5)}$$
$$= 0·787\,5 \times 10^8$$
$$= 0·787\,5 \times 10 \times 10^7$$
$$= 7·875 \times 10^7$$
$$= 7·9 \times 10^7 \text{ to 2 s.f.}$$

Exercise R1c

1 Express the following in standard form.
   a 526 000   b 0·000 706 3

2 Express the following in standard form.
   a 0·001 45   b 14·500

3 Change the following to ordinary form.
   a $1·67 \times 10^4$ b $4·55 \times 10^{-2}$

4 Express $1·56 \times 10^4$ as a whole number correct to 2 significant figures.

5 $0·000 005 257 = a \times 10^n$, where a is between 1 and 10 and n is an integer.
Write down the values of a and n, giving a correct to 3 significant figures.

6 If $\dfrac{3 \times 10^4}{8 \times 10^{-2}} = 3·75 \times 10^n$, what is the value of n?

7 Find the value of $25 \times 0·005\,3$, giving the answer in standard form correct to 3 significant figures.

8 Simplify $2.5 \times 10^3 \times 8.0 \times 10^5$ and give the answer in standard form.

9 Calculate the following, giving each answer in standard form.
   a 375×260
   b 600^2
   c $7 \times 10^9 \times 3.2 \times 10^{-3}$
   d $(4.8 \times 10^3) \div (5 \times 10^{-3})$

10 Calculate $4.355 \div 0.25$ and express your answer in standard form.

R1-4 Personal arithmetic (shopping, interest, tax)

Exercise R1d

1 Table R1.1 gives the market prices of gari and melon seed for four towns.

	local measure	Benin	Auchi	Agbor	Sapele
gari	*adana*	₦65	₦65	₦60	₦75
melon seed	milk cup	₦30	₦30	₦40	₦40

Table R1.1

   a Find the cost of buying 1 *adana* of gari and 4 milk cups of melon seed i in Benin, ii in Agbor.
   b In Auchi a woman buys 1 *adana* of gari and 2 milk cups of melon seed. How much change does she get from ₦200?
   c A Sapele woman visits Benin for the day. She brings back 5 *adana* of gari. How much does she save?
   d Approximately how many milk cups of melon seed can be bought for the cost of 1 *adana* of gari?
   e Find the average cost of 1 *adana* of gari for the four towns.
   f Find the average cost of 1 milk cup of melon seed for the four towns.

2 Tins of insect killer sell at ₦200 for 200 g and ₦340 for 400 g. A house uses about 200 g each week. Find how much is saved in a year if the bigger tins are used.

3 A parcel of land is sold for ₦180 000. The buyer pays 30% of the cost from his savings and borrows the rest. How much money does he borrow?

4 Calculate the simple interest on ₦20 000 for 4 years at 3% per annum.

5 What will ₦100 000 amount to if it is saved for $8\frac{1}{2}$ years at 7% per annum simple interest?

6 A man invests £2 500 at 5% simple interest for 4 years. How much does his investment come to by the end of this period?

7 The simple interest on ₦20 000 for 2 years is ₦2 000. Find the percentage rate per annum at which the interest is charged.

8 I bought an article for ₵1 240 in Ghana. I paid an import duty of 50% when I returned to Nigeria. If ₦1 = ₵4, what was the total cost of the article in Nigerian money?

9 The quarterly readings of an electricity meter are as follows:

1st quarter	2nd quarter	3rd quarter	4th quarter
7 537	12 659	15 938	21 365

The reading at the beginning of the 1st quarter was 3 398. Find the number of units of electricity used in each quarter.

10 The cost of electricity per month is calculated on a two-part rate: ₦600 fixed charge and ₦85 for each unit used. If a house uses 40 units, what is the bill?

11 Income tax allowances are given as follows:

personal	₦24 000
children	₦2 500 per child
dep. relative	maximum of ₦4 000

A person with four children has a salary of ₦216 320. Calculate
   a the total allowances assuming an allowance of ₦3 500 for a dependent relative,
   b the taxable income.

12 Tax is paid on taxable income as follows:

first ₦25 000	5%
next ₦25 000	10%
next ₦50 000	15%
next ₦50 000	20%
any further income	25%

Calculate the tax paid by a person with a taxable income of ₦177 160.

13 Use the data in questions 11 and 12 to find the 'take home' salary of the following:
  a a single person with a salary of ₦300 000 per annum:
  b the person in question 11;
  c someone with three children and no dependent relative, whose annual salary is ₦97 040.

14 A bicycle costs ₦17 700. A 10% discount is given for cash. On the other hand, the bicycle can be bought by paying 52 weekly instalments of ₦426.
  a Find the cash price.
  b Find the instalment price.
  c Hence find the saving by paying cash.

15 Palm oil sells at ₦1 296 for a kerosene tin and ₦75 for a bottle. A kerosene tin holds 18 bottles. Two women share a kerosene tin of oil equally.
  a How many bottles of oil does each get?
  b What is the saving for each woman on this amount?

16 Find the compound interest on ₦50 000 for 2 years at 7% per annum.

17 A man borrows ₦300 000. He is charged compound interest at 8% per annum. He repays ₦120 000 at the end of the first year and at the end of the second year. How much does he owe at the beginning of the third year?

18 A car depreciates in value by about 25% of its value at the beginning of each year. If a car cost ₦500 000 two years ago, find its value now, to the nearest ₦1 000.

R1-5 Commercial arithmetic (profit and loss, discount, hire purchase, commission)

Example 11

A trader makes a gain of 5% when he sells a motor bike for ₦336 000. If he sells it for ₦307 200, what is his gain or loss per cent?

₦336 000 includes a 5% gain.

$$105\% \text{ of cost price} = ₦336 000$$

$$1\% \text{ of cost price} = ₦\frac{336 000}{105}$$

$$100\% \text{ of cost price} = ₦\frac{336 000}{105} \times 100$$

$$= ₦320 000$$

$$\text{Cost price} = ₦320 000$$

$$\text{Second selling price} = ₦307 200$$

$$\text{Loss} = ₦320 000 - ₦307 200$$

$$= ₦12 800$$

$$\text{Loss \%} = \frac{12 800}{320 000} \times 100$$

$$= \frac{128}{32} = 4$$

He makes a 4% loss when he sells for ₦307 200.

Example 12

A gas cooker costs ₦31 500. During a sale, the price is reduced by 11k in the ₦ and rounded to the nearest ₦100. Find the sale price.

$$\text{Reduction} = 31 500 \times 11k$$

$$= 346 500k$$

$$= ₦3 465$$

$$\text{Sale price} = ₦31 500 - ₦3 465$$

$$= ₦28 035$$

$$= ₦28 000 \text{ to the nearest ₦100}$$

Exercise R1e

1 A trader buys five electric fans for a total of ₦10 600. He sells them all at ₦2 700 each. Find a his actual profit, b his percentage profit.

2 By selling an article for ₦560, a trader gained 12%. How much money did she gain?

③ By selling a cup of beans for ₦60, a trader makes a profit of 20%.
For how much did she buy the beans?

④ A trader makes a loss of 10% when he sells a TV set for ₦54 000. If he had sold it for ₦57 600, what would have been his percentage loss or gain?

⑤ By selling an article for ₦3 500, a shopkeeper lost 30%. How much should she have sold it for to gain 30%?

⑥ A trader fixes his selling prices by adding a basic charge of ₦500 to a 10% gain on cost price.
  a Find the selling price and profit on an article costing ₦7 000.
  b Find the profit and cost price on an article selling for ₦12 600.

⑦ A trader gives a 10% discount for cash payments. How much would a customer pay in cash for a television that originally cost ₦24 000?

⑧ A trader gives a 5% discount for cash payments. What cash discount will she give on a bill of ₦3 040?

⑨ A trader asks ₦2 300 for a large tin of groundnut oil. After bargaining with a woman customer, he agrees to sell it for four-fifths of his asking price. How much money does she save by bargaining?

⑩ A refrigerator costs ₦28 500. During a sale, the price is reduced by 15k in the naira and then rounded to the nearest ₦100.
Find the sale price.

⑪ The hire purchase price of a home cinema is ₦78 000. 20% of this is paid as a deposit. The rest is spread over 24 equal monthly instalments. Calculate
  a the amount of the deposit,
  b the remainder to be paid,
  c the amount of each monthly instalment.

⑫ The price of a small bus is ₦796 400. To pay by hire purchase requires a 20% deposit and 36 monthly payments of ₦22 120. On the other hand, if cash is paid, the dealer takes ₦47 400 off the price.

  a Find the cash price.
  b Find the total cost when paying by hire purchase.
  c Find the saving by paying in cash.

⑬ A furniture salesman gets a commission of 12k in the naira. In one week he sells three tables at ₦4 620 each and two beds at ₦6 360 each.
How much is his total commission?

⑭ A saleswoman is paid ₦3 200 per week plus 4k in the ₦ commission on her sales. How much does she get for a week in which she sells ₦77 000 worth of goods?

⑮ A rent collector gets a basic wage of ₦2 800 per week. To this is added $4\frac{1}{2}$% of the rents that he collects. Find his pay for a week in which he collects ₦58 400 in rents.

R1-6 Number bases

Example 13

Convert 46_{ten} to a number in base two.

```
2 | 46
2 | 23 + 0  ↑
2 | 11 + 1  |
2 |  5 + 1  |
2 |  2 + 1  |
2 |  1 + 0  |
      0 + 1  |
```

101110_{two}

$46_{ten} = 101110_{two}$

Example 14

Change 11101_{two} to a number in base ten.

$$11101_{two} = 1 \times 2^4 + 1 \times 2^3 + 1 \times 2^2$$
$$+ 0 \times 2 + 1$$
$$= 16 + 8 + 4 + 0 + 1$$
$$= 29$$

Exercise R1f

① Convert the following base ten numbers to numbers in base two:
a 41, b 65, c 88, d 121, e 256.

2 Convert the following base two numbers to
  numbers in base ten:
  a 1111_{two}, b 111011_{two}, c 11111_{two},
  d 1110011_{two}.

3 Convert each of the following numbers to
  numbers in base ten:
  a 35_{six}, b 124_{five}, c 27_{eight}, d 1032_{four}, e 212_{three}

4 Add:
  a $1110_{two} + 1101_{two}$
  b $123_{four} + 302_{four}$
  c $304_{five} + 1243_{five}$

5 Find the value of the following:
  a $111_{two} \times 101_{two}$
  b $(11_{two})^2$
  c $101_{two} \times 11_{two}$

Counting Cattle

A herdboy counts his cattle. When he
counts them in 3's, there is one left
over. When he counts them in 5's there
are two left over.
a) How many cattle might he have?
b) Investigate the possible numbers of
   cattle he could have.
c) Suggest a rule.

Highest Product?

We can use the digits 1, 2, 3, 4, 5 to
make various products:

  321 x 54, 543 x 21, 42 x 531,
  5 x 43 x 21, 5 x 4 x 13 x 2

and so on.
a) Use a calculator to find the
   arrangement of these digits that
   gives the highest product.
b) Extend the digits to 1, 2, 3, 4, 5, 6.
c) Try to find a rule.

R2-1 Use of letters

Exercise R2a

1. A herdsman sells x rams and y goats. He makes a profit of ₦1 100 on a ram and ₦800 on a goat. Write down an expression in x and y for his total profit.

2. A girl is x years old. Her mother's age is 10 years more than twice her age.
   What is the mother's age in terms of x?

3. Express n metres k cm in a cm, b metres.

4. A baker makes 120 loaves and sells them all for x naira each.
   How much money does the baker make?

5. The price of rice is ₦x per kg.
   How many kg can be bought for ₦2 000?

6. In a class of p students, the average mark is n. Find the total number of marks scored.

7. The perimeter of a square is p cm. Find an expression for its area in terms of p.

8. The area of a square is A cm². Find an expression for its perimeter in terms of A.

9. Rice costs t cents per cup. How many cups can I buy with p dollars?

10. From a piece of wire, L metres long, 25 pieces, each of length m cm are cut. What length of wire, in metres, is left?

11. A boy lives 4 km from school. Find the time, in minutes, that he takes to walk to school if his average speed is $\frac{6x}{11}$ km/h.

12. A car travels with an average speed of u km/h. How far does it travel in t hours?

13. Two cars start together and travel in the same direction along a road. The faster car has an average speed of u km/h and the other, v km/h.
    How far ahead is the faster car after t hours?

14. Express the mean of $2x$, $x - 2$ and 17 as simply as possible.

15. The perimeter of a rectangle is 30 cm and its length is x cm.
    Find a its breadth, b its area in terms of x.

R2-2 Linear equations and inequalities

Example 1

Solve $\dfrac{1}{1 - 2x} - \dfrac{3}{24 + x} = 0$.

The common denominator of the two fractions is $(1 - 2x)(24 + x)$. Multiply each term by $(1 - 2x)(24 + x)$.

$$\frac{1 \times (1 - 2x)(24 + x)}{(1 - 2x)} - \frac{3 \times (1 - 2x)(24 + x)}{(24 + x)}$$

$$= 0 \times (1 - 2x)(24 + x)$$
$$1 \times (24 + x) - 3 \times (1 - 2x) = 0$$

Clear brackets

$$24 + x - 3 + 6x = 0$$

Collect terms

$$21 + 7x = 0$$
$$7x = -21$$

Divide both sides by 7

$$x = -3$$

Example 2

x is a whole number. When 64 is divided by twice x, the result is greater than 5. Find the three highest values of x.

Twice x is $2x$.

64 divided by twice x is $\frac{64}{2x}$.

$\frac{64}{2x} > 5$ (from the 2nd sentence)

Multiply both sides by $2x$.

$$64 > 10x$$
$$\text{or } 10x, < 64$$

thus, $x, < \frac{64}{10}$

$$x, < 6\cdot4$$

Since x is a whole number, the three highest values of x are 4, 5 and 6.

Exercise R2b

① Solve the following equations.

a $x + 9 = 14$ b $x - 9 = 2$
c $20 = 7 + x$ d $1 = x - 10$
e $2 = x + 2$ f $2 = x - 2$

② Solve the following equations.

a $8x = 48$ b $3x = 39$
c $8x + 3 = 51$ d $3x - 2 = 37$
e $19 = 5x + 4$ f $6x - 9 = 17$
g $5 + 3d = 26$ h $3 = 7b - 11$
i $2x - 3 = 7$ j $2x - 3 = 0$

③ Solve the following equations.

a $5x + 7 = 10$ b $4x - 3 = 5$
c $1 = 7a - 5$ d $3 + 14x = 38$

④ Solve the following equations.

a $7 + 8a = a$
b $7 - 5y = 22$
c $5x = x + 20$
d $4c - 12 = c$
e $9x + 4 = 2x + 25$
f $10y + 8 = y - 19$
g $3a + 3 = 35 - 5a$
h $17 - 4f = 3f + 3$

⑤ Solve the following equations.

a $2(x - 5) = 8$
b $3(x + 5) = 18$
c $21 = 7(2f - 5)$
d $4(x + 9) = 0$
e $2(x - 5) = x - 7$
f $x - 9 = 5(x + 3)$
g $2(x - 2) + 5(x - 9) = 0$
h $7(x - 1) = 4(x + 2)$
i $9(x + 7) = 4(5x + 2)$
j $2(2 + 5x) - 7(1 + x) - 3 = 0$

⑥ Solve the following equations.

a $\frac{x}{9} = 2$ b $\frac{x}{4} = \frac{1}{2}$

c $\frac{7 + x}{2} = 1$ d $3 = \frac{x - 8}{6}$

e $\frac{x}{5} - \frac{x}{8} = 6$ f $\frac{35}{27} = \frac{2x}{3} + \frac{x}{9}$

g $\frac{x + 2}{3} + 2x = 10$

h $\frac{3x + 2}{5} - \frac{2x + 3}{3} = 3$

⑦ Solve the following equations.

a $\frac{45}{72} = \frac{40}{x}$ b $\frac{42}{x} = \frac{12}{20}$

c $\frac{3}{10} = \frac{1}{x} + \frac{1}{10}$ d $\frac{7}{2x} - \frac{1}{x} = \frac{1}{4}$

e $\frac{5}{2 + x} = 2$ f $8 = \frac{24}{1 - b}$

g $\frac{1}{x} = \frac{5}{4x + 7}$ h $\frac{2}{3a + 2} = \frac{1}{a + 3}$

i $\frac{8 - d}{2d - 1} = \frac{4}{7}$ j $\frac{2}{t + 1} - \frac{5}{3t - 1} = 0$

⑧ Find the range of values of x for which each of the following inequalities holds.

a $x + 2 > 0$ b $x + 2 < 0$
c $5 - 2x > 0$ d $5 - 2x < 0$
e $2x - 3 < 7$ f $x - 2 < 6 - 3x$

g $3x - 5 < 5x - 3$ **h** $2x + 6 < 5(x - 3)$

i $2x - 2 < \dfrac{x + 5}{2}$

j $\dfrac{x + 2}{5} \geqslant \dfrac{x - 3}{3} + 1$

⑨ I think of a number. I take away 14. The result is 13. What number am I thinking of?

⑩ Charles has ₦500. He buys six mangoes and gets ₦20 change.
Find the average cost of one mango.

⑪ The length of a rectangle is three times its width. The perimeter of the rectangle is 72 cm. Calculate the width of the rectangle.

⑫ I think of a number. I multiply it by 7. I add 12. The result is 40.
What is the number I am thinking of?

⑬ A book has 18 chapters of equal length. Each chapter has six pages.
How many pages does the book have?

⑭ A mother is 28 years older than her son. The mother's age is 10 years more than twice her son's age. What is the son's age?

⑮ A knife has a mass of m grammes. It is 20 g heavier than a spoon. The mass of a knife and four spoons is 330 g.
Find the mass of the knife.

⑯ A roll of cloth contains x metres. A woman who buys $\frac{2}{3}$ of the cloth gets 20 m more than a woman who buys $\frac{1}{4}$ of the cloth.
Find the value of x.

⑰ 54 is divided by the sum of 5 and x. The result is 3. Find x.

⑱ A brother is five years older than his sister. Four years ago the ratio of their ages was 4 : 3. Find their present ages.

⑲ n is a whole number. Write down any three values of n such that $n > 7$ and $n < 12$.

⑳ x is a whole number. Five times x is subtracted from 84. The result is less than −10. Find the three lowest values of x.

R2-3 Simplification, expansion, factorisation

Example 3

Simplify $\dfrac{3(4a - 5) - 2(a - 5)}{6a - 3}$.

Remove brackets from the numerator.

given expression $= \dfrac{12a - 15 - 2a + 10}{6a - 3}$

Collect terms.

given expression $= \dfrac{10a - 5}{6a - 3}$

Factorise numerator and denominator.

given expression $= \dfrac{5(2a - 1)}{3(2a - 1)}$

Divide numerator and denominator by $(2a - 1)$.

given expression $= \dfrac{5}{3} = 1\frac{2}{3}$

$\dfrac{3(4a - 5) - 2(a - 5)}{6a - 3}$ simplifies to $1\frac{2}{3}$.

Example 4

Expand $(x + 7)(x - 3)$.

$$(x + 7)(x - 3) = x(x + 7) - 3(x + 7)$$
$$= x^2 + 7x - 3x - 21$$
$$= x^2 + 4x - 21$$

Example 5

If $V = 503^2 - 497^2$, *use factorisation to find the value of* V.

$503^2 - 497^2$ is a difference of two squares.
Thus, $V = 503^2 - 497^2$
$$= (503 + 497)(503 - 497)$$
$$= 1\,000 \times 6$$
$$= 6\,000$$

Example 6

Factorise $a^2 + 2a - 15$.

$a^2 + 2a - 15 = (a + 5)(a - 3)$
Chapter 9 explains how to factorise quadratic expressions.

Exercise R2c

(1) Simplify the following.

  a $4a + 5a$

  b $7a - 3a$

  c $5x - 2x + 8x$

  d $x - 9x + 4x$

  e $3y \times 2$

  f $7 \times 5y$

  g $4r \times 6s$

  h $8ab \times 2a$

  i $-2a \times -5b$

  j $\dfrac{14a}{7}$

  k $\dfrac{32x^2}{8x}$

  l $\dfrac{-22xy}{2y}$

(2) Simplify the following.

  a $5x - x + 3$

  b $4x - 7 - 2x$

  c $11p + 3q - 5p - 2q$

  d $4h + 8k - 3k - 2h$

  e $3y \times 3 + 6y$

  f $7a \times 3 + 5 \times 2a - 9a \div 3$

  g $a + (b + 2a)$

  h $5x - (2x - y)$

  i $(10a - 3) - (4 - 5a)$

  j $8 - a - (3 + 2a)$

(3) Remove brackets from the following.

  a $4(x + 2y)$

  b $2(a - 5)$

  c $3(5 - 9x)$

  d $(2x + b)5$

  e $(6c - 5)9$

  f $-3(a + 4b)$

  g $-8(x - 2y)$

  h $(3y - z)(-6)$

(4) Remove brackets and simplify the following.

  a $5 + 2(x + 3)$

  b $7z - 5(z - 4)$

  c $2a - 6(1 - 2a)$

  d $4(a - 3b) - b$

  e $2(3x - y) + 3(x + 5y)$

  f $5(a + 2b) - 4(a - 2b)$

  g $a(a + 2) + 5(a + 2)$

  h $x(x - 3) - 5(x - 3)$

(5) Expand the following.

  a $(x + 5)(x + 4)$

  b $(n - 6)(n + 3)$

  c $(c - 3)(c + 7)$

  d $(b - 3)(b - 8)$

  e $(x + 5)^2$

  f $(y - 3)^2$

  g $(3a - b)(2a + 5b)$

  h $(a + 2b)(a - 2b)$

(6) Factorise the following.

  a $8x + 6y$

  b $9a + 3$

  c $ab - ac$

  d $15a - 10b$

  e $2xy + 12xz$

  f $7a^2 - a$

  g $7d^2 + 13d^2e$

  h $24p^2q - 36pq^2$

(7) Simplify the following.

  a $\dfrac{7a}{5} - \dfrac{2z}{5}$

  b $\dfrac{4}{d} + \dfrac{2}{d}$

  c $\dfrac{1}{2y} + \dfrac{2}{y}$

  d $\dfrac{3}{k} + \dfrac{5}{3k}$

  e $\dfrac{6a + 1}{4} + \dfrac{a - 5}{4}$

  f $\dfrac{d - 2}{6} + \dfrac{d + 3}{3}$

(8) Factorise the following.

  a $x(3x + y) - 2(3x + y)$

  b $2a(5 - r) - 5 + r$

  c $x^2 + 3x + 6x + 18$

  d $ac + 2bc + ad + 2bd$

  e $ab - by + b^2 - ay$

  f $ax - a + x - 1$

(9) Factorise the following.

  a $x^2 + 8x + 7$

  b $a^2 + 7a + 10$

  c $b^2 - 18b + 17$

  d $a^2 - 11a + 24$

  e $x^2 + 7x - 18$

  f $x^2 + x - 12$

  g $a^2 - 6a - 7$

  h $x^2 - 2x - 15$

(10) Factorise the following.

  a $x^2 + 6x + 9$

  b $y^2 + 20y + 100$

  c $a^2 - 8a + 16$

  d $d^2 - 14d + 49$

  e $9a^2 - b^2$

  f $c^2 - 81r^2$

  g $4p^2 - 25q^2$

  h $36k^2 - 49t^2$

(11) Simplify $2a - [4a - (5a - 7)]$.

(12) Simplify $\dfrac{5}{2cd} + \dfrac{4}{3de}$.

(13) Simplify $\dfrac{-2x - 6}{3x + 9}$.

(14) a Expand $2a(b + c) - b(c + 2a)$.

   b Simplify, then factorise the result.

(15) Multiply $(3 + a)$ by $(5 - 2a)$.

(16) Simplify $\dfrac{x^2 - y^2}{x + y}$.

(17) Factorise completely $108 - 3x^2$.

(18) a Factorise $x^2 - 4y^2$.

   b Evaluate $49^2 - 39^2$, using factors to help.

   c Evaluate $47^2 + 47 \times 53$, using factors to help.

(19) What value of k will make $x^2 - 18x + k$ a perfect square?

(20) a Expand $(a - b)^2$.

   b Using the fact that $49 \cdot 999 = 50 - 0 \cdot 001$, calculate $49 \cdot 999^2$ correct to one decimal place.

R2-4 Graphs of points and equations

Exercise R2d

① Name the coordinates of the points in Fig. R2.1.

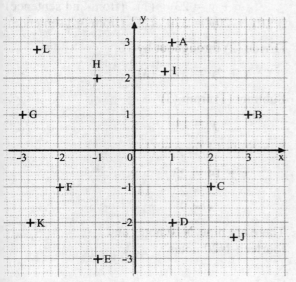

Fig. R2.1

② a Draw a pair of axes, Ox, Oy, such that the origin is near the middle of a page of graph paper.

b Use a scale of 1 cm to 1 unit on both axes and plot the following points.
A(0, −10), B(1, −6), C(1, −4), D(0, 8), E(−2, 6), F(−1, 2), G(−3, 6), H(−2, 8), I(−4, 6), J(−4, 2), K(−5, 7), L(−1, 10), M(−4, 9), N(0, 11), P(2, 11), Q(5, 9), R(6, 4), S(5, 7), T(2, 9), U(4, 6), V(3, 2), W(3, 6), X(1, 8), Y(2, −4), Z(2, −10)

c Join up the points in alphabetical order. What picture have you drawn?

③ a On a new sheet of graph paper, draw axes Ox, Oy such that O is near the middle of the paper.

b Use a scale of 2 cm to 1 unit on both axes and plot the points
A(1, $3\frac{1}{2}$), B($-2\frac{1}{2}$, $5\frac{1}{2}$), C(-3, $1\frac{1}{2}$), D($2\frac{1}{2}$, $-4\frac{1}{2}$).

c Draw quadrilateral ABCD. What kind of quadrilateral is it?

d Draw the diagonals of ABCD. Find the coordinates of their point of intersection.

e Find the coordinates of a point E, such that ABCE is a rhombus.

④ Table R2.1 gives corresponding values of x and y for the equation $y = 2 - 5x$.

x	−3	0	3
y	17	2	−13

Table R2.1

a Using a scale of 2 cm to 1 unit on the x-axis and 2 cm to 5 units on the y-axis, draw the line representing the equation $y = 2 - 5x$.

b Find the value of y when $x = 2\cdot6$.

c Find the value of x when $y = 7\frac{1}{2}$.

⑤ a If $y = 3x - 7$, copy and complete Table R2.2, giving corresponding values of x and y.

x	0	1	2	3	4	5
y	−7	−4				

Table R2.2

b Using a scale of 1 cm to 1 unit on both axes, draw the graph of the equation $y = 3x - 7$.

c Find the value of y when $x = 3\cdot4$.

d Write down the coordinates of the points where the line cuts the axes.

⑥ a Make y the subject of the equation $x + 2y = 2$.

b Hence copy and complete Table R2.3 for the equation $x + 2y = 2$.

x	−4	0	4
y			

Table R2.3

c Using a scale of 2 cm to 1 unit on both axes, draw the graph of $x + 2y = 2$.

d If the line cuts the x and y axes at A and B respectively, measure the size of OÂB.

⑦ a Draw the graph of $y = 2x - 1$ for values of x from -1 to $+3$. Use a scale of $2\,cm$ to 1 unit on both axes.

b On the same axes draw the line $y = 2x$.

c On the same axes, draw the line $2y = 1 - x$.

d What do you notice about the lines you have drawn?

⑧ a On the same axes, draw the lines $y = x + 4$ and $3x + 2y = 3$, using values which correspond to $x = -3, 0, 2$.

b Find the coordinates of the point where the lines cross.

R2-5 Simultaneous equations

Example 7

Solve the simultaneous equations
$3b + 8a - 1 = 0$ *and* $12 - a + 2b = 0$.

Arrange the equations with unknowns in alphabetical order on the LHS of the equals sign.

$$8a + 3b = 1 \qquad (1)$$
$$a - 2b = 12 \qquad (2)$$

Multiply (2) by 8

$$8a - 16b = 96 \qquad (3)$$

Subtract (1) from (3)

$$8a - 16b = 96 \qquad (3)$$
$$8a + 3b = 1 \qquad (1)$$

subtracting, $-19b = 95$

$$b = -\frac{95}{19}$$

$$b = -5$$

Substitute -5 for b in (2)

$$a - (-10) = 12$$
$$a + 10 = 12$$
$$a = 12 - 10$$
$$a = 2$$

$a = 2$ and $b = -5$ are the solutions.

Example 8

I have some ₦10 notes and ₦20 notes in my pocket. I have 23 notes altogether. Their value is ₦370. How many of each note do I have?

Let there be x ₦10 notes and y ₦20 notes.

$$x + y = 23 \qquad (1) \quad \text{(from 2nd sentence)}$$
$$10x + 20y = 370 \qquad (2) \quad \text{(from 3rd sentence)}$$

Divide (2) throughout by 10

$$x + 2y = 37 \qquad (3)$$

Subtract (1) from (3)

$$y = 14$$

Substitute 14 for y in (1)

$$x + 14 = 23$$
$$x = 23 - 14$$
$$x = 9$$

There are nine ₦10 notes and fourteen ₦20 notes.

Exercise R2e

① a If $2x - 3y = 8$, copy and complete Table R2.4.

x	1		0
y		-1	

Table R2.4

b Find which one of the pairs of values in the table is also a solution of $x + y = -1$.

② Draw graphs, or use calculation, to solve the following.

a $3x + y = 7$
  $x + y = 5$

b $x - y = 2$
  $2x + y = 7$

c $5x + y = 3$
  $2x + y = 0$

d $p + q = 8$
  $p - q = 5$

③ Solve the following.

a $x + 2y = 0$
  $2x + y = 3$

b $4a + 2y = 13$
  $3a - y = 6$

c $2x + y = 1$
  $x - 3y = 1$

d $p + q = \frac{1}{4}$
  $5p + 2q = 2$

e $2a - 3b + 2 = 0$ f $2x + 3y - 5 = 0$
  $3a + 2b - 23 = 0$ $5x - 2y + 16 = 0$

④ A boy is 3 years older than his sister. The sum of their ages is 31 years. Find their ages.

⑤ A rectangle is 5 cm longer that it is broad. Its perimeter is 26 cm. Find the length and breadth of the rectangle.

⑥ Three books and two pencils have a mass of 430 g. One of the books and four of the pencils have a mass of 210 g. Find the mass of each book and each pencil.

⑦ Four knives and six forks cost ₦520. Six knives and five forks cost ₦620. Find the cost of a a knife, b a fork.

⑧ A girl buys some ₦20 stamps and some ₦50 stamps. They cost ₦230 altogether and she gets seven stamps. Find how many of each stamp she gets.

R2-6 Formulae, substitution, variation

Exercise R2f

① Find the value of the following when $x = 3$, $y = 5$ and $z = -2$.
   a $x + y$ b $x + z$ c $x - y$
   d $y + z$ e $y - z$ f $2x + 3z$

   g $\dfrac{z}{x + y}$ h $\dfrac{4x + z}{y}$ i $\dfrac{1}{x} + \dfrac{1}{z}$

   j xyz k $xy - yz$ l $\sqrt{x(y + z)}$

② Find the value of the following when $x = -7$ and $y = 3$.

   a $\dfrac{x + y}{x - y}$ b $xy - 5x$ c $\dfrac{x^2 + y^2}{2}$

③ If $y = \dfrac{3x + 2}{x + 3}$, find y when $x = 4$.

④ Evaluate $\dfrac{1}{a} + \dfrac{2}{b} + \dfrac{3}{c}$ when $a = 2$, $b = 4$ and $c = \frac{2}{3}$.

⑤ Find the value of $2\pi \sqrt{\dfrac{l}{g}}$ when $\pi = 3\frac{1}{7}$, $l = 98$ and $g = 32$.

⑥ If $p^2 = q^2 + r^2$, what is the value of r when $p = 61$ and $q = 60$?

⑦ If $\dfrac{1}{f} = \dfrac{1}{u} + \dfrac{1}{v}$, use reciprocal tables to find f when $v = 3 \cdot 9$ and $u = 5 \cdot 2$.

⑧ If $\dfrac{1}{R} = \dfrac{1}{X} + \dfrac{1}{Y}$, use reciprocal tables to find R when $X = 215$ and $Y = 445$.

⑨ After t hours, a cyclist's distance, s km, from his starting point is given by $s = 15t$. Find a his distance after 3 hours, b how long it takes him to cycle 20 km.

⑩ If $L = \dfrac{kn^2}{d}$, express n in terms of d, k and L.

⑪ If $H = \dfrac{mv^2}{2gx}$, express v in terms of H, m, g and x.

⑫ If $I = \dfrac{E}{WL}$, obtain an expression for W in terms of I, E and L.

⑬ Make t the subject of the formula $a = \dfrac{k \sqrt{t}}{s}$.

⑭ Make t the subject of the formula $\dfrac{3vT}{t} = u$.

⑮ If $4q - qr = 1$, express q in terms of r.

⑯ Make C the subject of the formula $p^2 = Ct - k^2t^2$.

⑰ The length of the hypotenuse of a right-angled triangle is 1 cm and the length of one of the other two sides is x cm. Express the length of the remaining side in terms of x.

⑱ The formula $F = \dfrac{9C}{5} + 32$ shows the relationship between temperature in degrees Fahrenheit (F) and degrees Celsius (C).
   a Find F when $C = 40$.
   b Find C when $F = 100$.

⑲ The area, A, of $\triangle XYZ$ is given by the formula $A = \frac{1}{2}xy \sin Z$.
   a Make $\sin Z$ the subject of the formula.
   b Find $\sin Z$ when $A = 20$, $x = 10$ and $y = 8$.

⑳ W varies directly with d. If $W = 5$ when $d = 35$, find W in terms of d.

㉑ The time, t seconds, taken to travel a given distance varies inversely with the speed, v m/s. If $t = 2$ when $v = 5$, find t in terms of v.

㉒ If x varies directly with y and inversely with

z, use symbols to write a statement about the variation between x, y and z.

23 Two quantities, P and Q, are connected by the relationship $P = kQ + c$, where k and c are constants. $Q = 60$ when $P = 10$ and $Q = 240$ when $P = 100$.
Find the equation connecting P and Q.

24 The speed, V km/h, of a train t seconds after the brakes are put on, is given by
$V = a + bt$, where a and b are constants.
When $t = 0$, $V = 40$ and when $t = 8$, $V = 30$.
a Find a and b.
b Hence calculate V when $t = 10$.
c Calculate t when $V = 24$.

25 The cost of hiring a taxi is partly constant and partly varies directly with the distance travelled. It costs ₦500 for a journey of 10 km and ₦650 for a journey of 15 km.
a Find the formula connecting the cost, ₦C, with the distance travelled, d km.
b Hence find the cost of a 7 km taxi journey.

Bottle Packing Problem

Here is a plan view of a crate that can hold 24 soda bottles:

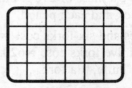

a) Place 18 bottles in the crate so that each row and each column has an even number of bottles in it.
b) Find 3 different ways of doing this.
c) Is it possible to do it with 17 bottles?

Boys, girls, chairs

Place 7 chairs in a row and get 3 boys and 3 girls to sit on them as shown~:

Problem: change over the boys and girls according to these rules:
a) a student can move into an adjacent empty chair,
b) a student can jump over one adjacent student of the opposite sex into an empty chair,
c) no backward moves are allowed.

What is the minimum number of moves needed?

R3 Geometry and mensuration

CHAPTER COVERAGE

The first part of this book contains detailed coverage of the following topics in geometry and mensuration:

R3-1 Length, area, volume

Example 1

The diagonals of a rhombus are 14 cm *and* 10 cm *long. Calculate its area.*

Fig. R3.1 shows that the diagonals divide the rhombus into four equal right-angled triangles.

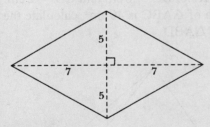

Fig. R3.1

Area of any one triangle $= \frac{1}{2} \times 5 \times 7\,\text{cm}^2$

Area of rhombus $= 4 \times \frac{1}{2} \times 5 \times 7\,\text{cm}^2$

$\qquad\qquad\quad = 70\,\text{cm}^2$

Example 2

In Fig. R3.2, calculate the area of QRST.

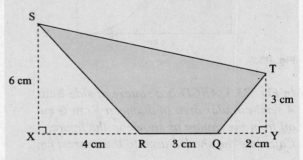

Fig. R3.2

Area of QRST = area of trapezium TYXS
$\qquad\qquad$ − (area of △SXR + area of △TYQ)

Area of trapezium TYXS

$\qquad\qquad = \frac{1}{2}(3 + 6) \times \text{XY cm}^2$

$\qquad\qquad = \frac{1}{2}(3 + 6) \times 9\,\text{cm}^2$

$\qquad\qquad = \frac{1}{2} \times 9 \times 9\,\text{cm}^2$

$\qquad\qquad = 40\frac{1}{2}\,\text{cm}^2$

Area of △SXR $= \frac{1}{2} \times 4 \times 6\,\text{cm}^2$

$\qquad\qquad\;\; = 12\,\text{cm}^2$

Area of △TYQ $= \frac{1}{2} \times 2 \times 3\,\text{cm}^2$

$\qquad\qquad\;\; = 3\,\text{cm}^2$

Area of QRST $= 40\frac{1}{2}\,\text{cm}^2 - (12 + 3)\,\text{cm}^2$

$\qquad\qquad\;\; = 40\frac{1}{2}\,\text{cm}^2 - 15\,\text{cm}^2$

$\qquad\qquad\;\; = 25\frac{1}{2}\,\text{cm}^2$

Example 3

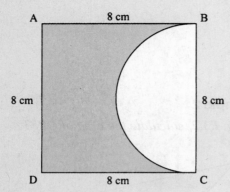

Fig. R3.3

In Fig. R3.3, ABCD is a square of side 8 cm. A semi-circular area of diameter 8 cm is cut off from the square as shown in the figure. Calculate the shaded area to the nearest cm².

Area of square $= 8 \times 8 \text{ cm}^2$
$$= 64 \text{ cm}^2$$

Area of semi-circular shape
$$= \tfrac{1}{2}\pi \left(\tfrac{8}{2}\right)^2 \text{cm}^2$$
$$= 8\pi \text{ cm}^2$$
$$= \frac{8 \times 22}{7} = 25 \cdot 14 \text{ cm}^2$$

Shaded area $= (64 - 25\cdot14)\text{ cm}^2$
$$= 39 \text{ cm}^2 \text{ (to the nearest cm}^2\text{)}$$

Exercise R3a

Use the value $\frac{22}{7}$ for π unless told otherwise.

1. A bicycle wheel has a diameter of 63 cm. Find **a** its circumference, **b** the distance the wheel travels in 1 000 revolutions.

2. A car wheel has a radius of 28 cm. How many revolutions does it make in going 4·4 km?

3. If the circumference of a circle is 11 m, calculate its radius.

4. What is the area of the shape in Fig. R3.4?

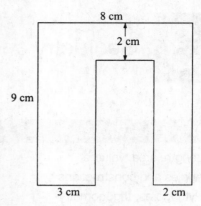

Fig. R3.4

5. The height, width and length of a closed rectangular box are 10 cm, 4 cm and 5 cm respectively.
Find the total surface area of the box.

6. The diagonals of a rhombus are 8 cm and 6 cm long. What is the area of the rhombus?

7. If the diagonals of a square are 8 cm long, what is the area of the square?

8. In Fig. R3.5, PQRS is a rectangle. Calculate **a** ST, **b** the area of PQRT.

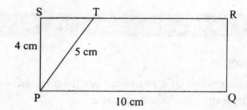

Fig. R3.5

9. In Fig. R3.6, BC = 8 cm and CD = 2 cm. If the area of △ABC is 40 cm², calculate the area of △ABD.

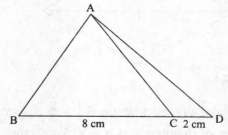

Fig. R3.6

10 The floor of a round house is a circle of radius 2·1 m.
  a Calculate the area of the floor.
  b Find the cost of covering the floor with matting costing ₦500 per m².

11 Calculate the shaded area in Fig. R3.7.

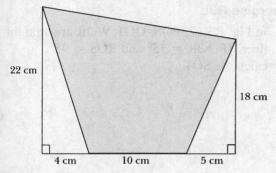

22 cm

18 cm

4 cm   10 cm   5 cm

Fig. R3.7

12 Fig. R3.8 shows a square of side 14 cm. The shaded part is a quadrant of a circle of radius 14 cm. What is the area of the unshaded part of the figure?

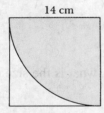

14 cm

Fig. R3.8

13 In Fig. R3.9, PQRS is the plan of a field with the dimensions as shown.
Calculate the area of the field.

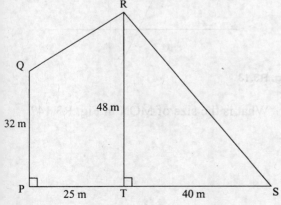

R

Q

48 m

32 m

P   25 m   T   40 m   S

Fig. R3.9

14 How many square tiles of side 20 cm are needed to cover a floor 3·8 m by 2·8 m?

15 A rectangular tank is 760 cm long, 50 cm wide and 40 cm high.
How many litres of water can it hold?

16 Calculate the capacity, in litres, of a tank 3·2 m long, 2·1 m wide and 0·75 m deep.

17 A circular cylinder of radius 2 cm has a height of 9 cm. Calculate the volume of the cylinder in terms of π.

18 Calculate, in terms of π, the total surface area of a solid cylinder of radius 3 cm and height 4 cm.

19 A paper label just covers the curved surface area of a cylindrical tin of diameter 16 cm and height $17\frac{1}{2}$ cm.
Calculate the area of the label.

20 Two circles have radii of a cm and b cm $(a > b)$.
  a Write down a formula for the difference between their areas.
  b Factorise the result.
  c If $a = 19$ and $b = 9$, calculate the difference in area between the two circles.

21 Calculate the area of the trapezium in Fig. R3.10.

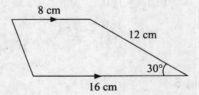

8 cm

12 cm

30°

16 cm

Fig. R3.10

22 The parallel sides of a trapezium are 11 cm and 13 cm. The area of the trapezium is 84 cm². Calculate the distance between the parallel sides.

23 The volume of a cone is 44 cm³. What is the height of the cone if its base radius is 3 cm?

24 A rectangular garden, 30 m by 20 m, consists of a plot 28 m by 18 m surrounded by a path.
  a Calculate the area of the path in m².
  b The path is to be made of cement 8 cm

thick. Calculate the volume of cement required in m³.

25) From a cylinder of diameter 70 cm and height 84 cm, a cone, having as its base one of the circular ends of the cylinder and height 84 cm, is removed. Calculate the volume of the remaining object.

R3-2 Angles and constructions

Example 4

Find the value of d in Fig. R3.11.

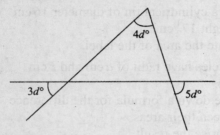

Fig. R3.11

One of the angles of the triangle is $4d°$.
By vertically opposite angles, the other two angles of the triangle are $3d°$ and $5d°$.

$4d + 3d + 5d = 180$ (sum of angles of △)
$$12d = 180$$

$$d = \frac{180}{12} = 15$$

Example 5

If the angles of a polygon are 90°, 4y°, 100°, 120° and (7y − 34)°, find the value of y.

For an *n*-sided polygon,
Sum of angles $= (n - 2) \times 180°$
The given polygon has five angles, thus it has five sides.

Sum of angles $= (5 - 2) \times 180°$
$$= 3 \times 180°$$
$$= 540°$$

Thus, $90 + 4y + 100 + 120 + (7y - 34)$
$$= 540$$

Collecting terms, $11y + 276 = 540$
$$11y = 540 - 276$$
$$11y = 264$$

$$y = \frac{264}{11} = 24$$

Exercise R3b

1) In Fig. R3.12, POS, QOT, WOR are straight lines. If QÔR = 35° and RÔS = 95°, calculate SÔT.

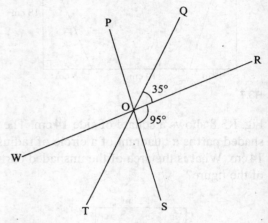

Fig. R3.12

2) In Fig. R3.13, what is the size of the angle marked *x*?

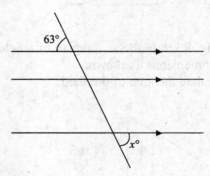

Fig. R3.13

3) What is the size of MÔN in Fig. R3.14?

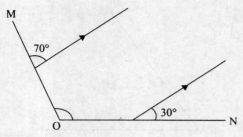

Fig. R3.14

④ Given the data of Fig. R3.15, find the value of *x*.

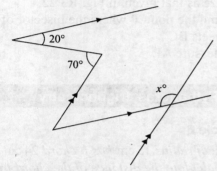

Fig. R3.15

⑤ In Fig. R3.16 find *x*.

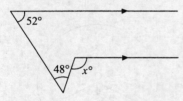

Fig. R3.16

⑥ In Fig. R3.17, AB = AC and BC = BD. If Â = 64°, find the angles marked *a, b, c, d, e*.

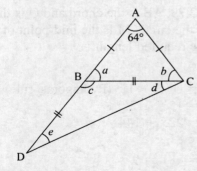

Fig. R3.17

⑦ In Fig. R3.18, YX = YZ, ZX = ZH and Ŷ = 52°. Calculate ZĤX.

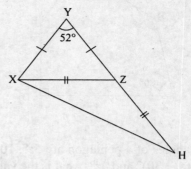

Fig. R3.18

⑧ Calculate the value of *k* in Fig. R3.19.

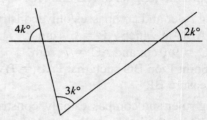

Fig. R3.19

⑨ In Fig. R3.20, what is the value of *x*?

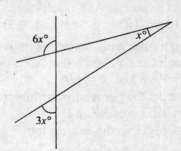

Fig. R3.20

⑩ Calculate the size of each angle of a regular 12-sided polygon.

⑪ In Fig. R3.21, Â = D̂ = 90°, Ĉ = 80° and B̂ = Ê = *x*°. Find *x*.

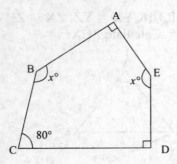

Fig. R3.21

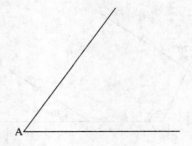

Fig. R3.22

12. If the angles of a pentagon are $5z°$, $100°$, $110°$, $(z - 30)°$ and $4z°$, what is the value of z?

13. $\triangle ABC$ is such that $BC = 10\,cm$, $A\hat{B}C = 30°$ and $A\hat{C}B = 80°$. Construct the triangle and measure the lengths of AB and AC.

14. Using ruler and compasses only, construct
   a $\triangle ABC$ in which $AB = 6\cdot4\,cm$, $BC = 9\cdot0\,cm$ and $AC = 7\cdot5\,cm$,
   b a point P on BC such that $P\hat{A}B = P\hat{A}C$.
   c Measure BP.

15. Using ruler and compasses only, construct $\triangle ABC$ in which $AB = 8\,cm$, $\hat{A}$ $45°$ and $\hat{B} = 30°$. Measure BC.

16. Using a ruler and a pair of compasses only, construct a triangle ABC such that $AC = 10\,cm$, $BC = 8\cdot5\,cm$ and $A\hat{C}B = 135°$.

17. a Using a ruler and compasses only, construct $\triangle XYZ$ such that $XY = 4\,cm$, $XZ = 7\,cm$ and $\hat{X} = 60°$.
   b Construct the perpendicular bisector of YZ such that it cuts XZ at P.
   c Measure XP to the nearest mm.

18. a Using ruler and compasses only, construct rhombus ABCD in which each side is 8 cm and $A\hat{B}C = 150°$.
   b Measure the length of the shorter diagonal to the nearest mm.

19. a Use ruler and compasses only to construct a quadrilateral ABCD in which $AB = BC = 3\,cm$, $\hat{B} = 120°$ and $AD = CD = 6\,cm$.
   b What kind of quadrilateral is ABCD?

20. a Use ruler and compasses to copy angle A in Fig. R3.22 into your exercise book.

   b Hence construct $\triangle ABC$ in which $AB = 5\,cm$, $AC = 8\,cm$ and $\hat{A}$ is the same size as that given in Fig. R3.22.
   c Find the point P where the bisector of $\hat{A}$ meets BC.
   d Measure AP.

R3-3 Pythagoras, trigonometry

Example 6

A circle of radius 15 cm *has a chord* 24 cm *long. Calculate the distance of the chord from the centre of the circle.*

Fig. R3.23 is a sketch of the information in the question.

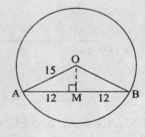

Fig. R3.23

In Fig. R3.23, AB is the chord and O is the centre of the circle. M is the mid-point of AB. OM is the required length.
In $\triangle OMA$,

$$15^2 = OM^2 + 12^2 \text{ (Pythagoras' rule)}$$
$$OM^2 = 15^2 - 12^2$$
$$= 225 - 144$$
$$= 81$$
$$OM = \sqrt{81} = 9$$

The chord is 9 cm from the centre of the circle.

Example 7

A student stands 30 m *from the foot of a flag-pole. The angle of elevation of the top of the flag-pole from a point* 1·7 m *above the ground is* 18°. *Calculate the height of the flag-pole to the nearest* $\frac{1}{2}$ *metre.*

Fig. R3.24 is a sketch of the information in the question.

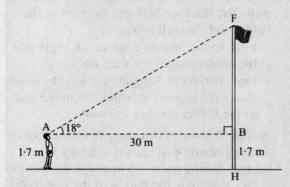

Fig. R3.24

In Fig. R3.24, FH represents the flag-pole.
In △ABF,

$$\tan 18° = \frac{FB}{30}$$

$$FB = 30 \times \tan 18°$$
$$= 30 \times 0·3249 \text{ (from tables)}$$
$$= 9·747$$
$$FH = FB + BH$$
$$= 9·747\,m + 1·7\,m$$
$$= 11·447\,m$$
$$= 11·5\,m \text{ to nearest } \tfrac{1}{2} \text{ metre}$$

Exercise R3c

① Use Pythagoras' rule to find the value of *x* in each of the figures in Fig. R3.25. All dimensions are in cm.

a

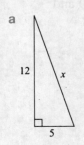

b

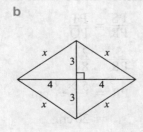

c

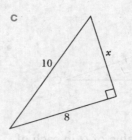

d

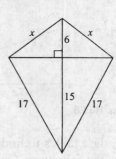

Fig. R3.25

② In Fig. R3.26, $\hat{C} = 90°$, AC = 5 cm and AB = 13 cm.
Calculate **a** BC, **b** the area of △ABC.

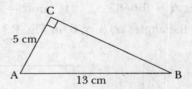

Fig. R3.26

③ A chord of a circle is 24 cm long. If the chord is 5 cm from the centre of the circle, calculate the radius of the circle.

④ A chord is drawn 3 cm away from the centre of a circle of radius 5 cm.
Calculate the length of the chord.

⑤ A man starts from Q. He walks 5 km northwards and then 8 km westwards. Find his distance from Q to the nearest 100 m.

⑥ Given the data of Fig. R3.27, **a** find AC and hence **b** find the value of cos $\hat{C}$.

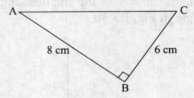

Fig. R3.27

⑦ In Fig. R3.28, find **a** AB, **b** tan $\hat{A}$.

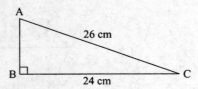

Fig. R3.28

(8) Use tables to find the value of α in each of the following. Give all answers to the nearest 0·1 of a degree.

a $\tan \alpha = 0·781$ b $\tan \alpha = 1·2$
c $\tan \alpha = 3·85$ d $\sin \alpha = 0·927$
e $\sin \alpha = 0·402$ f $\sin \alpha = 0·3818$
g $\cos \alpha = 0·927$ h $\cos \alpha = 0·661$
i $\cos \alpha = 0·0682$ j $\tan \alpha = 45·8$

(9) Find the angles α, β, γ, δ, in Fig. R3.29.

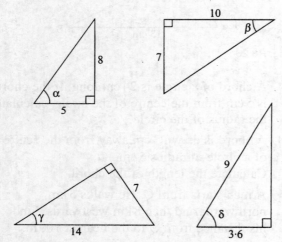

Fig. R3.29

(10) Calculate the size of the smallest angle of the triangle in Fig. R3.30.

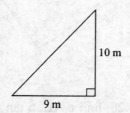

Fig. R3.30

(11) A triangle has sides 8 cm and 5 cm and an angle of 90° between them. Calculate the smallest angle of the triangle.

(12) From a place 400 m north of X, a man walks eastwards to Y which is 800 m from X. What is the bearing of X from Y?

(13) A ladder AB, 8 m long, has its end B on horizontal ground and its end A against a vertical wall. AB makes an angle of 76° with the ground. Calculate the height the ladder reaches up the wall.

(14) A ladder 20 m long rests against a vertical wall. The distance between the foot of the ladder and the wall is 9 m.
   a Find, to the nearest degree, the angle that the ladder makes with the wall.
   b Find, correct to 1 decimal place, the height above the ground at which the upper end of the ladder touches the wall.

(15) A student stands 20 m away from the foot of a tree. The angle of elevation of the top of the tree from a point 1·5 m above the ground is 24°. Calculate the height of the tree to the nearest $\frac{1}{2}$ metre.

R3-4 Similarity

Example 8

With the data as given in Fig. R3.31, calculate TR.

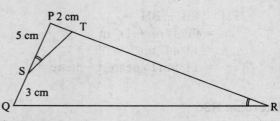

Fig. R3.31

$\triangle$PST and $\triangle$PRQ have $\hat{P}$ in common and $\hat{S} = \hat{R}$. Hence $\triangle$PST is similar to $\triangle$PRQ and

$$\frac{PS}{PR} = \frac{PT}{PQ}$$

$$\frac{5}{PR} = \frac{2}{8}$$

$$PR = \frac{5 \times 8}{2} \text{ cm}$$

$$= 20 \text{ cm}$$

$$TR = PR - 2\,cm$$
$$= 20 - 2\,cm$$
$$= 18\,cm$$

Example 9

A lake is represented on a map of scale 1 : 20 000 by an area of 7·8 cm². Find the area of the lake to the nearest hectare.

Scale factor $= 20\,000$
Area factor $= (20\,000)^2$
$= 400\,000\,000$
Area of lake $= 400\,000\,000 \times 7\cdot8\,cm^2$

$$= \frac{400\,000\,000 \times 7\cdot8}{100 \times 100}\,m^2$$

$$= \frac{400\,000\,000 \times 7\cdot8}{10\,000 \times 100 \times 100}\,ha$$

$$= 4 \times 7\cdot8\,ha$$
$$= 31\cdot2\,ha$$
$$= 31\,ha \text{ to the nearest ha}$$

Exercise R3d

① Which of the triangles in Fig. R3.32 are similar?

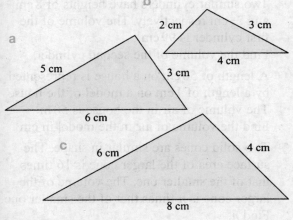

Fig. R3.32

② △ABC is similar to △XYZ. If AC = 9 cm, BC = 5 cm and YZ = 7 cm, find the length of XZ.

③ In Fig. R3.33, a wire is tightly stretched from the top of a pole 6 m high to a point on level ground 4 m from the bottom of the pole.

What is the height of the wire above the ground at a point 1 m from the base of the pole?

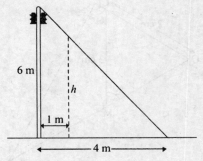

Fig. R3.33

④ In Fig. R3.34, rectangle ABCD is similar to rectangle AXYZ.
  a From the dimensions in the figure, calculate the length of YZ.
  b Hence find the area shaded.

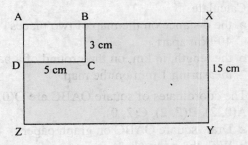

Fig. R3.34

⑤ In Fig. R3.35, calculate the length of BC.

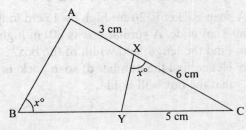

Fig. R3.35

6. In Fig. R3.36, calculate the length of QR.

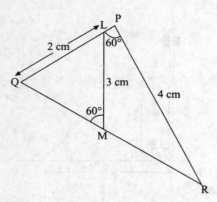

Fig. R3.36

7. The scale of a map is 1 cm to 18 km. The distance between two towns is 12 cm on the map. What is their real distance apart?

8. The scale of a map is 1 cm to 100 km. Calculate
   a the distance on the map of two places 400 km apart,
   b the length, in km, on the ground of a path measuring 1 mm on the map.

9. The coordinates of square OABC are O(0, 0), A(0, 2), B(2, 2), C(2, 0).
   a Draw square OABC on graph paper.
   b With the point (1, 3) as centre of enlargement, enlarge square OABC by scale factor 3.
   c Write down the coordinates of the vertices of the enlarged square O′A′B′C′.

10. A soap packet is 20 cm high by 15 cm long by 8 cm wide. A similar box is 80 cm high.
    a Find the length and width of the box.
    b Hence find the number of soap packets that the box will hold.

11. The area of a circle of radius r cm is A cm². What is the area of a circle of radius $3r$ in terms of A?

12. Two similar cones have heights of 6 cm and 11 cm respectively. Find the ratio of the curved surface area of the first cone to that of the second.

13. The volumes of two cubes are in the ratio 27 : 125. Find the ratio of their heights.

14. A map of a region is drawn to a scale of 1 cm to 100 m. Find the area on the map, in cm², which corresponds to a rectangular plot of the region 250 m by 160 m.

15. A circular lake is represented on a map by a circle of radius $3\frac{1}{2}$ cm. The scale of the map is 2 cm to 1 km. What is the actual area of the lake? (Use the value $\frac{22}{7}$ for π.)

16. The area of a State in a country is represented on a map of scale 1 : 25 000 by an area of 11·5 cm². Find the area of the State to the nearest hectare.

17. A square plot of land is drawn on a map using a scale of 1 cm : 5 m. The side of the plot is represented by 40 cm on the map. Find the area of the plot in m².

18. Two similar cylinders have heights of 8 cm and $2\frac{2}{3}$ cm respectively. The volume of the first cylinder is 99 cm³.
    Find the volume of the second cylinder.

19. A length of 50 cm on a house is represented by a length of 1 cm on a model of the house. The volume of air in the house is 50 m³. Find the volume of air in the model in cm³.

20. Two solid cones are similar in shape. The surface area of the larger cone is 16 times that of the smaller one. The volume of the larger cone is n times that of the smaller one. Find n.

R4 Statistics, averages, probability, graphs, tables

CHAPTER COVERAGE

R4-1 Pictograms, bar charts, pie charts

R4-2 Cost, travel and conversion graphs

R4-3 Reading tables

R4-4 Mean, median, mode, range, mixtures

R4-5 Probability

The first part of this book contains detailed coverage of the following topic in statistics (including averages):

Everyday statistics   (Chapter 16)

R4-1 Pictograms, bar charts, pie charts

Exercise R4a

1 Fig. R4.1 shows the mark distribution for a class test.

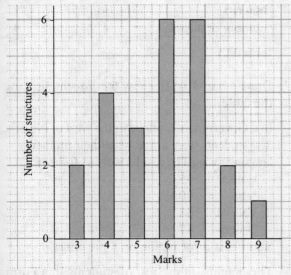

Fig. R4.1

  a What is the highest mark?

  b What is the lowest mark?

  c How many students scored 3 marks?

  d How many students scored 7 marks?

  e How many students took the test?

2 Fig. R4.2 shows the rainfall in mm for the days of a week.

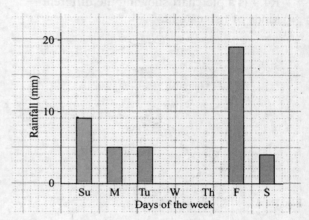

Fig. R4.2

  a On how many days did rain fall?

  b On which day(s) was there no rain?

  c Which day had the greatest rainfall?

  d 5 mm of rain fell on which day(s)?

  e How much rain fell on Sunday?

  f How much rain fell during the week?

3 Fig. R4.3 is a pictogram showing the numbers of users of electricity in a city for the years 2002 to 2008. Each light bulb represents 1 000 users.

Fig. R4.3

a Did the use of electricity increase or decrease with time?

b How many users, to the nearest 1 000, were there in 2002?

c Starting in 2002, how many years did it take for the number of users to double?

d Each user paid an average of ₦24 000 per year for electricity. How much money, to 2 s.f., was collected altogether in 2006?

④ 72 fish were caught in a river one day. Fig. R4.4 is a pie chart showing the different kinds of fish caught.

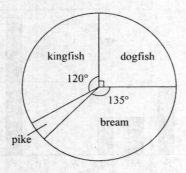

Fig. R4.4

a What percentage of fish were dogfish?

b What fraction of the fish were bream?

c How many kingfish were caught?

d How many pike were caught?

⑤ Fig. R4.5 represents the number of times the letters C, D, F, G, I appear in a paragraph of a book.

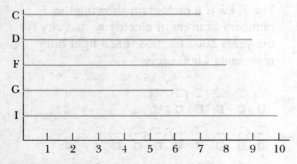

Fig. R4.5

a How many times did D appear?

b Which letter appeared eight times?

c Which of the letters appeared most often?

d Which of the letters appeared least often?

e What is the ratio of the least frequent letter to the most frequent letter?

⑥ The bar chart in Fig. R4.6 shows the distribution of Primary Classes 1–6 in a school.

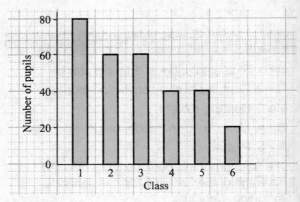

Fig. R4.6

a How many pupils are in the school?

b If each pupil gets three exercise books for the term, how many exercise books are needed?

c If an exercise book costs ₦60, how much is spent altogether on exercise books?

⑦ Table R4.1 gives the ages of a group of pupils in a school.

age (yr)	13	14	15	16	17
number of pupils	1	4	2	2	1

Table R4.1

Draw a bar chart to show the information in the table.

⑧ In a Government College in the west of Nigeria, 360 students were asked what their mother language was. The results were as follows:

Hausa   45

Igbo   60

Yoruba   168

Others   87

Show this information on a pie chart.

⑨ The heights, in metres, of students in a Form 1 class are given below.

1·7 1·5 1·6 1·4 1·5 1·4 1·6
1·4 1·7 1·6 1·5 1·5 1·8 1·8
1·4 1·5 1·6 1·6 1·3 1·7

a Copy and complete Table R4.2.

height (m)	1·3	1·4	1·5	1·6	1·7	1·8
frequency						

Table R4.2

b Draw a bar chart to show the data.

In a school week, a class has nine periods of English, six periods of mathematics, five periods of science and 20 periods of other subjects. Show this information on a pie chart.

R4-2 Cost, travel and conversion graphs

Exercise R4b

A finance company gives loans to people to buy motorcycles. The loans are repaid in 36 monthly instalments. Fig. R4.7 is a graph showing the monthly payments for loans up to ₦50 000.

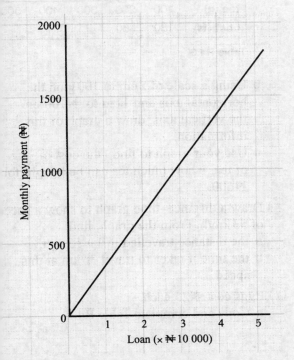

Fig. R4.7 Monthly payments for loans up to ₦50 000

a Find the size of the monthly payments for a loan of i ₦40 000, ii ₦26 000.
b Find the size of the loan if the monthly payment is i ₦1 050, ii ₦550.
c Find the profit the company makes on a loan of ₦50 000.

2 Fig. R4.8 shows the journeys of a car travelling from Kaduna to Gusau and a lorry travelling from Gusau to Kaduna.

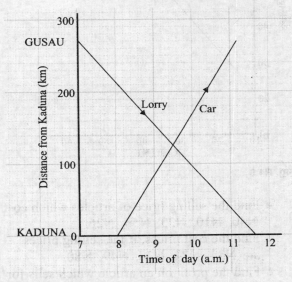

Fig. R4.8 Travel graphs to and from Kaduna

a How far is it from Kaduna to Gusau?
b How long did the car take?
c What is the average speed of the car?
d How long did the lorry take?
e What is the average speed of the lorry?
f At what time did the lorry and car pass each other?
g How far were they from Kaduna when this happened?
h When the car reached Gusau, how far was the lorry from Kaduna?

3 Fig. R4.9 is a conversion graph that a trader uses to change cost price to selling price. For example, the dotted line shows that if an article costs ₦50, the selling price is ₦70.

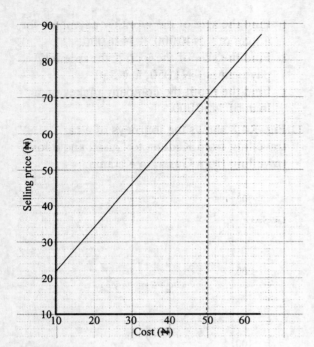

Fig. R4.9

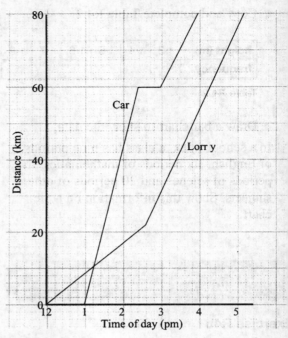

Fig. R4.10

a Find the selling price of articles which cost
₦40, ₦10, ₦23, ₦56, ₦26.

b Find the cost prices, if the selling prices
are ₦34, ₦74, ₦38, ₦49, ₦80.

c Find the profit on an article which sells for
₦65.

④ Fig. R4.10 shows the journeys of a car and a
lorry both travelling from the same place to
the same destination. The car stopped for a
punctured tyre to be replaced.

a How long did the lorry take for the
journey?

b When did the car stop to replace the tyre?

c How long did it take to replace the tyre?

d How far were the lorry and car apart when
the car started off again?

⑤ Tea costs ₦180 for 100 g.

a Copy and complete Table R4.3.

tea (g)	100	200	300	400	500
cost (₦)	180	360			

Table R4.3

b Using a scale of 2 cm to 100 g on the
horizontal axis and 1 cm to ₦100 on
the vertical axis, draw a graph of this
information.

c Use your graph to find i the cost of $\frac{1}{4}$ kg
of tea, ii how much tea can be bought for
₦600.

⑥ Draw a distance–time graph to show a speed
of 53 km/h. From the graph, find

a the distance travelled in 1 h 15 min,

b the time it takes to travel 36 km at this
speed.

⑦ Eggs cost ₦25 each.

a Copy and complete Table R4.4.

number of eggs	10	20	30	40	50	60
cost (₦)	250	500	750			

Table R4.4

b Using a scale of 2 cm to 10 eggs on the horizontal axis and 1 cm to ₦100 on the vertical axis, draw a graph showing the information in your table.

c Is your graph continuous or discontinuous? (Give reasons.)

d Use your graph to *estimate* the cost of i 2 dozen eggs, ii $3\frac{1}{2}$ dozen eggs.

Construct a conversion graph for changing marks in a test out of 60 into percentages. Use your graph to change the following marks out of 60 to percentages.

a 45   b 24   c 39   d 51   e 35

At 4 p.m., Ireneh leaves her office to cycle home. She rides steadily for 10 min and covers 2 km. She then stops and talks to a friend for 20 min. She then cycles the remaining 3 km, arriving home at 4.40 p.m.

a Show the above information on a distance–time graph.

b How far was she from home at 4.35 p.m.?

c Find her average speed for the first part of the journey.

d Find her average speed for the whole journey.

Boni started at 6 a.m. to walk from Oja to Jebako, 30 km away, at a steady speed of 6 km/h.

a Copy and complete Table R4.5.

time (a.m.)	6	7	8	9	10	11
distance (km)	0	6	12	18		

Table R4.5

b Using a scale of 2 cm to 1 hour on the horizontal axis and 2 cm to 5 km on the vertical axis, plot the graph of Boni's journey.

c At 9 a.m. Tunde sets out on his bicycle from Oja to Jebako at an average speed of 25 km/h. Plot Tunde's journey on the same axes as Boni's journey.

d When did Tunde pass Boni?

e How long did Tunde have to wait for Boni at Jebako?

R4-3 Reading tables

Exercise R4c

This exercise contains a number of numerical tables. Read the titles and column headings very carefully. These tell you what they are about.

1 Use the table of squares on page 273 to find the following correct to 3 s.f.:

a $8\cdot4^2$ b 84^2 c 1783^2
d 5350^2 e $2\cdot528^2$ f $0\cdot2524^2$

2 Use the tables of square roots on pages 274 and 275 to find the following:

a $\sqrt{2\cdot674}$ b $\sqrt{26\cdot78}$ c $\sqrt{2672}$
d $\sqrt{4400}$ e $\sqrt{84\cdot35}$ f $\sqrt{1093}$

3 A square plot has a perimeter of 79·2 m. Find the area of the plot to the nearest 10 m².

4 A square plot has an area of 3 230 m². Use square root tables to find the length of one of its sides correct to the nearest metre.

5 a Use square root tables to find n if
$n = \sqrt{38\cdot52}$.

b Using the value of n from a), find the value of n^2 from the table of squares.

c Explain why $n^2 \neq 38\cdot52$.

Table R4.6 is a timetable for flights daily between Lagos, Kano and London.

VN 800	↓	Flight number	↑	VN 801
1100	d	Lagos	a	0600
1220	a	Kano	d	0440
1315	d	Kano	a	0335
1900	a	London	d	2200

Table R4.6

Use Table R4.6 to answer questions 6 and 7.

6 A man flies from Lagos to London on flight VN 800.

   a What time does he leave Lagos?

   b How long is the plane on the ground in Kano?

   c What time does the plane land in London?

   d How long does it take to fly from Kano to London?

7 A woman leaves London on Monday 23 June to fly to Lagos on flight VN 801.

   a What time does she leave London?

   b What is the time and date when she arrives in Lagos?

   c What fraction of the journey times does the aircraft spend on the ground?

Table R4.7 is a distance chart, giving the straight line distances, in km, between some of the main cities of West Africa.

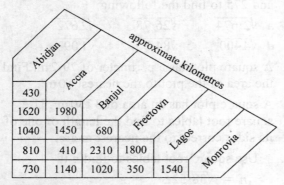

Table R4.7

Use Table R4.7 to answer questions 8 and 9.

8 **a** Which two cities are closest together?

   b Which two cities are furthest apart?

   c How far is Abidjan from Lagos?

   d What is the distance between Monrovia and Banjul?

9 **a** Find the distance from Lagos to Freetown
   i directly, **ii** via Accra.

   b Find the total distance travelled on the following round trip.
   Lagos → Banjul → Freetown → Accra → Lagos

10 Using a calculator, find the value of the following:

   a $125 \times 8 - 569$

   b $312 + 57 \times 19$

   c $832 \cdot 9 + 135 \cdot 2 \div 24 \cdot 6$

   d $(437 \cdot 8 - 10 \cdot 9) \div 1 \cdot 3$

   e $29 \cdot 296 - 2 \cdot 342 \times 7 \cdot 895$

   f $198 \cdot 4 \div (37 \cdot 6 - 23 \cdot 45)$

R4-4 Mean, median, mode, range, mixtures

Example 1

Table R4.8 shows the amount of money which some students have in their pockets.

amount (₦)	1	5	10	20	50	100
number of students	1	5	4	5	2	1

Table R4.8

Find to the nearest kobo, a the mean, b the median, c the modal amounts of money, d the range.

a Mean

$$= \frac{\text{total amount of money}}{\text{number of students}}$$

$$= ₦\frac{1 \times 1 + 5 \times 5 + 4 \times 10 + 5 \times 20 + 2 \times 50 + 1 \times 100}{1 + 5 + 4 + 5 + 2 + 1}$$

$$= ₦\frac{1 + 25 + 40 + 100 + 100 + 100}{18}$$

$$= ₦\frac{366}{18} = ₦\frac{61}{3} = ₦20\frac{1}{3}$$

$$= ₦20.33 \text{ to the nearest kobo}$$

b Median = the amount of money which the middle student has, when the students are arranged in order.

In this case, there are 18 students. The median is the mean of the money that the 9th and 10th students have.
In Table R4.8, the 1st student has ₦1, the 2nd to 6th students have ₦5, and so on. Counting on, the 9th and 10th students both have ₦10.

   Median = ₦10

c Mode = the amount of money which most students have.

In Table R4.8, more students have ₦5 and ₦20 than any other amount. There are two modes. This is an example of **bimodal** data.
  Mode = ₦5 and ₦20

d Range = ₦100 − ₦1 = ₦99

Example 2

Six girls have an average age of 16 years 3 months. When another girl is added to the group, the average age becomes 16 years 4 months. How old is the last girl?

Total age of the first 6 girls = $6 \times (16\,\text{yr}\,3\,\text{mo})$
$$= 6 \times 16\tfrac{1}{4}\,\text{yr}$$
$$= 97\tfrac{1}{2}\,\text{yr}$$

Total age of all 7 girls = $7 \times (16\,\text{yr}\,4\,\text{mo})$
$$= 7 \times 16\tfrac{1}{3}\,\text{yr}$$
$$= 114\tfrac{1}{3}\,\text{yr}$$

Age of last girl = $114\tfrac{1}{3} - 97\tfrac{1}{2}\,\text{yr}$
$$= 16\tfrac{5}{6}\,\text{yr}$$
$$= 16\,\text{yr}\,10\,\text{mo}$$

Example 3

Two bowls of white beans are mixed with four bowls of brown beans. If white beans cost ₦136 per bowl and brown beans cost ₦94 per bowl, find the average cost of one bowl of the mixture.

Total cost of white beans = $2 \times ₦136$
$$= ₦272$$
Total cost of brown beans = $4 \times ₦94$
$$= ₦376$$
Cost of 6 bowls of mixture = ₦272 + ₦376
$$= ₦648$$
Cost of 1 bowl of mixture = $\dfrac{₦648}{6}$
$$= ₦108$$

Exercise R4d

1. In a Biology class, the lengths of some bean plants were measured to the nearest cm. The results are given in Table R4.9.

length (cm)	17	18	19	20	21	22
frequency	3	6	15	17	14	12

Table R4.9

What is the mode of this distribution?

2. The scores obtained by ten students in a test are:
   1, 3, 5, 6, 4, 7, 6, 7, 5, 6
   What is the mode of the scores?

3. In a class test, the marks of a student in eight subjects were as follows.
   71, 30, 42, 96, 92, 62, 84, 70
   Find the median of the marks.

4. A group of students measured a certain angle. They obtained the following results.
   75°, 76°, 72°, 73°, 74°
   74°, 79°, 72°, 72°, 77°
   72°, 71°, 70°, 78°, 73°
   Find **a** the mode, **b** the median, **c** the range.

5. The scores of ten students in a test are 8, 4, 5, 10, 9, 8, 6, 5, 8, 6.
   a What is the modal score?
   b What is the median score?

6. For the following set of numbers:
   2, 3, 3, 4, 7, 7, 8, 8, 8, 10
   a state the median,   **b** state the mode,
   c calculate the mean,   **d** find the range.

7. A zoologist caught 10 snakes. Their lengths in cm were as follows.
   37, 39, 50, 64, 81, 43, 56, 43, 73, 59
   Find **a** the mean, **b** the median and **c** the modal lengths of the snakes.

8. Table R4.10 gives the ages of a group of students.

age (yr)	12	13	14	15	16	17	18
frequency	2	0	1	3	4	3	2

Table R4.10

a What is the modal age of the students?

b What is the mean age of the students?

c What is the range?

9 From the data in Table R4.1 (page 226), find

a the mean age,

b the modal age of the pupils.

10 A die is thrown 20 times with the following results.

6, 1, 6, 5, 4, 3, 3, 6, 1, 6

4, 1, 2, 5, 6, 5, 3, 6, 2, 1

a Make a frequency table.

b Find the mean, median and mode from the table.

11 The ages of eight students are as follows:

15 years 3 months

15 years 9 months

14 years 10 months

15 years

15 years 7 months

14 years 4 months

15 years 5 months

16 years

Calculate a the median age, b the mean age of the students correct to the nearest month.

12 Marks out of 10 were given to 15 students as follows:

5, 8, 7, 9, 3, 6, 2, 5, 8, 10, 6, 8, 9, 4, 8

a Write down the marks in ascending order of size.

b Write down the median.

c Write down the mode.

d Work out the mean, to one decimal place.

13 Coffee is sold in jars. The label on each jar states, 'Contents: at least 250 g'. The coffee in 10 jars was weighed. The results are given in Table R4.11.

mass (g)	248	249	250	251	252	253
frequency	1	0	2	2	3	2

Table R4.11

a Find the mean, median and modal amounts of coffee in the jars.

b Is the statement on the label true?

14 The following heights, in metres, were obtained for 12 pupils in a class.

1·5   1·59   1·47   1·62   1·74   1·53

1·44   1·5   1·71   1·53   1·68   1·56

Calculate the mean height to the nearest cm.

15 A factory employs 100 people.

14 earn ₦1 800 per day

20 earn ₦1 550 per day

31 earn ₦1 240 per day

The rest earn ₦960 per day

What is the average daily wage to the nearest naira?

16 The mean of the numbers 6, 9, 13, 15, 17, 19, 23, 31, 47 is 20. Hence find the mean of the numbers 66, 96, 136, 156, 176, 196, 236, 316, 476.

17 Find x, if the mean of the numbers 5, $3x$, 0 and 3 is 5.

18 Five students have a mean age of 15 years 4 months. When another student joins the group, the mean age becomes 15 years 6 months.

How old is the student who joins the group?

19 The average age of five girls is 16 years. The average age of four of them is $16\frac{1}{2}$ years. What is the age of the fifth girl?

20 The average mass of 29 boys in a class is 40 kg. A new boy, of mass 55 kg, joins the class. Find the new average mass of the class.

21 A man walks at an average speed of 6 km/h. He averages 125 paces per minute. Find the average length of one pace in metres.

22 On a journey, a motorist travels the first 40 km in $\frac{1}{2}$ hour, the next 34 km in 25 min and the last 7 km in 5 min. What is her average speed for the whole journey?

23 Ten students took an examination. John scored 500 marks. If he had scored 700 marks, the average score of the students would have been 410.

What was the total score for the group?

24 The average age of a football team of 11 players is 32 years. One man aged 45 years is replaced by another aged 23 years. What is the new average age of the team?

25 Twelve boys and n girls sat for a test. The mean of the boys' scores and that of the girls were 5 and 8 respectively. Find n if the total score was 180.

26 8 kg of coffee costing ₦1 200 a kg is mixed with 12 kg of another kind of coffee costing ₦1 800 a kg.
What is the cost of the mixture per kg?

27 Three bags of imported rice, costing ₦4 800 per bag, are mixed with five bags of local rice, costing ₦3 600 per bag. What is the average cost of one bag of the mixture?

28 Village A has 200 families with an average of 3·9 children each. Village B has 300 families with an average of 4·4 children each.
Find the average number of children per family for the two villages.

29 A lorry driver travelled 96 km between two towns at an average speed of 24 km/h. He travelled at an average speed of 36 km/h on 40 km of good road. For how long did he travel on the bad part of the road?

30 A girl walked 12 km at 3 km/h and cycled 18 km at 9 km/h. What was her average speed for the whole journey?

R4-5 Probability

Example 4

A number is chosen at random from the whole numbers 30 to 39. Find the probability that it is
a *divisible by 3,*
b *a prime number.*

$$\text{Probability} = \frac{\text{number of required outcomes}}{\text{number of possible outcomes}}$$

There are 10 possible outcomes:

30, 31, 32, 33, 34, 35, 36, 37, 38, 39.

a Of the 10 outcomes, the numbers 30, 33, 36, 39 are divisible by 3.
number of required outcomes = 4
$$\text{probability} = \frac{4}{10} = \frac{2}{5}$$

b Of the 10 outcomes, only the numbers 31 and 37 are prime.
number of required outcomes = 2
$$\text{probability} = \frac{2}{10} = \frac{1}{5}$$

Exercise R4e

1 A fair six-sided die is thrown. Find the possibility of getting the following.
a a 3　　　b a 4
c a 9　　　d a 1 or a 2
e an even number
f a number less than 5

2 A letter is chosen at random from the alphabet. Find the probability that it is
a N
b either A or B
c one of the letters of the word RANDOM
d one of the letters of the word CHOICE

3 A man has three white shirts, two blue shirts and five red shirts. He picks one at random. What is the probability that it is
a white, b blue, c red, d *not* red?

4 What is the probability that an integer chosen at random between and including 1 and 10 is even?

5 A number is chosen at random from the set of numbers 41, 42, …, 55, 56. What is the probability that it is a a multiple of 9, b a prime number?

6 A box contains 20 bottles of Fanta and four bottles of Sprite. A bottle is chosen at random. What is the probability that it is
a Fanta, b Sprite, c either Fanta or Sprite, d neither Fanta nor Sprite?

7 In a school of 500 students, one student is selected at random to represent the school in a debate. There are 25 students in the final year class.
What is the probability that the student chosen will be from the final year?

8 Given the data in question 15, Exercise R4d, what is the probability that a person chosen at random from the factory earns more than ₦1 200 per day?

9 Given the data in Table R4.11 (question 13, Exercise R4d), what is the probability that a new jar of coffee will contain less than 250 g?

10 A shop sells eggs in boxes of six. 25 boxes of eggs are examined. Table R4.12 gives the numbers of broken eggs in the boxes.

broken eggs	0	1	2	3	4	5	6
number of boxes	12	7	3	2	1	0	0

Table R4.12

a Show the information in a bar chart.
b Calculate the mean number of broken eggs in a box.
c What is the median and modal number of broken eggs in a box?
d What is the probability that a box chosen at random has less than two broken eggs in it?

Rectangles in a Square
Here are two ways of cutting a 4 x 4 square grid into rectangles:

In each case:
a) all the rectangles are different,
b) the edges of the rectangles are a whole number of units.
Find other ways of cutting a 4 x 4 grid according to these rules.

[Remember that {squares} ⊂ {rectangles}]

Three-colour Grid
Make a copy of the grid below:

Colour the squares either black, white or red so that:

Each red square touches a white.
Each white square touches a black.
Each black square touches a red.

Who took it?
A teacher popped out of the classroom, leaving a test paper on her desk. When she came back, it was missing. Four students were in the room: Ku, Lu, Mu and Nu. Of these, only one tells the truth.

Ku said, "Mu took it."
Lu said, "I didn't take it."
Mu said, "Lu is lying."
Nu said, "Mu is lying."
Who took the test paper?

Your teacher will tell you when to do this test.

1. What is the value of the digit 5 in the number 624·95?
   A 5 hundreds   B 5 tens   C 5 units
   D 5 tenths   E 5 hundredths

2. The highest common factor of 36, 72 and 90 is
   A 9   B 18   C 36
   D 90   E 360

3. 486 kg expressed in tonnes is
   A 48·6 t   B 4·86 t   C 0·486 t
   D 0·0486 t   E 0·00486 t

4. If 0·68 is expressed as a fraction in its lowest terms, its denominator will be
   A 17   B 25   C 34
   D 50   E 68

5. When $x = 9$, the value of $3x - 5$ is
   A 7   B 12   C 22
   D 32   E 34

6. The number which is 3 greater than n is
   A $n + 3$ B $3n$ C $n - 3$
   D $\frac{1}{3}n$ E $3 - n$

7. A prism has three rectangular faces. Its other faces are in the shape of a
   A rectangle   B square
   C pentagon   D triangle   E hexagon

8. The obtuse angle between the hands of a clock at 2.30 a.m. is
   A 105°   B 120°   C 135°
   D 150°   E 165°

9. $490 \div 10\,000 =$
   A 0·000049   B 0·00049   C 0·0049
   D 0·049   E 0·49

10. The sum of ₦x and y kobo expressed in kobo is
    A $\frac{x}{100} + y$ B $x + 100y$ C $x + y$
    D $100x + y$ E $x + \frac{y}{100}$

11. Which of the following statements about diagonals is (are) true for all rectangles?
    I they are equal in length
    II they cross at right angles
    III they bisect each other
    A I only   B I and II only   C II only
    D I and III only   E III only

12. $8 - 9 - (-5) =$
    A -6 B -4 C $+4$
    D $+6$ E $+12$

13. The perimeter of a rectangle is 20 cm. If the breadth of the rectangle is 2 cm, its area is
    A 16 cm²   B 18 cm²   C 20 cm²
    D 32 cm²   E 40 cm²

14. Laraba has x naira. Kunle has 15 naira less than Laraba. Together, the number of naira they have is
    A $x - 15$ B $2x$ C $2x - 15$
    D $2x + 15$ E 15

15. An equilateral triangle of side 16 cm has the same perimeter as a square. The area of the square, in cm², is
    A 48   B 64   C 96
    D 144   E 256

16. A thread is wound 200 times round a reel of diameter 5 cm. Use the value 3 for π to find the approximate length of the thread in metres.
    A 15   B 30   C $37\frac{1}{2}$
    D 60   E 75

Use the following set of numbers to answer questions 17, 18, 19:

8, 9, 5, 6, 2, 4, 8, 0

17. The mode of the above numbers is
    A 4   B 5   C 6
    D 7   E 8

18. The median of the above numbers is
    A 5   B 5·5   C 6
    D 6·5   E 7

19 The mean of the above numbers is
A 4　　　　B 5·5　　　　C 6
D 7　　　　E none of these

20 If $2x + 1 = 15$, then $x =$
A 7　　　　B 8　　　　C 12
D 14　　　　E 16

21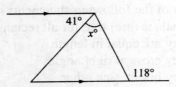

Fig. RT1

In Fig. RT1, $x =$
A 41　　　　B 49　　　　C 62
D 77　　　　E 139

22 8·048 to the nearest tenth is
A 10　　　　B 8　　　　C 8·0
D 8·1　　　　E 8·05

23 Four lines meet at a point. The sum of three of the angles at the point is 267°. The size of the other angle is
A 87°　　　　B 89°　　　　C 90°
D 91°　　　　E 93°

24 Solve $15 = 3y + 7$. $y =$
A $2\frac{2}{3}$　　　　B 5　　　　C $7\frac{1}{3}$
D 8　　　　E 24

25 250 g of sugar costs ₦150 at shop X. 100 g of sugar costs ₦95 at shop Y. The difference in cost per kg is
A ₦55　　　　B ₦220　　　　C ₦250
D ₦260　　　　E ₦350

26 The next term in the sequence
1, 4, 10, 19, 31, ... is
A 32　　　　B 34　　　　C 43
D 46　　　　E 50

27 The square root of $5\frac{4}{9}$ is
A $\frac{7}{9}$　　　　B $2\frac{1}{3}$　　　　C $2\frac{13}{18}$
D $5\frac{2}{3}$　　　　E $16\frac{1}{3}$

28 482 000 in standard form is
A $4·82 \times 10^{-6}$　B $4·82 \times 10^{-5}$　C $4·82 \times 10^{3}$
D $4·82 \times 10^{5}$　E $4·82 \times 10^{6}$

29 0·009 238 to 3 significant figures is
A 0·01　　　　B 0·009　　　　C 0·009 23
D 0·009 24　　　　E 0·923

30 In Fig. RT2, ABCD is a rhombus and AXCD is a kite.

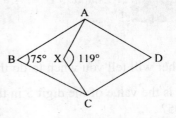

Fig. RT2

What is the size of XÂD?
A 77°　　　　B 83°　　　　C 97°
D 103°　　　　E 105°

31 In Fig. RT3, PQRS is a parallelogram and STUP is a square.

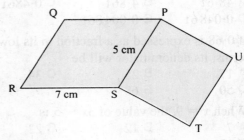

Fig. RT3

If PS = 5 cm and RS = 7 cm, the perimeter of PQRSTU is
A 24 cm　　　　B 29 cm　　　　C 34 cm
D 39 cm　　　　E not enough information

32 Find the value of $\dfrac{a - 3b}{a}$ when $a = 2$ and $b = -8$.
A −18　　　　B −11　　　　C $12\frac{1}{2}$
D 13　　　　E 24

33 Simplify $3(x - 2y) - 4(x - 5y)$.
A $7x - 26y$　　B $14y + x$　　C $-x - 26y$
D $14y - x$　　E $x + 26y$

34 In an exam 35 out of 125 students failed. What percentage passed?
A 28　　　　B 35　　　　C 65
D 72　　　　E 90

35 How much simple interest does ₦6 000 mak in 3 years at 7% per annum?

A N70   B N180   C N210
D N420   E N1 260

36) There are 180 girls in a mixed school. If the ratio of girls to boys is 4 : 3, the total number of students in the school is
A 225   B 315   C 360
D 405   E 420

37) Express $\frac{a}{3} + \frac{4}{b}$ as a single fraction.

A $\frac{3a + 4b}{3b}$ B $\frac{a + 4}{3 + b}$ C $\frac{ab + 12}{3b}$

D $\frac{ab + 12}{3 + b}$ E $\frac{a + 4}{3b}$

38) Solve $\frac{2x - 1}{5} + 2x = 19.$ $x =$

A $1\frac{2}{3}$ B $2\frac{1}{2}$ C 5
D 8   E 24

39) A man is four times as old as his son. In 5 years' time he will be three times as old as his son.
What is the present age of the son in years?
A 8   B 9   C 10
D 12   E 15

40) Which of the points in Fig. RT4 has coordinates $(-4, 1)$?

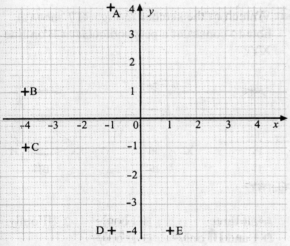

Fig. RT4

41) Use tables to find the value of $\sqrt{940}$.
A 3·070   B 9·695   C 30·66
D 32·06   E 96·95

42) A map is drawn to a scale 2 cm to 100 km.

On the map the distance between two towns is 2·5 cm. What is their true distance apart?
A 40 km   B 80 km   C 125 km
D 250 km   E 500 km

43) ABCD is a rectangle with sides 6 cm and 8 cm. If its diagonals cross at X, the length of AX is
A 5 cm   B 6 cm   C 7 cm
D 8 cm   E 10 cm

44) Which of the following gives the volume of a cylinder of height h and base radius r?
A $2\pi r^2 h$ B $\frac{1}{3}\pi r^2 h$ C πrh
D $\pi r^2 h$ E $2\pi rh$

Fig. RT5 is a graph giving the cost of hiring a car in terms of distance travelled. Use Fig. RT5 to answer questions 45, 46, 47.

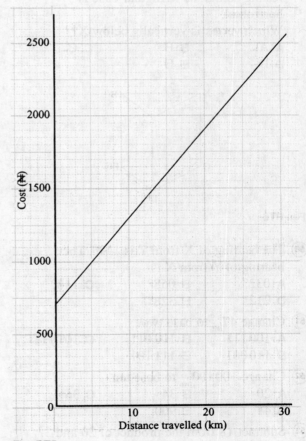

Fig. RT5

237

(45) How much does it cost to hire the car for a 15 km journey?

A ₦1 500   B ₦1 600   C ₦1 700
D ₦1 750   E ₦1 800

(46) If the cost of hiring the car is ₦2 350, the approximate distance travelled is

A 24 km   B 25 km   C 27 km
D 29 km   E 30 km

(47) How much does it cost to hire the car even if no distance is travelled?

A 0   B ₦500   C ₦700
D ₦750   E ₦900

(48) Find the range of values of x for which $7 - 2x < 19$.

A $x > 6$ B $x > -6$ C $x < 6$
D $x < -6$ E $x > -13$

(49) Fig. RT6 shows a right triangular prism resting so that its triangular base is horizontal.

Which vertex is vertically below X?

A A   B B   C C
D D   E E

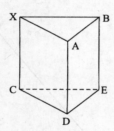

Fig. RT6

(50) The bearing of X from Y is 148°. The bearing of Y from X is

A 032°   B 058°   C 148°
D 212°   E 328°

(51) Change 47_{ten} to base two.

A 100 111   B 100 011   C 101 111
D 110 001   E 111 101

(52) Change $100 100_{two}$ to base ten.

A 20   B 34   C 36
D 44   E 900

(53) Subtract 18 from the product of 20 and 3.

A 1   B 5   C 6
D 42   E 78

(54) Calculate $(4 \times 10^3) \times (8 \times 10^2)$, giving the answer in standard form.

A $3 \cdot 2 \times 10^2$ B $3 \cdot 2 \times 10^4$ C $3 \cdot 2 \times 10^5$
D $3 \cdot 2 \times 10^6$ E $3 \cdot 2 \times 10^7$

(55) Calculate $0 \cdot 126 \div 36$, giving the answer in standard form.

A $3 \cdot 5 \times 10^{-4}$ B $3 \cdot 5 \times 10^{-3}$
C $3 \cdot 5 \times 10^{-2}$ D $3 \cdot 5 \times 10^2$ E $3 \cdot 5 \times 10^3$

(56) Which of the following is (are) factor(s) of $15pr - 10qs - 30\,qr + 5ps$?

I 5
II $(3r - s)$
III $(p - 2q)$

A I only   B I and II only   C II only
D I and III only   E III only

(57) If $f = \dfrac{uv}{u + v}$, find f when $u = 20$ and $v = -30$.

A -60 B -12 C -1
D 12   E 60

(58) If $I = \dfrac{E}{X + Y}$, express X in terms of I, E and Y.

$X =$

A $\dfrac{E}{I + Y}$ B $\dfrac{Y - E}{IY}$ C $\dfrac{E - IY}{I}$
D $\dfrac{E - I}{IY}$ E $\dfrac{EI - Y}{I}$

(59) Which of the sketches in Fig. RT7 show(s) how to construct a perpendicular at P on line XY?

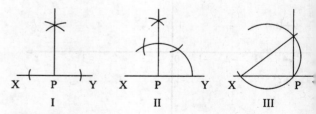

Fig. RT7

A all three   B I only   C III only
D I and III only   E II only

(60) Given the data of Fig. RT8, find the length of XQ.

238

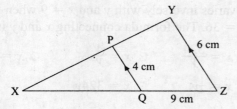

Fig. RT8

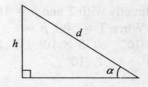

Fig. RT9

A 6 cm   **B** 7 cm   **C** 11 cm
D 15 cm   **E** 18 cm

61. Find cos 55·55° from tables.
    A 0·5650   **B** 0·5657   **C** 0·5664
    D 0·5671   **E** 0·5736

62. Use tables to find the angle whose tangent is $4\frac{4}{9}$.
    A 24°   **B** 55·2°   **C** 77·2°
    D 77·3°   **E** impossible

63. Factorise $x^2 - 7x - 30$.
    A $(x + 1)(x - 30)$ **B** $(x + 2)(x - 15)$
    C $(x + 3)(x - 10)$ **D** $(x + 5)(x - 6)$
    E $(x + 6)(x - 5)$

64. If $\frac{9}{2x} = 10 - \frac{8}{x}$, then $x =$

    A $\frac{7}{20}$ **B** $1\frac{1}{4}$ **C** $1\frac{1}{2}$

    D $1\frac{4}{5}$ **E** $1\frac{7}{10}$

65. If $3x - y = 14$ and $7x - y = 46$, then $x =$
    A 6   **B** 8   **C** 15
    D 22   **E** 28

66. When 27 people share a sack of rice, they each get 4 kg of rice. When 12 people share the same sack of rice, how much does each get?
    A 3 kg   **B** 8 kg   **C** 9 kg
    D 10 kg   **E** 12 kg

67. The average mass of six people is 58 kg. The lightest person has a body mass of 43 kg. What is the average mass of the other five people?
    A 58 kg   **B** 59 kg   **C** 61 kg
    D 64 kg   **E** 68 kg

68. In Fig. RT9, which one of the following is an expression for h in terms of d and α?
    A $d \sin \alpha$ **B** $\frac{d}{\sin \alpha}$ **C** $d \cos \alpha$
    D $\frac{d}{\cos \alpha}$ **E** $d \tan \alpha$

69. ₦10 000 is saved at compound interest of 11% per annum. The interest after 2 years is
    A ₦1 100   **B** ₦1 221   **C** ₦2 200
    D ₦2 321   **E** ₦2 442

70. The reciprocal of 173 is
    A 0·005 78   **B** 0·0578   **C** 0·578
    D 57·8   **E** 578

71.

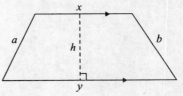

Fig. RT10

Which of the following expressions gives the area of the trapezium in Fig. RT10?
    A $\frac{1}{2}(a + b)h$ **B** $\frac{1}{2}(x + y)h$ **C** $\frac{1}{2}(a + b)x$
    D $\frac{1}{2}(a + b)y$ **E** $ay + xb$

72. The surface area of a cylinder is 31 cm². The surface area of a similar cylinder three times as high is
    A 34 cm²   **B** 62 cm²   **C** 93 cm²
    D 124 cm²   **E** 279 cm²

73. The scale of a model aeroplane is 1 : 20. The area of the wings on the model is 600 cm². Find the area of the wings of the aeroplane in m².
    A 12 m²   **B** 24 m²   **C** 48 m²
    D 72 m²   **E** 120 m²

74. p varies directly with T and $p = 10^5$ when T = 400. When T = 500, $p =$

A $1 \cdot 25 \times 10^4$ B 8×10^4 C $1 \cdot 25 \times 10^5$

D 8×10^5 E 10^6

75. x varies inversely with y and $x = 9$ when $y = 36$. The formula connecting x and y is

A $x = \dfrac{324}{y}$ B $x = \dfrac{4}{y}$ C $x = \dfrac{1}{4y}$

D $x = \tfrac{1}{4}y$ E $x = 324y$

JSCE practice examinations in mathematics

The following pages contain four full-scale practice examinations, each containing a Section I with 80 multiple choice objective questions, and a Section II with 3 essay/theory questions. They are part of the end of course review of the *New General Mathematics* course and provide practice in examinations technique. Attempt each examination under examination conditions, i.e. observe the time given and do not use the textbook, other than the four-figure tables.

The practice examinations in this section are in the style of the Federal JSCE examination at the time of going to press. Remember however, that the examination authorities, whether Federal or State, may change the format of the examination at any time.

General advice

1   Work out how much time you can afford to spend on each question. For example, in Section I of the examination, 80 questions in two hours = $1\frac{1}{2}$ minutes/question! Allow time for reading the question and checking your answer.
2   When a Section II question involves drawing, make a rough sketch first, whether it is a graph or a construction. Always follow the given instructions. For example, if a question says *Give your answer to two significant figures*, you will lose marks if you forget to do this. If a question says *Calculate*, then you must not measure, and vice versa.
3   In Section II, show all your working beside the question. Do not worry about your rough working. Examiners may give credit marks for such working – but only if they see it on the paper. Do not carry valuable work out of the examination room written on scraps of paper, or on your hands!
4   Always check your answers to see if they are sensible. For example, a car costing ₦200 or a walking speed of 6 000 km/h indicate that you have made a slip.

Tables and calculators

Mathematical tables, like those on pages 269 to 275 of this book, are provided in the examination room.

Section I: Multiple choice
          objective questions

Time allowed: 2 hours

1. Which pair of angles are complementary?
   A 47°, 83°   B 60°, 60°   C 90°, 90°
   D 38°, 52°   E 160°, 20°

2. How many edges has a cube?
   A 4   B 6   C 8
   D 10   E 12

3. Round off ₦81 253 to the nearest ₦100.
   A ₦81 300   B ₦81 250   C ₦813
   D ₦81 200   E ₦81 000

4. Write 1424 in Roman numerals.
   A MXMXXIV B MCDXXIV C MCMXIV
   D MCDCXXIV E MCMXXIV

5. Fig. E1 is a net of:

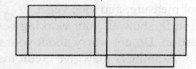

Fig. E1

   A a cube   B a pyramid   C a cuboid
   D a triangular prism   E a cylinder

6. Find x in Fig. E2.

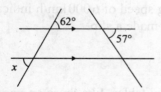

Fig. E2

   A 122°   B 119°   C 118°
   D 62°   E 57°

7. Solve for *m* in the equation 16 − *m* = 9.
   A 25   B 15   C 7
   D 27   E −25

8. Two right angles measure
   A 360°   B 180°   C 120°
   D 90°   E 40°

9. Round off 2·654 8 correct to one decimal place.
   A 2·6   B 2·65   C 2·66
   D 2·7   E 3

10. A salesgirl earns ₦3 000 per week. Each week she spends ₦3x on food and ₦2x on rent and saves the rest. How much does she save in a week?
    A ₦(3 000 − 3x)   B ₦(3 000 − 2x)
    C ₦(3 000 − 5x)   D ₦(1 500 − 5x)
    E ₦(2 000 − 6x)

The pie chart in Fig. E3 shows the different kinds of fish caught during a fishing competition. A total of 72 fishes were caught. Use the pie chart to answer questions 11–13.

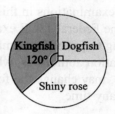

Fig. E3

11. How many were dogfish?
    A 18   B 12   C 10
    D 9   E 6

12. What fraction of the fishes were shiny rose?
    A $\frac{5}{6}$ B $\frac{1}{2}$ C $\frac{5}{12}$
    D $\frac{1}{3}$ E $\frac{1}{12}$

13. How many shiny rose were caught?
    A 60   B 36   C 30
    D 24   E 12

14. In Fig. E4, AB and CE are straight lines which cross at O. Find angle BOE.
    A 117°   B 75°   C 73°
    D 65°   E 42°

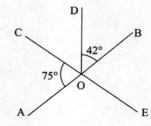

15 In Fig. E5, |AB| = |AD|; find x.

A 54°   B 72°   C 90°

D 108°   E 128°

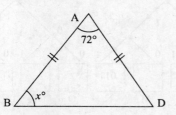

Fig. E5

16 Each angle of a regular polygon is 156°. How many sides has the polygon?

A 20   B 15   C 12

D 10   E 8

17 Find the size of the unknown angle in the triangle in Fig. E6.

A 132°   B 72°   C 68°

Γ 48°   F 40°

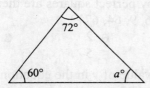

g. E6

18 The perimeter of a rectangle is 20 cm. If the breadth is 4 cm, find its area.

A 16 cm²   B 18 cm²   C 20 cm²

D 24 cm²   E 40 cm²

19 Which is a name of the shape in Fig. E7?

A triangle   B rectangle   C kite

D trapezium   E parallelogram

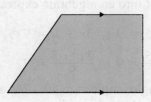

Fig. E7

20 Simplify $6x - 3y - (3x - 7y)$.

A $3x - 10y$ B $9x + 4y$ C $3x - 10y$

D $9x - 4y$ E $3x + 4y$

Fig. E8 shows the rainfall in mm for the days of a week in October.

Use the information to answer questions 21–24.

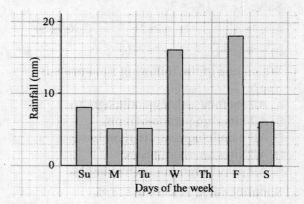

Fig. E8

21 Which day has a rainfall of 6 cm?

A Saturday   B Sunday   C Monday

D Tuesday   E Thursday

22 Which is the wettest day?

A Wednesday   B Sunday   C Friday

D Thursday   E Tuesday

23 How much rain fell on Sunday?

A 0 cm   B 5 cm   C 6 cm

D 7 cm   E 8 cm

24 On which day was there no rain?

A Sunday   B Monday   C Tuesday

D Wednesday   E Thursday

25 Identify the alternate angles in Fig. E9.

A c and f B c and e C b and d

D f and e E a and e

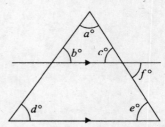

Fig. E9

26) The ratio of the radii of two cylinders whose heights are equal is 2 : 3. If the volume of the smaller cylinder is $32\,cm^2$, find the volume of the bigger one.

A $27\,cm^3$ B $72\,cm^3$ C $81\,cm^3$
D $108\,cm^3$ E $216\,cm^3$

27) Solve $3x + 18 \geqslant 7$.

A $x \geqslant 8\frac{1}{3}$ B $x \geqslant 3\frac{2}{3}$ C $x \leqslant 3\frac{2}{3}$
D $x \leqslant -3\frac{2}{3}$ E $x \geqslant -3\frac{2}{3}$

28) Which one of the following statements is true?

A All rhombuses are parallelograms
B All kites are parallelograms
C All parallelograms are rhombuses
D All kites are rhombuses
E All parallelograms are rectangles

29) Simplify $64 \times 3{\cdot}8 + 36 \times 3{\cdot}8$

A 280   B 300   C 380
D 400   E 3 800

30) Find the value of x when $\frac{2x}{7} - 5 = 9$.

A 14   B 28   C 34
D 49   E 63

In Fig. E10, to go from X to N, move along the arrowed paths. These paths are numbered 0, 1, 1 in order. The number 011 is written in box N.

Using the information in Fig. E10, answer questions 31–33.

31) Starting at X, find the number which should be written in box L.

A 001   B 010   C 011
D 100   E 101

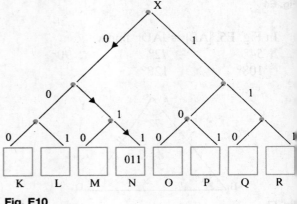

Fig. E10

32) Starting at X, which number goes into box Q?

A 000   B 011   C 101
D 110   E 111

33) Starting at X, find the box in which number 101 is written.

A L   B O   C P
D Q   E R

34) How many perfect squares are there in the se {1, 3, 4, 6, 9, 64, 67}?

A 1   B 2   C 3
D 4   E 5

35) Find the value of y in the equation $81 - 9y = 27$.

A -9 B -6 C 6
D 9   E 12

36) Which of the following plane shapes has no line of symmetry?

A kite   B rhombus   C trapezium
D square   E parallelogram

37) The sum of three times a number and 5 was divided by 7 to give 9. Translate this statement into an algebraic expression.

A $\frac{3x}{7} + 5 = 9$ B $3x + \frac{5}{7} = 9$ C $\frac{3x + 5}{9} =$?
D $\frac{3x + 5}{7} = 9$ E $\frac{3x - 5}{9} = 7$

38) In a triangle, angles are 40°, 76° and $2x$°. Find the value of x.

A 20°   B 30°   C 32°
D 38°   E 68°

244

39. How many lines of symmetry has an equilateral triangle?
    A 0   B 1   C 2
    D 3   E 4

40. Factorise the expression $6k + 2 - 6kh - 2h$.
    A $2(1 + h)(3k + 1)$ B $2(1 - h)(3k + 1)$
    C $(1 - 2h)(3k + 1)$ D $(3k + 1)(2k - h)$
    E $(2 + 3h)(3k - 1)$

41. Round off $0.008\,251$ to 2 significant figures.
    A 0.82 B 0.83 C 0.008
    D $0.008\,3$ E $0.008\,2$

42. Simplify $3x + x^2y + 2x + 3xy^2$.
    A $5x + 4x^2y$ B $5x + x^2y + 3xy^2$
    C $8x^3y$ D $5x + 3xy$
    E $5x + 4y^2x$

43. Find the size of each interior angle of a regular pentagon.
    A $135°$ B $128°$ C $120°$
    D $108°$ E $90°$

44. Find the value of $(101_{two})^2$ in base two.
    A $1\,001$ B $10\,001$ C $10\,111$
    D $11\,001$ E $11\,011$

45. If $\sqrt{52} = 7.211$ and $\sqrt{520} = 23.02$, find $\sqrt{5\,200}$.
    A 721.1 B 230.2 C 72.11
    D 23.02 E $2\,302$

46. If $a = \sqrt{4 \times 9 \times 16}$, find the value of a.
    A 96 B 48 C 36
    D 24 E 16

47. Expand $(3a + b)(3a - b)$.
    A $9a^2 + b^2$ B $9a^2 - 6ab + b^2$
    C $9a^2 + 6ab + b^2$ D $9a^2 - b^2$
    E $9a^2 - 3ab + b^2$

A shop sells eggs in boxes of six. 25 boxes of eggs are examined. Table E1 gives the numbers of broken eggs in the boxes.

number of broken eggs	0	1	2	3	4	5	6
number of boxes	12	6	4	2	1	0	0

Table E1

Use the information in Table E1 to answer questions 48–51.

48. What is the median number of broken eggs?
    A 0   B 1   C 2
    D 3   E 4

49. Find the modal number of broken eggs.
    A 0   B 1   C 2
    D 3   E 4

50. Calculate the mean number of broken eggs.
    A 0   B 0.24 C 0.48
    D 0.96 E 1

51. Find the probability that a box of eggs chosen at random has fewer than two broken eggs.
    A $\frac{22}{25}$ B $\frac{21}{25}$ C $\frac{18}{25}$
    D $\frac{16}{25}$ E $\frac{7}{25}$

52. Write $0.000\,54$ in standard form
    A 54×10^3 B 5.4×10^2
    C 0.54×10^3 D 5.4×10^{-4}
    E 5.4×10^{-3}

53. Write down the inequality which represents the graph shown in Fig. E11.
    A $-2 \leqslant x \leqslant 1$ B $-2 \leqslant x < 1$ C $-2 < x < 1$
    D $-1 \leqslant x < 2$ E $-2 < x \leqslant 1$

Fig. E11

54. Which of the following is an obtuse angle?
    A $86°$ B $136°$ C $236°$
    D $336°$ E $354°$

55. Which of these expressions is a factor of $x^2 + 3x - 54$?
    A $x - 9$ B $x - 6$ C $x - 18$
    D $x + 6$ E $x + 3$

56. Find the square root of $7\frac{1}{9}$.
    A $49\frac{1}{3}$ B $4\frac{2}{3}$ C $2\frac{2}{3}$
    D $2\frac{1}{3}$ E $\frac{8}{9}$

57. Solve $\dfrac{1}{6-b} = \dfrac{1}{b-5}$.

  A $5\frac{1}{2}$ B $1\frac{3}{4}$ C $\frac{1}{2}$

  D $-\frac{9}{2}$ E $-\frac{11}{2}$

58. $173^2 - 127^2$ is equal to

  A 13 800   B 13 080   C 10 380

  D 346   E 300

59. Change the decimal fraction 0·016 to a common fraction.

  A $\frac{8}{5}$ B $\frac{4}{25}$ C $\frac{2}{125}$

  D $\frac{4}{125}$ E $\frac{1}{625}$

60. A letter is chosen at random from the alphabet. What is the probability that it is one of the letters of the word AUNTY?

  A $\frac{1}{5}$ B $\frac{5}{26}$ C $\frac{4}{5}$

  D $\frac{2}{3}$ E $\frac{1}{6}$

61. What is the reciprocal of 0·003 7?

  A 0·270 3   B 2·703   C 27·03

  D 270·3   E $2·7 \times 10^2$

62. Find the tangent of angle 48·5°.

  A 13·03   B 7·490   C 6·826

  D 1·130 3   E 0·749 0

63. Which of the following quadrilaterals do not have their diagonals perpendicular to each other?

  A a square   B a kite

  C a rhombus   D a parallelogram

  E none of these

64. A telephone company charges for the number of units used as follows: a fixed charge of ₦1 000, and ₦15 per unit for the number of units used. If VAT of 5% is also added, find the charge for 200 units.

  A ₦2 655   B ₦3 150   C ₦3 200

  D ₦4 000   E ₦4 200

65. If $D = \sqrt{\dfrac{3h^2}{2}}$, make h the subject of the relation.

  A $h = \sqrt{\dfrac{2D}{3}}$ B $h = \sqrt{\dfrac{4D}{9}}$

  C $h = \dfrac{4D^2}{9}$ D $h = \sqrt{\dfrac{2D^2}{3}}$

  E $h = \sqrt{\dfrac{4D^2}{9}}$

66. 14 is added to $\frac{2}{3}$ of a number x. The result is $1\frac{1}{4}$ times the original number. Which of the following represents the statement?

  A $14 + \frac{2}{3} = 1\frac{1}{4}$ B $14 + \frac{2}{3}x = 1\frac{1}{4}$

  C $14 + \frac{2}{3}x = 1\frac{1}{4}x$

  D $\left(14 + \frac{2}{3}\right)x = 1\frac{1}{4}x$ E $14x + \frac{2}{3} = \frac{1}{4}x$

67. Which one of the following is *not* true of a parallelogram?

  A opposite sides are parallel

  B opposite sides are equal

  C diagonals are equal

  D opposite angles are equal

  E diagonals bisect each other

68. An open cylindrical drum has a circular base of radius $1\frac{3}{4}$ m. Its height is 1·5 m. Calculate the total surface area. (Take π to be $\frac{22}{7}$.)

  A 11 m²   B 18 m²   C 20 m²

  D 22 m²   E 26 m²

69. In Fig. E12, OAB and OPQ are similar triangles. If OP = 5 cm and OA = 2 cm, find the length of AB if PQ = 3 cm.

  A 7·5 cm   B 7 cm   C 3 cm

  D 2·5 cm   E 1·2 cm

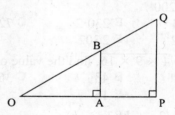

Fig. E12

70. Calculate to one decimal place the angle of elevation of the top of a flag-pole 31·9 m high from a point 55 m away on the ground level.

  A 30°   B 30·1°   C 32·4°

  D 59·9°   E 60°

71. If p varies directly as q and inversely as s, write down this relationship.

  A $p \propto q$ B $p \propto qs$ C $p \propto \frac{1}{s}$

  D $p \propto \frac{q}{s}$ E $p \propto \frac{1}{qs}$

(72) The bearing of A from P is 243°. Find the bearing of P from A.

A 333°   B 153°   C 117°

D 63°   E 47°

(73) A fair 6-faced die is thrown. What is the probability of obtaining an even number?

A 1   B $\frac{1}{2}$ C $\frac{1}{3}$

D $\frac{1}{6}$ E 0

(74) Which of the following is an irrational number?

A $\sqrt{121}$ B $\sqrt{19}$ C 2·5

D 3·$\dot{3}$ E $\frac{5}{7}$

(75) If $V = \pi(\frac{d}{2})^2h$, then $d =$

A $2\sqrt{\pi h V}$ B $\sqrt{\frac{2V}{\pi h}}$ C $\frac{4\pi}{hV}$

D $2\sqrt{\frac{\pi V}{h}}$ E $2\sqrt{\frac{V}{\pi h}}$

(76) If the range of a set of numbers is 3, and the highest number is 12, find the least number.

A 12   B 9   C 6

D 3   E 2

(77) Solve the simultaneous equations $y = x + 1$, $x + y = 3$, and find $x + 2y$.

A 6   B 5   C 4

D 3   E 2

(78) Convert 107_{ten} to a number in base two.

A 1 100 011   B 1 100 111   C 111 011

D 1 101 011   E 1 101 111

(79) The following numbers are rational except

I $\sqrt{3}$ II $\sqrt{\frac{4}{9}}$ III $\frac{30}{2}$

A I only   B II only   C III only

D II and III   E I and II

(80) Calculate the length of the side of a square whose area is 1 089 cm².

A 21 cm   B 23 cm   C 32 cm

D 33 cm   E 103 cm

Section II: Essay-theory questions

Attempt all questions
Time Allowed: 1 hour

(1) a Convert $110\,111_{two}$ to base ten.

   b Multiply $10\,110_{two}$ by 110_{two}.

   c The sum of two numbers is 21. Two-thirds of one number is added to three-quarters of the other number to give 15. Find the two numbers, showing clearly your working.

(2) a The monthly charge, C, of an electricity company is made up as follows: a constant charge a and a charge which varies directly as N the number of units used. When $N = 80$, $C = $₦820. When $N = 124$, $C = $₦1 040.

    i Find the relationship between C and N.

    ii Find C when $N = 180$.

   b Calculate the compound interest on ₦20 000 for 2 years at 9% per annum.

(3) Use a scale of 2 cm to 1 unit on both axes and draw the graphs of the equations $x - y = 1$ and $x + 2y = 7$. Hence obtain from the graphs the solution of the simultaneous equations $x - y = 1$ and $x + 2y = 7$.

Examination 2

Section I: Multiple choice
            objective questions

Time allowed: 2 hours

(1) What number do the tally marks represent?

卌 卌 卌 卌 卌 卌 |||

A 63   B 28   C 33

D 23   E 18

(2) Approximate 12 256 to 3 significant figures.

A 12 260   B 12 300   C 12·3

D 12 200   E 122

(3) Find the value of x in $x \times 4 = 12$.

A 2   B 3   C 4

D 5   E 6

(4) Which of the following is *not* a property of all parallelograms?

A Adjacent sides are equal

B Opposite angles are equal

C Opposite sides are equal

D The diagonals bisect each other

E Opposite sides are parallel.

5. The number of lines of symmetry in a parallelogram is

A 0   B 1   C 2
D 3   E 4

6. The sum of two consecutive even numbers is 34. Find the smaller number.

A 20   B 16   C 14
D 12   E 10

7. A trader bought a book for ₦500 and sold it for ₦360. Calculate the percentage loss.

A 12%   B 18%   C 24%
D 28%   E $33\frac{1}{3}$%

8. In Fig. E13, PQRS is a parallelogram where PQ = QR and $\hat{P} \neq \hat{Q}$. What name can be given to the parallelogram?

A square   B rectangle   C rhombus
D trapezium   E quadrilateral

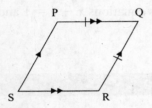

Fig. E13

9. Solve the equation $5(x + 1) - 15 = 0$.

A $x = -9$ B $x = -6$ C $x = 2$
D $x = 3$ E $x = 5$

10. Write 394 in Roman numerals.

A CCIXIV   B CCCIV   C CCIX
D CCCICV   E CCCXCIV

11. In Fig. E14, what is the value of x in terms of y?

A $90° + y°$ B $270° - y°$ C $180° + y°$
D $360° - y°$ E $270° + y°$

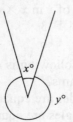

Fig. E14

12. If $a = 2$, $b = -3$, and $x = 0$, which of the following is correct?

A $ab < x$ B $ab > x$ C $ab = x$
D $ab \leqslant x$ E $ab \geqslant x$

13. Express 72 as the product of its factors, leaving your answer in index form.

A $2^2 \times 3^3$ B $2^3 \times 3^2$ C $2^4 \times 3^2$
D $2^2 \times 3^2$ E $2^3 \times 3^3$

14. In Fig. E15, RT and SQ are parallel lines. What is the size of the angle marked $x°$?

A $130° - x°$ B $130°$ C $65°$
D $50°$ E $25°$

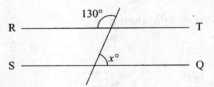

Fig. E15

15. A trader gets ₦80 for every tray of eggs sold. At the end of a week, she makes a total of ₦5 600. How many trays of eggs did she sell?

A 7   B 35   C 50
D 70   E 80

16. If $m = 2$, $n = 5$ and $y = 3$, evaluate $\dfrac{m(n + y)}{nm}$.

A 1·6   B 1·66   C 2·5
D 16   E 16·6

17. Convert 57_{ten} to a number in base two.

A 100 111   B 111 110   C 111 001
D 111 101   E 110 011

18. Find the unknown angle $x°$ in Fig. E16.

A $40°$ B $50°$ C $60°$
D $80°$ E $100°$

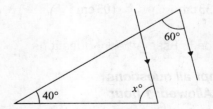

Fig. E16

19. If $x = -2$, find the value of $8 - 3x^2$.
   A −4   B 4   C 5
   D 12   E 20

20. Find the unknown angle in Fig. E17.
   A 40°   B 50°   C 60°
   D 70°   E 110°

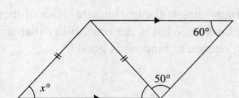

Fig. E17

21. Simplify $(5a + 3b) - (2a - 7b)$.
   A $3a - 4b$ B $3a - 10b$ C $3a + 4b$
   D $3a + 10b$ E $7a + 10b$

22. What is the multiplicative inverse of -0.04?
   A $-\frac{1}{25}$ B −4   C −25
   D 0·06   E 0·25

23. Calculate the area of the shape in Fig. E18.
   A 40 cm²   B 50 cm²   C 60 cm²
   D 100 cm²   E 120 cm²

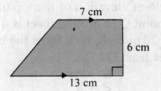

Fig. E18

24. Simplify $\frac{1}{a} + \frac{1}{3a}$.
   A $\frac{4}{3a}$ B $\frac{2}{3a}$ C $\frac{1}{3a^2}$
   D $\frac{1}{4a}$ E $\frac{2}{4a}$

25. Find the length of the unknown side in the triangle in Fig. E19.
   A 2·6 cm   B 3 cm   C 6·5 cm
   D 10 cm   E 12 cm

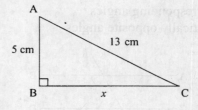

Fig. E19

26. Which of the fractions is equivalent to $\frac{12xy}{8x^2a}$?
   A $\frac{3y}{2x^2a}$ B $\frac{3xy}{2a}$ C $\frac{3y}{2xa}$
   D $\frac{2y}{3xa}$ E $\frac{2y}{3a^2}$

27. If $p^2 - q^2 = (p + q)(p - q)$, evaluate $121^2 - 79^2$.
   A 9 559   B 8 404   C 8 400
   D 4 206   E 1 764

28. Calculate the area of a circle whose diameter is 7 cm. (Take π to be $\frac{22}{7}$.)
   A 22 cm²   B 38 cm²   C 38·5 cm²
   D 44 cm²   E 154 cm²

29. Factorise $4x^2 - 1$.
   A $(2x + 1)(2x - 1)$ B $(2x - 1)(2x - 1)$
   C $(4x + 1)(x - 1)$ D $(4x + 1)(x + 1)$
   E $(2x - 2)(2x + 1)$

30. The bearing of a tree from a house is 295°. Find the bearing of the house from the tree.
   A 0·25°   B 095°   C 115°
   D 295°   E 475°

31. What kind of triangle has only two sides equal?
   A equilateral   B isosceles
   C right-angled   D scalene
   E acute-angled

32. Find the range of the following set of numbers: 10, 10, 11, 11, 5, 6, 13, 7, 6.
   A 1   B 2   C 3
   D 7   E 8

33. In Fig. E20, if AB//CD and PQ is a transversal, then $x°$ and $y°$ are called:
   A allied angles
   B alternate angles
   C angles on a straight line

D corresponding angles

E vertically opposite angles

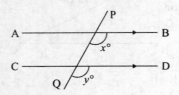

Fig. E20

34. Find the value of $2\,004^2 - 16$.

A 4 016 000   B 401 600   C 40 160

D 4016   E 401

35. Factorise $2a^2 - bc + 2ac - ab$.

A $(a + c)(2a + b)$ B $(a - c)(2a - b)$

C $(a - c)(2ab + b)$ D $(a + c)(2a - b)$

E $(a + c)(2b - a)$

36. Two alternate angles formed on parallel lines are:

A complementary   B corresponding

C equal   D supplementary

E vertically opposite

37. What type of angle lies between 0° and 90°?

A acute   B obtuse   C reflex

D scalene   E right angle

38. Esther is three times as old as her sister Janet. If the sum of their ages is 20 years, find the difference between their ages.

A 3 years   B 8 years   C 10 years

D 12 years   E 16 years

39. The sum of two numbers is 43, and their difference is 7. Find the smaller number.

A 50   B 36   C 18

D 10   E −8

40. A circle has a circumference of 77 cm. Calculate the radius of the circle. (Take π to be $\frac{22}{7}$.)

A 49 cm   B $24\frac{1}{4}$ cm   C $12\frac{1}{2}$ cm

D $12\frac{1}{4}$ cm   E 7 cm

41. If $0\cdot007\,25$ is written as $7\cdot25 \times 10^n$, the value of n is

A −4   B −3   C −2

D −1   E 3

42. What is the size of one interior angle of a regular octagon?

A 45°   B 90°   C 108°

D 120°   E 135°

43. If the angles of a quadrilateral are $5x$, $4x$, $3x$ and $6x$, what is the value of x?

A 10°   B 15°   C 18°

D 20°   E 90°

44. A trader has 100 eggs for sale. Four of them are broken. What is the probability that an egg chosen at random is good?

A $\frac{24}{25}$ B $\frac{4}{5}$ C $\frac{18}{25}$

D $\frac{9}{20}$ E $\frac{1}{25}$

45. In Fig. E21, POQ and OR are straight lines. Find the value of x.

A 96°   B 60°   C 36°

D 30°   E 6°

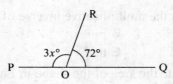

Fig. E21

46. The angle of elevation of the top of a tower from a point Q at ground level is 45°. If the tower is 20 m high, how far is the bottom of the tower from Q?

A 40 m   B 30 m   C 20 m

D 10 m   E 5 m

47. Bimbo spent a quarter of her pocket money on Monday and $\frac{3}{8}$ on Wednesday. What fraction of her money is left?

A $\frac{3}{4}$ B $\frac{5}{8}$ C $\frac{3}{8}$

D $\frac{1}{4}$ E $\frac{1}{8}$

48. If one ruler and three pencils cost ₦120 and two rulers and one pencil cost ₦140, find the cost of one ruler and one pencil.

A (₦60, ₦20)   B (₦10, ₦70)

C (₦20, ₦60)   D (₦14, ₦20)

E (₦54, ₦20)

49. In Fig. E22, the angle of elevation of Y from X is 40°. What is the angle of depression of X from Y?

A 140°   B 100°   C 60°

D 50°   E 40°

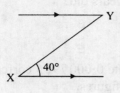

Fig. E22

50 What type of triangles are PST and PQR in Fig. E23?
A congruent   B equilateral
C symmetrical   D similar
E equal

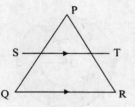

Fig. E23

51 One factor of $x^2 - 2x - 8$ is $x + 2$.
Find the other factor.
A $x + 4$ B $x - 2$ C $x - 4$
D $x + 1$ E $x - 8$

52 What is the value of x which satisfies the equation $\frac{21}{2x - 1} = 3$?
A $10\frac{1}{2}$ B 10   C 7
D 4   E $3\frac{1}{2}$

53 The circular base of a cylinder has a diameter of 14 cm. Its height is 7 cm. Taking π to be $\frac{22}{7}$, find its volume to 2 significant figures.
A 3 300 cm³   B 1 100 cm³   C 1 000 cm³
D 31 cm³   E 1 500 cm³

54 Find the difference between 16 and -2.
A 32   B 18   C 16
D 14   E 8

55 How long is the diagonal of a rectangle 4 cm long and 3 cm wide?
A 4 cm   B 5 cm   C 6 cm
D 7 cm   E 12 cm

56 Express 100011_{two} as a base ten number.
A 32   B 33   C 34
D 35   E 36

57 If $3x + 4y = 5$, make y the subject of the equation.
A $y = 5 - 3x$ B $y = \frac{5 + 3x}{4}$ C $y = \frac{5 - 3x}{4}$
D $y = \frac{5 - 4x}{3}$ E $y = \frac{5 - 3x}{5}$

58 Make v the subject of the formula $\frac{1}{f} = \frac{1}{v} + \frac{1}{u}$.
A $v = \frac{1}{f} + \frac{1}{u}$ B $v = \frac{1}{f} - \frac{1}{u}$
C $v = f - u$ D $v = \frac{fu}{u - f}$
E $v = \frac{u - f}{fu}$

59 A cylinder has radius 14 cm and length 10 cm. Find its curved surface area. (Take π to be $\frac{22}{7}$.)
A 220 cm²   B 280 cm²   C 440 cm²
D 880 cm²   E 1 760 cm²

60 Solve the inequality $3 - 2x > 5$.
A $x > -1$ B $x < -1$ C $x > -2$
D $x < -2$ E $x > 1$

61 The sum of all the interior angles of a regular polygon is 1 260°. Find the number of sides of the polygon.
A 10   B 9   C 8
D 7   E 6

62 If equations $3x - 2y = 4$ and $2x + 3y = -6$ are solved simultaneously, then $y =$
A -2 B -1 C 1
D 2   E 3

63 Express $\frac{2}{a} + \frac{5}{b}$ as a single fraction.
A $\frac{2b + 5a}{a + b}$ B $\frac{7}{ab}$ C $\frac{7}{a + b}$
D $\frac{2a + 5b}{ab}$ E $\frac{2b + 5a}{ab}$

64 The area of a triangle ABC is 18 cm² and the base BC is 6 cm. Calculate the height of the triangle.
A 2 cm   B 4 cm   C 6 cm
D 9 cm   E 18 cm

65 How many years will it take to earn ₦8 100 simple interest on ₦180 000 at 9% per annum?
A 2 yr   B $1\frac{1}{2}$ yr   C 1 yr
D $\frac{1}{2}$ yr   E $\frac{1}{4}$ yr

66. When the number x is trebled and 7 is subtracted from it, the result is equal to 8. Represent this statement algebraically.
   A $3(x - 7) = 8$ B $7 - 3x = 8$
   C $3x = 7 - 8$ D $3x - 7 = 8$ E $\frac{x}{3} - 7 = 8$

67. A girl travels 2 km at a speed of x km/h. How many hours, in terms of x, does the journey take?
   A $2x$ B $\frac{2}{x}$ C $\frac{x}{2}$
   D $\frac{1}{2x}$ E $(x + 2)$

68. Calculate the area of a circular field of diameter 6 metres correct to 2 significant figures. (Take $\pi = 3.14$.)
   A $9.4\,m^2$ B $28\,m^2$ C $28.3\,m^2$
   D $29\,m^2$ E $112\,m^2$

69. Find the area of a circular metal washer, given that the outer radius and the inner radius are $4\frac{1}{2}$ cm and $2\frac{1}{2}$ cm respectively. (Take $\pi = \frac{22}{7}$.)
   A $154\,cm^2$ B $77\,cm^2$ C $44\,cm^2$
   D $33\,cm^2$ E $14\,cm^2$

70. A box contains four blue balls and six red balls. If a ball is selected at random, what is the probability of selecting a blue ball?
   A 0 B $\frac{1}{4}$ C $\frac{1}{3}$
   D $\frac{2}{5}$ E $\frac{1}{2}$

Table E2 gives the distribution of the ages (in years) of 30 students in a school club. Use the information to answer questions 71–74.

age (years)	10	11	12	13	14	15
frequency	4	12	7	4	2	1

Table E2

71. Obtain the mode.
   A 11 years   B 12 years   C 13 years
   D 14 years   E 15 years

72. Find the median.
   A 11 years   B 11.5 years   C 12 years
   D 12.5 years   E 13 years

73. Calculate the mean.
   A 5 years   B 6 years   C 7 years
   D 11 years   E 11.7 years

74. What is the probability that a student in the club is 11 years old?
   A 0 B $\frac{2}{15}$ C $\frac{8}{15}$
   D $\frac{2}{5}$ E $\frac{3}{5}$

75. Approximate 0.0007925 correct to 3 significant figures.
   A 0.001 B 0.000793 C 0.0008
   D 0.793 E 0.00079

76. Fig. E24 shows a washer. If the external radius is R and the internal radius is r, find its area.
   A πR^2 B $2\pi(R - r)$ C $\pi(R - r)^2$
   D $\pi(R - r)(R + r)$ E $\pi(R + r)^2$

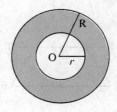

Fig. E24

77. Make r the subject of the formula $V = \pi r^2 h$.
   A $r = \dfrac{V}{\sqrt{\pi h}}$ B $r = \sqrt{\dfrac{V}{\pi h}}$ C $r = \sqrt{\dfrac{Vh}{\pi}}$
   D $r = \dfrac{V}{\pi h}$ E $r = \sqrt{\dfrac{\pi h}{V}}$

78. If y varies inversely as x^2 and $y = 3$ when $x = 4$, find y.
   A $y = \dfrac{16}{3x^2}$ B $y = \dfrac{16}{8x^2}$ C $y = \dfrac{48}{x^2}$
   D $y = 48x^2$ E $y = \dfrac{3}{16x^2}$

79. The angle of elevation of the top of a building is 25° from a point 80 m away on level ground. Calculate the height of the building to 2 significant figures.
   A $3.70\,m$ B $37.0\,m$ C $370\,m$
   D $373\,m$ E $3700\,m$

80. Factorise $ax - ay - bx + by$.
   A $ab(x - y)$ B $ay(b - x)$
   C $(a - b)(x - y)$ D $(a - b)(x + y)$
   E $(a + b)(x - y)$

Attempt all questions
Time allowed: 1 hour

1 a A car costs ₦1·8 million. Its value depreciates by 25% in its first year and 20% in the second year. Calculate its value after 2 years.

  b The diagonals of a rectangle are 10 cm long. They intersect at an angle of 120°. Make a sketch of the rectangle. Use trigonometry to calculate the perimeter of the rectangle.

2 Table E3 gives the ages of a group of students in a school club.

age (years)	12	13	14	15	16
number of students	4	6	4	4	2

Table E3

  a Calculate the mean age.
  b Find the median.
  c Obtain the mode.
  d If a student is selected at random, what is the probability that the student is 14 years old?

3 Using a pair of compasses and ruler only, construct $\triangle$PQR in which |PQ| = 7 cm, |PR| = 10 cm and $\hat{Q}$ = 120°. Measure |RQ| and $\hat{P}$.

Examination 3

Section I: Multiple choice
objective questions

Time allowed: 2 hours

1 What is the reciprocal of −0·9?

  A 9
  B $\frac{-10}{9}$
  C 0·9
  D −0·9
  E $\frac{10}{9}$

2 Express 9 126 to the nearest thousand.

  A 91 000
  B 10 000
  C 9 120
  D 9 100
  E 9 000

3 What number does CXIV represent?

  A 94
  B 106
  C 110
  D 114
  E 116

4 What is 0·021 728 to 3 significant figures?

  A 0·021
  B 0·022
  C 0·0217
  D 0·021 8
  E 0·021 73

5 A girl cycles at the rate of 10 km/h for $1\frac{1}{2}$ hours. How far does she travel?

  A 5 km
  B 10 km
  C 15 km
  D 18 km
  E 20 km

6 Simplify $(-4) \times (-6) \times (2)$.

  A 48
  B 24
  C 12
  D −24
  E −48

7 The length of a board is twice its width. If its perimeter is 3·60 m, what is its width in cm?

  A 60
  B 100
  C 120
  D 150
  E 240

8 What is the sum of the following numbers in base two: 1101, 1110, 1001?

  A 10 000
  B 100 010
  C 100 100
  D 100 110
  E 100 111

9 A car travels 42 km on 6 litres of petrol. How far will it travel on 9 litres?

  A 49 km
  B 63 km
  C 70 km
  D 72 km
  E 84 km

10 A bicycle wheel has a diameter of 42 cm. Find its circumference. (Take π to be $\frac{22}{7}$.)

  A 1 386 cm
  B 264 cm
  C 132 cm
  D 66 cm
  E 21 cm

11 Solve for a in the equation $4 - 6a = -2$.

  A 3
  B 1
  C $\frac{1}{3}$
  D −1
  E −3

12 If x varies directly as y and inversely as z, write down this relationship.

  A $x \propto y$
  B $x \propto \frac{1}{z}$
  C $x \propto yz$
  D $x \propto \frac{y}{z}$
  E $x \propto \frac{1}{yz}$

13 Find the value of $2y^2 - 3$ if $y = 5$.

  A 7
  B 17
  C 47
  D 53
  E 97

14 Express 4 570 000 in standard form.

  A 457×10^4
  B $45·7 \times 10^5$
  C $4·57 \times 10^6$
  D $4·5 \times 10^6$
  E $4·0 \times 10^6$

15 Fig. E25 shows a square of side 7 cm. The shaded part is a quadrant of a circle of radius

7 cm. What is the area of the unshaded part of the figure? (Take π to be $\frac{22}{7}$.)

A $154\,cm^2$ B $84\cdot5\,cm^2$ C $49\,cm^2$

D $38\cdot5\,cm^2$ E $10\cdot5\,cm^2$

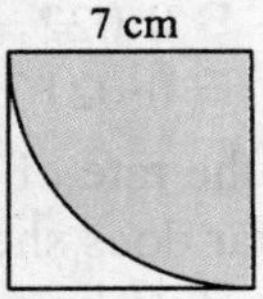

7 cm

Fig. E25

(16) A square has a perimeter of 24 cm. Find its area in cm^2.

A $96\,cm^2$ B $72\,cm^2$ C $48\,cm^2$

D $36\,cm^2$ E $24\,cm^2$

(17) $2x + 3 = 7$, what is x?

A 5   B 4   C $3\frac{1}{2}$

D 2   E -2

(18) Simplify $2 \times 3y + 6y \div 3$.

A $9y$ B $8y$ C $6y$

D $4y$ E $2\frac{1}{2}y$

(19) The area of a rectangle is $40\,cm^2$ and one side is 8 cm long. Find its perimeter.

A 40 cm   B 32 cm   C 26 cm

D 20 cm   E 16 cm

(20) What is x in the simultaneous equations $x - y = 1, x + y = 3$?

A 4   B 3   C 2

D 0   E -3

(21) Calculate the area of the triangle ABC shown in Fig. E26.

A $30\,cm^2$ B $20\,cm^2$ C $18\,cm^2$

D $15\,cm^2$ E $9\,cm^2$

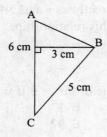

A

6 cm

3 cm

B

5 cm

C

Fig. E26

(22) 9 was subtracted from a certain number and the result was divided by 4. If the final answer is 5, what was the original number?

A 4   B 5   C 18

D 20   E 29

(23) Factorise $81 - 4x^2$.

A $(81 - 2x)(81 + 2x)$ B $(9 - 2x)(9 + 2x)$

C $(9 + 2x)^2$ D $(9 - x)(9 + x)$

E $(81 - 2x)(81 + x)$

(24) Convert 71_{ten} to a number in base two.

A 100 111   B 1 000 101   C 1 000 111

D 1 100 010   E 1 000 011

(25) Find the price if a discount of 20% is given on an article costing ₦27 000.

A ₦20 000   B ₦20 600   C ₦21 600

D ₦24 300   E ₦25 000

(26) A board measures 3 m by 2 m and costs ₦450. Calculate the cost of $1\,m^2$ of the board

A ₦45   B ₦60   C ₦75

D ₦80   E ₦90

(27) A cuboid is 24 cm long, 20 cm wide and 15 cm high. A similar cuboid is 16 cm long. What is its height?

A 6 cm   B $7\frac{1}{2}$ cm   C 8 cm

D 10 cm   E $12\frac{1}{2}$ cm

(28) In a basket of 100 oranges, 26 are bad. What percentage is good?

A 26   B 40   C 64

D 70   E 74

(29) Reduce $\frac{48}{72}$ to its lowest form.

A $\frac{6}{9}$ B $\frac{4}{6}$ C $\frac{2}{3}$

D $\frac{4}{9}$ E $\frac{2}{6}$

(30) If today is Tuesday, what day of the week will it be after 18 days?

A Tuesday   B Wednesday   C Thursday

D Friday   E Saturday

(31) Find the compound interest on ₦30 000 for 2 years at 7% per annum.

A ₦2 100   B ₦4 200   C ₦4 347

D ₦6 300   E ₦8 400

(32) Which of the following is a non-rational number?

A $20\cdot4$ B $\sqrt{15\cdot8}$ C $\sqrt{\frac{20}{5}}$

D $\frac{22}{7}$ E $\sqrt{1\cdot44}$

(33) What is the value of $\sqrt{\frac{27}{48}}$?

A $\frac{3}{4}$ B $\frac{3}{16}$ C $\frac{9}{16}$

D $\frac{9}{32}$ E $\frac{18}{32}$

34 Calculate the perimeter of a football field which measures 60 m by 40 m.
A 20 m   B 100 m   C 120 m
D 200 m   E 2 400 m

35 A rectangular room 6 m long and 4 m wide contains 72 m³ of air. Calculate the height of the room.
A 36 m   B 24 m   C 18 m
D 12 m   E 3 m

36 Find the size of the angle marked x in Fig. E27.
A 115°   B 109°   C 75°
D 65°   E 37°

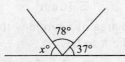

Fig. E27

37 A pyramid has five triangular faces. Its other face is in the shape of a
A rectangle   B triangle   C pentagon
D hexagon   E square

38 ABC is a triangle in which B = 90°. What is the length of side AC if AB = 5 cm and BC = 12 cm?
A $\sqrt{5}$ cm   B $\sqrt{60}$ cm   C 12 cm
D 13 cm   E 24 cm

39 Expand $(2a - 3)^2$.
A $4a^2 + 12a + 9$ B $4a^2 - 12a - 9$
C $4a^2 - 12a + 9$ D $4a^2 - 6a + 9$
E $4a^2 - 6a - 9$

40 Make W the subject of the relation $I = \dfrac{E}{WL}$.

A $W = \dfrac{E}{I}$ B $W = \dfrac{E}{LI}$ C $W = ILE$

D $W = \dfrac{LI}{E}$ E $W = \dfrac{L}{IE}$

41 Solve for b if $\frac{1}{b} + \frac{1}{3} = \frac{1}{2}$.
A 2   B 3   C 5
D 6   E 7

42 The ratio of the areas of two similar rectangles is 8:50. Find the ratio of their lengths.
A 4:25   B 16:625   C 2:5
D 8:625   E 2:3

43 What is the length of a diagonal of a rectangle 24 cm by 10 cm?
A 14 cm   B 26 cm   C 34 cm
D 48 cm   E 60 cm

The graph in Fig. E28 shows the cost of a certain cloth in metres. Use the graph to answer questions 44 and 45.

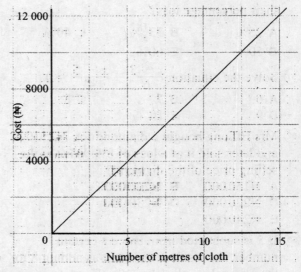

Fig. E28

44 What is the cost of 4 m of the cloth?
A ₦2 400   B ₦3 000   C ₦3 200
D ₦4 000   E ₦5 000

45 What length of the cloth can be bought for ₦8 400?
A 12 m   B $10\frac{1}{2}$ m   C 10 m
D 9 m   E $9\frac{1}{2}$ m

46 If a is directly proportional to b, and $a = -1$ while $b = -4$, the formula connecting a and b is
A $a = \frac{1}{4}b$ B $a = \frac{1}{2}b$ C $a = b$
D $a = 2b$ E $a = 4b$

47 Which of the following groups of numbers forms a Pythagorean triple?
A 2, 4, 6   B 4, 6, 8   C 6, 8, 10
D 8, 10,12   E 10, 12, 14

48 If two pencils cost y naira, what is the cost of 12 pencils?

A $\frac{2}{12}$ naira   B $\frac{2y}{12}$ naira   C $2y$ naira

D $6y$ naira   E $10y$ naira

49. Calculate the volume of a cylindrical steel bar which is 7 cm long and 6 cm in diameter.
A $21\pi\,cm^3$ B $42\pi\,cm^3$ C $63\pi\,cm^3$
D $126\pi\,cm^3$ E $252\pi\,cm^3$

50. Mr and Mrs Samuel bought a generator for ₦120 000. They sold it for ₦80 000. What is their percentage loss?

A 25%   B $33\frac{1}{3}$%   C 40%

D 50%   E 60%

51. Solve the equation $\dfrac{x-3}{6} - \dfrac{x-5}{4} = 0$.

A 6   B 7   C 8

D 9   E 10

52. Mrs Effiong bought a diamond for ₦250 000 and later sold it at a loss of 8%. What is the selling price of the diamond?
A ₦150 000   B ₦200 000
C ₦220 000   D ₦230 000
E ₦240 000

53. If 5 is subtracted from twice a certain number, the result is the same as adding 8 to the original number. Express this statement as an equation.
A $5 - 2x = x + 8$ B $2(5 - x) + 8 = x$
C $2x - 5 = x + 8$ D $x - 2 \times 5 = 8 + x$
E $2x + 5 = x - 8$

54. Divide $100\,001_{two}$ by 11_{two}.
A 1 001   B 1 011   C 1 110
D 1 101   E 10 111

55. Write $5\cdot48 \times 10^{-4}$ as a decimal fraction.
A 0·054 8   B 0·005 48   C 0·000 548
D 0·000 054 8   E 0·000 005 48

56. Simplify $\dfrac{x^2 - y^2}{x + y}$.

A $x + y$ B $x - y$ C $2x - y$

D $\dfrac{1}{(x - y)}$ E $x^2 + y^2$

57. A six-faced die numbered 1, 2, 3, 4, 5 and 6 is thrown. What is the probability of getting a number not less than 5?

A $\frac{1}{4}$ B $\frac{1}{3}$ C $\frac{1}{2}$

D $\frac{2}{3}$ E $\frac{5}{6}$

58. $x \propto \frac{1}{y}$ and $x = 3$ when $y = 2$. Find x when $y = 4$.
A 1   B $1\frac{1}{3}$ C $1\frac{1}{2}$
D 2   E 6

59. Expand $(t + 1)(t - 2)$.
A $t^2 + t - 2$ B $t^2 - t + 2$ C $t^2 + t + 2$
D $t^2 - t - 2$ E $t^2 - 2t - 2$

60. Find the area of a square with side 7 cm.
A $10\,cm^2$ B $14\,cm^2$ C $35\,cm^2$
D $49\,cm^2$ E $343\,cm^2$

61. What is the area of a triangle with base 3 cm and height 6 cm?
A $3\,cm^2$ B $6\,cm^2$ C $9\,cm^2$
D $12\,cm^2$ E $16\,cm^2$

62. What is the area of a circle with radius $3\frac{1}{2}$ cm? (Take π to be $\frac{22}{7}$.)
A $7\,cm^2$ B $11\,cm^2$ C $22\,cm^2$
D $38\frac{1}{2}\,cm^2$ E $134\frac{3}{4}\,cm^2$

63. Factorise completely $2a^2 - 18$.
A $(a + 3)(a - 3)$ B $2(a + 3)(a - 3)$
C $2(a + 3)(a + 3)$ D $2(a - 3)(a - 3)$
E $(2a + 3)(2a - 3)$

64. A cuboid with volume $64\,cm^3$ has a height of 8 cm. What is its base area?
A $4\,cm^2$ B $8\,cm^2$ C $16\,cm^2$
D $32\,cm^2$ E $64\,cm^2$

65. If the circumference of a circle is 44 cm, calculate its radius. (Take π to be $\frac{22}{7}$.)
A 21 cm   B 14 cm   C 7 cm
D 5 cm   E 3·5 cm

66. Solve for x in the simultaneous equations $x + y = 1$, $x - y = 3$.
A 2   B 1   C 0
D -1 E -2

67. In a test, 154 out of 175 candidates passed. What percentage pass is this?
A 12%   B 15%   C 88%
D 90%   E 92%

68. Solve the equation $\dfrac{3}{y + 1} = \dfrac{2}{y}$.

A 1   B $1\frac{1}{2}$ C 2
D 5   E 6

69. Write $6\cdot73 \times 10^5$ in full.
A 0·000 673   B 0·006 73   C 0·067 3
D 67 300   E 673 000

⑦⓪ Find the size of an exterior angle of a regular octagon.
  A 30°   **B** 45°   **C** 60°
  D 120°   **E** 135°

⑦① Write 0·000 054 9 in standard form.
  A $5·49 \times 10^{-5}$ **B** $5·49 \times 10^{-4}$
  C $0·549 \times 10^{-3}$ **D** $54·9 \times 10^{4}$
  E $5·49 \times 10^{5}$

⑦② What is the bearing of Q from P in Fig. E29?
  A 52°   **B** 114°   **C** 206°
  D 256°   **E** 276°

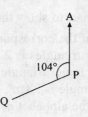

Fig. E29

⑦③ In Fig. E30, SP = 12 cm, RQ = 3 cm and QP = 4 cm. What is the length of RS?
  A 7 cm   **B** 10 cm   **C** 13 cm
  D 15 cm   **E** 19 cm

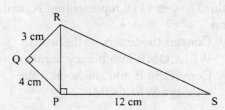

Fig. E30

⑦④ Simplify $\dfrac{-24}{(-3) \times (-4)}$.

  A 4   **B** 2   **C** $\frac{1}{2}$
  D $-\frac{1}{2}$ **E** -2

⑦⑤ Find the value of y in Fig. E31.
  A 86°   **B** 75°   **C** 56°
  D 51°   **E** 35°

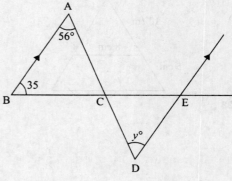

Fig. E31

⑦⑥ There are three red balls and six blue balls in a box and each is equally likely to be picked. What is the probability of picking a red ball?
  A 1   **B** 0   **C** $\frac{1}{2}$
  D $\frac{1}{3}$ **E** $\frac{3}{10}$

⑦⑦ Calculate the volume of the prism in Fig. E32.
  A 24 cm³   **B** 48 cm³   **C** 96 cm³
  D 144 cm³   **E** 192 cm³

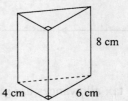

Fig. E32

⑦⑧ What is the length (in cm) of the side of a square equal in area to a rectangle measuring 24·5 cm by 18 cm?
  A 14 cm   **B** 21 cm   **C** 28 cm
  D 42·5 cm   **E** 85 cm

⑦⑨ Find 18% of ₦30 000.
  A ₦3 000   **B** ₦5 400   **C** ₦5 600
  D ₦54 000   **E** ₦72 000

⑧⓪ Fig. E33 shows two similar triangles. Calculate the length of the side marked x.
  A 25 cm   **B** 15 cm   **C** 12 cm
  D 4 cm   **E** 2·5 cm

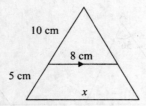

Fig. E33

Section II: Essay-theory questions

Attempt all questions
Time allowed: 1 hour

① a Fig. E34 shows a trapezium with AB parallel to EC. The dimensions are given in metres, and the angles are as shown. Find, to the nearest metre, the perimeter of the shape.

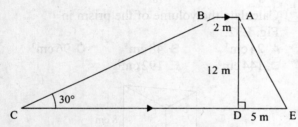

Fig. E34

b Income tax allowances are given as follows:

Personal   ₦6 000
Children (not   ₦2 500 per child
exceeding 4)
Dependent relative Not more than
                    ₦4 000

i Calculate the personal allowance of a nurse with 3 children and a dependent relative for whom she claims ₦3 500.

ii If income tax is paid as follows:
first ₦40 000   10%
next ₦40 000   15%
next ₦40 000   20%
calculate the tax paid by the nurse on an income of ₦120 000.

② a Solve $\dfrac{3x + 2}{5} - \dfrac{2x + 3}{3} = 3$.

b Simplify $\dfrac{2\frac{1}{5} - 1\frac{1}{2} + 1\frac{7}{10}}{\frac{1}{3} \text{ of } 2\frac{2}{5}}$.

c A company makes different perfumes A, B, C, D and E. Sales of the perfume are as shown in Table E4.

perfume	A	B	C	D	E
sale in thousands ₦	5·6	4·8	7·5	8·1	10

Table E4

Draw a pie chart to show the sales.

③ a The ratio of the corresponding sides of two similar triangles is 2 : 5. Calculate the area of the larger triangle if the area of the smaller triangle is 28 m².

b Letters of the alphabet $a, b, c, d, \ldots, z$ are converted to binary numbers such that $a = 1, b = 10, c = 11, d = 100, \ldots,$ $z = 11010$ in that order. In Fig. E35 Tape A shows the message 'BANKER' in which the first row is 10 representing B, the second row is 01 representing A, the third row is 1110 representing N, and so on.

i Convert the letters of the word WELCOME into binary numbers.

ii Copy Tape B and shade on it the message WELCOME.

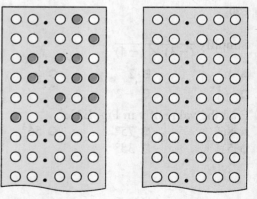

Tape A   Tape B

Fig. E35

Time allowed: 2 hours

① How many edges has a cube?
  A 4   B 6   C 8
  D 12   E 16

② Convert $11\,100_{two}$ to a number in base ten.
  A 24   B 28   C 29
  D 48   E 56

③ If a six-faced die is thrown, what is the probability of getting a number not greater than 2?
  A 1   B $\frac{1}{2}$ C $\frac{1}{3}$
  D $\frac{1}{6}$ E 0

④ What is the place value of 5 in the number 249·056?
  A five tenths   B five hundredths
  C five units   D fifty
  E five thousandths.

⑤ Find the simple interest on a loan of ₦45 000 at the rate of $3\frac{1}{2}$% for 2 years.
  A ₦1 350   B ₦3 150   C ₦3 350
  D ₦4 050   E ₦4 500

⑥ What are the prime factors of 60?
  A 1, 20, 30   B 3, 5   C 2, 3, 4, 5
  D 2, 3, 5   E 1, 2, 3, 5

⑦ The sum of the interior angles of an octagon is equal to
  A 1 440°   B 1 080°   C 720°
  D 540°   E 360°

⑧ R varies directly as S and inversely as T. If $R = 8$ when $S = 4$ and $T = 3$, then R is equal to
  A $32\frac{S}{T}$ B $\frac{6S}{T}$ C $\frac{3S}{2T}$
  D $\frac{3T}{2S}$ E $\frac{6T}{S}$

⑨ Write 0·072 58 correct to 3 significant figures.
  A 0·070   B 0·072   C 0·073
  D 0·072 5   E 0·072 6

Table E5 is a record of the favourite games of some students in a school.

type of games	wrestling	tennis	football	table tennis	athletics
number of students	1	2	12	8	2

Table E5

Use this information to answer questions 10–12.

⑩ What game was the favourite of most students?
  A wrestling   B tennis   C football
  D table tennis   E athletics

⑪ What game was least liked by the students?
  A wrestling   B tennis   C football
  D table tennis   E athletics

⑫ What is the probability that a student picked from the class at random liked tennis most?
  A 0·48   B 0·2   C 0·16
  D 0·08   E 0·02

⑬ Find the value of x if $x - 25 = 6x$.
  A −5   B $-4\frac{1}{6}$ C −3
  D −2   E 3

⑭ Find the value of x if $9x^2 = 4$.
  A 4   B $\frac{9}{4}$ C $\frac{3}{2}$
  D $\frac{4}{9}$ E $\frac{2}{3}$

⑮ What is the coefficient of y in the equation $3y^2 - \frac{4}{5}y + 6 = 0$?
  A 3   B $\frac{4}{5}$ C $-\frac{4}{5}$
  D 6   E −6

⑯ Give the number 29 542 correct to the nearest ten.
  A 31 000   B 30 000   C 29 600
  D 29 540   E 29 500

⑰ The lowest common multiple of 2, 5 and 6 is …
  A 10   B 12   C 15
  D 30   E 60

(18)

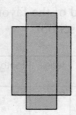

Fig. E36

Which of the following shapes has a net as shown in Fig. E36?
A an open cube   B a closed cube
C an open cylinder   D an open cuboid
E a closed cuboid.

(19) Round off 0·004 365 correct to 2 significant figures.
A 0·004   B 0·0044   C 0·00437
D 0·0043   E 0·44

(20) Find the multiplicative inverse of $\frac{10}{9}$.
A $\frac{10}{9}$ B $\frac{9}{10}$ C $\frac{1}{9}$
D $-\frac{9}{10}$ E $-\frac{10}{9}$

(21) If three coins are tossed once, how many different outcomes are possible?
A 27   B 9   C 8
D 6   E 3

(22) Which of the following is *not* a pair of equivalent fractions?
A $\frac{12}{20}, \frac{3}{5}$ B $\frac{20}{30}, \frac{2}{3}$ C $\frac{3}{5}, \frac{8}{10}$
D $\frac{1}{2}, \frac{12}{24}$ E $\frac{7}{9}, \frac{21}{27}$

(23) Factorise $2x^2 - 18xy$.
A $2x(x + 9y)$ B $2x(x - 9y)$
C $2x^2(1 - 9y)$ D $x(9y^2 - 2x)$ E $x(x - 9y)$

(24) A car travelled 80 km in 48 minutes. Find the speed of the car in km/h.
A 120 km/h   B 110 km/h
C 100 km/h   D 90 km/h   E 80 km/h

(25) The graph in Fig. E37 represents the inequality
A $-3 < x < -1$ B $-3 < x < 1$
C $3 < x < -1$ D $-2 < x < 1$
E $-3 < x < -1$

-4 -3 -2 -1 0 1 2 3 4

Fig. E37

(26) A bowl contains 30 eggs, five of which are broken. If an egg is chosen at random, what is the probability that it is not broken?
A $\frac{6}{5}$ B $\frac{5}{6}$ C $\frac{1}{5}$
D $\frac{1}{6}$ E 1

(27) Convert 57_{ten} to a number in base two.
A 111001   B 110111   C 111000
D 111011   E 101111

(28) Which of the following is a rational number?
A $\sqrt{3}$ B π C $3 \cdot \dot{3}$
D $\sqrt{7}$ E $\sqrt{91}$

(29) Find x in Fig. E38.
A 18°   B 36°   C 54°
D 72°   E 77°

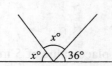

Fig. E38

(30) If $p = \dfrac{E}{x + y}$, express x in terms of p, E and y.
A $x = \dfrac{E - py}{p}$ B $x = \dfrac{y - E}{py}$ C $x = \dfrac{E}{p + y}$
D $x = \dfrac{E - p}{py}$ E $x = \dfrac{E + py}{p}$

The bar chart in Fig. E39 shows the distribution of Primary Classes 1 to 6 in a UBE school. Use this information to answer questions 31–34.

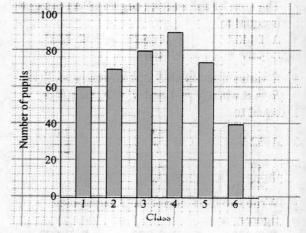

Fig. E39

(31) How many pupils are in Class 4?
    A 90   B 80   C 70
    D 60   E 50

(32) Find the total number of pupils in the primary section.
    A 400   B 414   C 420
    D 422   E 424

(33) Which class has the largest number of pupils?
    A 1   B 2   C 3
    D 4   E 5

(34) If a pupil is chosen at random, what is the probability that she belongs to Primary Class 3?
    A $\frac{80}{400}$ B $\frac{80}{414}$ C $\frac{74}{400}$
    D $\frac{80}{424}$ E $\frac{90}{400}$

(35) Find the perimeter of the shaded part of Fig. E40.
    A 39 cm   B 32 cm   C 31 cm
    D 28 cm   E 18 cm

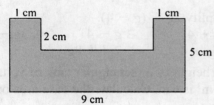

Fig. E40

(36) A trader accepts ₦60 000 for goods whose selling price was ₦65 000. What was the percentage discount?
    A 5%   B $7\frac{9}{13}$%   C $8\frac{1}{2}$%
    D 10%   E $12\frac{1}{2}$%

(37) A woman is four times as old as her son. In 5 years' time, she will be three times as old as her son. How old is the woman?
    A 50 years   B 45 years   C 40 years
    D 35 years   E 30 years

(38) Calculate the area of the parallelogram in Fig. E41.
    A 10 cm²   B 20 cm²   C 40 cm²
    D 60 cm²   E 80 cm²

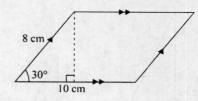

Fig. E41

(39) Find the range of the following numbers:
    6, 4, 5, 9, 4, 4, 3, 6, 5, 4, 5.
    A 3   B 4   C 5
    D 6   E 9

(40) Simplify $5a - 3b - a + 2b$.
    A $6a + 5b$ B $6a - b$ C $4a + b$
    D $4a - 5b$ E $4a - b$

(41) If $S = (5 \cdot 42)^2 - (4 \cdot 58)^2$, find S.
    A 10   B 9·9   C 8·4
    D 8·16   E 0·8

(42) If p varies directly as q, and q varies inversely as r, then
    A p varies directly as r
    B p varies inversely as r
    C p varies partially as r
    D p varies jointly as r
    E p does not vary as r

A rectangular tray is 30 cm long, 20 cm wide and 6 cm high. A similar tray is 12 cm long. Use this information to answer questions 43 and 44.

(43) What is the scale factor of the enlargement of the smaller tray to the bigger tray?
    A $\frac{1}{2}$ B $\frac{2}{3}$ C $\frac{5}{3}$
    D $\frac{3}{2}$ E $\frac{5}{2}$

(44) What is the height of the smaller tray?
    A 2 cm   B 2·4 cm   C 2·5 cm
    D 3 cm   E 4·8 cm

(45) Fig. E42 shows two similar triangles (not drawn to scale). What is the scale factor of the smaller triangle in relation to the bigger one?
    A $\frac{5}{12}$ B $\frac{5}{120}$ C $\frac{1}{5}$
    D $\frac{1}{10}$ E $\frac{1}{100}$

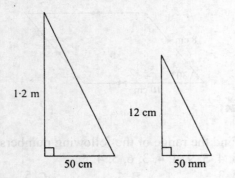

Fig. E42

Table E6 shows the favourite drinks of some groups of students in a school.

type of beverage	Bovin	Ovalto	Milotine	Prono	Samilk
number of students	3	6	5	2	2

Table E6

Use this information to answer questions 46–48.

46 How many students were in the group?
   A 10   B 15   C 16
   D 18   E 20

47 Which of the drinks is preferred by most students?
   A Bovin   B Milotine   C Ovalto
   D Prono   E Samilk

48 What is the probability that a student, chosen at random, will prefer Ovalto?
   A $\frac{2}{3}$ B $\frac{1}{2}$ C $\frac{1}{3}$
   D $\frac{1}{6}$ E 0·6

49 The larger angle between the hands of a clock at 10·30 a.m. is
   A 105°   B 195°   C 210°
   D 225°   E 240°

50 Sarah has x naira and David has ₦15 more than Sarah. Together the number of naira they have is
   A ₦$(x - 15)$ B ₦$2x$
   C ₦$(2x - 15)$ D ₦$(2x + 15)$ E ₦$15x$

51 The square root of $42\frac{1}{4}$ is

   A $3\frac{1}{4}$ B $6\frac{1}{4}$ C $6\frac{1}{2}$
   D $7\frac{1}{2}$ E $8\frac{1}{2}$

52 In an examination, 350 out of 1 250 students failed. What percentage passed?
   A 35%   B 50%   C 65%
   D 72%   E 90%

53 Find the square root of 590·8 using four-figure tables.
   A 2·431   B 7·686   C 23·8
   D 24·31   E 76·86

54 A nurse is paid ₦4 000 for a 10-day job. What will be her pay for x days?
   A ₦$\frac{40\,000}{x}$ B ₦$4\,000x$ C ₦$\frac{4\,000}{x}$
   D ₦$40\,000x$ E ₦$\frac{400\,000}{x}$

55 What is the sum of the exterior angles of any polygon?
   A 540°   B 360°   C 180°
   D 90°   E 60°

56 Calculate the mean of the following numbers: 10, 2, 3, 6 and 4.
   A 3   B 4   C 5
   D 6   E 7

57 Simplify $2g - (g - 4)$.
   A $g + 4$ B $g - 4$ C $3g - 4$
   D $3g + 4$ E $2g^2 + 8g$

58 The height of a rectangular tank of volume 480 m³ is 6 m. Calculate the base area of the tank.
   A 2 880 m²   B 486 m²   C 80 m²
   D 60 m²   E 48 m²

59 Fig. E43 is made up of a semicircle of diameter 14 m and an equilateral triangle. Calculate the perimeter of the figure. (Take π to be $\frac{22}{7}$.)
   A 72 cm   B 64 cm   C 50 cm
   D 43 cm   E 42 cm

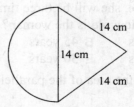

Fig. E43

60 How much simple interest does ₦3 000 yield in 2 years at $8\frac{1}{3}$% per annum?

A ₦1 000   B ₦600   C ₦500
D ₦300   E ₦200

The marks scored by some students in a test are 4, 6, 7, 8, 9, 9, 4, 9.
Use these data to answer questions 61–63.

61) Find the mean score.
A 5   B 6   C 7
D 8   E 9

62) Find the modal score.
A 9   B 8   C 7
D 4   E 6

63) Find the range.
A 2   B 3   C 4
D 5   E 6

64) Which one of the following is *not* a solid?
A cube   B cone   C cylinder
D trapezium   E prism

65) The figure representing a front elevation of the cylinder in Fig. E44 is

Fig. E44

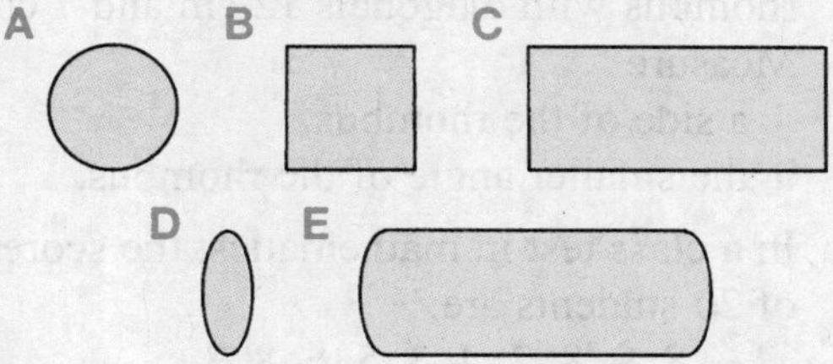

A   B   C

D   E

66) Which of the following is true of a cube?
A It has eight equal faces
B It has six vertices
C It has 12 equal edges
D All the faces are parallel to one another
E All the edges are parallel to one another

67) In Fig. E45, angle RQP is an alternate angle to one of the following.
A TP̂Q   B RT̂S   C PT̂S
D RŜT   E PR̂Q

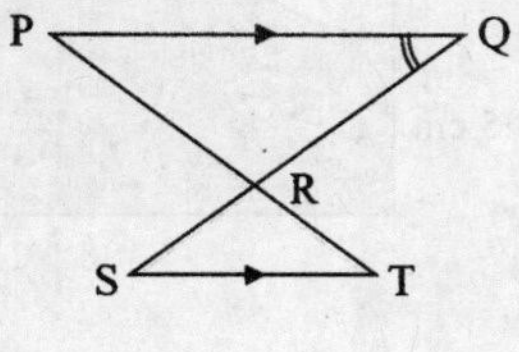

Fig. E45

68) Find the value of x in Fig. E46.
A 95°   B 80°   C 65°
D 50°   E 15°

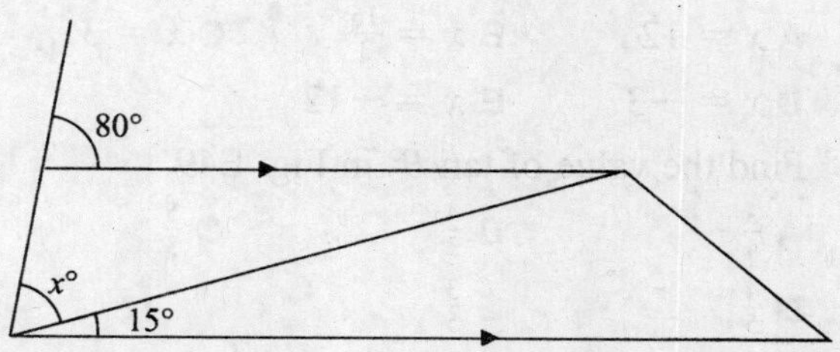

Fig. E46

69) Calculate the perimeter of the shape in Fig. E47.
A 34 cm   B 27 cm   C 25 cm
D 24 cm   E 22 cm

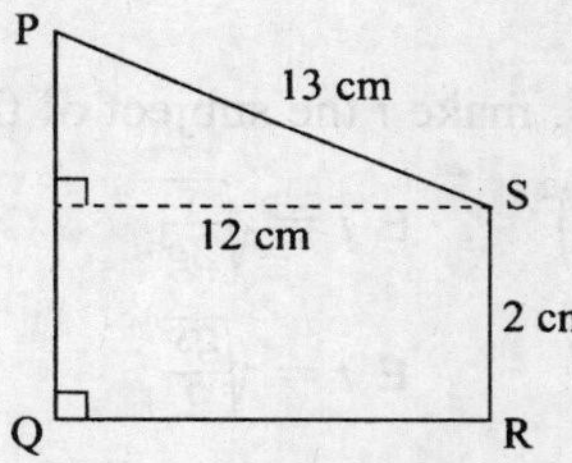

Fig. E47

70) Calculate the radius of a circle whose area is $38\frac{1}{2}$ cm^2 . (Take π to be $\frac{22}{7}$.)
A 77 cm   B $19\frac{1}{4}$ cm   C 14 cm
D 7 cm   E $3\frac{1}{2}$ cm

71) Find the value of a in Fig. E48.
A 124°   B 112°   C 56°
D 28°   E 14°

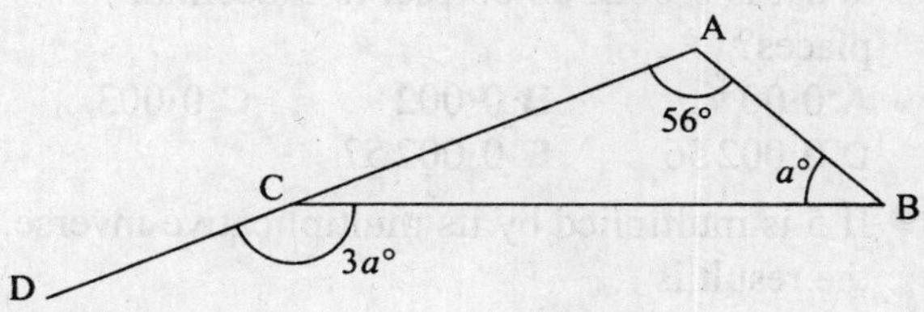

Fig. E48

72) It costs ₦37 800 to cover the floor of a room of length 12 m and width 10·5 m with a straw mat.
What was the cost per m^2 of the straw mat?

A ₦400   B ₦350   C ₦325
D ₦300   E ₦250

A $\frac{1}{10}$ B $\frac{1}{5}$ C $\frac{3}{10}$
D $\frac{3}{5}$ E $\frac{7}{10}$

(73) Solve the equation $\frac{2}{3}x + 5 = -3$.

A $x = 12$ B $x = \frac{16}{3}$ C $x = 3$

D $x = -3$ E $x = -12$

(74) Find the value of tan $\theta°$ in Fig. E49.

A $\frac{3}{4}$ B $\frac{4}{3}$ C $\frac{5}{3}$

D $\frac{4}{5}$ E $\frac{3}{5}$

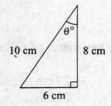

Fig. E49

(75) If $s = \frac{1}{2}gt^2$, make t the subject of the formula.

A $t = \left(\frac{g}{2s}\right)^2$ B $t = \sqrt{\frac{s}{2g}}$ C $t = \left(\frac{2s}{g}\right)^2$

D $t = \sqrt{\frac{2s}{g}}$ E $t = \sqrt{\frac{gs}{2}}$

(76) Calculate the volume of a cylinder of diameter 1 m and height $1\frac{3}{4}$ m. (Take π to be $\frac{22}{7}$.)

A $5\frac{1}{2}$ m³   B $2\frac{5}{8}$ m³   C $2\frac{3}{8}$ m³

D $1\frac{1}{2}$ m³   E $1\frac{3}{8}$ m³

(77) Calculate the simple interest on ₦6 000 for 3 years at 12% per annum.

A ₦2 500   B ₦2 160   C ₦2 000
D ₦1 080   E ₦7 200

(78) What is 0·002 568 correct to 3 decimal places?

A 0·00   B 0·002   C 0·003
D 0·002 56   E 0·002 57

(79) If 5 is multiplied by its multiplicative inverse, the result is …

A 1   B $\frac{1}{5}$ C −5

D $\frac{1}{5}$ E 25

(80) A number is picked at random from the numbers 1 to 10. What is the probability that it is a perfect square?

Section II: Essay-theory questions

Attempt all questions
Time Allowed: 1 hour

(1) a Solve the equation $\frac{6}{x + 3} = \frac{11}{x - 2}$.

b A closed tin of milk has diameter 10 cm and height 16 cm. Find the total surface area of the tin. (Take π to be $\frac{22}{7}$.)

c Make r the subject of the formula $V = \pi r^2 h$.

(2) a A trader opens a bank account with ₦250 000. In one month, she pays out two cheques for ₦49 000 and ₦34 000 and pays in one cheque for ₦14 000. How much money does she have in her account after one month?

b The diagonals of a rhombus are perpendicular bisectors of each other. Using this information, construct a rhombus with diagonals 12 cm and 7 cm. Measure
  i a side of the rhombus,
  ii the smaller angle of the rhombus.

(3) a In a class test in mathematics, the scores of 20 students are:
  8, 9, 8, 7, 4, 3, 5, 6, 8, 3,
  6, 8, 8, 7, 7, 5, 9, 6, 8, 7
  i Present the information in a frequency table.
  ii Find the mode.
  iii Calculate the mean score.

b Calculate the area of the shaded part of Fig. E50. (Take π to be $3\frac{1}{7}$.)

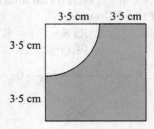

Fig. E50

Mensuration tables and formulae, money

Mass
The **gramme** is the basic unit of mass.

unit	abbreviation	basic units
1 kilogramme	1 kg	1 000 g
1 hectogramme	1 hg	100 g
1 decagramme	1 dag	10 g
1 gramme	1 g	1 g
1 decigramme	1 dg	0·1 g
1 centigramme	1 cg	0·01 g
1 milligramme	1 mg	0·001 g

The **tonne** (t) is used for large masses. The most common measures of mass are the milligramme, the gramme, the kilogramme and the tonne.

$$1\,g\ =\ 1\,000\,mg$$
$$1\,kg\ =\ 1\,000\,g\ =\ 1\,000\,000\,mg$$
$$1\,t\ =1\,000\,kg\ =\ 1\,000\,000\,g$$

Time
The **second** is the basic unit of time. Units of time are not in multiples of ten.

unit	abbreviation	basic units
1 second	1 s	1 s
1 minute	1 min	60 s
1 hour	1 h	3 600 s

Length
The metre is the basic unit of length.

unit	abbreviation	basic units
1 kilometre	1 km	1 000 m
1 hectometre	1 hm	100 m
1 decametre	1 dam	10 m
1 metre	1 m	1 m
1 decimetre	1 dm	0·1 m
1 centimetre	1 cm	0·01 m
1 millimetre	1 mm	0·001 m

The most common measures are the millimetre, the metre and the kilometre.
$$1\,m\ =\ 1\,000\,mm$$
$$1\,km\ =\ 1\,000\,m\ =\ 1\,000\,000\,mm$$

Area
The **square metre** is the basic unit of area. Units of area are derived from units of length.

unit	abbreviation	relation to other units of area
square millimetre	mm^2	
square centimetre	cm^2	1 cm^2 = 100 mm^2
square metre	m^2	1 m^2 = 10 000 cm^2
square kilometre	km^2	1 km^2 = 1 000 000 m^2
hectare (for land measure)	ha	1 ha = 10 000 m^2

Volume

The **cubic metre** is the basic unit of volume.
Units of volume are derived from units of length.

unit	abbreviation	relation to other units of volume
cubic millimetre	mm³	
cubic centimetre	cm³	1 cm³ = 1 000 mm³
cubic metre	m³	1 m³ = 1 000 000 cm³

Capacity

The **litre** is the basic unit of capacity. 1 litre
takes up the same space as 1 000 cm³.

unit	abbreviation	relation to other units of capacity	relation to units of volume
millilitre	mℓ		1 mℓ = 1 cm³
litre	ℓ	1 ℓ = 1 000 mℓ	1 ℓ = 1 000 cm³
kilolitre	kℓ	1 kℓ = 1 000 ℓ	1 kℓ = 1 m³

Remember this poem:

> Thirty days have September,
> April, June and November.
> All the rest have thirty-one,
> Excepting February alone;
> This has twenty-eight days clear,
> And twenty-nine in each Leap Year.

For a Leap year, the year date must be divisible
by 4.
Thus, 2008 was a Leap Year.
Century year dates, such as 1900 and 2000, are
Leap Years only if they are divisible by 400.
Thus, 1900 was not a Leap Year but 2000 was a
Leap Year.

Money

Some divided currencies

Europe	100 cents (c)	= 1 euro (€)
Ghana	100 pesewas (p)	= 1 cedi (₵)
South Africa	100 cents (c)	= 1 rand (R)
UK	100 pence (p)	= 1 pound (£)
USA	100 cents (c)	= 1 dollar ($)

Some undivided currencies

Francophone countries	franc (CFA)
Japan	yen (¥)
Nigeria	naira (₦)
Uganda	shilling (USh).

Divisibility tests

Any whole number is exactly divisible by
2 if its last digit is even or zero
3 if the sum of its digits is divisible by 3
4 if its last two digits form a number divisible by 4
5 if its last digit is 5 or 0
6 if its last digit is even and the sum of its digits is divisible by 3
8 if its last three digits form a number divisible by 8
9 if the sum of its digits is divisible by 9
10 if its last digit is 0

Multiplication table

×	1	2	3	4	5	6	7	8	9	10
1	1	2	3	4	5	6	7	8	9	10
2	2	4	6	8	10	12	14	16	18	20
3	3	6	9	12	15	18	21	24	27	30
4	4	8	12	16	20	24	28	32	36	40
5	5	10	15	20	25	30	35	40	45	50
6	6	12	18	24	30	36	42	48	54	60
7	7	14	21	28	35	42	49	56	63	70
8	8	16	24	32	40	48	56	64	72	80
9	9	18	27	36	45	54	63	72	81	90
10	10	20	30	40	50	60	70	80	90	100

Mensuration formulae

	perimeter	area	volume
square side s	$4s$	s^2	
rectangle length l, breadth b	$2(l + b)$	lb	
circle radius r	$2\pi r$	πr^2	
trapezium height h, parallels of length a and b		$\frac{1}{2}(a + b)h$	
triangle base b, height h		$\frac{1}{2}bh$	
parallelogram base b, height h		bh	
cube edge s		$6s^2$	s^3
cuboid length l, breadth b, height h			lbh
triangular prism height h, base area A			Ah
sphere radius r		$4\pi r^2$	$\frac{4}{3}\pi r^3$
cylinder base radius r, height h		$2\pi rh + 2\pi r^2$	$\pi r^2 h$
cone base radius r, height h, slant height l		$\pi rl + \pi r^2$	$\frac{1}{3}\pi r^2 h$

Angle and length

In an n-sided polygon,
sum of angles $= (n - 2) \times 180°$

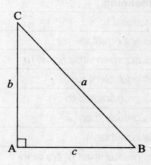

Fig. T1

In the right-angled triangle shown in Fig. T1,
$a^2 = b^2 + c^2$ (Pythagoras' rule)

$$\tan B = \frac{b}{c} \qquad \tan C = \frac{c}{b}$$

$$\sin B = \frac{b}{a} \qquad \sin C = \frac{c}{a}$$

$$\cos B = \frac{c}{a} \qquad \cos C = \frac{b}{a}$$

symbol	meaning
=	is equal to
≠	is not equal to
≃	is approximately equal to
≡	is equivalent to
∝	is proportional to
>	is greater than
<	is less than
⩾	is greater than or equal to
⩽	is less than or equal to
°	degrees (size of angle)
°C	degrees Celsius (temperature)
A, B, C, …	points
AB	the line joining the point A and the point B *or* the distance between points A and B
△ABC	triangle ABC
AB̂C	the angle ABC
⊥	lines meeting at right angles
AB//CD	line AB is parallel to line CD
π	pi (3·14…)
%	per cent

Sines of angles (x in degrees)

$x \to \sin x$

x = 45° to 89°

x	.0	.1	.2	.3	.4	.5	.6	.7	.8	.9	1	2	3	4	5	6	7	8	9
45	0.7071	7083	7096	7108	7120	7133	7145	7157	7169	7181	1	2	4	5	6	7	9	10	11
46	0.7193	7206	7218	7230	7242	7254	7266	7278	7290	7302	1	2	4	5	6	7	8	10	11
47	0.7314	7325	7337	7349	7361	7373	7385	7396	7408	7420	1	2	4	5	6	7	8	9	11
48	0.7431	7443	7455	7466	7478	7490	7501	7513	7524	7536	1	2	4	5	6	7	8	9	10
49	0.7547	7559	7570	7581	7593	7604	7615	7627	7638	7649	1	2	3	5	6	7	8	9	10
50	0.7660	7672	7683	7694	7705	7716	7727	7738	7749	7760	1	2	3	4	6	7	8	9	10
51	0.7771	7782	7793	7804	7815	7826	7837	7848	7859	7869	1	2	3	4	5	7	8	9	10
52	0.7880	7891	7902	7912	7923	7934	7944	7955	7965	7976	1	2	3	4	5	6	8	9	10
53	0.7986	7997	8007	8018	8028	8039	8049	8059	8070	8080	1	2	3	4	5	6	7	8	9
54	0.8090	8100	8111	8121	8131	8141	8151	8161	8171	8181	1	2	3	4	5	6	7	8	9
55	0.8192	8202	8211	8221	8231	8241	8251	8261	8271	8281	1	2	3	4	5	6	7	8	9
56	0.8290	8300	8310	8320	8329	8339	8348	8358	8368	8377	1	2	3	4	5	6	7	8	9
57	0.8387	8396	8406	8415	8425	8434	8443	8453	8462	8471	1	2	3	4	5	6	7	8	8
58	0.8480	8490	8499	8508	8517	8526	8536	8545	8554	8563	1	2	3	4	5	5	6	7	8
59	0.8572	8581	8590	8599	8607	8616	8625	8634	8643	8652	1	2	3	4	4	5	6	7	8
60	0.8660	8669	8678	8686	8695	8704	8712	8721	8729	8738	1	2	3	3	4	5	6	7	8
61	0.8746	8755	8763	8771	8780	8788	8796	8805	8813	8821	1	2	2	3	4	5	6	7	8
62	0.8829	8838	8846	8854	8862	8870	8878	8886	8894	8902	1	2	2	3	4	5	6	6	7
63	0.8910	8918	8926	8934	8942	8949	8957	8965	8973	8980	1	2	2	3	4	5	5	6	7
64	0.8988	8996	9003	9011	9018	9026	9033	9041	9048	9056	1	1	2	3	4	5	5	6	7
65	0.9063	9070	9078	9085	9092	9100	9107	9114	9121	9128	1	1	2	3	4	4	5	6	7
66	0.9135	9143	9150	9157	9164	9171	9178	9184	9191	9198	1	1	2	3	4	4	5	6	6
67	0.9205	9212	9219	9225	9232	9239	9245	9252	9259	9265	1	1	2	3	3	4	5	5	6
68	0.9272	9278	9285	9291	9298	9304	9311	9317	9323	9330	1	1	2	3	3	4	4	5	6
69	0.9336	9342	9348	9354	9361	9367	9373	9379	9385	9391	1	1	2	2	3	4	4	5	6
70	0.9397	9403	9409	9415	9421	9426	9432	9438	9444	9449	1	1	2	2	3	3	4	5	5
71	0.9455	9461	9466	9472	9478	9483	9489	9494	9500	9505	1	1	2	2	3	3	4	4	5
72	0.9511	9516	9521	9527	9532	9537	9542	9548	9553	9558	1	1	2	2	3	3	4	4	5
73	0.9563	9568	9573	9578	9583	9588	9593	9598	9603	9608	0	1	1	2	2	3	3	4	4
74	0.9613	9617	9622	9627	9632	9636	9641	9646	9650	9655	0	1	1	2	2	3	3	4	4
75	0.9659	9664	9668	9673	9677	9681	9686	9690	9694	9699	0	1	1	2	2	3	3	4	4
76	0.9703	9707	9711	9715	9720	9724	9728	9732	9736	9740	0	1	1	2	2	2	3	3	4
77	0.9744	9748	9751	9755	9759	9763	9767	9770	9774	9778	0	1	1	2	2	2	3	3	3
78	0.9781	9785	9789	9792	9796	9799	9803	9806	9810	9813	0	1	1	1	2	2	2	3	3
79	0.9816	9820	9823	9826	9829	9833	9836	9839	9842	9845	0	1	1	1	2	2	2	3	3
80	0.9848	9851	9854	9857	9860	9863	9866	9869	9871	9874	0	1	1	1	2	2	2	2	3
81	0.9877	9880	9882	9885	9888	9890	9893	9895	9898	9900	0	0	1	1	1	2	2	2	2
82	0.9903	9905	9907	9910	9912	9914	9917	9919	9921	9923	0	0	1	1	1	1	2	2	2
83	0.9925	9928	9930	9932	9934	9936	9938	9940	9942	9943	0	0	1	1	1	1	1	2	2
84	0.9945	9947	9949	9951	9952	9954	9956	9957	9959	9960	0	0	1	1	1	1	1	1	2
85	0.9962	9963	9965	9966	9968	9969	9971	9972	9973	9974	0	0	0	1	1	1	1	1	1
86	0.9976	9977	9978	9979	9980	9981	9982	9983	9984	9985	0	0	0	1	1	1	1	1	1
87	0.9986	9987	9988	9989	9990	9990	9991	9992	9993	9993	0	0	0	0	0	1	1	1	1
88	0.9994	9995	9995	9996	9996	9997	9997	9998	9998	9998	0	0	0	0	0	0	0	1	1
89	0.9998	9999	9999	9999	9999	1.0000	1.0000	1.0000	1.0000	1.0000	0	0	0	0	0	0	0	0	0

x = 0° to 44°

x	.0	.1	.2	.3	.4	.5	.6	.7	.8	.9	1	2	3	4	5	6	7	8	9
0	0.0000	0017	0035	0052	0070	0087	0105	0122	0140	0157	2	3	5	7	9	10	12	14	16
1	0.0175	0192	0209	0227	0244	0262	0279	0297	0314	0332	2	3	5	7	9	10	12	14	16
2	0.0349	0366	0384	0401	0419	0436	0454	0471	0488	0506	2	3	5	7	9	10	12	14	16
3	0.0523	0541	0558	0576	0593	0610	0628	0645	0663	0680	2	3	5	7	9	10	12	14	16
4	0.0698	0715	0732	0750	0767	0785	0802	0819	0837	0854	2	3	5	7	9	10	12	14	16
5	0.0872	0889	0906	0924	0941	0958	0976	0993	1011	1028	2	3	5	7	9	10	12	14	16
6	0.1045	1063	1080	1097	1115	1132	1149	1167	1184	1201	2	3	5	7	9	10	12	14	16
7	0.1219	1236	1253	1271	1288	1305	1323	1340	1357	1374	2	3	5	7	9	10	12	14	16
8	0.1392	1409	1426	1444	1461	1478	1495	1513	1530	1547	2	3	5	7	9	10	12	14	16
9	0.1564	1582	1599	1616	1633	1650	1668	1685	1702	1719	2	3	5	7	9	10	12	14	15
10	0.1736	1754	1771	1788	1805	1822	1840	1857	1874	1891	2	3	5	7	9	10	12	14	15
11	0.1908	1925	1942	1959	1977	1994	2011	2028	2045	2062	2	3	5	7	9	10	12	14	15
12	0.2079	2096	2113	2130	2147	2164	2181	2198	2215	2233	2	3	5	7	8	10	12	14	15
13	0.2250	2267	2284	2300	2317	2334	2351	2368	2385	2402	2	3	5	7	8	10	12	14	15
14	0.2419	2436	2453	2470	2487	2504	2521	2538	2554	2571	2	3	5	7	8	10	12	14	15
15	0.2588	2605	2622	2639	2656	2672	2689	2706	2723	2740	2	3	5	7	8	10	12	13	15
16	0.2756	2773	2790	2807	2823	2840	2857	2874	2890	2907	2	3	5	7	8	10	12	13	15
17	0.2924	2940	2957	2974	2990	3007	3024	3040	3057	3074	2	3	5	7	8	10	12	13	15
18	0.3090	3107	3123	3140	3156	3173	3190	3206	3223	3239	2	3	5	7	8	10	12	13	15
19	0.3256	3272	3289	3305	3322	3338	3355	3371	3387	3404	2	3	5	7	8	10	12	13	15
20	0.3420	3437	3453	3469	3486	3502	3518	3535	3551	3567	2	3	5	7	8	10	11	13	15
21	0.3584	3600	3616	3633	3649	3665	3681	3697	3714	3730	2	3	5	6	8	10	11	13	15
22	0.3746	3762	3778	3795	3811	3827	3843	3859	3875	3891	2	3	5	6	8	10	11	13	14
23	0.3907	3923	3939	3955	3971	3987	4003	4019	4035	4051	2	3	5	6	8	10	11	13	14
24	0.4067	4083	4099	4115	4131	4147	4163	4179	4195	4210	2	3	5	6	8	10	11	13	14
25	0.4226	4242	4258	4274	4289	4305	4321	4337	4352	4368	2	3	5	6	8	9	11	13	14
26	0.4384	4399	4415	4431	4446	4462	4478	4493	4509	4524	2	3	5	6	8	9	11	12	14
27	0.4540	4555	4571	4586	4602	4617	4633	4648	4664	4679	2	3	5	6	8	9	11	12	14
28	0.4695	4710	4726	4741	4756	4772	4787	4802	4818	4833	2	3	5	6	8	9	11	12	14
29	0.4848	4863	4879	4894	4909	4924	4939	4955	4970	4985	2	3	5	6	8	9	11	12	14
30	0.5000	5015	5030	5045	5060	5075	5090	5105	5120	5135	2	3	5	6	8	9	11	12	14
31	0.5150	5165	5180	5195	5210	5225	5240	5255	5270	5284	1	3	4	6	7	9	10	12	13
32	0.5299	5314	5329	5344	5358	5373	5388	5402	5417	5432	1	3	4	6	7	9	10	12	13
33	0.5446	5461	5476	5490	5505	5519	5534	5548	5563	5577	1	3	4	6	7	9	10	12	13
34	0.5592	5606	5621	5635	5650	5664	5678	5693	5707	5721	1	3	4	6	7	9	10	11	13
35	0.5736	5750	5764	5779	5793	5807	5821	5835	5850	5864	1	3	4	6	7	8	10	11	13
36	0.5878	5892	5906	5920	5934	5948	5962	5976	5990	6004	1	3	4	6	7	8	10	11	13
37	0.6018	6032	6046	6060	6074	6088	6101	6115	6129	6143	1	3	4	6	7	8	10	11	12
38	0.6157	6170	6184	6198	6211	6225	6239	6252	6266	6280	1	3	4	5	7	8	10	11	12
39	0.6293	6307	6320	6334	6347	6361	6374	6388	6401	6414	1	3	4	5	7	8	9	11	12
40	0.6428	6441	6455	6468	6481	6494	6508	6521	6534	6547	1	3	4	5	7	8	9	11	12
41	0.6561	6574	6587	6600	6613	6626	6639	6652	6665	6678	1	3	4	5	7	8	9	10	12
42	0.6691	6704	6717	6730	6743	6756	6769	6782	6794	6807	1	3	4	5	6	8	9	10	12
43	0.6820	6833	6845	6858	6871	6884	6896	6909	6921	6934	1	3	4	5	6	8	9	10	11
44	0.6947	6959	6972	6984	6997	7009	7022	7034	7046	7059	1	2	4	5	6	7	9	10	11

Cosines of angles (x in degrees)

x → cos x

x	·0	·1	·2	·3	·4	·5	·6	·7	·8	·9	1	2	3	4	5	6	7	8	9
0	1·0000	1·000	1·000	1·000	1·000	1·000	·9999	·9999	·9999	·9999									
1	·9998	·9998	·9998	·9997	·9997	·9997	·9996	·9996	·9995	·9995	0	0	0	0	0	0	0	0	0
2	·9994	·9993	·9993	·9992	·9991	·9990	·9990	·9989	·9988	·9987	0	0	0	0	0	0	0	1	1
3	·9986	·9985	·9984	·9983	·9982	·9981	·9980	·9979	·9978	·9977	0	0	0	0	0	1	1	1	1
4	·9976	·9974	·9973	·9972	·9971	·9969	·9968	·9966	·9965	·9963	0	0	0	1	1	1	1	1	1
5	·9962	·9960	·9959	·9957	·9956	·9954	·9952	·9951	·9949	·9947	0	0	0	1	1	1	1	1	2
6	·9945	·9943	·9942	·9940	·9938	·9936	·9934	·9932	·9930	·9928	0	0	1	1	1	1	1	2	2
7	·9925	·9923	·9921	·9919	·9917	·9914	·9912	·9910	·9907	·9905	0	0	1	1	1	1	2	2	2
8	·9903	·9900	·9898	·9895	·9893	·9890	·9888	·9885	·9882	·9880	0	1	1	1	1	2	2	2	2
9	·9877	·9874	·9871	·9869	·9866	·9863	·9860	·9857	·9854	·9851	0	1	1	1	1	2	2	2	3
10	·9848	·9845	·9842	·9839	·9836	·9833	·9829	·9826	·9823	·9820	0	1	1	1	2	2	2	2	3
11	·9816	·9813	·9810	·9806	·9803	·9799	·9796	·9792	·9789	·9785	0	1	1	1	2	2	2	3	3
12	·9781	·9778	·9774	·9770	·9767	·9763	·9759	·9755	·9751	·9748	1	1	1	2	2	2	3	3	3
13	·9744	·9740	·9736	·9732	·9728	·9724	·9720	·9715	·9711	·9707	1	1	1	2	2	2	3	3	4
14	·9703	·9699	·9694	·9690	·9686	·9681	·9677	·9673	·9668	·9664	1	1	1	2	2	3	3	3	4
15	·9659	·9655	·9650	·9646	·9641	·9636	·9632	·9627	·9622	·9617	1	1	1	2	2	3	3	4	4
16	·9613	·9608	·9603	·9598	·9593	·9588	·9583	·9578	·9573	·9568	1	1	2	2	2	3	3	4	4
17	·9563	·9558	·9553	·9548	·9542	·9537	·9532	·9527	·9521	·9516	1	1	2	2	3	3	4	4	5
18	·9511	·9505	·9500	·9494	·9489	·9483	·9478	·9472	·9466	·9461	1	1	2	2	3	3	4	4	5
19	·9455	·9449	·9444	·9438	·9432	·9426	·9421	·9415	·9409	·9403	1	1	2	2	3	3	4	5	5
20	·9397	·9391	·9385	·9379	·9373	·9367	·9361	·9354	·9348	·9342	1	1	2	2	3	4	4	5	5
21	·9336	·9330	·9323	·9317	·9311	·9304	·9298	·9291	·9285	·9278	1	1	2	3	3	4	4	5	6
22	·9272	·9265	·9259	·9252	·9245	·9239	·9232	·9225	·9219	·9212	1	1	2	3	3	4	5	5	6
23	·9205	·9198	·9191	·9184	·9178	·9171	·9164	·9157	·9150	·9143	1	1	2	3	3	4	5	5	6
24	·9135	·9128	·9121	·9114	·9107	·9100	·9092	·9085	·9078	·9070	1	1	2	3	4	4	5	6	6
25	·9063	·9056	·9048	·9041	·9033	·9026	·9018	·9011	·9003	·8996	1	2	2	3	4	4	5	6	7
26	·8988	·8980	·8973	·8965	·8957	·8949	·8942	·8934	·8926	·8918	1	2	2	3	4	5	5	6	7
27	·8910	·8902	·8894	·8886	·8878	·8870	·8862	·8854	·8846	·8838	1	2	2	3	4	5	6	6	7
28	·8829	·8821	·8813	·8805	·8796	·8788	·8780	·8771	·8763	·8755	1	2	2	3	4	5	6	7	7
29	·8746	·8738	·8729	·8721	·8712	·8704	·8695	·8686	·8678	·8669	1	2	3	3	4	5	6	7	8
30	·8660	·8652	·8643	·8634	·8625	·8616	·8607	·8599	·8590	·8581	1	2	3	3	4	5	6	7	8
31	·8572	·8563	·8554	·8545	·8536	·8526	·8517	·8508	·8499	·8490	1	2	3	4	4	5	6	7	8
32	·8480	·8471	·8462	·8453	·8443	·8434	·8425	·8415	·8406	·8396	1	2	3	4	5	6	6	7	8
33	·8387	·8377	·8368	·8358	·8348	·8339	·8329	·8320	·8310	·8300	1	2	3	4	5	6	7	8	9
34	·8290	·8281	·8271	·8261	·8251	·8241	·8231	·8221	·8211	·8202	1	2	3	4	5	6	7	8	9
35	·8192	·8181	·8171	·8161	·8151	·8141	·8131	·8121	·8111	·8100	1	2	3	4	5	6	7	8	9
36	·8090	·8080	·8070	·8059	·8049	·8039	·8028	·8018	·8007	·7997	1	2	3	4	5	6	7	8	9
37	·7986	·7976	·7965	·7955	·7944	·7934	·7923	·7912	·7902	·7891	1	2	3	4	5	6	7	9	10
38	·7880	·7869	·7859	·7848	·7837	·7826	·7815	·7804	·7793	·7782	1	2	3	4	5	7	8	9	10
39	·7771	·7760	·7749	·7738	·7727	·7716	·7705	·7694	·7683	·7672	1	2	3	4	5	7	8	9	10
40	·7660	·7649	·7638	·7627	·7615	·7604	·7593	·7581	·7570	·7559	1	2	3	5	6	7	8	9	10
41	·7547	·7536	·7524	·7513	·7501	·7490	·7478	·7466	·7455	·7443	1	2	4	5	6	7	8	9	11
42	·7431	·7420	·7408	·7396	·7385	·7373	·7361	·7349	·7337	·7325	1	2	4	5	6	7	8	10	11
43	·7314	·7302	·7290	·7278	·7266	·7254	·7242	·7230	·7218	·7206	1	2	4	5	6	7	8	10	11
44	·7193	·7181	·7169	·7157	·7145	·7133	·7120	·7108	·7096	·7083	1	2	4	5	6	7	8	10	11

SUBTRACT Differences

x	·0	·1	·2	·3	·4	·5	·6	·7	·8	·9	1	2	3	4	5	6	7	8	9
45	0·7071	·7059	·7046	·7034	·7022	·7009	·6997	·6984	·6972	·6959	1	2	4	5	6	7	9	10	11
46	0·6947	·6934	·6921	·6909	·6896	·6884	·6871	·6858	·6845	·6833	1	3	4	5	6	8	9	10	11
47	0·6820	·6807	·6794	·6782	·6769	·6756	·6743	·6730	·6717	·6704	1	3	4	5	6	8	9	10	12
48	0·6691	·6678	·6665	·6652	·6639	·6626	·6613	·6600	·6587	·6574	1	3	4	5	7	8	9	11	12
49	0·6561	·6547	·6534	·6521	·6508	·6494	·6481	·6468	·6455	·6441	1	3	4	5	7	8	9	11	12
50	0·6428	·6414	·6401	·6388	·6374	·6361	·6347	·6334	·6320	·6307	1	3	4	5	7	8	9	11	12
51	0·6293	·6280	·6266	·6252	·6239	·6225	·6211	·6198	·6184	·6170	1	3	4	5	7	8	10	11	12
52	0·6157	·6143	·6129	·6115	·6101	·6088	·6074	·6060	·6046	·6032	1	3	4	6	7	8	10	11	13
53	0·6018	·6004	·5990	·5976	·5962	·5948	·5934	·5920	·5906	·5892	1	3	4	6	7	8	10	11	13
54	0·5878	·5864	·5850	·5835	·5821	·5807	·5793	·5779	·5764	·5750	1	3	4	6	7	8	10	11	13
55	0·5736	·5721	·5707	·5693	·5678	·5664	·5650	·5635	·5621	·5606	1	3	4	6	7	9	10	11	13
56	0·5592	·5577	·5563	·5548	·5534	·5519	·5505	·5490	·5476	·5461	1	3	4	6	7	9	10	12	13
57	0·5446	·5432	·5417	·5402	·5388	·5373	·5358	·5344	·5329	·5314	1	3	4	6	7	9	10	12	13
58	0·5299	·5284	·5270	·5255	·5240	·5225	·5210	·5195	·5180	·5165	1	3	4	6	7	9	10	12	13
59	0·5150	·5135	·5120	·5105	·5090	·5075	·5060	·5045	·5030	·5015	1	3	4	6	7	9	11	12	13
60	0·5000	·4985	·4970	·4955	·4939	·4924	·4909	·4894	·4879	·4863	2	3	5	6	8	9	11	12	14
61	0·4848	·4833	·4818	·4802	·4787	·4772	·4756	·4741	·4726	·4710	2	3	5	6	8	9	11	12	14
62	0·4695	·4679	·4664	·4648	·4633	·4617	·4602	·4586	·4571	·4555	2	3	5	6	8	9	11	12	14
63	0·4540	·4524	·4509	·4493	·4478	·4462	·4446	·4431	·4415	·4399	2	3	5	6	8	9	11	13	14
64	0·4384	·4368	·4352	·4337	·4321	·4305	·4289	·4274	·4258	·4242	2	3	5	6	8	9	11	13	14
65	0·4226	·4210	·4195	·4179	·4163	·4147	·4131	·4115	·4099	·4083	2	3	5	6	8	10	11	13	14
66	0·4067	·4051	·4035	·4019	·4003	·3987	·3971	·3955	·3939	·3923	2	3	5	6	8	10	11	13	14
67	0·3907	·3891	·3875	·3859	·3843	·3827	·3811	·3795	·3778	·3762	2	3	5	6	8	10	11	13	14
68	0·3746	·3730	·3714	·3697	·3681	·3665	·3649	·3633	·3616	·3600	2	3	5	6	8	10	11	13	15
69	0·3584	·3567	·3551	·3535	·3518	·3502	·3486	·3469	·3453	·3437	2	3	5	7	8	10	11	13	15
70	0·3420	·3404	·3387	·3371	·3355	·3338	·3322	·3305	·3289	·3272	2	3	5	7	8	10	12	13	15
71	0·3256	·3239	·3223	·3206	·3190	·3173	·3156	·3140	·3123	·3107	2	3	5	7	8	10	12	13	15
72	0·3090	·3074	·3057	·3040	·3024	·3007	·2990	·2974	·2957	·2940	2	3	5	7	8	10	12	13	15
73	0·2924	·2907	·2890	·2874	·2857	·2840	·2823	·2807	·2790	·2773	2	3	5	7	8	10	12	13	15
74	0·2756	·2740	·2723	·2706	·2689	·2672	·2656	·2639	·2622	·2605	2	3	5	7	8	10	12	13	15
75	0·2588	·2571	·2554	·2538	·2521	·2504	·2487	·2470	·2453	·2436	2	3	5	7	8	10	12	14	15
76	0·2419	·2402	·2385	·2368	·2351	·2334	·2317	·2300	·2284	·2267	2	3	5	7	8	10	12	14	15
77	0·2250	·2233	·2215	·2198	·2181	·2164	·2147	·2130	·2113	·2096	2	3	5	7	9	10	12	14	15
78	0·2079	·2062	·2045	·2028	·2011	·1994	·1977	·1959	·1942	·1925	2	3	5	7	9	10	12	14	15
79	0·1908	·1891	·1874	·1857	·1840	·1822	·1805	·1788	·1771	·1754	2	3	5	7	9	10	12	14	15
80	0·1736	·1719	·1702	·1685	·1668	·1650	·1633	·1616	·1599	·1582	2	3	5	7	9	10	12	14	15
81	0·1564	·1547	·1530	·1513	·1495	·1478	·1461	·1444	·1426	·1409	2	3	5	7	9	10	12	14	16
82	0·1392	·1374	·1357	·1340	·1323	·1305	·1288	·1271	·1253	·1236	2	3	5	7	9	10	12	14	16
83	0·1219	·1201	·1184	·1167	·1149	·1132	·1115	·1097	·1080	·1063	2	3	5	7	9	10	12	14	16
84	0·1045	·1028	·1011	·0993	·0976	·0958	·0941	·0924	·0906	·0889	2	3	5	7	9	10	12	14	16
85	0·0872	·0854	·0837	·0819	·0802	·0785	·0767	·0750	·0732	·0715	2	3	5	7	9	10	12	14	16
86	0·0698	·0680	·0663	·0645	·0628	·0610	·0593	·0576	·0558	·0541	2	3	5	7	9	10	12	14	16
87	0·0523	·0506	·0488	·0471	·0454	·0436	·0419	·0402	·0384	·0366	2	3	5	7	9	10	12	14	16
88	0·0349	·0332	·0314	·0297	·0279	·0262	·0244	·0227	·0209	·0192	2	3	5	7	9	10	12	14	16
89	0·0175	·0157	·0140	·0122	·0105	·0087	·0070	·0052	·0035	·0017	2	3	5	7	9	10	12	14	16

SUBTRACT Differences

Tangents of angles (x in degrees)

x → tan x

x = 0 to 44

x	.0	.1	.2	.3	.4	.5	.6	.7	.8	.9	1	2	3	4	5	6	7	8	9
0	0.0000	.0017	.0035	.0052	.0070	.0087	.0105	.0122	.0140	.0157	2	3	5	7	9	10	12	14	16
1	.0175	.0192	.0209	.0227	.0244	.0262	.0279	.0297	.0314	.0332	2	3	5	7	9	10	12	14	16
2	.0349	.0367	.0384	.0402	.0419	.0437	.0454	.0472	.0489	.0507	2	3	5	7	9	11	12	14	16
3	.0524	.0542	.0559	.0577	.0594	.0612	.0629	.0647	.0664	.0682	2	4	5	7	9	11	12	14	16
4	.0699	.0717	.0734	.0752	.0769	.0787	.0805	.0822	.0840	.0857	2	4	5	7	9	11	12	14	16
5	.0875	.0892	.0910	.0928	.0945	.0963	.0981	.0998	.1016	.1033	2	4	5	7	9	11	12	14	16
6	.1051	.1069	.1086	.1104	.1122	.1139	.1157	.1175	.1192	.1210	2	4	5	7	9	11	13	14	16
7	.1228	.1246	.1263	.1281	.1299	.1317	.1334	.1352	.1370	.1388	2	4	5	7	9	11	13	14	16
8	.1405	.1423	.1441	.1459	.1477	.1495	.1512	.1530	.1548	.1566	2	4	5	7	9	11	13	15	16
9	.1584	.1602	.1620	.1638	.1655	.1673	.1691	.1709	.1727	.1745	2	4	5	7	9	11	13	15	16
10	.1763	.1781	.1799	.1817	.1835	.1853	.1871	.1890	.1908	.1926	2	4	5	7	9	11	13	15	16
11	.1944	.1962	.1980	.1998	.2016	.2035	.2053	.2071	.2089	.2107	2	4	5	7	9	11	13	15	16
12	.2126	.2144	.2162	.2180	.2199	.2217	.2235	.2254	.2272	.2290	2	4	6	7	9	11	13	15	16
13	.2309	.2327	.2345	.2364	.2382	.2401	.2419	.2438	.2456	.2475	2	4	6	7	9	11	13	15	17
14	.2493	.2512	.2530	.2549	.2568	.2586	.2605	.2623	.2642	.2661	2	4	6	7	9	11	13	15	17
15	.2679	.2698	.2717	.2736	.2754	.2773	.2792	.2811	.2830	.2849	2	4	6	8	9	11	13	15	17
16	.2867	.2886	.2905	.2924	.2943	.2962	.2981	.3000	.3019	.3038	2	4	6	8	10	11	13	15	17
17	.3057	.3076	.3096	.3115	.3134	.3153	.3172	.3191	.3211	.3230	2	4	6	8	10	11	13	15	17
18	.3249	.3269	.3288	.3307	.3327	.3346	.3365	.3385	.3404	.3424	2	4	6	8	10	12	13	15	18
19	.3443	.3463	.3482	.3502	.3522	.3541	.3561	.3581	.3600	.3620	2	4	6	8	10	12	14	16	18
20	.3640	.3659	.3679	.3699	.3719	.3739	.3759	.3779	.3799	.3819	2	4	6	8	10	12	14	16	18
21	.3839	.3859	.3879	.3899	.3919	.3939	.3959	.3979	.4000	.4020	2	4	6	8	10	12	14	16	18
22	.4040	.4061	.4081	.4101	.4122	.4142	.4163	.4183	.4204	.4224	2	4	6	8	10	12	14	16	19
23	.4245	.4265	.4286	.4307	.4327	.4348	.4369	.4390	.4411	.4431	2	4	6	8	11	13	15	17	19
24	.4452	.4473	.4494	.4515	.4536	.4557	.4578	.4599	.4621	.4642	2	4	6	8	11	13	15	17	19
25	.4663	.4684	.4706	.4727	.4748	.4770	.4791	.4813	.4834	.4856	2	4	6	9	11	13	15	17	20
26	.4877	.4899	.4921	.4942	.4964	.4986	.5008	.5029	.5051	.5073	2	4	7	9	11	13	15	18	20
27	.5095	.5117	.5139	.5161	.5184	.5206	.5228	.5250	.5272	.5295	2	4	7	9	11	13	15	18	20
28	.5317	.5340	.5362	.5384	.5407	.5430	.5452	.5475	.5498	.5520	2	5	7	9	11	14	16	18	20
29	.5543	.5566	.5589	.5612	.5635	.5658	.5681	.5704	.5727	.5750	2	5	7	9	12	14	16	18	21
30	.5774	.5797	.5820	.5844	.5867	.5890	.5914	.5938	.5961	.5985	2	5	7	9	12	14	16	19	21
31	.6009	.6032	.6056	.6080	.6104	.6128	.6152	.6176	.6200	.6224	2	5	7	10	12	14	17	19	22
32	.6249	.6273	.6297	.6322	.6346	.6371	.6395	.6420	.6445	.6469	2	5	7	10	12	15	17	20	22
33	.6494	.6519	.6544	.6569	.6594	.6619	.6644	.6669	.6694	.6720	3	5	8	10	13	15	18	20	23
34	.6745	.6771	.6796	.6822	.6847	.6873	.6899	.6924	.6950	.6976	3	5	8	10	13	16	18	21	24
35	.7002	.7028	.7054	.7080	.7107	.7133	.7159	.7186	.7212	.7239	3	5	8	11	13	16	18	21	24
36	.7265	.7292	.7319	.7346	.7373	.7400	.7427	.7454	.7481	.7508	3	5	8	11	14	16	19	22	24
37	.7536	.7563	.7590	.7618	.7646	.7673	.7701	.7729	.7757	.7785	3	6	8	11	14	17	19	22	25
38	.7813	.7841	.7869	.7898	.7926	.7954	.7983	.8012	.8040	.8069	3	6	9	11	14	17	20	23	26
39	.8098	.8127	.8156	.8185	.8214	.8243	.8273	.8302	.8332	.8361	3	6	9	12	15	18	20	23	26
40	.8391	.8421	.8451	.8481	.8511	.8541	.8571	.8601	.8632	.8662	3	6	9	12	15	18	21	24	27
41	.8693	.8724	.8754	.8785	.8816	.8847	.8878	.8910	.8941	.8972	3	6	9	12	16	19	22	25	28
42	.9004	.9036	.9067	.9099	.9131	.9163	.9195	.9228	.9260	.9293	3	6	10	13	16	19	22	26	29
43	.9325	.9358	.9391	.9424	.9457	.9490	.9523	.9556	.9590	.9623	3	7	10	13	17	20	23	27	30
44	.9657	.9691	.9725	.9759	.9793	.9827	.9861	.9896	.9930	.9965	3	7	10	14	17	21	24	27	31
x	.0	.1	.2	.3	.4	.5	.6	.7	.8	.9	1	2	3	4	5	6	7	8	9

ADD Differences

x = 45 to 89

x	.0	.1	.2	.3	.4	.5	.6	.7	.8	.9	1	2	3	4	5	6	7	8	9
45	1.000	1.003	1.007	1.011	1.014	1.018	1.021	1.025	1.028	1.032	0	1	1	1	2	2	2	3	3
46	1.036	1.039	1.043	1.046	1.050	1.054	1.057	1.061	1.065	1.069	0	1	1	1	2	2	3	3	3
47	1.072	1.076	1.080	1.084	1.087	1.091	1.095	1.099	1.103	1.107	0	1	1	2	2	2	3	3	4
48	1.111	1.115	1.118	1.122	1.126	1.130	1.134	1.138	1.142	1.146	0	1	1	2	2	2	3	3	4
49	1.150	1.154	1.159	1.163	1.167	1.171	1.175	1.179	1.183	1.188	0	1	1	2	2	3	3	3	4
50	1.192	1.196	1.200	1.205	1.209	1.213	1.217	1.222	1.226	1.230	0	1	1	2	2	3	3	3	4
51	1.235	1.239	1.244	1.248	1.253	1.257	1.262	1.266	1.271	1.275	0	1	1	2	2	3	3	4	4
52	1.280	1.285	1.289	1.294	1.299	1.303	1.308	1.313	1.317	1.322	0	1	1	2	2	3	3	4	4
53	1.327	1.332	1.337	1.342	1.347	1.351	1.356	1.361	1.366	1.371	0	1	1	2	2	3	3	4	4
54	1.376	1.381	1.387	1.392	1.397	1.402	1.407	1.412	1.418	1.423	1	1	2	2	3	3	4	4	5
55	1.428	1.433	1.439	1.444	1.450	1.455	1.460	1.466	1.471	1.477	1	1	2	2	3	3	4	4	5
56	1.483	1.488	1.494	1.499	1.505	1.511	1.517	1.522	1.528	1.534	1	1	2	2	3	3	4	5	5
57	1.540	1.546	1.552	1.558	1.564	1.570	1.576	1.582	1.588	1.594	1	1	2	3	3	4	4	5	5
58	1.600	1.607	1.613	1.619	1.625	1.632	1.638	1.645	1.651	1.658	1	1	2	3	3	4	4	5	6
59	1.664	1.671	1.678	1.684	1.691	1.698	1.704	1.711	1.718	1.725	1	1	2	3	3	4	5	5	6
60	1.732	1.739	1.746	1.753	1.760	1.767	1.775	1.782	1.789	1.797	1	1	2	3	4	4	5	6	6
61	1.804	1.811	1.819	1.827	1.834	1.842	1.849	1.857	1.865	1.873	1	2	2	3	4	5	5	6	7
62	1.881	1.889	1.897	1.905	1.913	1.921	1.929	1.937	1.946	1.954	1	2	2	3	4	5	6	6	7
63	1.963	1.971	1.980	1.988	1.997	2.006	2.014	2.023	2.032	2.041	1	2	3	3	4	5	6	7	8
64	2.050	2.059	2.069	2.078	2.087	2.097	2.106	2.116	2.125	2.135	1	2	3	4	5	6	7	8	9
65	2.145	2.154	2.164	2.174	2.184	2.194	2.204	2.215	2.225	2.236	1	2	3	4	5	6	7	8	9
66	2.246	2.257	2.267	2.278	2.289	2.300	2.311	2.322	2.333	2.344	1	2	3	4	5	7	8	9	10
67	2.356	2.367	2.379	2.391	2.402	2.414	2.426	2.438	2.450	2.463	1	2	4	5	6	7	8	10	11
68	2.475	2.488	2.500	2.513	2.526	2.539	2.552	2.565	2.578	2.592	1	3	4	5	6	8	9	10	11
69	2.605	2.619	2.633	2.646	2.660	2.675	2.689	2.703	2.718	2.733	1	3	4	5	7	8	10	11	13
70	2.747	2.762	2.778	2.793	2.808	2.824	2.840	2.856	2.872	2.888	2	3	5	6	8	9	11	13	14
71	2.904	2.921	2.937	2.954	2.971	2.989	3.006	3.024	3.042	3.060	2	3	5	7	9	11	12	14	16
72	3.078	3.096	3.115	3.133	3.152	3.172	3.191	3.211	3.230	3.251	2	4	6	7	9	11	13	15	17
73	3.271	3.291	3.312	3.333	3.354	3.376	3.398	3.420	3.442	3.465	2	4	6	9	11	13	15	17	19
74	3.487	3.511	3.534	3.558	3.582	3.606	3.630	3.655	3.681	3.706	2	5	7	10	12	14	17	20	22
75	3.732	3.758	3.785	3.812	3.839	3.867	3.895	3.923	3.952	3.981	3	5	8	11	14	16	19	22	25
76	4.011	4.041	4.071	4.102	4.134	4.165	4.198	4.230	4.264	4.297	3	6	10	13	16	19	22	26	29
77	4.331	4.366	4.402	4.437	4.474	4.511	4.548	4.586	4.625	4.665									
78	4.705	4.745	4.787	4.829	4.872	4.915	4.959	5.005	5.050	5.097						differences unreliable:			
79	5.145	5.193	5.242	5.292	5.343	5.396	5.449	5.503	5.558	5.614									
80	5.671	5.730	5.789	5.850	5.912	5.976	6.041	6.107	6.174	6.243									
81	6.314	6.386	6.460	6.535	6.612	6.691	6.772	6.855	6.940	7.026									
82	7.115	7.207	7.300	7.396	7.495	7.596	7.700	7.806	7.916	8.028									
83	8.144	8.264	8.386	8.513	8.643	8.777	8.915	9.058	9.205	9.357									
84	9.514	9.677	9.845	10.02	10.20	10.39	10.58	10.78	10.99	11.20									
85	11.43	11.66	11.91	12.16	12.43	12.71	13.00	13.30	13.62	13.95									
86	14.30	14.67	15.06	15.46	15.89	16.35	16.83	17.34	17.89	18.46									
87	19.08	19.74	20.45	21.20	22.02	22.90	23.86	24.90	26.03	27.27									
88	28.64	30.14	31.82	33.69	35.80	38.19	40.92	44.07	47.74	52.08									
89	57.29	63.66	71.62	81.85	95.46	114.6	143.2	191.0	286.5	573.0									
x	.0	.1	.2	.3	.4	.5	.6	.7	.8	.9	1	2	3	4	5	6	7	8	9

ADD Differences

Reciprocals

$x \rightarrow \dfrac{1}{x}$

Table (x = 55–99)

x	0	1	2	3	4	5	6	7	8	9		SUBTRACT Differences							
											1	2	3	4	5	6	7	8	9
55	1818	1815	1812	1808	1805	1802	1799	1795	1792	1789	0	1	1	1	2	2	2	3	3
56	1786	1783	1779	1776	1773	1770	1767	1764	1761	1757	0	1	1	1	2	2	2	3	3
57	1754	1751	1748	1745	1742	1739	1736	1733	1730	1727	0	1	1	1	2	2	2	2	3
58	1724	1721	1718	1715	1712	1709	1706	1704	1701	1698	0	1	1	1	1	2	2	2	3
59	1695	1692	1689	1686	1684	1681	1678	1675	1672	1669	0	1	1	1	1	2	2	2	3
60	1667	1664	1661	1658	1656	1653	1650	1647	1645	1642	0	1	1	1	1	2	2	2	3
61	1639	1637	1634	1631	1629	1626	1623	1621	1618	1616	0	1	1	1	1	2	2	2	2
62	1613	1610	1608	1605	1603	1600	1597	1595	1592	1590	0	1	1	1	1	2	2	2	2
63	1587	1585	1582	1580	1577	1575	1572	1570	1567	1565	0	0	1	1	1	1	2	2	2
64	1562	1560	1558	1555	1553	1550	1548	1546	1543	1541	0	0	1	1	1	1	2	2	2
65	1538	1536	1534	1531	1529	1527	1524	1522	1520	1517	0	0	1	1	1	1	2	2	2
66	1515	1513	1511	1508	1506	1504	1502	1499	1497	1495	0	0	1	1	1	1	2	2	2
67	0.1493	1490	1488	1486	1484	1481	1479	1477	1475	1473	0	0	1	1	1	1	2	2	2
68	1471	1468	1466	1464	1462	1460	1458	1456	1453	1451	0	0	1	1	1	1	2	2	2
69	1449	1447	1445	1443	1441	1439	1437	1435	1433	1431	0	0	1	1	1	1	1	2	2
70	1429	1427	1425	1422	1420	1418	1416	1414	1412	1410	0	0	1	1	1	1	1	2	2
71	1408	1406	1404	1403	1401	1399	1397	1395	1393	1391	0	0	1	1	1	1	1	2	2
72	1389	1387	1385	1383	1381	1379	1377	1376	1374	1372	0	0	1	1	1	1	1	2	2
73	1370	1368	1366	1364	1362	1361	1359	1357	1355	1353	0	0	1	1	1	1	1	2	2
74	1351	1350	1348	1346	1344	1342	1340	1339	1337	1335	0	0	1	1	1	1	1	1	2
75	1333	1332	1330	1328	1326	1325	1323	1321	1319	1318	0	0	1	1	1	1	1	1	2
76	1316	1314	1312	1311	1309	1307	1305	1304	1302	1300	0	0	1	1	1	1	1	1	2
77	1299	1297	1295	1294	1292	1290	1289	1287	1285	1284	0	0	1	1	1	1	1	1	2
78	1282	1280	1279	1277	1276	1274	1272	1271	1269	1267	0	0	1	1	1	1	1	1	2
79	1266	1264	1263	1261	1259	1258	1256	1255	1253	1252	0	0	0	1	1	1	1	1	1
80	1250	1248	1247	1245	1244	1242	1241	1239	1238	1236	0	0	0	1	1	1	1	1	1
81	1235	1233	1232	1230	1229	1227	1225	1224	1222	1221	0	0	0	1	1	1	1	1	1
82	1220	1218	1217	1215	1214	1212	1211	1209	1208	1206	0	0	0	1	1	1	1	1	1
83	1205	1203	1202	1200	1199	1198	1196	1195	1193	1192	0	0	0	1	1	1	1	1	1
84	1190	1189	1188	1186	1185	1183	1182	1181	1179	1178	0	0	0	1	1	1	1	1	1
85	1176	1175	1174	1172	1171	1170	1168	1167	1166	1164	0	0	0	1	1	1	1	1	1
86	1163	1161	1160	1159	1157	1156	1155	1153	1152	1151	0	0	0	1	1	1	1	1	1
87	1149	1148	1147	1145	1144	1143	1142	1140	1139	1138	0	0	0	0	1	1	1	1	1
88	1136	1135	1134	1133	1131	1130	1129	1127	1126	1125	0	0	0	0	1	1	1	1	1
89	1124	1122	1121	1120	1119	1117	1116	1115	1114	1112	0	0	0	1	1	1	1	1	1
90	1111	1110	1109	1107	1106	1105	1104	1103	1101	1100	0	0	0	0	1	1	1	1	1
91	1099	1098	1096	1095	1094	1093	1092	1090	1089	1088	0	0	0	0	1	1	1	1	1
92	1087	1086	1085	1083	1082	1081	1080	1079	1078	1076	0	0	0	0	1	1	1	1	1
93	1075	1074	1073	1072	1071	1070	1068	1067	1066	1065	0	0	0	0	1	1	1	1	1
94	1064	1063	1062	1060	1059	1058	1057	1056	1055	1054	0	0	0	0	1	1	1	1	1
95	1053	1052	1050	1049	1048	1047	1046	1045	1044	1043	0	0	0	0	1	1	1	1	1
96	1042	1041	1039	1038	1037	1036	1035	1034	1033	1032	0	0	0	0	1	1	1	1	1
97	1031	1030	1029	1028	1027	1026	1025	1024	1022	1021	0	0	0	0	1	1	1	1	1
98	1020	1019	1018	1017	1016	1015	1014	1013	1012	1011	0	0	0	0	1	1	1	1	1
99	1010	1009	1008	1007	1006	1005	1004	1003	1002	1001	0	0	0	0	1	1	1	1	1

Table (x = 10–54)

x	0	1	2	3	4	5	6	7	8	9		SUBTRACT Differences							
											1	2	3	4	5	6	7	8	9
10	1000	9901	9804	9709	9615	9524	9434	9346	9259	9174	9	18	28	37	46	55	64	74	83
11	9091	9009	8929	8850	8772	8696	8621	8547	8475	8403	8	15	23	31	38	46	53	61	69
12	8333	8264	8197	8130	8065	8000	7937	7874	7813	7752	6	13	19	26	32	39	45	52	58
13	7692	7634	7576	7519	7463	7407	7353	7299	7246	7194	6	11	17	22	28	33	39	44	50
14	7143	7092	7042	6993	6944	6897	6849	6803	6757	6711	5	10	14	19	24	29	34	38	43
15	6667	6623	6579	6536	6494	6452	6410	6369	6329	6289	4	8	13	17	21	25	29	34	38
16	6250	6211	6173	6135	6098	6061	6024	5988	5952	5917	4	7	11	15	19	22	26	30	33
17	5882	5848	5814	5780	5747	5714	5682	5650	5618	5587	3	7	10	13	16	20	23	26	29
18	5556	5525	5495	5464	5435	5405	5376	5348	5319	5291	3	6	9	12	15	18	21	24	26
19	5263	5236	5208	5181	5155	5128	5102	5076	5051	5025	3	5	8	11	13	16	19	21	24
20	5000	4975	4950	4926	4902	4878	4854	4831	4808	4785	2	5	7	10	12	14	17	19	22
21	4762	4739	4717	4695	4673	4651	4630	4608	4587	4566	2	4	7	9	11	13	15	17	20
22	4545	4525	4505	4484	4464	4444	4425	4405	4386	4367	2	4	6	8	10	12	14	16	18
23	4348	4329	4310	4292	4274	4255	4237	4219	4202	4184	2	4	5	7	9	11	13	15	16
24	4167	4149	4132	4115	4098	4082	4065	4049	4032	4016	2	3	5	7	8	10	12	13	15
25	4000	3984	3968	3953	3937	3922	3906	3891	3876	3861	2	3	5	6	8	9	11	12	14
26	3846	3831	3817	3802	3788	3774	3759	3745	3731	3717	1	3	4	6	7	9	10	11	13
27	3704	3690	3676	3663	3650	3636	3623	3610	3597	3584	1	3	4	5	7	8	9	11	12
28	3571	3559	3546	3534	3521	3509	3497	3484	3472	3460	1	2	4	5	6	7	9	10	11
29	3448	3436	3425	3413	3401	3390	3378	3367	3356	3344	1	2	3	5	6	7	8	9	10
30	3333	3322	3311	3300	3289	3279	3268	3257	3247	3236	1	2	3	4	5	6	8	9	10
31	3226	3215	3205	3195	3185	3175	3165	3155	3145	3135	1	2	3	4	5	6	7	8	9
32	3125	3115	3106	3096	3086	3077	3067	3058	3049	3040	1	2	3	4	5	6	7	8	9
33	3030	3021	3012	3003	2994	2985	2976	2967	2959	2950	1	2	3	4	4	5	6	7	8
34	2941	2933	2924	2915	2907	2899	2890	2882	2874	2865	1	2	3	3	4	5	6	7	8
35	2857	2849	2841	2833	2825	2817	2809	2801	2793	2786	1	2	2	3	4	5	6	6	7
36	2778	2770	2762	2755	2747	2740	2732	2725	2717	2710	1	2	2	3	4	5	5	6	7
37	2703	2695	2688	2681	2674	2667	2660	2653	2646	2639	1	1	2	3	4	4	5	6	6
38	2632	2625	2618	2611	2604	2597	2591	2584	2577	2571	1	1	2	3	3	4	5	5	6
39	2564	2558	2551	2545	2538	2532	2525	2519	2513	2506	1	1	2	3	3	4	5	5	6
40	2500	2494	2488	2481	2475	2469	2463	2457	2451	2445	1	1	2	2	3	4	4	5	6
41	2439	2433	2427	2421	2415	2410	2404	2398	2392	2387	1	1	2	2	3	3	4	5	5
42	2381	2375	2370	2364	2358	2353	2347	2342	2336	2331	1	1	2	2	3	3	4	4	5
43	2326	2320	2315	2309	2304	2299	2294	2288	2283	2278	1	1	2	2	3	3	4	4	5
44	2273	2268	2262	2257	2252	2247	2242	2237	2232	2227	1	1	2	2	3	3	4	4	5
45	2222	2217	2212	2208	2203	2198	2193	2188	2183	2179	0	1	1	2	2	3	3	4	4
46	2174	2169	2165	2160	2155	2151	2146	2141	2137	2132	0	1	1	2	2	3	3	4	4
47	2128	2123	2119	2114	2110	2105	2101	2096	2092	2088	0	1	1	2	2	3	3	4	4
48	2083	2079	2075	2070	2066	2062	2058	2053	2049	2045	0	1	1	2	2	3	3	3	4
49	2041	2037	2033	2028	2024	2020	2016	2012	2008	2004	0	1	1	2	2	2	3	3	4
50	2000	1996	1992	1988	1984	1980	1976	1972	1969	1965	0	1	1	2	2	2	3	3	4
51	1961	1957	1953	1949	1946	1942	1938	1934	1931	1927	0	1	1	2	2	2	3	3	3
52	1923	1919	1916	1912	1908	1905	1901	1898	1894	1890	0	1	1	1	2	2	3	3	3
53	1887	1883	1880	1876	1873	1869	1866	1862	1859	1855	0	1	1	1	2	2	2	3	3
54	1852	1848	1845	1842	1838	1835	1832	1828	1825	1821	0	1	1	1	2	2	2	3	3

$x \rightarrow x^2$

Squares ($x = 55$ to 99)

x	0	1	2	3	4	5	6	7	8	9		Differences 1	2	3	4	5	6	7	8	9
55	3025	3036	3047	3058	3069	3080	3091	3102	3114	3125		1	2	3	4	6	7	8	9	10
56	3136	3147	3158	3170	3181	3192	3204	3215	3226	3238		1	2	3	4	6	7	8	9	10
57	3249	3260	3272	3283	3295	3306	3318	3329	3341	3352		1	2	3	4	6	7	8	9	10
58	3364	3376	3387	3399	3411	3422	3434	3446	3457	3469		1	2	4	5	6	7	8	10	11
59	3481	3493	3505	3516	3528	3540	3552	3564	3576	3588		1	2	4	5	6	7	8	10	11
60	3600	3612	3624	3636	3648	3660	3672	3684	3697	3709		1	2	4	5	6	7	8	10	11
61	3721	3733	3745	3758	3770	3782	3795	3807	3819	3832		1	2	4	5	6	7	8	10	11
62	3844	3856	3869	3881	3894	3906	3919	3931	3944	3956		1	2	4	5	6	7	8	10	11
63	3969	3982	3994	4007	4020	4032	4045	4058	4070	4083		1	3	4	5	7	8	9	10	12
64	4096	4109	4122	4134	4147	4160	4173	4186	4199	4212		1	3	4	5	7	8	9	10	12
65	4225	4238	4251	4264	4277	4290	4303	4316	4330	4343		1	3	4	5	7	8	9	10	12
66	4356	4369	4382	4396	4409	4422	4436	4449	4462	4476		1	3	4	5	7	8	9	10	12
67	4489	4502	4516	4529	4543	4556	4570	4583	4597	4610		1	3	4	5	7	8	9	10	12
68	4624	4638	4651	4665	4679	4692	4706	4720	4733	4747		1	3	4	6	7	8	10	11	13
69	4761	4775	4789	4802	4816	4830	4844	4858	4872	4886		1	3	4	6	7	8	10	11	13
70	4900	4914	4928	4942	4956	4970	4984	4998	5013	5027		1	3	4	6	7	8	10	11	13
71	5041	5055	5069	5084	5098	5112	5127	5141	5155	5170		1	3	4	6	7	8	10	11	13
72	5184	5198	5213	5227	5242	5256	5271	5285	5300	5314		1	3	4	6	7	8	10	11	13
73	5329	5344	5358	5373	5388	5402	5417	5432	5446	5461		2	3	5	6	8	9	11	12	14
74	5476	5491	5506	5520	5535	5550	5565	5580	5595	5610		2	3	5	6	8	9	11	12	14
75	5625	5640	5655	5670	5685	5700	5715	5730	5746	5761		2	3	5	6	8	9	11	12	14
76	5776	5791	5806	5822	5837	5852	5868	5883	5898	5914		2	3	5	6	8	9	11	12	14
77	5929	5944	5960	5975	5991	6006	6022	6037	6053	6068		2	3	5	6	8	9	11	12	14
78	6084	6100	6115	6131	6147	6162	6178	6194	6209	6225		2	3	5	6	8	10	11	13	14
79	6241	6257	6273	6288	6304	6320	6336	6352	6368	6384		2	3	5	6	8	10	11	13	14
80	6400	6416	6432	6448	6464	6480	6496	6512	6529	6545		2	3	5	6	8	10	11	13	14
81	6561	6577	6593	6610	6626	6642	6659	6675	6691	6708		2	3	5	6	8	10	11	13	14
82	6724	6740	6757	6773	6790	6806	6823	6839	6856	6872		2	3	5	6	8	10	11	13	14
83	6889	6906	6922	6939	6956	6972	6989	7006	7022	7039		2	3	5	7	9	10	12	14	15
84	7056	7073	7090	7106	7123	7140	7157	7174	7191	7208		2	3	5	7	9	10	12	14	15
85	7225	7242	7259	7276	7293	7310	7327	7344	7362	7379		2	3	5	7	9	10	12	14	15
86	7396	7413	7430	7448	7465	7482	7500	7517	7534	7552		2	3	5	7	9	10	12	14	15
87	7569	7586	7604	7621	7639	7656	7674	7691	7709	7726		2	3	5	7	9	10	12	14	15
88	7744	7762	7779	7797	7815	7832	7850	7868	7885	7903		2	4	5	7	9	11	13	14	16
89	7921	7939	7957	7974	7992	8010	8028	8046	8064	8082		2	4	5	7	9	11	13	14	16
90	8100	8118	8136	8154	8172	8190	8208	8226	8245	8263		2	4	5	7	9	11	13	14	16
91	8281	8299	8317	8336	8354	8372	8391	8409	8427	8446		2	4	5	7	9	11	13	14	16
92	8464	8482	8501	8519	8538	8556	8575	8593	8612	8630		2	4	5	7	9	11	13	14	16
93	8649	8668	8686	8705	8724	8742	8761	8780	8798	8817		2	4	6	8	10	11	13	15	17
94	8836	8855	8874	8892	8911	8930	8949	8968	8987	9006		2	4	6	8	10	11	13	15	17
95	9025	9044	9063	9082	9101	9120	9139	9158	9178	9197		2	4	6	8	10	11	13	15	17
96	9216	9235	9254	9274	9293	9312	9332	9351	9370	9390		2	4	6	8	10	11	13	15	17
97	9409	9428	9448	9467	9487	9506	9526	9545	9565	9584		2	4	6	8	10	11	13	15	17
98	9604	9624	9643	9663	9683	9702	9722	9742	9761	9781		2	4	6	8	10	12	14	16	18
99	9801	9821	9841	9860	9880	9900	9920	9940	9960	9980		2	4	6	8	10	12	14	16	18

Squares ($x = 10$ to 54)

x	0	1	2	3	4	5	6	7	8	9		Differences 1	2	3	4	5	6	7	8	9
10	1000	1020	1040	1061	1082	1103	1124	1145	1166	1188		2	4	6	8	11	13	15	17	19
11	1210	1232	1254	1277	1300	1323	1346	1369	1392	1416		2	5	7	9	12	14	16	18	21
12	1440	1464	1488	1513	1538	1563	1588	1613	1638	1664		3	5	8	10	13	15	18	20	23
13	1690	1716	1742	1769	1796	1823	1850	1877	1904	1932		3	5	8	11	14	16	19	22	24
14	1960	1988	2016	2045	2074	2103	2132	2161	2190	2220		3	6	9	12	15	17	20	23	26
15	2250	2280	2310	2341	2372	2403	2434	2465	2496	2528		3	6	9	12	16	19	22	25	28
16	2560	2592	2624	2657	2690	2723	2756	2789	2822	2856		3	7	10	13	17	20	23	26	30
17	2890	2924	2958	2993	3028	3063	3098	3133	3168	3204		4	7	11	14	18	21	25	28	32
18	3240	3276	3312	3349	3386	3423	3460	3497	3534	3572		4	7	11	15	19	22	26	30	33
19	3610	3648	3686	3725	3764	3803	3842	3881	3920	3960		4	8	12	16	20	23	27	31	35
20	4000	4040	4080	4121	4162	4203	4244	4285	4326	4368		4	8	12	16	21	25	29	33	37
21	4410	4452	4494	4537	4580	4623	4666	4709	4752	4796		4	9	13	17	22	26	30	34	39
22	4840	4884	4928	4973	5018	5063	5108	5153	5198	5244		5	9	14	18	23	27	32	36	41
23	5290	5336	5382	5429	5476	5523	5570	5617	5664	5712		5	9	14	19	24	28	33	38	42
24	5760	5808	5856	5905	5954	6003	6052	6101	6150	6200		5	10	15	20	25	29	34	39	44
25	6250	6300	6350	6401	6452	6503	6554	6605	6656	6708		5	10	15	20	26	31	36	41	46
26	6760	6812	6864	6917	6970	7023	7076	7129	7182	7236		5	11	16	21	27	32	37	42	48
27	7290	7344	7398	7453	7508	7563	7618	7673	7728	7784		6	11	17	22	28	33	39	44	50
28	7840	7896	7952	8009	8066	8123	8180	8237	8294	8352		6	11	17	23	29	34	40	46	51
29	8410	8468	8526	8585	8644	8703	8762	8821	8880	8940		6	12	18	24	30	35	41	47	53
30	9000	9060	9120	9181	9242	9303	9364	9425	9486	9548		6	12	18	24	31	37	43	49	55
31	9610	9672	9734	9797	9860	9923	9986	1005	1011	1018										
32	1024	1030	1037	1043	1050	1056	1063	1069	1076	1082		1	1	2	2	3	4	4	5	5
33	1089	1096	1102	1109	1116	1122	1129	1136	1142	1149		1	1	2	3	4	4	5	6	6
34	1156	1163	1170	1176	1183	1190	1197	1204	1211	1218		1	1	2	3	4	4	5	6	6
35	1225	1232	1239	1246	1253	1260	1267	1274	1282	1289		1	1	2	3	4	4	5	6	6
36	1296	1303	1310	1318	1325	1332	1340	1347	1354	1362		1	1	2	3	4	4	5	6	6
37	1369	1376	1384	1391	1399	1406	1414	1421	1429	1436		1	1	2	3	4	4	5	6	6
38	1444	1452	1459	1467	1475	1482	1490	1498	1505	1513		1	2	2	3	4	5	6	6	7
39	1521	1529	1537	1544	1552	1560	1568	1576	1584	1592		1	2	2	3	4	5	6	6	7
40	1600	1608	1616	1624	1632	1640	1648	1656	1665	1673		1	2	2	3	4	5	6	6	7
41	1681	1689	1697	1706	1714	1722	1731	1739	1747	1756		1	2	2	3	4	5	6	6	7
42	1764	1772	1781	1789	1798	1806	1815	1823	1832	1840		1	2	2	3	4	5	6	6	7
43	1849	1858	1866	1875	1884	1892	1901	1910	1918	1927		1	2	3	4	5	5	6	7	8
44	1936	1945	1954	1962	1971	1980	1989	1998	2007	2016		1	2	3	4	5	5	6	7	8
45	2025	2034	2043	2052	2061	2070	2079	2088	2098	2107		1	2	3	4	5	5	6	7	8
46	2116	2125	2134	2144	2153	2162	2172	2181	2190	2200		1	2	3	4	5	5	6	7	8
47	2209	2218	2228	2237	2247	2256	2266	2275	2285	2294		1	2	3	4	5	5	6	7	8
48	2304	2314	2323	2333	2343	2352	2362	2372	2381	2391		1	2	3	4	5	6	7	8	9
49	2401	2411	2421	2430	2440	2450	2460	2470	2480	2490		1	2	3	4	5	6	7	8	9
50	2500	2510	2520	2530	2540	2550	2560	2570	2581	2591		1	2	3	4	5	6	7	8	9
51	2601	2611	2621	2632	2642	2652	2663	2673	2683	2694		1	2	3	4	5	6	7	8	9
52	2704	2714	2725	2735	2746	2756	2767	2777	2788	2798		1	2	3	4	5	6	7	8	9
53	2809	2820	2830	2841	2852	2862	2873	2884	2894	2905		1	2	3	4	6	7	8	9	10
54	2916	2927	2938	2948	2959	2970	2981	2992	3003	3014		1	2	3	4	6	7	8	9	10

Square roots from 1 to 10

$x \rightarrow \sqrt{x}$

x	0	1	2	3	4	5	6	7	8	9		Differences 1	2	3	4	5	6	7	8	9
1.0	1.000	1.005	1.010	1.015	1.020	1.025	1.030	1.034	1.039	1.044		0	1	1	2	2	3	3	4	4
1.1	1.049	1.054	1.058	1.063	1.068	1.072	1.077	1.082	1.086	1.091		0	1	1	2	2	3	3	4	4
1.2	1.095	1.100	1.105	1.109	1.114	1.118	1.123	1.127	1.131	1.136		0	1	1	2	2	3	3	4	4
1.3	1.140	1.145	1.149	1.153	1.158	1.162	1.166	1.171	1.175	1.179		0	1	1	2	2	3	3	3	4
1.4	1.183	1.187	1.192	1.196	1.200	1.204	1.208	1.212	1.217	1.221		0	1	1	2	2	3	3	3	4
1.5	1.225	1.229	1.233	1.237	1.241	1.245	1.249	1.253	1.257	1.261		0	1	1	2	2	2	3	3	4
1.6	1.265	1.269	1.273	1.277	1.281	1.285	1.288	1.292	1.296	1.300		0	1	1	2	2	2	3	3	4
1.7	1.304	1.308	1.312	1.315	1.319	1.323	1.327	1.330	1.334	1.338		0	1	1	2	2	2	3	3	3
1.8	1.342	1.345	1.349	1.353	1.357	1.360	1.364	1.368	1.371	1.375		0	1	1	1	2	2	3	3	3
1.9	1.378	1.382	1.386	1.389	1.393	1.396	1.400	1.404	1.407	1.411		0	1	1	1	2	2	3	3	3
2.0	1.414	1.418	1.421	1.425	1.428	1.432	1.435	1.439	1.442	1.446		0	1	1	1	2	2	2	3	3
2.1	1.449	1.453	1.456	1.460	1.463	1.466	1.470	1.473	1.477	1.480		0	1	1	1	2	2	2	3	3
2.2	1.483	1.487	1.490	1.493	1.497	1.500	1.503	1.507	1.510	1.513		0	1	1	1	2	2	2	3	3
2.3	1.517	1.520	1.523	1.526	1.530	1.533	1.536	1.539	1.543	1.546		0	1	1	1	2	2	2	3	3
2.4	1.549	1.552	1.556	1.559	1.562	1.565	1.568	1.572	1.575	1.578		0	1	1	1	2	2	2	3	3
2.5	1.581	1.584	1.587	1.591	1.594	1.597	1.600	1.603	1.606	1.609		0	1	1	1	2	2	2	2	3
2.6	1.612	1.616	1.619	1.622	1.625	1.628	1.631	1.634	1.637	1.640		0	1	1	1	2	2	2	2	3
2.7	1.643	1.646	1.649	1.652	1.655	1.658	1.661	1.664	1.667	1.670		0	1	1	1	2	2	2	2	3
2.8	1.673	1.676	1.679	1.682	1.685	1.688	1.691	1.694	1.697	1.700		0	1	1	1	2	2	2	2	3
2.9	1.703	1.706	1.709	1.712	1.715	1.718	1.720	1.723	1.726	1.729		0	1	1	1	1	2	2	2	3
3.0	1.732	1.735	1.738	1.741	1.744	1.746	1.749	1.752	1.755	1.758		0	1	1	1	1	2	2	2	3
3.1	1.761	1.764	1.766	1.769	1.772	1.775	1.778	1.780	1.783	1.786		0	1	1	1	1	2	2	2	2
3.2	1.789	1.792	1.794	1.797	1.800	1.803	1.806	1.808	1.811	1.814		0	1	1	1	1	2	2	2	2
3.3	1.817	1.819	1.822	1.825	1.828	1.830	1.833	1.836	1.839	1.841		0	1	1	1	1	2	2	2	2
3.4	1.844	1.847	1.849	1.852	1.855	1.857	1.860	1.863	1.866	1.868		0	1	1	1	1	2	2	2	2
3.5	1.871	1.874	1.876	1.879	1.882	1.884	1.887	1.889	1.892	1.895		0	1	1	1	1	2	2	2	2
3.6	1.897	1.900	1.903	1.905	1.908	1.911	1.913	1.916	1.918	1.921		0	1	1	1	1	2	2	2	2
3.7	1.924	1.926	1.929	1.931	1.934	1.937	1.939	1.942	1.944	1.947		0	1	1	1	1	2	2	2	2
3.8	1.949	1.952	1.955	1.957	1.960	1.962	1.965	1.967	1.970	1.972		0	1	1	1	1	2	2	2	2
3.9	1.975	1.977	1.980	1.982	1.985	1.988	1.990	1.993	1.995	1.998		0	1	1	1	1	2	2	2	2
4.0	2.000	2.002	2.005	2.007	2.010	2.012	2.015	2.017	2.020	2.022		0	0	1	1	1	1	2	2	2
4.1	2.025	2.027	2.030	2.032	2.035	2.037	2.040	2.042	2.045	2.047		0	0	1	1	1	1	2	2	2
4.2	2.049	2.052	2.054	2.057	2.059	2.062	2.064	2.066	2.069	2.071		0	0	1	1	1	1	2	2	2
4.3	2.074	2.076	2.078	2.081	2.083	2.086	2.088	2.091	2.093	2.095		0	0	1	1	1	1	2	2	2
4.4	2.098	2.100	2.102	2.105	2.107	2.110	2.112	2.114	2.117	2.119		0	0	1	1	1	1	2	2	2
4.5	2.121	2.124	2.126	2.128	2.131	2.133	2.135	2.138	2.140	2.142		0	0	1	1	1	1	2	2	2
4.6	2.145	2.147	2.149	2.152	2.154	2.156	2.159	2.161	2.163	2.166		0	0	1	1	1	1	2	2	2
4.7	2.168	2.170	2.173	2.175	2.177	2.179	2.182	2.184	2.186	2.189		0	0	1	1	1	1	2	2	2
4.8	2.191	2.193	2.195	2.198	2.200	2.202	2.205	2.207	2.209	2.211		0	0	1	1	1	1	2	2	2
4.9	2.214	2.216	2.218	2.220	2.223	2.225	2.227	2.229	2.232	2.234		0	0	1	1	1	1	2	2	2
5.0	2.236	2.238	2.241	2.243	2.245	2.247	2.249	2.252	2.254	2.256		0	0	1	1	1	1	2	2	2
5.1	2.258	2.261	2.263	2.265	2.267	2.269	2.272	2.274	2.276	2.278		0	0	1	1	1	1	2	2	2
5.2	2.280	2.283	2.285	2.287	2.289	2.291	2.294	2.296	2.298	2.300		0	0	1	1	1	1	2	2	2
5.3	2.302	2.304	2.307	2.309	2.311	2.313	2.315	2.317	2.320	2.322		0	0	1	1	1	1	2	2	2
5.4	2.324	2.326	2.328	2.330	2.332	2.335	2.337	2.339	2.341	2.343		0	0	1	1	1	1	1	2	2

x	0	1	2	3	4	5	6	7	8	9		Differences 1	2	3	4	5	6	7	8	9
5.5	2.345	2.347	2.350	2.352	2.354	2.356	2.358	2.360	2.362	2.364		0	0	1	1	1	1	1	2	2
5.6	2.366	2.369	2.371	2.373	2.375	2.377	2.379	2.381	2.383	2.385		0	0	1	1	1	1	1	2	2
5.7	2.388	2.390	2.392	2.394	2.396	2.398	2.400	2.402	2.404	2.406		0	0	1	1	1	1	1	2	2
5.8	2.408	2.410	2.412	2.415	2.417	2.419	2.421	2.423	2.425	2.427		0	0	1	1	1	1	1	2	2
5.9	2.429	2.431	2.433	2.435	2.437	2.439	2.441	2.443	2.445	2.447		0	0	1	1	1	1	1	2	2
6.0	2.449	2.452	2.454	2.456	2.458	2.460	2.462	2.464	2.466	2.468		0	0	1	1	1	1	1	2	2
6.1	2.470	2.472	2.474	2.476	2.478	2.480	2.482	2.484	2.486	2.488		0	0	1	1	1	1	1	2	2
6.2	2.490	2.492	2.494	2.496	2.498	2.500	2.502	2.504	2.506	2.508		0	0	1	1	1	1	1	2	2
6.3	2.510	2.512	2.514	2.516	2.518	2.520	2.522	2.524	2.526	2.528		0	0	1	1	1	1	1	2	2
6.4	2.530	2.532	2.534	2.536	2.538	2.540	2.542	2.544	2.546	2.548		0	0	1	1	1	1	1	2	2
6.5	2.550	2.551	2.553	2.555	2.557	2.559	2.561	2.563	2.565	2.567		0	0	1	1	1	1	1	1	2
6.6	2.569	2.571	2.573	2.575	2.577	2.579	2.581	2.583	2.585	2.587		0	0	1	1	1	1	1	1	2
6.7	2.588	2.590	2.592	2.594	2.596	2.598	2.600	2.602	2.604	2.606		0	0	1	1	1	1	1	2	2
6.8	2.608	2.610	2.612	2.613	2.615	2.617	2.619	2.621	2.623	2.625		0	0	1	1	1	1	1	1	2
6.9	2.627	2.629	2.631	2.632	2.634	2.636	2.638	2.640	2.642	2.644		0	0	1	1	1	1	1	1	2
7.0	2.646	2.648	2.650	2.651	2.653	2.655	2.657	2.659	2.661	2.663		0	0	1	1	1	1	1	1	2
7.1	2.665	2.667	2.668	2.670	2.672	2.674	2.676	2.678	2.680	2.681		0	0	1	1	1	1	1	1	2
7.2	2.683	2.685	2.687	2.689	2.691	2.693	2.694	2.696	2.698	2.700		0	0	1	1	1	1	1	1	2
7.3	2.702	2.704	2.706	2.707	2.709	2.711	2.713	2.715	2.717	2.719		0	0	1	1	1	1	1	1	2
7.4	2.720	2.722	2.724	2.726	2.728	2.729	2.731	2.733	2.735	2.737		0	0	1	1	1	1	1	1	2
7.5	2.739	2.740	2.742	2.744	2.746	2.748	2.750	2.751	2.753	2.755		0	0	1	1	1	1	1	1	2
7.6	2.757	2.759	2.760	2.762	2.764	2.766	2.768	2.769	2.771	2.773		0	0	1	1	1	1	1	1	2
7.7	2.775	2.777	2.778	2.780	2.782	2.784	2.786	2.787	2.789	2.791		0	0	1	1	1	1	1	1	2
7.8	2.793	2.795	2.796	2.798	2.800	2.802	2.804	2.805	2.807	2.809		0	0	1	1	1	1	1	1	2
7.9	2.811	2.812	2.814	2.816	2.818	2.820	2.821	2.823	2.825	2.827		0	0	1	1	1	1	1	1	2
8.0	2.828	2.830	2.832	2.834	2.835	2.837	2.839	2.841	2.843	2.844		0	0	1	1	1	1	1	1	2
8.1	2.846	2.848	2.850	2.851	2.853	2.855	2.857	2.858	2.860	2.862		0	0	1	1	1	1	1	1	2
8.2	2.864	2.865	2.867	2.869	2.871	2.872	2.874	2.876	2.877	2.879		0	0	1	1	1	1	1	1	1
8.3	2.881	2.883	2.884	2.886	2.888	2.890	2.891	2.893	2.895	2.897		0	0	1	1	1	1	1	1	2
8.4	2.898	2.900	2.902	2.903	2.905	2.907	2.909	2.910	2.912	2.914		0	0	1	1	1	1	1	1	2
8.5	2.915	2.917	2.919	2.921	2.922	2.924	2.926	2.927	2.929	2.931		0	0	1	1	1	1	1	1	2
8.6	2.933	2.934	2.936	2.938	2.939	2.941	2.943	2.944	2.946	2.948		0	0	1	1	1	1	1	1	1
8.7	2.950	2.951	2.953	2.955	2.956	2.958	2.960	2.961	2.963	2.965		0	0	1	1	1	1	1	1	1
8.8	2.966	2.968	2.970	2.972	2.973	2.975	2.977	2.978	2.980	2.982		0	0	1	1	1	1	1	1	2
8.9	2.983	2.985	2.987	2.988	2.990	2.992	2.993	2.995	2.997	2.998		0	0	1	1	1	1	1	1	1
9.0	3.000	3.002	3.003	3.005	3.007	3.008	3.010	3.012	3.013	3.015		0	0	0	1	1	1	1	1	1
9.1	3.017	3.018	3.020	3.022	3.023	3.025	3.027	3.028	3.030	3.032		0	0	0	1	1	1	1	1	1
9.2	3.033	3.035	3.036	3.038	3.040	3.041	3.043	3.045	3.046	3.048		0	0	0	1	1	1	1	1	1
9.3	3.050	3.051	3.053	3.055	3.056	3.058	3.059	3.061	3.063	3.064		0	0	0	1	1	1	1	1	1
9.4	3.066	3.068	3.069	3.071	3.072	3.074	3.076	3.077	3.079	3.081		0	0	0	1	1	1	1	1	1
9.5	3.082	3.084	3.085	3.087	3.089	3.090	3.092	3.094	3.095	3.097		0	0	0	1	1	1	1	1	1
9.6	3.098	3.100	3.102	3.103	3.105	3.106	3.108	3.110	3.111	3.113		0	0	0	1	1	1	1	1	1
9.7	3.115	3.116	3.118	3.119	3.121	3.123	3.124	3.126	3.127	3.129		0	0	0	1	1	1	1	1	1
9.8	3.131	3.132	3.134	3.135	3.137	3.139	3.140	3.142	3.143	3.145		0	0	0	1	1	1	1	1	1
9.9	3.146	3.148	3.150	3.151	3.153	3.154	3.156	3.158	3.159	3.161		0	0	0	1	1	1	1	1	1

Square roots from 10 to 100 $x \rightarrow \sqrt{x}$

Left table (x = 10 to 54)

x	0	1	2	3	4	5	6	7	8	9		1	2	3	4	5	6	7	8	9
10	3.162	3.178	3.194	3.209	3.225	3.240	3.256	3.271	3.286	3.302		2	3	5	6	8	9	11	12	14
11	3.317	3.332	3.347	3.362	3.376	3.391	3.406	3.421	3.435	3.450		1	3	4	6	7	9	10	12	13
12	3.464	3.479	3.493	3.507	3.521	3.536	3.550	3.564	3.578	3.592		1	3	4	6	7	8	10	11	13
13	3.606	3.619	3.633	3.647	3.661	3.674	3.688	3.701	3.715	3.728		1	3	4	5	7	8	10	11	12
14	3.742	3.755	3.768	3.782	3.795	3.808	3.821	3.834	3.847	3.860		1	3	4	5	7	8	9	11	12
15	3.873	3.886	3.899	3.912	3.924	3.937	3.950	3.962	3.975	3.988		1	3	4	5	6	8	9	10	11
16	4.000	4.012	4.025	4.037	4.050	4.062	4.074	4.087	4.099	4.111		1	2	4	5	6	7	9	10	11
17	4.123	4.135	4.147	4.159	4.171	4.183	4.195	4.207	4.219	4.231		1	2	4	5	6	7	8	10	11
18	4.243	4.254	4.266	4.278	4.290	4.301	4.313	4.324	4.336	4.347		1	2	3	5	6	7	8	9	10
19	4.359	4.370	4.382	4.393	4.405	4.416	4.427	4.438	4.450	4.461		1	2	3	5	6	7	8	9	10
20	4.472	4.483	4.494	4.506	4.517	4.528	4.539	4.550	4.561	4.572		1	2	3	4	6	7	8	9	10
21	4.583	4.594	4.604	4.615	4.626	4.637	4.648	4.658	4.669	4.680		1	2	3	4	5	6	8	9	10
22	4.690	4.701	4.712	4.722	4.733	4.743	4.754	4.765	4.775	4.785		1	2	3	4	5	6	7	8	9
23	4.796	4.806	4.817	4.827	4.837	4.848	4.858	4.868	4.879	4.889		1	2	3	4	5	6	7	8	9
24	4.899	4.909	4.919	4.930	4.940	4.950	4.960	4.970	4.980	4.990		1	2	3	4	5	6	7	8	9
25	5.000	5.010	5.020	5.030	5.040	5.050	5.060	5.070	5.079	5.089		1	2	3	4	5	6	7	8	9
26	5.099	5.109	5.119	5.128	5.138	5.148	5.158	5.167	5.177	5.187		1	2	3	4	5	6	7	8	9
27	5.196	5.206	5.215	5.225	5.235	5.244	5.254	5.263	5.273	5.282		1	2	3	4	5	6	7	8	9
28	5.292	5.301	5.310	5.320	5.329	5.339	5.348	5.357	5.367	5.376		1	2	3	4	5	6	7	8	9
29	5.385	5.394	5.404	5.413	5.422	5.431	5.441	5.450	5.459	5.468		1	2	3	4	5	5	6	7	8
30	5.477	5.486	5.495	5.505	5.514	5.523	5.532	5.541	5.550	5.559		1	2	3	4	5	5	6	7	8
31	5.568	5.577	5.586	5.596	5.604	5.612	5.621	5.630	5.639	5.648		1	2	3	4	4	5	6	7	8
32	5.657	5.666	5.675	5.683	5.692	5.701	5.710	5.718	5.727	5.736		1	2	3	3	4	5	6	7	8
33	5.745	5.753	5.762	5.771	5.779	5.788	5.797	5.805	5.814	5.822		1	2	3	3	4	5	6	7	8
34	5.831	5.840	5.848	5.857	5.865	5.874	5.882	5.891	5.899	5.908		1	2	3	3	4	5	6	7	8
35	5.916	5.925	5.933	5.941	5.950	5.958	5.967	5.975	5.983	5.992		1	2	2	3	4	5	6	7	7
36	6.000	6.008	6.017	6.025	6.033	6.042	6.050	6.058	6.066	6.075		1	2	2	3	4	5	6	6	7
37	6.083	6.091	6.099	6.107	6.116	6.124	6.132	6.140	6.148	6.156		1	2	2	3	4	5	6	6	7
38	6.164	6.173	6.181	6.189	6.197	6.205	6.213	6.221	6.229	6.237		1	2	2	3	4	5	6	6	7
39	6.245	6.253	6.261	6.269	6.277	6.285	6.293	6.301	6.309	6.317		1	2	2	3	4	5	6	6	7
40	6.325	6.332	6.340	6.348	6.356	6.364	6.372	6.380	6.387	6.395		1	2	2	3	4	5	5	6	7
41	6.403	6.411	6.419	6.427	6.434	6.442	6.450	6.458	6.465	6.473		1	2	2	3	4	5	5	6	7
42	6.481	6.488	6.496	6.504	6.512	6.519	6.527	6.535	6.542	6.550		1	2	2	3	4	5	5	6	7
43	6.557	6.565	6.573	6.580	6.588	6.595	6.603	6.611	6.618	6.626		1	2	2	3	4	5	5	6	7
44	6.633	6.641	6.648	6.656	6.663	6.671	6.678	6.686	6.693	6.701		1	1	2	3	4	4	5	6	7
45	6.708	6.716	6.723	6.731	6.738	6.745	6.753	6.760	6.768	6.775		1	1	2	3	4	4	5	6	7
46	6.782	6.790	6.797	6.804	6.812	6.819	6.826	6.834	6.841	6.848		1	1	2	3	4	4	5	6	7
47	6.856	6.863	6.870	6.878	6.885	6.892	6.899	6.907	6.914	6.921		1	1	2	3	4	4	5	6	7
48	6.928	6.935	6.943	6.950	6.957	6.964	6.971	6.979	6.986	6.993		1	1	2	3	4	4	5	6	6
49	7.000	7.007	7.014	7.021	7.029	7.036	7.043	7.050	7.057	7.064		1	1	2	3	4	4	5	6	6
50	7.071	7.078	7.085	7.092	7.099	7.106	7.113	7.120	7.127	7.134		1	1	2	3	3	4	5	6	6
51	7.141	7.148	7.155	7.162	7.169	7.176	7.183	7.190	7.197	7.204		1	1	2	3	3	4	5	6	6
52	7.211	7.218	7.225	7.232	7.239	7.246	7.253	7.259	7.266	7.273		1	1	2	3	3	4	5	5	6
53	7.280	7.287	7.294	7.301	7.308	7.314	7.321	7.328	7.335	7.342		1	1	2	3	3	4	5	5	6
54	7.349	7.355	7.362	7.369	7.376	7.382	7.389	7.396	7.403	7.410		1	1	2	3	3	4	5	5	6

Right table (x = 55 to 99)

x	0	1	2	3	4	5	6	7	8	9		1	2	3	4	5	6	7	8	9
55	7.416	7.423	7.430	7.436	7.443	7.450	7.457	7.463	7.470	7.477		1	1	2	3	3	4	5	5	6
56	7.483	7.490	7.497	7.503	7.510	7.517	7.523	7.530	7.537	7.543		1	1	2	3	3	4	5	5	6
57	7.550	7.556	7.563	7.570	7.576	7.583	7.589	7.596	7.603	7.609		1	1	2	3	3	4	5	5	6
58	7.616	7.622	7.629	7.635	7.642	7.649	7.655	7.662	7.668	7.675		1	1	2	3	3	4	5	5	6
59	7.681	7.688	7.694	7.701	7.707	7.714	7.720	7.727	7.733	7.740		1	1	2	3	3	4	5	5	6
60	7.746	7.752	7.759	7.765	7.772	7.778	7.785	7.791	7.797	7.804		1	1	2	3	3	4	4	5	6
61	7.810	7.817	7.823	7.829	7.836	7.842	7.849	7.855	7.861	7.868		1	1	2	3	3	4	4	5	6
62	7.874	7.880	7.887	7.893	7.899	7.906	7.912	7.918	7.925	7.931		1	1	2	3	3	4	4	5	6
63	7.937	7.944	7.950	7.956	7.962	7.969	7.975	7.981	7.987	7.994		1	1	2	3	3	4	4	5	6
64	8.000	8.006	8.012	8.019	8.025	8.031	8.037	8.044	8.050	8.056		1	1	2	3	3	4	4	5	6
65	8.062	8.068	8.075	8.081	8.087	8.093	8.099	8.106	8.112	8.118		1	1	2	2	3	4	4	5	6
66	8.124	8.130	8.136	8.142	8.149	8.155	8.161	8.167	8.173	8.179		1	1	2	2	3	4	4	5	6
67	8.185	8.191	8.198	8.204	8.210	8.216	8.222	8.228	8.234	8.240		1	1	2	2	3	4	4	5	5
68	8.246	8.252	8.258	8.264	8.270	8.276	8.283	8.289	8.295	8.301		1	1	2	2	3	4	4	5	5
69	8.307	8.313	8.319	8.325	8.331	8.337	8.343	8.349	8.355	8.361		1	1	2	2	3	4	4	5	5
70	8.367	8.373	8.379	8.385	8.390	8.396	8.402	8.408	8.414	8.420		1	1	2	2	3	4	4	5	5
71	8.426	8.432	8.438	8.444	8.450	8.456	8.462	8.468	8.473	8.479		1	1	2	2	3	4	4	5	5
72	8.485	8.491	8.497	8.503	8.509	8.515	8.521	8.526	8.532	8.538		1	1	2	2	3	4	4	5	5
73	8.544	8.550	8.556	8.562	8.567	8.573	8.579	8.585	8.591	8.597		1	1	2	2	3	3	4	5	5
74	8.602	8.608	8.614	8.620	8.626	8.631	8.637	8.643	8.649	8.654		1	1	2	2	3	3	4	5	5
75	8.660	8.666	8.672	8.678	8.683	8.689	8.695	8.701	8.706	8.712		1	1	2	2	3	3	4	5	5
76	8.718	8.724	8.729	8.735	8.741	8.746	8.752	8.758	8.764	8.769		1	1	2	2	3	3	4	5	5
77	8.775	8.781	8.786	8.792	8.798	8.803	8.809	8.815	8.820	8.826		1	1	2	2	3	3	4	5	5
78	8.832	8.837	8.843	8.849	8.854	8.860	8.866	8.871	8.877	8.883		1	1	2	2	3	3	4	4	5
79	8.888	8.894	8.899	8.905	8.911	8.916	8.922	8.927	8.933	8.939		1	1	2	2	3	3	4	4	5
80	8.944	8.950	8.955	8.961	8.967	8.972	8.978	8.983	8.989	8.994		1	1	2	2	3	3	4	4	5
81	9.000	9.006	9.011	9.017	9.022	9.028	9.033	9.039	9.044	9.050		1	1	2	2	3	3	4	4	5
82	9.055	9.061	9.066	9.072	9.077	9.083	9.088	9.094	9.099	9.105		1	1	2	2	3	3	4	4	5
83	9.110	9.116	9.121	9.127	9.132	9.138	9.143	9.149	9.154	9.160		1	1	2	2	3	3	4	4	5
84	9.165	9.171	9.176	9.182	9.187	9.192	9.198	9.203	9.209	9.214		1	1	2	2	3	3	4	4	5
85	9.220	9.225	9.230	9.236	9.241	9.247	9.252	9.257	9.263	9.268		1	1	2	2	3	3	4	4	5
86	9.274	9.279	9.284	9.290	9.295	9.301	9.306	9.311	9.317	9.322		1	1	2	2	3	3	4	4	5
87	9.327	9.333	9.338	9.343	9.349	9.354	9.359	9.365	9.370	9.375		1	1	2	2	3	3	4	4	5
88	9.381	9.386	9.391	9.397	9.402	9.407	9.413	9.418	9.423	9.429		1	1	2	2	3	3	4	4	5
89	9.434	9.439	9.445	9.450	9.455	9.460	9.466	9.471	9.476	9.482		1	1	2	2	3	3	4	4	5
90	9.487	9.492	9.497	9.503	9.508	9.513	9.518	9.524	9.529	9.534		1	1	2	2	3	3	4	4	5
91	9.539	9.545	9.550	9.555	9.560	9.566	9.571	9.576	9.581	9.586		1	1	2	2	3	3	4	4	5
92	9.592	9.597	9.602	9.607	9.613	9.618	9.623	9.628	9.633	9.638		1	1	2	2	3	3	4	4	5
93	9.644	9.649	9.654	9.659	9.664	9.670	9.675	9.680	9.685	9.690		1	1	2	2	3	3	4	4	5
94	9.695	9.701	9.706	9.711	9.716	9.721	9.726	9.731	9.737	9.742		1	1	2	2	3	3	4	4	5
95	9.747	9.752	9.757	9.762	9.767	9.772	9.778	9.783	9.788	9.793		1	1	2	2	3	3	4	4	5
96	9.798	9.803	9.808	9.813	9.818	9.823	9.829	9.834	9.839	9.844		1	1	1	2	3	3	4	4	5
97	9.849	9.854	9.859	9.864	9.869	9.874	9.879	9.884	9.889	9.894		0	1	1	2	2	3	3	4	4
98	9.900	9.905	9.910	9.915	9.920	9.925	9.930	9.935	9.940	9.945		1	1	1	2	2	3	3	4	4
99	9.950	9.955	9.960	9.965	9.970	9.975	9.980	9.985	9.990	9.996		0	1	1	2	2	3	3	4	4

275

Answers

Preliminary chapter

Review test 1 [page 3]

1. a 70   b 36   c 63   d 75
2. a 5×10^6 b 4×10^4
   c 5×10^{-4} d 7×10^{-6}
3. a i 9000   ii 9400   iii 9410
   b i 20000   ii 20000   iii 20100
   c i 30   ii 30   iii 29·6
   d i 0·005   ii 0·0052   iii 0·00521
4. a i 14·9   ii 14·90   iii 14·903
   b i 0·0   ii 0·01   iii 0·007
   c i 3·9   ii 3·88   iii 3·877
   d i 0·0   ii 0·01   iii 0·008
5. a 18   b −44   c −2   d 5
6. 40 tonnes
7. a ₦500 : ₦1000   b 320 mm : 80 mm
   c 28 oranges : 16 oranges
8. a ₦450   b ₦3 300
9. a 36 100   b 68 890 000
   c 63·23   d 26·55
10. a i 1   ii 1·1   iii 1·05
    b i 90   ii 89·8   iii 89·85

Review test 2 [page 4]

1. a 60   b 72   c 66   d 81
2. a 8×10^3 b 2×10^8
   c 4×10^{-5} d 9×10^{-3}
3. a i 500   ii 550   iii 547
   b i 8   ii 8·0   iii 8·03
   c i 40 000   ii 39 000   iii 39 400
   d i 0·04   ii 0·045   iii 0·0446
4. a i 35·2   ii 35·23   iii 35·229
   b i 2·1   ii 2·10   iii 2·097
   c i 0·1   ii 0·06   iii 0·058
   d i 0·0   ii 0·01   iii 0·009
5. a 648   b −60   c −13   d 10
6. 20 mins
7. a ₦250 : ₦50   b 36 ml : 54 ml
   c 25 eggs : 35 eggs
8. a ₦1 900   b ₦336

9. a 3 249   b 1 103 000
   c 89·47   d 25·77
10. a i 1   ii 1·0   iii 0·98
    b i 6   ii 6·3   iii 6·30

Review test 3 [page 6]

1. a +5   b −14   c +514   d $-\frac{3}{7}$
2. a $+\frac{1}{7}$ b $-\frac{7}{6}$ c $+\frac{1}{34}$ d −6·67
3. a $9b - a$ b $y^2 - 9y + 18$
4. a $18 - 3x - xy + 6y$ b $5x^2 - 16xy + 3y^2$
5. a $5x^2$ b $3ax$
6. a pqr b $24a^2b$
7. a $a(2a - 9b)$ b $-6p(3q + 2)$
8. a 6   b $3\frac{1}{8}$
9. a >   b <
10. a $x < 4\frac{1}{2}$ b $x < -2\frac{2}{5}$ c $x > -4$

Review test 4 [page 6]

1. a −3   b +7   c −118   d +0·27
2. a $\frac{1}{4}$ b 5   c $-\frac{1}{9}$ d −1·43
3. a $x^2 - x + 10$ b $a^2 - b^2$
4. a $xy - 9x + 6y - 54$ b $3x^2 + x - 14$
5. a $6xy$ b $3xy$
6. a $12ab$ b $18xy$
7. a $3a(b + 2c)$ b $5y(3 - x)$
8. a 5·4   b 1
9. a >   b <
10. a $x > 5$ b $x > -1\frac{3}{4}$ c $x \leqslant 3$

Review test 5 [page 10]

1. 61°, 61°, 119°   2. 1
3. $m = 53°, n = 27°, p = 71°, q = 85°,$
   $s = 100°$
4. c 5, 12, 13   5. 36 mm
6. a 288 cm², 1 152 cm³   b 528 cm², 1 452 cm³
   c 3 cm, 297 cm³   d 7 cm, 168 cm²
7. a 40°   b 105°
8. a 046°   b 135°   c 215°   d 282°
9. a 125 cm²   b 32 cm²   c 450 cm³   d 160 cm³

Review test 6   [page 11]

① 42°, 138°, 138°   ② 4

③ $p = 72°$, $q = 108°$, $r = 72°$, $s = 128°$, $t = 62°$, $x = 73°$

④ b 3, 4, 5   ⑤ 3·2 m

⑥ a 240 cm², 480 cm³   b 180 cm², 225 cm³
   c 3 cm, 189 cm³   d 4 cm, 120 cm²

⑦ a 75°   b 36°

⑧ a 081°   b 158°
   c 224°   d 335°

⑨ a 112 cm²   b 28·1 cm²
   c 980 cm³   d 147 cm³

Review test 7   [page 13]

① a 9   b 11   c 6   d 6

② a i 7   ii 9   iii 10
   b i 5   ii 5   iii 4·3
   c i 8   ii 9   iii 9
   d i 5   ii 5   iii 6

③ a 50   b 0·56   c 0·44   d 0·2

Review test 8   [page 13]

① a 11   b 7   c 4   d 13

② a i 5   ii 6   iii 6·5
   b i 12   ii 11   iii 10
   c i 1   ii 5·5   iii 7
   d i 4   ii 2·5   iii 2·5

③ a 400   b 248   c 62%   d 0·6

Exercise 1a   [page 14]

① a 2, 3, 7, 9,   b 5, 3, 3,   c 2, 4, 1, 0,3
   d 3, 0, 2, 1, 3   e 1, 0, 0, 1, 1

② a 10^3, 10^2, 10^1, 10^0 b 8^2, 8^1, 8^0
   c 6^4, 6^3, 6^2, 6^1, 6^0 d 2^3, 2^2, 2^1, 2^0
   e 3^4, 3^3, 3^2, 3^1, 3^0

③ a $3 \times 5^3 + 4 \times 5^2 + 0 \times 5^1 + 2 \times 5^0$
   b $2 \times 4^4 + 2 \times 4^3 + 0 \times 4^2 + 1 \times 4^1 + 1 \times 4^0$
   c $3 \times 8^4 + 5 \times 8^3 + 7 \times 8^2 + 3 \times 8^1 + 2 \times 8^0$
   d $1 \times 2^3 + 0 \times 2^2 + 1 \times 2^1 + 1 \times 2^0$
   e $4 \times 6^3 + 3 \times 6^2 + 1 \times 6^1 + 2 \times 6^0$
   f $3 \times 10^4 + 4 \times 10^3 + 2 \times 10^2 + 0 \times 10^1 + 8 \times 10^0$
   g $1 \times 2^5 + 0 \times 2^4 + 1 \times 2^3 + 1 \times 2^2 + 0 \times 2^1 + 1 \times 2^0$
   h $2 \times 3^4 + 0 \times 3^3 + 2 \times 3^2 + 0 \times 3^1 + 1 \times 3^0$
   i $6 \times 7^2 + 0 \times 7^1 + 3 \times 7^0$

   j $1 \times 2^4 + 1 \times 2^3 + 1 \times 2^2 + 1 \times 2^1 + 0 \times 2^0$

Exercise 1b   [page 16]

① a 17_{eight} b 33_{eight}
   c 200_{eight} d 1071_{eight}
   e 2327_{eight} f 11666_{eight}

② a 40_{five} b 301_{five}
   c 344_{five} d 430_{five}
   e 2011_{five} f 10413_{five}

③ a 1011_{two} b 10010_{two}
   c 100011_{two} d 11001_{two}
   e 10001_{two} f 11111_{two}
   g 11101   h 100111   i 10001
   j 101011   k 10111   l 11011

④ a 20_{six} b 51_{six}
   c 121_{six} d 152_{six}
   e 3205_{six} f 4344_{six}

⑤ a 111111_{two} b 1000000_{two}
   c 1000001_{two} d 110001_{two}
   e 1100100_{two} f 10000001_{two}
   g 110110   h 1001000   i 1100101
   j 1111000   k 1011001   l 1011110

Exercise 1c   [page 16]

① 15   ② 25   ③ 153
④ 314   ⑤ 409   ⑥ 45
⑦ 33   ⑧ 69   ⑨ 165
⑩ 307   ⑪ 14   ⑫ 28
⑬ 45   ⑭ 49   ⑮ 75
⑯ 23   ⑰ 44   ⑱ 69
⑲ 7   ⑳ 8   ㉑ 10
㉒ 30   ㉓ 20   ㉔ 27

Exercise 1d   [page 18]

① a 0001, 0010, 0100, 1000
   b 0011, 0101, 1001, 0110, 1010, 1100
   c 0111, 1011, 1101, 1110
   d 1111
   e 0001, 0010, 0011, 0100, 0101, 0110, 0111, 1000, 1001, 1010, 1011, 1100, 1101, 1110, 1111

② The 11th and 20th binary numbers are:
   1011, 1100, 1101, 1110, 1111, 10000, 10001, 10010, 10011, 10100

③ a 1010   b 1100100

④ a 11100   b 11011
   c 100110   d 101001

e 110010   f 111011
g 111111   h 1001101

⑤ a 9   b 11   c 21
  d 30   e 26   f 53

⑥ a 62_ten   b 76_eight

⑦ a 110001   b 1111001

⑧ a 1000   b 1001

Exercise 1e [page 19]

① a 11000   b 11101
  c 10010   d 10111
  e 10001000   f 110
  g 100100   h 1011111
  i 1011010   j 11111101

② a 10101111   b 100011

Exercise 1f [page 20]

① a It gives a quick way of checking that all the cards are stacked correctly in the box.
  b

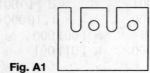

Fig. A1

  c i football, hockey, tennis   ii hockey
    iii football, volleyball, tennis
    iv football, tennis

② a 1011   b

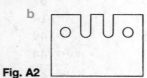

Fig. A2

  c B, C, F

④ b i 1100   ii 1000   iii 0011
    iv 0000   v 0001

⑤ f The cards should be in correct numerical order.

Exercise 1g [page 21]

① Notice that the binary numbers from one to twenty are given in the answer to question 1, Exercise 1d.

② REMOVE MULTIPLES

③ a PRIME NUMBERS
  b COMMON FACTORS
  c ADD RECIPROCAL
  d COMPUTER PROGRAM

④ BINARY CODE

⑤ a i   ii

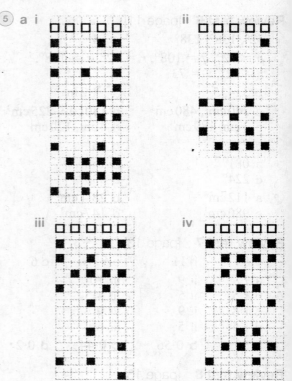

iii   iv

Fig. A3

Exercise 2a [page 23]

① 21   ② 230   ③ 11
④ 83   ⑤ 3·1   ⑥ 75
⑦ 1½   ⑧ 2·0   ⑨ $1\frac{13}{28}$
⑩ −5·4   ⑪ 5   ⑫ 18
⑬ 4   ⑭ 7·6   ⑮ 17
⑯ 20, 21, 22   ⑰ 17, 19, 21, 23,   ⑱ 14
⑲ 18 or 7·2   ⑳ +5 or −11

Exercise 2b [page 24]

① 48   ② 54   ③ +28   ④ +90
⑤ 0·2   ⑥ 0·09   ⑦ 12   ⑧ 3
⑨ 11   ⑩ 45   ⑪ 2   ⑫ −3
⑬ 26   ⑭ 2⅓   ⑮ 0·6

Exercise 2c [page 25]

① 13   ② 45   ③ 40   ④ 42
⑤ 30   ⑥ 0·5   ⑦ 42   ⑧ 6
⑨ 105   ⑩ $\frac{5}{12}$ ⑪ 1   ⑫ 0·76
⑬ 21   ⑭ 45   ⑮ 54

Exercise 2d [page 26]

(1) 4 (2) 6 (3) 20 (4) 7

(5) 3 (6) 7 (7) 4 (8) $1\frac{1}{2}$

(9) 12 (10) 4 (11) 2 (12) 9

(13) 11 (14) 7 (15) 2·8 (16) +2

(17) 0·32 (18) 4 (19) 6 (20) 3

Exercise 2e [page 27]

(1) the sum of 19 and 8

(2) the sum of −7 and −3

(3) the sum of −8, 2 and 5

(4) the positive difference between 16 and 2

(5) the positive difference between −5 and −20

(6) the negative difference between 6 and 11

(7) the product of 3 and 14

(8) the product of −6 and 5

(9) the product of 5, 4 and 9

(10) the product of 4 and the sum of 2 and 7

(11) the product of 5 and the positive difference between 8 and 3

(12) 8 times the sum of 7 and 9

(13) from the sum of 5 and 8, subtract 2

(14) subtract the sum of 3 and 9 from 20

(15) the positive difference between the product of 5 and 4 and the sum of 8 and 11

(16) 4 divided by the sum of 9 and 2

(17) 10 divided by the product of 6 and 5

(18) 13 divided by the positive difference between 12 and 7

(19) one-third of the positive difference between the sum of 9 and 14 and the number 8

(20) one-quarter of the sum of 9 and the product of 5 and 11

Exercise 2f [page 28]

(1) 4 (2) 8 (3) 3 (4) 6

(5) 11 (6) 10 (7) 15 (8) 13

(9) 5 (10) 8, 13 (11) 14 (12) 26, 12

(13) 24 (14) $4\frac{2}{7}$ (15) 12, 9 (16) 15, 16

(17) 6 (18) $2\frac{2}{17}$ (19) 28 (20) 14

Exercise 3a [page 29]

(1) $2x + 2y$ (2) $35 - 5a$

(3) $3n + 27$ (4) $16a - 8b$

(5) $-5x - 15y$ (6) $-12p + 4q$

(7) $-2m - 2n$ (8) $-3a + 3b$

(9) $-4p - 4q$ (10) $-21d + 14$

(11) $18k + 27r$ (12) $-42s + 6t$

(13) $x^2 + 2x$ (14) $y^2 - y$

(15) $a^2 + ab$ (16) $3n^2 - 2n$

(17) $2ps + 3pt$ (18) $5m - 3mn$

(19) $10a^2 - 16ab$ (20) $3x^2 + 27x$

(21) $45pr - 40ps$ (22) $-12a^2 + 42ab$

(23) $9ab - 12b^2$ (24) $2\pi r^2 + 2\pi rh$

Exercise 3b [page 29]

(1) 5 (2) 3 (3) mp (4) $5x$

(5) $4a$ (6) $13b$ (7) ab (8) $3de$

(9) $8p$ (10) $2ax$ (11) 3 (12) $2a$

Exercise 3c [page 30]

(1) $5(a + z)$ (2) $3(2x - 5y)$

(3) $mp(7n - 1)$ (4) $5x(y + 3)$

(5) $4a(3 + 2a)$ (6) $13b(a - 2)$

(7) $ab(b - a)$ (8) $3de(2d - e)$

(9) $8p(q + 3p)$ (10) $2ax(5x + 7a)$

(11) $5m(a - 4b)$ (12) $a^2(5a - 3b)$

(13) $\pi r(r + s)$ (14) $d(7d - 1)$

(15) $3d(11b - e)$ (16) $3(3pq + 4t)$

(17) $b(a - 2)$ (18) $3d(h + 5k)$

(19) $x(x + 9y)$ (20) $2a(a + 5)$

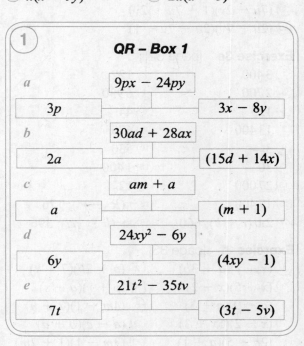

(1) QR – Box 1

a | $9px - 24py$

$3p$ | $3x - 8y$

b | $30ad + 28ax$

$2a$ | $(15d + 14x)$

c | $am + a$

a | $(m + 1)$

d | $24xy^2 - 6y$

$6y$ | $(4xy - 1)$

e | $21t^2 - 35tv$

$7t$ | $(3t - 5v)$

Exercise 3d [page 31]

1. $m(3 + u - v)$
2. $a(2 - 3x - y)$
3. $x(3 - a + b)$
4. $p(4m - 3n - 5)$
5. $(m + 1)(a + b)$
6. $(n + 2)(a - b)$
7. $x(a - b + 4c)$
8. $(a - b)(5x - 2y)$
9. $(5u - v)(3h + 2k)$
10. $m(u - v + m)$
11. $d(3h + k - 4d)$
12. $a(5a + b - c)$
13. $x(4x - 3y - 2z)$
14. $d^2(3d - e + 4f)$
15. $a(4u + v)$
16. $2a(x - 3y)$
17. $(3u + 2v)(3 - a)$
18. $(4a - b)(3x + 2y)$
19. $(2a - 7b)(h - 3k)$
20. $m(5m - 2)$
21. $a^2(2a - 3b)$
22. $4x(x - 1)$
23. $(3m - 4n)(2d - 3e)$
24. $(x - y)(a + 2b - 3)$
25. $(2m + n)(p + q - r)$
26. $(h + k)(2r - s)$
27. $(u + v)(4x + y)$
28. $(b - c)(2d + 3e)$
29. $(a + 2b)(a + 2b - 3)$
30. $(3m - 2n)(3m - 2n + 5p)$
31. $2(2u - 3v)(m - 3n)$
32. $(x + 2y)(a + x + 2y)$
33. $(2x + y(3u - 2x - y)$
34. $(f - g)(4e - f + g)$
35. $3(a - 3b)(u + 2v)$
36. $5(5m + 2n)(a + b)$
37. $(x + 3y)(m - n + 1)$
38. $(2a - 3b)(c + d - 1)$
39. $(7u - 2v)(1 + 7u - 2v)$
40. $(2u - 7v)(2u - 7v - 1)$

Exercise 3e [page 32]

1. 3400
2. 122
3. 2700
4. 6930
5. 125
6. 44
7. 13400
8. 670
9. $3\frac{1}{7}$
10. 530
11. 30
12. 1400
13. 27000
14. $12\frac{4}{7}$
15. 17400
16. $\pi(R^2 - r^2)$; 176
17. $2\pi r(r + h)$; 660
18. $\pi r^2(h + \frac{1}{3}H)$; 396

Exercise 3f [page 33]

1. $(x + y)(a + 3b)$
2. $(a + 2b)(7 + x)$
3. $(x + 5)(x + 2)$
4. $(p + r)(q + s)$
5. $(a - 9)(a + 3)$
6. $(4m - 1)(2 + n)$
7. $(x - 2)(5x + 3)$
8. $(a - c)(b + d)$
9. $(2b - 5)(a + 1)$
10. $(3m - 1)(1 + 2m)$

Exercise 3g [page 33]

1. $(a + c)(b - m)$
2. $(3x + 2)(3 - x)$
3. $(x - y)(2a - 3b)$
4. $(x - 7)(x - 2)$
5. $(a - b)(5 - c)$
6. $(q + 4r)(3p - y)$
7. $(a - 3)(a - 3)$
8. $(2s + 5t)(p - r)$
9. $(x - 6)(x - 1)$
10. $(3k + 1)(1 - h)$

Exercise 3h [page 33]

1. $(a + b)(6 + m)$
2. $(p + q)(r + s)$
3. $(3 + y)(5 - x)$
4. $(a - b)(c + d)$
5. $(a + x)(x - y)$
6. $(d - m)(a + c)$
7. $(x - 3)(x - 5)$
8. $(2a + 3y)(4 + 5b)$
9. $(a - b)(3 + c)$
10. $(t + 3s)(1 + 2z)$

Exercise 3i [page 34]

1. $(m + n)(x + y)$
2. $(x - y)(a + b)$
3. $(u + v)(h - k)$
4. $(a - b)(u - v)$
5. $(a + 2b)(m + n)$
6. $(c - d)(x + 2y)$
7. no factors
8. $(a - 2x)(b - 2y)$
9. $(m - n)(a + 1)$
10. no factors
11. $(a + 1)(a^2 + 1)$
12. $(h + k)(2m - 3n)$
13. $(x - y)(3s + 5t)$
14. $(ax + y)(bx + y)$
15. $(h - 2m)(k + 3n)$
16. no factors
17. $(g + h)(2k - 3l)$
18. $(f + 2g)(2h - k)$
19. no factors
20. $(h + 2k)(l - 3m)$
21. $(e - 2f)(3c - 2d)$
22. $(x - 2n)(y + 3n)$
23. $(a + 2b)(b - 2c)$
24. no factors
25. $(4u - v)(2v + 3w)$
26. $(m - 2n)(n + 3p)$
27. $(3x + 2y)(y - a)$
28. $3(a - u)(b + v)$
29. no factors
30. $(2c + 3d)(4e - f)$
31. $(mu + v)(nu - v)$
32. $5(m - n)(x - y)$
33. $(3a - c)(b - 3d)$
34. $(2a - 5c)(3b + 2d)$
35. $2a(m + n)(u - v)$
36. $(am + 2)(bm - 3)$
37. $2(2a + b)(x + 2y)$
38. $(7m - x)(3n + y)$
39. no factors
40. $(2a - 3m)(m + 2n)$
41. $(5u - 1)(2v + 1)$
42. $(a + m)(am - n)$
43. $(xy + a)(2x - y)$
44. $(1 - 5a)(1 + 3x)$
45. $(d + 2xy)(2dx - 3y)$

Exercise 4a [page 37]

2.
   a M is the mid-point of AC.
   b PM is the perpendicular bisector of AC.
3.
   e The 3 folds meet at a point.
   f Each fold is a perpendicular bisector of one of the sides of $\triangle$ABC.

④ b The 3 perpendicular bisectors meet at a point.

⑤ b Both perpendicular bisectors meet at the centre of the circle.

⑥ b a diameter   c a square

⑦ d MN = $\frac{1}{2}$AC   ⑧ c 7·1 cm

Exercise 4b   [page 39]

② a BÂR = CÂR

   b the bisector of BÂC

③ e The 3 folds meet at a point.

④ d The 3 bisectors meet at a point.

⑤ d In isosceles △XYZ the bisector of Ŷ is the same line as the perpendicular bisector of XZ.

⑤ e $\frac{1}{8}$

⑤ c 2·7 cm, 3·3 cm

⑤ d octagon   e 57 mm

Exercise 4c   [page 41]

③ b 117 mm

④ b 12·7 cm

⑤ b 7·8 cm

⑥ c AC passes through the centre of the circle, i.e. it is a diameter.

⑦ b 5·7 cm

⑧ b 6·9 cm

Exercise 4d   [page 42]

④ d 5 cm

⑤ 7·9 cm, 13·1 cm

⑥ b 7·3 cm, 9·5 cm

⑦ b 91 mm, 53 mm

⑧ b 7·4 cm

---

② **QR – Box 2**

a 30°	b 120°	c 135°	d 75°
e 105°	f 67$\frac{1}{2}$°	g 22$\frac{1}{2}$°	h 15°

Exercise 4f   [page 45]

① b 71 mm

② d 4·7 cm; yes

③ c 69 mm

④ d yes   e 2 : 1

---

⑤ b yes

⑥ c 8·8 cm

⑦ c each 59 mm

⑧ c 6·6 cm

⑨ d 57 mm

⑩ b 52 mm

⑪ b 5·8 cm

⑫ b 7·9 cm

Exercise 5a   [page 47]

① $3·24 \times 10^1$ ② $4·71 \times 10^{-1}$

③ $3·472 \times 10^6$ ④ $6·131 \times 10^{-4}$

⑤ $4·576 \times 10^3$ ⑥ $5·172 \times 10^4$

⑦ $4·381 \times 10^{-2}$ ⑧ $2·31 \times 10^{-7}$

⑨ $6·23 \times 10^8$ ⑩ $3·471\,21 \times 10^{-3}$

⑪ 313   ⑫ 0·783 4

⑬ 0·042 9   ⑭ 914 000

⑮ 86·7   ⑯ 0·005 73

⑰ 13 600   ⑱ 0·000 647 4

⑲ 0·000 002 43   ⑳ 82 500 000

Exercise 5b   [page 48]

① $9·6 \times 10^3$ ② $7·5 \times 10^8$

③ $8·37 \times 10^9$ ④ $5·2 \times 10^4$

⑤ $1·5 \times 10^2$ ⑥ $2·86 \times 10^4$

⑦ $1·67 \times 10^6$ ⑧ 1×10^7

⑨ $1·101 \times 10^4$ ⑩ 6×10^3

⑪ 5×10^8 ⑫ 5×10^4

⑬ $7·6 \times 10^{-2}$ ⑭ $6·4 \times 10^{-4}$

⑮ $4·4 \times 10^{-3}$ ⑯ $2·89 \times 10^{-5}$

⑰ $2·35 \times 10^4$ ⑱ $8·367 \times 10^6$

⑲ $7·4 \times 10^{-2}$ ⑳ $7·337 \times 10^3$

㉑ $6·25 \times 10^5$ ㉒ $5·49 \times 10^{-4}$

㉓ $1·004\,8 \times 10^0$ ㉔ $2·3 \times 10^{-4}$

Exercise 5c   [page 49]

① 6×10^{11} ② 2×10^4

③ 8×10^{-7} ④ 3×10^{-6}

⑤ 4×10^8 ⑥ 6×10^3

⑦ $2·8 \times 10^3$ ⑧ 4×10^6

⑨ $4·5 \times 10^{-2}$ ⑩ 6×10^{-15}

⑪ $3·6 \times 10^{-5}$ ⑫ 2×10^4

⑬ $4·35 \times 10^5$ ⑭ $1·2 \times 10^1$

⑮ $2·5 \times 10^0$ ⑯ $2·47 \times 10^{-1}$

⑰ 7×10^0 ⑱ $2·31 \times 10^{-9}$

(19) $1 \cdot 2 \times 10^{-3}$ (20) $6 \cdot 25 \times 10^{1}$

(21) $5 \cdot 022 \times 10^{2}$ (22) $5 \cdot 4 \times 10^{4}$

(23) $2 \cdot 7216 \times 10^{4}$ (24) $2 \cdot 3 \times 10^{-2}$

(3) QR – Box 3

a	3×10^{2}	$+$	$4 \cdot 5 \times 10^{2}$	$=$	$7 \cdot 5$	$\times$	10^{2}	
b	8×10^{-4}	$-$	6×10^{-4}	$=$	2	$\times$	10^{-4}	
c	$6 \cdot 2 \times 10^{-6}$	$+$	$2 \cdot 7 \times 10^{-6}$	$=$	$8 \cdot 9$	$\times$	10^{-6}	
d	7×10^{5}	$-$	$4 \cdot 3 \times 10^{5}$	$=$	$2 \cdot 7$	$\times$	10^{5}	
e	4×10^{3}	$\times$	6×10^{7}	$=$	$2 \cdot 4$	$\times$	10^{11}	
f	$8 \cdot 8 \times 10^{-3}$	$\div$	4×10^{-3}	$=$	$2 \cdot 2$	$\times$	10^{0}	
g	3×10^{-2}	$\times$	5×10^{-2}	$=$	$1 \cdot 5$	$\times$	10^{-3}	
h	$1 \cdot 8 \times 10^{4}$	$\div$	9×10^{9}	$=$	2	$\times$	10^{-6}	

Exercise 5d [page 51]

(1) $9 \cdot 2 \times 10^{9}$ (2) $9 \cdot 24 \times 10^{5} \, km^{2}$

(3) a $100 \, ha = 1 \, km^{2}$ (4) a ₦645 233 000
     b $9 \cdot 24 \times 10^{7} \, ha$ b ₦$6 \cdot 45 \times 10^{8}$

(5) $2 \cdot 11 \times 10^{6}$ (6) $2 \cdot 8 \times 10^{4} \, km$

(7) $1 \cdot 9878 \times 10^{4} \, m$ (8) $5 \cdot 893 \times 10^{-7} \, m$

(9) $1 \cdot 0 \times 10^{6}, \ 1 \cdot 0 \times 10^{4}, \ 100 : 1$

(10) $1 \, h = 3 \cdot 6 \times 10^{3}$ seconds

(11) $1 \cdot 08 \times 10^{9} \, km$

(12) $5 \cdot 1 \times 10^{4}$ newton/m^{2}

(13) $3 \times 10^{7} \, cm^{3}$ (14) $39 \, kg$

(15) $3 \times 10^{-6} : 1$ (16) $1 \cdot 1 \times 10^{7} \, m^{3}$

(17) a 661 b $1 \times 10^{-4} \, m$

(18) a $1 \cdot 78 \times 10^{8}$
     b The Gambia   140
       Ghana   120
       Liberia   33
       Nigeria   150
       Sierra Leone   74

Exercise 6a [page 54]

(1) a $309 \, K$ b $127°C$

(2) a $12 \cdot 8 \, cm$ b $3 \cdot 5 \, cm$

(3) a $y = 7$ b $x = \frac{7}{9}$

(4) a $15 \, m^{2}$ b $8 \, cm$
     c $18 \, cm$ d $2 \cdot 5 \, m$

(5) a ₦30 000   b ₦46 000

(6) a 3 amps   b 3 volts   c 90 ohms

(7) a $11 \, m$ b $7 \, m$

(8) a $60 \, 000 \, kg$ b $2 \, m$ c $\frac{2}{3} \, m$

(9) a $44 \, cm$ b $3 \cdot 5 \, m$
     c $6 \frac{2}{7} \, m$ d $0 \cdot 4375 \, m$

(10) a $60 \, km/h$ b $6 \frac{1}{4} \, s$

Exercise 6b [page 55]

(1) $y = 4, 3, 2, 1, 0$

(2) $d = 1, 2, 3, 4, 5$

(3) $y = 1, 3, 5, 7, 9$

(4)

x	-1	0	1	2	3
$3x$	-3	0	3	6	9
$+2$	$+2$	$+2$	$+2$	$+2$	$+2$
y	-1	$+2$	$+5$	$+8$	$+11$

(5)

x	0	1	2	3	4	5
17	17	17	17	17	17	17
$-6x$	0	-6	-12	-18	-24	-30
y	17	11	5	-1	-7	-13

(6) a ₦2950   b $146 \, km$

(7) a $1 \, h \, 13 \, min$ b $2 \cdot 6 \, kg$

(8) a $\$150$ b $\$1\,195$ c $\$2\,500$

(9) a 38 litres   b $4\frac{1}{2} \, h$ c $6 \cdot 3 \, h$

(10) a $440 \, cm^{2}$ b $16 \, cm$

Exercise 6c [page 56]

(1) a $y = 0, 40, 160, 360, 640, 1\,000$
     b $x = \pm\frac{1}{2}, \pm3, \pm5, \pm10$

(2) a $y = 0, 12, 16, 12, 0$
     b $x = \pm4, \pm3, \pm2, \pm1$

(3) a $m = 100, 4, 1, \frac{1}{4}$
     b $n = \pm10, \pm5, \pm3\frac{1}{3}, \pm2$

(4) a $154 \, m^{2}$ b $14 \, cm$ c $3 \cdot 5 \, m$

(5) a $308 \, cm^{3}$ b $14 \, cm$ c $2\frac{1}{3} \, cm$

(6) a $44 \cdot 1 \, m$ b $6 \cdot 4 \, m$ c $10 \, s$
     d $5 \, s$ e $44 \cdot 1 \, m$

(7) a $95 \, min$ b 5

(8) a $12 \cdot 5 \, m$ b $5 \cdot 5 \, m$ c $50 \, km$

a $6\frac{1}{2}$ cm   b 14

a 1275   b 13   c 10

Exercise 6d   [page 58]

1) $x = y - 8$ 2) $x = y + 3$

3) $a = b - c, c = b - a$ 4) $x = \dfrac{y}{3}$

5) $x = 4y$ 6) $a = \dfrac{b}{c}, c = \dfrac{b}{a}$

7) $a = \dfrac{n}{5x}, x = \dfrac{n}{5a}$ 8) $x = 9y$

9) $x = \dfrac{y}{2}$ 10) $m = np, n = \dfrac{m}{p}$

11) $x = \dfrac{y - 11}{6}$ 12) $x = \dfrac{y + 2}{7}$

13) $a = \dfrac{b + c}{5}$

14) $x = 13 - y, y = 13 - x$

15) $q = 2p, p = \frac{1}{2}q$

16) $x = \dfrac{d + y}{2}, y = 2x - d$

17) $d = \dfrac{p}{4}$ or $\frac{1}{4}p$ 18) $r = \dfrac{c}{2\pi}$

19) $\theta = T - 273$ 20) $V = \dfrac{W}{I}, I = \dfrac{W}{V}$

21) $r = \dfrac{A}{\pi l}, l = \dfrac{A}{\pi r}$

22) $l = \dfrac{V}{bh}, b = \dfrac{V}{lh}, h = \dfrac{V}{lb}$

23) $r = \dfrac{A}{2\pi h}, h = \dfrac{A}{2\pi r}$

24) $v = \dfrac{2s}{t}, t = \dfrac{2s}{v}$

25) $b = \dfrac{2A}{h}, h = \dfrac{2A}{b}$

26) $l = \dfrac{2V}{bh}, b = \dfrac{2V}{lh}, h = \dfrac{2V}{lb}$

27) $R = \dfrac{100I}{PT}$

28) $V = IR, R = \dfrac{V}{I}$

29) $l = \dfrac{s - 2b}{2}, b = \dfrac{s - 2l}{2}$

30) $u = v - at, a = \dfrac{v - u}{t}, t = \dfrac{v - u}{a}$

Exercise 6e   [page 59]

1) a $x = \dfrac{y + 9}{2}$ b $x = 7$

2) a $x = \dfrac{d - y}{3}$ b $x = -4$

3) a $h = \dfrac{A}{2\pi r}$ b $h = 6$

4) a $b = \dfrac{2A}{h}$ b $b = 15$

5) a $r = \dfrac{w - 5\,900}{200}$ b $11\frac{1}{2}h$

6) a $P = \dfrac{100I}{RT}$ b ₦85 000

7) a $T = \dfrac{100I}{PR}$ b $3\frac{1}{2}$ years

8) a $R = \dfrac{100I}{PT}$ b $3\frac{1}{3}\%$

9) a $d = \dfrac{c}{p}$ b 1·9

10) a $V = IR$, 12 volts

    b $R = \dfrac{V}{I}$, 2 400 ohms

Exercise 6f   [page 60]

1) a x^2y^2 b $\dfrac{a^2}{t^2}$ c $\dfrac{x^4}{y^2}$

    d $(x + y)^2$ e $\dfrac{d}{g}$ f a^2m

    g $4\pi^2a$ h $\dfrac{9}{b}$ i $\dfrac{2\pi^2g}{9}$

2) Positive square roots only are given:

    a $3b$ b bx c $m\sqrt{3}$

    d $\frac{4}{3}tm$ e $\sqrt{xy}$ f $\sqrt{(a - b)}$

    g $\sqrt{(a^2 + b^2)}$ h $\sqrt{\dfrac{A}{\pi}}$ i $\sqrt{\dfrac{2s}{g}}$

3) a $\dfrac{1}{x}$ b $\dfrac{y}{x}$ c x

    d xy e $\dfrac{3}{m}$ f $3m$

    g $\dfrac{b}{b - 1}$ h $\dfrac{a + b}{ab}$ i $\dfrac{fv}{2f - v}$

Exercise 6g   [page 60]

1) $x = a^2$ 2) $x = \frac{1}{2}a^2$

3) $x = \frac{1}{4}a^2$ 4) $x = \sqrt{a}$

5) $x = \sqrt{\dfrac{y}{4a}}$ 6) $b = \dfrac{ad}{c}$

7) $b = \dfrac{5a}{3}$ 8) $a = \dfrac{x^2}{b - x}$

9) $x = \dfrac{a}{c - b}$ 10) $a = \dfrac{b}{b + 1}$

⑪ $N = PD - 2$ ⑫ $h = \dfrac{2D^2}{3}$

⑬ $I = \sqrt{\dfrac{W}{R}}$ ⑭ $t = \sqrt{\dfrac{2s}{g}}$

⑮ $d = 5\sqrt{\dfrac{h}{2}}$ ⑯ $r = \sqrt{\dfrac{V}{\pi h}}$

⑰ $u = \dfrac{2s}{t} - v$ ⑱ $h = \dfrac{S}{2\pi r} - r$

⑲ $z = \sqrt{x^2 - y^2}$ ⑳ $u = \dfrac{vf}{2v - f}$

Exercise 6h   [page 61]
① a $a = 2m - b$ b $a = 15$
② a $y = 16ax^2$ b $y = 12$
③ a $r = \sqrt{\dfrac{A}{\pi}}$ b $3\frac{1}{2}$ cm
④ a $r = \sqrt{\dfrac{S}{4\pi}}$ b 7 cm
⑤ a $h^2 = f^2 + g^2$ b $f = \sqrt{h^2 - g^2}$
   c $f = 1\frac{1}{2}$ cm
⑥ a $n = \sqrt{4m + 1}$ b $n = \pm7$
⑦ a $v = \sqrt{\dfrac{2E}{m}}$ b $14\,\text{ms}^{-1}$
⑧ a $r = \sqrt{\dfrac{3V}{\pi h}}$ b $2\frac{1}{2}$ cm
⑨ a $y = \dfrac{xR}{x - R}$ b $14\frac{2}{5}$
⑩ a $h = \sqrt{\left(\dfrac{A}{\pi r}\right)^2 - r^2}$ b 24 cm

Exercise 7a   [page 64]
① The ratios in parts a and b should be the same.
② The angles in one triangle are equal to the angles in the other.
③ In each case the ratio is 5 : 2.
④ a All angles = 90°
   b $\dfrac{AB}{BC} = \dfrac{4}{3}$, $\dfrac{PQ}{QR} = \dfrac{8}{1}$. The ratios are different.
⑤ a It is unlikely that they will be similar.
⑥ It is unlikely that these cuboids will be similar.

```
┌─────────────────────────────────┐
│ 4        QR – Box 4             │
│                                 │
│   Similar: a, d, f, g, h        │
│   Not similar: b, c, e          │
└─────────────────────────────────┘
```

```
┌──────────────────────────────────────┐
│ 5             QR – Box 5              │
│                                        │
│  a  PQ, QR, RP respectively           │
│  b  EF, FD, DE respectively           │
│  c  KL, LM, MK respectively           │
│  d  EF, FD, DE respectively           │
│  e  LM, MN, NL respectively           │
│  f  AE, ED, DA respectively           │
└──────────────────────────────────────┘
```

Exercise 7b   [page 68]
① 1 $\triangle PQR$ 2 $\triangle EFD$
   3 $\triangle KLM$ 4 $\triangle EFD$
   5 $\triangle LMN$ 6 $\triangle AED$
② $\hat{H} = 55°$, $\hat{Q} = 73°$; the triangles are equiangular: $\triangle FGH$ is similar to $\triangle QPR$.
③ a QR   b PR   c FD   d QP
④ a side OP   b side DA   c diagonal N
   d diagonal DB   e side NM
⑤ $\triangle MKL$

Exercise 7c   [page 69]
① $\triangle CBA$, $104\frac{1}{2}°$, 6 cm, $4\frac{1}{2}$ cm
② $\triangle EFD$, $37°$, 8 m, 10 m, $53°$
③ $\triangle HKG$, $58\frac{1}{2}°$, $35°$, $86\frac{1}{2}°$
④ $\triangle MLN$, $49°$, $22°$, 8 cm, 15 cm
⑤ $\triangle RQP$, $44°$, $6\frac{2}{3}$ m, $9\frac{1}{3}$ m
⑥ $\triangle VWU$, $36\frac{1}{2}°$, $26°$, $5\frac{1}{3}$ m, 4 m
⑦ $\triangle CBA$, $90°$, 20 cm, 15 cm
⑧ $\triangle FED$, $21°$, $32°$, $127°$
⑨ $\triangle HKG$, $41°$, $60°$, $7\frac{1}{2}$ m, $11\frac{1}{4}$ m
⑩ $\triangle LNM$, $62°$, $36°$, 9 cm, $6\frac{2}{3}$ km

Exercise 7d   [page 71]
① a $\frac{2}{3}$ b $\frac{2}{3}$ c $\frac{2}{3}$
② $\dfrac{AB}{EF} = \dfrac{BC}{FD} = \dfrac{CA}{DE} = \dfrac{1}{2}$
③ $\dfrac{AB}{KL} = \dfrac{BC}{LM} = \dfrac{CA}{MK} = 2$
④ $\dfrac{AB}{EF} = \dfrac{BC}{FD} = \dfrac{CA}{DE} = \dfrac{5}{8}$
⑤ $\dfrac{AB}{LM} = \dfrac{BC}{MN} = \dfrac{CA}{NL} = \dfrac{4}{3}$
⑥ $\dfrac{AC}{AD} = \dfrac{CB}{DE} = \dfrac{BA}{EA} = 2$
⑦ $\dfrac{AB}{PQ} \simeq \dfrac{8.7}{10.7} \simeq 0.8$; $\dfrac{AC}{PR} \simeq \dfrac{4.7}{5.8} = 0.8$

a $\frac{AB}{BC} \simeq \frac{6\cdot5}{6} \simeq 1\cdot1$, $\frac{PQ}{QR} \simeq \frac{9\cdot8}{9} \simeq 1\cdot1$

b $\frac{AC}{BC} \simeq \frac{3\cdot8}{6} \simeq 0\cdot63$, $\frac{PR}{QR} \simeq \frac{5\cdot7}{9} \simeq 0\cdot63$

c $\frac{AB}{AC} \simeq \frac{6\cdot5}{3\cdot8} \simeq 1.7$, $\frac{PQ}{PR} \simeq \frac{9\cdot8}{5\cdot7} \simeq 1\cdot7$

37°, 53°, 90° in both triangles. The triangles are similar.

$13\frac{1}{2}$ m, 9 m

$12\frac{1}{2}$ cm, 5 cm

△XOP, $5\frac{1}{4}$ m, 3 m

10 cm, $3\frac{3}{5}$ cm

△OKH, $4\frac{4}{5}$ cm, $4\frac{1}{5}$ cm

$10\frac{1}{2}$ m, $1\frac{1}{2}$ m

Exercise 7e [page 72]

The rectangles in set (b) are similar.

20 cm

No : $\frac{AB}{BC} = \frac{1}{3}$, $\frac{WX}{XY} = \frac{4}{9}$; the ratios are different

10 cm long, $17\frac{1}{2}$ cm wide

18 cm

All cubes are similar.

1·04 cm

1·8 m wide, 2·4 m long

18 cm or 2 cm

true: a, c, d, f false: b, e, g

Exercise 7f [page 74]

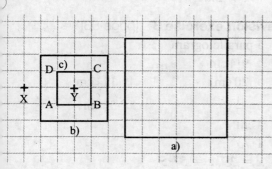

g. A4

a A   b $\frac{4}{3}$

a 0   b $\frac{5}{3}$ c $3\frac{1}{3}$ cm

c A′(2, 2), B′(6, 2), C′(2, 8)

⑤ b 2, (4, 3)

Exercise 7g [page 75]

①

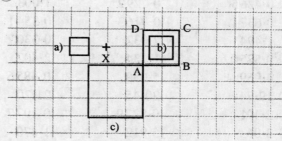

Fig. A5

② −3   ③ c P′(2, 3), Q′(4, 5), R′(6, $2\frac{1}{2}$)

④ a $-1\frac{1}{4}$ b 15 cm

⑤ b $-\frac{1}{3}$, ($2\frac{1}{2}$, $\frac{1}{2}$)

Exercise 8a [page 78]

① tan 30° ≃ 0·58

② tan 51° ≃ 1·23

Exercise 8b [page 78]

① 0·9	② 1·9	③ 0·78
④ 2·9	⑤ 1·0	⑥ 0·51
⑦ 4·3	⑧ 0·25	⑨ 0·65

Exercise 8c [page 79]

① 29°	② 16°	③ 53°
④ 58°	⑤ 70°	⑥ 32°
⑦ 42°	⑧ 48°	⑨ $35\frac{1}{2}$°

Exercise 8d [page 79]

All answers are corrected to 2 s.f.

① a 6·3	b 15	c 5·1
② a 12	b 8·4	c 6·0
③ a 11	b 11	c 5·2
④ 1·6 m	⑤ 110 m	⑥ 37 m

Exercise 8e [page 81]

All answers are corrected to 2 s.f.

① a 14	b 10	c 13
② a 4·7	b 4·9	c 1·7
③ a 36	b 53	c 12
④ 110 m	⑤ 41 m	⑥ 11 km
⑦ 38·7°	⑧ 48·8°	⑨ 16 km

Exercise 8f [page 83]

① 0·2309	② 2·050	③ 0·7002
④ 1·483	⑤ 3·487	⑥ 28·64
⑦ 0·4265	⑧ 0·7292	⑨ 1·003
⑩ 0·6371	⑪ 0·9163	⑫ 0·3541
⑬ 1·494	⑭ 2·032	⑮ 0·3307
⑯ 0·5250	⑰ 1·134	⑱ 2·402
⑲ 4·959	⑳ 5·050	㉑ 0·4856
㉒ 19·74	㉓ 20·45	㉔ 21·20
㉕ 2·491	㉖ 0·8229	㉗ 0·1977
㉘ 3·063	㉙ 5·912	㉚ 1·470
㉛ 13·00	㉜ 6·940	㉝ 0·0573
㉞ 0·2222	㉟ 0·9137	㊱ 1·019

Exercise 8g [page 83]

① 43°	② 24°	③ 29°
④ 62°	⑤ 67°	⑥ 87°
⑦ 57·5°	⑧ 41·4°	⑨ 41·5°
⑩ 65·5°	⑪ 3°	⑫ 59·7°
⑬ 19·7°	⑭ 74·4°	⑮ 88·4°
⑯ 5·8°	⑰ 84·4°	⑱ 85·6°
⑲ 32°	⑳ 58°	㉑ 37·88°
㉒ 68·2°	㉓ 21·8°	㉔ 62·1°
㉕ 26·55°	㉖ 34·33°	㉗ 70·12°
㉘ 43·23°	㉙ 43·26°	㉚ 89·6°

Exercise 8h [page 84]

① a 11 m   b 4·9 m   c 6·7 m
   d 6·1 m   e 4·8 m   f 170 m

② a 21·8°   b 42°   c 33·7°
   d 59·1°   e 37·4°

③ a $\alpha = 53 \cdot 1°, \beta = 36 \cdot 9°$
   b $\alpha = 67 \cdot 4°, \beta = 22 \cdot 6°$
   c $\alpha = 61 \cdot 9°, \beta = 28 \cdot 1°$

④ 9·6 cm	⑤ 2·5 cm	⑥ 30·1°
⑦ 12·5°	⑧ 25 m	⑨ 28·4°
⑩ 15·4°	⑪ 032°	⑫ 56·3°
⑬ 2 m	⑭ 3·9 cm	⑮ 270 m
⑯ 34 m	⑰ 87 m	⑱ 7·6 m
⑲ 11 m	⑳ 23·2°	

Revision exercise 1 [page 87]

① $10101_{two} (= 21_{ten})$

②
```
00110    10101
01001    01110
01110    01011
```
```
00100    01110
         01111
         10111
         01110
```

③ a STOCK   b CONTROL

④ 50

⑤ 16

⑥ $A = 1 \cdot 11, n = -7$

⑦ $1 \cdot 27 \times 10^4$

⑧ a $2 \cdot 9 \times 10^4$ b $7 \cdot 93 \times 10^3$
   c $6 \cdot 76 \times 10^3$ d $6 \cdot 2 \times 10^{-3}$

⑨ a $7 \cdot 6 \times 10^5$ b 5×10^3
   c $3 \cdot 2 \times 10^2$ d 6×10^4

⑩ $6 \cdot 8 \times 10^7$

Revision exercise 2 [page 88]

① a $9(a - 3)$ b $r(3 - 8t)$
   c $14x(3x - 2y)$ d $3ab(14a - 17b)$

② a $x(1 - 7x)$ b $(x + a)(5y - 2b)$

③ a $(m + n)(a - 3)$ b $(a - 7)(a + 3)$
   c $(y - 2z)(3x - 5a)$

④ a $(3a + 2x)(y - b)$ b $(s - t)(d - r)$

⑤ 3 700

⑥ a 8   b −22

⑦ a 12   b 7

⑧ a $17\frac{1}{2}$ cm^2 b 11 cm

⑨ a $x = \dfrac{y}{8}$ b $x = 3z$

   c $x = \dfrac{y + 3}{5}$ d $x = \dfrac{c}{2\pi}$

⑩ a $r = \dfrac{A}{2\pi h}$ b $r = 3$

Revision exercise 3 [page 88]

② a parallelogram

③ b 9·4 cm

④ a 20 cm   b $11\frac{2}{3}$ cm

⑤ a $1\frac{1}{3}$ b $5\frac{1}{3}$ cm

⑥ 4 cm

⑦ 1·73

⑧ $x = 39, z = 57 \cdot 5$

⑨ 165 cm

⑩ 5·6 cm

Exercise 9a [page 92]

① $a^2 + 5a + 6$ ② $c^2 + 5c - 6$

③ $e^2 - e - 6$

④ $d^2 - 3d - 18$

⑤ $x^2 - 3x + 2$

⑥ $a^2 + 6a + 9$

⑦ $b^2 - 10b + 25$

⑧ $m^2 - 16$

⑨ $n^2 + n - 20$

⑩ $d^2 - 4d - 21$

⑪ $b^2 + b - 30$

⑫ $p^2 - 8p + 15$

⑬ $q^2 - 9$

⑭ $u^2 - 4u - 45$

⑮ $v^2 - 13v + 36$

⑯ $2a^2 + 7a + 3$

⑰ $3b^2 + 14b + 8$

⑱ $2c^2 - 11c + 15$

⑲ $2d^2 - 15d - 27$

⑳ $4x^2 + 4x + 1$

㉑ $10x^2 - 11x - 6$

㉒ $6y^2 - 7y - 5$

㉓ $m^2 + 8mn + 16n^2$

㉔ $u^2 + 5uv + 6v^2$

㉕ $9d^2 - 4e^2$

㉖ $6b^2 + bc - 2c^2$

㉗ $6s^2 - 13st - 5t^2$

㉘ $4c^2 - 12cd + 9d^2$

㉙ $12m^2 - 15mn + 3n^2$

㉚ $8c^2 - 16ce - 45e^2$

Exercise 9b [page 93]

① $a^2 + 3a + 2$

② $a^2 + 5a + 6$

③ $a^2 + 7a + 12$

④ $b^2 - b - 2$

⑤ $b^2 - b - 6$

⑥ $b^2 - b - 12$

⑦ $c^2 - 7c + 12$

⑧ $d^2 + 8d + 7$

⑨ $e^2 + 11e + 18$

⑩ $f^2 - 9f + 20$

⑪ $x^2 - 8x + 7$

⑫ $y^2 - 11y + 18$

⑬ $h^2 + 12h + 36$

⑭ $k^2 - 10k + 25$

⑮ $z^2 - 7z - 18$

⑯ $a^2 + 10a + 24$

⑰ $a^2 - 10a + 24$

⑱ $a^2 + 2a - 24$

⑲ $a^2 - 2a - 24$

⑳ $b^2 + 3b - 18$

㉑ $c^2 - 3c - 2$

㉒ $m^2 - 2m + 1$

㉓ $n^2 + 2n + 1$

㉔ $f^2 + 20f + 99$

㉕ $e^2 - 8e + 15$

㉖ $d^2 + 8d - 20$

㉗ $h^2 - 5h - 24$

㉘ $a^2 + 6a + 9$

㉙ $a^2 - 6a + 9$

㉚ $a^2 - 9$

㉛ $b^2 - 25$

㉜ $c^2 - 49$

Exercise 9c [page 94]

① a $+9$ b $+2$ c -4 d -5 e $+14$

② a -1 b -3 c $+2$ d 0 e -10

③ a $+7$ b -7 c -5 d -38 e -24

④ a $+7$ b -5 c $+3$ d 0 e -6

Exercise 9d [page 95]

① $(x + 5)(x + 1)$

② $(x + 11)(x + 1)$

③ $(a + 13)(a + 1)$

④ $(b + 7)(b + 1)$

⑤ $(y + 8)(y + 1)$

⑥ $(z + 4)(z + 2)$

⑦ $(c + 5)(c + 3)$

⑧ $(d + 11)(d + 2)$

⑨ $(n + 6)(n + 2)$

⑩ $(r + 5)(r + 4)$

⑪ $(s + 8)(s + 2)$

⑫ $(t + 4)(t + 4)$

Exercise 9e [page 96]

① $(x - 3)(x - 1)$

② $(y - 2)(y - 1)$

③ $(z - 17)(z - 1)$

④ $(a - 7)(a - 1)$

⑤ $(b - 3)(b - 2)$

⑥ $(c - 6)(c - 1)$

⑦ $(d - 7)(d - 2)$

⑧ $(n - 5)(n - 2)$

⑨ $(p - 8)(p - 3)$

⑩ $(q - 7)(q - 3)$

⑪ $(f - 14)(f - 2)$

⑫ $(x - 5)(x - 5)$

Exercise 9f [page 97]

① $(x + 5)(x - 1)$

② $(a - 5)(a + 1)$

③ $(x + 7)(x - 1)$

④ $(b - 7)(b + 1)$

⑤ $(n + 2)(n - 1)$

⑥ $(r - 3)(r + 1)$

⑦ $(x - 11)(x + 1)$

⑧ $(y + 13)(y - 1)$

⑨ $(x - 5)(x + 3)$

⑩ $(x + 15)(x - 1)$

⑪ $(s + 6)(s - 1)$

⑫ $(t - 6)(t + 1)$

⑬ $(u - 3)(u + 2)$

⑭ $(v + 3)(v - 2)$

⑮ $(z + 5)(z - 4)$

⑯ $(c - 10)(c + 2)$

⑰ $(x + 7)(x - 7)$

⑱ $(x + 2)(x - 2)$

Exercise 9g [page 97]

① $a^2 + 8a + 16$

② $b^2 - 6b + 9$

③ $25 + 10c + c^2$

④ $4 - 4d + d^2$

⑤ $1 + 2m + m^2$

⑥ $4n^2 + 4n + 1$

⑦ $9x^2 + 6xy + y^2$

⑧ $u^2 - 4uv + 4v^2$

⑨ $25h^2 - 10hk + k^2$

⑩ $p^2 + 8pq + 16q^2$

⑪ $4a^2 + 12ad + 9d^2$

⑫ $9b^2 - 30bc + 25c^2$

⑬ $49e^2 - 28ef + 4f^2$

⑭ $100x^2 - 20x + 1$

⑮ $1 + 24y + 144y^2$

⑯ $9a^2 + 42ab + 49b^2$

⑰ $c^2 - 16cd + 64d^2$

⑱ $81u^2 + 18uv + v^2$

Exercise 9h [page 98]

① $10\,201$

② $9\,801$

③ $10\,609$

④ $9\,604$

⑤ $1\,002\,001$

⑥ $998\,001$

⑦ $1\,010\,025$

⑧ $992\,016$

⑨ $990\,025$

⑩ $5\,184$

⑪ $6\,889$

⑫ $6\,241$

Exercise 9i [page 98]

① $(a + 5)^2$

② $(b + 4)^2$

③ $(c + 3)^2$

④ $(d + 10)^2$

⑤ $(m - 3)^2$

⑥ $(n - 6)^2$

⑦ $(x - 2)^2$

⑧ $(y - 1)^2$

⑨ $(z + 8)^2$

⑩ $(k - 7)^2$

⑪ $(2 - b)^2$

⑫ $(9 + d)^2$

13. $(x + 3y)^2$ 14. $(2u - 3)^2$

15. $(1 - a)^2$ 16. $(5n - 3v)^2$

17. $(3a - 4b)^2$ 18. $(11 - y)^2$

Exercise 9j   [page 99]

1. $(x + 1)(x - 1)$ 2. $(1 + y)(1 - y)$

3. $(2m - n)(2m + n)$ 4. $(u + 4v)(u - 4v)$

5. $(1 - ab)(1 + ab)$ 6. $(3 - 2c)(3 + 2c)$

7. $(2d + 3e)(2d - 3e)$ 8. $3(1 - f)(1 + f)$

9. $4(g + 1)(g - 1)$ 10. $(2h + 5)(2h - 5)$

11. $(5k - 4)(5k + 4)$ 12. $(7m - n)(7m + n)$

13. $(pq - 3)(pq + 3)$ 14. $(5 + uv)(5 - uv)$

15. $(9 - w)(9 + w)$ 16. $(10x + 1)(10x - 1)$

17. $4(2y + z)(2y - z)$ 18. $(4h - k)(4h + k)$

19. $(2c + 7d)(2c - 7d)$ 20. $(e + 2f)(e - 2f)$

21. $(6a + 7b)(6a - 7b)$ 22. $5(c - 3d)(c + 3d)$

23. $(xy + z)(xy - z)$ 24. $(10 - w)(10 + w)$

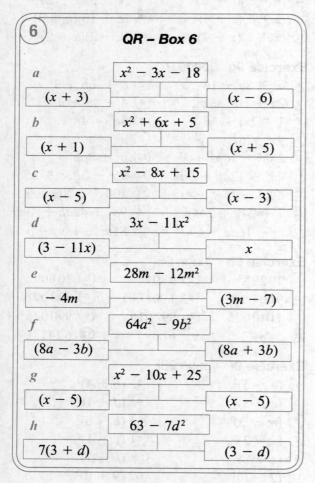

6

QR – Box 6

a $x^2 - 3x - 18$

$(x + 3)$ $(x - 6)$

b $x^2 + 6x + 5$

$(x + 1)$ $(x + 5)$

c $x^2 - 8x + 15$

$(x - 5)$ $(x - 3)$

d $3x - 11x^2$

$(3 - 11x)$ x

e $28m - 12m^2$

$-4m$ $(3m - 7)$

f $64a^2 - 9b^2$

$(8a - 3b)$ $(8a + 3b)$

g $x^2 - 10x + 25$

$(x - 5)$ $(x - 5)$

h $63 - 7d^2$

$7(3 + d)$ $(3 - d)$

Exercise 9k   [page 100]

1. $9\,200$ 2. $13\,600$

3. 288 4. $9\,600$

5. $10\,600$ 6. 400

7. $2\,600$ 8. 224

9. $1\,008\,000$ 10. $994\,000$

11. $39\,\text{cm}^2$ 12. $495\,\text{mm}^2$

13. 219 14. $125{\cdot}6\,\text{mm}^2$

15. $2\,640\,\text{cm}^3$

Exercise 9l   [page 100]

1. $(a + 1)(a + 3)$ 2. $(b + 2)(b + 3)$

3. $(c + 1)(c + 2)$ 4. $(d + 2)(d + 5)$

5. $(e + 3)(e + 4)$ 6. $(f - 1)(f - 5)$

7. $(g - 1)(g - 2)$ 8. $(h - 3)(h - 5)$

9. $(m - 3)(m - 4)$ 10. $(n - 1)(n - 7)$

11. $(p - 1)(p + 3)$ 12. $(q + 1)(q - 3)$

13. $(r - 2)(r + 5)$ 14. $(s + 2)(s - 5)$

15. $(t + 2)(t - 3)$ 16. $(u - 2)(u + 3)$

17. no factors   18. $(w + 2)(w - 7)$

19. $(x - 2)(x + 7)$ 20. no factors

21. $(z - 1)(z + 6)$ 22. $(z + 1)(z - 6)$

23. $(m + 1)(m + 12)$ 24. $(n - 1)(n + 12)$

25. $(a - 3)(a + 4)$ 26. no factors

27. $(b - 2)(b - 6)$ 28. $(x + 2)(x - 6)$

29. no factors   30. no factors

31. $(b - 4)(b - 5)$ 32. $(a - 2)(a - 10)$

33. $(e + 4)(e - 5)$ 34. no factors

35. $(x - 2)(x + 10)$ 36. $(y + 1)(y + 20)$

37. $(z + 3)^2$ 38. $(m - 4)^2$

39. no factors   40. $(p - 2)(p + 8)$

41. $(q - 3)(q + 6)$ 42. $(b + 2)(b - 9)$

43. $(c + 5)^2$ 44. $(a - 7)^2$

45. $(f - 3)(f - 7)$ 46. $(x + 3)(x - 3)$

47. $(y + 5)(y - 5)$ 48. $(h + 5)(h - 7)$

49. no factors   50. $(u - 4)(u - 8)$

51. $(v + 4)(v + 9)$ 52. no factors

53. no factors   54. $(b + 4)(b - 4)$

55. $(c + 6)(c - 6)$ 56. $(d + 4)(d + 10)$

57. $(e + 5)(e + 8)$ 58. $(f - 4)(f + 12)$

59. $(g + 6)(g - 8)$ 60. $(h - 2)(h - 24)$

Exercise 10a   [page 102]

1. $x = 18$ 2. $a = 15$ 3. $d = 17$

4. $h = 9$ 5. $n = 3$ 6. $r = 5$

$x = 21$ $\quad$ ⑧ $x = -4$ $\quad$ ⑨ $x = 7$
⑩ $x = 11$

Exercise 10b [page 103]

① $x = 5$ $\quad$ ② $r = 9$ $\quad$ ③ $m = 4$
④ $y = 3\frac{1}{2}$ $\quad$ ⑤ $s = \frac{2}{5}$ $\quad$ ⑥ $n = -\frac{4}{11}$
⑦ $t = 3\frac{2}{3}$ $\quad$ ⑧ $z = 3\frac{1}{2}$ $\quad$ ⑨ $p = 4\frac{1}{2}$
⑩ $a = 1\frac{1}{2}$ $\quad$ ⑪ $x = 2\frac{1}{2}$ $\quad$ ⑫ $q = -2\frac{1}{3}$
⑬ $b = 6$ $\quad$ ⑭ $y = 5$ $\quad$ ⑮ $r = 8$
⑯ $c = \frac{2}{9}$ $\quad$ ⑰ $d = 15$ $\quad$ ⑱ $s = -\frac{3}{4}$
⑲ $z = \frac{2}{15}$ $\quad$ ⑳ $r = 5\frac{1}{4}$ $\quad$ ㉑ $t = \frac{2}{3}$
㉒ $x = 3$ $\quad$ ㉓ $y = 7\frac{1}{2}$ $\quad$ ㉔ $d = 6$
㉕ $f = 3$ $\quad$ ㉖ $x = 1\frac{1}{2}$ $\quad$ ㉗ $h = 7$
㉘ $x = 9$ $\quad$ ㉙ $x = 4$ $\quad$ ㉚ $x = \frac{3}{4}$

Exercise 10c [page 104]

① a $\dfrac{15}{n}$ kg $\quad$ b 20 fish
② a ₦$6\dfrac{720}{x}$ $\quad$ b 7 calculators
③ a $\dfrac{3}{v}$ hours $\quad$ b $5\frac{1}{7}$
④ 82 books
⑤ 35 mangoes
⑥ 48 km/h
⑦ a $\dfrac{100}{x}$ $\quad$ b $\dfrac{100}{4x}\left(\text{or } \dfrac{25}{x}\right)$ $\quad$ c ₦5
⑧ ₦1 600
⑨ a $\dfrac{8}{v}$ $\quad$ b $\dfrac{15}{2v}$ $\quad$ c 6 km/h
⑩ 45 km/h
⑪ a $\dfrac{14 \cdot 5}{n}$ kg $\quad$ c $\dfrac{21}{2n}$ kg $\quad$ c 40 oranges
⑫ 28 fish

Exercise 10d [page 106]

① $x = 5$ $\quad$ ② $x = 3$ $\quad$ ③ $y = 1\frac{1}{2}$
④ $t = 3\frac{1}{3}$ $\quad$ ⑤ $z = -3$ $\quad$ ⑥ $r = -2$
⑦ $x = -9$ $\quad$ ⑧ $k = 2\frac{1}{2}$ $\quad$ ⑨ $a = 1$
⑩ $x = \frac{4}{5}$ $\quad$ ⑪ $x = 2$ $\quad$ ⑫ $a = 10$
⑬ $y = 7$ $\quad$ ⑭ $b = -9$ $\quad$ ⑮ $e = -6$
⑯ $c = 12\frac{1}{2}$ $\quad$ ⑰ $n = 4\frac{1}{6}$ $\quad$ ⑱ $d = -1$
⑲ $a = \frac{1}{2}$ $\quad$ ⑳ $x = 6$

Exercise 10e [page 107]

① $a - 3$ $\quad$ ② $y - 15$ $\quad$ ③ $x = -4$

④ $a = 1\frac{1}{8}$ $\quad$ ⑤ $n = -3$ $\quad$ ⑥ $n = 1$
⑦ $x = 27$ $\quad$ ⑧ $x = 10$ $\quad$ ⑨ $x = 4$
⑩ $x = -9$ $\quad$ ⑪ $x = \frac{1}{4}$ $\quad$ ⑫ $t = -8$
⑬ $k = 2$ $\quad$ ⑭ $a = 5$ $\quad$ ⑮ $a = 6$
⑯ $x = -14$ $\quad$ ⑰ $n = 2$ $\quad$ ⑱ $a = 6\frac{1}{2}$
⑲ $y = -9$ $\quad$ ⑳ $c = -\frac{1}{2}$ $\quad$ ㉑ $x = -6$
㉒ $t = 29$ $\quad$ ㉓ $a = -4\frac{1}{2}$ $\quad$ ㉔ $d = -38$
㉕ $r = -13$ $\quad$ ㉖ $p = 3\frac{1}{4}$ $\quad$ ㉗ $w = 1$
㉘ $a = 5$ $\quad$ ㉙ $x = 7$ $\quad$ ㉚ $b = 2\frac{1}{5}$

Exercise 10f [page 108]

① 3
② 11
③ 23
④ a $d - 18$ $\quad$ b ₦$\dfrac{12\,800}{d - 18}$ $\quad$ c 50 m
⑤ a $\dfrac{38\,400}{n - 280}$ $\quad$ b 600
⑥ a $(k - 15)$ litres $\quad$ b $\dfrac{344}{k - 15}$ km $\quad$ c $k = 58$
⑦ 16 games
⑧ AC = 8 cm, PR = 10 cm
⑨ 9 cm by 14 cm
⑩ a $(x + 24)$ years $\quad$ b 16 years
⑪ 72 kg and 45 kg
⑫ a $\dfrac{156}{v}$ h $\quad$ b $(v + 8)$ km/h
  c $\dfrac{180}{v + 8}$ h $\quad$ d $v = 52$
⑬ 73 km/h and 82 km/h
⑭ a 87 km/h $\quad$ b 45 km/h
⑮ a $(y + 20)$ years $\quad$ b $(y - 4)$ years
  c $(y + 16)$ years $\quad$ d 19 years
⑯ 17 years and 14 years
⑰ a $\dfrac{100}{t - 4}$ m/s $\quad$ b $\dfrac{200}{t + 1}$ m/s
  c $t = 9$, 20 m/s
⑱ a $\dfrac{200}{V + 6}$ g/cm³ $\quad$ b $\dfrac{120}{V - 4}$ g/cm³
  c 19 cm³, 8 g/cm³
⑲ a ₦$\dfrac{5\,700}{n - 3}$ $\quad$ b ₦$\dfrac{7\,500}{n + 3}$
  c $n = 22$, ₦300 each
⑳ 65 mangoes

Exercise 11a [page 111]

① ₦960 $\quad$ ② ₦1 820 $\quad$ ③ ₦810

289

(4) ₦300	(5) ₦336	(6) ₦1 140
(7) ₦3 690	(8) ₦2 160	(9) ₦688
(10) $123.30	(11) ₦4 242	(12) ₦5 855
(13) $178.20	(14) $212.49	(15) $39.51

Exercise 11b   [page 112]

(1) ₦530	(2) ₦864	(3) ₦4 720
(4) ₦8 050	(5) ₦52 200	(6) ₦337 500
(7) ₦498·60	(8) ₦1 512	(9) $104.30
(10) ₦31 950	(11) ₦7 648	(12) ₦53 630
(13) $176.25	(14) $218.31	(15) $489.88

Exercise 11c   [page 113]

(1) a ₦46 656	b ₦6 656
(2) a ₦68 694	b ₦8 694
(3) a ₦56 180	b ₦6 180
(4) a ₦34 992	b ₦4 992
(5) a ₦6 615	b ₦615
(6) a ₦105 270	b ₦18 270
(7) a ₦13 230	b ₦1 230
(8) a ₦39 326	b ₦4 326
(9) a ₦5 832	b ₦832
(10) a $88.20	b $8.20
(11) a ₦1 331	b ₦331
(12) a ₦6 945.75	b ₦945.75
(13) a ₦6 298.56	b ₦1 298.56
(14) a ₦12 250.43	b ₦2 250.43
(15) a ₦3 367.43	b ₦1 067.43

Exercise 11d   [page 114]

(1) ₦27 478	(2) ₦11 910
(3) ₦4 981	(4) ₦53 870
(5) ₦98 100	(6) ₦25 920
(7) ₦5 701 440	(8) $1 199.40
(9) 474 000	(10) ₦345 600
(11) $27 750	(12) ₦4 912
(13) ₦115 166	
(14) a ₦701 006	b ₦1 006 greater
(15) 33·1%	(16) ₦13 225

(17) Cost is 219·7 units after 3 years

(18) ₦6 900

Exercise 12a   [page 120]

(1) Keep trying!

(2) c The outcomes in the **Totals**, **Average** and **% Female** cells change automatically to

reflect the new data. This is because the underlying formulae remain unchanged.

(3) a

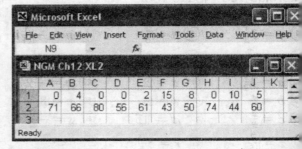

Fig. A6

b 61

c

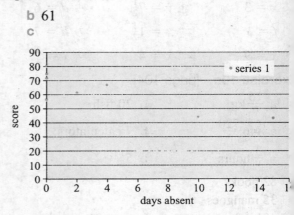

Fig. A7

The graph shows the following trend: the more days absent, the lower the test score

(4) a

	A	B	C	D
1	TEST A (25)	TEST B (100)	TEST A (100)	
2	5	48	20	
3	8	42	32	
4	12	57	48	
5	12	55	48	
6	13	60	52	
7	14	60	56	
8	16	58	64	
9	18	70	72	
10	18	67	72	
11	20	88	80	
12				

C2   fx =A2*4

Fig. A8

b

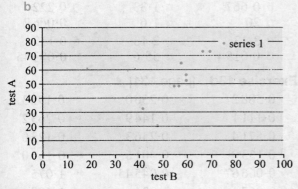

Fig. A9

c In general, the scores on Test B were better than those on Test A, indicating that the geography teacher was effective.

5 a, b, c

	A	B	C	D	E	F
1	ITEM	Unit Cost (N)	No of Units	Cost (N)	VAT (5%)	Cost + VAT (N)
2						
3	A4 Ream	600	125	75000	3750	78750
4	Rulers	50	250	12500	625	13125
5	Exercise books	60	750	45000	2250	47250
6	Wallet folder	240	250	60000	3000	63000
7	Box file	300	325	97500	4875	102375
8						

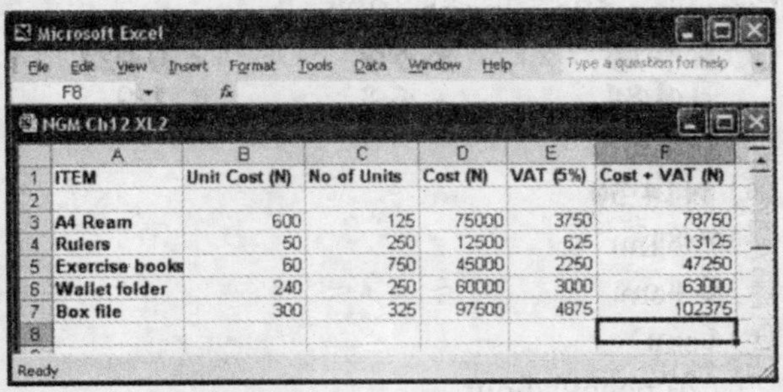

Fig. A10

d The formula would be =D3*0.12

6

1	4	3	2
2	3	4	1
3	2	1	4
4	1	2	3

Fig. A11

Exercise 13a [page 123]

1 a direct b direct c inverse
d direct e inverse f inverse
g direct h inverse

2 a directly b ₦216

3 a inversely b 10 cups

4 a

length (m)	2	4	8
cost (₦)	900	1800	3600

b directly

5 a

cost (₦)	200	300	600
number	15	10	5

b inversely

6 a

mass (g)	200	125	50
number	10	16	40

b inversely

7 a 10 pieces b $\frac{1}{2}$ m (50 cm)

8 a

time (h)	2	5	10
speed (km/h)	25	10	5

b $16\frac{2}{3}$ km/h

9 a

speed (km/h)	10	15	20
time (h)	3	2	$1\frac{1}{2}$

b 1 h 40 min ($1\frac{2}{3}$ h)

10 a

length (m)	5	8	20
number	8	5	2

b $2\frac{1}{2}$ m

11 72 km 12 30 13 10
14 1680 15 250 16 50 min ($\frac{5}{6}$ h)

Exercise 13b [page 126]

1 a 131 fr CFA, 288 fr CFA
b ₦19, ₦45

2 b 17·5 km, 52·5 km, 63 km

3 b 2 h, 1·6 h, 1·2 h

4 a ₦935, ₦2720, ₦3825
b 19, 27, 41 litres

5 a 94 g, 163 g
b 39 cm^3, 82 cm^3

6 a

speed (km/h)	30	60	90
time (h)	4	2	$1\frac{1}{3}$
$\frac{1}{\text{time}}$	0·25	0·5	0·75

c $2\frac{1}{2}$ h

(7) a

speed (km/h)	6	12	60
time (h)	10	5	1
$\frac{1}{\text{time}}$	0·1	0·2	1

  c i 4 h
    ii 8 km/h

(8) a

time (h)	8	4	2
speed (km/h)	10	20	40
$\frac{1}{\text{speed}}$	0·1	0·05	0·025

  c i 16 km/h
    ii 3·2 h

(9) a

price/item	₦300	₦600	₦1 000
n	20	10	6
$\frac{1}{n}$	0·05	0·1	0·17

  c i 25
    ii ₦40

(10) a

share (₦)	2 000	4 000	5 000
n	10	5	4
$\frac{1}{n}$	0·1	0·2	0·25

  c i 8
    ii ₦2 222

Exercise 13c [page 129]

(1)

n	$\frac{1}{n}$	n	$\frac{1}{n}$	n	$1/n$
1	1	10	0·1	0·1	10
2	0·5	20	0·05	0·2	5
3	0·333	30	0·0333	0·3	3·33
4	0·25	40	0·025	0·4	2·5
5	0·2	50	0·02	0·5	2
6	0·167	60	0·0167	0·6	1·67
7	0·143	70	0·0143	0·7	1·43
8	0·125	80	0·0125	0·8	1·25
9	0·111	90	0·0111	0·9	1·11

(2) a 0·5   b 5   c 50
  d 0·125   e 0·0125   f 0·00125
  g 1·5   h 0·6   i 0·15
  j 4   k 0·8   l 0·16

m 0·667   n 1·33   o 0·222
p 20   q 1·6   r 0·0667
(3) a 3·13   b 2·13   c 0·112
  d 0·0154   e 55·6   f 0·00345

Exercise 13d [page 131]

(1) 0·5882   (2) 0·2500   (3) 0·1923
(4) 0·1111   (5) 0·1449   (6) 0·2632
(7) 0·5714   (8) 0·2463   (9) 0·1230
(10) 0·1330   (11) 0·4016   (12) 0·1650
(13) 0·06667   (14) 0·04545   (15) 1·075
(16) 2·857   (17) 1·724   (18) 1·408
(19) 0·3456   (20) 0·0003454   (21) 345·5
(22) 0·02067   (23) 0·0002064   (24) 2·066
(25) 0·1290   (26) 7·700   (27) 0·3160
(28) 1·115   (29) 0·8956   (30) 3·299

Exercise 13e [page 132]

(1) a 0·76   b 5·9   c 0·024
  d 0·84   e 6·3   f 1·9
(2) 68 km/h
(3) ₦14·30
(4) 7·8 km
(5) 6·4 cm
(6) 6 cm
(7) 120 pencils/hour
(8) 180 litres/hour
(9) $f = 11$
(10) $R = 1·9$
(11) ₦25
(12) 16
(13) 2·5
(14) a 4·3   b 6·0   c 57
(15) ₦2·83

Exercise 14a [page 134]

(1) b $y = 5$ c $x = 21$ d (0, 2) and (−2, 0)
(3) c the lines are parallel
(4) b (0, 0·5) and (−0·3, 0)
(5) b $(1\frac{1}{2}, 2\frac{1}{2})$
(6) b (−1, 3)
(7) b (−1, 2)   c 90°
(8) a (2, −1)   b (3, 1)   c $(2, 1\frac{1}{2})$
  d (−2·2, 3·4)

Exercise 14b [page 136]

(1) $x = 1, y = 2$ (2) $x = 3, y = 2$

③ $x = 1, y = 0$ ④ $x = 0, y = 2$

⑤ $x = -1, y = 2$ ⑥ $x = 3, y = -1$

⑦ $x = -1, y = -1$ ⑧ $x = 2\frac{1}{2}, y = 1\frac{1}{2}$

⑨ $x = 1\cdot6, y = 1\cdot4$ ⑩ $x = 1\cdot3, y = -1\cdot2$

⑪ $x = -1\cdot7, y = 2\cdot3$ ⑫ $x = -0\cdot8, y = -2\cdot5$

⑬ $x = -1, y = 7$ ⑭ $x = 2, y = 8$

⑮ $x = -3, y = -1$ ⑯ $x = 6, y = 8$

⑰ $x = 0, y = -3$ ⑱ $x = 2, y = -3$

⑲ $x = 8, y = 0$ ⑳ $x = 2, y = -1$

Exercise 14c   [page 137]

① $x = 1, y = 2$ ② $x = 3, y = 2$

③ $a = -1, b = 3$ ④ $m = -1, n = 2$

⑤ $x = 3, y = 1$ ⑥ $x = -1, y = -1$

⑦ $a = 5, b = -2$ ⑧ $x = 2, y = 2$

⑨ $x = 1, y = 3$ ⑩ $a = 7, b = 5$

⑪ $x = -2, y = -3$ ⑫ $x = 1, y = -3$

⑬ $a = 6, b = -9$ ⑭ $x = 2, y = 2$

⑮ $x = 1\frac{1}{2}, y = 0$ ⑯ $m = \frac{4}{5}, n = \frac{3}{5}$

⑰ $a = \frac{1}{3}, b = \frac{2}{3}$ ⑱ $x = -2, y = -1$

⑲ $m = 1, n = \frac{1}{2}$ ⑳ $x = 2, y = 1$

Exercise 14d   [page 139]

① $a = 4, b = 3$ ② $p = 3, q = -1$

③ $x = 7, y = -2$ ④ $x = 2, y = -4$

⑤ $x = 2, y = -3$ ⑥ $x = 0, y = 3$

⑦ $a = 2\frac{1}{2}, b = 1$ ⑧ $x = 5, y = -2$

⑨ $x = 0, y = -2$ ⑩ $h = 2, k = 1\frac{1}{2}$

⑪ $p = -1, q = -2$ ⑫ $r = -2, s = 11$

⑬ $x = -3, y = 0$ ⑭ $x = 12, y = -5$

⑮ $a = 3, b = 4$ ⑯ $u = -2, v = 1$

⑰ $d = -2, e = 2$ ⑱ $x = 1\frac{1}{3}, y = 3$

⑲ $f = 2\frac{1}{3}, g = 1\frac{1}{2}$ ⑳ $y = 2\frac{1}{2}, z = -3\frac{1}{4}$

Exercise 14e   [page 140]

① $12, 7$ ② $39 \,\text{yr}, 14 \,\text{yr}$

③ $11, 6$ ④ ₦420, ₦180

⑤ ₦20, ₦90   ⑥ ₦30, ₦24

⑦ $5 \times$ ₦5 notes   ⑧ $14 \,\text{yr}, 11 \,\text{yr}$
$3 \times$ ₦10 notes

⑨ $x = 3, y = 2$; $150 \,\text{cm}^2$ ⑩ $x = 2, y = 5$; $24 \,\text{cm}$

⑪ ₦28, ₦22   ⑫ $4 \,\text{g}, 10 \,\text{g}$

⑬ $13, 9$ ⑭ $x = 3, y = 2$

⑮ $40 \,\text{yr}, 15 \,\text{yr}$ ⑯ $x = 2, y = 3$; $24 \,\text{cm}$

⑰ $x = 2, y = 3$; $81 \,\text{cm}^2$ ⑱ 73

⑲ $24 \,\text{cm}, 18 \,\text{cm}$ ⑳ 48

Exercise 15a   [page 144]

① a $0\cdot34, 0\cdot94$ b $0\cdot64, 0\cdot77$ c $0\cdot91, 0\cdot42$

② a $30°$ b $68°$ c $37°$
d $18°$ e $15°$ f $70°$

Exercise 15b   [page 145]

① a $5 \,\text{cm}$ b $6\cdot1 \,\text{m}$ c $2\cdot3 \,\text{km}$

② a $4\cdot1 \,\text{m}$ b $4\cdot2 \,\text{km}$ c $5\cdot2 \,\text{cm}$

③ a $4\cdot5 \,\text{m}$ b $1\cdot9 \,\text{km}$ c $3\cdot5 \,\text{cm}$

④ $4\cdot3 \,\text{m}$ ⑤ $6\cdot4 \,\text{km}$ ⑥ $14 \,\text{cm}$

⑦ $9\cdot0 \,\text{cm}$ ⑧ $11 \,\text{cm}, 16 \,\text{cm}$

Exercise 15c   [page 146]

① $0\cdot8290$ ② $0\cdot9848$ ③ $0\cdot0872$

④ $0\cdot7547$ ⑤ $0\cdot2079$ ⑥ $0\cdot9781$

⑦ $0\cdot2756$ ⑧ $0\cdot2756$ ⑨ $0\cdot6157$

⑩ $0\cdot6157$ ⑪ $0\cdot3584$ ⑫ $0\cdot3584$

⑬ $0\cdot6884$ ⑭ $0\cdot8729$ ⑮ $0\cdot2453$

⑯ $0\cdot9421$ ⑰ $0\cdot1599$ ⑱ $0\cdot8358$

⑲ $0\cdot7147$ ⑳ $0\cdot4370$ ㉑ $0\cdot9890$

㉒ $0\cdot8612$ ㉓ $0\cdot1417$ ㉔ $0\cdot5567$

㉕ $0\cdot5770$ ㉖ $0\cdot5788$ ㉗ $0\cdot4793$

㉘ $0\cdot4775$ ㉙ $0\cdot3997$ ㉚ $0\cdot4011$

Exercise 15d   [page 147]

① a $36°$ b $54°$

② a $53°$ b $37°$

③ a $21°$ b $69°$

④ a $37°$ b $53°$

⑤ a $32°$ b $58°$

⑥ a $24°$ b $66°$

⑦ a $56\cdot5°$ b $33\cdot5°$

⑧ a $9\cdot7°$ b $80\cdot3°$

⑨ a $31\cdot1°$ b $58\cdot9°$

⑩ a $36\cdot8°$ b $53\cdot2°$

⑪ a $46\cdot98°$ b $43\cdot02°$

⑫ a $4\cdot23°$ b $85\cdot77°$

⑬ a $22\cdot03°$ b $67\cdot97°$

⑭ a $51\cdot06°$ b $38\cdot94°$

⑮ a $23\cdot58°$ b $66\cdot42°$

⑯ a $41\cdot82°$ b $48\cdot18°$

⑰ a $21\cdot1°$ b $68\cdot9°$

18 a 34·85°   b 55·15°
19 a 12·91°   b 77·09°
20 a 34·39°   b 55·61°
21 a 39·25°   b 50·75°

Exercise 15e   [page 148]

1. $a = 4·0\,cm$ $b = 3·0\,cm$
   $c = 1·3\,cm$ $d = 1·5\,cm$
   $e = 6·1\,cm$ $f = 19\,cm$
   $g = 5·1\,cm$ $h = 3·1\,cm$
2. $\alpha = 17·5°, \beta = 44·4°, \gamma = 48·2°, \delta = 61°$
3. $x = 3·5\,cm, y = 13\,cm, z = 16\,cm$
4. $BC = 4·2\,m, XY = 4·9\,cm, PQ = 13\,m$
5. $a = 69·5°, \beta = 53·1°, \gamma = 48·2°, \delta = 18·2°$
6. 7·4 m   7. a 19 km   b 35 km
8. 71·8°   9. 3·8 m   10. 23·6°
11. 45·6°   12. 510 m   13. 4·4 m
14. a 34·8°   b 2·9 m   15. 6·0 cm

Exercise 15f   [page 150]

1. a $\sin \theta = \dfrac{c}{a} = \dfrac{d}{e} = \dfrac{e}{b + d}$

   b $\cos \theta = \dfrac{b}{a} = \dfrac{c}{e} = \dfrac{a}{b + d}$

   c $\tan \theta = \dfrac{c}{b} = \dfrac{d}{c} = \dfrac{e}{a}$

2. 154 cm (1·54 m)
3. $\alpha = 55°, \beta = 61·7°, A\hat{B}C = 116·7°$
4. 112·3° (41·8° + 70·5°)
5. a 620 km   b 500 km
6. a $\sqrt{3} = 1·73\,m$ b 1·732 m
7. a 7·27 m   b 61·2°
8. 5·3 cm
9. 6·7 cm, 7·4 cm
10. 1·1 m, 2·3 m

Exercise 16a   [page 153]

1. a bicycles   b motor bikes
   c 85   d 25
2. a 5 900 m   b 6 200 m
   c Blanc   d 1 800 m
3. a $\frac{1}{3}$ b 25%
   c 25 min
4. a 1 400 000   b 3 000 000
   c $\frac{1}{30}$ d 30%

5.

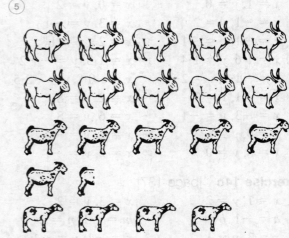

Fig. A12

6.

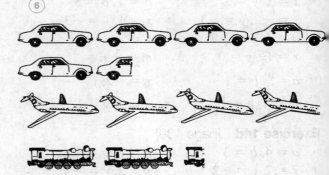

Each symbol represents 10 people
Fig. A13

7.

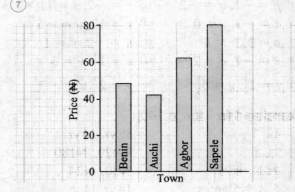

Fig. A14

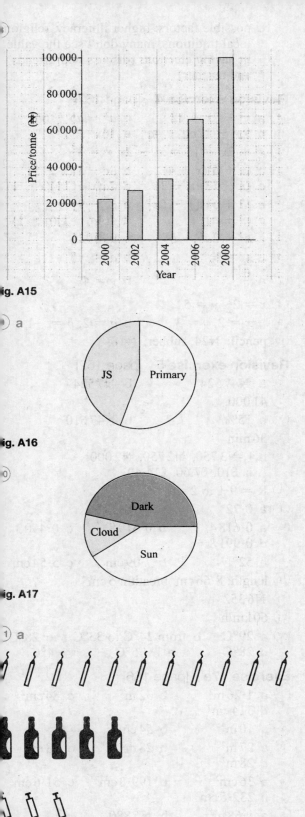

Fig. A15

Fig. A16

Fig. A17

Each symbol represents 10 people.

b

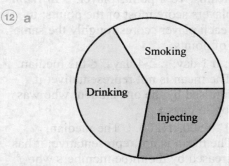

Fig. A18

⑫ a

Fig. A19

b i smoking,   ii drug injection

Exercise 16b [page 156]

① mean ② median ③ mode
④ a 8, 7, 7   b 4, 4, 3
  c $4\frac{1}{3}$, $4\frac{1}{2}$, 1   d 5, 4, 3
  e 0·55, 0·35, 0   f 156·4, 155·8, 155·8
⑤ a ₦4 746   b ₦4 618   ⑥ 83·3 kg
⑦ a 1·15 kg   b 1 kg   ⑧ 23 yr 3 mo
⑨ 59 kg   ⑩ ₦164/kg   ⑪ 32·5 mm
⑫ ₦600 000   ⑬ 12·5, 12·8, 9·1
⑭ 48 km/h   ⑮ 50 km/h   ⑯ 64 km/h
⑰ 46 km/h   ⑱ 61·4
⑲ a 24   b 4   c 4   d 3·5
⑳ a Rose 58, Sola 67, Tayo 61, Uche 28, Vera 41
  b Eng. 52, Hist. 52, Maths 49, Sci. 51
  c Eng. 52, Hist. 60, Maths 49, Sci. 48

Exercise 16c [page 159]

① a range: from 1 to 9, mean: 5; b range: from 1 to 9, mean: 6. The sets of numbers have the same range but different means.

2 a range: from 35 to 48, mean: 40; b range: from 21 to 95, mean: 40. The sets of numbers have different ranges but the same mean.

3 a ₦260. b No; the two types of pen are of such different value that it is not sensible to find their mean cost.

4 a ₦7333. b No; this average is misleading.

5 a Both weeks: 13 mm/day. b Although the averages are the same, the weather is different during the two weeks. Rain falls steadily each day during *Week 1*. *Week 2* begins very wet and finishes with dry weather.

6 a Both teams: 16·4 points/player. b In *Team A*, two players score most of the points; in *Team B* each player scores roughly the same number of points.

7 a 0 day; b 1 day; c 2·4 days; d the median, 1 day. (The mean is not representative; it has been raised by the one student who was absent for 35 days.)

8 a ₦880, ₦500, ₦200. b The median, ₦500. The mean is not representative; it has been increased by the three members who gave ₦5000.

9 a 39·6, 39·5, 40. b Yes. The mode is 40; the mean and median, to the nearest whole number of matchsticks, are also 40.

10 a

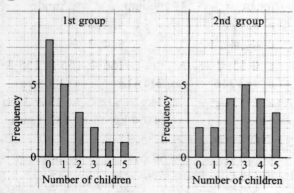

Fig. A20

b

	mode	mean
1st group	0	1·3
2nd group	3	2·8

c The first group may have contained young and unmarried women. The second group may have contained older married women.

11 a 81%
b women (85%) (men: 78%)

c possible factors: higher illiteracy, religion, local traditions, many don't see the value in having elections (discuss with friends and teacher)

Revision exercise 4 [page 162]

1 a $x^2 - 7x + 12$ b $a^2 - ab - 6b^2$
c $9p^2 - 12pq + 4q^2$ d $16x^2 - 1$

2 $x^2 + 2x - 15 = x^2 - 2x$, $x = 3\frac{3}{4}$

3 a $(x + 6)(x + 4)$ b $(x - 3)(x - 5)$
c $(x - 13)(x + 2)$ d $2a(x - 11)(x - 1)$

4 a $(1 + 5x)(1 - 5x)$ b $(x - 9)^2$
c $(3 + a)^2$ d $4(4a - 1)(a - 1)$

5 a $a^2 - 2ab + b^2$ b 990 025

6 a $x = 3\frac{1}{2}$ b $a = -3$

7 a $\frac{6}{v}$ b $v = 4\frac{1}{2}$

8 $x = 2\frac{1}{2}$, $y = 5$

9 a $x = 2$, $y = 3$ b $a = 2$, $b = -1$

10 pencil: ₦24, rubber: ₦18

Revision exercise 5 [page 162]

1 a ₦47 524   b ₦7 524

2 41 000

3 a 15%   b ₦47 610

4 36 min

5 b i ₦3 750, ₦2 750, ₦2 000.
ii £10, £7.60, £14.40

6 R = 9·1 to 2 s.f.

7 a 0·72   b 53'

8 a 0·6184   b 0·6198   c 0·4503
d 0·9918

9 a 52°   b 7·09 cm   c 5·54 cm

10 length: 8·66 cm, breadth: 5 cm

11 ₦6352

21 60 km/h

13 a 29°C   b from 24°C to 33°C   c 28°C
d 28°C   e i +5°C   ii −4°C

Exercise 17a [page 166]

1 a 1·26 m²   b 32 m²   c 84 cm²
d 314 cm²

2 a 10 m²   b 54 cm²

3 a 27 m²   b 28 m²   c 28 m²
d 28 m²

4 a 36 cm²   b 199·8 cm² c 51·6 cm²
d 232·5 cm²

5 a 1·68 m²   b ₦5880

(6) 384 cm²   (7) 308 mm² (3·08 cm²)   (13) 16·5 m²   (14) 10·4 cm²

(8) 550 min (9 h 10 min)   (8) ₦420 000   (15) 907·5 cm²   (16) 100

(10) a 231   b 2 566 cm²   (17) 0.495 ha (roughly half a hectare)

(18) 16.2 ha   (19) 380 ha

Exercise 17b   [page 168]

(20) 5 500 m²

(1) a 15 cm²   b 26 cm²   c 40 cm²

d 37½ cm²   e 5·31 cm²

Exercise 18a   [page 178]

(2) a 5   b 4   c 6½

(1) 100 : 9   (2) 16 : 49

d 7   e 5½

(3) a 4 : 25   b 24 cm²

Exercise 17c   [page 170]

(4) a $\frac{2}{3}$ b 18 cm

The answers are given to 3 s.f. as a check on calculation. Round each answer to the nearest whole number to give a suitable degree of accuracy.

(5) a $\frac{2}{3}$ b 73·5 cm

(6) a $\frac{121}{81}$ b 243 cm²

(1) a 17·6 cm²   b 4·22 cm²   c 4·53 cm²

(7) 200 ha   (8) 24 cm²   (9) ₦275

d 20·4 cm²   e 16·2 cm²

(10) ₦250   (11) 72 cm   (12) 220 cm by 55 cm

(2) a 28·7 cm²   b 26·5 cm²   c 15·9 cm²

d 31·1 cm²   e 25·8 cm²

(3) a 26·7 m²   b 5·80 m²   c 17·6 m²

d 38·1 m²   e 31·5 m²

(8)   **QR – Box 8**

Exercise 17d   [page 173]

a

(1) a 22 m²   b 66 cm²   c 148·5 m²

d 5·28 cm²

	$\frac{3}{4}$	
$\frac{9}{16}$		$\frac{27}{64}$

(2) a 38·5 cm²   b 770 m²   c 18·48 cm²

d 36·96 cm²   e 513⅓ m²   f 70 cm

b

g 21 cm   h 45°   i 9 m   j 72°

	$\frac{4}{5}$	
$\frac{16}{25}$		$\frac{64}{125}$

(3) a 10·5 cm²   b 14 cm²   c 10·5 cm²

(4) a 7 cm   b 21 cm   c 5·25 m

c

d 140 m

	$\frac{5}{3}$	
$\frac{25}{9}$		$\frac{125}{27}$

(5) 5 cm

d

(7)   **QR – Box 7**

a → r and a → v
b → p, c → t, d → u
e → q, f → t, g → s

	$\frac{4}{7}$	
$\frac{16}{49}$		$\frac{64}{343}$

e

	$\frac{5}{6}$	
$\frac{25}{36}$		$\frac{125}{216}$

Exercise 17e   [page 174]

(1) a 280   b 120   c 238   d 630

e 952   f 252   g 120   h 240

(2) a 135   b ₦17 550

f

(3) 1 320 tiles   (4) ₦432

	$\frac{2}{3}$	
$\frac{4}{9}$		$\frac{8}{27}$

(5) 187   (6) 14

(7) 1 132 tiles   (8) 1395

(9) 11 sheets   (10) ₦2 406

Exercise 18b   [page 181]

(11) 352 cm²   (12) 71·5 cm²

(1) 8 : 27   (2) 1 : 8   (3) 1 : 8

④ a $1:27$ b $324\,g$
⑤ a $3:2$ b $24\,cm$
⑥ $3\cdot072$ litres   ⑦ $6\cdot4$ litres
⑧ ₦216   ⑨ $\frac{1}{24}\,m^3$ ⑩ $12\,cm$

Exercise 18c   [page 182]
① ₦400   ② ₦200   ③ $405\,ml$
④ ₦1 080   ⑤ $2\cdot7\,t$ ⑥ $4\cdot608\,kg$
⑦ $12\,500$ litres   ⑧ a $1:1375$ b $38\cdot5\,m$
⑨ a $1:80$ b $1\,296\,m^2$ ⑩ $675\,kg$

Exercise 19a   [page 184]
① $25x\,g$ ② ₦$4y$ ③ $15t\,km$ ④ ₦$25n$
⑤ $8d\,ml$ ⑥ $C = 7n$ ⑦ $D = 16t$ ⑧ $x = \frac{1}{4}y$
⑨ $d = 4s$ ⑩ $a = 0\cdot8b$
⑪ a $D = 4S$ b 44
⑫ a $x = 2\frac{1}{2}y$ b 25 c $5\cdot6$
⑬ a $P = \frac{3}{8}Q$ b 6 c $6\cdot4$
⑭ a $0\cdot9$ b $3\frac{1}{3}$
⑮ a $0\cdot36$ b 55

Exercise 19b   [page 185]
① $d \propto \frac{1}{t}$
② a inversely   b $n \propto \frac{1}{l}$
③ a $l = \frac{A}{b}$ b $b = \frac{A}{l}$ c inversely
④ $x = \frac{66}{y}$ ⑤ $R = \frac{32}{T}$ ⑥ $m = \frac{7\,000}{n}$
⑦ a $T = \frac{120}{S}$ b $1\frac{1}{3}$ c 48
⑧ a 3 b $1\frac{1}{3}$
⑨ a $0\cdot4$ b 150
⑩ a 10 c 160

Exercise 19c   [page 186]
① ₦260 = £1, ₦7 280   ② $D = 54T$, $270\,km$
③ $h = 0\cdot15T$, $11\cdot4\,cm$ ④ $0\cdot432\,cm$
⑤ $276\,km$ ⑥ $b = \frac{56}{n}$, 16 bricks
⑦ $m = \frac{13\,500}{a}$, 18 months   ⑧ $13\frac{1}{3}\,kg$
⑨ ₦700   ⑩ $2\cdot4\,h$ ($2\,h\ 24\,min$)
⑪ $1\cdot25\,m^3$ ⑫ $2\cdot5 \times 10^4\,N/m^2$

Exercise 19d   [page 187]
① a $x = 5yz$ b 120

② a $x = \frac{6y}{z}$ b 7
③ a $A = \frac{BC}{6}$ b 5 c 8
④ a $T = \frac{12S}{t}$ b 22
⑤ a $M = 0\cdot8At$ b $960\,g$
⑥ a $V = \frac{90T}{11p}$ b $1\cdot7 \times 10^5\,N/m^2$

Exercise 19e   [page 189]
① a $x = 20 + 5y$ b 35
② a $x = 2 + 3y$ b 32
③ a $x = 5 + \frac{2}{3}y$ b $7\frac{2}{3}$
④ a $D = 30 + 3V$ b 249
⑤ ₦2 400
⑥ a $C = 5\,000 + 800T$ b ₦11 000
⑦ a ₦960   b ₦1 100   c ₦2 364
⑧ a ₦1·80   b $T = 50 + 1\cdot8n$
⑨ a ₦2 110   b ₦2 215.50
⑩ a ₦40   b $E = 375 + 40N$

Exercise 20a   [page 191]
① The following are non-rational: j), k), o), p), r), z)
The others are rational.
② a $\frac{25}{3}$ b $\frac{20}{3}$ c $\frac{43}{9}$
   d $\frac{316}{99}$ e $\frac{325}{99}$ f $\frac{160}{99}$

Exercise 20b   [page 193]
① a 4 b 2 c 5 d 7 e 3 f 8
  g 6 h 9 i 1
② a $1\cdot7$ b $2\cdot8$ c $3\cdot6$ d $4\cdot8$
  e $7\cdot2$ f $8\cdot3$

Revision exercise 6   [page 195]
① $90\,cm^2$ ② $9\cdot9\,cm^2$ ③ $58\,cm^2$
④ 154 ⑤ $88\,m^2$ ⑥ $26\cdot4\,cm^2$
⑦ a $2:5$ b $27\cdot5\,cm$ ⑧ $19\,m^2$
⑨ $5\frac{1}{3}\,kg$ ⑩ $6\,kg$

Revision exercise 7   [page 196]
① $x = \frac{1}{5}y$ ② $I = \frac{E}{80}$, $I = 5$
③ a $104\,000$ b $25\,h$ ④ $I = \frac{240}{R}$
⑤ a $n = 20$ b $d = 1\frac{1}{2}$ ④ $3\frac{4}{5}$ hours
⑦ a $p = \frac{2m}{5n}$ b $p = \frac{3}{4}$

a $c = -6 + 3n$ b 75

$\frac{524}{99}$ (10) 8·6

Exercise R1a   [page 200]

a $5\frac{3}{10}$ b $2\frac{5}{12}$ c $8\frac{13}{24}$ d $1\frac{13}{24}$

a 9   b 7   c 2   d $4\frac{2}{3}$

a 4   b $\frac{4}{5}$ c $\frac{6}{7}$ d $\frac{3}{5}$

a $\frac{14}{15}$ b 3   c $\frac{5}{21}$ d 4

a ₦615   b 5·202   c 5·83   d ₦551

a 4·5   b ₦7560   c 16·9   d 1·7248

a 20   b 400   c 0·18   d 28

a 189   b $1\frac{1}{4}$ c ₦220   d 150 g

a 60%   b 76%   c $62\frac{1}{2}$%   d $66\frac{2}{3}$%

  e 54%   f 3%   g $22\frac{1}{2}$%   h $33\frac{1}{3}$%

a 45%   b 3%   c $16\frac{1}{2}$%   d $16\frac{2}{3}$%

a $\frac{11}{40}$ b 135

a $37\frac{1}{2}$%   b 96

a 15   b 1

a 20   b $2\frac{3}{4}$

a $\frac{19}{24}$ b 12%

(6) $\frac{3}{4}, \frac{4}{5}, \frac{17}{20}, \frac{9}{10}$

(7) $\frac{1}{6}$ (18) $\frac{7}{15}$

(9) $8\frac{3}{4}$%   (20) 150%

a 2·75   b 35·29   c 157·06

a 0·0035   b 59   c 2·2   d 61 000

a 60   b 20   c 20 000   d 0·07

a 0·00244   b 54 300   c 0·0216

a 7·385   b 56·06   c 100
  d 43·6   e 44

Exercise R1b   [page 201]

(1) 28 kg, 22 kg   (2) 12 eggs, 42 eggs

(3) 630 students   (4) $n = 500\,000$

(5) 11 : 5   (6) ₦17 280, ₦34 560

(7) 818 g   (8) $37\frac{1}{2}$ litres

(9) US$47.50   (10) 1·458 kg

(11) 16 kg   (12) 40 min

(13) a 52·5 m   (14) $x = 7$
   b 137 min

(15) 720 km   (16) 15 days

(17) 4 days   (18) 16 pieces

(19) 20 children   (20) 2 h 40 min

Exercise R1c   [page 202]

(1) a $5·26 \times 10^5$ b $7·063 \times 10^{-4}$

(2) a $1·45 \times 10^{-3}$ b $1·45 \times 10^1$

(3) a 16 700   b 0·0455

(4) 16 000

(5) $a = 5·26, n = 26$

(6) $n = 5$

(7) $1·33 \times 10^{-1}$

(8) 2×10^9

(9) a $9·75 \times 10^4$ b $3·6 \times 10^5$
   c $2·24 \times 10^7$ d $9·6 \times 10^5$

(10) $1·742 \times 10^2$

Exercise R1d   [page 203]

(1) a i ₦185   ii ₦220   b ₦75
   c ₦50   d 2   e ₦66·25   f ₦35

(2) ₦1 560   (3) ₦126 000

(4) ₦2 400   (5) ₦159 500

(6) £3 000   (7) 5%   (8) ₦465

(9) 4 139, 5 122, 3 279, 5 427 respectively

(10) ₦4 000

(11) a ₦37 500   b ₦78 820

(12) ₦28 040

(13) a ₦241 250   b ₦150 365   c ₦85 859

(14) a ₦15 930   b ₦22 152   c ₦6 222

(15) a 9 bottles   b ₦27

(16) ₦7 245   (17) ₦100 320   (18) ₦280 000

Exercise R1e   [page 204]

(1) a ₦2 900   b 27·4

(2) ₦60   (3) ₦50

(4) 4% loss   (5) ₦6 500

(6) a ₦8 200, profit of ₦1 200
   b profit of ₦1 600, cost = ₦11 000

(7) ₦21 600   (8) ₦152

(9) ₦460   (10) ₦24 200

(11) a ₦15 600   b ₦62 400   c ₦2 600

(12) a ₦749 000   b ₦955 600   c ₦206 600

(13) ₦3 189·60   (14) ₦6 280   (15) ₦5 428

Exercise R1f   [page 205]

(1) a 101001_{two} b 1000001_{two}
   c 1011000_{two} d 1111001_{two}
   e 100000000_{two}

② a 15　b 59　c 31　d 115
③ a 23　b 39　c 23　d 78　e 23
④ a 11011_{two}　b 1031_{four}　c 2102_{five}
⑤ a 100011_{two}　b 1001_{two}　c 1111_{two}

Exercise R2a　[page 207]

① ₦$(1\,100x + 800y)$　② $2x + 10$ years

③ a $100n + k$　b $n + \dfrac{k}{100}$

④ ₦$120x$　⑤ $\dfrac{2\,000}{x}$ kg

⑥ pn marks　⑦ $\dfrac{p^2}{16}$ cm²

⑧ $4\sqrt{A}$ cm　⑨ $\dfrac{100p}{t}$ cups

⑩ $(L - \frac{1}{4}m)$ metres　⑪ $\dfrac{440}{x}$ min

⑫ ut km　⑬ $t(u - v)$ km

⑭ $x + 5$　⑮ a $15 - x$ cm　b $x(15 - x)$ cm²

Exercise R2b　[page 208]

① a $x = 5$　b $x = 11$
　c $x = 13$　d $x = 11$
　e $x = 0$　f $x = 4$
② a $x = 6$　b $x = 13$
　c $x = 6$　d $x = 13$
　e $x = 3$　f $x = 4\frac{1}{3}$
　g $d = 7$　h $b = 2$
　i $x = 5$　j $x = 1\frac{1}{2}$
③ a $x = \frac{3}{5}$　b $x = 2$
　c $a = \frac{6}{7}$　d $x = 2\frac{1}{2}$
④ a $a = -1$　b $y = -3$
　c $x = 5$　d $c = 4$
　e $x = 3$　f $y = -3$
　g $a = 4$　h $f = 2$
⑤ a $x = 9$　b $x = 1$
　c $f = 4$　d $x = -9$
　e $x = 3$　f $x = -6$
　g $x = 7$　h $x = 5$
　i $x = 5$　j $x = 2$
⑥ a $x = 18$　b $x = 2$
　c $x = -5$　d $x = 26$
　e $x = 80$　f $x = 1\frac{2}{3}$
　g $x = 4$　h $x = -54$
⑦ a $x = 64$　b $x = 70$
　c $x = 5$　d $x = 10$
　e $x = \frac{1}{2}$　f $b = -2$

g $x = 7$　h $a = 4$
i $d = 4$　j $t = 7$
⑧ a $x > -2$　b $x < -2$
　c $x < 2\frac{1}{2}$　d $x > 2\frac{1}{2}$
　e $x < 5$　f $x < 2$
　g $x > -1$　h $x > 7$
　i $x < 3$　j $x \leqslant 3$
⑨ 27　⑩ ₦80
⑪ 9 cm　⑫ 4
⑬ 108 pages　⑭ 18 years
⑮ 82 g　⑯ 48 m
⑰ $x = 13$　⑱ 24 yr, 19 yr
⑲ 8, 9, 10 or 11　⑳ 19, 20, 21

Exercise R2c　[page 210]

① a $9a$　b $4a$
　c $11x$　d $-4x$
　e $6y$　f $35y$
　g $24rs$　h $16a^2b$
　i $10ab$　j $2a$
　k $4x$　l $-11x$
② a $4x + 3$　b $2x - 7$
　c $6p + q$　d $2h + 5k$
　e $15y$　f $28a$
　g $3a + b$　h $3x + y$
　i $15a - 7$　j $5 - 3a$
③ a $4x + 8y$　b $2a - 10$
　c $15 - 27x$　d $10x + 5b$
　e $54c - 45$　f $-3a - 12b$
　g $-8x + 16y$　h $-18y + 6z$
④ a $2x + 11$　b $2z + 20$
　c $14a - 6$　d $4a - 13b$
　e $9x + 13y$　f $a + 18b$
　g $a^2 + 7a + 10$　h $x^2 - 8x + 15$
⑤ a $x^2 + 9x + 20$　b $n^2 - 3n - 18$
　c $c^2 + 4c - 21$　d $b^2 - 11b + 24$
　e $x^2 + 10x + 25$　f $y^2 - 6y + 9$
　g $6a^2 + 13ab - 5b^2$　h $a^2 - 4b^2$
⑥ a $2(4x + 3y)$　b $3(3a + 1)$
　c $a(b - c)$　d $5(3a - 2b)$
　e $2x(y + 6z)$　f $a(7a - 1)$
　g $d^2(7 + 13e)$　h $12pq(2p - 3q)$
⑦ a a　b $\dfrac{6}{d}$

　c $\dfrac{5}{2y}$　d $\dfrac{14}{3k}$

　e $\dfrac{7a - 4}{4}$　f $\dfrac{3d + 4}{6}$

⑧ a $(3x + y)(x - 2)$ b $(5 - r)(2a - 1)$
c $(x + 3)(x + 6)$ d $(a + 2b)(c + d)$
e $(a + b)(b - y)$ f $(x - 1)(a + 1)$
⑨ a $(x + 7)(x + 1)$ b $(a + 5)(a + 2)$
c $(b - 17)(b - 1)$ d $(a - 8)(a - 3)$
e $(x + 9)(x - 2)$ f $(x + 4)(x - 3)$
g $(a - 7)(a + 1)$ h $(x - 5)(x + 3)$
⑩ a $(x + 3)^2$ b $(y + 10)^2$
c $(a - 4)^2$ d $(d - 7)^2$
e $(3a + b)(3a - b)$ f $(c + 9r)(c - 9r)$
g $(2p + 5q)(2p - 5q)$ h $(6k + 7t)(6k - 7t)$
⑪ $3a - 7$
⑫ $\dfrac{15e + 8c}{6cde}$
⑬ $-\dfrac{2}{3}$
⑭ a $2ab + 2ac - bc - 2ab$
b $c(2a - b)$
⑮ $15 - a - 2a^2$
⑯ $x - y$
⑰ $3(6 + x)(6 - x)$
⑱ a $(x + 2y)(x - 2y)$ b 880 c 4700
⑲ 81
⑳ a $a^2 - 2ab + b^2$ b $2499 \cdot 9$

Exercise R2d   [page 211]

① A(1, 3), B(3, 1), C(2, −1), D(1, −2)
E(−1, −3), F(−2, 21), G(−3, 1), H(−1, 2)
I(0·8, 2·2), J(2·6, −2·4), K(−2·8, −2),
L(−2·6, 2·8)
② c a palm tree
③ c a kite   d $(-1, 2\frac{1}{2})$ e $E(\frac{1}{2}, -\frac{1}{2})$
④ b -11 c $-1 \cdot 1$
⑤ a

x	0	1	2	3	4	5
y	−7	−4	−1	2	5	8

c 3.2 d $(0, -7)$ and $(2 \cdot 3, 0)$
⑥ a $y = \frac{1}{2}(2 - x)$
b

x	−4	0	4
y	3	1	−1

c $26\frac{1}{2}°$

⑦ d Lines a and b are parallel to each other.
Line c is perpendicular to lines a and b.
⑧ b $(-1, 3)$

Exercise R2e   [page 212]

① a

x	1	$2\frac{1}{2}$	0
y	−2	−1	$-2\frac{2}{3}$

b $x = 1, y = -2$

② a $x = 1, y = 4$ b $x = 3, y = 1$
c $x = 1, y = -2$ d $p = 6\frac{1}{2}, q = 1\frac{1}{2}$
③ a $x = 2, y = -1$ b $a = 2\frac{1}{2}, y = 1\frac{1}{2}$
c $x = \frac{4}{7}, y = 2\frac{1}{7}$ d $p = \frac{1}{2}, q = -\frac{1}{4}$
e $a = 5, b = 4$ f $x = -2, y = 3$
④ 17 yr, 14 yr
⑤ 9 cm long, 4 cm broad
⑥ book: 130 g, pencil: 20 g
⑦ a ₦70,   b ₦40
⑧ 4 ₦20 stamps, 3 ₦50 stamps

Exercise R2f   [page 213]

① a 8 b 1 c -2
d 3 e 7 f 0
g $-\frac{1}{4}$ h 2 i $-\frac{1}{6}$
j -30 k 25 l 3
② a $\frac{2}{5}$ b 14 c 29
③ 2 ④ $5\frac{1}{2}$ ⑤ 11
⑥ 11 ⑦ $2 \cdot 23$ ⑧ 145
⑨ a 45 km   b 1 h 20 min
⑩ $n = \sqrt{\dfrac{ld}{k}}$ ⑪ $v = \sqrt{\dfrac{2gHx}{m}}$
⑫ $W = \dfrac{E}{IL}$ ⑬ $t = \left(\dfrac{as}{k}\right)^2$
⑭ $t = \dfrac{3vT}{u}$ ⑮ $q = \dfrac{1}{4 - r}$
⑯ $C = \dfrac{p^2 + k^2t^2}{t}$ ⑰ $\sqrt{1 - x^2}$
⑱ a $F = 104$ b $C = 37\frac{7}{9}$
⑲ a $\sin Z = \dfrac{2A}{xy}$ b $\sin Z = \frac{1}{2}$
⑳ $W = \frac{1}{7}d$ ㉑ $t = \dfrac{10}{v}$
㉒ $x \propto \dfrac{y}{z}$ ㉓ $P = \frac{1}{2}Q - 20$
㉔ a $a = 40, b = -1\frac{1}{4}$ b $V = 27\frac{1}{2}$ c $t = 12 \cdot 8$
㉕ a $C = 200 + 30d$ b ₦410

Exercise R3a   [page 216]

① a 198 cm   b $1 \cdot 98$ km
② 2500 ③ $1\frac{3}{4}$ m

301

④ 51 cm²

⑤ 220 cm²

⑥ 24 cm²

⑦ 32 cm²

⑧ a 3 cm

b 34 cm²

⑨ 50 cm²

⑩ a 13·86 m²

b ₦6930

⑪ 291 cm²

⑫ 42 cm²

⑬ 1960 m²

⑭ 266 tiles

⑮ 1520 litres

⑯ 5040 litres

⑰ 36π cm³

⑱ 42π cm²

⑲ 880 cm²

⑳ a πa² − πb²
 b π (a + b)(a − b)
 c 880 cm²

㉑ 72 cm²

㉒ 7 cm

㉓ 4⅔ cm

㉔ a 96 m²

b 7·68 m³

㉕ 215600 cm³

Exercise R3b [page 218]

① 50°

② 63°

③ 100°

④ 130°

⑤ 100°

⑥ a = b = 58°, c = 122°, d = e = 29°

⑦ 32°

⑧ 20

⑨ 18

⑩ 150°

⑪ 140

⑫ 36

⑬ AB = 10·5 cm, AC = 5·3 cm

⑭ c BP ≃ 4·1 cm

⑮ BC ≃ 5·9 cm

⑯ c XP ≃ 3·3 cm

⑰ b 4·1 cm

⑱ b a kite

⑲ d AP ≃ 5·4 cm

Exercise R3c [page 221]

① a 13   b 5   c 6   d 10

② a 12 cm   b 30 cm²

③ 13 cm   ④ 8 cm   ⑤ 9·4 km

⑥ a 10 cm   b 0·6

⑦ a 10 cm   b 2·4

⑧ a 38°   b 50·2°   c 75·4°   d 68°
 e 23·7°   f 22·4°   g 22°   h 48·6°
 i 86·1°   j 88·7°

⑨ α = 58°, β = 35°, γ = 30°, δ = 66·4°

⑩ 42°   ⑪ 32°   ⑫ 240°

⑬ 7·76 m   ⑭ a 27°   b 17·9 m

⑮ 10½ m

Exercise R3d [page 223]

① b and c

② 12·6 cm

③ 4·5 m

④ a 25 cm   b 360 cm²

⑤ 10·8 cm   ⑥ 2⅔ cm

⑦ 216 km

⑧ a 4 cm   b 10 km

⑨ c O′(−2, −6), A′(−2, 0), B′(4, 0), C′(4, −6)

⑩ a 60 cm long, 32 cm wide   b 64

⑪ 9A   ⑫ 36 : 121

⑬ 3 : 5   ⑭ 4 cm²

⑮ 9⅝ km²   ⑯ 72 ha

⑰ 40000 m²   ⑱ 3⅔ cm³

⑲ 400 cm³   ⑳ n = 64

Exercise R4a [page 225]

① a 9   b 3   c 2   d 6   e 24

② a 5   b Wednesday, Thursday
 c Friday   d Monday, Tuesday
 e 9 mm   f 42 mm

③ a increased   b 6000   c 6 years
 d ₦240 million

④ a 25%   b ⅜   c 24   d 3

⑤ a 9   b F   c I   d G   e 3 : 5

⑥ a 300   b 900   c ₦54000

⑨ a frequencies: 1, 4, 5, 5, 3, 2

Exercise R4b [page 227]

① a i ₦1400   ii ₦900
 b i ₦30000   ii ₦16000   c ₦13000

② a 270 km   b 3 hours   c 90 km/h
 d 4½ h   e 60 km/h   f 9·24 a.m.
 g 125 km   h 30 km

③ a ₦58, ₦22, ₦62, ₦77, ₦41
 b ₦20, ₦53, ₦23, ₦33, ₦58·50
 c ₦19

④ a 5 hours   b 2·30 p.m.   c ½ hour
 d 28 km

⑤ c i ₦250   ii 330 g

⑥ a 66 km   b 41 min

⑦ c discontinuous: it is impossible to buy a fraction of an egg.
 d i ₦600   ii ₦1050

⑧ a 75% b 40% c 65% d 85% e 58%

⑨ b 1½ km   c 12 km/h   d 7½ km/h

Exercise R4c   [page 229]

① a 70·6   b 7060   c 3 180 000
   d 28 600 000   e 6·39   f 0·063 7
② a 1·635   b 5·175   c 51·69
   d 66·33   e 9·184   f 33·06
③ 390 m²   ④ 57 m
⑤ a $n = 6·206$ b $n^2 = 38·51$
   c Square root tables are rounded to 4
     significant figures; thus they are not fully
     accurate.
⑥ a 1100   b 55 min   c 1900   d 5$\frac{3}{4}$ hours
⑦ a 2200   b 0600, Tuesday 24th June
   c $\frac{13}{96}$
⑧ a Freetown and Monrovia
   b Banjul and Lagos
   c 810 km   d 1 020 km
⑨ a i 1 800 km,   ii 1 860 km   b 4 850 km
⑩ a 431   b 1 395   c 838·395 93
   d 328·384 62   e 10·805 91   f 14·021 201

Exercise R4d   [page 231]

① 20 cm   ② 6   ③ 70·5 marks
④ a 72°   b 73°   c 9°
⑤ a 8   b 7
⑥ a 7   b 8   c 6   d 8
⑦ a 54·5 cm   b 53 cm   c 43 cm
⑧ a 16 yr   b 15·6 yr   c 6 yr
⑨ a 14·8 yr   b 14 yr
⑩ a

number	1	2	3	4	5	6
frequency	4	2	3	2	3	6

   b mean = 3·8, median = 4, mode = 6
⑪ a 15 yr 4 mo   b 15 yr 3 mo
⑫ a 2, 3, 4, 5, 5, 6, 6, 7, 8, 8, 8, 8, 9, 9, 10
   b 7   c 8   d 6·5
⑬ a mean = 251·2 g, median = 251·5 g, mode
     = 252 g
   b No. One of the jars has contents less than
     250 g.
⑭ 1·57 m   ⑮ ₦1 282   ⑯ 206
⑰ $x = 4$ ⑱ 16 yr 4 mo   ⑲ 14 yr
⑳ 40·5 kg   ㉑ 0·8 m   ㉒ 81 km/h
㉓ 3 900   ㉔ 30 yr   ㉕ $n = 15$
㉖ ₦1 560   ㉗ ₦4 050   ㉘ 4·2

Exercise R4e   [page 233]

① a $\frac{1}{6}$ b $\frac{1}{6}$ c 0   d $\frac{1}{3}$ e $\frac{1}{2}$ f $\frac{2}{3}$
② a $\frac{1}{26}$ b $\frac{1}{13}$ c $\frac{3}{13}$ d $\frac{5}{26}$
③ a $\frac{3}{10}$ b $\frac{1}{5}$ c $\frac{1}{2}$ d $\frac{1}{2}$
④ $\frac{1}{2}$ ⑤ a $\frac{1}{8}$ b $\frac{1}{4}$
⑥ a $\frac{5}{6}$ b $\frac{1}{6}$ c 1   d 0
⑦ $\frac{1}{20}$ ⑧ $\frac{13}{20}$ ⑨ $\frac{1}{10}$
⑩ b 0·92 eggs
   c median = 0·14 eggs, mode = 0 eggs
   d $\frac{19}{25}$

Examination 1   [pages 242–247]
Section I

① D   ② C   ③ A   ④ B   ⑤ C   ⑥ D
⑦ C   ⑧ B   ⑨ D   ⑩ C   ⑪ A   ⑫ C
⑬ C   ⑭ B   ⑮ A   ⑯ B   ⑰ D   ⑱ D
⑲ D   ⑳ E   ㉑ A   ㉒ C   ㉓ E   ㉔ E
㉕ D   ㉖ B   ㉗ E   ㉘ A   ㉙ C   ㉚ D
㉛ A   ㉜ B   ㉝ C   ㉞ D   ㉟ E   ㊱ C
㊲ D   ㊳ C   ㊴ D   ㊵ B   ㊶ D   ㊷ B
㊸ D   ㊹ D   ㊺ C   ㊻ D   ㊼ D   ㊽ B
㊾ A   ㊿ D   51 C   52 D   53 B   54 B
55 B   56 C   57 A   58 A   59 C   60 B
61 D   62 D   63 D   64 E   65 D   66 C
67 C   68 E   69 E   70 B   71 D   72 D
73 B   74 B   75 E   76 B   77 B   78 D
79 A   80 D

Section II

① a 55   b 1 000 100   c 12, 9
② a i $C = 420 + 5N$, ii ₦1 320   b ₦23 762
   3 $x = 3, y = 2$

Examination 2   [pages 247–253]
Section I

① C   ② B   ③ B   ④ A   ⑤ A   ⑥ B
⑦ D   ⑧ C   ⑨ C   ⑩ E   ⑪ D   ⑫ A
⑬ B   ⑭ D   ⑮ D   ⑯ A   ⑰ C   ⑱ D
⑲ A   ⑳ D   ㉑ D   ㉒ C   ㉓ C   ㉔ A
㉕ E   ㉖ C   ㉗ C   ㉘ C   ㉙ A   ㉚ C
㉛ B   ㉜ E   ㉝ D   ㉞ A   ㉟ D   ㊱ C
㊲ A   ㊳ C   ㊴ C   ㊵ D   ㊶ B   ㊷ E

43 D 44 A 45 C 46 C 47 C 48 A
49 E 50 D 51 C 52 D 53 B 54 B
55 B 56 D 57 C 58 D 59 D 60 A
61 B 62 A 63 D 64 C 65 D 66 D
67 B 68 B 69 C 70 D 71 A 72 A
73 E 74 D 75 B 76 D 77 B 78 C
79 B 80 C

3 W = 10111
E = 000101
L = 01100
C = 00011
O = 01111
M = 01101
E = 00101

Section II

1 a ₦1·08 million   b 27·3 cm
2 a 13·7 yr   b 13·5 yr   c 13 yr   d 0·2
3 |RQ| ≈ 4·5 cm, P̂ ≈ 23°

Examination 3 [pages 253–258]
Section I

1 B 2 E 3 D 4 C 5 C 6 A
7 C 8 C 9 B 10 C 11 B 12 D
13 C 14 C 15 E 16 D 17 D 18 B
19 C 20 C 21 E 22 E 23 B 24 C
25 C 26 C 27 D 28 E 29 C 30 E
31 C 32 B 33 A 34 D 35 E 36 D
37 C 38 D 39 C 40 B 41 D 42 C
43 B 44 C 45 B 46 A 47 C 48 D
49 C 50 B 51 B 52 D 53 C 54 B
55 C 56 B 57 B 58 C 59 D 60 D
61 C 62 D 63 B 64 B 65 C 66 A
67 C 68 C 69 E 70 B 71 A 72 D
73 C 74 E 75 C 76 D 77 C 78 B
79 B 80 C

Section II

1 a 56 m   b i ₦17100,   ii ₦14780
2 a x = 254   b 3
  c Pie chart with angles of 56° (A), 48° (B),
    75° (C), 81° (D), 100° (E)

Examination 4 [pages 259–264]
Section I

2 C 2 B 3 C 4 B 5 B 6 D
7 B 8 B 9 E 10 C 11 A 12 D
13 A 14 E 15 C 16 D 17 D 18 D
19 B 20 B 21 C 22 C 23 B 24 C
25 A 26 B 27 A 28 C 29 D 30 A
31 A 32 B 33 D 34 B 35 B 36 A
37 C 38 C 39 D 40 E 41 C 42 B
43 E 44 B 45 D 46 D 47 C 48 C
49 D 50 D 51 C 52 D 53 D 54 B
55 B 56 C 57 A 58 C 59 C 60 C
61 C 62 A 63 D 64 D 65 C 66 C
67 D 68 C 69 A 70 E 71 D 72 D
73 E 74 A 75 D 76 E 77 B 78 B
79 A 80 C

Section II

1 a $x = -9$ b 660 cm²   c $r = \sqrt{\dfrac{V}{\pi h}}$
2 a ₦181000   b i 6·9 cm,   ii 60° (approx)
3 a i

score	3	4	5	6	7	8	9
frequency	2	1	2	3	4	6	2

  ii mode = 9,   iii mean = 6·6
b) 39·4 cm²

Index

Numbers in italics indicate where subject is referred to in chapter summaries.